CULTURE'S CONSEQUENCES

CULTURE'S CONSEQUENCES

International Differences in Work-Related Values

Geert Hofstede

 SAGE PUBLICATIONS Beverly Hills London

For information address:

SAGE Publications
275 South Beverly Drive
Beverly Hills, California 90212

SAGE Publications Ltd
28 Banner Street
London EC1Y 8QE, England

Printed in the United States of America

Library of Congress Cataloging in Publication Data

Hofstede, Geert
    Culture's consequences: international differences
      in work-related values.
    (Cross cultural research and methodology series; 5)
    Bibliography: p.
    Includes indexes.
    1. Ethnopsychology.   2. National characteristics.
I. Title.
GN502.H63   155.8   80-16327
ISBN 0-8039-1444-X

FIRST PRINTING

CONTENTS

ABOUT THE SERIES

The Sage Series on Cross-Cultural Research and Methodology was created to present comparative studies on cross-cultural topics and interdisciplinary research. Inaugurated in 1975, the *Series* is designed to satisfy a growing need to integrate research method and theory and to dissect issues in comparative analyses across cultures. The recent ascent of the cross-cultural method in social and behavioral science has largely been due to a recognition of methodological power inherent in the comparative perspective; a truly international approach to the study of behavioral, social, and cultural variables can be done only within such a methodological framework.

Each volume in the *Series* presents substantive cross-cultural studies and considerations of the strengths, interrelationships, and weaknesses of its various methodologies, drawing upon work done in anthropology, political science, psychology, and sociology. Both individual researchers knowledgeable in more than one discipline and teams of specialists with differing disciplinary backgrounds have contributed to the *Series.* While each individual volume may represent the integration of only a few disciplines, *the cumulative totality of the* Series *will reflect an effort to bridge gaps of methodology and conceptualizations across all disciplines and many cultures.*

As co-editors, it is our pleasure to present *Culture's Consequences* (Volume 5) by Geert Hofstede, which breaks new ground by moving into the domain of international organizations. Hofstede's book is the result of a prodigious effort in scholarship and methodology, and will be heralded as a major source of information about value differences around the world. Imagine the task which Hofstede took on with such enthusiasm: He analyzes data collected in detailed questionnaire format from hundreds of individuals in 40 countries, and at *two* points in time. At the same time, he pays attention to all of the attendant methodological pitfalls associated with research of this kind. Finally, he makes the entire effort relevant, understandable, and sound from both a theoretical and practical standpoint. Hofstede has succeeded in doing all of these things, and has uncovered four value dimensions that may be so fundamental to human activity that they will serve as necessary criteria in much future culture-comparative work. The book is an invaluable addition to the *Series* and to a truly international and interdisciplinary audience of cross-cultural researchers.

—Walter J. Lonner
Western Washington University

—John W. Berry
Queen's University

[7]

*"Vérité en-deça des Pyrénées,
erreur au-delà"*

Blaise Pascal, 1623–1662*

*from Pensées, 60 (294). My translation: "There are truths on this side of the Pyrenees which are falsehoods on the other."

PREFACE

The survival of mankind will depend to a large extent on the ability of people who think differently to act together. International collaboration presupposes some understanding of where others' thinking differs from ours. Exploring the way in which nationality predisposes our thinking is therefore not an intellectual luxury. A better understanding of invisible cultural differences is one of the main contributions the social sciences can make to practical policy makers in governments, organizations, and institutions—and to ordinary citizens.

Highlighting culture-dependent differences in thinking and acting is not always a welcome intervention. My general experience in discussing the topics of this book with various audiences is that the amount of international exposure within the group strongly affects the way the subject is received. Internationally experienced audiences have little trouble seeing its importance and tolerating a certain amount of introspection into their own cultural constraints. Internationally naive audiences have difficulty seeing the points, and some members even feel insulted when their own culture is discussed.

Readers of the book may go through the same kind of experiences. Multicultural readers and those who have earlier gone through one or more culture shocks in their lives may find that the book expresses in formal terms much that they already intuitively knew. For readers whose activities have so far been confined within a single national culture, the book itself may have a certain culture-shock effect: They will find question marks attached to the universal validity of much that they have taken for granted so far and of much that has become dear to them.

Nevertheless, I hope the book will find both multicultural and monocultural readers in many of the countries described and in others as well; and that many of these readers will respond to the author's request of feedback and descriptions of experiences (See Appendix 6). The book aims at a readership of policy makers in public and private organizations and scholars and students from various disciplines: comparative management, anthropology, economics, political science, psychology, sociology, comparative law, history, and social geography.

The research project which forms the basis of this book has a long history, going back to the preparation of the first international HERMES survey in 1966. I could not foresee then that my involvement with this survey should eventually lead to my spending five years, from late 1973 to the end of 1978, on in-depth research on *Culture's Consequences*. Some of us suspected the scientific importance of the HERMES data as early as 1968. My colleagues of those days went on to other tasks; I alone remained to follow the intellectual track offered by this unique data base. It led

[9]

me from psychology into sociology and then into political science and anthropology; it also led us to living as a family in three countries, while surviving on money from five. To a large extent it has determined our lives over the past eight years. It was not always smooth and easy, but we have not regretted it. Never a dull moment.

A preface is the place for paying tribute to one's supporters. My primary tribute goes to the HERMES Corporation and its unnamed management, who believed us when we claimed that these were useful data to collect and who afterwards made the data available to general research; while from 1975–1978 they also supplied a research grant to support my work. Then there is a long list of persons who at some time contributed to the progress of the project. Among the pioneers of the HERMES study I must mention David Sirota, who created many of the questions that afterwards proved so important as indicators of culture, and somewhat later Paul de Koning and Allen Kraut. There are the data processors who managed my requests for handling the unwieldy data bank for the world's largest survey; in particular, Frits Claus and Jack Zandstra. There are the statistics experts who helped with some phases of the analysis: Peter Van Hoesel at Leyden University, Klaus Brockhoff at Kiel University, and Zvi Maimon at Tel Aviv University. There are my colleagues at the European Institute for Advanced Studies in Management at Brussels who stimulated me and acted as critical discussion partners; in particular, Alan Dale, Claude Faucheux, André Laurent, and Bengt Stymne. There are those who critically read through the manuscript and commented upon it: Torbjörn Stjernberg, Steven Velds (who read everything), Harry Triandis, Alberto Marradi, Robert Marsh, Seenu Srinivasan, and Wilfrid Dixon (who read parts). There is the competent staff of the European Institute—in particular Gerry Dirickx, who supplied library assistance, and my most essential supporter, Christiane Merckaert, who first turned 18 almost unreadable manuscripts into working papers and then typed the book.

Finally, there is a team of interested discussion partners and critics, experienced in multicultural living, sharing their observations, the younger among them even willing (if properly compensated) to act as research associate or administrative assistant. I mean Maaike Hofstede-Van den Hoek, Gert-Jan Hofstede, Rokus Hofstede, Bart Hofstede, and Gideon Hofstede. This is more their book than they will believe.

SUMMARY OF THE BOOK

This book explores the differences in thinking and social action that exist between members of 40 different modern nations. It argues that people carry "mental programs" which are developed in the family in early childhood and reinforced in schools and organizations, and that these mental programs contain a component of national culture. They are most clearly expressed in the different values that predominate among people from different countries.

Cross-cultural studies proliferate in all the social sciences, but they usually lack a theory of the key variable: culture itself. Names of countries are usually treated as residues of undefined variance in the phenomena found. *Culture's Consequences* aims at being specific about the elements of which culture is composed. It identifies four main dimensions along which dominant value systems in the 40 countries can be ordered and which affect human thinking, organizations, and institutions in predictable ways.

The data used for the empirical part of the research were extracted from an existing bank of paper-and-pencil survey results collected within subsidiaries of one large multinational business organization in 40 countries, and covering among others many questions about values. The survey was held twice, around 1968 and around 1972, producing a total of over 116,000 questionnaires; respondents can be matched by occupation, age, and sex. Additional data were collected among managers participating in international management development courses and unrelated to the first multinational business organization. The four main dimensions on which country cultures differ were revealed by theoretical reasoning and statistical analysis. They were labeled Power Distance, Uncertainty Avoidance, Individualism, and Masculinity. Each of the 40 countries could be given a score on these four dimensions.

The book shows that the same four dimensions are reflected in data from completely different sources, both survey studies of various kinds and nonsurvey comparative studies like McClelland's Achievement Motivation analysis based on a content analysis of children's books. Altogether, data from 38 other studies comparing from five to 39 countries are significantly correlated with one or more of the four dimensions. With few exceptions, these other studies so far had not been related to each other by their authors or by anyone else. In addition, the four dimensions show some significant and meaningful correlations with geographic, economic, demographic, and political national indicators.

The book shows how countries on the basis of their scores on the four dimensions can be divided into culture areas and in some cases is able to point to historical reasons that are likely to have led to the cultural differentiation between the areas.

The fact that the survey data were collected twice over a four-year interval allows an analysis of value developments over this period; it shows no convergency between countries but some worldwide or almost worldwide value shifts.

The differences demonstrated in this book have profound consequences for the validity of the transfer of theories and working methods from one country to another. In the last chapter, the findings are interpreted on behalf of policy makers in national but especially in international and multinational organizations who are confronted daily with the problems of collaboration of members of their staff carrying different culturally influenced mental programs.

—Geert Hofstede

Chapter 1

VALUES AND CULTURE

SUMMARY OF THIS CHAPTER

This is an introductory chapter which deals with basic questions of the definition and measurement of *"mental programs"* in people in general, and *values* and *culture* in particular. Mental programs can be found at the universal, the collective, and the individual level. They must be operationalized in order to be measured; four different strategies of operationalization are discussed. Values are distinguished into *values as the desired* and *values as the desirable,* and a review is presented of ways of measuring both types of values. Culture is defined as collective programming of the mind. The word is reserved for describing entire societies; for groups within societies, "subculture" is used. A diagram suggests how culture patterns are rooted in value systems of major groups of the population and how they are stabilized over long periods in history.

The chapter then goes into the study of culture and its specific methodological problems: We change the level of analysis from the individual to society. It refers to the "ecological fallacy" and signals a not infrequent "reverse ecological fallacy." It shows the dangers of ethnocentrism and disciplinary parochialism; and it lists the multitude of different disciplines that can contribute to the comparative study of national cultures. Special attention is paid to the relatively new field of "comparative management." Problems of language and the translation of research instruments are discussed, as well as problems of matching samples in different cultures to obtain functional equivalence. It is shown how marginal phenomena in societies can be as meaningful for comparison as modal phenomena.

The concept of *dimensions of culture* is introduced by an inquiry into the philosophical opposition between the specific and the general, the different and the similar. On the basis of this, four strategies for comparative multisociety studies are distinguished, of which the search for dimensions of culture represents one particular choice. A survey is presented of existing literature about dimensions of culture, both theory-based and empirically derived through factor analysis. From the dimensions found in the literature, those suggested by Inkeles and Levinson in a 1969 review article come close to those that have been found empirically in the study on which this book is based.

DEFINITIONS AND DISTINCTIONS

Mental Programs

Social systems can only exist because human behavior is not random, but to some extent predictable. I predict that Mrs. X will be in the office at 8:25 a.m. tomorrow; that the taxi driver will take me to the station and not somewhere else if I ask him; that all members of the family will come if I ring the dinner bell. We make such predictions continuously, and the vast majority of them are so banal that they pass completely unnoticed. But for each prediction of behavior, we try to take both the *person* and the *situation* into account.[1] We assume that each person carries a certain amount of mental programming which is stable over time and leads to the same person showing more or less the same behavior in similar situations. Our prediction may never prove true: Mrs. X may not turn up, the taxi driver may take me to the wrong destination, family member Y may refuse to come for dinner. But the more accurately we know a person's mental programming and the situation, the more sure our prediction will be.[2]

It is possible that our mental programs are physically determined by states of our brain cells. Nevertheless, we cannot directly observe mental programs. What we can observe is only behavior, words, or deeds. When we observe behavior, we infer from it the presence of stable mental programs. This type of inference is not unique to the social sciences; it exists, for example, in physics, where the intangible concept of "forces" is inferred from its manifestations in the movement of objects.[3] Like "forces" in physics, "mental programs" are intangibles, and the terms we use to describe them are *constructs*. A construct is "not directly accessible to observation but inferable from verbal statements and other behaviors and useful in predicting still other observable and measurable verbal and nonverbal behavior" (Levitin, 1973: 492). Constructs do not "exist" in an absolute sense: We define them into existence.

One unfortunate consequence of our dealing with constructs is that their definition contains of necessity an element of subjectivity on the side of the definer. For the intangibles in the physical sciences there are usually definitions on which there is virtual consensus among scholars. However, in comparison to the physical sciences, the social sciences deal with systems at a much higher level of complexity, where consensus is more difficult. To see why this is so, I find it helpful to refer to the General Hierarchy of Systems (Boulding, 1956a: 202–205; Von Bertalanffy, 1968: 28–29). In this General Hierarchy, the "systems" that we find around us and that are studied by the various sciences are ordered in nine levels of complexity: (1) static frameworks; (2) dynamic systems with predetermined motions; (3) closed-loop control or cybernetic systems; (4) homeostatic, self-controlling systems like the biological cell; (5) the living plant; (6) the animal; (7) man; (8) human organizations and society; and (9) transcendental systems. Each higher level adds a dimension of complexity to the previous one.

The object of the social sciences is at level 8, where the complexity is overwhelming (physics deals with levels 1–3, biology with 4–6). Man-the-social-scientist is at level 7; he is less complex than his object. He can never completely grasp what goes on at the level of social systems, and therefore his perception of them will never be exactly the same as his colleague's perception. I disagree with those authors who describe the social sciences as "not yet" sciences: we can "not yet" reach the same precision, consensus, and understanding as do the physical sciences. I think their "not yet" is naïve; the object of the social sciences is different in kind, not in degree. Social scientists approach the social reality as the blind men from the Indian fable approached the elephant; the one who gets hold of a leg thinks it is a tree, the one who gets the tail thinks it is a rope, but none of them understand what the whole animal is like. We will never be more than blind men in front of the social elephant; but by joining forces with other blind men and women and approaching the animal from as many different angles as possible, we may find out more about it than we could ever do alone. In other words, there is no such thing as objectivity in the study of social reality: We will always be subjective, but we may at least try to be "intersubjective," pooling and integrating a variety of subjective points of view of different observers.

What we do, in fact, when we try to understand social systems is use models. Models are lower-level systems which we can understand better and which we substitute for what we cannot understand. We simplify because we have no other choice. It is in this simplification that our subjectivity enters the process. What it means for the use of constructs is that definitions of constructs in social science reflect not only its object, but also the specific mental programming of the scholar who makes or borrows them. Therefore, no single definition of a construct in social science is likely to do justice to its complexity (Williams, 1968: 283).

Let us come back to the issue of mental programs. Every person's mental programming is partly unique, partly shared with others. We can distinguish broadly three levels of uniqueness in mental programs, as pictured in Figure 1.1. The least unique but most basic is the *universal* level of mental programming which is shared by all, or almost all, mankind. This is the biological "operating system" of the human body, but it includes a range of expressive behaviors such as laughing and weeping and associative and aggressive behaviors which are also found in higher animals. This level of our programming has been popularized by ethologists (biologists specialized in animal behavior) such as Morris (1968), Lorenz (1970), and Eibl-Eibesfeldt (1976). The *collective* level of mental programming is shared with some but not with all other people; it is common to people belonging to a certain group or category, but different among people belonging to other groups or categories. The whole area of subjective human culture (called "subjective" to distinguish it from "objective" human artifacts; see Triandis, 1972: 4) belongs to this level. It includes the language in which we express ourselves, the deference we show to our elders, the physical distance from other people we maintain in order to feel comfortable, the way we perceive general human activities like eating, making love, or defecating and the ceremonials surrounding them.

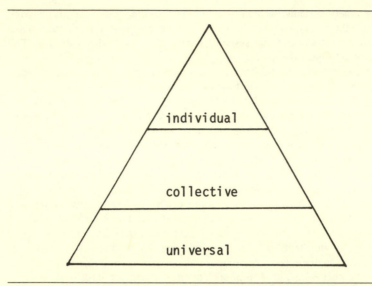

FIGURE 1.1   Three Levels of Uniqueness in Human Mental Programming

The *individual* level of human programming is the truly unique part—no two people are programmed exactly alike, even if they are identical twins raised together. This is the level of individual personality, and it provides for a wide range of alternative behaviors within the same collective culture. The borderlines in Figure 1.1 are a matter of debate among anthropologists; it is difficult to draw sharp dividing lines between individual personality and collective culture or to distinguish exceptional individuals from their cultural system. Also still an open issue is which phenomena are culture-specific—that is, collective—and which are human universals (Redfield, 1962: 439ff; Albert, 1968: 291).

Mental programs can be inherited—transferred in our genes—or they can be learned after birth. From the three levels in Figure 1.1, the bottom "universal" level is most likely entirely inherited: It is that part of our genetic information which is common to the entire human species. Eibl-Eibesfeldt (1976) calls it our *Vorprogrammierung* (preprogramming). On the top "individual" level at least part of our programming must be inherited; it is difficult to explain otherwise the differences in capabilities and temperament between children of the same parents raised in very similar environments. It is at the middle, collective level that most or all of our mental programming is learned, which is shown by the fact that we share it with people who went through the same learning process but who do not have the same genes. The existence of the American people as a phenomenon is one of the clearest illustrations of the force of learning: With a multitude of genetic roots, it shows a collective mental programming which is striking to the non-American. The transfer of collective mental programs is a social phenomenon which, following Durkheim (1937 [1895]: 107), we should try to explain socially and not to reduce to something else like race. Societies, organizations, and groups have ways of conserving and passing on mental programs from generation to generation with an obstinacy which many people tend to underestimate.[4]

The learning transferring collective mental programs goes on during our entire lives, but as most of it deals with fundamental facts of life, we tend to learn it when we are very young: When the mind is still relatively empty, programs are most easily registered.[5]

Operationalizing Mental Programs

In empirical research, we look for measures of the constructs that describe mental programs: that is, we have to *operationalize* them. We need to find observable phenomena from which the construct can be inferred. In some types of research our operationalization leads to quantitative measures; in other types, to descriptive, nonquantitative measures. Whichever we aim for, any operationalization of mental programs has to use forms of behavior or outcomes of behavior. The behavior we use can be either "provoked" (stimulated by the researcher for the purpose of the research) or "natural" (taking place or having taken place regardless of the research and the researcher). Also, the behavior we use can be verbal (words) or nonverbal (deeds). The combination of these two classifications leads to the diagram in Figure 1.2, which pictures four types of strategies of operationalization.[6]

FIGURE 1.2　Four Available Strategies for Operationalizing Constructs about Human Mental Programs

	provoked	natural
words	1) interviews questionnaires projective tests	2) content analysis of speeches discussions documents
deeds	3) laboratory experiments field experiments	4) direct observation use of available descriptive statistics

Strategies using provoked behavior inevitably contain a "Heisenberg effect,"[7] in that the researcher interferes with the behavior observed. This means that such behavior cannot always be extrapolated to circumstances where the researcher is not present. The general problem of all operationalizations is how to achieve *validity;* that is, correspondence between the observed behavior and the underlying constructs. Some constructs are directly conceptually related to specific behavior: This is in particular the case for *intentions,* people's subjective probabilities that they will perform some behavior (Fishbein and Ajzen, 1975: 288). In this case, the operationalization can be subjected to *pragmatic validation:* establishing the relationship between expressed intentions and actual behavior following them. Other constructs, among which are attitudes and values, are not directly conceptually related to specific behavior, but only through other constructs, according to some assumed set of relationships. In this case pragmatic validation is not possible, and we should be satisfied with *construct validation,* which means that the measures used for our construct relate to the measures used for other, related constructs in the way pre-dicted by our theory. To achieve good construct validity we therefore need both good measurements *and* good theory.

From the strategies pictured in Figure 1.2, those in Cell 1 are the easiest and therefore the most frequently used: especially paper-and-pencil "instruments." These produce provoked verbal behavior, which is used to predict other behavior, both verbal in other situations and nonverbal. Frequently, the validity of these predictions is assumed without further proof, as *face validity;* whereas a rigid test has to include the *predictive validity;* that is, a comparison between predicted and observed behav-ior. Deutscher (1973) has collected an impressive set of material to show the risk in relying on "words" to predict "deeds"; in fact, verbal and other behavior may be consistent in some situations, unrelated in others, or even inversely related. Argyris and Schon (1974) have demonstrated the difference between "espoused theories" of people and their "theories in use." Reviewing the U.S. literature on the relationship between attitudes (words) and behavior (deeds), Eagly and Himmelfarb (1978: 527ff) conclude that in the late 1960s many studies showed poor predictability of behavior from attitudes, but that in the mid-1970s it had become clear that good predictability can be obtained from words to deeds, if these words and deeds are selected so that they make theoretical sense.[8] A proper theoretical understanding of the relationship between words and deeds implies that the situation is taken into account. Cultural factors may also affect the relationship between attitudes and behavior. A good example of this is a study by Noesjirwan (1977), who compared the behavior of patients in doctor's waiting rooms in Jakarta, Indonesia, and Sydney, Australia. After having been observed, some of the patients were interviewed; 62 percent of the Indonesians and 43 percent of the Australians said they would be unlikely to initiate a conversation with a stranger. However, the previous observa-tions had shown that 56 percent of the Indonesians against 76 percent of the Austra-lians had actually been silent. Relying on the interviews, the researcher would predict the Australians to be more talkative; in fact, the situation was the reverse. The cultural factor involved seems to be a greater social desirability to be seen as sociable in Australia than in Indonesia.[9]

Face validity of an operationalization is therefore not sufficient. On the other hand, rigid predictive solutions are not often available. The next best solution is to avoid putting all one's eggs into one basket: to use more than one approach to operationalization simultaneously, and look for convergence between these ap-proaches. Webb et al. (1966: 3) call this process "triangulation," a term used in celestial navigation or land surveying. If we want to determine our distance to a point where we cannot go, we choose two base points where we can go and measure the position of the third point from there. The wider apart our base points, the more accurate our measurement. Thus, in social science where we cannot measure con-structs directly, we should use at least two measurement approaches as different as possible (with different error sources) and only go ahead if we find convergence in their results. In practice this means that it is undesirable to use Cell 1 measurements like paper-and-pencil instruments (see Figure 1.2) only; where possible, they should be supported by, for example, direct observation or available descriptive statistics (Cell 4). If we have to rely on Cell 1 measurements only, we should try to "triangulate" within them—for example, by approaching the same issue through Cell 1 measurements from different informants.

It is, of course, equally undesirable to use Cell 2, 3, or 4 measurements *only*. Measures based on deeds (actions, nonverbal behavior) have to be interpreted to find the underlying constructs—those expressed in words. Measures based on content analysis also have to be interpreted. If we collect nothing else but data about deeds, we should question whether we gain any insight by postulating mental programs at all—whether we cannot keep our analysis entirely at the level of behavior.[10] Cell 1 measurements, once they are collected, speak more for themselves and take less subjective interpretation from the researcher than Cell 2, 3, or 4 measurements. The best strategy, therefore, is to use Cell 1 measurement plus at least one other type.

In this book, I shall make an extensive use of Cell 1 measurements. For validation purposes, I shall use data collected by others: mainly Cell 1 measurements from different informants (various survey data) and Cell 4 measurements (available descriptive statistics).

Values

The key constructs to be used in this book for describing mental programs are *values* and *culture*. Values are an attribute of individuals as well as of collectivities; culture presupposes a collectivity. I define a value as "a broad tendency to prefer certain states of affairs over others." This is a simplified version of the more precise anthropological definition by Kluckhohn (1951b: 395): "a value is a conception, explicit or implicit, distinctive of an individual or characteristic of a group, of the desirable which influences the selection from available modes, means and ends of actions." It is also in line with the definition of Rokeach (1972: 159–160): "to say that a person 'has a value' is to say that he has an enduring belief that a specific mode of conduct or end-state of existence is personally and socially preferable to alternative modes of conduct or end-states of existence." These definitions reserve the word "value" for mental programs that are relatively unspecific: the same "value" can be activated in a variety of situations. Rokeach counts that an adult possesses "only several dozens of instrumental values and perhaps only a few handfuls of terminal values" (1968: 162). For mental programs that are more specific, Rokeach and others use the terms "attitudes" and "beliefs."

Because our values are programmed early in our lives, they are non-rational (although we may subjectively feel ours to be perfectly rational!). In fact, values determine our subjective definition of rationality. "Values are ends, not means, and their desirability is either nonconsciously taken for granted . . . or seen as a direct derivation from one's experience or from some external authority" (Bem, 1970: 16).[11] Our values are mutually related and form value systems or hierarchies, but these systems need not be in a state of harmony: Most people simultaneously hold several conflicting values, such as "freedom" and "equality." Our internal value conflicts are one of the sources of uncertainty in social systems: Events in one sphere of life may activate latent values which suddenly affect our behavior in other spheres of life. A change in our perception of a situation may swing the balance in an internal value conflict: in particular, the extent to which we perceive a situation as "favorable" or "critical."[12]

The term "value" or "values" is used in all social sciences (anthropology, economics, political science, psychology, and sociology) with different though not completely unrelated meanings; "value" is nearly as much an interdisciplinary term as "system" and therefore a natural choice as a central construct for a book like this which borrows from several disciplines. Nearly all our other mental programs (such as attitudes and beliefs) carry a value component. Man is an evaluating animal (Kluckhohn, 1951b: 403). Christian, Judaic, and Moslem biblical mythology puts the choice between good and evil right at the beginning of mankind's history—with Adam and Eve—thus indicating the fundamental impossibility for man to escape from choice based on value judgments.

Values have both *intensity* and *direction* (Kluckhohn, 1951b: 413–414 uses "intensity" and "modality"). Mathematically, values have a size and a sign; they can be represented by arrows along a line. If we "hold" a value, this means that the issue involved has a certain relevance for us (intensity) and that we identify certain outcomes as "good" and others as "bad" (direction). For example, "having money" may be highly relevant to us (intensity) and we consider "more" as good and "less" as bad (direction). Someone else may differ from us as to the intensity, the direction, or both. A person who takes the Christian Bible (St. Mark 10: 21–25) seriously could consider having money equally relevant, but with a reversed direction sign—"more" is bad and "less" is good. For still another person, the entire issue of having money may be less relevant. In some primitive societies, "witchcraft" is both relevant and good; in medieval Europe, it was relevant and bad; to most of us today, it is simply irrelevant.

We should further distinguish between values as the *desired* and the *desirable:* what people actually desire versus what they think ought to be desired. Whereas the two are of course not independent, they should not be equated; equating them is a "positivistic fallacy" (Levitin, 1973: 497) and in research leads to a confusion between reality and social desirability. In most of the psychological and sociological research literature, "social desirability" is treated as something undesirable to the researcher. The term is used in two ways: as a quality of certain measurement items, or as a personality construct of the respondents (Phillips and Clancy, 1972: 923). In both senses, it usually represents "noise" in the measurement. In the study of values, however, asking for the desirable is perfectly respectable; it is part and parcel of the phenomenon studied. So in this case, "social desirability" in our measurements is not undesirable; we should only realize that we deal with values of two different natures.

Avoiding the positivistic fallacy is especially important if we try to relate values to behavior. Responding to questionnaires or interviews is also a form of behavior, but, as argued above, we should distinguish "words" (questionnaires, interviews, meetings, speeches) from "deeds" (nonverbal behavior). Values should never be equated with deeds, for the simple reason that behavior depends on both the person and the situation. However, values as the desired are at least closer to deeds than values as the desirable. The desired-desirable distinction relates to several other distinctions made, listed in Figure 1.3.

Figure 1.3 refers to *norms* of value. We can speak of norms as soon as we deal with a collectivity. In the case of the desired, the norm is statistical: it indicates the values actually held by the majority.[13] In the case of the desirable, the norm is

FIGURE 1.3   Distinction Between the Desired and the Desirable and
              Associated Distinctions

nature of a value	the desired	the desirable
dimension of value	intensity	direction
nature of corresponding norm of value	statistical, phenomeno-logical, pragmatic	absolute, deontological, ideological
corresponding behavior	choice and differential effort allocation	approval or disapproval[a]
dominant outcome	deeds and/or words	words
terms used in measuring instrument	important, successful, attractive, preferred	good, right, agree, ought, should
affective meaning of this term	activity *plus* evaluation	evaluation only
person referred to in measuring instrument	me, you	people in general

[a]The distinction between approval and choice, etc. is based on Kluckhohn (1951b: 404–405).

absolute or deontological (pertaining to what is ethically right). The desired relates more to pragmatic issues, the desirable to ideology.

The association between the various lines in Figure 1.3 should be seen as probabilistic, not rigid: For example, we may approve with deeds rather than words, or what is desired may never become expressed in deeds. There remains a discrepancy between actual behavior (deeds) and the desired, but there is another discrepancy between the desired and the desirable. Norms for the desirable can be completely detached from behavior (Adler, 1956: 277). The tolerable size of the discrepancies may differ from person to person and from group to group, based on both personality and culture. In Catholicism, the practice of confessing can be seen as a device to cope with both discrepancies and thus make them tolerable. Ideological indoctrination will more easily affect the desirable than the desired; it is possible that it widens the gap between the two without changing the desired.

The inescapability of value judgments applies to the student of values as much as to anyone else. First, we have to distinguish between a phenomenological study of values (which is the area of social science) and a deontological approach (which belongs to ethics, ideology, or theology). But even in purely phenomenological research the values of the researcher determine to a large extent the way he or she observes, describes, classifies, understands, and predicts reality. There is no way out of this dilemma but to (1) expose oneself and one's work to the work of others with different value systems and (2) try to be as explicit as possible about one's own value system. Both, to a certain extent, go against our nature. For the interested reader I have composed a picture of my own value system and its origins in Appendix 5. More about it, however, probably will be readable "between the lines" of the book.

A related issue is whether there are absolute values at all or only relative ones. Anthropologists have tried to identify absolute values in the form of cultural universals from the phenomenological side (Bidney, 1962: 450). The systems philosopher

Ervin Laszlo (1973) concludes that such cultural universals exist and argues from the deontological side that "good" in absolute terms is what contributes to the survival of the world system, and that error tolerance for the world has become so small that relativism is obsolete. However, his position itself reflects a value choice. The problem is that man is at the same time the source of values and their instrument; for which, as far as I know, systems theory has no solution. A comparative study of human values presupposes in the student a certain amount of relativism or, at least, tolerance of deviant values.

Measuring Values

Questionnaires designed to measure values abound in the U.S. social science literature, as a logical consequence of U.S. empiricism.[14] Besides, other questionnaires not designed for measuring values but for measuring such constructs as beliefs, attitudes, or personality can be used to *infer* values.

In order to investigate the convergency of various value-measuring instruments, I have administered eight of them to groups of managers from about 20 different countries attending executive development programs at IMEDE, Lausanne, Switzerland.[15] The highest correlation found between conceptually related scores on different instruments was $r = .49$ (across 64 respondents; see also Chapter 2). This, although statistically significantly different from zero, is not high; which means that measures of values depend strongly on the instrument used—a proof of the subjectivity referred to earlier. Also, where I could compare the patterns of correlations between scores of an instrument for my international respondent sample with the correlations reported for American samples, these correlation patterns were usually quite different. This shows that the scores did not carry the same meaning for the two samples, and that it is a doubtful practice to use instruments developed in one country (in this case, the United States) in another cultural environment, assuming they carry the same meaning there.

Inspection of a number of instruments designed to measure human values makes it clear that the universe of all human values is not defined and that each author has made his or her own subjective selection from this unknown universe, with little consensus among authors. This means that the *content validity* of measurements of values (their representativeness for the universe of values) is necessarily low. In the United States Bales and Couch (1969) have collected nearly 900 different formulations of values used in different instruments, in theoretical literature, or in group discussions they had organized. Using 500 U.S. students as test persons, they showed statistically (through factor analysis) that the statements could be meaningfully reduced to four basic issues: authority, self-restraint, equality, and individuality. But this only applies to U.S. students and it is unlikely that other members of the human race will not have additional basic value issues. Bales and Couch did not consider, nor did they weed out, issues on which all or most of the American students agreed. These, however, may be precisely the ones that are most revealing in comparison with other countries and social groups.

Eysenck (1953, 1954) used the same statistical method (factor analysis) to show that political attitudes (I would also call them "values") of British, U.S., Swedish, and German respondents could all be regarded as being determined by two main principles: Radicalism-Conservatism (dealing, among other things, with equalitarianism) and Tough-mindedness-Tender-mindedness (dealing with aggression and intolerance of ambiguity). Eysenck related these to voting behavior: Communists were tough-minded radicals, fascists were tough-minded conservatives, (British) conservatives were tender-minded conservatives, and socialists were tender-minded radicals. The statistical proof for Eysenck's theory was weak, however, for which he has been criticized.[16] Much later, Rokeach (1973: 165ff) presented another two-dimensional classification system of political values which does not use factor analysis of survey data but a content analysis of the writings of four types of politicians. He showed that the two dimensions on which their ideas can be distinguished are *Equality* and *Freedom*. The writings of Lenin (communist) are high on Equality, low on Freedom; of Hitler (fascist), low on both; of Goldwater (conservative), low on Equality, high on Freedom; and of various socialist writers (who are rare in the United States), high on both.

Various authors have divided the universe of values according to theoretical criteria. Rokeach (1972) divides them into terminal values (end states) and instrumental values (ways to get there); Levitin (1973: 494), into telic values (ultimate means and ends), ethical (good or evil), aesthetic (beautiful or ugly), intellectual (true or false), and economic values. Reviewing the value-measuring instruments in the U.S. literature, I find three types of values: those dealing with our relationship with (1) other people, (2) things (our nonhuman environment), and (3) our own inner selves and God.

In the previous section, I stressed that values (by their very nature) have both intensity and direction. However, we rarely find value-measurement instruments that ask for both. Some focus on intensity and take direction for granted, some focus on direction and take intensity for granted, and some even confuse them.[17] The focus is determined by the words used to express the values. The work of Osgood and his associates (1957, 1975) with the "semantic differential" has shown that across a large variety of languages, three basic dimensions appear regularly in the affective meaning of words: *evaluation* (good-bad), *potency* (strong-weak), and *activity* (active-passive). Osgood et al. (1961) applied the semantic differential to a set of 13 terminal values (Morris' "Ways to Live"; see Morris, 1956) and found that in this case, the three dimensions collapsed into one: the preferred "Ways to Live" were felt to be good, strong, and active. However, the words used in questionnaire scales rarely tap all these meanings. They are often of the type good-bad, right-wrong, agree-disagree, which is purely evaluation and deals with the *direction of the value;* or they are of the type important-unimportant, successful-unsuccessful, meaningful-meaningless, which, according to Osgood et al. (1957: 62–63), represents activity as well as evaluation. In this case, they deal with the *intensity* of the value with an implicit direction.

The intensity-direction distinction has been associated in Figure 1.3 with the distinction between "values as the desired" and "values as the desirable." In the lower part of Figure 1.3 I have indicated what this means for the design of measuring instruments. Values as the desired are measured by such words as important-unimportant, expressing activity as well as evaluation, and usually refer to the respondent in the first or second person. Values as the desirable are measured by such words as agree-disagree, expressing evaluation only, and usually refer to people in general.

Value measurements are quantified either through scale-rating or through ranking. Various instruments use ratings of individual items on scales of between 2 and 11 points. Others use ranking of items relative to one another, with a minimum number of 2 and a maximum of 18 (Rokeach's Value Survey).

Rating and ranking lead to similar but not identical results. An indication of this is found in the results of one study in which 22 different "work goals" (work values as the desired) were scored by 1196 respondents in five European laboratories. Respondents had to rate every single value on a five-point scale and also to select the first, second, and third most important item from the entire list. The order of the 22 work goals based on ratings is rank-correlated (Spearman) .58 with the order of the same 22 goals based on selecting rank 1, 2 and 3 (Hofstede, 1976b: 13–15).

When the intensity of values is measured (that is, for values as the desired) the interpretation of the scores always implies some kind of ranking of one value versus other values. A rating of one value is as meaningful as the sound of one hand clapping. Most of us will value both "freedom" and "equality," but the difference between people will only appear when we look at the relative value attached to freedom over equality, or vice versa, in case of conflict.

All measures of values discussed so far are Cell 1 measurements (provoked words). Moreover, all are based on self-descriptions (values as the desired) or ideological statements (values as the desirable). There is another technique which is still Cell 1 but avoids the distorting effects of self-descriptions and ideological statements. This technique (which is too seldom used) is to infer values from the way respondents describe specific third people, recognizing that our perceptions are colored by our values. An instrument using this technique is F. E. Fiedler's Least Preferred Co-Worker questionnaire (Fiedler, 1967), in which a respondent describes the other person with whom he or she can work least well. Some respondents describe their least-preferred co-worker in relatively favorable terms (high LPC-score), others in extremely unfavorable terms (low LPC-score). Fiedler interprets high LPC scorers as interpersonally oriented, low LPC as task-oriented. However, it appears that if the LPC questionnaire is given together with self-descriptions of values, high LPC scorers tend to describe themselves as task-oriented and low LPC scorers as interpersonally oriented: the reverse of what could be expected at face value (Hofstede, 1974b: 14).

Fiedler and Chemers (1974: 103) interpret this paradox by referring to the influence of the situation. They have shown that the behavioral consequences of a high or low LPC score depend on the degree of criticalness of the situation, and that people who behave one way in an uncritical situation may show quite different behavior when the situation is critical. Self-descriptions of values are typically collected assuming "normal"—that is, non-critical—circumstances. LPC, however, refers to the perception of someone else under dramatically critical circumstances: the impossibility to get a job done. It should be no surprise, then, that LPC and self-descriptions of values are not, or even negatively, related. Deutscher (1973: 45) concludes that, in general, laboratory experimental studies show a positive correlation between attitudes and behavior, while field observational studies do not show such a correlation.

This suggests the same phenomenon: (attitude) self-description measurements only give valid predictions for behavior under favorable (laboratory) circumstances.

In paper-and-pencil questionnaires, people very rarely describe themselves under crisis circumstances. They will, however, easily describe *others* under crisis circumstances. On top of this, we all are better observers of others than we are observers of ourselves; but as the experience with the LPC questionnaire shows, in observing others we reveal something about ourselves too. Therefore, paper-and-pencil measures of values through perceptions of third persons can be expected to have greater behavioral validity than those based on self-descriptions—this is what Fiedler proves extensively for LPC. In this book, the measure that will be used for the value complex "Power Distance" will be partly based on the perception of the behavior of others: one's boss and one's colleagues (Chapter 3).

Cell 2, 3, and 4 measures of values are rarer in the literature. Nevertheless, almost any behavior which is systematically observable—verbal and nonverbal—can be used to infer mental programs in general and values in particular. Examples on the cross-cultural level are (Cell 2)—McClelland's (1961) content analysis of children's stories from 41 countries; (Cell 3)—Schachter et al.'s (1954) laboratory experiments with group discussions by schoolboys in seven European countries; and (Cell 4)—Adelman and Morris' (1967) factor analysis of national statistical data from 74 developing countries.

Culture

Culture has been defined in many ways. Kluckhohn (1951a: 86, 5) quotes as a consensus of anthropological definitions:

> Culture consists in patterned ways of thinking, feeling and reacting, acquired and transmitted mainly by symbols, constituting the distinctive achievements of human groups, including their embodiments in artifacts; the essential core of culture consists of traditional (i.e. historically derived and selected) ideas and especially their attached values.

Kroeber and Parsons (1958: 583) arrive at a cross-disciplinary definition of culture as "transmitted and created content and patterns of values, ideas, and other symbolic-meaningful systems as factors in the shaping of human behavior and the artifacts produced through behavior." Triandis (1972: 4) distinguishes "subjective" culture from its expression in "objective" artifacts and defines the former as "a cultural group's characteristic way of perceiving the man-made part of its environment." In this book I treat culture as "the collective programming of the mind which distinguishes the members of one human group from another." This is not a complete definition (see Kluckhohn above), but it covers what I have been able to measure. Culture, in this sense, includes systems of values; and values are among the building blocks of culture.

Culture is to a human collectivity what personality is to an individual. Personality has been defined by Guilford (1959) as "the interactive aggregate of personal characteristics that influence the individual's response to the environment." Culture could be defined as the interactive aggregate of common characteristics that influence a human group's response to its environment. Culture determines the identity of a human group in the same way as personality determines the identity of an individual. Moreover, the two interact; "culture and personality" is a classic name for psychological anthropology (Bohannan, 1969: 3; Barnouw, 1973). Cultural traits sometimes can be measured by personality tests.

In the English language, "culture" has a number of other meanings, all deriving from its original Latin meaning: the cultivation of soil (the same applies in French and German). The other meaning which leads to most confusion, especially in communication with the French is "the training and refining of the mind, manners, taste etc. or the result of this" (Webster's dictionary, concise edition, 1964). "He/she has no culture" is almost as bad as "he/she has no personality." To avoid this confusion, it is necessary to explain that in the social sciences the most humble people and the most menial acts still reflect "culture."

The word "culture" is usually reserved for societies (in the modern world we speak of "nations") or for ethnic or regional groups, but it can be applied equally to other human collectivities or categories: an organization, a profession, or a family. In this book, to avoid confusion I shall reserve the word "culture" for societies and in other cases use "subculture." Societies merit special consideration in the study of cultures because they are the most "complete" human groups that exist; a society is a social system "characterized by the highest level of self-sufficiency in relation to its environments" (Parsons, 1977: 6). Collectivities within societies tend to be more interdependent with other collectivities. The degree of cultural integration varies between one society and another, and may be especially low for some of the newer nations (Geertz, 1973: 255ff); few of these, however, are in the sample of nations studied in this book. Most subcultures within a society still share common traits with other subcultures, which make their members recognizable to foreigners as belonging to that society.

This book is about differences in national culture among 40 modern nations. It will show evidence of differences and similarities among the culture patterns of countries; differences and similarities that have very old historical roots (some, for example, going back as far as the Roman Empire). There must be mechanisms in societies which permit the maintenance of stability in culture patterns across many generations. I suggest that such mechanisms operate like Figure 1.4.[18]

In the center is a system of societal norms, consisting of the value systems (the mental programs) shared by major groups of the population. Their origins are in a variety of ecological factors (in the sense of factors affecting the physical environment). The societal norms have led to the development and pattern maintenance of institutions in society with a particular structure and way of functioning. These include the family, education systems, politics, and legislation. These institutions, once they have become facts, reinforce the societal norms and the ecological conditions that led to them. In a relatively closed society, such a system will hardly change at all. Institutions may be changed, but this does not necessarily affect the societal norms; and when these remain unchanged, the persistent influence of a majority value system patiently smoothes the new institutions until their structure and functioning is again adapted to the societal norms. An example of this process is the history of France since Louis XIV (Peyrefitte, 1976). Change comes mainly from the outside, through forces of nature (changes of climate, silting up of harbors) or forces

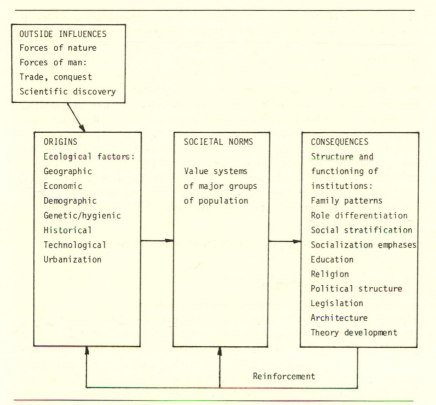

FIGURE 1.4   The Stabilizing of Culture Patterns

of man (trade, conquest, colonization, scientific discovery). The arrow of outside influences is deliberately directed at the origins, not at the societal norms themselves. I believe that norms change rarely by direct adoption of outside values, but rather through a shift in ecological conditions: technological, economical, and hygienic. In general, the norm shifts will be gradual unless the outside influences are particularly violent (such as in the case of military conquest or deportation).

One of the most effective ways of changing mental programs of individuals is changing behavior first (Bem, 1970: 60). That value change has to precede behavior change is an idealistic assumption which neglects the contribution of the *situation* to actual behavior. This applies on the level of societies as well. Kunkel (1970: 76), dealing with the economic development of societies, concludes that "the major problem of economic development is not the alteration of character, values or attitudes, but the change of those selected aspects of man's social environment which are relevant to the learning of new behavior patterns." In this case I would omit the word "social."

The system of Figure 1.4 is in a homeostatic (self-regulating) quasi-equilibrium. History has shown cases of peoples that through such a system have maintained an identity over hundreds and thousands of years, even in the face of such sweeping changes as loss of independence, deportation, or loss of language; examples are Jews, Gypsies, and Basques (Spicer, 1971). Other peoples in similar conditions have disappeared, however, when their self-regulating cycle was too far disturbed by outside influences. Obviously, both the strength of the existing self-regulation and the strength of the outside forces have played a role in these cases.

As nearly all our mental programs are affected by values, nearly all are affected by culture, and this is reflected by our behavior. The cultural component in all kinds of behavior is difficult to grasp for people who remain embedded in the same cultural environment; it takes a prolonged stay abroad and mixing with nationals there to recognize the numerous and often subtle differences in the way they and we behave, because that is how our society has programmed us. If I take the train from Brussels to Rotterdam, I can tell the Belgian passengers from the Dutch; most Dutch people greet strangers when entering a small, closed space like a train compartment, elevator, or doctor's waiting room, but most Belgians do not.

METHODOLOGICAL ISSUES IN THE STUDY OF CULTURE

Comparing Cultures:
Changing the Level of Analysis

In studying "values" we compare individuals; in studying "culture" we compare societies. When we base our study of culture on quantified data which have to be statistically treated, we meet a problem which the study of values of individuals did not present: the simultaneous analysis of data at the individual and at the societal level.[19] Some data are collected at the level of the society, such as its population density or per capita gross national product. Other data are still collected from individuals, such as responses on questionnaires; these stem from individuals within societies.

Let us suppose we want to study the relationship between two variables which belong to the latter category: stemming from individuals within societies. We want to measure this relationship through a mathematical measure, the correlation coefficient. However, we have the choice between:

—a global correlation between all individuals regardless of the society they are in;
—a number of within-society correlations, one for each society, between those individuals belonging to that society; and
—a between-society correlation, based on the mean scores of the variables for each society.

For data collected at the level of the society, we obviously have only a between-society correlation.

The problem of data from individuals within societies is that the various types of correlations referred to above most likely are not equal. First, the within-society correlations may be significantly different from one society to the other. For example, Kagitcibasi (1970) has shown that questionnaire item scores that correlate in the United States and together form the F-scale (used to determine the "authoritarian personality") are not correlated in Turkey. In societies where the culture imposes strong behavioral norms, certain attitudes and behaviors show such small variance that they do not correlate with other attitudes and behaviors; this is the case for some of the F-scale items in Turkey.[20] It is precisely these differences in within-society correlations which are of interest from a culture point of view; when these exist, the use of global correlations is misleading.

Even if the within-society correlations are not significantly different from each other, they are not at all the same as the between-society correlations. I shall call the latter "ecological correlations": they are calculated either from mean values of variables for each society or (in the case of yes-no variables) from percentages. It is easy to see why ecological correlations are not the same as within-society correlations if we consider some extreme cases. One extreme is that for one of the variables the mean value is the same for any single society; in this case we find only within-society correlations, and the ecological correlation is zero. The other extreme is that one of the variables is a constant for all members within a society, but differs from one society to another. In this case the within-society correlations are all zero, and we find only an ecological correlation. Usually, of course, for neither variable the societies or the people are entirely equal, so we find both types of correlations. However, they are not of equal magnitude; they can even have opposite signs.

A confusion between within-system and ecological correlations is known as the "ecological fallacy." The classical example is from Robinson (1950: 352) and deals with the relationship between skin color and illiteracy in the United States. Between percentages of Negro population and percentages of illiterates across nine geographic divisions of the United States (1930 data) the *ecological* correlation is .95. Across 48 states, the ecological correlation is .77. Across 97 million individuals, the *individual* correlation is .20. The ecological fallacy is committed when authors interpret the ecological correlations (.95 or .77: strong association between skin color and illiteracy) as if they applied to individuals. This is attractive, because ecological correlations are often stronger than individual correlations.[21]

The fact that ecological correlations should not be confused with individual correlations does not mean that they are meaningless. In a comment on Robinson's article, Menzel (1950) has drawn attention to the unique meaning of ecological correlations per se because these reflect properties of larger social structures, not of individuals. Later, American sociologists such as Blau (1960), Meltzer (1963), and Tannenbaum and Bachman (1964) have drawn attention to the merits of analyzing "structural" effects in data separately from individual effects. Meltzer, for example, used data from a survey of 539 members of voluntary committees in the United States, divided over 79 groups. He showed that in many cases, individuals' attitudes could be better predicted from their group's mean scores on related issues than from their own individual scores on these issues. The cases where the group results best predicted the individuals' attitudes were those in which group processes played a role: attitudes toward the organization's programs or attitudes about the group chairman, for example.

The ecological fallacy is a special temptation for political scientists. In cross-cultural studies by social psychologists, however, I find another type of confusion between the individual and the ecological level: I shall call it the *"reverse ecological fallacy."* The reverse ecological fallacy is committed in the construction of ecological *indices* from variables correlated at the individual level. Indices are, for example, constructed by adding the scores on two or more questionnaire items. In constructing indices for the individual level, we make sure (or ought to make sure) that the items correlate across individuals: For example, if we want an overall appreciation index of school results, we may add up the marks obtained for mathematics and language (which are usually positively correlated) but not the marks for mathematics with the number of days of absence (which are, if anything, probably negatively correlated). The reverse ecological fallacy in cross-cultural studies consists in comparing cultures on indices created for the individual level.

Let us take an example. Bass and Franke (1972) administered an "Organizational Success Questionnaire" to 1009 students from six countries. The questionnaire consisted of 12 items, six expressing "social" and six "political" approaches to success. For the "social" and "political" scales, the mean internal consistency found on a pretest with Americans was .72, which indicates that items forming one scale were highly positively correlated across individuals. Bass and Franke calculated mean scores for each of the 12 items for each of the six countries (each score measured on a six-point scale) and averaged the six "social" item scores to obtain a country "social" index score, and the six "political" items to obtain a "political" index score. Country "social" and "political" index scores were subsequently correlated with country-level indices like GNP/capita, population density, and the like. The authors did not look at the ecological correlations of their items: the correlations of country means for each item (across n = 6 countries). I have calculated these correlations using Bass and Franke's published data. The 15 correlations between the six social items vary from −.48 to .72 with a median of .28. For the six "political" item scores, the 15 ecological correlations vary from −.86 to .78 with a median of .14, which means that the ecological scores have hardly any internal consistency at all. The country indices used were nevertheless made up by averaging country item scores of which several are negatively correlated (the two items correlated −.86 have been *added* in calculating the country "political" index).

There are two fallacies in this case. First, Bass and Franke pretested their scales on Americans only and did not prove their internal consistency for each of the other five national groups. This could be important for determining whether the test can in fact discriminate between more socially and more politically oriented Frenchmen or between more socially and more politically oriented Swedes in the same way as it can discriminate between Americans. Second, the internal consistency across individuals within whichever nation is irrelevant if we mean to compare nations with our items. The only thing that counts, in this case, is the internal consistency of the ecological (country mean) scores. Bass and Franke's purpose is not to compare individuals; rather, it is to compare nations, as is testified by their correlating their indices with GNP/capita and other such indices. For this purpose, individually based indices simply make no sense.

What, then, can be done? Bass and Franke's data allow a clustering of items on the basis of country mean scores. If we do this, we find that for purposes of ecological comparison, the items should be divided into *three* clusters, each composed of both "social" and "political" variables. The clusters can be meaningfully interpreted, but not in terms of "social" and "political". I shall refer to them in Chapter 5.

The reverse ecological fallacy is not only a matter of inadequate data treatment; this is only its outcome. At the root of it is an inadequate research paradigm,[22] in which cultures are treated and categorized as if they were individuals. Cultures are not individuals: they are wholes, and their internal logic cannot be understood in the terms used for the personality dynamics of individuals. Eco-logic differs from individual logic. Industrial social psychologists performing studies sometimes try to classify cultures according to Herzberg et al.'s (1959) distinction between intrinsic and extrinsic motivation, or according to Maslow's (1970) hierarchy of human needs. For example, an early and pioneering study of managers' values in 14 countries (Haire et al., 1966) used the Maslow framework. Country scores on 11 questionnaire items dealing with needs and satisfactions were condensed into five indices based on levels in Maslow's hierarchy. In their condensation, the authors have not tested whether the items lumped together were correlated at the ecological level. Had they done this, they would have found that, cross-culturally, the 11 items do *not* group themselves according to Maslow's theory (see Chapter 5). Within the imposed Maslow framework, their results do not make much sense. Had the authors not been caught in the Maslow paradigm, they might have been able to discover the truly *cultural* dimensions in their data which would have made sense.

One reason the reverse ecological fallacy occurs easily is that studies with data from more than a few societies have been rare. It is not obvious to compute ecological correlations if we have only two or three cases (societies), although even in this case the reverse ecological fallacy can occur and can be avoided. For example, when we compare within a population the subcultures of men and women (an ecological n = 2), we should mistrust theories which force us to add characteristics or items for which the men-women difference does not carry the same sign. Caught in the Herzberg dichotomy between intrinsic and extrinsic motivation, U.S. researchers have tried to determine whether men were more "intrinsically" interested than women. Such studies have not shown consistent sex differences in intrinsic motivation (Crowley et al., 1973: 446), but have indicated that some "intrinsic" factors appealed more to women, others to men (see Chapter 6). In such a case, we need another set of concepts than intrinsic-extrinsic to explain why these female and male subcultures differ.

Ecological dimensions can more clearly be detected when we have data from more—for example, 10 or 15—societies (Allerbeck, 1977: 391). This is one reason such multicultural studies are highly desirable (Albert, 1968: 290; Frijda and Jahoda, 1969: 45).

Ethnocentrism

Ethnocentrism has been defined as an "exaggerated tendency to think the characteristics of one's own group or race superior to those of other groups or races" (Drever, 1952: 86). Faucheux (1976: 309) compares ethnocentrism with egocentrism: Egocentrism is a phase in the development of a child before it can take the viewpoint of an Other; so Faucheux sees ethnocentrism as a phase in the development of a social science—in the case he refers to, of social psychology. In the history of anthropology there has been an ethnocentric phase which has subsequently been overcome. Other social science disciplines in which cross-cultural contacts play a less major role than in anthropology are less developed in this respect.

Ethnocentrism can be very subtle, and it is certainly easier to recognize it in contributions from other cultures than from one's own. Let us take an example. In the previous section of this chapter I referred to Haire et al.'s (1966) study of managers' values in 14 countries, deploring that the authors forced their data into a classification according to Maslow's hierarchy of human needs. Maslow's hierarchy implies that needs appear in an order; some, like "security," are lower, more basic; when a lower-level need is satisfied, the next higher need takes its place, and so on. Haire et al. order their five need categories as follows: security—social—esteem—autonomy—self-actualization. The latter is Maslow's supreme category, and in Haire et al.'s operationalization it includes three items: personal growth, self-fulfillment, and accomplishment.

Haire et al. show the mean scores for 14 countries on the five need categories for need satisfaction (1966: 89) and need importance (1966: 100). The rank orders of these mean scores are extremely interesting. For three countries (Italy, England, and the United States) the *satisfaction* mean scores appear exactly in the Maslow order: security most satisfied, self-actualization least. From these, the United States is the one for which the spread between the need category scores is widest. For need *importance,* no country follows exactly the Maslow order, but the United States comes closest: the rated importance of the five need categories rank-correlates (Spearman) .90 with Maslow. The next highest rank correlations are .80 for Italy and .70 for England and Norway. The direction of the correlation in these countries shows that self-actualization is most important, security least.

The authors of the study never looked at their data in this way, but the data show that if we follow the categorization of Maslow (who was an American), the scores from U.S. managers follow the hierarchy of Maslow's theory more than those from other countries' managers. My interpretation is that this tells us more about Maslow than about the other countries' managers. Maslow categorized and ordered his human needs according to the U.S. middle-class culture pattern in which he was embedded himself—he could not have done otherwise. American theories fit American value patterns, and French theories will fit French value patterns. If we recognize culture as an all-encompassing influence on our mental programming, this should be no surprise. In taking Maslow's theory and applying it to other cultures, however, Haire et al. have unconsciously and unintentionally been ethnocentric, besides committing the reverse ecological fallacy as described earlier.[23]

Ethnocentrism is already present in the instruments used for the collection of data. The 1960s and 1970s have seen an increase in comparative research on values by industrial social psychologists and business Ph.D. candidates, which consists of taking a questionnaire designed and pretested in the United States on students or business managers, sometimes translating it, and administering it in other countries. Popular instruments are the Allport-Vernon-Lindzey Study of Values and G. W. England's Personal Values Questionnaire.[24] In this case the ethnocentrism starts at the data collection: Questions are only about issues raised by the U.S. designers of the instrument which proved relevant to their test population and for which the American language has words.

To avoid ethnocentrism in data collection, instruments for cross-cultural use should be developed cross-culturally. A good example of how an instrument for cross-cultural use can be developed nonethnocentrically is given by Triandis et al.

(1972). The purpose of this study was to map cognitive structures in Greece, India, Japan, and the United States. Twenty concepts were selected from a list of culturally unspecific words developed empirically around the world by Osgood et al. (1975): these included "freedom," "power," "respect," and "wealth." The 20 concepts were translated into the four languages and back-translated by others for a check. Then 100 male students in each country wrote down three "antecedents" and three "consequents" for each word (antecedents: "If you have . . . then you have FREEDOM"; consequents: "If you have FREEDOM then you have . . ."). Thus, 6000 antecedents and 6000 consequents were collected and double-translated into English. The total material was then used to select 30 antecedents and 30 consequents for each of the 20 words, which formed the basis for a series of predetermined choice questionnaires suitable for use in all four countries.

The ethnocentrism still present in this case is in the decision that such research is worthwhile doing—in the project design and its coordination and funding. The very idea of cross-cultural research probably reflects a western universalist value position. This, I am afraid, we have to live with (it applies to anthropology as well). Taft (1976: 327) writes,

> By the very act of engaging in cross-cultural research, the western scholar has automatically imposed his own values into his transaction with his subjects, and if he wishes to go through with the exercise, they must accept the element of ethnocentrism that is inherent in this.

Ethnocentrism is found not only in research design, data collection, and data analysis; it is also present in the divulging of research results. Articles published in foreign languages are completely out of most researchers' conceptual worlds; in this respect multilingual Asians and Europeans are better off than most Americans. In the English language, professional journals usually publish articles following their own implicit research paradigm and style of communication. I have noticed that the comments of American journal reviewers on innocently submitted European manuscripts show a similar embarrassment as the comments of French management students on translated American textbooks.

The primitive ethnocentrism of many cross-cultural studies of organizational behavior has been, I believe, one of the main reasons for the lack of advance of the art. We cannot avoid ethnocentrism completely, but we can do a lot better than we do now. Data-collection methods can be culturally decentered; even ethnocentrically collected older data can be analyzed anew without ethnocentric or reverse ecological fallacies. Research teams can be expanded with bi- or multicultural researchers—that is, people who were brought up, lived, and/or worked in more than one cultural environment. I believe the latter is more fruitful than composing teams of monocultural researchers from different cultures who get stuck in misunderstandings or passively submit to the chief researcher and his or her paradigms.

The Need for a Multidisciplinary Approach

Cross-cultural studies presuppose a systems approach, by which I mean that any element of the total system called "culture" should be eligible for analysis, regardless of the discipline that usually deals with such elements. At the level of (national) cultures, these are phenomena on all levels: Individuals, groups, organizations, or society as a whole may be relevant. There is no excuse for overlooking any vital factor because it is usually treated in someone else's department at the university.

The literature shows, unfortunately, a fair amount of disciplinary parochialism. Inspection of citations in journal articles shows that references to the literature of other disciplines are rare. Highly relevant studies belonging to neighboring disciplines are often ignored. This situation is perpetuated by the promotion system in academic establishments which seldom rewards a free crossing of disciplinary boundaries, and by the review criteria of many journals. However, a number of multidisciplinary bibliographies of comparative multisociety studies have appeared which can lead the student into unfamiliar but relevant disciplines. Four of these bibliographies covering the English language area and the period since 1950 each list about 100 entries per year.[25]

In this book I shall refer to cross-cultural or cross-national studies from the disciplines of psychology (and, in particular, cross-cultural psychology), sociology (particularly organization sociology), anthropology, political science, economics, geography, history, comparative law, comparative medicine, and international market research. I also refer to many stúdies which can be classified under the label "comparative management"; this is an object-oriented field of research and teaching, rather than a discipline, borrowing from comparative organization psychology, comparative organization sociology, and microeconomics. The quality of "comparative management" studies varies widely; the field has quickly become very popular and attracted many amateurs. This in itself is not bad at all, but these amateurs have not always realized the specific problems which this type of research poses, and recognized standards for good research were missing. Early studies in the field were based on travel impressions and interviews by U.S. business school professors.[26] Other authors used personal insight obtained as practitioners in different countries or multicultural settings.[27] Later, questionnaire surveys of individual managers across a number of countries became popular, starting with Haire et al.'s (1966) survey of managerial thinking in 14 countries, to which I referred earlier. Still later, studies were published based on interviews with managers in their organizational context, which called for a considerably more sophisticated research design.[28] Several review articles and readers cover more or less the entire "comparative management" area.[29]

Language and Translation

Language is both the vehicle of most of cross-cultural research and part of its object. Culture, as I use the word in this book, includes language.[30] Language is the most clearly recognizable part of culture and the part that has lent itself most readily to systematic study and theory-building. Language is very evidently a learned characteristic (not an inherited one), and people are able to learn additional languages beyond their first. It seems that the second language is most difficult to master; once people have learned to switch their minds between two languages they absorb more easily additional ones. Some people demonstrate that the human mind can master up to 10 or more languages more or less fluently.

Language is not a neutral vehicle. Our thinking is affected by the categories and words available in our language. This has been recognized at least since Von Humboldt (mid-nineteenth-century Germany); Sapir and Whorf in the United States in the 1920s and 1930s stated in various ways what has become known at the "Whorfian hypothesis." One of its formulations is that "observers are not led by the same picture of the universe, unless their linguistic backgrounds are similar or can in some way be calibrated" (Fishman, 1974: 65). Differences in categories for thinking about the universe can be found in many fields and are larger for languages that are structurally further apart. Some examples are the way in which the color spectrum is divided (several languages have no separate words for "blue" and "green"); the way various aspects of "time" are distinguished (with consequences for behavior); and the way relatives are classified.[31] Translators of American literature have noticed that French and many other modern languages have no adequate equivalent for the English "achievement"; Japanese has no equivalent for "decision-making." Modern linguists struggle with the issue of what, if any, are common basic categories of thought across all languages.

If equivalents of a concept in another language are missing, often we can still transfer the desired meaning by circumlocution. People whose language does not distinguish "blue" and "green" are able to discern the two shades, but need additional words to describe this difference (Hoijer, 1962: 263–264). "Languages differ not so much as to what *can* be said in them, but rather as to what is *relatively easily* said in them" (C. F. Hockett, quoted in Fishman, 1974: 81). Modern languages borrow extensively from each other to avoid the need for circumlocution for useful terms for which the own language has no equivalent. Words are borrowed for concrete objects ("sauna" from Finnish, "computer" from English) but also for concepts with a flavor related to the cultural context of their country of origin: "laissez-faire" and "savoir-vivre" from French; "verboten" and "Weltanschauung" from German; "business" and "manager" from English.

The problems with the use of language in research about culture start before the actual translation of questions. The researchers and their informants may hold different normative expectations about the use of language.[32] In some cultures and subcultures, being polite to the other person is more important than supplying objectively correct information; in some, respondents will never use "no." In a comparative experiment in Iran and England, it was shown that in Iran, 20 percent of people in the street pointed a foreigner the way to a place even if that place did not exist; in England this never happened (Collett and O'Shea, 1976: 453).

In few cross-cultural studies can we escape the need for translating research instruments, like questionnaires, and back-translating non-precoded responses and analytic conclusions. This translation is rarely simple, and the less so, the wider apart the structures of the two languages. Where exact equivalents do not exist a "contextual transposition" (Gasse, 1973) must be found; apparent equivalents sometimes do not express the meaning intended by the researcher. From an extensive experiment with translations from English into 10 Pacific and Asian languages and back, Brislin (1970) draws the not surprising conclusion that the crucial factor is the quality of the translators, who should be familiar not only with both languages but with the context of the material to be translated as well.[33]

Translators are obviously bilinguals, if not multilinguals. Most bilinguals still have one dominant or preferred language, in which they express themselves more easily; this depends, among other things, on the order in which the languages were learned (Anderson, 1967: 135– 136). If at all possible, translators should be chosen such that they translate *into* their preferred language, as it takes greater familiarity with a language to *express* nuances of meaning than to *understand* them. As soon as we have a preferred language, however, we are culturally not neutral: the translator is the first exponent of the foreign culture we meet in the research process, and the impact of culture on our findings starts in his or her mind. In the translation of questions about values for the project this book is about, I have noticed, for the languages which I can read, at least two cases in which translators left out some words of the English original in their translation because they considered them redundant. Subsequent research results showed in both cases through the answers to other questions that the values associated with the omitted words were particularly opposed in the translators' countries. In other words, translators filtered meanings according to their countries' dominant value systems.

The recommended remedy against nonequivalence in translation is back-translation by a second bilingual, comparing the back-translated text with the original and resolving differences by discussion. This is certainly a wise safeguard against translation errors, but it is costly and time-consuming and does not detract from the fact that the quality of the translation still depends on the insight and skill of the translators. I prefer a one-shot translation by a gifted translator familiar with the content matter of the document over the result of a back-translation exercise using two or more mediocre bilinguals. A translation may have passed a back-translation filter and still look clumsy in the other language (as questionnaire designers are not necessarily selected on their stylistic abilities, even untranslated questionnaires look clumsy at times).

Some research has been done on the equivalence of different language versions of the same questionnaire using bilingual respondents as a test population. For two instruments, the Job Descriptive Index and the Index of Organizational Reactions, Katerberg et al. (1977) collected scores from 128 U.S. residents of Puerto Rican and Cuban origin on both an English and a Spanish version. Differences in scores between the two language versions were small and for practical purposes negligible. Bennett (1977a) administered a questionnaire based on eight organizational variables identified by Likert (1967) to 51 Filipino managers both in English and in Tagalog and to 71 Chinese managers in Hong Kong both in English and in Chinese. Scores on some questions were equivalent between the pairs of languages, but scores on other questions differed significantly depending on the language used. In particular, this was the case for questions on communication and interaction processes, for which native language scores were more positive than English scores. Bennett concludes that the language evokes a reference group and that because these people communicate and interact more easily with others speaking their native language than with superiors speaking only English, they give more favorable responses about·these issues in their own languages. The contradictory results of the studies by Katerberg et al. and by Bennett can be attributed to at least three factors: (a) the difference in questionnaire content; (b) the fact that Katerberg's subjects lived in an English-speaking environment, had to use English all day, and were probably more intimately familiar with it than Bennett's subjects, who lived in their native countries; and (c) possibly the quality of the translations.

For the practice of cross-cultural research, the previous paragraphs imply that translation is a source of error. The error can be reduced by a careful selection of translators and by the use of a back-translation procedure, although the latter is no guarantee of a perfect translation. I might add that it helps considerably if the researcher is multilingual. For a deeper understanding of a foreign culture and for the avoidance of ethnocentric blunders, some familiarity with the language is indispensable. Anthropologists would hardly dare to study a tribe without some mastery of its language. Something can also be done in the composition of the questionnaire. Questions destined for translation should be plain, free from home-country local color—almost unimaginative. The questionnaire should contain a certain amount of redundancy, so that key issues are approached from several angles and a weak translation of one question does not spoil all information on the issue.

Questionnaire translations can be tested in ways other than back-translations. A careful check by a panel of bilingual readers familiar with the content matter is less time-consuming and may be as effective. More time-consuming but revealing is a separate correlation and/or factor analysis of pretest (or even of final) data for each language version and a comparison of the patterns of correlations found. Convergencies and divergencies between factor structures not only show where meanings have been similar or different but often suggest what other meanings were attributed. However, samples of respondents in the different languages should be matched on other criteria (occupation, age, sex) because these, too, affect the meanings of answers (Hofstede et al., 1976: 21ff).

Finally, translation errors are randomized if we are able to increase the number of languages used. One bad translation may invalidate a two-country study but it is unlikely that systematic translation errors affect the conclusions of a 40-country, 18-language study like the one described in this book. Language, in this case, becomes a variable in the analysis and not just a source of bias.

Matching Samples: Functional Equivalence

Anthropologists have studied nonliterate cultures on the basis of small samples of informants studied in great depth. In this case,

> the validity of the sample depends not so much on the number of cases as upon the proper specification of the informant, so that he or she can be accurately placed, in terms of a very large number of variables: age, sex, order of birth, family background, life-experience, temperamental tendencies (such as optimism, habit of exaggeration, etc.), political and religious position, exact situation relationship to the investigator, configurational relationship to every other informant, and so forth. Within this very extensive degree of specification, each informant is studied as a perfect example, an organic representation of his complete cultural experience [Mead, 1962b: 408–409].

From such in-depth sample studies, anthropologists draw conclusions on the culture as a whole, including its "modal personality" or "national character."[34] Comparisons between cultures by anthropologists are based on comparisons of aspects of these inferred wholes.

Modern nations are too complex and subculturally heterogeneous for their national characters or modal personalities to be determined in this way. The study of the "national characters" of modern nations therefore has not developed very much beyond the speculative, impressionistic stage; we could even wonder whether modern nations possess national characters. The present book shows that modern nations do have dominant national character traits which can be revealed by survey studies and by the comparison of measurable data on the society level. The mental programs of members of the same nation tend to contain a common component.

Other components of the mental programs of people are subcultural; that is, shared only by others of the same educational level, socioeconomic status, occupation, sex, or age group. Of course, some countries are more culturally homogeneous than others: Students of culture should be aware of linguistic, regional, verbal, ethnic, religious, or caste cleavages within nations which can make data nonrepresentative for the whole of the nation. But apart from such specific cleavages, when we compare cultural aspects of modern nations, we should try to match for subculture. It is obviously not very meaningful to compare Spanish nurses with Swedish policemen.

Depending on the nature of the characteristics we want to compare, we can compose matched samples of individuals, situations (like Noesjirwan's doctors' waiting rooms quoted earlier), institutions (like families) or organizations. A good example of the latter is Tannenbaum et al.'s (1974) study of hierarchy in 10 industrial companies, matched for size and product, in each of five countries. One strategy of matching is to make the samples very broad, so that subcultural differences are randomized out. We find this in comparisons of the results of public opinion polls using representative samples of national populations. The opposite strategy is to make the samples very narrow, so that we draw from similar subcultures but in different countries. We can compare Spanish nurses with Swedish nurses, or Spanish policemen with Swedish policemen. In the case of such narrow samples, we have to be careful about generalizing to the nation as a whole: Are police departments and hospitals functionally equivalent in both nations? That is, do they fulfill the same function in society?[35] A more solid research strategy, if we have to use narrow samples, is to take several from different parts of society. With a fourfold sample of Spanish and Swedish nurses and Spanish and Swedish policemen we can test not only the nationality effect but also the occupation effect (nurses versus policemen) and the possible interaction between the two which can give clues as to functional equivalence. The quality of the matching of narrow samples often can only be proved ex post facto: If the differences we find between cultures in one sample set, are confirmed by those found by others in other matched samples, our matching was adequate.

The practical problems involved in getting access to matched samples in different cultures can be enormous, and researchers have to accept compromises in order to obtain data at all. However, the problems of both matching and access are reduced when we can use as a setting for the research organizations which are by their very nature multisocietal; the number of such organizations is increasing in the modern world. Possibilities are available in international professional associations (an example is Rubenowitz, 1968), international schools and training centers (Hofstede, 1976a), national organizations employing personnel from different nationalities (Hofstede and Kranenburg, 1974) or, as in the present book, multinational business corporations. Some people welcome and some deplore the growth of multinational business; but this growth is a fact, and for the student of differences in national cultures these new organizations represent a unique and until now insufficiently exploited setting for research. The fact that these organizations have similarly structured subsidiaries in many countries provided matched settings in which many factors are equal except the nationality of the actors. A common objection against studying subsidiaries of multinational corporations is that these are atypical for their country. This is true; they are just as atypical as samples of policemen or samples of nurses. Studying subsidiaries of multinational corporations represents a *narrow-sample strategy,* but with the advantage that the functional equivalence of the samples is clear. That these samples are atypical does not matter as long as they are atypical in the same way from one country to another. Multinational corporations have subcultures of their own; to the extent that these subcultures reduce the variability in the data from one country to another, the remaining variability will be a conservative estimate of the true variability among countries, which only speaks in favor of this setting for cross-cultural research.

Modal and Marginal Phenomena

In order to learn about differences among societies we need not necessarily study what is modal in each society; we can also learn from a comparison of marginal phenomena. Focusing on what is modal has been the concern of social psychologists and sociologists. Anthropologists are more naturally attracted to what is marginal or unique. In recent years, anthropologists have reduced their predilection for nonliterate societies and increasingly included modern industrial society in their field of research.[36] Bovenkerk and Brunt (1976) claim that the special vocation of the anthropologist in modern society is to highlight society's marginal phenomena. Some of these can characterize a society more clearly than modal phenomena. Ever since Durkheim (1937 [1895]), suicide percentages have been used to draw conclusions about societies as a whole, even though only a marginal fraction of people actually took their own lives.

There is a good statistical reason why extreme phenomena differentiate more between cultures than modal ones; this is pictured schematically in Figure 1.5. Let us assume a characteristic x (of individuals, institutions, or organizations) which is normally distributed across the nation, but with a cultural difference between society A and society B, so that the two normal distributions do not quite overlap. The shift in Figure 1.5 is chosen of the size σ or equal to the within-country standard deviations. Such a characteristic at the individual level could be "aggressiveness." The percentage of individuals with an aggressiveness level beyond the common average p in this case would be 30.9 in society A and 69.1 in society B, a ratio between the two societies of 2.2. However, the percentage with an aggressiveness level beyond an extreme value q, representing a distance of 2σ from the mode of B and 3σ from the mode of A, would occur in .14 percent of individuals in society A but in 2.27 percent in society B, a ratio between the two societies of 16.8, or eight times as large as the ratio of those beyond level p. Now if an aggressiveness level beyond q is likely to lead to individually committed criminal offenses, such offenses are 16.8 times as likely to occur in society B. For collective phenomena, the difference becomes even larger. Suppose that a criminal gang is likely to be created where two persons with an

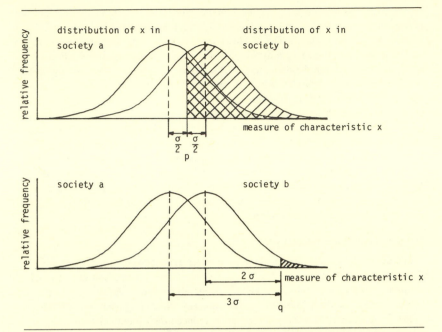

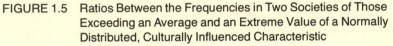

FIGURE 1.5   Ratios Between the Frequencies in Two Societies of Those
Exceeding an Average and an Extreme Value of a Normally
Distributed, Culturally Influenced Characteristic

aggressiveness level beyond q meet. This is $16.8^2 = 282$ times as likely to occur in society B as in society A.

The example is, of course, grossly oversimplified, but it shows how small modal differences between societies can become manifest in large differences in marginal phenomena. The study of the marginal and unique in society is justified by more than curiosity alone.

The Specific and the General

The comparison of cultures presupposes that there is something to be compared; that each culture is not so unique that any parallel with another culture is meaningless. Throughout the history of the study of culture there has been a dispute between those stressing the unique aspects and those stressing the comparable aspects. The first hold that "you cannot compare apples and oranges," while the second argue that apples and oranges are both fruits and can be compared on a multitude of aspects, such as weight, color, nutritive value, or durability. The selection of these aspects obviously necessitates an a priori theory about what is important in fruits.

The distinction between the unique and the comparable, the specific and the general, was made by Windelband in late-nineteenth-century Germany when he defined "idiographic" versus "nomothetic" styles of scientific inquiry. The idiographic style was mainly found in "historical" disciplines looking for wholes or *"Gestalten"*, unique configurations of events, conditions, or developments; the nomothetic style mainly in natural sciences looking for general laws or *"Gesetze"* (Lammers, 1976: 31). In their subsequent development, the social sciences have moved between both styles. In the 1960s, anthropologist Goldschmidt labeled the choice between the two styles the "Malinovskian dilemma" (Berry, 1969: 120; Lammers, 1976: 28) after Bronislav Malinovski, who introduced functionalism in anthropology in the 1920s. Functionalism stresses the purposive nature of institutions in society; but the purpose is derived from the particular culture of that society, which is a unique whole. Therefore, institutions can only be understood in terms of their own culture; functional equivalence with institutions in other societies cannot be proven; and, according to Malinovski, "cross-cultural comparison of institutions is essentially a false enterprise, for we are comparing incomparables." Similar points of view, stressing the need for understanding of social systems from the inside and through the definitions of their members, have been labeled by others "ethnoscience" and "ethnomethodology." While few scholars take the extreme position attributed to Malinowski, there is a wide range of points of view as to the importance of understanding-from-within versus measuring-from-without.

While the terms "idiographic" and "nomothetic" are probably better known among sociologists, cross-cultural psychologists have adopted another set of terms from anthropology which, however, covers more or less the same distinction: "emic" versus "etic." These terms were introduced into anthropology in the 1960s by the linguist K. L. Pike. In linguistics, a distinction is made between phonemic and phonetic classification. The phonetic classification is universal and allows characterizing any sound in any language. In a particular language, only certain sound units are actually used; these are called phonemes, and in combination with other phonemes they are the carriers of meaning (Bright, 1968: 19). Thus, the phonemic is the specific; the phonetic, the general. The suffixes -emic and -etic have been promoted to independent terms in anthropology for distinguishing the study of unique and specific wholes from the application of general, polycultural classification schemes.

The fact of engaging in a comparative study of culture at all presupposes at least an etic point of departure. Berry (1969: 125) suggests an approach which tries to combine a concern for the general with a concern for the specific, and which can be applied where functional equivalence of behaviors in two cultures can be demonstrated (or, I would add, reasonably assumed): (a) Existing descriptive categories and concepts are applied tentatively, as an imposed etic; (b) These are then modified so that they represent an adequate emic description from within each system; (c) Shared categories can then be used to build up new categories valid for both systems as a derived etic, and can be expanded if desired until they constitute a universal. This derived etic or universal is then used as the basis for new measurement instruments and techniques.[37]

Lammers (1977: 10) makes another distinction related to the idiographic-emic versus nomothetic-etic dilemma. In the (nomothetic-etic) search for general classification schemes, some search for "lawlike theories" whereas others search for "configurations." The first approach aims at determining variables which relate to other variables in a certain lawlike way; the second approach aims at establishing ideal types which are wholes in themselves and which the cases studied can be shown to resemble. "Pure" nomothetes will follow the variables approach, whereas those with an inclination toward the idiographic side will find the type approach more useful.

One's position or flexibility in the specific versus general spectrum will strongly affect one's choice of data treatment. The pure idiographer will probably shy away from quantitative data and the use of statistics. Those collecting comparative data that lend themselves to statistical analysis will be attracted to different statistical methods according to their degree of nomotheticity. A greater idiographic concern will express itself in a focus on relation betweeen variables *within* cultures, followed by a comparison of the patterns found from one culture to another; this can be used for a type approach. Looking at the variances and covariances of variables *between* cultures is a step more toward the nomothetic side: It presupposes data on a greater number of cultures and means a study of ecological correlations as described earlier in this chapter.[38] Matrices of ecological correlations between variables can be used again for a type approach through some form a Q-factor or cluster analysis which shows which cultures have similar ecological correlations. Probably the most nomothetic data treatment is using matrices of ecological correlations for a factor analysis or similar multivariate technique subsuming the original variables into dimensions which can enter laws of the greatest generality, but which are at the same time least sensitive to the uniqueness of each culture. This is the approach this book will be using.

DIMENSIONS OF CULTURE

The Search for Dimensions of Culture
as One Research Strategy

In the process of comparing phenomena, similarity and differences are two sides of the same coin; one presupposes the other. Nevertheless, research designs usually favor either the search for similarities or the search for differences. Lammers and Hickson (1979) signal a bias either way in comparative studies of organizations. Some studies want to show that different organizations are in reality "brothers under the skin"; other studies want to show that superficially similar organizations are really "birds of a *different* feather." The predilection for one or the other is ideologically related to the previously described choice between the general and the specific: who looks for brothers under the skin looks for the general; who is convinced of specificity finds birds of a different feather.

The distinction between a focus on similarities and a focus on differences can be fruitfully combined with the distinction between levels of analysis as we met it earlier in this chapter into a fourfold classification of research strategies. Although this classification can be extended to other types of comparative studies as well, I will apply it only to the comparison of phenomena in different societies. These phenomena can be behaviors of individuals or situations, institutions, or organizations. The classification is drawn in Figure 1.6.

In Cells 1 and 2 of Figure 1.6 we find those studies which focus on either similarities or differences among societies but which are concerned with micro-level variables and their relationships, measured *within* societies. In Cell 1 we find studies with a nomothetic-etic orientation, which try to prove the universality of micro-level laws. Examples are the study of managerial thinking in 14 countries by Haire et al. (1966) and extension to other countries of the "Aston" studies about the relationship

FIGURE 1.6   Four Available Research Strategies for Comparative
                       Multisociety Studies

concerned with micro-level variables within societies culture as black box	1) prove universality of micro-level laws	2) illustrate uniqueness of each society
concerned with ecological variables between societies culture specified	3) determine types or subsets of societies	4) determine dimensions of societies and macro-level laws
	focus on similarities between societies	focus on differences between societies

between organization structure and context which try to confirm the "culture-free thesis" (Hickson et al., 1974). In Cell 2 we find studies with a more idiographic-emic orientation which, through showing differences among societies, illustrate the uniqueness of each. This includes field studies by anthropologists which are only implicitly comparative but also explicitly comparative studies, such as the extensive work of Osgood et al. (1975) in showing the different affective meanings of words for individuals in different cultures, and studies of organizations in the "Aston" tradition aiming at refuting the "culture-free" thesis (Child and Kieser, 1979).

Studies in Cells 1 and 2 go across cultures, but without necessarily specifying what "culture" stands for. Culture is often treated in these studies as a "black box" which we know is there but not what it contains. In Cell 1, we hope it can be proven to make no difference, and then it does not matter what is in the black box; in Cell 2, we hope it does matter, but we argue that our black box is a Pandora's box containing so much that it is impossible to be more specific. In Cells 1 and 2 we deal with societies as names, not as variables; and as "names" they are "residua of variables that influence the phenomenon being explained but have not yet been considered" (Przeworski and Teune, 1970: 29)—or, I would add, are too complex to be considered.

In Cells 3 and 4 we find studies which focus on either similarities or differences among societies on the basis of ecological variables and their relationships—that is, variables measured at the level of societies. In Cell 3 we find studies that use ecological variables to determine types or subsets of cultures that are similar among themselves but differ from other types or subsets. For example, Adelman and Morris (1967) used factor analysis of a matrix of 41 ecological variables for 74 developing nations, but they created subsets of nations of lowest, intermediate, and high development level. Russett (1968) used data from the World Handbook of Political and Social Indicators, the first edition of which he edited, to cluster countries through a Q-analysis. He arrived at an Afro-Asian, Western, Latin American, and Eastern European cluster. In Cell 4, finally, we find studies concerned with determining dimensions of societies and laws at the level of societal variables, identifying the variables that can replace the names of societies in our analysis.[39]

Przeworski and Teune (1970: 31ff), writing from a political science background, are mainly concerned with the distinction between Cell 1 and Cell 4 studies. They normatively suggest for Cell 1 studies a "most different systems design": If we want to prove universality of micro-level laws, it is more meaningful to test them in Sweden, Japan, and Zambia than in Sweden, Denmark, and Norway. For Cell 4 studies they suggest a "most similar systems design": taking societies that are similar in many respects except a few, which enables us to see more clearly what differences those few societal aspects are related to. If we are interested in which societal influences affect suicide rates, it is meaningful to study Denmark, Sweden, and Norway, which are similar in many respects but of which the latter has a strikingly lower suicide rate (Rotterstol, 1975).

Cell 1 studies are most vulnerable to ethnocentricity. This is less the case for other cells; Cells 2 and 3 studies are by their nature "polycentric," and Cell 4 studies "geocentric."[40] In order to avoid the inherent danger of ethnocentricity in Cell 1 studies we have to expand our strategy with Cell 2 and Cell 4 methods[41]; focus on differences even if what we want to prove is similarities—that is, be the devil's advocate. Lammers (1976: 37) recommends "loading the dice" as much as possible against the thesis that our relevant propositions are culture-free. Przeworski and Teune's "most different systems design" for Cell 1 is also a way of being the devil's advocate.

The present book deals with dimensions of national culture and therefore represents clearly a Cell 4 approach. The number of societies covered—40—is large enough to include similar as well as different ones and to make a "geocentric" approach possible.

Dimensions of Culture in the Literature: Theory-Based

In an article first published in 1952, anthropologist Clyde Kluckhohn argued that there should be universal categories of culture:

> In principle . . . there is a generalized framework that underlies the more apparent and striking facts of cultural relativity. All cultures constitute so many somewhat distinct answers to essentially the same questions posed by human biology and by the generalities of the human situation. . . . Every society's patterns for living must provide approved and sanctioned ways for dealing with such universal circumstances as the existence of two sexes; the helplessness of infants; the need for satisfaction of the elementary biological requirements such as food, warmth, and sex; the presence of individuals of different ages and of differing physical and other capacities [Kluckhohn, 1962: 317–318].

The kind of framework meant by Kluckhohn must consist of empirically verifiable, more or less independent dimensions on which cultures can be meaningfully ordered. Hall (1965: 45–46) has described 10 "Primary Message Systems" which occur in each culture and which expand on Kluckhohn's list of universal circumstances with which every society has to cope: interaction, association (with others), subsistence, bisexuality, territoriality, temporality, learning, play, defense, exploitation (of materials). These are conceptual categories, not dimensions found in the real world, but it is likely that dimensions found empirically will be associated with these issues.

The most common dimension used for ordering societies is their degree of economic evolution or modernity. A one-dimensional ordering of societies from traditional to modern fitted well with the nineteenth- and twentieth-century "evolutionism" and belief in progress; a late offspring of it is the "convergency theory" in comparative management which implies that management philosophy and practice around the world will become more and more alike.[42] Naroll (1970: 1242ff) has reviewed over 150 comparative anthropological studies of primitive societies and, quoting archaeological as well as present-day evidence, identifies a number of characteristics in the ecology and the institutions of societies[43] that evolve together:

—the command of the environment from weak to strong;
—occupational specialization from generalists to specialists;
—organizations from simple to complex;
—population patterns from rural to urban;
—the distribution of goods from wealth-sharing to wealth-hoarding;
—the leadership from consensual to authoritative;
—the behavior of elites from responsible to exploitative; and
—the function of war from vengeance to political.

Driver (1973: 356ff) adds to these characteristics that are tied to the evolution of societies the increases in population density, gross national or tribal product, knowledge, and the number of words in the language (since the advent of writing). Lomax and Berkowitz (1972) have combined data from Murdock's World Ethnographic Sample out of the Human Relations Area Files for 148 cultures with an analysis of song patterns in these cultures ("cantometrics"): They arrive at a taxonomy for the evolution of (primitive) cultures in which the main factor which increases monotonously with evolution is called *differentiation*. Differentiation means control of the environment through an increased complexity of society. Marsh (1967: 329ff) has constructed a single "Index of Differentation" which orders societies from primitive to differentiated and which he has been able to compute for 467 primitive societies (with data from Murdock's World Ethnographic Sample) and for 114 contemporary nations.[44]

There can be little doubt that economic evolution (modernity, differentiation) is an important dimension which is bound to be reflected in the evolution of societal norms, along the lines pictured in Figure 1.4. On the other hand, there is no reason why economic and technological evolution should suppress cultural variety (Maurice, 1976). In fact, we see in the 1970s an increasing tendency among new nations to affirm their unique cultural identity against the inroads made by a western-type modernization. After political independence and a largely unsuccessful struggle for economic independence, the focus is now on cultural independence; the new nations want to be both modern *and* culturally themselves (Poirier, 1978). This means that there exist other dimensions of culture, unrelated to economic evolution (Triandis, 1973: 170; see also Chapter 8).

One multidimensional classification is offered by Parsons and Shils (1951: 77) in their "General Theory of Action." They claim that all human action is determined by five "pattern variables," which they see as choices between pairs of alternatives (the explanations between parentheses are mine):

(1) Affectivity (need gratification) versus Affective neutrality (restrain of impulses);
(2) Self-orientation versus Collectivity-orientation;[45]
(3) Universalism (applying general standards) versus Particularism (taking particular relationships into account);

(4) Ascription (judging others by who they are) versus Achievement (judging them by what they do);

(5) Specificity (limiting relations to others to specific spheres) versus Diffuseness (no prior limitations to nature of relations).

Parsons and Shils claim these choices are present at the individual (personality) level, at the social system (group or organization) level, and at the cultural (normative) level. They do not take into account that different variables could operate at different levels.

Parsons (1951: 182ff) uses his variables 3 and 4 (Universalism-Particularism and Ascription-Achievement) for a fourfold taxonomy of countries in which he places China, Germany, Latin America, and the United States (see also Chapter 7). On the other hand, Parsons (1977: 14) suggests that the evolution of societies replaces particularism by universalism and ascription by achievement. This would mean that evolution would eventually push all societies to join the United States in the universal-ist-achievement corner of his taxonomy! However, Parsons is less outspoken about the relationship between evolution and the other pattern variables, and acknowledges that throughout evolution, cultural systems continue to differ (1977: 235, 237) so there should not be one-way traffic on all five variables.

Another multidimensional classification of cultures is offered by Kluckhohn and Strodtbeck (1961: 12), on the basis of a field study in five geographically close, small communities in the Southwestern United States: Mormons, Spanish Americans, Texans, Navaho Indians, and Zuni Indians. They found that the communities differed on the following value orientations:

(1) an evaluation of human nature (evil-mixed-good);

(2) the relationship of man to the surrounding natural environment (subjugation-harmony-mastery);

(3) the orientation in time (toward past-present-future);

(4) the orientation toward activity (being-being in becoming-doing); and

(5) relationships among people (lineality [that is, hierarchically ordered positions]–collaterality [that is, group relationships]–individualism).

If we take the relationship orientation as an example, they found Texans and Mormons to value individualism over collaterality over lineality, but with greater stress on individualism for the Texans; Spanish Americans stressed individualism over lineality over collaterality; both groups of Indians stressed collaterality over lineality over individualism. The difference between Kluckhohn and Strodbeck's value orientations and Parsons and Shil's pattern variables is that the former formulate their orientations around basic human problems which allow different solutions; these solutions then direct the actions. The latter merely describe the dominant modes of action.

Ackoff and Emery (1972: 131) use another typology which they assume to be valid for the individual level, the group level, and the cultural level. Their two dimensions are: (1) the extent to which a culture (group, individual) is affected by its environment—high ("objectiversion") versus low ("subjectiversion"); and (2) the extent to which a culture (group, individual) affects its environment—high ("ex-ternalization") versus low ("internalization"). They classify a number of countries in the fourfold taxonomy based on these two dimensions, and illustrate their classification with statements about the institutionalization of drinking in those countries. I find their arguments difficult to follow and full of gratuitous assumptions.

Finally, Douglas (1973a, 1978) proposes a two-dimensional ordering of "cosmologies" (ways of looking at the world): (1) "group" or inclusion—the claim of groups over members, and (2) "grid" or classification—the degree to which interaction is subject to rules. Douglas sees these as relating to a wide variety of beliefs and social actions: views of nature, traveling, spatial arrangements, gardening, cookery, medicine, the meaning of time, age, history, sickness, and justice. However, Douglas herself applies the "grid" and "group" dimensions on the level of subcultures of groups and categories of people rather than on the level of national cultures.

The four two- or more-dimensional classifications above represent subjective reflective attempts to order a complex reality. Each of them is, however, strongly colored by the subjective choices of their authors. They show little overlap; and the mixing of levels (individual-group-culture) in some of them is a severe methodological weakness (see, earlier in this chapter the section on "changing the level of analysis"). More helpful than these subjective classifications I find an "intersubjective" approach by Inkeles and Levinson (1969). In an extensive review article about national character and modal personality, these authors have summarized a number of studies. What I have labeled "dimensions" they call "standard analytic issues" (1969: 447). They propose

> to concentrate, for purposes of comparative analysis, on a limited number of psychological issues . . . . that meet at least the following criteria. First, they should be found in adults universally, as a function both of maturational potentials common to man and of sociocultural characteristics common to human societies. Second, the manner in which they are handled should have functional significance for the individual personality as well as for the social system."

Then Inkeles and Levinson distill from the literature three standard analytic issues that meet these criteria:

(1) relation to authority;
(2) conception of self, including the individual's concepts of masculinity and femininity; and
(3) primary dilemmas or conflicts, and ways of dealing with them, including the control of aggression and the expression versus inhibition of affect.

Inkeles and Levinson's three standard analytic issues will be shown to be amazingly similar to the dimensions empirically found in the study this book is about, described in Chapters 3 through 6. "Power Distance" relates to the first, "Individualism" and "Masculinity" to the second, and "Uncertainty Avoidance" to the third standard analytic issue.

Dimensions of Culture in the Literature:
Factor-Analytic

Studies using statistical methods for determining the relationship among quantified variables across a number of cultures have been called "hologeistic."[46] Hologeistic data matrices, showing the values of a number of variables for a number of cultures, are eminently suitable for the statistical determination of underlying dimensions. The most common method used for this purpose is *factor analysis;* more modern methods, which sometimes need fewer assumptions about the characteristics of the data, are cluster analysis, multidimensional scaling, and smallest-space analysis. All of these are methods of data reduction: They replace a number of original variables by a smaller number of new variables (called *factors* in the case of factor analysis) which explain as much of the total variance in the original matrix as possible in as few factors as possible.

Apart from the interpretation of the factors which is subjective, there are three arbitrary decisions the user of factor analysis and similar techniques has to make. The first is which variables and cases to include in the analysis and which to leave out. This is vital; the "garbage in-garbage out" rule applies entirely. If we include strongly intercorrelated trivial variables in our analysis, we will find strong but trivial factors. From a point of view of interpretation, the strength of a factor (its percentage of variance explained) tells nothing about its importance unless we are sure that the variables put in were important and representative of the phenomenon we wanted to study. The other two arbitrary decisions are the choice of the number of factors to be retained and, in the case of the ordinary factor analysis, whether to look for mutually independent factors ("orthogonal rotation") or for mutually correlated factors ("oblique rotation"). Often, users will run an analysis trying several numbers of factors in succession in order to find the one for which factors are most clearly interpretable.[47]

In hologeistic studies, we analyze data at the level of cultures or societies; if we use factor analysis, this is an *ecological* factor analysis. Earlier in this chapter we saw that correlations among variables across individuals usually differ from correlations of the mean scores of the same variables across countries. A factor analysis starts from a correlation matrix; therefore, ecological (country-level) factors are different from individual factors.[48] A particular problem in hologeistic studies is that the number of cases is usually small in relation to the number of variables. There is no objection to using a factor analysis for detecting the principal components (dimensions) in the data even if the number of cases is less than the number of variables (Allerbeck, 1977). However, the number of *factors* can never exceed the number of cases; and the smaller the number of cases, the more the factors found will be affected by the peculiarities of the individual cases.

From the extensive and mostly American literature of studies using factor analysis on ecological data I shall limit myself to studies using modern nations as units of analysis (cases) and that have been published in easily accessible sources. Such studies can be divided into two types: those dealing with variables selected according to a specific theoretical criterion, and what I shall call "catch-all" studies. I shall first discuss the theory-based studies.

Gregg and Banks (1965) are political scientists looking for dimensions of political systems. From data collected by Banks and Textor (1963), they used 68 political and historical variables for 115 nations and found seven factors, of which three together explain 51 percent of the variance in the data. These three factors are "access," opposing countries with multiparty systems to countries with one-party systems; "differentiation," opposing old and westernized to young and ex-colonial nations; and "consensus," opposing stable to unstable régimes.

Adelman and Morris (1967) are economists looking for social, political, and

economic factors that accompany economic development of less-developed countries. They collected data for 12 sociocultural, 12 political and 17 economic indicators for 74 developing nations. They showed selective factor analyses of national
wealth (per capita GNP in 1961) and economic growth (rate of growth of real per
capita GNP from 1950–1951 to 1963–1964) with different combinations of sociocultural, political, and economic indicators; they did this for all countries and for
subsections of their set of countries. Adelman and Morris showed that there are two
clusters of social and political conditions associated with wealth: one is differentiation in society, implying, for example, the decrease of the traditional agricultural
sector (also measured by Marsh's Index described above); the other is the existence
of pluralistic political systems. As we go from very poor to less poor countries, the
latter factor becomes more closely associated with wealth. Economic growth (increase in wealth) is more associated with economic than with social and political
conditions, except for the very poorest countries, where economic growth (or rather,
the lack of it) is associated with both economic and social conditions.

Lynn and Hampson (1975) are British psychologists who elaborated on earlier
work by Lynn (1971) looking for psychological dimensions of national character in
data from 18 modern nations on 12 medical and related indicators, such as the
frequency of chronic psychosis, average calorie intake, suicide rates, and cigarette
consumption. They found two main factors explaining, respectively, 34 and 24
percent of total variance, which they identify as the dimensions of "neuroticism" and
"extraversion" to which (among others) Eysenck (1954: 177) refers. In Chapters 3
and 4 I shall relate one of Gregg and Banks' dimensions and Adelman and Morris'
clusters of social and political conditions to Power Distance and Lynn and Hampson's
Neuroticism to Uncertainty Avoidance.

A number of "catch-all" factor-analytic studies of ecological variables have been
carried out in the United States. By "catch-all" I mean that these studies use all kinds
of variables that happen to be available, without a recognizable theoretical framework guiding their choice. The foundation for this type of analysis was laid by
psychologist Cattell, who had used factor analysis extensively in the development of
self-report tests of personality: Cattell (1949), Cattell et al. (1952), and Cattell and
Gorsuch (1965) are reports on factor-analytic studies of ecological variables (first
72, later 48) for large numbers of nations (first 69, then 40, then again 52). The
variables deal with geographical and demographical aspects and the supposed races
of inhabitants; historical and political aspects; social, legal and religious aspects; and
economical, medical, and "elite" aspects, such as the number of Nobel prizes. Cattell
looked for dimensions among nations of what he labeled "syntality," a parallel
concept to "personality" on the level of individuals. Cattell's factors are difficult to
interpret, however; the only obvious element which some of them reflect is economic
development. This difficulty is due to the unsystematic selection of variables of great
diversity and to the large number of factors which Cattell retained: not less than 12. If
he had been prepared to limit himself to fewer factors, he might have eliminated more
"noise" from his data. After Cattell, Russett (1968) factor-analyzed 54 variables for
82 countries. He found five factors: economic development (by far the strongest
factor), communism, size, catholic culture, and intensive agriculture.

The most ambitious continuation of Cattell's approach is the Dimensionality of

Nations (DON) project which started in 1962 at Northwestern University in Evanston, Illinois, and after various migrations settled at the University of Hawaii. A history of the project until 1972 has been published by Hilton (1973).

The two chief researchers whose names have been related successively to the project are J. Sawyer and R. J. Rummel. Sawyer and Levine (1966) published a factor-analytic study of data from primitive societies taken from Murdock's World Ethnographic Sample from the Human Relations Area Files (Murdock, 1949), with 30 variables and 565 societies. They found nine factors dealing mainly with means of existence (agriculture, animal husbandry, fishing) and family structure (nuclear family household, patrilineality, matrilineality). Sawyer (1967) subsequently published factor analysis results for a matrix of 236 variables for 82 modern nations (not entirely the same set of nations as used by Russett). Sawyer found that 40 percent of the total variance in his immense matrix could be explained by three factors: economic development, size, and political orientation. Rummel (1972: 217ff) has published four additional factors obtained from the same analysis: catholic culture, population density, foreign conflict behavior and domestic conflict behavior.

The factors found by Russett, Sawyer, and Rummel are certainly easier to interpret than those of Cattell, but the unavoidable question is: So what? That a country's level of economic development, its size, and its political allegiance are meaningful criteria which affect many other aspects of life in that country are conclusions so trivial that we hardly need a factor analysis to find them. The lack of a priori theory which has guided the selection of input variables has condemned the output to triviality. These studies have provided little insight into *why* some countries are more developed than others or *why* some have chosen communism and others have not.[49]

NOTES

1. In mathematical notation, our predictions can be expressed (following Kurt Lewin) by

$$B = f (P,S),$$

in which   B = predicted behavior,
          P = a contribution of the person,
          S = a contribution of the situation or environment,
and   f = some probabilistic interactive function, most likely not
          specifiable in more exact mathematical terms.

The function f is probabilistic because our prediction is not perfect and interactive because the relationship between B and P may be a different one for any new situation Si. If we know how Peter behaves when he meets Mary, how John behaves when he meets Mary, and how Peter behaves when he meets Mary's father, we still can not predict how John will react to Mary's father.

2. The formula in note 1 is in fact an expression of a double contingency of behavior, both on the person and on the situation. "Contingency" implies dependence on both known factors and uncertainty, side by side (Luhmann, 1976a: 97). Without our assumption of stable mental programming, we would face intolerable uncertainty; our assumption reduces uncertainty, but does not eliminate it.

3. This analogy is borrowed from Kluckhohn (1951b: 405).

4. Those with vested interest in societal inequality are fond of theories trying to prove that collective differences in behavior are due to heredity. The German Nazis had their race theories. In the United States many people continue to believe that Negroes are genetically less intelligent

than whites. Not so long ago this became the issue of a hot ideological debate among U.S. academicians; one professor defended the genetic inferiority of Negroes' intelligence (Jensen, 1969), against which the American Anthropologist Association took a public stand (for critiques of Jensen see the articles following Jensen, 1969, and also Brace and Livingstone, 1974). In Great Britain the heredity-versus-environment issue led to the disgrace of a once glorified psychologist suspected of having manipulated his data in favor of heredity (Sir Cyril Burt: see Wilmott, 1977). The opposite extreme has been found in the Soviet Union, where the dominant ideology involves the playing down of heredity in favor of environmental factors, which led to the now refuted biological theories of Lysenko.

5. It is likely that the development of values and culture in children goes along with the development of intelligence and personality traits. Intelligence-versus-age curves usually show a very rapid development of intelligence in the early years from two to about seven, with a slowing down after age nine (Bloom, 1964: 64). For personality development, adequate measures are harder to get at, but such characteristics as intellectual interest, dependency and aggression seem to a considerable extent to be developed before age five (1964: 177).

6. A similar but more detailed taxonomy is found in Galtung (1967: 110).

7. This term derives from nuclear physics and refers to Heisenberg's "principle of indeterminacy": one cannot observe a particle without disturbing it.

8. See also Triandis (1977: Chap. 7).

9. For a general review of cultural influences on the relationship of attitudes to behavior see Schuman and Johnson (1976: 201).

10. This is an application of the epistemological principle of parsimony, also known as "Ockham's razor" after William of Ockham (1300–1350).

11. Bem calls the first type of values (nonconsciously taken for granted) *zero-order beliefs,* and the second type (direct derivations) *first-order beliefs.*

12. In some theories of leadership (Fiedler, 1967; Mulder et al., 1971) the relative criticalness of the situation is therefore a key determining variable.

13. Dale (1974) and Dale and Spencer (1977) have further disentangled the definitions of norms. They show that the statistical norm of a "sentiment" such as a value may be different from the perception of this norm by the majority: there is such a thing as pluralistic ignorance.

14. A summary of the variety of approaches followed in these questionnaires, followed by a selection of 12 different instruments, has been composed by Levitin and published in Robinson and Shaver (1973: 489ff). Seven instruments dealing with "occupational values" are separately described in Robinson et al. (1969: 223ff).

15. The detailed results of the comparisons have been published in four working papers (Hofstede, 1972a, 1974a, 1974b, 1974c). See also Hofstede (1976a) and Chapter 2.

16. Basically benevolent critiques against which Eysenck has presented no effective defense are found in Rokeach and Hanley (1956), Eysenck (1956a), Hanley and Rokeach (1956), and in Christie (1956a), Eysenck (1956b), and Christie (1956b).

17. For a critique of an instrument that confuses intensity and direction see a working paper by the author (1974a).

18. The terminology in Figure 1.4 is party taken from Berry (1975). The diagram contains elements from the cybernetic hierarchy of Parsons (1977: 10); the system of societal norms in the center is Parsons' "cultural system." The idea of a central value system which feeds into different types of institutions is also found in Shils (1970); he argues that it is shared by at least the majority of the *elites,* not necessarily of the rest of the population.

19. For a clear exposé of the theory of analysis at different levels see Przeworski and Teune (1970: Chap. 3).

20. This phenomenon exists also on the level of subcultures: an example is given by Rosenberg (1955), who showed that female American students show a strong correlation between low "faith in people" and a desire to get ahead on their own, while for male American students the need to get ahead is so much culturally imposed that it is hardly modified by faith in

people. For still another example see Van Leent (1964: 73).

21. The ecological fallacy was already signaled by Thorndike (1939). Later studies on the subject are Scheuch (1966) and Langbein and Lichtman (1978).

22. A paradigm is a set of concepts used to build a theory. It is not a theory itself, but a basic way of ordering reality which inevitably has to precede any theory formation. The inadequate paradigm signaled is part of a "person-centered preoccupation and causal attribution bias" in U.S. psychological research (Caplan and Nelson, 1973).

23. Another example of ethnocentrism in data analysis is described in Faucheux (1976: 282ff). He makes an alternative analysis of the results of a comparative laboratory study by McClintock and McNeel (1966) in the United States and Belgium. The study used a pay-off game by students and concluded that Belgians were more competitive than Americans. Starting from a different value position, Faucheux uses the same data to show that Americans were more competitive than Belgians. Faucheux is French and identifies with the Belgians; McClintock and McNeel are American. There is no objective analysis in this case, and there may not be in many cases. Tannenbaum et al. (1974: Chap. 7) show how members of a research team from different countries interpret the same findings differently.

24. I myself used L. V. Gordon's Surveys of Personal and Interpersonal Values in this way (see Hofstede, 1976a).

25. For the period 1950–1963 Marsh (1967): over 1100 entries. For 1950–1966 with some earlier studies Rokkan et al. (1969): nearly 1000 entries. For 1962–1971 Roberts (1972): nearly 1000 entries. For 1967–1973 Almasy et al. (1976): nearly 500 entries. A selected bibliography of about 300 entries is found in Przeworski and Teune (1970: 135ff).

26. Harbison and Burgess (1954), Harbison and Myers (1959), Kerr et al. (1960), Granick (1962).

27. Nowotny (1964), Farmer and Richman (1965), Van der Haas (1967).

28. Examples are Negandhi and Prasad's (1971) study of U.S. subsidiaries versus local firms in Argentina, Brazil, India, the Philippines, and Uruguay, and Tannenbaum et al.'s (1974) study of hierarchy in five countries.

29. Some review articles are Nath (1968), Schollhammer (1969), Barrett and Bass (1970), Ajiferuke and Boddewyn (1970a), Roberts (1973), Negandhi (1974), and Kraut (1975b). A bibliography is by Peterson (1969). Readers and textbooks plus readers are by Harbison and Myers (1959), Webber (1969), Boddewyn (1969, 1970), Davis (1971), Graves (1973), and Weinshall (1977).

30. Bright (1968: 18) stresses that anthropologists use "culture" in two senses: either on a higher level of generality, including language, or on a more specific level, excluding verbal communication.

31. For example, in some tribes living in extended families, the same word is used for "mother" and "aunt." The Dutch language has only one word (neef) for "cousin" and "nephew." Swedish has different words for grandparents on the mother's side and on the father's side.

32. See Nagi (1977: 168): "(a) sub-cultures within societies and societies as wholes differentially evaluate the importance of speech skills and differentially value speech performances; (b) there are different norms, both within and across cultures and sub-cultures, about privacy, and its violation; (c) there are norms about proper ways of getting information."

33. A general reader on translation problems was edited by Brislin (1976).

34. Inkeles and Levinson (1969: 428) define "national character" as "relatively enduring personality characteristics and patterns that are modal among the adult members of the society."

35. For a discussion on functional equivalence see Berry (1969: 122).

36. This has led to a certain amount of soul-searching among anthropologists as to what is left in this case as the unique contribution of anthropology as opposed to, for example, sociology (Eisenstadt, 1961, and the comments following it; Banton, 1964; Despres, 1968, and the comments following it).

37. Berry's approach is more or less used by Triandis et al. (1972; see earlier in this chapter). Another example is found in Davidson (1977: 52ff). A critique of the approach is expressed by Jahoda (1977: 57ff).

38. The study of such correlations for primitive ethnic units was already undertaken in the late nineteenth century by Edward B. Tylor in Britain. His publication evoked a reaction by Sir Francis Galton, which became famous as "Galton's problem": How should such correlations be explained? Are they based on functional association of variables rooted in general laws of human society, or more simply on diffusion of patterns from one culture to another (Naroll, 1970: 1229; Driver, 1973: 338ff)?

39. We saw that Lammers and Hickson (1979), dealing with comparative studies on organizations, distinguish "brothers under the skin" and "birds of a different feather" approaches; these correspond mainly to Cells 1 and 2. Lammers (1976: 37ff) calls Cell 1 strategies "cross-cultural" and Cell 4 strategies "inter-cultural." In a review of cross-national methodology in sociology, Elder (1976) distinguishes three types of studies: (a) national uniqueness and cross-national contrasts, corresponding to Cell 2; (b) cross-national subsets and limited cross-national generalization, corresponding to Cell 3; and (c) cross-national comparisons and cross-national generalizations, which include both Cell 1 and Cell 4.

40. These terms were used to describe the structures of multinational enterprises by Perlmutter (1965). See Chapter 9.

41. Kluckhohn (1962: 314) has stated that "biological, psychological and sociosituational universals afford the possibility of comparing cultures in terms which are not ethnocentric, which depart from 'givens', begging no needless questions."

42. See Harbison and Myers (1959: 117); Inkeles (1960); Kerr et al. (1960); Likert (1963); and Webber (1969: 524).

43. A large research project on the modernity of *individuals* was carried out by Inkeles (1966, 1969) in 1962– 1964; about 1000 young men in each of six countries were interviewed: Argentina, Chile, India, Israel, Nigeria, and East Pakistan (later Bangladesh). More or less the same cluster of attitudes and behaviors related to "modernity" was found in all six countries, characterized by openness to new experience, independence of parental and traditional authority, interest in planning ahead, and interest in community affairs and news from the outside world.

44. For the latter, Marsh's Index of Differentiation is computed from the summed T-scores of the percentage of males in nonagricultural occupations, and of the gross energy consumption per capita; data around 1960.

45. In his later work, Parsons has dropped "self-orientation versus collectivity orientation" as a pattern variable; it did not fit into the tight paradigm he developed (Rocher, 1974: 52, 43).

46. From Greek *holos,* whole, and *gè,* earth. The term seems to have been coined by Gonggrijp in the Netherlands in the beginning of our century (Koebben, 1952: 131) but is now proposed anew by Shaefer (1977).

47. "Studying a factor analysis of a set of data with a step-by-step increasing of the number of factors rotated is like focussing a microscope on an object. At first, when the number of factors is small, the picture is blurred and not understandable. Then, gradually, factors start to dissolve themselves into interpretable components. After passing the optimal number of factors, components dissolve themselves still further, but now the interpretable relationships begin to disappear and the picture disintegrates and becomes unclear again" (Hofstede, 1967: 121).

48. Empirical proof of the different structures of within- and between-culture factors is collected in a working paper (Hofstede and Van Hoesel, 1976).

49. Rummel's original interest was in conflict behavior between and within nations (Rummel, 1963); in its later stages, the DON project under his supervision has taken a more theoretically guided turn trying to test models of behavior of one country versus another (Hilton, 1973: 12ff).

Chapter 2

DATA COLLECTION AND TREATMENT

SUMMARY OF THIS CHAPTER

A profile is drawn of the large multinational corporation HERMES. The story is told how HERMES got an international attitude survey program which between 1967 and 1973 produced a data bank with answers to about 117,000 survey questionnaires from 66 countries. Additional data were obtained from a Yugoslav worker-self-managed company which markets and services HERMES products in its country. The questionnaire translation process (in 20 languages) and the problems of administering so large a survey program are described. Part of the standardized questions in the HERMES data bank deal with values rather than with satisfactions and perceptions. In the history of the research project an important role is played by additional data collected by the author at IMEDE Business School in Lausanne between 1971 and 1973, which showed that country differences in values found within HERMES could be reproduced on a completely different international population, and with the English version of the questionnaire only. The chapter describes the statistical treatment of the HERMES data: frequency distributions, correlations, and factor analyses of data across individuals; analysis of variance using country, occupation, sex, and age as criteria; and, finally, ecological correlations and factor analyses. For reasons of stability of data, the latter were limited to 40 countries. The ecological dimensions of Power Distance and Uncertainty Avoidance were found through an eclectic analysis of data, based on theoretical reasoning and correlation analysis. In these two dimensions, work goal importance data had not been used. The processing of these needed an extra step: first, scores had to be standardized across goals in order to eliminate acquiescence. Then they were subject to ecological factor analyses of occupation scores and of country scores; the country analysis led to the identification of the ecological dimensions of Individualism and Masculinity. Finally, an ecological factor analysis of all data combined was used to fit the picture of the four dimensions together.

Subsequently, the country scores on the four dimensions found in HERMES were compared with country scores published by other authors based on data unrelated to HERMES but which showed some conceptual similarity to the HERMES dimensions. These included mean country scores of survey results as well as a variety of data measured at the country level. The similarity between these other data and the HERMES scores were determined by Spearman rank and/or product moment correlations; in some cases, multiple and stepwise regressions were calculated between the other data and all four HERMES dimensions. Seven geographic, demographic, and economic indicators of countries were selected as particularly meaningful in this respect: wealth, economic growth, geographical latitude, population size, population growth, population density, and HERMES organization size.

THE RESEARCH SETTINGS

The HERMES Corporation

The large multinational corporation which I shall call HERMES[1] is based in the United States with subsidiaries in all countries around the world which admit such subsidiaries. It manufactures and sells a range of high-technology products. In the period in which the data were collected, 1967 through 1973, the HERMES Corporation developed its products in seven countries, manufactured in 13 countries, and marketed and serviced in about a hundred countries.

The smaller marketing-plus-service subsidiaries of HERMES and the marketing-plus-service divisions of the larger subsidiaries which also had product development and/or manufacturing were organized along similar lines except for size. If the size of the operations justified it, there were branch offices in a country's main cities and a country head office in (usually) the capital. Branch offices employed managers and supervisors, salespersons, technical experts to advise customers on applications, service technicians to provide maintenance of the products after sales, and administrative staff. Head offices employed managers and supervisors and a professional and administrative headquarters staff.

Country organizations in HERMES employed almost exclusively nationals of the country, except in the first years of the creation of new subsidiaries. This applied all the way through the level of country general managers with few exceptions. Coordination of the subsidiaries of HERMES was not obtained through delegating nationals of the corporation's home country within the subsidiaries, but through a tight system of rules and controls and frequent personal contacts between higher managers in the country subsidiaries and personnel of international headquarters.

International headquarters operations were concentrated regionally at a few points on the globe, and their managerial and professional personnel were recruited from different countries. These persons usually served in headquarters for a restricted number of years, after which they returned to their country of origin. The top management of the corporation was located in the United States and almost entirely American.

Promotion in HERMES was usually from within; managers came from the ranks, rarely from outside. The company hired young people with good qualifications and encouraged them to continue developing themselves. The technical nature of the product made necessary frequent retraining and updating of personnel. Labor turnover varied strongly from country to country and from job to job; it was higher among young college-trained professionals than among most other groups.

The people employed in the company's marketing, service, and product development were essentially from the middle class rather than the working class. A sizable working-class population was found only in the manufacturing plants which represented a different sub-subculture within the company subculture, with more traditional industrial values than the marketing and product development divisions. The latter could be classified as service industries as much as manufacturing industries. The degree of union membership among employees varied according to the industrial relations patterns of the countries but was in general not high. In countries in which a sizable share of employees was represented by unions, the relationship between the company and the unions was usually good.

HERMES had a distinct corporate identity—a company subculture—and it encouraged successfully in its employees a sense of pride. In two cases, a subsidiary of HERMES participated in a countrywide attitude survey together with other companies in that country which made it possible to compare their employees' satisfaction pattern with that within other, mostly local national, companies. In both cases, HERMES people appeared above average in their satisfaction with their job content and earnings, but below average in their satisfaction with their managers. The latter can be attributed to a combination of three factors: (1) relatively young and inexperienced managers due to fast company growth in the 1960s; (2) a generally highly qualified work force which was handling difficult technical problems with a lot of de facto autonomy; and (3) the company's tight system of controls and rules. The relatively inexperienced managers acted as the friction point between employee autonomy and company controls.

All in all, the corporation employed more people in marketing and customer service than in manufacturing. A consequence of this was that about one out of every two HERMES employees had direct fact-to-face or voice-to-voice contact with customers. This contributed to employees' identification with the corporation which they represented. A curious difference in employee attitudes was shown in a special study (Hofstede, 1976c) among employees and managers in the branch offices who regularly faced the customers, and among employees and managers in the country and international head offices who did not. Branch office personnel of all levels were more satisfied with the content of their jobs and with their own personal contribution to the company's success. Country head office personnel were less satisfied in these respects, and international head office personnel least of all. However, a question on the image of the company as such, independent of the employee's contribution to it, showed the opposite result: in this case, people in international headquarters were most positive and those in the branch offices least. It is unlikely that this should be a specific HERMES phenomenon; it may well exist in many large decentralized organizations. It was interpreted as stronger intrinsic job motivation at the periphery of the organization and signs of alienation in the center.

Wherever in this book a comparison *among countries* has to be made, data will be used from HERMES' marketing-plus-service organization only, as this is the sole part of the company that operates in all countries where the company exists. Wherever the purpose is comparison *among occupations,* data will be used from product development, manufacturing plants, and marketing-plus-service organizations, but limited to a few large countries in which all three divisions of the corporation were represented.

The Use of Attitude Surveys in HERMES

A concern of managers with employee morale was a characteristic feature of the HERMES subculture. This could be justified partly by the intensity of HERMES employees' contacts with customers: How could the company maintain good relationships with customers if its people facing these customers were disgruntled? This argument is sound, but yet other organizations that depend as much on customer contact have not shown the same concern with employee morale as HERMES has. The deeper roots of HERMES' concern with employee morale were historical; it grew out of the convictions of HERMES' founder many decades ago and was made one of the pillars of the "HERMES" way of life in which newcomers were automatically socialized.

In this concern with employee morale, employee attitude surveys fitted as something natural. Incidental surveys of parts of the organization within certain countries had been done by consultants since the 1950s. Each of these used its own method and survey questions. As the number of such surveys increased and groups were surveyed a second time, some people in HERMES' personnel departments started to worry about the comparability of results, both over time and across groups. This comparability was easy to obtain as long as studies were carried out by the same researcher, but for comparison across researchers, some mutually agreed-upon standardization of research methods and instruments would be necessary.

Obtaining standardization through mutual agreement between researchers is not an easy task. Researchers tend to see themselves as independent, creative professionals, and the adoption of tools "not invented here" for the sake of standardization does not come naturally to them. Also, when an item has been used within a particular population, there will be a sacrifice in historical information when it is changed in the interest of standardization with other populations. It was only after HERMES had appointed its own personnel research experts at two international headquarters locations and in some of the main countries in which it operated that standardization became feasible. I was the first personnel researcher in HERMES' European headquarters. In 1966–1967 I headed up an international team of six researchers (three internal, three consultants) which prepared the first internationally standardized questionnaire for a simultaneous survey of the corporation's product development personnel in six countries. This first international questionnaire consisted of 180 standardized items which were chosen on the basis of open-ended pilot interviews in the six product development laboratories and of a selection from the questionnaires used in earlier incidental surveys. The questionnaire was issued in five languages and administered in June 1967. In November 1967 a second international survey was organized by a colleague; it covered the company's total personnel in 26 Asian, Latin-American, and Pacific countries, most of which had not been surveyed before and did not have their own researchers. Its questionnaire counted 183 standardized items including many from the previous laboratories survey; it was a condensation of a longer pilot version which was pretested on both a U.S. and a Latin American test population. The November 1967 questionnaire was issued in four language versions: English, Japanese, Portuguese, and Spanish, with small differences between the Spanish versions used in the Caribbean and southern Latin America.

These two pioneer international survey projects were followed by surveys of all European and Middle East marketing and administrative operations in 1968 and 1969 and of all manufacturing plants in 1970. By the end of that year most parts of the organization had been covered once by an international survey: a total of about 60,000 respondents from 53 countries around the world. The number of common question items was gradually reduced to 160, but in some cases supplements for certain countries and certain categories of personnel were added to this. The number of language versions had been increased to 18.

HERMES' home country, the United States, was formally not included in the surveys. The different divisions of HERMES in the United States had survey histories of their own and their own independent survey staffs. Through personal negotiation among researchers, the standardized international questions were administered to samples of personnel from HERMES-U.S.A., so that comparisons with the United States could be made.

The simple statement that so many people were surveyed in so many countries hides a complex process of decision-making, negotiation, and persuasion of a "political" nature. It did not occur that one day a top manager issued a decision that "from now on we shall survey." The initiative was not taken at the top of the organization; it came from two committed psychologists employed in two different international headquarters who at the right time conceived of an idea that fitted the company subculture and were able to mobilize their superiors for it. Country subsidiaries could not be told to participate; top managers in the countries had to be "sold" on the project. Some were known to have a spontaneous interest in applications of social science and they were approached first; some usually went along with projects that seemed to have the approval of their superiors in headquarters and they were approached second; some were expected to be difficult and they were approached last with the strong argument that all the other countries had decided to join. In a few cases this did not work, and the first survey round shows some blank spots for parts of country organizations that could not be surveyed. In the second survey round the idea had become so well accepted that almost everyone agreed to participate.

The international attitude surveys were not sold to HERMES as a research project but as a management tool for organization development. Considerable attention was given to data feedback to managers of different levels and to employees in order to avoid defensive reactions of managers whose departments showed unfavorable results. The reactions of nonmanagerial employees, after some initial suspicion, were invariably positive, although sometimes skeptical as to the likelihood of corrective action by managers. Various studies were devoted to factors that helped and hindered the use of survey data by managers (Sirota, 1970; Klein et al., 1971; Hofstede, 1975a). To go deeper into the potential of attitude surveys as organization development tools is beyond the purpose of this book. A list of practical aspects of the use of attitude surveys, based on the HERMES experience, is reprinted in Figure 2.1.

FIGURE 2.1   Practical Aspects of the Use of Employee Attitude Surveys

ASPECT OF SURVEY	MAIN POINTS AND ALTERNATIVES	REMARKS
purpose———————▶	research	motives and attitudes
	organization development	opinions and perceptions
	voting	majority decision
initiative———————▶	outside organization	mostly for research
	top management	may be seen as audit
	local management	best chances of utilization
	employee representatives	rank-and-file consultation
people surveyed———————▶	managers	easy but limited information
	all employees	always include managers
	sample only	random or non-random
organization of survey———▶	survey coordinator	always somebody inside the company
	planning method	plan everything including feedback and action phase in advance—use PERT or similar technique
	time needed	full time for coordinator—3 months or more
survey design and analysis———▶	outside expert	social science training. May have problems because he does not know company
	inside expert	social science training. Should be seen as independent from company politics
	inside lay analysts	line managers and employees, trained by expert

FIGURE 2.1 Continued

data collection method ➤	unstructured interviews	for survey design and follow-up phases; expensive
	structured interviews	
	unstructured questionnaires	not recommended
	structured questionnaires	for mass collection of data, computer-processable; cheap
feedback of results ➤	breakdown by organizational units	not less than 8, not more than 50 persons per unit
	written feedback to participants	necessary but not sufficient
	discussion with participants by line management	highly desirable if action on survey is expected
action phase ➤	line management responsibility	part of line management objectives
	action task force	useful but no substitute for line management responsibility
	follow-up in-depth research	useful if no excuse for inaction
re-survey ➤	essential if effect of actions taken is to be known	not less than 6 months, not more than 4 years after previous survey
	should ask questions about previous survey	perception of feedback and action on previous survey
cost (everything except ➤ cost of actions)	2–20 $ per participant	depends strongly on method used

With some modifications, taken from Hofstede (1975a: 11).

In 1970 the international surveys had become established in HERMES. Personnel departments of all major parts of the organization had appointed personnel research officers. The new personnel research fraternity met in order to plan the survey approach for the next four years. Some local researchers asked for more autonomy than they had had in the centrally controlled surveys of the first years; they wanted to have both the time and the freedom to try their own approach and work on their own research projects on behalf of the part of the organization for which they were appointed.

A task force of personnel researchers worked out a new approach to international survey projects which would mean a compromise between standardization (in the interest of comparison of results) and flexibility (in the interest of adaptation to locally felt needs). It was agreed that on the basis of the results obtained in the first survey round a core set of 60 question items would be selected which would remain compulsory for all surveys. The figure 60 was estimated as the minimum acceptable based on the number of factors found in factor analyses and on the desire for reliability of measurement by covering key factors by more than one question.

The section of the 60 core items has been described in detail elsewhere (Hofstede et al., 1976). It was made on the basis of an extensive study of the available literature and a number of factor analyses of the results obtained with the first survey rounds. Factor analyses were done separately on three sets of questions: 54 "satisfaction" questions, 50 "management" questions, and 42 "culture" questions; the latter dealing with preferences, values, and beliefs. For each set of questions, a separate within-subculture factor analysis was carried out for each of five very diverse subpopulations: technical experts in France, technical experts in Great Britain, clerks in Great Britain, unskilled manufacturing operators in Great Britain, and unskilled manufacturing operators in Japan.

Among the five subpopulations both similarities and differences in factor structure were found. In about 80 percent of cases, questions showed a first or a significant second loading on a common factor; the remaining 20 percent of cases represented relationships between a question and a factor which were specific to one or two subpopulations only (Hofstede et al., 1976: 10). Based on these factor analyses, a selection was made of the 60 "core" questions which were to be universally used in 1971–1974 and of 66 other questions used previously and recommended for further use on an optional basis.

It should be stressed that the 1970 selection of core and recommended questions was based on a factor analysis *within subcultures* only. A *between*-cultures (ecological) analysis had not been done at that time; first, because the main purpose of the survey operation was organization development—that is, use *within* parts of the organization—which made the within-analysis obvious, and second, I must confess that the difference between within- and between-culture analysis had not occurred to us at that time. If it had, we might have come to a different selection of, in particular, the "culture" survey items.

As it was, a resurvey of the product development laboratories of HERMES took place in 1971 with a transition questionnaire (partly old, partly new), and a resurvey of the marketing and administrative departments using the new questionnaire was spread over 1971, 1972, and 1973. In 1974, HERMES took a new approach to its surveys and considerably shortened the questionnaires used, eliminating at least temporarily the "culture" questions on which this book is based. For the analysis in this book I shall not look at data later than 1973.

The second survey round—which did not include the manufacturing plants—numbered, again, about 60,000 respondents, of whom about 30,000 who had earlier participated in the first survey round; 20,000 had joined the company since the first survey, and 10,000 were in groups and countries which had not been included the first time. The number of countries covered in either or both survey rounds had grown to 66; the number of languages stayed at 18. Figure 2.2 lists the countries and the languages.

In 1971 an opportunity arose to include data from Yugoslavia, a country in which HERMES has no subsidiary. I was asked to act as a consultant to a Yugoslav worker-self-managed import-export organization, which among other things

FIGURE 2.2   The Countries Surveyed with the HERMES Questionnaire
and the Languages Used

Code	Country	Language(s) of survey questionnaire	Code	Country	Language(s) of survey questionnaire
ARG	Argentina	Spanish	(LEB)	Lebanon	Arabic
AUL	Australia	English	(LYA)	Libya	Arabic
AUT	Austria	German	(MAL)	Malaysia	English
(BAH)	Bahamas	English	MEX	Mexico	Spanish
BEL	Belgium	Dutch/	(NAT)	Neth. Antilles	Dutch
		French	NET	Netherlands	Dutch
(BOL)	Bolivia	Spanish	(NIC)	Nicaragua	Spanish
BRA	Brazil	Portuguese	(NIG)	Nigeria	English
CAN	Canada	English	NOR	Norway	Norwegian
CHL	Chile	Spanish	NZL	New Zealand	English
COL	Colombia	Spanish	PAK	Pakistan	English
(COS)	Costa Rica	Spanish	(PAN)	Panama	Spanish
DEN	Denmark	Danish	PER	Peru	Spanish
(DOM)	Dominican Republic	Spanish	PHI	Philippines	English
(EGY)	Egypt	Arabic	POR	Portugal	Portuguese
(EQA)	Equador	Spanish	SAF	South Africa	English
FIN	Finland	Finnish	(SAL)	El Salvador	Spanish
FRA	France	French	SIN	Singapore	English
GBR	Great Britain	English	SPA	Spain	Spanish
GER	Germany (F.R.)	German	SWE	Sweden	Swedish
(GHA)	Ghana	English	SWI	Switzerland	French/
GRE	Greece	Greek			German
(GUA)	Guatemala	Spanish	TAI	Taiwan	English
HOK	Hong Kong	English	THA	Thailand	Thai
(HOD)	Honduras	Spanish	(TRI)	Trinidad	English
(IDO)	Indonesia	English	TUR	Turkey	Turkish
IND	India	English	(URU)	Uruguay	Spanish
IRA	Iran	Farsi	USA	United States	English
IRE	Ireland	English	VEN	Venezuela	Spanish
(IRQ)	Iraq	Arabic	(VIE)	South-Vietnam	English
ISR	Israel	Hebrew	(ZAM)	Zambia	English
ITA	Italy	Italian			
(JAM)	Jamaica	English		Outside	
JAP	Japan	Japanese		HERMES:	
(KEN)	Kenya	English	YUG	Yugoslavia	Serbo-Croatian
(KOR)	South Korea	English			Slovenian
(KUW)	Kuwait	Arabic			

There were small differences among the various Arabic, Dutch, English, French, German,
Portuguese, and Spanish versions due to local idiom.
Countries with codes shown in parentheses were eliminated from the analysis in this book
because of insufficient sample size.

marketed and serviced HERMES products in Yugoslavia. The Yugoslav company
was interested in measuring its employees' attitudes, and we surveyed those employees using largely the same questionnaire as that used in HERMES. It is thus possible
to add the Yugoslav data to our list, although they do not form part of the HERMES

data bank, and the different superstructure of the worker-self-managed Yugoslav company should be taken into account in the comparison.

Questionnaire Translation and Survey Administration

The master versions of the international questionnaires were always formulated in English. It had been noticed early that some words (for example, "achievement") were difficult to translate in many of the other languages; such words were henceforth avoided. In general, the master versions sought plain formulations without culturally loaded idiom.

The translations were made and checked by in-company personnel. It is a definite advantage that in an international organization whose lingua franca is English, capable bi- and multilingual persons are numerous. As the surveys were not meant to be scientific instruments but practical management tools, and as their preparation was subject to a tight business time schedule, back-translation was used only exceptionally. In most cases it was considered sufficient to have a draft translation made by the person who was going to act as the local survey coordinator or by another person selected by him or her for linguistic skills. The translators translated into their native language. The translations were then checked by some of the company's bilingual managers. In some cases, pilot runs of the translated versions were made with small panels of employees who were asked to signal any difficulties or ambiguities they met in answering.

In later stages of the analysis, I have done several back-translation checks on items that produced unexpected results in some countries. In all these cases the translation proved to be right. Comparative correlation and factor analysis between items in various language versions revealed some differences but again translation errors were ruled out as causes. In spite of the unscientific approach to the translation process, I feel reasonably confident about the quality of the translations. Only in two cases were translations recognized as weak and containing definite errors; in both cases they had been made by qualified psychologists who refused assistance in preparing the translations.

The administration of a survey in 67 countries is a heroic adventure which could never have succeeded without the help of the existing corporation infrastructure. After the initial approval of the country general manager had been obtained, the most suitable way of administering the surveys was determined separately for each country and each survey with the assistance of International Headquarters researchers. These issued for each survey a "Survey Administration Manual." In the larger subsidiaries which had their own personnel research person or staff, the latter handled the survey administration completely. In the medium-sized subsidiaries which lacked a personnel research person, a lay survey coordinator was nominated, trained by the International Headquarters researchers, and entrusted with the entire handling of the survey. In the smallest subsidiaries either a traveling regional headquarters person distributed the questionnaires and took the completed questionnaires with him or her, or everything was handled by mail.

The task of the local survey coordinators included advance information to managers and employees; some designed extensive and imaginative internal publicity campaigns in order to prepare employees for the survey. The actual filling out of the questionnaires was done (1) for employees who did not have desks (usually in the cafeteria, in groups); and (2) for employees who had desks (usually at their desks, individually).

The questionnaires were always anonymous and contained a reassurance that no attempt to identify respondents would be made and that they were free not to answer a question if they did not want to. Completed questionnaires were dropped in boxes which were supervised by a person who could be assumed to have the employees' confidence. The contents of the boxes were later bundled and sent to data processing. Employees in remote locations received and sent in questionnaires by mail.

Initially, data processing was done centrally in two places, but afterwards more and more subsidiaries handled their own data processing and sent in copies of their data on card or tape for the international data bank. Data were transferred to punched cards by manual key punching from the questionnaire, or from an answer sheet attached to the questionnaire, or by the use of machine-readable answer sheets. Results were printed out in data books with various degrees of specificity (by division in a country, by country, international) using special-purpose computer programs which allowed comparisons among groups and with previous surveys of the same group. An example of a page of such a data book shown in Figure 2–3.

The analysis of the data for organization development purposes was coordinated by the personnel research staff but entrusted as much as possible to line managers, sometimes assisted by analysis task forces of employee delegates. All employees were usually informed of their country or division results by a written brochure and by one or more group meetings with their colleagues and superiors. Managers were expected to develop strategies for corrective actions which the survey showed to be necessary. The effectiveness of this procedure varied widely.

Even with the help of the existing company infrastructure, the purely administrative aspects of such a survey remain delicate. Working through so many different persons in so many different cultures means a large number of sources of error, misunderstanding, and accidents. Questions were mysteriously missing in some countries, answer categories were inadvertently left out, packages of questionnaires got lost in the mail. Once a box containing the answer sheets of a thousand respondents was stolen from an airplane and never found. Questions were coded on the wrong number, so that, for example, the answers on the preferred type of manager (question A54, see Appendix 1) of country X showed up among the answers on the actually perceived manager (A55) of the other countries. Some groups were found coded on the wrong occupations. In international survey administration, as in any large human undertaking, the Law of Conservation of Misery[2] applies: If anything can go wrong, it will. A painful process of correcting, recoding, and discounting suspect information is necessary to arrive at results that make sense.

The HERMES Survey Data Bank

The computerized survey data bank contains the scores on all questions for all surveys held between November 1967 and 1973. The June 1967 product development survey is not part of the data bank because it had too many different questions. Some data, for example those from the U.S. are not integrated into the data bank, but available separately. With 65 countries (66 including the U.S.) and about 88,000 different respondents on about 117,000 questionnaires, the HERMES data bank represents probably the largest body of survey data ever collected with one instrument up to that time.

FIGURE 2.3 An Example of Information Output for HERMES Survey Feedback

PERSONNEL RESEARCH - PREFER PROGRAM
OPINION SURVEY 1972-73
NON MANAGERS

QUESTION LABEL A5
HOW IMPORTANT IS IT TO YOU TO HAVE CHALLENGING WORK TO DO   1-OF UTMOST IMP 2-VERY IMP 3-MODERATE IMP
                          4-LITTLE IMP 5-VERY LITTLE/NO IMP
ALLOWABLE RESPONSES 1 THROUGH 5   VALID RESPONSES 1 THROUGH 5

CATEGORY		MEAN	STD. DEV.	VALID RESP.	TOTAL RESP.	DISTRIBUTION OF RESPONSES - PER CENT					OTHER
						1	2	3	4	5	
(HEAD QUARTERS)											
BELGIUM	1973	1.92	0.66	415	423	31	50	12	1	0	2
BELGIUM	1969	1.95	0.75	285	297	28	52	19	1	1	4
DENMARK	1973	1.64	0.69	270	270	45	46	9	1	1	0
DENMARK	1969	1.88	0.79	171	174	34	47	16	2	1	2
FINLAND	1973	1.77	0.63	115	115	34	55	11	2	1	0
FINLAND	1969	1.98	0.77	107	110	29	46	23	2	0	3
IRELAND	1973	1.56	0.63	41	42	51	41	7	0	0	2
IRELAND	1969	1.65	0.68	26	28	46	42	12	0	0	7
NETHERLANDS	1973	1.85	0.72	263	258	32	53	13	2	0	2
NETHERLANDS	1969	1.73	0.64	215	218	37	53	9	0	0	2
NORWAY	1973	2.01	0.68	138	142	20	62	17	1	0	1
NORWAY	1969	2.02	0.74	96	99	23	55	19	3	1	3
SWEDEN	1973	1.77	0.66	350	351	34	57	8	1	1	0
SWEDEN	1969	1.61	0.62	343	358	45	51	3	1	0	4
AUSTRIA	1973	1.65	0.65	207	208	44	46	10	1	0	0
AUSTRIA	1969	1.59	0.71	213	213	53	36	10	1	0	0
ITALY	1973	NO VALID DATA FOR THIS UNIT									
ITALY	1969	1.51	0.65	487	493	56	39	4	1	0	1
PORTUGAL	1973	1.51	0.63	55	55	56	36	7	0	0	0
PORTUGAL	1969	1.79	0.82	24	25	42	42	13	4	0	4

[65]

The entries into the data bank are coded by country (65 countries) and by occupation (50 different occupations). This produces a matrix of $65 \times 50 = 3250$ cells, but many of these are empty; only about 1150 really occur, and then often with very small numbers of respondents. The part of the matrix that is full is L-shaped: Only a few large countries have all occupations, and only a few general occupations (such as sales representatives, service technicians, and office clerks) occur in all countries.

As stated earlier, 60 "core" questions and 66 "recommended" questions were standardized in 1971. According to their content, they can be divided into four types:

(1) *Satisfactions* supply a personal evaluation of an aspect of the work situation (for example: "How satisfied are you with . . . " but also "How do you like your job—the kind of work you do?" with answers from "very good" to "very poor").

(2) *Perceptions* are subjective descriptions of an aspect or problem of the work situation; about half of the "perception" questions deal with the behavior of various managers (for example: "How often does your manager expect a large amount of work from you?"). I include in this category the question about job stress (A37 in Appendix 1).

(3) *Personal goals and beliefs* are statements not about the job or the company as such but related to an ideal job or to general issues in industry. Personal goals (for example: "How important is it to you to have an opportunity for high earnings?") deal with the *desired* and beliefs (for example, "Competition between employees usually does more harm than good") with the *desirable;* there need not always be consistency between the two (see Chapter 1). This category includes the preferred manager (A54).

(4) *Demographics* deal with age, sex, years of education, years with the company, and so on.

The present study is concerned with questions that can be assumed to represent values—that is, people's more permanent mental programming—that reflect the contribution of the *person* more than the *situation.* For all questions except perhaps the demographics, the answers reflect both the person and the situation; but the situational component can be expected to be stronger for satisfactions than for personal goals and beliefs, with perceptions in between. The choice of the questions for further analysis reflects this: For the present study, one satisfaction question, 14 perception questions, and 44 personal goals and beliefs questions were used; the latter include 19 questions that had actually been dropped from the questionnaire in 1971 or before, but for which the results available on file still proved interesting (C1 through C19).

Four demographic questions served as controls; thus, the cross-cultural analysis of HERMES Survey data is based on $1 + 14 + 44 + 4 = 63$ questions. Their text can be found in Appendix 1.[3]

The use of the "personal goals" questions (Appendix 1: A5 through A18 and C1 through C8) and of the "beliefs" questions (B52 through B61 and C9 through C19) represents a feature of the HERMES questionnaires without which this book would not have been written. This type of question is not part of most standard attitude survey instruments.

The "personal goals" questions ask respondents "how important" they consider each of a list of aspects (facets) of the work situation, such as high earnings, job challenge, or good physical working conditions. This type of question has been used in many research studies in the U.S. in the 1950s and 1960s, mostly for testing theoretical models of job satisfaction. It fits a questionnaire sold as an organization development tool only to the extent that average work goal importance rankings can contribute to setting priorities for action: If people are equally dissatisfied on two work facets, then the one with the highest average importance rating should have action priority (Glennon et al., 1960; Youngberg et al., 1962; Hofstede, 1976c: 49). The "personal goals" questions were introduced in the international HERMES questionnaire from the first (1967) product development laboratories survey. The researchers' team that prepared the questionnaire felt that in an *international* survey these questions would help in understanding differences in mentality among countries. The action argument came only second, although it can be argued that different mentalities should lead to different action approaches after surveys.

The content of the "personal goals" questions derived from similar lists used in U.S. surveys and from open interviews with laboratory personnel in six European countries. The various versions used in HERMES counted between 26 and 14 goals. The content validity (representativeness of the universe of personal goals) of the various lists is doubtful; for greater content validity, initial open-ended interviews should have been held by a multicultural team of interviewers with different categories of employees in all countries. Let me illustrate this. The personal goal "Live in an area desirable to you and your family" (A6) was selected for inclusion in the list by this author (who is a native Dutchman) after pilot interviews in the Netherlands. Its inclusion was disputed several times—among others, by colleagues from Germany and Italy.

The results (Appendix 3, Table A3.2) show that the mean importance rank of "living in a desirable area" found among HERMES employees is 3 out of 22 in the Netherlands, 17 out of 22 in Italy, and 22 out of 22 in Germany. The "desirable area" item is one of the most culturally discriminating items on the masculinity-femininity axis (Chapter 6). Not developing items from multicultural sources or giving in to pressures of those who considered this item irrelevant would have led to suppressing the culturally relevant information. Fortunately, many culturally relevant questions were retained. In Chapter 9 I shall mention some issues that were not covered and that I believe should be included in future surveys of this kind (see also Appendix 4).

The "beliefs" questions were first introduced in the questionnaire in the November 1967 Asian, Latin American, and Pacific survey. The list then contained 19 items, of which 11 gradually were dropped, while two new items were added. Even less than the "personal goals" questions, this list of statements (to which responses should be given on an agree/disagree scale) has content validity. It is not based on interviews with employees, but derives from a brainstorming of International Headquarters personnel for beliefs which, according to their experience, distinguish HERMES people in one country from those in another—in view of the wide international experience of these informants, not a bad source at all. The "beliefs" items have no meaning for organization development, which is one of the reasons why their number has soon been reduced and they were not made "core" items. They are, however, extremely useful for providing insight in value patterns.

A Second Research Setting: IMEDE

IMEDE Management Development Institute in Lausanne, Switzerland, is a relatively small postgraduate and postexperience international business school. It was founded by the Nestlé Corporation in 1958, and provides training to managers from all over the world through courses whose length can vary from a few days to one year.

I taught courses in organizational behavior at IMEDE from 1971 to 1973. By that time it had become clear that certain questions in the HERMES questionnaire which could be expected to express values produced highly stable and predictable differences in answer patterns among countries. I included in my IMEDE courses the administration of a 17-item "Questionnaire on Work Goals and Preferences" which contained questions A5 through A18, A54, B46, and C1 of the HERMES questionnaire; I used the results as teaching material in the course itself. Answers on this questionnaire were obtained from 362 managers from about 30 different countries and from a variety of private and public organizations unrelated to the HERMES Corporation. As will be shown in Chapters 3 and 5, the major country differences found in HERMES are also visible in the IMEDE sample. The latter is based on a different population, and all respondents reacted to the *English* version of the questionnaire, whereas in HERMES every nationality received its own language version. The similarity between HERMES and IMEDE data rules out the hypothesis that the differences found among countries could be due to the translation of the questionnaire.

Unfortunately, at the time I arrived at IMEDE I had only a vague idea of what survey questions were most culturally relevant. Otherwise, my selection for the questionnaire used at IMEDE would have been somewhat different.

In addition to the HERMES questionnaire, I administered at IMEDE to participants in different courses other tests of values and personality, which enabled me to correlate the scores found with different instruments and to test their convergency. The other instruments used were

(1) The Allport-Vernon-Lindzey Study of Values (AVL)
(2) L. V. Gordon's Survey of Interpersonal Values (SIV)
(3) L. V. Gordon's Survey of Personal Values (SPV)
(4) L. V. Gordon's Personal Profile (GPP)
(5) G. W. England's Personal Values Questionnaire (PVQ)
(6) F. E. Fiedler's Least Preferred Co-Worker (LPC)
(7) W. C. Schutz's FIRO-B.

Detailed results of the comparisons have been published in a series of working papers (Hofstede, 1972a, 1974a, 1974b, 1974c). The highest correlation found between any two instruments was .49 (across 64 respondents, significant at the .001-level) between the "Recognition" Score of Gordon's SIV and a score computed out of the items "importance of recognition" (A11) and "importance of advancement" (A15) of the HERMES questionnaire. This at least showed that the HERMES questions did measure the same types of constructs as other values tests and that the convergency between their scores and other test scores was as good as any other correlation between different test scores; for example, the highest correlation found between SIV and AVL was .48 (SIV-Benevolence versus AVL-Social).

In addition to these comparisons between instruments, I have used the Gordon's SIV and SPV scores which were available for 372 IMEDE participants to determine value profile differences among 14 countries (Hofstede, 1976a). The results of this study will be used as comparative evidence in Chapter 3.

All in all, the IMEDE experience showed that the differences among countries found in the HERMES data could be reproduced at least partly with other respondents, that the HERMES questions on personal goals were acceptable as a test of values, and that it was worthwhile to continue the analysis of the HERMES data, as they contained evidence of broad differences in value systems between the respective countries which were not limited to HERMES employees.

The situation at the end of 1973 was thus: HERMES had completed its second survey round. I had served my term at IMEDE, which had proven further analysis of the data worthwhile, and HERMES was willing to make the data bank accessible for further study. Under the auspices of the European Institute for Advanced Studies in Management in Brussels, I started on the research project which has provided the data for this book, not aware that it would take five years.

DATA TREATMENT

Data Analysis: Frequency Distributions and Measures of Central Tendency

The first information obtained from the HERMES survey data bank consists typically of frequency distributions for the different answer categories of one question, as the one reproduced in Figure 2.3. The question analysed in the figure is A5: "How important is it to you to have challenging work to do—work from which you can get a personal sense of accomplishment?" Five valid answer categories follow. The page shown produces the frequency distribution in full percents for nonmanagers in country headquarters for a number of countries. For each country, the 1973 data are followed by the results of the same group in the previous survey round (1969) in order to provide historical comparison.

Every paper-and-pencil instrument produces invalid responses; blank answers, double answers (more than one answer checked for a question for which only one is allowed) and sometimes data entry errors which produce, for example, some answers "6" for a case where only five exist. In the HERMES surveys, invalid answers rarely exceed five percent of total (see the last column labeled "other" in Figure 2.3) and they are excluded for further analysis; which means that the percents in the frequency distribution are based on valid responses only.

Most questions in the HERMES questionnaire use five-point answer scales, and most frequency distributions are skewed; nearly all are unimodal. The vast majority use *ordinal* scales, which means that the answer categories show a natural and · unambiguous rank order from less to more important, satisfied to dissatisfied, or vice versa. They are not *interval* scales in the strict sense of the word, which would imply that the distance between, for example, answers 1 and 2 (such as from very good to good) is equal to the distance between answers 3 and 4 (such as from average to poor). A few questions (for example, A55) do not have ordinal scales but only *nominal* scales (no natural rank order for all answers).

For further processing of the information contained in the frequency distributions it is often necessary to reduce the information to a single number per frequency distribution. This can be done by dichotomizing or by using a measure of central tendency. Dichotomizing means retaining only the percent giving answer 1, or answers 1 and 2, or another combination. It will be obvious that a considerable amount of information is lost in this case. As measures of central tendency, the mean and the median are available. The mean loses the least information, is easier to compute, and plays a role in all parametric statistical calculations, such as product moment correlations. However, it formally presupposes interval scales which we do not have. The median is the theoretically more correct measure, but for short scales with many cases per answer category it approaches the mean closely.[4] In the analysis of the HERMES data the choice has been made to consider scales of the type "very good" to "very poor," "utmost" to "no importance," and "strongly agree" to "strongly disagree" as *quasi-interval scales* and to use the mean as a measure of central tendency for such scales. In the case of questions with different scales (A43, A54, A55) I shall not use a measure of central tendency, but instead dichotomize the frequency distributions at the most meaningful point.

Figure 2.3 shows, beside the means, the standard deviations which, however, are rarely used in the analysis; large standard deviations can be a warning that we are dealing with heterogeneous groups of respondents and that we should look for criteria to further break down our groups.

Within-Group Analysis

The data have been extensively analyzed within groups, "groups" being any sets of respondents that were assumed to be homogeneous as to certain external criteria. Usually a group for analysis represented one occupation (or set of similar occupations) in one country; sometimes one or more occupations across a set of countries.

The major analysis tools were cross-tabulations, correlation analysis, and factor analysis. For questionnaire items with quasi-interval scales, product moment correlations were based on question scores; missing data were eliminated. Questionnaire items with nominal scales have been included in some cases in the correlation analyses by making each answer category a yes/no variable.

An early study using within-group cross-tabulation dealt with the connotations of various leadership styles (Sadler and Hofstede, 1972). The "group" in this case was a multicountry sample including various managerial, professional, and technical occupations. The study showed, among other things, how employees who described their boss as having any of four different leadership styles described his behavior in other respects (see Chapter 7, Figure 7.6).

An example of an extensive application of correlation analysis is a study of the relationship among work goal importance, work facet satisfaction, and overall satisfaction, done separately for 18 different homogeneous groups (occupations in countries; see Chapter 6). An example of an extensive application of factor analysis is the study used to select the core and recommended questions of the 1971 version of the HERMES international questionnaire, described above (Hofstede et al., 1976; 14ff).

In the latter two cases the analysis is based on within-group data, but it includes a comparison of within-group characteristics (correlation coefficients, factor loadings) *between* groups. Groups are compared on the internal structure of relationships among their variables.

Variance Analysis:
Country, Occupation, Sex, and Age

The main criteria that can be responsible for group differences in the survey data and that apply to all data are country, occupation, sex, and age groups of the respondents. From these, occupation and sex are closely related; only a few occupations have sizable numbers of both men and women. Other possible criteria are length of service with the company and education level. Length of service with the company is obviously correlated with age. For a random sample of 12 subpopulations from the data bank, age group and length of service correlated across individuals between .52 and .76, with a median of .61. I shall not use length of service as a separate criterion, therefore. Educational level is closely related to occupation. For our international survey population, however, data about education levels are less accurate than data about occupations, as education systems vary from one country to another, but the occupation classification is standardized throughout the corporation. I shall use occupation as the main criterion, but where it is necessary to order the various occupations on a one-dimensional scale I shall order them according to the mean number of years of formal education of their incumbents.[5]

In order to test the relative contribution to the variance in the data of the four criterion variables country, occupation, sex, and age, I have performed a variance analysis (ANOVA) on a subsample of the data covering a wide range of respondents on all four criteria.[6] The subsample was taken from the 1970 survey in the manufacturing plants. It included ten countries (Argentina, Brazil, Canada, France, Great Britain, Germany, India, Japan, the Netherlands, and Sweden) and five occupational groups (managers, professionals, technicians plus skilled workers, clerks, and unskilled workers). The number of cases per cell of one country, one occupation, was randomly reduced for the larger plants so that it varied between 12 (professionals in India) and 181 (unskilled in Netherlands); the average number per cell was 64 (a total of 3220 cases for 50 cells). Sex and age group were taken as covariants. The variance analysis was done separately for the six questions A37, A43, A54, A55, B46, and B61 that will be used in Chapters 3 and 4 to form the Power Distance Index and the Uncertainty Avoidance Index. In addition, separate variance analyses were done on two composite scores computed for each respondent as the differences between the scores on two questions each: an Individualism score (A18-A9; see Chapter 5) and a Masculinity score (A7-A8; see Chapter 6). The reason for analyzing the difference between two questions in this case, rather than single questions, is that in this way I eliminate acquiescence (see below); otherwise the variance analysis would have shown mainly variance in acquiescence.

The outcome of the variance analysis is presented in Figure 2.4. We see that the country effect is highly significant (beyond the .001 level) in all eight cases. This is not surprising, because the eight questions were selected because of their ability to discriminate between countries. The occupation effect is also significant in all eight cases, although not always at the .001 level. Sex and age effects are each significant in five out of eight cases.[7]

The fact that the nationality of the respondents (and sometimes the other criterion variables occupation, sex, and age) affects the scores of these questions highly significantly does not mean, of course, that a respondent's answer is fully predictable from his or her nationality or any other identification. In fact, of the total variance in the answers of the 3220 respondents in the variance analyses, only 4.2% is accounted for by their belonging to one of the 10 nationalities in the sample. This, however, is 16 times as much as could be expected on the basis of pure chance. We should

FIGURE 2.4   Summary of Results of ANOVA on Data from 3220
Respondents from the 1970 Manufacturing Survey*

Question	F-Value and Significance of Effects for:				
	Country 9 d.f.	Occupation 4 d.f.	Country x Occupation 36 d.f.	Sex 1 d.f.	Age 1 d.f.
B46: employees afraid to disagree	7.1***	24.9***	2.3***	.4	.4
A54: preferred manager no.3	3.2***	19.8***	1.0	7.3**	.1
A55: perceived manager no.1 or 2	5.9***	5.8***	.7	1.6	2.0
A37: stress	46.7***	3.8**	1.5*	3.2	5.8*
A43: continue less than five years	8.8***	6.7***	1.8**	120.8***	92.7***
B60: company rules should not be broken	6.0***	19.8***	1.6*	3.9*	56.9***
A18–A9: importance personal time but not training (individualism)	12.9***	2.8*	1.6*	39.3***	21.5***
A7–A8: importance earnings but not cooperation (masculinity)	25.8***	6.0***	1.5*	11.7***	13.2***
significance limits for F:					
.001	3.1	4.6	2.1	10.8	10.8
.01	2.4	3.3	1.7	6.6	6.6
.05	1.9	2.4	1.3	3.8	3.8

*Ten countries, five occupations for six questions plus two composite scores.
significance levels: *** .001 level   ** .01 level   * .05 level

imagine the distribution of answer scores within and between countries as pictured by Figure 1.5: a broad dispersion across individuals and relatively small shifts of group means which, nevertheless, may have considerable consequences for group behavior and for institutions.

The main purpose of this book is a comparison by country. This will be supplemented with comparisons by occupation, sex, and age groups where such comparisons seem meaningful (for the effect of sex see Chapter 6; for the effect of age, see Chapter 8).

Comparison of Scores by Country:
Stability Over Time

In order to compose scores by country I had to control for occupation. The composition of occupational groups by sex and age varies only marginally among subsidiaries of HERMES, which makes it unnecessary to control for sex and age once we have controlled for occupation.

The scores to be composed by country are either mean scores on five-point quasi-interval scales or percentages of answers on nominal scales. The country comparison used only data from the marketing and service division of the corporation, not from product development or manufacturing. The marketing and service division was surveyed twice: in 1967–1969 and in 1971–1973. For each of the two surveys, a country score was computed as the arithmetical mean of the scores for seven occupational categories:

(1) managers (all levels), country head office;
(2) managers (all levels), branch offices, including sales, service, and technical managers[8];
(3) technical experts, branch offices;
(4) sales representatives B (high technology products), branch offices;
(5) service technicians B (highly qualified), branch offices;
(6) service technicians A (moderately qualified), branch offices; and
(7) administrative personnel, country head office, including clerks and professionals[9].

Each of these seven categories carries equal weight in the country score regardless of its actual number of respondents. The computer program used for data bank information output (Figure 2.3) did not print results for groups smaller than eight respondents. The use of smaller groups was seen as a threat to the anonymity of respondents, but it is also statistically undesirable. Many of the smaller subsidiaries, however, had less than eight respondents in one or more of the seven occupational categories. As a minimal criterion for including a country in the analysis, I used that at least four out of the seven categories should have eight or more respondents and therefore have data printed out. Data for missing occupational categories were extrapolated: (a) If data for this category were available in 1971–1973 but not in 1967–1969, the earlier data were derived from the later data by correcting for the mean shift which occurred in the country's other occupational categories between the two surveys; and vice-versa if data were available in 1967–1969 but not in 1971–1973; (b) if data for this category were missing in both surveys, they were derived from the other categories' data correcting for the occupational differences found in the total world data.[10] In this way, scores for 39 out of the 66 countries in the HERMES data bank could be used, from which 30 have been surveyed twice. Yugoslavia was the fortieth country. The total number of respondents involved is 31,218 for 1967–1969 and 40,997 for 1971–1973; the minimum per country per survey is 37 (Pakistan 1967–1969) and the maximum 7907 (Germany 1971–1973).[11]

The data from countries which were surveyed twice within a four-year interval allow a test of the stability of the between-country differences. It was argued that only questions should be retained for which the differences in score level from country to country would be relatively stable from the first to the second survey round (from about 1968 to about 1972), because:

(1) The purpose of the analysis is to find value differences among countries and to relate these to characteristics of the countries; we cannot expect to find meaningful relationships for measures that are not more or less stable over time.
(2) Country score levels reflect in general both the collective state of mind of the respondents and the collective situation in which these respondents find themselves. We are interested in the first more than in the second. Collective states of mind of the type that interests us change slowly; the situation, however, may change much faster, such as through a change in market conditions, company policy, or management practice. By weeding out questions for which score levels are unstable over time, we avoid such situationally determined issues.

The stability data for 44 questions selected for further analysis (the A and B questions from Appendix 1, but not the C questions, none of which were used twice) are shown in Figure 2.5. The stability coefficients are computed as (Spearman) rank correlations of mean country scores (based on seven occupations) between the first and the second survey rounds. They vary from .12 to .95. Arbitrarily, I consider scores as reasonably stable if the coefficient exceeds .50.[12] We find .39 for overall satisfaction; the questions dealing with perceptions have stabilities ranging from .12 to .94, with a median of .53; the coefficients for the group of "personal goals and beliefs" range from .40 to .95, with a median of .77; the stabilities of the demographics range from .56 to .78, with a median of .65. We see that country scores for personal goals and beliefs are the most stable over time, in accordance with my assumption that these will be least affected by situational factors. The satisfaction measure is fairly unstable; the stabilities for the perceptions vary strongly. It should be stressed that these stability coefficients are based on country mean scores—that is, *aggregate data*. For comparison purposes, I show in the last column of Figure 2.5 for those questions for which they are available stability (test-retest-reliability) data for *individual* answers. These were determined in a test-retest experiment with 62 managers in IMEDE and retest after two weeks (Hofstede, 1975b). There is no visible relationship between the two types of stability.[13]

Based on the stability coefficients in Figure 2.5, five questions from the perceptions group have been excluded from further analysis: A48, B39, B47, B49 and B51, with stabilities between .35 and .12. For the last four, the stability coefficients are not even significantly different from zero. For the remaining questions, the stability coefficients range from .39 to .94, with a median of .76. Five questions with stability coefficients between .39 and .49 have been provisionally retained (two of them were dropped later; see below). For the questions that were retained, country scores were computed as means between the values found in the two survey rounds. From a comparison between the two survey rounds, it became clear that there had been worldwide shifts on some questions (I shall go deeper into this in Chapter 8). For the countries surveyed only once, either in the first or in the second round, it was necessary to correct for these shifts. Scores for countries surveyed only once were therefore corrected, with half the worldwide shifts between 1968 and 1972 based on the countries surveyed twice. In this way, for all countries the country scores can be assumed to approximate as well as possible the situation around 1970.

FIGURE 2.5   Stability Coefficients of Country Mean Scores on 44
              Questions, from 1967–1969 to 1971–1973

Question Number	Question	Number of Countries Surveyed Twice	Stability Coefficient of Country Mean Scores	Stability of Individual Scores[c]
	Satisfaction			
A58	Overall satisfaction	28	.39	
	Perceptions			
A37	stress	29	.94	
A43	answer 1 + 2: continue less than five years	28	.70	
	answer 4: continue until retirement	28	.91	
A48	would complainer suffer?	28	.35[x]	
A52	manager helps ahead	29	.65	
A55	perceived manager 1 or 2	29	.82	
B9	prefer specialist career	13	.53	
B24	prefer foreign company	22	.77	
B25	other job available?	25	.48	
B39	manager insists on rules	23	.34[x]	
B44	prefer manager own nationality	21	.47	
B46	employees afraid to disagree	26	.70	.66
B47	unclear on duties	13	.12[x]	
B49	superiors involved in details	21	.18[x]	
B51	groups looking down on others	10	.28[x]	
	Personal Goals and Beliefs			
A5	importance challenge	19	.57	.46
A6	importance desirable area	19	.81	.66
A7	importance earnings	19	.74	.73
A8	importance cooperation	19	.66	.37
A9	importance training	19	.77	.51
A10	importance benefits	19	.90	.54
A11	importance recognition	19	.77	.53
A12	importance physical conditions	19	.76	.67
A13	importance freedom	19	.95	.31
A14	importance employment security	19	.69	.64
A15	importance advancement	19	.94	.63
A16	importance manager	19	.49	.33
A17	importance use of skills	19	.76	.36
A18	importance personal time	19	.89	.53
A54	preferred manager 1 or 2	29	.94	.53
B52	corporation responsible for employees	22	.79	.72
B53	interesting work as important as earnings	23	.90	.25
B54	competition harmful	21	.84	.76
B55	employees lose respect for consultative manager	20	.74	.09
B56	employees should participate more	0	a	.51
B57	individual decisions better	17	.79	.61

FIGURE 2.5   Continued

B58	corporation responsible for society	0	a	.58
B59	staying with one company desirable	21	.79	.56
B60	company rules should not be broken	20	.75	.57
B61	most employees avoid responsibility	20	.40	.55
	Demographics			
A1	percent female respondents	26	.65	
A2	seniority in company	29	.56	
A56	educational level number of years	0	b	
A57	age	29	.78	

[a]Question newly created in 1971.
[b]1967–1969 data not reliable.
[X]Excluded from further analysis.
[c]Determined on IMEDE data.

Eclectic Analysis: The Power Distance and Uncertainty Avoidance Index Formation

From the earliest surveys onward, it had been clear that questions dealing with hierarchical relationships received systematically different answers in different countries. An early publication (Sadler and Hofstede, 1972) explored the differences in preferred and perceived leadership styles (questions A54 and A55) in six countries. Later, for conceptual reasons related to Mulder's Power Distance Reduction Theory (Mulder, 1976, 1977), the question "How frequently are employees afraid to express disagreement with their managers?" (B46) was chosen as a central question measuring "Power Distance." Country scores on this question were correlated with those on six other conceptually related questions (A48, A52, A54, A55, B55, B56). Based on these ecological correlations, the three questions A54, A55, and B46 were selected to form a Power Distance Index (the exact computation of the index is described in Chapter 3).

The Uncertainty Avoidance Index was developed in an analogous way. I had an early theoretical interest in the phenomenon of stress which was measured by the question "How often do you feel nervous or tense at work?" (A37), but in stress differences by occupation rather than by country (Hofstede, 1978c). It then appeared that stress scores varied much more by country than by occupation (compare Figure 2.4). A subsequent analysis of stress differences by country showed these to be highly significantly correlated with anxiety factor scores based on national statistics from 18 countries, calculated by Lynn (1971). The ecological correlation of stress scores with power distance was weak enough (.30) to suppose that stress scores would reflect another ecological dimension. The search for this other dimension was guided by theoretical reasoning based on the findings of the Aston group in Great Britain (Pugh, 1976; Pugh and Hickson, 1976) with regard to dimensions of organizational structure. The Aston group found two main dimensions of structure: "concentration of authority" and "structuring of activities." The first is conceptually related to power distance; I argued that the second could be related to stress. A search in the HERMES questionnaire revealed three questions which could express structuring of activities, of which, however, only one showed stable country differences over time: the belief that "company rules should not be broken—even when the employee thinks it is in the company's best interests" (B60).[14] Country scores on this question proved significantly correlated with country stress scores. A final search of the ecological correlations of both "stress" and "company rules should not be broken" with all other questions for which country scores had proved stable over time led to the discovery of a third quesion for which country scores were correlated with both. This was, "How long do you think you will continue working for this company?" (A43). The combination of stress, need for fixed company rules, and need for continuing with the company was interpreted as expressing a level of "uncertainty avoidance" in the country, among other things conceptually related to the Aston "structuring of activities."Country scores on the three questions A37, A43, and B60 were then used to form an Uncertainty Avoidance Index (for a further explanation of the concept of Uncertainty Avoidance, as well as for the exact calculation of the index, see Chapter 4).

The phase of the analysis in which the Power Distance Index and Uncertainty Avoidance Index were developed can be called "eclectic" because questions were selected on the basis of theoretical reasoning (with the exception of A43), and statistics (ecological correlation analysis) was used only *after* theoretical reasoning had singled out certain questions as potentially relevant. That is, theory preceded the use of statistics. This as opposed to an alternative approach which simply would have taken all available questions regardless of their theoretical relevance and subjected their country scores to an ecological factor analysis right away. As I shall relate below, I did use an ecological factor analysis, but only at the very end of the analysis process, in order to fit the total picture together. The difference between using heavy statistical treatment (factor analysis) at the beginning or at the end of the analysis may look trivial, but this is not so: the atheoretical, statistics-first approach carries three substantial risks which the theory-first approach avoids. The first risk is that potentially important nuances in data are overlooked. For example, it is doubtful whether I would have discovered in a wholesale factor analysis the difference in cultural meaning of the 1967–1969 and 1970–1973 versions of manager 4 in question A54, the "preferred manager" (see Chapter 3). The second risk is the operation of a kind of Gresham's Law according to which "bad data drive out good": Many trivial variables in a factor analysis cloud the meaning of a few crucial ones. Finding a "strong factor" just means that many variables are intercorrelated, not that they mean anything (the correlation may be due to response set); a weak factor may hide an essential variable for which the questionnaire had no correlates due to the cultural bias of the people who composed it. For example, as authors of the HERMES questionnaire, we were strongly concerned with employee-manager relationships which led to many questions being related to "power distance." We were, however, naive with regard to issues of formal organization, which led to a lack of questions related to "uncertainty avoidance." The third risk of a statistics-first approach is that results rarely will be confronted with theory; once the results of the analysis are there, the researcher is seriously constrained in his search for theoretical clarification by his "findings" and tempted to be quickly satisfied with a few superficial interpretations. Studies of this kind often show remarkably little synergy with other studies.

The Analysis of Work Goal Importance Data: Eliminating Acquiescence

A potentially rich source of information was available in the "work goal importance" questions, which form a self-contained block. The 1968–1971 surveys contained 22 such questions[15]; after that the list was reduced to 14 (A5 through A18). A fundamental problem with these questions is that their answers are strongly affected by *acquiescence*. Acquiescence is the tendency to give a positive answer to any question, regardless of its content ("yesmanship"). In general, we find that the lower the status and educational level of a group of respondents, the stronger their acquiescence. This is clearly demonstrated in Figure 2.6.

For 38 occupations, gross mean work goal importance scores were computed taking 15 European countries [16] and all 22 work goals together (1968–1971 data). A low gross mean indicates that people in this occupation tend to score *all* goals more frequently as "of utmost importance" or "very important." We see in Figure 2.6 that gross means for the 38 occupations vary from 1.82 to 2.28, and that the rank correlation of the gross mean with the occupation's mean years of formal education is as high as .83. That is, the tendency of rating everything more important is for $.83^2 = 69$ percent a matter of the occupation's educational level. [17]

Greater acquiescence by less-educated, lower-status employee categories is probably due to both a desire to please the (higher-status) author of the questionnaire and to a less differentiated "cognitive map" in the respondents: They distinguish less clearly between goals. Acquiescence not only varies among occupations; it also varies among countries. The gross mean work goal importance score across 14 goals has been taken as the measure of acquiescence for each of the 40 countries. It is abbreviated IMP; we find its values in Appendix 3, Table A3.1.

Acquiescence is an interesting phenomenon per se, but it is irrelevant for determining the importance of a particular work goal for a certain category of respondents. It tends to distort the answers. In general we can say that the *absolute* importance score of a single goal is irrelevant: It is as meaningful as the sound of one hand clapping. Importance becomes meaningful only when we can compare at least two goals.[18] Earnings and cooperation are both important for almost anyone; only the relative importance of one over the other tells us something about the values of a person or group. This means that work goal importance scores for single goals should not be shown in their raw state—they should be shown relative to other goals. The simplest way to achieve this is replacing the mean importance scores for the different goals by rank numbers: 1 for the goal with the lowest mean (most important), 14, 22, or n for the goal with the highest mean (least important). In the ranking process, however, the information about the relative distances between the goals is lost. I have therefore used a more sophisticated procedure: *standardizing* the mean scores for each group across the n goals.[19] In standardizing, we express the scores in the distance from their common overall mean, measured in terms of their common standard deviations. Raw scores are now replaced by standard scores. The information about the relative distances of scores between goals is retained, but acquiescence is eliminated. The overall mean of the standard scores for the n goals for each group is zero.

The necessity of ranking or standardizing work goal importance scores before comparing them, unfortunately, is not always recognized in the literature; quite a few studies have obtained misleading results by comparing nonstandardized group means of work goal importance scores (see Chapter 5).

In this book, work goal importance scores will always be given in their standardized form (Appendix 3). In order to avoid negative scores and decimal points I have

FIGURE 2.6   Comparison Between Educational Level and Mean
"Importance" Scores Across 22 Work Goals for 38
Occupations, Europe or Worldwide, 1968–1971 Data
(n = 48,895)

Identi-fica-tion No.	Occupation	Mean Formal Educational Level Years	Mean Work Goal Impor-tance Score Over All 22 Goals
21	Unskilled Plant Workers B	10.4	1.86
46	Unskilled Plant Workers A	10.5	1.82
49	Unskilled Auxiliary Plant Workers	10.9	1.86
47	Skilled Plant Workers	11.0	1.87
11	Branch Office Service Managers A	11.2	2.02
12	Branch Office Service Technicians A	11.3	1.98
50	Plant Technicians	11.5	1.97
51	Plant Clerks	11.5	2.01
19	Plant Managers A	11.6	1.96
64	Laboratory Clerks A	11.6	2.04
31	Office Typists and Secretaries	11.7	2.04
14	Branch Office Clerks	11.8	1.98
7	Branch Office Service Managers B	11.9	2.14
63	Laboratory Technicians A	12.1	2.09
8	Branch Office Service Technicians B	12.2	2.13
9	Sales Department Managers A	12.3	1.90
74	Laboratory Clerks B	12.3	2.13
10	Sales Representatives A	12.4	1.90
18	Data Processing Operators	12.4	1.98
73	Laboratory Technicians B	12.7	2.15
26	Head Office Clerks	12.9	2.00
41	Plant Managers B, First-line	13.3	2.09
13	Branch Office Administration Managers	13.3	2.10
24	Head Office Managers	14.1	2.08
43	Plant Professionals	14.3	2.13
15	Data Processing Managers	14.4	2.09
42	Plant Managers B, Higher Level	14.4	2.10
25	Head Office Professionals	14.8	2.09
17	Data Processing Professionals	14.9	2.13
2	Sales Representatives B	15.6	2.11
1	Sales Department Managers B	15.6	2.16
62	Laboratory Professionals A	15.6	2.22
61	Laboratory Managers A	15.6	2.22
5	Branch Office Technical Experts	15.8	2.15
6	Trainee Professionals	15.9	2.19
71	Laboratory Managers B	15.9	2.27
72	Laboratory Professionals B	15.9	2.28

FIGURE 2.6 Continued

82	Research Professionals	16.5	2.27
	Mean of 38 Occupations	13.2	2.07
	Spearman rank correlation with educational level		.83***

Throughout this book, significance levels will be indicated as follows:
*** .001 level   ** .01 level   * .05 level

given the standardized scores a mean of 500 and a standard deviation of 100; also, their sign has been reversed, so that a very important goal (raw score 2 × s.d. below mean) now scores around 700 and the least important goals now score below 300.[20]

Standardizing as a way of controlling for acquiescence has been used only for the work goals questions. It is, of course, possible and even likely that the other questions will also show some acquiescence response set. However, most other questions have a clear midpoint on their answer scale (for example, "undecided" between "agree" and "disagree"). This provides more objective anchoring of responses than the very subjective "importance" scale (every respondent measures importance by his or her own standards); such anchoring reduces response set. Standardizing for the other questions was also difficult to carry out because they use varying answer formats which may be differentially affected by acquiescence. Only the "general beliefs" (B52 through B61 and C9 through C19) have the same format. The problem here is that because and B questions were optional there are many missing country data; but one cannot standardize if there are missing data. I have therefore left these other question scores in their raw state (Appendix 2), but afterwards corrected them for acquiescence tendencies where these were visible. I did this assuming that acquiescence in these questions will be a linear function of acquiescence in the "importance" questions. The latter is measured by IMP (Table A3.1). By computing partial correlation coefficients controlling for IMP, I have corrected for acquiescence (bottom lines in Appendix 2 for B and C questions).

Further Analysis of Work Goal Importance Data: Ecological Factor Analysis

In Chapter 1 I dealt at length with the problem of changing the level of analysis when comparing cultures rather than individuals. In the study of the HERMES data the need for changing the level of analysis has become particularly clear for the block of first 22, then 14 work goal importance questions. The issue is how to meaningfully reduce the amount of information contained in 22 (14) questions to a smaller number of underlying dimensions. In the earlier phases of the research we had used factor analysis of unstandardized individual within-country, within-occupation work goal importance scores. We usually met six factors, related to job content, reward, interpersonal relations, security, comfort, and company; sometimes—especially for less-educated employee categories—two or more of these factors collapsed into one. The selection of 14 goals made in 1972 aimed at achieving adequate representation of five dimensions of goals: job content, reward, interpersonal relations, security, and comfort (Hofstede et al., 1976: 48). These more or less fit the categorization of Maslow's (1970) hierarchy: self-actualization, esteem, belongingness, safety, and physiological needs. The "company" goals C3, C4 and C5 were not selected in 1971, although they did form a factor of their own; but they did not fit our paradigm of human needs, which had been strongly influenced by Maslow.

At that time I had not yet grasped the implications of changing the level of analysis from individuals to countries. I tried to use the five dimensions—job content, reward, interpersonal relations, security, and comfort—for comparing occupations and for comparing countries, drawing occupation and country profiles according to the relative importance of the five. The resulting picture was more easily understandable for occupations than for countries. Occupations could be interpreted as operating at different levels of the Maslow hierarchy (professionals near the top, clerks in the middle, unskilled near the bottom). As will be clear from this book (especially Chapter 5), I no longer interpret the data in this way, but at least this interpretation seemed to make some sense then. A theoretical base for the country comparisons was missing; geographically close countries, for example, those in Scandinavia or Latin America, produced similar profiles, but a Maslowian interpretation led nowhere.

One more satisfying approach was a study contrasting the work goal importance scores of a single country (the Netherlands) against those of a group of countries (Europe: see Hofstede, 1973, and Chapter 5). No attempt was made to cluster the 22 goals into "dimensions," but they were divided into two groups: those on which the Dutch tended to score greater importance and those on which they tended to score less importance than the average European. The differences between Dutch and average Europeans proved to be consistent across 21 different occupations, from unskilled operators to laboratory engineers.[21] The pattern of Dutch-versus-Europeans differences gave a meaningful picture of the Dutch national character of "being happy in a small way." Later, I attempted to compare 22 work goals in ten countries without clustering them into dimensions, but the resulting multitude of figures was not readily interpretable (Hofstede, 1974d).

Considerable progress was made after a methodological exploration with the help of the Department of Psychology of the University of Leyden, the Netherlands (Hofstede and Van Hoesel, 1976). For the first time, we recognized that factors based on between-group correlations might be different from those based on within-group correlations. We took (unstandardized) work goals data for 3600 respondents divided into 18 one-country, one-occupation groups, together covering eight different countries and nine different occupations and did factor analyses on three levels: total data, within groups, and between groups. The total and within-group factor analyses gave very similar results; the six factors we knew already explained about 50 percent of the variance. The between-group or ecological factor analysis was less clear; it took nine factors to explain 46 percent of the variance, and the factors were only partly similar to those in the total and within-group analyses. What we learned from this exercise was that between-group factors are different from within-group factors. The unclear between-group structure afterward appeared to be due to the fact that we used unstandardized data and that we had taken groups which differed according to two criteria (country and occupation) at the same time. It became evident that ecological correlations between countries are not the same as ecological correlations between occupations, and that if one mixes the two, chaos can result.

The next step was repeating the ecological factor analysis of the work goals data, but this time separately for occupations (controlling for country) and for countries (controlling for occupation). Data were available for 22 work goals in 38 occupations, for 22 work goals in 19 countries surveyed in 1968 and 1969, and for 14 work goals in all 40 countries. This time all data were standardized (Appendix 3). The factor analyses are shown in the statistical section of Chapter 5, showing that a Maslowian framework makes some sense for comparing occupations but not at all for comparing countries. Countries do not group themselves according to Maslowian categories: Their goal patterns can be classified according to two dimensions, an Individual-Collective dimension and an Ego-Social dimension. Basing myself on the 14 goals, 40 countries ecological factor analysis, I used the factor scores of the 40 countries on the axes corresponding to these two dimensions for constructing the indices of Individualism and Masculinity. The number of ecological dimensions in the data had thus been increased to four: Power Distance and Uncertainty Avoidance (each measured by an index composed of the scores on three questions) plus Individualism and Masculinity (both measured through factor scores in a factor analysis of 14 questions). The meaning of Individualism is explored in Chapter 5; of Masculinity, in Chapter 6.

An Ecological Factor Analysis of All Items:
Putting the Picture Together

The four dimensions of Power Distance, Uncertainty Avoidance, Individualism, and Masculinity were derived from partial studies of the data. Other dimensions did not readily offer themselves from the data, nor could they be inferred from theory. As a final check on whether the four dimensions adequately explain the ecological variations in the data, I ran a factor analysis[22] of all data. From the 44 items listed in Figure 2.5, 39 were retained (those not marked with x). For question A43 (intent to continue with company) two variables were created (see Figure 2.5): percent answering 1 or 2—continue less than five years, and percent answering 4—continue until retirement. For question A54 (preferred manager), four variables were created: percent answering 1 or 2, percent answering 3 (1967–1969 version only), percent answering 3 (1972–1973 version only), and percent answering 4 (1972–1973 version only). The rationale for this distinction is related in Chapter 3. For question A55 (perceived manager), the scores used are percent answering 1 or 2; autocratic or persuasive boss (see Appendix 2). For questions A5 through A18 (the work goals), the standardized scores were used which are listed in Appendix 3, Table A3.1. The number of variables had now been increased to 43 (39 + 1 + 3). Finally, the four indices for Power Distance, Uncertainty Avoidance, Individualism, and Masculinity were added to the matrix plus the mean raw Work Goal Importance score across 14 goals (IMP, used before as a measure of acquiescence). The resulting matrix was of the order 40 countries × 48 variables.[23]

The matrix was transformed into a 48 × 48 correlation matrix using a missing data correlation program (BMDP),[24] and the resulting ecological correlation matrix was used as the starting point for a factor analysis. The first four factors together explained 37 percent of the variance. Because correlations between some of the dimensions could not be excluded, an *oblique* rotation was chosen for separating the factors. The intercorrelations between the rotated factors, however, were very weak (the strongest being –.14 between Factors 1 and 4). Factor 1 combined Individualism with the reverse of Power Distance. Factor 2 was Uncertainty Avoidance; Factor 3,

Masculinity. Factor 4 was a weak second Power Distance factor which seemed to express a "capitalist" philosophy (employees should not participate more, a corporation is not responsible for society, and individual decisions are better than group decisions; but managers should be consultative and power distances are not perceived as large). For an analysis of this factor see Chapter 3.

The objection could be made that the factor analysis for 48 variables as described above has forced the appearance of the predetermined factors Power Distance, Uncertainty Avoidance, and so on by including indices that are in themselves composites of other variables in the matrix; by employing four variables for one "Power Distance" question (A54, the preferred manager), and so on. I have therefore created a new purified matrix by weeding out from the 48-variable matrix: the five indices; the four demographics which are, strictly speaking, not "values"; three of the four variables for question A54, the preferred manager (only the percent preferring manager 3, style 1967–1969, was maintained; this is the variable used in composing the Power Distance Index); one of the two variables for question A43, the intent to continue with the company (only the percent intending to continue less than five years was retained). Finally, three more questions were eliminated: B61, which did not load on any factor and showed marginal stability in Figure 2.5; B25, with a .49 loading on Factor 1, marginal stability in Figure 2.5 and which does not seem to relate conceptually to the other items on the factor (there is no real indication that it reflects much of a value); and A52, which only loaded .51 on Factor 4. The residual matrix now counted 32 variables. The 32 × 32 correlation matrix was again factor analyzed; this time, the first four factors together explained 57 percent of the variance.[25]

An oblique rotation with four factors was again tried, but it showed basically the same factors as the 48-variable matrix; factor intercorrelations were again low, and the fourth factor was weak, with loadings of .40 or above for only three variables which did not also load on Factor 1, 2, or 3 (Importance of advancement, Individual decisions better, and Does not prefer manager of own nationality). This factor did not seem to reflect a basic dimension of societal values.

Therefore, I have limited the analysis of the 32-variable matrix to three factors, together explaining 49 percent of the variance, using an orthogonal rotation. The following rotated factors were found (all loadings of .35 and over are shown):

Factor 1 (factor variance 24 percent)

.82	A18	Importance personal time
.82	B53	Interesting work *not* as important as earnings
.78	B52	Corporation *not* responsible for employees
−.76	A55	Low percentage perceived manager 1 or 2
.75	B46	Employees *not* afraid to disagree
.74	A54	High percentage preferred manager 3 (1967–1969)
.69	B59	Staying with one company *not* desirable
.63	B56	Employees should *not* participate more
−.62	A12	Low importance physical conditions
−.61	A9	Low importance training
.59	A13	Importance freedom
.59	B55	Employees *don't* lose respect for consultative manager

.59 B24   Does *not* prefer foreign company
−.58 A17   Low importance use of skills
.41 A5   Importance challenge (second loading)
.37 B58   Corporation *not* responsible for society
−.35 A15   Low importance advancement (third loading)

Factor 2 (factor variance 13 percent)
−.71 A16   Low importance manager
.68 A7   Importance earnings
−.67 A8   Low importance cooperation
.60 A11   Importance recognition
.54 A5   Importance challenge
−.53 A6   Low importance desirable area
−.51 A14   Low importance employment security
−.46 A37   High stress (second loading)
−.45 B57   Individual decisions better (second loading)
.43 A17   Importance use of skills (second loading)
.39 A15   Importance advancement (second loading)
−.35 B52   Corporation responsible for employees (second loading)
−.35 B58   Corporation responsible for society (second loading)

Factor 3 (factor variance 12 percent)
.76 B60   Company rules may be broken
.62 A37   Low stress
.59 A43   Continue less than five years
.56 B9   Prefers manager rather than specialist career
−.50 B57   Individual decisions better
.49 B44   Does *not* prefer manager of own nationality
.49 A58   Low overall satisfaction
.46 A15   Importance advancement
−.46 B55   Employees lose respect for consultative manager (second loading)
.45 B54   Competition *not* harmful
−.43 A9   Low importance training (second loading)
−.35 A10   Low importance benefits

All variables show a loading of at least .35 on one of these three factors.

Again, Factor 1 represents an Individualism-low Power Distance factor: it includes the Individual-Collective dimension of Work Goals (questions A18, A12, A9, A13, A17, and A5) and Power Distance with a negative sign (questions A55, A46, and A54). In addition, it shows loadings for six "beliefs" (B53, B52, B59, B56, B55, and B58, all with a positive sign) and with two other questions (B24 and A15). In spite of the fact that Power Distance and Individualism load on the same factor, I shall continue treating them as two dimensions because they are conceptually distinct; see Chapters 3 and 5.

Factor 2 is a Masculinity factor (with questions A16, A7, A8, A11, A5, A6, A14, A17, and A15). It has collected only four second loadings from other questions. This factor will be explored further in Chapter 6.

Factor 3 corresponds to Uncertainty Avoidance, again with reversed sign. The three highest loading items are the ones which together form the Uncertainty Avoidance Index. This factor will be explored further in Chapter 4.

The ecological factor analysis did not include the C questions, which were dropped after the 1968, 1969, or 1970 survey rounds and for which the data are therefore based on one survey only. However, for the "general beliefs" C9 through C19, ecological correlations with the four indices are listed in Appendix 2.[26] These correlations are used in Chapters 3 through 6 as supplementary information.

Comparing HERMES Data with Data From Other Sources

The result of the analysis of the HERMES data is the identification of four dimensions of national culture, plus index scores which locate each of 40 countries on each of these dimensions. All this is only moderately interesting unless it can be shown that the same dimensions can be found in non-HERMES data. My interest was not in HERMES employees as such, but in HERMES employees as narrow but extremely well-matched samples of their countries' middle class. Earlier in this chapter, I related how I collected additional data at IMEDE Management Development Institute in Lausanne, which showed that the same differences between country scores could be reproduced at least partly on a different population—and without translation of the questionnaire. After this encouraging start, I set out to look for other data that could be hypothesized to correlate with the HERMES dimensions.

The search for other data led me through the literature of all the disciplines listed in Chapter 1. I only considered those studies and sources which were somehow conceptually related to issues covered by the four HERMES dimensions and which yielded quantitative measures for a number of countries also represented in the HERMES sample. They were of three different kinds: (1) survey studies of other narrow but matched samples of populations, such as university students; (2) representative sample polls of entire national populations, and (3) characteristics of countries measured directly at the country level, such as government spending on development aid. All in all, I found data from 38 other studies comparing between five and 39 countries to be significantly correlated with one or more of the four dimensions; these studies are described in detail in Chapters 3 through 6 and summarized in Figures 7.8 and 7.9 in Chapter 7.

For comparing the country scores from these other studies with the HERMES country scores, I used either the Spearman rank correlation coefficient or the product moment correlation coefficient. For scores on scales of unknown properties, the Spearman rank correlation coefficient gives the safer estimate of a relationship, since individual observations cannot play an overpowering role in the result. However, the product moment correlation coefficient offers the possibility to compute a multiple regression (showing the relationship of the other data with all four HERMES indices together) and to follow a stepwise regression (showing how much more of the variance in the other data can be explained by adding one more HERMES dimension at the time). In cases where a multiple and stepwise regression looked desirable, I have therefore used the product moment correlation coefficient. As an emergency solution, for cases in which Spearman rank and product moment correlation led to considerably different results (which was rarely the case), I have used the fact that if we replace all observations by their rank numbers, the product moment and Spearman rank correlation coefficients are identical. In these cases I therefore first transformed all data into rank numbers and then carried out product moment correlations and multiple and stepwise regressions. This was the more justified because I am more interested in the *order* in which the four indices appear in the stepwise regression than in the precise level of their contribution to predicting the other data.

Economic, Geographic, and Demographic Indicators

In Chapters 3 through 6 I shall also explore the relationships among the four dimensions (Power Distance, Uncertainty Avoidance, Individualism, and Masculinity) and a number of geographic, demographic, and economic indicators of the 40 countries. On the basis of a literature search, I have selected in the first instance the nine indicators listed in Figure 2.7. The first seven are country-specific, the last two company-specific (that is, HERMES-specific).

FIGURE 2.7   Nine Indicators Considered for Relating to Value Dimensions

Code	Indicator	Definition	Source of Data
GNP	Wealth	1970 GNP per capita in $/10	World Bank Atlas, 1972
GNG	Economic growth	1960–1970 average annual growth rate of GNP per capita in %, × 10	World Bank Atlas, 1972
LAT	Latitude	Geographical latitude (either North or South) of the country's capital city, in degrees	Regular geographic atlas
POP	Population size	Decimal logarithm of number of inhabitants in 1970 in millions, × 100	World Bank Atlas, 1972
PGR	Population growth	1960–1970 average annual growth rate of population, × 10	World Bank Atlas, 1972
PDN	Population density	Population divided by area in sq. km. Values for the two city states Hong Kong and Singapore divided by eight	See POP and Oxford Economic Atlas, 4th ed., 1972
DIF	Differentiation index	Sum of T–scores of percent gainfully employed males in nonagricultural occupations around 1950 and of gross energy consumption per capita in 1952	Marsh (1967: Appendix 1) (Singapore missing: made equal to Hong Kong)
ORG	Organization size	Decimal logarithm of number of employees of HERMES as of 1/1/1970 (excluding manufacturing and product development) × 100	Company statistics
ROS	Relative organization size	Number of employees of HERMES divided by number of inhabitants in millions	See POP and ORG

Wealth (GNP per capita) is the most common measure of a country's economic development. It is a debatable measure (Morgenstern, 1975) but retained for lack of a better one. The same applies to *Economic growth* (GNG: 10-year average growth in GNP per capita). *Latitude* (LAT: determined for the country's capital city) is an unambiguous measure of the country's geographical position and a crude measure of climate (tropical-moderate-cold). *Population size* (POP) is an obvious demographic measure which in various factor analytic studies has appeared to be related to social and political variables (see Chapter 1). In view of its skewed distribution among the countries studied, it has been measured on a logarithmic scale. *Population growth* (PGR) is an obvious complement to population size. *Population density* (PDN) appears as an explanatory variable in various theories of cultural behavior. Its distribution is fairly normally shaped except for the two city-states Hong Kong and Singapore. In order to prevent these countries' data from dominating all correlations, the values for Hong Kong and Singapore were divided by eight, which puts them at the top of the list but within the range of values for the other countries. Marsh's (1967) *Index of Differentiation* (DIF) is an alternative to GNP per capita for measuring a country's economic development; Marsh has computed it for traditional as well as modern societies. It is based on data from about 1950 when Singapore did not yet exist as a country (it was part of Malaysia). I have substituted for Singapore the same value as for Hong Kong as an approximation.[27] The variables *Organization size* (ORG) and *Relative organization size* (ROS) have been added because it is reasonable to suppose that attitudes in a HERMES subsidiary could be determined more by the demographics of that subsidiary than by any nationwide indicators.

The values for the nine indicators for the 40 countries are listed in Figure 2.8. Their intercorrelations across the 40 countries are shown in Figure 2.9.

FIGURE 2.8   Country Scores on Nine Economic, Geographic, and Demographic Indicators

Country	GNP	GNG	LAT	POP	PGR	PDN	DIF	ORG	ROS
Argentina	116	25	35	137	15	8	45	298	41
Australia	282	31	36	110	20	2	73	324	139
Austria	201	39	48	87	5	88	51	298	128
Belgium	272	40	51	99	6	318	75	323	160
Brazil	42	24	23	197	29	11	26	320	17
Canada	370	36	46	133	18	2	90	380	288
Chile	72	16	33	99	23	13	41	254	35
Colombia	34	17	5	133	32	19	25	250	15
Denmark	319	37	56	69	7	114	56	301	224
Finland	239	39	60	67	6	14	48	274	116
France	310	46	49	171	10	92	58	398	195
Great Britain	227	22	52	175	6	243	85	385	127
Germany (F.R.)	293	35	51	179	10	248	68	409	199
Greece	109	66	38	95	7	67	31	230	22
Hong Kong	97	84	22	60	25	500	38	216	36
India	11	12	29	273	23	164	20	277	1
Iran	38	54	36	146	29	18	17	219	5
Ireland	136	36	53	46	4	42	43	229	67

FIGURE 2.8   Continued

Country	GNP	GNG	LAT	POP	PGR	PDN	DIF	ORG	ROS
Israel	196	47	32	46	32	140	48	260	138
Italy	176	46	42	173	8	178	41	360	75
Japan	192	96	36	201	10	282	42	365	44
Mexico	67	37	19	171	35	26	29	295	17
Netherlands	243	39	52	111	13	387	58	340	194
Norway	286	41	60	59	8	12	55	281	167
New Zealand	270	21	41	45	17	10	58	259	139
Pakistan	10	24	25	211	27	138	17	189	1
Peru	45	14	12	113	31	11	23	237	17
Philippines	21	29	15	157	30	124	21	251	9
Portugal	66	53	39	98	9	105	30	260	41
South Africa	76	30	26	135	30	18	45	292	38
Singapore	92	52	1	32	24	438	38	205	53
Spain	102	61	40	153	11	67	31	316	44
Sweden	404	38	59	90	7	18	63	327	232
Switzerland	332	25	47	80	15	152	52	326	288
Taiwan	39	71	25	115	29	388	32	215	10
Thailand	20	49	14	156	31	70	14	221	5
Turkey	31	39	40	155	25	45	24	214	4
U.S.A.	476	32	41	231	12	22	110	478	280
Venezuela	98	23	10	102	35	11	39	274	53
Yugoslavia	65	43	45	131	11	80	26	248	15
Mean of 40									
Countries	162	39	36	126	18	117	45	290	92

For explanation of abbreviations see Figure 2.7.

We find correlations of .90 and over between *Wealth* and *Differentiation Index,* and between *Wealth* and *Relative organization size*. As HERMES markets advanced technological products, the size of its subsidiary in a country reflects almost perfectly the country's economic development. The correlations are so high that I have dropped *Differentiation Index* and *Relative organization size* as indicators, as they merely duplicate the *Wealth* variable.

The seven remaining variables show one cluster of four variables (wealth, latitude, less population growth, and organization size) with a weak link to a fifth (population size); another cluster of economic growth and population density is completely separate. The cluster of four splits into two subclusters: wealth plus organization size and latitude plus less population growth. Across the 40 countries, the correlation between population growth and economic growth is an insignificant − .19 (Kuznets, 1973: 43, finds − .31 for all noncommunist countries in the 1950–1960s).

The correlations of these seven indicators with the HERMES indices will complement the correlations between HERMES indices and other data in Chapters 3 through 6; a summary and a test of multiple and stepwise correlations of the indicators on the four indices is presented in Chapter 7, Figure 7.10.

FIGURE 2.9   Product Moment Intercorrelations Across 40 Countries of
              Nine Geographic, Economic, and Demographic Indicators

GNP	GNG	LAT	POP	PGR	PDN	DIF	ORG	ROS	
	−.03	.68***	−.17	−.60***	−.03	.90***	.74***	.96***	GNP
		.06	−.14	−.19	.50***	−.11	−.08	−.13	GNG
			−.14	−.84***	−.09	.55***	.47***	.63***	LAT
				.15	−.08	−.08	.39**	−.19	POP
					−.08	−.51***	−.46***	−.51***	PGR
						.04	−.04	−.00	PDN
							.77***	.85***	DIF
								.70***	ORG
									ROS

NOTES

1. Hermes is the Greek god of commerce. McClelland (1961: 301ff) sees in him the personification of achievement motivation.

2. Also known as Murphy's Law.

3. In Appendix 1, "core" questions are numbered A1–A60, as in the official HERMES questionnaire, but only those analyzed in this book are reproduced. For the other questions, see Hofstede et al. (1976). Appendix 1, however, includes the core "satisfaction" questions A19–A32 which were not analyzed cross-culturally but to which I shall still refer in Chapter 6. Also included are the "recommended" questions (numbered B1–B66 but only reproduced inasfar as they are analyzed in this book) and the 19 "other" personal goals and beliefs questions (numbered C1–C19).

4. In a random sample of 100 five-point frequency distributions from the HERMES data, the median could be shown never to differ more than .10 points from the mean; the mean difference between the two was .02 points (the median lower).

5. In the 1967–1969 survey round, education data were not reliable due to coding differences among countries and between subsequent versions of the questionnaire. For the occupations surveyed twice, educational levels have been determined on the basis of 1971–1973 data only.

6. This analysis was made possible by the kind help of Professor Dr. Klaus Brockhoff of Kiel University, Germany, and his computer staff.

7. For the work goal importance questions (A5 through A18), Hinrichs and Ferrario (1974) did an ANOVA on unstandardized manager data, using country (type of managerial) occupation and age as criterion variables. They found a country effect for both "intrinsic" and "extrinsic" goals, but an occupation effect for intrinsic goals only. It will be evident from the discussion later in this chapter that I dispute the meaningfulness of the use of unstandardized goal data; I also dispute the use of the categories "intrinsic" and "extrinsic" when it comes to comparing countries. For the work goal importance data of the 1969–1970 U.S. Survey of Working Conditions, Quinn (1973: 244) and Crowley et al. (1973: 452–453) have calculated chi-squares for the relative contribution to the scores of education level (closely related to occupation level), age, race, and sex. The educational level effect is the strongest, followed by sex and age; the race effect is marginal. A survey among about 1000 Canadian civil servants by Taylor and

Thompson (1976) using 23 items (goals, beliefs, and preferences) shows that scores depend most on educational level, next on age, and finally on sex (p. 530).

8. Actually a combination of five occupation codes: Sales Department Managers A and B, Branch Office Technical Managers, and Branch Office Service Managers A and B.

9. A combination of two occupation codes: Head Office Clerks and Head Office Professionals. The ratio between these two varies only slightly between countries.

10. For the "work goals" and "general beliefs" this was simplified by substituting the data of occupational category 1 for 2 or 2 for 1 if either were missing; 3 for 4 or 4 for 3, and 5 for 6 or 6 for 5.

11. See Appendix 2. The data from Pakistan 1969 are exceptionally based on only three occupational categories, the remaining ones being extrapolated back from 1972.

12. In this case the reliability of the measurement of country differences based on the mean of *both* surveys, according to the Spearman-Brown formula, will be .67.

13. Across 24 questions for which both types of stability are available, the median stability for country mean scores over four years is .77; for individual scores over two weeks it is .55. The rank correlation between the two sets of stability coefficients is .03.

14. I called agreement with this belief "Rule Orientation." Lammers and Hickson (1979) in their last chapter use a classification of countries according to my Power Distance and Rule Orientation scores. At the time their chapter was written, I had not yet developed the label "Uncertainty Avoidance."

15. The 1967 laboratories survey used 26 goals; the 1967 Asia-Pacific-Latin America survey, 16 goals. The questions eliminated in 1971 are C1 through C8.

16. For manufacturing and product development, the available occupation data are worldwide data (excluding the United States). In these, however, European countries dominated strongly numerically.

17. Data reported by Friedlander (1965: 10) also show lower-status employees to attach higher average importance to work goals than higher-status employees.

18. This argument applies to values in general. It even applies to the concept of "value" in economics. Pareto pointed out that for economic value, only ordinal utility, not cardinal utility, is relevant (Bannock et al., 1972: 310).

19. The standardization across the n goals can be carried out on the scores of individuals or on the mean scores of groups. The result is not necessarily the same: Standardizing individual scores before calculating a group mean in general will lead to a somewhat different rank order of goals than calculating a group mean first, before standardizing. Ritti (1964: 317–318) recommends *double* standardization of individual scores as a preparation for factor analysis: first across goals, then across individuals (the reverse makes no sense, because the subsequent factor analysis starts with a correlation matrix which is invariant to standardization across goals). Ritti states, however, that single standardization across individuals has largely the same effect as double standardization (1964: 307). In my analysis I have single-standardized group means across goals (first calculating group means, then standardizing) because this is much simpler to carry out; also, I am interested in eliminating acquiescence as a *group* phenomenon, before comparing groups, not as an individual phenomenon.

20. In the composition of the data in Table A3.1, a problem existed for two countries (Chile and India) surveyed only in 1967. In the 1967 surveys a partly different list of goals was used, so that data on "desirable area," "cooperation," "manager," and "use of skills" are missing. In order not to lose Chile and India completely from the data, the values of Argentina were substituted for the missing data from Chile, and for India those of Pakistan were substituted, after correcting for differences in overall score level (acquiescence) between each pair of countries, visible in the scores for the remaining 10 goals.

21. In this study the work goal scores were not yet standardized but the scores were corrected to make the mean across all 22 goals for the Dutch equal to that for total Europe.

Standardization equalizes not only the means but also the standard deviations.

22. In various phases of the research I have tried other methods of multivariate analysis: for example, cluster analysis and smallest space analysis. As these led to very similar results as factor analysis, I continued to use the latter, with which I am most familiar. See also Chapter 7.

23. Several times in this book I refer to factor analyses in which the number of observations (countries) is less than the number of variables. This makes statistical inference invalid (it inflates the percentage of variance "explained") but it is still valid as a way of detecting the *structure* in the data: which variables are most strongly associated.

24. Some data in the matrix are missing, because some questions were not used in some countries (two questions, B56 and B58, were only used in 28 countries; for the other questions the number of countries varied between 33 and 40; in all, 65 cells in the matrix, or three percent, of all cells were empty).

25. See Note 23. The number of variables has become smaller than the number of countries; the percentage of variance explained is no longer inflated.

26. The scores for C9 through C14 are means across the usual seven occupations. For C15 through C19 (dropped after 1968) they are means across five occupations; they do not include headquarters managers and headquarters clerks, as in the European countries these were surveyed in 1969 only.

27. Another alternative measure of economic development has been constructed by Eitzen (1967) on the basis of data from Banks and Textor (1963); it is a nine-point Guttman scale. I have not used it because the distribution of the HERMES countries on the scale is very skewed with 15 countries in the highest scale class and only 11 in the six lowest classes.

Chapter 3

POWER DISTANCE

SUMMARY OF THIS CHAPTER[1]

The first of the four dimensions of national culture which the HERMES data reveal is called Power Distance. The basic issue involved, to which different societies have found different solutions, is human inequality. Inequality can occur in areas such as prestige, wealth, and power; different societies put different weights on status consistency among these areas. Inside organizations, inequality in power is inevitable and functional. This inequality is usually formalized in hierarchical boss-subordinate relationships. According to Mulder's Power Distance Reduction theory, subordinates will try to reduce the power distance between themselves and their bosses and bosses will try to maintain or enlarge it. The present study, however, suggests that the level of power distance at which both tendencies will find their equilibrium is societally determined. It can be expressed in a Power Distance Index (PDI), which is derived from country mean scores on three questions in the HERMES survey. These questions deal with perceptions of the superior's style of decision-making and of colleagues' fear to disagree with superiors, and with the type of decision-making which subordinates prefer in their boss. PDI scores differ strongly across occupations as well, especially in countries where the country PDI is low. Differences on PDI between the sexes are inconsistent. The meaning of PDI is validated against a number of other survey data: other questions in the HERMES survey, the same questions used at IMEDE, and other questions used with other populations. From this a description has been distilled of the "Power Distance norm" as a value system held by the majority of a country's middle class. Correlations of PDI with geographic, economic, and demographic country indicators, comparisons of educational systems, and consideration of historical factors lead to a suggested causal chain for the origins of national differences. An analysis of political systems, religious life, and philosophical and ideological thinking in various countries shows differences which are interpreted as consequences of power distance norm differences, but which feed back into the norm and support it. Finally, the consequences of PDI differences for organizations are explored; the Power Distance dimension is associated with the "concentration of authority" dimension in the Aston studies of organization structures.

INEQUALITY AND POWER DISTANCE

On Animal and Human Inequality

A pet food manufacturer keeps 30 cats as a consumer panel. At the time of feeding, the cats cue up in a definite order, always the same. Only when a new cat enters is there some disorder: It tries to take a place in the cue and is bitten by every neighbor until it has found a place where henceforth it is tolerated.

Similar orders of inequality expressed in "dominance behavior" have been found among chickens (hence the term "pecking order") and among many other animals: species of apes, birds, and fish. On the other hand, some species do not show consistent dominance behavior: for example, gorillas, ducks, and carp (Bohannan, 1969: 164).

From a biological point of view, the human species belongs to the category that shows dominance behavior. Human pecking orders are part of the "universal" level of human mental programming (Figure 1.1). How the basic fact of dominance is worked out in human social existence, however, varies from one society to another and from one group to another: It belongs to the "collective," cultural level. Some societies have elaborate formal systems of dominance; others go to great lengths to deemphasize dominance. The great diversity of forms in which human societies deal with inequality and stratification has been described for nonliterate societies by anthropologists and modern societies by sociologists.[2] The general conclusion to be drawn from these descriptions is that stratification systems are extremely culturally dependent and that we should be very careful about extrapolating experience from one culture or subculture to another.

Inequality is one of the oldest concerns of human thinking. The following is a quote from Plato's *The Laws* written about 350 B.C.:

> [E]ven if you proclaim that a master and his slave shall have equal status, friendship between them is inherently impossible. The same applies to the relations between an honest man and a scoundrel. Indiscriminate equality for all amounts to *in*equality, and both fill a state with quarrels between its citizens. How correct the old saying is that "equality leads to friendship"! It's right enough and it rings true, but what kind of equality has this potential is a problem which produces ripe confusion. This is because we use the same term for two concepts of "equality" which in most respects are virtual opposites. The first sort of equality (of measures, weights and numbers) is within the competence of any state and any legislator; that is, one can simply distribute equal awards by lot. But the most genuine equality, and the best, is not so obvious. . . . . The general method I mean is to grant much to the great and less to the less great, adjusting what you give to take account of the real nature of each. [Saunders, 1970: 229–230].

The ambiguity of "the real nature of each" is precisely the reason why equality before and after Plato has always remained problematic. It is striking that Plato already plays on two meanings of the word "equality," which points to a semantic confusion which has forever existed and sometimes been exploited, as immortalized by George Orwell in *Animal Farm:* "All animals are equal but some are more equal than others." (In)equality is a multifaceted phenomenon.

Inequality in Society

Inequality can occur in a variety of areas:

—physical and mental characteristics—this is a basic fact of human existence;
—social status and prestige,
—wealth;
—power;
—laws, rights, and rules—"privileges" are private laws.

Inequality in these areas need not go together[3]: social inequality is multidimensional (Runciman, 1969). Successful athletes, artists, or scientists who show unique physical and/or mental characteristics usually enjoy status, but only in some societies do they enjoy wealth as well, and rarely do they have power. Politicians in some countries can enjoy status and power without wealth; businessmen, wealth and power without status. In general, in every society we can distinguish two opposing forces. One tries to eliminate status inconsistencies between the various areas (Lenski, 1966: 86). Sportsmen become professionals to gain access to wealth; politicians exploit their power to achieve the same; in some traditional societies, whoever is strong and smart gains prestige, wealth, power, and privileges. The counterforce tries to maintain equality by offsetting rank in one area against another. The stress in the Christian Bible and in Buddhism on the merits of poverty is a manifestation of this force[4]; so is Marx's plea for a "dictatorship of the proletariat." Universalistic legal systems deny privileges on the basis of status, wealth, or power.

The battle between the two forces—status consistency versus overall equality—is one of the basic issues in any human society. We find it in the quote from Plato above, in which he clearly defends status consistency. The opposite point of view is taken by Rousseau in his *Contrat Social* (1762[1972]):

> [L]e pacte fondamental substitue . . . . une égalité morale et légitime à ce que la nature avait pu mettre d'inégalité physique entre les hommes, et . . . . pouvant être inégaux en force ou en génie, ils deviennent tous égaux par convention et de droit.[5]

Rousseau proposes a distinction between "moral" and "natural" inequality, and he rejects the first while accepting the second as a fact of human existence. Béteille (1977: 10, 166) shows that this does not resolve the problem, because natural inequalities acquire meaning only by a process of evaluation which is culturally defined; it differs among societies and among epochs in history.

In a country in which people were not equal before the law (eighteenth-century France), Rousseau expected too much from establishing this formal legal equality. For a modern discussion of the same topic, consider the following quote from a U.S. newspaper:

> President Carter took issue yesterday with former President Richard Nixon's claim that
> the chief executive has an inherent power to order burglaries and other illegal actions
> against dissidents. President Carter does not feel any president has a right to break the
> law, said White House Deputy Press Secretary Rex Granum. He feels very strongly that
> it is a tragic mistake to follow that philosophy, as past events have shown so dramati-
> cally. He does feel there are adequate judicial means to prevent danger to the country.
> Mr. Nixon, defending some of the illegal acts that took place in his administration, made
> the assertion during the third of his televised interviews with David Frost, broadcast last
> night [*International Herald Tribune,* May 21–22, 1977: 3].

Carter in this case defends equality before the law against Nixon, who wants to let the
law yield to power.

In the manifestation of the dilemma of status consistency versus equality we
should distinguish sharply between the ideological and the pragmatic level, the level
of the desirable versus the desired as described in Chapter 1 (Figure 1.3). Plato,
Rousseau, and Carter all operate on the ideological level; Nixon is trying to justify
his acts and is therefore operating exceptionally on the pragmatic level; it is extremely unlikely that he would have made the same statement in other circumstances.
The reactions of the public to the Watergate affair, to which the Carter-Nixon quote
refers, can be seen as an attempt in American society to close the gap between the
desired and the desirable. Other societies at other moments in history have shown
even larger gaps in this respect. The "liberté, égalité, fraternité"[6] of the French
Revolution of 1789 was an ideological statement which did not cover the behavior of
the revolutionaries at all.[7] Lammers (1978a) distinguishes ideological "democrats"
and "oligocrats," but shows that different ideological positions may lead to the same
types of pragmatic action so that, for example, "constitutional oligocrats" can act as
"functional democrats" (1978a: 11).

In practice no society has ever obtained equality in the form of complete inconsistency between different areas of rank. What has been obtained in some societies is
what Galtung (1966) calls "criss-cross" in social structure: the existence of individuals who belong to disparate groups in the structure and can thus serve as bridges in
case of conflict. These individuals form a middle layer in society in between the "top
dogs" and the "underdogs." The stabilizing role in society of middle strata is an age-
old truth:

> Thus it is manifest . . . that those states are likely to be well-administered, in which the
> middle class is large . . . for the addition of the middle class turns the scale, and prevents
> either of the extremes from being dominant [Aristotle "The Politics," approximately 330
> B.C., reprinted in Bendix and Lipset, 1966: 1].

Societies with criss-cross structures can be called "pluralist"; societies without criss-
cross but with status consistency, "elitist" (Blais, 1974). Pluralist societies are less
unequal than elitist societies but still maintain large inequalities (Playford, 1976). In
all modern societies, probably without exception, there are disadvantaged groups
which are behind in physical and mental abilities, having been undernourished and
undereducated, who earn less and enjoy life less and who die younger (Sauvy, 1966:
80ff; Desplanques, 1973; Berthoud, 1976).

Related to the pluralist-elitist distinction is the aspect of social mobility. Other factors being equal, in pluralist societies new members will be more easily admitted into elites than in elitist societies, because the middle groups in the pluralist society are stepping stones to the top dog ranks.

Societies differ in the implications of rank inequalities for social functioning. Bohannan (1969: 198ff) distinguishes between caste, estate, and class. *Castes,* as existed formally in preindependence India, are organized associations of extended families, membership in which determines a person's rank in all areas of life. In modern India castes formally have been abolished; but they continue to affect daily life very deeply (Srinivas, 1969; Béteille, 1977: 28ff). *Estates,* as existed in feudal Europe (nobility, yeomanry, and serfs), are legal categories of people with specific rights and obligations but without organizations uniting members of the same category. *Classes* in modern sociology are categories of people who are not necessarily organized as such (Marx wanted them to organize) or legally identified but which share characteristics on which they can be ranked: prestige, wealth, power. Class members are usually identified by their economic activity and/or educational background, and they can be shown to share the same values, forming subcultures. Aron (1969) distinguishes between a "nominalist" definition of class, which is typical for U.S. sociology, and a "realist" definition, which is typical for French sociology. In the nominalist definition, the central concept is the "deference" present in the mind of the individual member of the lower classes. In the realist definition, there is a collective consciousness of the members of a class of belonging together. Behind this difference in definitions is a difference in societies; "class" in France is much more a reality than in the United States.

Inkeles (1960) has reviewed data on attitudes and values from a large number of studies, each comparing different classes within one society from a variety of societies, and concludes, "the average proportion of persons holding particular view may be distinctive of a given country, but within all modern societies the order or structure of response is the same, following the typical status ladders of occupation, income, and education" (1960: 1). Parkin (1971:81ff) distinguishes between a dominant value system, a subordinate value system (which is accommodating to the dominant one and held by the nonelites; both support the status quo), and a radical value system which promotes opposition to the existing inequalities.

Castes, estates, and classes represent more or less integrated systems; one class presupposes other classes. However, societies may also contain unintegrated groups. Bohannan (1969: 183) calls these the "pariahs" after the untouchables of India. Racial minorities or even majorities may be such pariahs; the migrant workers in Western Europe (12 million in 1976) represent another pariah group. "Pariahs are, by definition, kept outside the recognized major institutions of the social structure, although they usually have an economic link with them" (1963: 184). In the case of pariahs, the inequality is total.

Inequality in Organizations

Within organizations as units of society, we inevitably find inequality of members' abilities and inequality of power. An unequal distribution of power over members is the essence of organization. Without it we get something like "a flock of birds, in which the only rule of behaviour for each bird is to change the direction of its flight so that, relatively, it always sees its fellows in the same position and thus never leaves the group" (Cotta, 1976: 178). Inequality of power in organizations is essential for temporarily overcoming the Law of Entropy, which states that disorder will increase (p. 176). Even organizations designed to be equalitarian, such as political parties, develop their power elites; this is Michels' Iron Law of Oligarchy (Michels, 1915 [1962]: 342ff).

In most utilitarian organizations, the distribution of power is formalized in a hierarchy.[8] The basic element from which hierarchical pyramids are built is the relationship between a boss B and a subordinate S. If we know that S "reports to B," we know certain formal aspects of their relationship; it is likely that B can set priorities for S's work and possible that B has some influence on S's rewards and career. Luhmann (1975: 104) feels that power in organizations is mainly exercised through influence on people's careers, but this may be more true in societies and groups in which careers are more important (as in Germany; see Chapter 6). Beyond the few formal aspects, we know little about the actual power relationship between B and S. A boss and a subordinate can fill in their formal hierarchical relationship in very different ways (Crozier, 1964a: 160; Hofstede, 1967: 9ff; Luhmann, 1975; 111). Objective factors play a role, such as the expertise of both parties, the history of their relationship, the task at hand, and the relative criticalness of the situation (Mulder et al., 1971). Then there are the subjective factors of the way in which B and S choose to play their hierarchical roles, which depends on their mental programming and their psychological impact on each other. Their mental programming contains their personalities and their values, affected by the societal norms which they respect.

The boss-subordinate relationship is a basic human relationship which bears resemblance to even more fundamental relationships earlier in life: that of parent and child (Levinson et al., 1962: 69; Kakar, 1971) and of teacher and pupil. Both as bosses and as subordinates, people can be expected to carry over values and norms from their early life experiences as children and school pupils. As family and school environments differ strongly among cultures, we can expect to find the traces of these differences in the exercise of power in hierarchies.

Differences in the exercise of power in a hierarchy relate to the value systems of both bosses *and* subordinates and not to the values of the bosses only, even through they are the more powerful partners. The popular management literature on "leadership" often forgets that leadership can only exist as a complement to "subordinateship."[9] In the same way that patterns of inequality between groups in society are supported by both dominant and subordinate value systems, patterns of power inequality within organizations reflect the values of both parties. Subordinates as a group are accessary to the exercise of power in a hierarchical system: The way the system functions reflects their collective complicity and the role relationship to which both parties contribute. Authority only exists where it is matched by obedience. In France, Etienne de La Boétie wrote in 1548 (1976) in his *Discours de la Servitude Volontaire* that a tyrant has no other power than that which is given to him, and that the problem is less the tyrant than the "voluntary servitude" of his subjects.[10] On the psychological level, the need for independence in people is matched by a need for dependence, and the need for power by a need for security; dependence and security needs stem from early childhood and are common to all mankind; independence and power are only developed later in our lives, if they are developed at all (McGregor, 1960: 26; Levinson et al., 1962: 43).

The Concept of Power Distance

In order to describe meaningfully the relationship between boss B and subordinate S in a hierarchy, including its values component, I shall use the concept of Power Distance. Power Distance is a measure of the interpersonal power or influence between B and S as perceived by the least powerful of the two, S. The term "power distance" is taken from the work of Mulder (et al., 1971; Mulder, 1976, 1977); Mulder's theory is based on a long series of laboratory and field experiments with simple social structures. Mulder defines "power" as "the potential to determine or direct (to a certain extent) the behaviour of another person/other persons more so than the other way round," and "power distance" as "the degree of inequality in power between a less powerful Individual (I) and a more powerful Other (O), in which I and O belong to the same (loosely or tightly knit) social system" (Mulder, 1977: 90). He has proved about 20 hypotheses, of which the most relevant to this study are the following (p. 92):

1. The mere exercise of power will give satisfaction
2. The more powerful individual will strive to maintain or to increase the power distance to the less powerful person.
3. The greater this distance from the less powerful person, the stronger the striving to increase it.
4. Individuals will strive to reduce the power distance between themselves and more powerful persons.
5. The smaller this distance from the more powerful person, the stronger the tendency to reduce it.
3/5. The "downward" tendencies of the powerful to maintain the power distance, and the "upward" power distance reduction of the less powerful reinforce each other.

The implication of hypothesis 5 is that the strongest power distance reduction tendency "will not be found in the powerless, but in people whose power striving is partly satisfied. *The power striving is not fed by dissatisfaction* but by satisfaction. Having power feeds the need, making it comparable to the need for hard drugs. An individual can become addicted to "power distance reduction" (1977: 46).

Mulder makes it plausible that the hypotheses proved in his laboratory setting are valid for (Dutch) societal settings such as labor-management relationships. In the United States, Kipnis (1972) independently carried out laboratory experiments similar to Mulder's and arrived at similar conclusions. Kipnis shows that more powerful persons tend to devalue the worth of the performance of less powerful ones and to attribute the cause of the less powerful's efforts to themselves. Kipnis et al. (1976) show that this even applies between partners in marriage and for U.S. housewives employing maids. The conclusions from Mulder's and Kipnis' psychological experiments converge with those from sociological studies on the forming of power elites, such as Michels' Iron Law of Oligarchy, to which I referred earlier in this chapter; Michels' "law" is based on an analysis of the German Social Democratic Party before

World War I and of other European socialist parties. There is therefore evidence from a number of western countries which supports the validity of Mulder's hypotheses. This evidence shows how inequality confirms and perpetuates itself. Boulding (1978: 282, 283) refers to the "Matthew principle" (from the Christian New Testament, Matthew 13: 12: "for he who has, to him shall more be given"); Boulding finds the Matthew principle present both in the concentration of power and in the concentration of wealth.

In the poorer countries, historical events point strongly to the confirmation and perpetuation of inequality in power, so that it is very likely that here, too, Mulder's Power Distance Theory applies. However, where cultural differentiation comes in is in determining the level of power distance at which the tendency of the powerful to maintain or increase power distances and the tendency of the less powerful to reduce them will find their equilibrium. My definition of power distance (which does not differ substantially from Mulder's) is as follows:

> The power distance between a boss B and a subordinate S in a hierarchy is the difference between the extent to which B can determine the behavior of S and the extent to which S can determine the behavior of B.[11]

What I shall try to show in this chapter is that the *power distance, thus defined, which is accepted by both B and S and supported by their social environment is to a considerable extent determined by their national culture.*

Power Distance and Human Inequality

If different cultures can be shown to maintain consistently different power distances in hierarchies, the Power Distance norm can be used as a criterion for characterizing cultures (without excluding other criteria). In fact, various authors have referred to such a criterion. For example, Gasse (1976: 6) argues that "each culture justifies authority using its major values" and then proceeds to picture a continuum of which the two poles are "monolithism" and "pluralism." At the monolithic pole, cultures are characterized by power held by few people; at the pluralistic pole, competition between groups and leaders is encouraged, control by leaders is limited since members can join several organizations, democratic politics are fostered and information sources are independent of a single organization.

In Chapter 1, ways of dealing with hierarchy and authority as a proposed criterion for ordering cultures were mentioned in reference to the work of Kluckhohn and Strodtbeck (1961) and of Inkeles and Levinson (1969). A summary is given by Albert (1968: 289):

> [I]n a number of societies as remote from each other as imperial China and the Central African kingdom of Burundi, the model of filial piety, associated with a rigidly hierarchical ordering of all social relations, draws together in a single formula masses of verbal and behavioral data. In parent-child relations, husband-wife relations, politics, religion, and economics, the same superordinate-subordinate pattern applies.

This latter quote suggests that a Power Distance norm spills over from one sphere of life—work organizations—into others; in fact, it helps us to find the origin of a Power Distance norm in the early socialization by the family, the school, and the other institutions of society. However, it is then likely that larger inequalities in *power* are also reflected in larger inequalities in the other areas referred to earlier in this chapter: in particular, social status and prestige, wealth, and rights. There is empirical evidence for this: For example, Tannenbaum et al. (1974) have shown in their study of hierarchy in industrial organizations in five countries that greater differences in power are associated with greater differences ("gradients") of rewards, privileges, and opportunities between bosses and subordinates. Such differences in other areas in their turn feed back into the power distance and reinforce it. We can therefore expect to find differences in the Power Distance norm between societies associated with degrees of inequality in other areas.

So far we have applied the term "power distance" rather indiscriminately regardless of the level of aggregation of phenomena: to the small group (Mulder's experiments) and to society as a whole. We may, however, have to become more precise as to the level at which our hypotheses apply. In particular, we may find different norms as to power distances *within groups* and *between groups* in society. It is possible that within certain groups small power distances between "bosses" and "subordinates" are maintained, while from one group to another the power and other inequalities are very large (Béteille, 1977: 44). Moreover, power in the relationships between groups and organizations is not just a replication of power between people within groups and organizations (Crozier, 1973: 225). Whether norms of power distance between groups co-vary with norms for power distance within groups is a matter for empirical research.

MEASURING NATIONAL DIFFERENCES IN
POWER DISTANCE IN HERMES

Organization of Chapters 3 Through 6

The remainder of this chapter will be devoted to the analysis of research evidence: first, of data collected within the HERMES Corporation, and second, of the relationship between the HERMES data and data from a wide range of other sources. This analysis uses a fair amount of statistical argumentation, applying factor analysis, product moment and Spearman rank correlations, multiple and stepwise regression, and significance tests. In the interest of the readability of the book, the purely statistical part has been assembled in a separate section at the end of Chapter 3 ("Statistical Analysis of Data Used"). The same procedure will be followed in Chapters 4 through 6, which deal with the other dimensions of national culture. In the main body of each chapter, the results of the statistical analysis will be reported, while the reader is referred to the statistical sections for proof.

A Power Distance Index
for HERMES Countries

I chose as the central questionnaire item for exploring power distance differences between countries, "How frequently, in your experience, does the following problem occur: employees being afraid to express disagreement with their managers?" (B46 in Appendix 1, with a five-point answer scale from "very frequently" to "very seldom"). Of all the questions in the questionnaire, this one seems most clearly to express power distance. It is a projective question: respondents are not asked how frequently they *themselves* are afraid to disagree, but their answers can be expected to reflect a projection of their own feelings.

Fear of disagreement has been used as a measure by others. In a series of surveys in the United States Patchen (1965: 48– 54) used an index of "willingness to disagree with supervisors." Across individual respondents, it correlated with employee control over work goals, interest in work innovation, and (in most cases) the supervisor's ranking of employees in order of readiness to disagree. A reference to fear of disagreement as part of a country's culture is found in Whyte (1969: 37), who deals with an example from Venezuela:

> In a highly stratified society where all powers are concentrated in the hands of the superior, the subordinate learns that it can be dangerous to question a decision of the superior. In this type of situation, people learn to behave submissively—at least in the presence of the boss. They do not learn to thrash things out with him, face-to-face. Then, when there is no reason to fear, they still do not feel that it is natural to speak up.

This attitude occurs not only among lower-level employees. Negandhi and Prasad (1971: 128) quote a senior Indian executive with a Ph.D. from a prestigious American university:

> What is most important for me and my department is not what I do or achieve for the company, but whether the Master's (i.e., an owner of the firm) favor is bestowed on me . . . This I have achieved by saying "yes" to everything the Master says or does . . . [T]o contradict him is to look for another job. . . . I left my freedom of thought in Boston.

In the HERMES data on the "employees afraid" question (Appendix 2), Venezuela and India (the two countries from which the quotes above originate) are among the top five most "afraid" countries.

Two other questions in the HERMES questionnaire, A54 and A55, provide unique information about power distances in boss-subordinate relationships. They use a description of four types of decision-making behavior by managers and ask subordinates to indicate (a) their preferred type and (b) their perception of their boss' actual type. The descriptions of the four types were originally taken from Tannenbaum and Schmidt (1958). In the version of the questionnaire used from 1967 to 1969, the four decision-making styles are (1) autocratic ("tells"), (2) persuasive/paternalistic ("sells"), (3) consultative ("consults"), and (4) democratic (majority vote, "joins"). Since 1970 the description of the fourth type was changed to a participative (consensus) style, more or less conforming to Likert (1967)'s "System 4." This was done because the actual occurrence of the old type 4 was perceived as very rare, and offering a possibility to choose the "participative" style was seen as desirable for organization development purposes. This change obviously affects the response distribution; it can be expected to affect especially the distribution of responses between managers 3 and 4, less the choices for 1 and 2.[12]

Whereas the "employees afraid" question asked for a perception of the behavior of fellow employees, the "perceived manager" question asks for a perception of the behavior of the boss. It is a subjective description of the boss' decision-making behavior; but in order to understand the boss' impact on subordinate behavior, a subjective description by the subordinate is probably more relevant than would be any objective description (assuming we would be able to obtain such a description).

There is a significant correlation across the 40 countries of the mean "employees afraid" scores and the mean percentage of employees perceiving a manager 1 or 2 (autocratic or persuasive/paternalistic): If managers are more often seen as autocratic, employees are more often seen as afraid to disagree with them, and vice versa (see the statistical section, Figure 3.11).

As opposed to the "employees afraid" and "perceived manager" questions, which deal with perceptions rather than values, the "preferred manager" question directly expresses a value; in the terminology of Chapter 1, I call this a "value as the desired." The statistical analysis shows that across the 40 HERMES countries, the percentages of employees preferring a certain type of manager are correlated with the perceptions both of employees being afraid and of managers being autocratic or persuasive/paternalistic. The correlations, however, are much higher for the 1967–1969 data (using a manager 4 = democratic, majority vote) than for the 1971–1973 data (manager 4 = participative, consensus). This is why for the HERMES Power Distance Index I have used only the 1967–1969 data for the "preferred manager" question. Interestingly, the pattern of correlations (Figure 3.10) opposes the preference for manager 3 (consultative) to all others (1, 2, or 4: autocratic, persuasive, *or democratic*). In countries in which few employees are perceived as afraid, many employees prefer a "consultative" manager. In countries in which many employees are perceived as afraid, employees tend *not* to prefer the consultative manager but to vote for the autocratic, the persuasive, *or* the democratic, majority vote manager.

The correlation between a preference for a consultative manager and "employees not afraid" shows that a particular power relationship is established through the values of *both* partners, the superiors as well as the subordinates. In systems in which superiors maintain large power distances, subordinates *prefer* such superiors *(dependent reaction)* or go to the other extreme—that is, they prefer a superior who does not decide at all but who governs by a majority vote of his subordinates. This latter type of decision-making is unlikely to be effective in work organizations: it would be feasible only if departments were completely autonomous and independent of other departments, while in fact modern work organizations are complex interdependent systems. Therefore, the preference for a majority vote decision type is unrealistic; I interpret it as a *counterdependent reaction* to a situation of large power distance. So we see that where superiors maintain a large power distance, subordinates tend to polarize into dependence and counterdependence.[13] On the other hand, where superiors maintain a smaller power distance, subordinates tend to prefer the consultative decision style; this can be interpreted as an *interdependence* between superior and subordinate. This interdependent relationship is more in line with the requirements of modern work organizations as complex systems.

The participative manager (number 4, 1971–1973) does not collect "counterdependence" votes. The preference for this type is unrelated to the country's Power Distance level. In an unpublished study of HERMES' manufacturing employees, it has been shown that a preference for a participative manager related partly to the respondents' age: across countries, 37 percent of those between 25 and 30 chose a participative manager, but only 25 percent of those between 40 and 50 chose such a manager.

A Power Distance Index for each of the 40 countries has now been computed on the basis of the country mean scores for the three questions:

(a) Nonmanagerial employees' perception that employees are afraid to disagree with their managers (B46).

(b) Subordinates' perception that their boss tends to take decisions in an autocratic (1) or persuasive/paternalistic (2) way (A55).

(c) Subordinates' preference for anything but a consultative (3) style of decision-making in their boss: that is, for an autocratic (1), a persuasive/paternalistic (2), *or* a democratic (4) style (A54).

The actual computation of the country Power Distance Index (PDI) uses mean percent values for question b and c: in the case of b, for 1967–1969 plus 1971–1973 data; in the case of c, for 1967–1969 data only. It uses mean scores on a five-point scale (1 = very frequently, 5 = very seldom) for question a; these mean scores have been multiplied by 25 to make their range, and therefore their contribution to the PDI, roughly equal to the range in percentage values of questions b and c. The actual formula used is:

PDI = 135 − 25 (mean score empl. afraid)
   + (% perceived mgr. 1 + 2)
   − (% preferred mgr. 3—1967–1969).

The constant 135 has been added to give the country index values a range between zero (small Power Distance) and 100 (large Power Distance). The theoretical range of the index is from − 90 (no one afraid, no manager 1 + 2, everyone prefers 3) to +210 (everyone afraid, all managers 1 + 2, no one prefers 3).

The computation of the PDI values for the 40 countries can be reconstructed from the values in Appendix 2 (for the filling in of missing data, see the statistical section). The resulting values are listed in Figure 3.1 (first column).

Country Index values range from 11 for Austria (small Power Distance) to 94 for Philippines (large Power Distance), with an overall mean for 39 HERMES countries of 51 (52 across all 40 countries, including Yugoslavia). The ranking of the countries suggests immediately certain clusters of similar countries, to which I shall come back later in this chapter and in Chapter 7.

The Power Distance Index is a measure of *values* found in the HERMES subsidiaries, but it differs from classical values tests in several respects. First, it applies to entire subsidiaries, not to individuals: It is an *ecological* index (for the difference between individual and ecological measures, see Chapter 1). Second, all three questions are asked of the subordinates rather than the superiors—that is, asked of the least powerful partners in the relationship who can be supposed to be better judges of power distance than their more powerful superiors. Third, only question c asks for a value in the strict sense: a preference for one state of affairs over others. Question b deals with a characteristic of the organizational "regime" (the superior's style of decision-making) and question a with an aspect of the organizational "climate" (the extent to which employees are afraid to disagree). Obviously, the scores on questions a and b represent perceptions which are in the beholder as well as in the objective situation, but this is true for any measure of regime or climate. People are more accurate in describing others than in describing themselves.[14] As the statistical analysis shows (Figure 3.11), the correlations among the country scores on the three questions across the 40 countries are well over .50, so that in this case value, regime, and climate go together, forming a coherent pattern which differentiates between one

FIGURE 3.1   Power Distance Index (PDI) Values by Country Based on the
Scores on Three Attitude Survey Questions for a Stratified
Sample of Seven Occupations at Two Points in Time

Country	PDI Actual	PDI Predicted	Country	PDI Actual	PDI Predicted
Philippines	94	73	South Africa	49	62
Mexico	81	70	Argentina	49	56
Venezuela	81	66	U.S.A.	40	42
India	77	78	Canada	39	36
Singapore	74	64	Netherlands	38	38
Brazil	69	72	Australia	36	44
Hong Kong	68	56	Germany (F.R.)	35	42
France	68	42	Great Britain	35	45
Colombia	67	75	Switzerland	34	32
Turkey	66	60	Finland	33	30
Belgium	65	36	Norway	31	27
Peru	64	69	Sweden	31	23
Thailand	64	74	Ireland	28	37
Chile	63	56	New Zealand	22	35
Portugal	63	53	Denmark	18	28
Greece	60	51	Israel	13	44
Iran	58	61	Austria	11	40
Taiwan	58	63			
Spain	57	56	Mean of 39 countries	51	52
Pakistan	55	74	(HERMES)		
Japan	54	57			
Italy	50	53	Yugoslavia (same industry)	76	53

Actual values and values predicted on the basis of multiple regression on latitude, population size,
and wealth.

country and another. Across 38 occupations, the mean scores on the three questions
are also highly correlated (see below). However, the correlations among the three
questions across *individuals* are virtually zero. It is not necessarily the individual
who sees his boss as autocratic, who will also describe his colleagues as afraid, and
who will prefer an autocratic boss. The lack of individual correlations should remind
us that Power Distance as measured here can be used only as a characteristic of *social
systems,* not of *individuals.* It cannot be used to measure, for example, the authoritarianism of individuals; however, it can be used to measure the "authoritarianism" of
whole societies and their dominant supervision styles (Glaser, 1971: 96-98).

Power Distance Index Scores by Occupation

The high correlations among the *occupation* scores for the three PDI questions
which are shown in Figure 3.11 mean that a Power Distance Index also can be
meaningfully computed by occupation. This has been done elsewhere (Hofstede,
1977c); a summary of the scores found (using the same formula as for countries) is
listed in Figure 3.2.

FIGURE 3.2   Power Distance Index Values for Six Categories of
              Occupations

Categories of occupations	Number of occupations in this category	PDI		
		Range		
		From	to	Mean
Unskilled and semiskilled workers	3	85	97	90
Clerical workers and nonprofessional salesmen	8	57	84	71
Skilled workers and technicians	6	33	90	65
Managers of the previous categories	8	22	62	42
Professional workers	8	−22	36	22
Managers of professional workers	5	−19	21	8
Total	38	−22	97	47

Stratified sample of data from France, Germany, and Great Britain. This is a summary of Table 2 in Hofstede (1977c).

In the same way as country scores had to be computed for a stratified sample of occupations, occupation scores had to be computed for a stratified sample of countries. The data in Figure 3.2 are based on responses from the three large countries, France, Germany, and Great Britain, giving equal weight to each.

We see that the lower-education, lower-status occupations tend to produce high PDI values and the higher-education, higher-status occupations tend to produce low PDI values. Education is by far the dominant factor: The correlation of the occupation's PDI with the average years of formal education is an amazing $r = -.90$. Every additional year of formal school education needed for an occupation reduces the occupation's PDI score by about 18 points.[15]

There is also a tendency for managers to produce lower PDI values than non-managers.[16] The multiple correlation of PDI with education and hierarchical level is $R = .94$, showing that the occupation's PDI is highly predictable from these two factors (88% of the variance in occupational PDI is explained).

The conclusions of the occupational data analysis so far are as follows:

(1) Power distances between less educated and nonmanagerial employees and their superiors tend to be larger than between more educated and managerial employees and their superiors.
(2) The range of PDI scores among different countries (Figure 3.1), holding occupation and thereby education constant, is still nearly as large as among different occupations (Figure 3.2). The differences in hierarchial power distance found between equally educated employees in different countries are therefore of the same magnitude as those between unskilled workers and college-trained professionals within one country.

We have now studied the country and the occupation effect on Power Distance, but not yet their interaction. Some insight into country-occupation interactions can be obtained from Figure 3.3.

FIGURE 3.3   Power Distance Index Values for Four Occupations in Each of 11 Countries

	All occupations	B.O. technical experts	H.O. clerks	B.O. service techn. B	Unskilled plant workers B	Δ Occupations (highest–lowest)	Spearman correlation with Occupation PDI
Country	PDI	29	61	63	97		
Mexico	81	83	97	99	99	16	.95
India	77	80	81	87	88	8	1.00*
Brazil	69	64	90	96	115	51	1.00*
France	68	58	84	86	108	50	1.00*
Colombia	67	48	94	95	106	58	1.00*
Japan	54	58	57	84	92	35	.80
Argentina	49	57	96	77	106	49	.80
Canada	39	24	42	55	80	56	1.00*
Netherlands	38	17	59	41	83	66	.80
Germany (F.R.)	35	14	53	62	90	76	1.00*
Great Britain	35	15	50	42	102	87	.80
Δ countries (highest–lowest)	46	69	55	58	35		.80
Spearman rank correlation with country PDI		.96***	.70**	.90***	.35	−.82***	

Each cell (one country, one occupation) counts at least 20 respondents.

In Figure 3.3, PDI scores are shown for 44 one-country, one-occupation subpopulations. Four nonmanagerial occupations are covered:

(1) branch office technical experts, average educational level 15.8 years;
(2) head office clerks, average educational level 12.9 years;
(3) branch office service technicians B, average educational level 12.2 years; and
(4) unskilled plant workers B, average educational level 10.5 years.

Occupation 1 is college level and can be rated upper middle class; 2 and 3 are high school level and lower middle class; 4 is less than high school and working class. Data on occupation 4 are only available for 11 countries from the 13 in which HERMES has manufacturing plants. The PDI scores for the other three occupations are shown only for these same 11 countries. These three are included in the seven occupational categories that were used to compute country PDI-scores; occupation 4, evidently, was not.

We see in Figure 3.3 that the ranking of the four occupations in order of Power Distance is largely retained for each country and that the ranking of the 11 countries is similar across the first three occupations (which contributed to the country scores) but less between these and the unskilled workers. The most striking conclusion from the table is an interaction effect between country and occupation: The country differences are much larger for the more-educated than for the less-educated occupations, and the occupation differences are much larger in the small power distance countries than in the large power distance countries. The theoretical maximum PDI score is 210, but it looks as if there is a practical maximum of around 100 and all respondents in high power distance countries (regardless of educational level) and all respondents in unskilled jobs (regardless of country) are pushed against this ceiling. Low PDI values occur only for highly educated occupations in low power distance countries. Class differences in Power Distance scores are particularly high in Great Britain and Germany. Such differences are low in India and Mexico because in these countries power distances are large for everyone, regardless of class. Japan takes a middle position with middle-range Power Distance scores for all four occupations.

The fact that less-educated, lower-status employees hold more "authoritarian" values has been signaled before—for example, for employees in banking, insurance, and government administration in France by Crozier (1964b); for automobile workers in Detroit by Kornhauser (1965: 267); and for parents of 10–11-year-old children in the United States and Italy by Kohn (1969: passim). The latter two studies started from an interest in mental health and show that among less-educated, lower-status people there is also a greater frequency of mental health problems (compare Chapter 4). Kohn (1969) goes deeply into the relationship between these phenomena. For his U.S. data, he combines educational and occupational level into a social class index (Hollingshead's Index of Social Position); his study relates this social class index to the respondents' values and behavior. The main conclusion of his book is that parents higher on the social class scale "are more likely to emphasize children's self-direction, and working-class parents to emphasize their conformity to external authority" (1969: 34).

> The essence of higher class position is the expectation that one's decisions and actions can be consequential; the essence of lower class position is the belief that one is at the mercy of forces and people beyond one's control, often beyond one's understanding [1969: 189].

> The class relationships are built on the cumulative effects of educational training and occupational experience. The former is present insofar as it provides or fails to provide the capacity for self-direction, the latter insofar as it provides or fails to provide the experience of exercising self-direction in so consequential a realm of life as work [1969: 188].

Kohn also shows, however, that social class and national environment interact in the maintenance of authoritarian values. Working-class fathers put high value on their children's obedience in both Italy and the United States, but middle-class fathers stress this point much more in Italy than in America (p. 42). As Italy is a higher PDI country than the United States, this is in line with the trend of Figure 3.3. Interestingly, Kohn's data for *mothers* also show a class effect and a country effect but not an interaction between the two, as for the fathers.

What we have seen in the PDI data so far is that class differences in values about power distance are more clearly present in some countries than in others; especially in less economically developed countries such as Mexico and India, even the middle classes seem to feel at the mercy of forces beyond their control. I shall continue to identify countries as "low PDI" or "high PDI," but the reader should remember that this distinction refers to my middle-class sample and applies much less to working-class respondents.

Sex Differences in Power Distance

Besides country and occupation, the two other universal criteria by which the HERMES survey data can be differentiated are the sex and the age group of the respondents. As age group differences can also reveal shifts over time, they will be discussed in Chapter 8. Sex and occupation are highly interdependent, so the analysis by sex makes sense only for occupations which are filled by sizable numbers of both men and women doing the same work.

In Figure 3.4 the computation of PDI by sex is shown for one professional and one clerical occupation which more or less fulfil these criteria. As the relative numbers of men and women in these occupations vary only modestly among the larger country subsidiaries, I have, for simplicity, taken total world data in Figure 3.4 (all respondents together, regardless of country); I also took the mean of the two survey rounds, at least for questions a and b. We should first check whether comparing the sexes on a Power Distance *Index* makes sense. That is, do the three questions that make up the PDI differentiate in the same direction between the sexes? The table shows that questions a and c differentiate and that b does not differentiate at all.[17] Only one difference is statistically significant: Female clerks have less preference for a consultative manager than their male colleagues. We saw earlier in the analysis of variance of the manufacturing data (Figure 2.4) that in this case, too, only the preference for a consultative manager shows a significant sex effect; and inspection of the data (not visible in the table) shows that this effect is in the same direction: Female manufacturing employees prefer less a consultative manager. In Figure 3.4 I have computed

FIGURE 3.4   Power Distance Index Computation for Men and Women in the Same Occupations.

Occupations (2 surveys, total world data)	(a) Not perceiving employees afraid mean score	(b) % Perceiving superior as autocratic or paternalistic	(c) % Preferring consultative manager (1967–1969)	Power Distance Index = 135–25 a + b – c
Branch office technical experts				
men (n = 9917)	3.32	43	67	28
women (n = 591)	3.26	43	64	33
Head office clerks				
men (n = 7665)	2.98	48	52	57
women (n = 5496)	2.96	48	41***	68

The differences between men and women on question a, tested by the t-test for differences of means, do not reach statistical significance.

The differences between men and women on question c, tested by the Kolmogorov-Smirnov test, are not significant for Branch Office technical experts but significant at the .001 level for Head Office clerks.

PDI values, which are higher for women than for men (especially in the case of the less educated group, the clerks). It is, however, questionable whether one statistically significant difference out of six justifies the use of PDI for comparing between the sexes. PDI is not the proper index for this: Using it would mean a reverse ecological fallacy (see Chapter 1).

Country Power Distance Index Scores
and Other HERMES Survey Questions

The three questions making up the PDI are only a small fraction of the questions in the HERMES questionnaire conceptually related to values. As can be read from the correlations across countries between PDI and the other questions (see Appendix 2), respondents in high PDI countries, compared with those in low PDI countries, endorse significantly more frequently the following items:[18]

(1) Employees lose respect for a consultative manager (B55); and a good manager gives detailed instructions (C9).
(2) My manager is not concerned with helping me get ahead (A52); and an employee should not ask for a salary increase (C18).
(3) However, employees in industry should participate more in the decisions taken by management (B56).
(4) The average human being has an inherent dislike of work and will avoid it if he can (C13).
(5) There are few qualities in a man more admirable than dedication and loyalty to his company (C12), and most employees want to make a real contribution to the success of it (C14).
(6) By and large, companies change their policies and practices much too often (C16).
(7) Finally, for the same occupations, respondents in higher PDI countries tend to have more years of education (A56).

It may strike the reader that these statements are partly contradictory (for example, 1 and 3, 4 and the second question in 5). However, eco-logic differs from personal logic.

Points 1 and 2 in the list (questions B55, C9, A52, and C18) are consistent. The manager in a high PDI environment is more of an initiator. Factor analytic studies of leadership behavior, such as the classic Ohio State studies (Stogdill and Coons, 1957), typically show two dimensions: a "people" and a "task" dimension (in the Ohio State studies these are labeled "consideration" and "initiating structure"). In HERMES, the question "manager helps ahead" has been shown to be the most central "consideration" question (Hofstede et al., 1976: 25). A high PDI environment stands for more initiating structure and less consideration.

Point 3, the agreement that "employees should participate more" in higher PDI countries (B56, correlation with PDI: $r = -.65$) shows that the images of the ideal manager and of the ideal control structure (participation/nonparticipation in the decisions taken by management) are not complementary. We can interpret this as a conflict between values as the desirable (employee participation as an ideology) and values as the desired (my own interaction with my boss in day-to-day matters). The ideological statement acts to some extent as a compensation for what happens on the pragmatic level. In low PDI countries where there is not only a more delegating manager ideal but more de facto delegation, people are less emphatic about a need for more employee participation. In high PDI countries there will be a stronger ideological push toward models of formal participation (for example, through works councils, boardroom representation, or even nationalization), but also more resistance against de facto participation. The paradox is that it is more difficult to realize ideological ideals of participation if people at the same time desire and expect powerful persons to maintain large power distances toward them. Practice has shown that not only informal consultation but also formal participation has advanced more easily in some low PDI countries, such as Sweden and Norway, than in high PDI countries, such as Yugoslavia, Peru, or Chile.

Point 4, "the average human dislikes work" (C13; correlation with PDI; r = .75) is directly taken from McGregor's Theory X (McGregor, 1960: 33). The strong ecological correlation between high PDI and more agreement with Theory X throws additional light on the nature of McGregor's distinction. In his book, *The Human Side of Enterprise* (1960), McGregor called his Theories X and Y "theoretical assumptions of management." An entire management development business has interpreted this in such a way that if managers could only learn the new theory (Y) they would adopt different leadership strategies and become more effective. McGregor, in the meantime, seems to have become more and more aware of the cultural nature of the distinction. In his posthumous book, *The Professional Manager* (1967), he calls Theories X and Y "managerial cosmologies" (theories about the nature of the world) and continues:

> Theory X and Theory Y are *not* managerial strategies. They are underlying beliefs about the nature of men that *influence* managers to adopt one strategy rather than another [1967: 79].

Earlier in the same book (p. 17) he has related cosmology to selective perceptions of reality. He also uses the word "values":

> The values that I have stated are part of my identity. I perceive my role as a human being and as a behavioral scientist to include the promotion of them. I share them with some of my colleagues, and not with others. They certainly affect my interpretation of objective scientific evidence. I do not believe it is possible for me to eliminate their influence on my views concerning appropriate managerial strategies [1967: 78].

The PDI-Theory X correlation across a number of countries (in this case, 30) provides empirical proof that we are dealing with a values complex, a true cosmology which is embedded in the social system as much as in the minds of the people. It also shows that Theory X, like PDI, is in the minds of respondents in every category in a country, *not only of managers* (the HERMES scores are mainly based on answers by nonmanagers). A psychologistic interpretation of Theory X-Y as a set of assumptions of individuals which can be changed by training neglects the profound sociocultural roots of the phenomenon.

What remains to be seen is whether all that is covered by McGregor's Theory X is part of a single cosmology on which country cultures differ. A second statement which also belongs to Theory X was used in the HERMES questionnaire as well. This is B61: "Most employees in industry prefer to avoid responsibility, have little ambition, and want security above all." This is *not* correlated with PDI (r = − .07) and only weakly with the first statement (rho = .34 across 30 countries). It seems that at least on the level of country cultures, liking work for its own sake (the perceived work ethic) and ambition are two different things. The two may be associated within the American middle-class culture from which McGregor writes, but they do not extend from one culture to another. There are cultures which are characterized by a lower perceived work ethic but not by a lower perceived level of ambition and in which people will try to meet their ambition in other ways than by working hard. The perceived work ethic is negatively correlated with PDI. The perceived level of ambition is not; in fact, it is weakly negatively correlated with the Uncertainty Avoidance Index (r = −.31; see Appendix 2).

Point 5 (items C12 and C14) seems to express that anything that stresses the relationship between employee and company is endorsed more strongly in higher PDI countries (see also Chapter 5). Point 6 (item C16) shows a resistance to change in higher PDI countries which will be shown to be related also to uncertainty avoidance (Chapter 4). Point 7, finally, shows that the correlation between PDI and educational level can be positive across countries (r = .44), whereas we saw earlier that it was strongly negative across occupations (r = −.90). In higher PDI countries, HERMES employees in the particular set of occupations (managerial, professional, technical, and clerical) tend to have *more* years of formal education than in lower PDI countries. This is a consequence of both the labor market situation and the educational system in many less-developed countries: a large offer of candidates with long but impractical formal schooling. Within the schools and universities, the communication is one-way from the teachers to the students, with a considerable amount of rote learning. This reinforces the high PDI value system.

COMPARING THE HERMES POWER DISTANCE INDEX VALUES WITH OTHER DATA

Survey Studies Outside HERMES: Significant Correlations with PDI

Four studies of matched samples of respondents, completely unrelated to the HERMES Corporation, show significant and meaningful correlations with the Power Distance Index. These studies cover between 14 and 19 countries from the HERMES set. The relevant statistical proof can be found on pages 139ff.

(1) Managers at IMEDE answering HERMES questions (see Chapter 2). In order not to lose all information from the IMEDE participants, I had to accept very small samples in this case. Normally, I would only consider as reliable data from 50 or more participants per country (Hofstede, 1975b). In the IMEDE case, this would have left me with data from only one country, so I accepted a minimum sample size of seven participants per country: The effect of this is a strong reduction in the level of correlations expected, as the IMEDE data contain a high level of random variation.

From the two HERMES PDI questions used at IMEDE, the "preferred manager" shows, nevertheless, a rank correlation across 15 countries of rho = .71 between IMEDE managers and HERMES employees. This is amazingly high, if we also take into account the fact that IMEDE managers answered the question in English and HERMES employees in a multitude of local languages.

The question on "employees afraid to disagree" shows a positive but nonsignificant rank correlation (rho = .27) between IMEDE managers and HERMES employees. In fact, this is not a good question with which to test the values of *managers;* in answering it, they refer to their subordinates, while nonmanagers, in answering the same question, refer to their colleagues. It is known that perceptions of the feelings of subordinates are often distorted. The HERMES country scores for the "employees afraid to disagree" were exceptionally calculated *without* the answers by managers (see the Statistical Analysis at the end of this chapter). The lack of a significant correlation between IMEDE managers and HERMES employees in this case, therefore, is not surprising.

(2) Managers at IMEDE, answering L. V. Gordon's Value Surveys (see also Chapter 2). The same restriction to very small samples as we found in the previous section exists in this case as well. I used an ecological factor analysis to summarize the results of 12 value scales (six from Gordon's Survey of Personal Values, six from Gordon's Survey of Interpersonal Values) into three factors. We find, across 14 countries, a highly significant rank correlation (rho = .79) between PDI and a factor "Decisiveness versus Practical-Mindedness." This means that IMEDE managers from high PDI countries, compared with those from low PDI countries, tend to score their own values on the Gordon tests as follows:

—Greater Decisiveness: To have strong and firm convictions, to make decisions quickly, to always come directly to the point, to make one's position on matters very clear, to come to a decision and stick to it.
—Greater Benevolence: Doing things for other people, sharing with others, helping the unfortunate, being generous.
—Less Practical-Mindedness: *Not* to always get one's money's worth, to take good care of one's property, to get full use out of one's possessions, to do things that will pay off, to be very careful with one's money.
—Less Support: *Not* being treated with understanding, receiving encouragement from other people, being treated with kindness and consideration.
—Less Orderliness: *Not* to have well-organized work habits, to keep things in their proper place, to be a very orderly person, to follow a systematic approach in doing things, to do things according to a schedule.

We should remember that these are self-descriptions of values. The self-image of the IMEDE manager from a high PDI country is that of a benevolent decisionmaker. The self-image of the IMEDE manager from a low PDI country is rather that of the practical, orderly person who likes to be treated with understanding. It is doubtful whether others would also see them like this; but this is at least how they would *like* to be seen (self-descriptions always contain a lot of wishful thinking; see Sadler and Hofstede, 1972: Table 5 and its analysis).

(3) Samples of students, answering L. V. Gordon's Survey of Interpersonal Values. Mean country scores for the six scales of this values test have been published by Gordon (1976); for 17 countries in the HERMES set, samples are available that meet my minimum criteria of 50 respondents per country. We find high ecological correlations across these 17 countries between PDI in HERMES and the following answers by students:

—Greater Conformity (r = .80): Doing what is socially correct, following regulations closely, doing what is accepted and proper, being a conformist.
—Less Independence (r = −.79): *Not* having the right to do whatever one wants to do, being free to make one's own decisions, being able to do things in one's own way.

In addition, for the students as well, we find in higher PDI countries less endorsement of Support and more of Benevolence, the same as for the IMEDE managers (see the previous section). The self-images of the male students in high versus low PDI countries are nowhere opposed to those of the IMEDE managers, but they place different accents: Managers did not differentiate significantly on Conformity and Independence, whereas students do. It is likely that managers attending courses at IMEDE form a selected population with regard to values about conformity and independence so that the cultural variance is suppressed.

(4) Samples of managers in 19 countries, answering to Haire et al.'s "management attitudes and assumptions." In this case, the comparison with the HERMES indices is seriously hampered by the fact that Haire et al. do not report the country scores on their individual items, only the combined scores of two items at the time whose combination *on the country level* may be irrelevant (a "reverse ecological fallacy"). As it is, we find one significant (r = .54) positive correlation across the 19 countries between PDI and the Haire et al. subscale on "Capacity for leadership and initiative":

(a) The average human being prefers to be directed, wishes to avoid responsibility, and has relatively little ambition (disagree).
(b) Leadership skills can be acquired by most people regardless of their particular inborn traits and abilities (agree).

This looks paradoxical: In countries which are high in PDI how can respondents be more optimistic about people's capacity for leadership and initiative?

The paradox was recognized in Southeast Asian data (which Haire et al. did not have) by Martyn-Johns (1977). The latter discusses the case of Indonesia in depth (a country not in my sample) and attributes a high belief in "capacity for leadership and initiative" simultaneously with low internal control and absolute management authority to the Asian way of obtaining consensus before deciding. This looks rather a far-fetched explanation, and the paradoxical finding also is not confined to Asian countries. In fact, Haire et al. already signaled a paradox in the country mean scores for their subscales (without looking at ecological correlations): on "capacity for leadership and initiative" the majority in nearly all countries scored "traditional"; on sharing information and objectives, participation, and internal control the majority scored "modern." Haire et al. note that

it would seem illogical to install a set of procedures for sharing information, allowing self-control, and practising participation, unless subordinates were capable of handling these types of situations. Yet, this is what the managers in our sample seem to be advocating [1966: 24].

They find that the paradox is strongest for the European countries; it would be the European rather than the Asian data which need explanation. My general explanation of the apparent paradox is that we should again distinguish between "values as the desirable" and "values as the desired" (Chapter 1). An essential difference between the two items dealing with "capacity for leadership and initiative" and the six other items is that the former are about "the average human being" and "most people." They are ideological statements, "values as the desirable." The latter are formulated in terms of interaction between superiors and subordinates and more pragmatic, closer to "values as the desired." The two levels of values may be in line, may be independent, or may be negatively correlated across countries. An example of the latter we found on the issue of employee participation in decisionmaking (ideological) versus being consulted by one's boss (pragmatic). In the present case the negative correlation can be explained as follows: when answering about "the average human being" and "most people," respondents are unconsciously selecting a reference group. In societies more affected by caste and class differences, the managers who answered the question are more likely to have taken as a reference group their own class; the others are completely out of their picture. The more this is the case, the more an optimistic picture of man's capacities will result, and vice versa. However, the opposite applies to pragmatic rules about the interaction between superiors and subordinates.[19]

PDI Scores and Survey Studies of a
Smaller Numbers of Countries

Comparison of PDI scores with comparative studies of smaller numbers of countries—less than 10, for example—will not easily show statistically significant correlations of ecological data but may supply more depth and additional insight into the power distance phenomenon. In this section I will refer to a selected set of such studies which are meaningful to our theme.

Kohn's (1969) study, "Class and Conformity," supplies insight about the roots of PDI differences in the family. I referred to his study earlier in this chapter for the relationship between working-class status and conformity to external authority. Kohn's work is partly based on interview data collected from the parents of 10–11-year-old children in Turin, Italy and in Washington, D.C. The data show that for both middle class and working class, fathers and mothers in Italy (higher PDI) put higher value on children obeying them than in the United States (lower PDI; see Kohn, 1969: 42; compare also page 107). We need look not just at the official sociological literature, of course, to learn that parents in different countries hold different values for their children. For example, Ledda's (1977) autobiography *Padre Padrone* (from Sardinia) is one of the clearest illustrations of the transfer of a high PDI syndrome across generations.

Meade and Whittaker (1967) give information about the incidence of authoritarian values among students. They performed a comparative study with the F-scale (authoritarianism scale) developed in the United States by Adorno et al. (1950). They administered the F-scale to students in Brazil, Hong Kong, India, Lebanon, Rhodesia, and the United States. Across the four countries for which comparison with HERMES data is possible, their F-scale scores rank-correlate (Spearman) .80 with PDI (which is not significant but encouraging; the correlations with the other HERMES indices are lower). However, the use of a ready-made U.S. scale like this means a reverse ecological fallacy, as Kagitcibasi (1970) has shown. She administered the F-scale to male and female high school students in the United States (lower

PDI) and Turkey (higher PDI). She shows that higher intercorrelations of the various components of authoritarianism were found among Americans than among Turks: The relatively coherent "authoritarian personality" syndrome exists in the United States but not in Turkey, although Turks tend to score higher on most authoritarian values. She concludes that in international comparisons, *norm* authoritarianism should be distinguished from *personal* authoritarianism. Norm authoritarianism applies to the culture level and cannot be explained in terms of personality dynamics. It is evident that PDI is a measure of norm authoritarianism. The F-scale is not the best measure for determining norm authoritarianism cross-culturally, as it lumps it together with other attitudes not ecologically correlated with it.[20]

About management in industry we have a descriptive study by Harbison and Burgess (1954), who compared U.S. with "European" management, but their European sample consisted of France, Belgium, and Italy—three countries from the high PDI group. Their conclusions are predictable:

> Workers in European plants seldom talk back to their bosses. Upward communication is neither expected nor encouraged. . . . In these countries, the paternalistic employer appears to develop in the working forces a feeling of gratitude and dependence mingled with resentment. Socially irresponsible management creates active opposition and outright hatred [1954: 19–20].

Harbison and Burgess gave an insightful description of the large power distance syndrome, but their extrapolation to "Europe" was not justified. In a later study by Harbison and Myers (1959) which collected qualitative evidence on management processes in 12 countries, European countries were no longer placed in one category. In fact, Harbison and Myers (1959: 65) introduce a dimension from paternalism to pluralism which closely resembles an inverted PDI: They put Japan, Italy, and France on the paternalist side; Sweden, England, and the United States on the pluralist side.

That more autocratic management styles are not only more common among managers but also more appreciated by subordinates in high PDI countries is shown by Williams et al. (1966), who compared workers in two large electrical utility companies, one in Peru (high PDI) and one in the United States (lower PDI). Among both white- and blue-collar employees, the correlations between perceived closeness of supervision and general satisfaction with the boss were small but significantly *positive* in Peru and *negative* in America. The same differences were found for correlations between perceived pressure for production and satisfaction with the boss. On the issue of worker consultation, Williams et al. conclude that "although Peruvians are just as concerned as U.S. workers about having some power and influence over their work, they are not nearly so inclined to see this power and influence as being related to the participative communication practices of the supervisor" (1966: 108). In an attempt to probe beneath the reaction patterns observed, Williams et al. showed that these were related to differences in *faith in people,* or interpersonal trust. Whyte had earlier found that in comparison to U.S. students, Peruvian high school boys in a survey scored a very low level of interpersonal trust. Williams et al. administered the "faith in people" questions to 202 Peruvian white-collar workers and found the same low level of interpersonal trust. When the Peruvian respondents were divided into high, medium, and low trust groups, it appeared that for the high trust group, satisfaction with the supervisor was associated more with the supervisor's social leadership (as in America), but for the low trust group, satisfaction with the supervisor was associated more with his technical leadership.

Williams et al. have thus established an important conceptual link between superior-subordinate relationship patterns (levels of power distance) on the one side and relationships between people in general (and between subordinates in particular) on the other. They also show evidence that the Peruvians less than the U.S. respondents perceive themselves as members of a (cohesive) work group, and that, again, in this case the high trust Peruvians are more like the U.S. respondents. Williams et al. conclude that for the Peruvian, "his organizational relations tend to be polarized in relation to a more authoritarian management, which seems to result in isolation of the individual worker from his fellows" (1966: 117).

Low interpersonal trust and low cooperativeness among subordinates were also found by Negandhi and Prasad (1971: 105ff) in Argentina, Brazil, Uruguay, and the Philippines; only in India was the level of cooperativeness among employees slightly better.[21]

The issue of interpersonal trust and group cohesiveness will be taken up again in Chapter 5. For the time being, we have seen that for a variety of high PDI countries, studies have shown lower interpersonal trust than for the United States, which is lower in PDI. Unfortunately, the HERMES questionnaire lacks questions dealing with interpersonal trust, so I am unable to find confirmation of the negative relationship between PDI and interpersonal trust there.

With regard to the issue of subordinates' appreciation of leadership styles, Cascio (1974) has published data obtained with the exercise "Supervise," designed by B. M. Bass and distributed by IRGOM (the International Research Group on Management). In role-playing exercises, managers had to play the role of subordinates with three different superiors: among these superiors one was instructed to act in a directive, one in a persuasive, and one in a participative way. The percentage of subordinates who afterwards declared themselves to have been most satisfied in their decision-making meeting with the participative superior varied from 29 in India to 65 in Western Europe. Unfortunately, Cascio's results are not published by country, but by country cluster. Across six clusters, his percent most satisfied with a participative superior and the cluster's mean PDI rank correlate with rho $= -.78$ (which for this small number of cases stays below the .05 significance level).

With regard to the societal implications of differences in power and wealth, we can use the study about the cognitive structures of male students in Greece, India, Japan, and the United States by Triandis et al. (1972) described in Chapter 1. From the 20 concepts used in this research project, "freedom," "power," "respect" and "wealth" are conceptually related to the issue of power distance.[22] From the frequency scores of the 30 "antecedents" and 30 "consequents" per concept I have isolated those which show a rank correlation of 1.00 with the PDI (the PDI ranking of the four countries is U.S.A.—Japan—Greece—India). Such a perfect rank agreement (if it would have been predicted) has less than a five percent probability of occurring by chance. The antecedents and consequents which appear in this order of frequency (and with a minimum frequency of 40 in at least one culture) are listed in Figure 3.5.

Figure 3.5 shows a convincing picture of two types of society—a welfare society

FIGURE 3.5   Antecedents and Consequents of Four Concepts as
              Measured among Male Students by Triandis et al. (1972)

Low Power Distance Index	High Power Distance Index
Antecedents of "Freedom"	
Respect of individual	Tact
Equality	Servitude
	Money
Consequents of "Freedom"	
	Industrial Production
	Disorderly Society
	Wealth
Antecedents of "Power"	
Leadership	Wrestling
Knowledge	
Consequents of "Power"	
	Cruelty
Antecedents of "Wealth"	
Happiness	Inheritance
Knowledge	Ancestral property
Love	High interest charges
	Stinginess
	Crime
	Deceit
	Theft
Consequents of "Wealth"	
Satisfaction	Fear of Thieves
Happiness	Arrogance
	Unhappiness
Antecedents of "Respect"	
Love	Old age
Consequents of "Respect"	
Friendship	
Recognition of superiority	
Liking	

Frequency across four countries is perfectly rank correlated with the Power Distance Index.

on the low PDI side (no negative antecedents or consequents scored at all), and a class society on the high PDI side, where money leads to freedom and freedom to a disorderly society, where power is acquired by wrestling and leads to cruelty, where wealth is inherited and threatened and leads to arrogance, and where old age leads to respect. On the low PDI side, all associations with "Power" and "Wealth" are favorable; on the high PDI side, nearly all are unfavorable. To students on the high PDI side (which in this case means especially India), wealth and power are conflict-ridden issues; to U.S. students they are not.

Finally, Tannenbaum et al. conducted a study which highlights the differences in practice between formal employee participation structures and informal consultation

(*Hierarchy in Organizations*, 1974). It covered five very small manufacturing plants (30–130 employees) in Austria, Italy, the United States, and Yugoslavia, 10 in Israeli kibbutzim, and five medium-sized plants (200–1500 employees) in the first four countries, all in matched industries. The study produced a large number of indices of hierarchy and of gradients of decision-making, opportunities and advantages, and reaction and adjustment across the hierarchy. As we have only five cases to compare, significant correlations with PDI are unlikely. It appears, however, that where Tannenbaum et al. measure *formal* elements of hierarchy, there is no correlation between their data and PDI at all (such as for a summary measure of "emphasis placed on hierarchy": 1974: 118). Where they measure *informal* elements of hierarchy, the correlations with PDI are generally strong (such as in their questions 33, "What do workers communicate to their superior?" and 42, "Is your immediate superior inclined to take into account your opinions and suggestions?"; both are negatively correlated with PDI). As in the case of the HERMES statement in favor of employee participation (B56), we see here that the formal and the informal levels should be sharply distinguished. Italy scores low on both types of participation, Yugoslavia high on formal but low on informal, Israel high on both, and Austria and the United States low on formal but higher on informal participation.

A Summary of Connotations of
the Power Distance Index
Found in Survey Material

At this point, the reader may feel a need for an integration of the large amount of detail in the attitudes somehow found to be related to the Power Distance Index. This integration is supplied in the summary table of Figure 3.6, which assembles the connotations of PDI found in the various survey data: what the societal norm which I called Power Distance stands for.

Figure 3.6 opposes "low PDI countries" to "high PDI countries." This is a dichotomy which serves to clarify the distinctions, but it should be kept in mind that (1) PDI is a continuum, so that countries are not just polarized between "high" and "low" but may be anywhere in between; (2) not all connotations apply with equal strength to a given country; and (3) individuals in countries show a wide range of variation around the country's societal norms (compare Figure 1.5).

With these provisos, we find in Figure 3.6 a picture of two types of societal norms which start from the values parents hold for their children. It is likely that especially the father-child relationship is the model for the degree of power distance which a society expects, although the corresponding values are also held by mothers (Kohn, 1969: 42). Corresponding differences in attitudes of young people (students)—for example, conformity versus independence and higher versus lower authoritarianism—show that the parental values have been internalized by these young people. In work organizations, we find that managers model their decision-making behavior in accordance with these values, and that subordinates feel more comfortable with managers who correspond to the model. Subordinates' feelings about close or loose supervision are complemented by the prevalent image of man as someone who likes or dislikes work as an activity per se. Subordinates' preferences for the decision-making style of their boss reflect the kind of supervision the majority of them feels most comfortable with, with one exception. In the high PDI countries,

FIGURE 3.6   Summary of Connotations of Power Distance Index
Differences found in Survey Research

See page	Low PDI Countries	High PDI Countries
114	Parents put less value on children's obedience.	Parents put high value on children's obedience.
113	Students put high value on independence.	Students put high value on conformity.
115	Authoritarian attitudes in students are a matter of personality.	Students show authoritarian attitudes as a social norm.
102 115	Managers seen as making decisions after consulting with subordinates.	Managers seen as making decisions autocratically and paternalistically.
115	Close supervision negatively evaluated by subordinates.	Close supervision positively evaluated by subordinates.
111	Stronger perceived work ethic; strong disbelief that people dislike work.	Weaker perceived work ethic; more frequent belief that people dislike work.
116	Managers more satisfied with participative superior.	Managers more satisfied with directive or persuasive superior.
102	Subordinates' preference for manager's decision-making style clearly centered on consultative, give-and-take style.	Subordinates' preference for manager's decision-making style polarized between autocratic-paternalistic and majority rule.
112	Managers like seeing themselves as practical and systematic; they admit a need for support.	Managers like seeing themselves as benevolent decision makers.
100	Employees less afraid of disagreeing with their boss.	Employees fear to disagree with their boss.
116	Employees show more cooperativeness.	Employees reluctant to trust each other.
109	Managers seen as showing more consideration.	Managers seen as showing less consideration.
117	Students have positive associations with "power" and "wealth."	Students have negative associations with "power" and "wealth."
109	Mixed feeling about employees' participation in management.	Ideological support for employees' participation in management.
113	Mixed feelings among managers about the distribution of capacity for leadership and initiative.	Ideological support among managers for a wide distribution of capacity for leadership and initiative.
118	Informal employee consultation possible without formal participation.	Formal employee participation possible without informal consultation.
106	Higher-educated employees hold much less authoritarian values than lower-educated ones.	Higher- and lower-educated employees show similar values about authority.

some subordinates switch to the other extreme and express a preference for a majority rule decision-making system in which the manager does not manage at all. I interpreted this earlier as a counterdependent subordinate reaction, which means that in high PDI countries, subordinates tend to polarize between dependence and counterdependence versus their boss; in low PDI countries, they center on interdependence (consultative decision-making). The societal norm affects the self-image which managers prefer, but also the emotional distance between superior and subordinate and the amount of consideration which subordinates find in their superiors. All these differences point to a greater power inequality in high than in low PDI countries, which is not only maintained by the more powerful but also desired by many of the less powerful. Still, great inequality is considered problematic at the same time, and students in higher PDI countries show negative associations not only with "power" but also with "wealth" (in the following sections we shall go deeper into the association of power inequality and wealth inequality). People in higher PDI countries are more open to ideological solutions to an inequality which is felt as problematic, but for which daily interactions between more and less powerful people offer no alternative. Ideas of worker participation in management are more strongly endorsed on the "desirable" level. Managers in high PDI countries are more ready to admit a wide distribution of capacities for leadership and initiative among people, but this may be because their reference group is more narrowly limited to their own class. As the Yugoslav example shows, formal employee participation in management is possible in high PDI countries, but it does not affect the pattern of informal employee consultation. Finally, it is in the low PDI countries that attitudes toward power distance are most class-dependent; in the high PDI countries all classes share the high PDI norm. In the low PDI countries it is really only the middle and perhaps the upper classes that hold low PDI values; the lower classes do not.

THE POWER DISTANCE NORM,
ITS ORIGINS AND CONSEQUENCES

The Power Distance Norm

It is time now to step back from the data and try to describe the general societal norm which is behind the "low PDI" and "high PDI" syndromes. This is an exercise in induction, which means that I have completed the picture with elements based on intuition rather than on empirical evidence, much like an archaeologist completes ancient pottery from which shards are missing. The total picture is given in Figure 3.7. The societal norm is meant to be a value system shared by a majority in the middle classes in a society. It contains both values as the desirable and values as the desired and is only at some distance followed by reality. All the provisos of the previous section apply: Most countries are in between, not all statements apply equally strongly in all countries, and individuals in countries vary widely around the norm.

The PDI norm deals with the desirability or undesirability of inequality and of dependence versus interdependence in society. Both low and high PDI countries have hierarchies, but they mean something else: The basic values with regard to inequality are projected onto the hierarchical relationship and make it into a convenience arrangement on one side, and an existential arrangement on the other.

The values about inequality are coupled with values about the exercise of power. The statement that in high PDI countries power is a basic fact of society which antedates good or evil and whose legitimacy is irrelevant is taken from Martyn-Johns (1977: 350), who compares a "European" with a "Javanese" (Indonesian) concept of power, and who has been inspired by B. R. Anderson. This may, in fact, be true in *all* societies. Crozier (1973: 223) states: "[P]ower in its noble aspects arises out of dubious negotiations, and has to rely on blackmail in its exercise. The established order of things is merely the ratified outcome of prior relationships in which black-mail played a major role." Mulder (1977: 15) has shown in his laboratory experi-ments that people react to illegitimate power in the same way they react to legitimate power. However, I propose that in some societies (which I call high PDI) power needs less legitimation than in others (which I call low PDI). The difference is more clearly visible on the next issue in Figure 3.7: whether powerholders should obey the same rules as others. Does the president of the company use a time-clock card if the workers do so? Does he have a private toilet? Should the general legitimate himself to the sentry? In low PDI countries, power is something of which power holders are almost ashamed and which they will try to underplay. I heard a Swedish university official state that in order to exercise power, he tries not to look powerful. This theory definitely does not hold in Belgium or France. I once met the Dutch prime minister with his caravan on a camping site in Portugal; I could not very well see his French or Italian colleague in that situation.

We owe to French and Raven (1959) a well-known classification of the bases of social power into five types: reward power, coercive power, legitimate power (based on rules), referent power (based on personal charisma of the powerful and identifica-tion with him or her by the less powerful), and expert (specialist) power. I surmise that, other things being equal, there will be more coercive and referent power used in the high PDI societies and more reward, legitimate, and expert power in the low PDI societies.

The statement that in high PDI countries the underdog is the first to be blamed for anything wrong in the system whereas in low PDI countries the system is blamed is inspired by a research review about Latin America and India from Negandhi and Prasad (1971: 105). I have noticed this tendency in some European countries as well. On the other hand, the blame may revert to the powerful, and this is the "revolution" philosophy on the high PDI side: Change the top person and you change the system. This is a popular "solution" in organizations, although in reality problems often survive after leaders fall.

The final statement in Figure 3.7 recognizes a latent conflict between the power-ful and the powerless on the high PDI side; a basic mistrust which may never explode but is always present. On the low PDI side, there is an ideal model of harmony between the powerful and powerless which in practice may be as "latent" as the conflict on the other side; that is, it does not exclude de facto conflict, but the conflict tends to be pragmatic rather than fundamental.

Predictors of PDI:
Latitude, Population Size, and Wealth

The statistical analysis shows that across the 40 countries, 43 percent of the variance in PDI can be predicted from the geographical latitude (of the country's

FIGURE 3.7   The Power Distance Societal Norm

Low PDI	High PDI
• Inequality in society should be minimized.	• There should be an order of inequality in this world in which everyone has his rightful place; high and low are protected by this order.
• All should be interdependent.	• A few should be independent; most should be dependent.
• Hierarchy means an inequality of roles, established for convenience.	• Hierarchy means existential inequality.
• Subordinates are people like me.	• Superiors consider subordinates as being of a different kind.
• Superiors are people like me.	• Subordinates consider superiors as being of a different kind.
• The use of power should be legitimate and is subject to the judgment between good and evil.	• Power is a basic fact of society which antedates good or evil. Its legitimacy is irrelevant.
• All should have equal rights.	• Powerholders are entitled to privileges.
• Powerful people should try to look less powerful than they are.	• Powerful people should try to look as powerful as possible.
• Stress on reward, legitimate and expert power.	• Stress on coercive and referent power.
• The system is to blame.	• The underdog is to blame.
• The way to change a social system is by redistributing power.	• The way to change a social system is by dethroning those in power.
• People at various power levels feel less threatened and more prepared to trust people.	• Other people are a potential threat to one's power and rarely can be trusted.
• Latent harmony between the powerful and the powerless.	• Latent conflict between powerful and the powerless.
• Cooperation among the powerless can be based on solidarity.	• Cooperation among the powerless is difficult to bring about because of low faith in people norm.

capital) alone; 51 percent can be predicted from a combination of latitude and population size, and 58 percent from latitude, population size, plus wealth (1970 GNP/capita). The second column in Figure 3.1 lists the values of PDI which would be predicted in this latter case. The mean absolute prediction error is 10 points; the maximum error, 31 points (for Israel).

That geographical latitude is the strongest predictor of PDI (with negative sign) may be surprising. However, a country's geographical position is a fundamental fact which is bound to have a strong effect on the subjective culture of its inhabitants, as this culture was shaped over many generations. Even when people migrate, they usually prefer migrating to a climatic zone not very different from the one they leave, which means a roughly similar latitude (north or south). The logic of the relationship between latitude (by definition an independent variable) and power distance is, of course, a matter of educated speculation. In any case, latitude should be seen as a rough global indicator of climate (tropical—moderate—cold). In my interpretation of the latitude–power distance relationship, the key intervening variable is the need for technology as a condition for survival. Human survival in colder climates presupposes protection against the hardships of nature, which means that only those people survived who were able to master the minimal technical skills necessary for survival. In warmer climates the need for technology was less. This difference is at the beginning of a causal chain which is pictured in Figure 3.8 and which leads to two different dominant types of social structure.

Some would probably attribute the effect of climate on human society primarily to its impact on man's physical performance; a tropical climate would make people less inclined to work (Myrdal, 1968: 2136; Bandyopadhyaya, 1978). I rather believe that in the long term with which we are dealing here, the human species is highly adaptable; if man performs less in tropical countries this is not because he could not become a high performer there, but because there was less of a need for it.

The (positive) relationship between PDI and our second predictor, population size, can be interpreted in two ways; large population size can be classified both as a consequence and as an origin of large Power Distance. The question is, why have some small nations remained independent while others have been absorbed into larger states? Obviously, military accidents have played an important role, but the will to be independent is an indispensable ingredient which in the long term has often proved stronger than military violence. It is not difficult to see a link between the will to be independent as a small nation and the maintenance of small power distances in other institutions. Thus, small population size can be a consequence of a small power distance norm. On the other hand, once a large nation exists, its members will have to accept a political power which is more distant and less accessible than for a small nation (Dahl and Tufte, 1974: 87). This should then reinforce a norm in society of less questioning of authority in general—that is, a larger power distance.

Wealth, itself highly correlated with latitude, is the third predictor of PDI, with negative sign, after the effects of latitude and population size have been eliminated. Wealth, too, can be interpreted as both a consequence and an origin of smaller power distances. National wealth is obviously associated with a whole complex of other factors. A study by Adelman and Morris (1967) in which they factor-analyzed 24 economic, social, and political indicators for 74 noncommunist developing countries found a first factor with a .73 loading on GNP per capita in 1961 and with, among others, the following other loadings:

- −.89 (small) size of the traditional agricultural sector
- .88 extent of mass communication
- .86 extent of social mobility
- .86 extent of literacy
- .84 extent of urbanization
- .82 importance of the middle class
  [Adelman and Morris, 1967: Table IV-1].

Adelman and Morris also showed a separate factor analysis for the 25 relatively most developed countries out of their set, including (from our set) Argentina, Brazil,

See pages	Causal chain	Origins of Power Distance norm	
		Low PDI	High PDI
123		Moderate to cold climates	Tropical and subtropical climates
123		Survival and population growth more dependent on man's intervention with nature	Survival and population growth less dependent on man's intervention with nature
123 125		More need for technology	Less need for technology
127 128		Historical events: early legislation applied to rulers; one-son inheritance	Historical events: early legislation not applied to rulers; divided inheritance
123 128		Less traditional agriculture, more modern industry, more urbanization	More traditional agriculture, less modern industry, less urbanization
123 126		More need for education of lower strata (literacy, mass communication)	Less need for education of lower strata
123		Greater social mobility and strong development of middle class	Less social mobility and weak development of middle class
123		Greater national wealth	Less national wealth
125		Wealth more widely distributed	Wealth concentrated in hands of small elite
125		Political power based on system of representation	Political power concentrated in hands of oligarchy or military
123		Strong will to be independent: smaller size of population	Little popular resistance to integration into a large state: large size of population
127ff		Historical events: independence, federalism, negotiation	Historical events: occupation, colonialism, imperialism
125		Less centralization of political power	Centralization of political power
128		Faster population increase in wealthy countries	Slower population increase in wealthy countries
126		Technological momentum of change	More static society
126		Children learn things which elders never learned: less dependent	Children dependent on parents and elders
127		Some teaching is two-way	Teachers are omniscient, teaching is one-way
122		More questioning of authority in general	Less questioning of authority in general

FIGURE 3.8 Origins of National Power Distance Index Differences

Chile, Colombia, Greece, Israel, Japan, Mexico, Peru, Taiwan, Turkey, and Venezuela. This time they found a first factor with a .82 loading on GNP per capita in 1961
and with loadings above .60 on the same variables as mentioned above (except
urbanization, which was left out of the analysis), plus the following:

    .85 level of modernization of techniques in agriculture
    .72 strength of the labor movement
  −.70 extent of centralization of political power
  −.70 political strength of the military
    .69 degree of modernization of outlook
    .61 level of modernization of industry
        [Adelman and Morris, 1967: Table VII-5].

This analysis adds to our list for these more developed countries three more items
dealing with technological development (level of modernization in agriculture, degree of modernization of outlook, and level of modernization of industry) as well as
three items directly related to the role of the elites: Centralization of political power
and political strength of the military are negatively related to wealth, and strength of
the labor movement—that is, a countervailing power—is positively related to
wealth. All three, evidently, are conceptually related to power distance; the first two
positively, the third negatively. I have fitted them into the causal chain of Figure 3.8.

Power Distance and Income Inequality

A linking variable between wealth and small power distance is most likely also
"small wealth distance," or the distribution of wealth among the strata of the population. Greater wealth presupposes higher technology; higher technology calls for
higher-educated but also better-paid lower and middle strata; so wealth will be more
equally distributed and power also will be more equally distributed. In order to test
this I looked for data on income inequality by country and found three studies
covering between eight and 12 of the HERMES countries each. As the statistical
section shows, all three show significant rank correlations between income inequality and PDI (but in the most recent study, this was only true for income inequality
after tax). The correlation coefficients are .89, .86, and .57.

Brossard and Maurice (1974) have published data for carefully matched pairs of
industrial manufacturing units in France and Germany. Wage differentials (upper
percentile divided by lower decile) were between 3.7 and 5.5 in France, and between
2.0 and 2.3 in Germany. This is in line with the PDI difference between the two
countries.

It seems that on the level of societies, inequality in power and inequality in wealth
go hand in hand. The greater the power inequality, the greater the wealth inequality,
and vice versa. Larger or smaller inequality in wealth is one of the elements in the
causal chain that helps to explain the power distance syndrome (Figure 3.8).

Power Distance and Educational Systems

We have seen that across occupations in HERMES, PDI and average years of
formal education are strongly negatively related (Figure 3.2). Across countries in
HERMES (and keeping occupations constant), PDI and years of formal education

are *positively* correlated (see page 111). However, this is a different story: Within the same occupations, the educational levels of HERMES employees vary only marginally, and in the poorer (high PDI) countries there is a relative oversupply of people with long formal schooling for these jobs. We can still assume PDI to be correlated with the average level of education in the country at large, not within HERMES. In the causal chain of Figure 3.8, education appears more in lower PDI countries because it is needed more. It is associated with a need for mastery of technology, which is a characteristic of the social system.

One measure of the mastery of technology in a country is the number of Nobel prize winners in the physical sciences which this country has produced. Moulin (1961) has composed a "Nobel Index" which divides the number of Nobel prizewinners between 1901 and 1960 in physics, chemistry, medicine, and physiology by the average number of inhabitants of the country in millions. On Moulin's list 20 countries appear, from which 17 are in the HERMES sample,[23] but I have eliminated those with a 1970 GNP/capita below $1300 because these poorer countries are unlikely to have had adequate laboratories to really compete. However, I have added wealthy countries not on the list because they never had a Nobel prizewinner. The only country in this category is Norway, which makes us wonder about possible biases in the Nobel prize's Swedish judges![24] Across 14 countries,[25] the Nobel Index rank correlates with rho = −.50 with PDI.[26] Thus there tends to have been more mastery of the sciences in the twentieth century in countries which in 1970 showed lower PDI values (Peyrefitte, 1976: 194, quotes Moulin's study to illustrate "the French disease": high PDI France only appears ninth on the Nobel Index list).

In spite of this evidence of a correlation of PDI with peak scientific performance, the crucial aspect of a country's educational system which is logically linked with the Power Distance norm is not the relative number of top educated scholars. They could just form another elite. The crucial aspect is the educational level of the rank and file which contribute to the middle strata in society. Mulder (1976: 92) argues that in order to learn power distance reduction it is necessary that there be intermediary levels in between the powerful and the powerless (compare page 95). Gaspari and Millendorfer (1978: 198) use the ratio between the number of secondary school students and the number of university students as a measure of the development of middle strata. Northern and Western European countries show over time a development toward higher ratios (more secondary school students), while Eastern European countries (but also Italy) show permanent low ratios (a relative predominance of higher education—that is, the formation of a relative elite). The other indicator used by Gaspari and Millendorfer (1978: 199) is the average number of nurses per doctor in a country. Across 15 countries this rank-correlates −.52 with PDI (but it correlates even more with UAI and IDV; thus, I shall deal with it in Chapter 4 rather than here).

Education is, of course, not only a matter of numbers: numbers of years at school or numbers of students. It is very important what is taught and how. On the high PDI side where children are more dependent on parents we will find more frequently that students are dependent on teachers. There is more rote learning, and the asking of questions by the student is seldom encouraged; teachers are more often supposed to be omniscient, even if they do not like it. This is by no means limited to children; as a professor in international institutes of learning, I am less challenged by my French than by my Swedish doctoral students. In my classes for middle managers, participation in the discussion depends, of course, on people's mother tongues; but on the average, Englishmen or Danes participate more even if the course is in French than do French or French Swiss if the course is in English. The influence of the French educational system on the maintenance of large power distances has been widely commented upon (see for example Schonfeld, 1976; Marceau, 1977; Maurice et al., 1978). In French organizations, the educational difference between lower- and higher-level employees is confirmed and perpetuated in their different legal status: higher-educated employees become "cadres" and lower-educated "non-cadres," and the transfer between the two groups is very difficult. In one of my classes for French managers, a participant described the difference between "cadres" and "non-cadres" as follows: *"Les cadres ont la logique de l'efficacité, les non-cadres de la contestation."*[27]

PDI and Historical Factors

Latitude, population size, and wealth leave 42 percent of the variance in Power Distance Index unexplained. This unexplained part of the variance contains the part due to measurement error, to idiosyncracies of the sample of multinational company respondents (nonrepresentativeness for the population of their country), and to factors working on the level of national systems but unrelated to latitude, population size, and wealth.

Figure 3.1 shows that the countries deviating most from the predicted values of PDI (more than 15 points above or below) are Belgium ($+$ 29), France ($+$ 26), Yugoslavia ($+$ 23), Philippines ($+$ 21), Israel ($-$ 31), Austria ($-$ 29), and Pakistan ($-$ 19). Yugoslavia is a special case because the PDI data used are from another organization with a different subculture. It is likely that the multinational organization's subculture is characterized by a relatively more open communication with superiors than most other work organizations. Therefore, other work organizations in the same countries can be expected to show higher PDI values.[28] That in Yugoslavia, in spite of worker-self-management, the *informal* relationship between subordinates and superiors is not so participative has been shown by Tannenbaum et al. (1974: 77; compare page 118).

The high scores for Belgium and France make them fit well into a cluster of Latin countries, which includes both those in Latin Europe and Latin America. All Latin countries in Europe show higher PDI values, while all Germanic countries (including the English-speaking ones) show lower PDI values. Latin languages indicate the cultural inheritance of the Roman Empire. Half of Belgium speaks Dutch, a Germanic language, but until recently the French language and culture in this country have been strongly dominant. (I shall deal in more detail with the value differences between the linguistic groups in Belgium in Chapter 7).

In the Latin countries of Europe, the Roman Empire was the first large and effective state to be established. In the same way as early childhood experiences have a major impact on personality, these early societal experiences must have had a lasting impact on polity, affecting all institutions that have followed. In the Roman Empire, the emperor had absolute authority and stood above the law: "[B]y an implied contract the people confer upon the emperor all power and authority over them so that his will has the force of the law" (Smith, 1964: 272).[29] When the Roman Empire disintegrated, this absolute authority of the ruler was also taken over by the Germanic invaders of France who mixed with the Romanized population (Pirenne, 1939: 32), but not by the Germanic Anglo-Saxon invaders of Britain who chased the Romanized Celts without mixing with them. In the Germanic tradition, the power of the king was subordinate to the assembly of free men. In this tradition, an absolutist rule could never settle in Britain; when the Norman kings attempted to establish it, they were forced to recognize the rights of the people in the Magna Charta of 1214 (1939: 257). In Germany up until the nineteenth century, a central authority could never be established, and the country was composed of small principalities.

Jordan (1973: 69) claims that the Roman and Germanic traditions also divided Europe by their different inheritance laws. In the former Roman Empire, the practice of divided inheritance was long dominant; land and other possessions were divided equally among all heirs, leading to all children remaining on ever-smaller farms and a need for birth control. In Germanic and English common law, land was usually inherited by the oldest son only, with the remaining offspring being compensated in other ways, if at all (a familiar picture from several of Grimm's German fairytales). This led in a much later stage of history to emigration and urbanization of the younger children.[30] "The younger sons have made England great" (Sauvy, 1966: 26). The differences in population growth among the four largest European countries between 1720 and 1970 are startling (Jordan, 1973: 72): France—19 to 50 million, growth factor 2.6; Italy—13 to 53 million, growth factor 4.1; Germany (East and West)—14 to 77 million, growth factor 5.5; and Great Britain—seven to 55 million, growth factor 7.9.

France had by far the slowest population increase (at the same time, it supplied fewer overseas migrants than the other countries); this has been a matter of lower birthrates (that is, of voluntary birth prevention), as death rates in France were not systematically different from those in other countries (Sauvy, 1966: 54). The French-speaking part of Belgium had an equally slow population increase. In the causal chain of Figure 3.8 I have linked slower population increases with a more static society (Sauvy, 1966: 30; this applies at least for the wealthier countries—see the signs of the correlations with population growth in Figure 3.20). It is also likely that smaller family sizes mean that parental authority weighs heavier on the children who remain more dependent.

The difference in inheritance laws between Germanic and Latin Europe also exists between Japan and China (Hsu, 1971: 38). The existence of one-son inheritance in Japan is used to explain the faster rate of modernization by the energy of the younger sons who had to find other activities. On the other hand, in the Chinese tradition, the people had the right to judge the ruler; in the Japanese tradition the emperor was unimpeachable (Azumi, 1974: 517). In this respect Japan is more like the Latin; China, like the Germanic countries. On the PDI scale we see that, all in all, the scores for Japan and the part of China on which data were available—Taiwan—are about the same, in spite of the much lower wealth of the latter. Unfortunately we lack data on mainland China; however, a recent perceptive study by Laaksonen (1977) describes work relationships as quite participative but party relationships as strongly hierarchical, which leads to estimating for China a total Power Distance score somewhere in the middle of the scale—not very far from Taiwan and Japan.

The Chinese settlements of Singapore and Hong Kong show much higher PDIs, but these are (ex-)colonies. Two other recently independent states, India and the Philippines, also show high PDI values. Modern organizations in the colonial countries were set up by the colonial rulers. Even rulers like the British, who practiced democracy and lower power distance society at home, did not practice equality between themselves and the colonial populations. This kind of inconsistency of values is quite common in human society (Béteille, 1969). The Power Distance Index definitely does *not* measure tolerance toward other races, religions, and so on; this is rather a matter of Uncertainty Avoidance (see Chapter 4). In the ex-colonies of Asia, the places of the colonists were taken by local managers who adopted the existing management style (Kakar, 1971). However, traditional pre-colonial relationships also contained elements of large inequality: There is no better example than the Indian caste system. Kumar and Singh (1976: 22) conclude that in India's highly stratified society, "constructs regarding superiority-subordinacy tend to dominate alternate patterns of categorization. " Heginbotham (1975) in the Indian State of Tamil Nadu finds four different and conflicting "cognitive models of organization" from which both the traditional Indian and the British colonial model stress vertical relationships.

Among the former colonies, the Philippines show an extremely high PDI score; contrary to the others, it used to be a Latin (Spanish) rather than a British colony, which may explain the additional stress on inequality. Pakistan, on the other hand, scores relatively low and lower than predicted. It may be that the Pakistani sample, one of the smallest in the data set, is particularly enlightened compared with its environment; although it is predictable that Pakistan, the Muslim part of the former British Colonial subcontinent, would stress stratification less than the predominantly Hindu part, India: in Islam, all believers are equal before God.

The other countries that deviate particularly from their predicted PDI values are Israel and Austria. There are cultural links between the two: The modern state of Israel was founded by an Austrian, Theodor Herzl, and in the intellectual life in Austria until the Nazi period the Jewish part of the intelligentsia played a key role. The low PDI score for Israel makes intuitive sense for a society which developed the kibbutz system. The very low score for Austria is surprising, but the position of Austria becomes clearer if we also take its Uncertainty Avoidance score into account (which is fairly high: see Chapter 4). The equalitarian ethos in Austria is recognizable in its stable socialist majority (see the next section).[31]

The historical factors mentioned fill some missing links in the hypothesized causal chain of Figure 3.8.

PDI and Political Systems

In Chapter 1 I described various large factor-analytical studies of country data. The one focusing specifically on political systems is by Gregg and Banks (1965). Their factor analysis used 68 aspects of political systems for 115 countries. They found a strong first factor (explaining 25 percent of the total variance) which they called "access." It has, among others, the following loadings:

.94 electoral system
.93 constitutional regime
.92 group opposition
.86 horizontal power distribution
.85 representativeness of regime
.80 press freedom
− .81 *not* a totalitarian regime

This main dimension of political systems corresponds to Aron's (1965) distinction between constitutional-pluralistic and monopolistic regimes, or to Cutright's (1967) "Political Representativeness Index."

A measure for the 40 countries on this measure around 1970 was not available, but I could, without much ambiguity, dichotomize the 40 countries into 20 with "balanced power in government" and 20 with "unbalanced power," basing the dichotomy on historical events in the period 1950–1975. As the statistical analysis shows, the "balanced versus unbalanced power" split is highly significantly associated with PDI. We could add "politics": balanced power = 1, unbalanced = 2, as a fourth variable to the explanations of PDI beyond latitude, population size, and wealth. In this way we can explain another five percent of the variance (up to a total of 63 percent). However, the question is whether the country's political system really "explains" the PDI or whether both the political system and the PDI scores are symptoms of the same underlying societal norm. I hold the latter interpretation more reasonable. Eisenstadt (1974) has stressed that the world shows a great variety of political systems without signs of convergence and subject to the influence of historical and cultural continuities; the main dimensions of national culture, of which Power Distance is only one, should also be reflected in differences in political systems. Political decision-making depends to a large extent on factors other than political systems. Haniff (1976) has shown, for example, that social policy outputs, as measured by the expenditure of funds for citizen welfare, across 125 sovereign states could be predicted from wealth and literacy rather than from political variables.

Political systems, unless imposed by foreign violence, reflect something about the values and the behavior of the population. Low power distances are more likely to be associated with a certain consensus among the population which reduces disruptive conflicts. In the statistical section, I have correlated the HERMES indices with three independent measures of domestic political violence across 37, 37, and 10 countries.[32] All correlations with PDI are highly significantly positive (.39, .71, and .93). In the two studies covering 37 countries each, we can see that especially the countries in the lower third of the PDI range show less political violence and are responsible for the correlation; more violence is found both in the middle and in the upper third of PDI countries (such as Argentina, Brazil, Chile, Colombia, France, India, Iran, Italy, Pakistan, Peru, Portugal, South Africa, Spain, Thailand, Turkey, and Venezuela). In the more recent history of the 1970s it looks as if countries in the *middle* part of the PDI scale had the most problems of governmental instability: Argentina, Chile, Greece, Iran, Italy, Pakistan, Peru, Portugal, South Africa, Spain, and Thailand. Countries higher in the PDI range tend to have relatively stable, authoritarian governments; those lower in PDI, relatively stable, pluralist systems (an exception may be India). In the middle-range countries, governments can no longer count on the dependence needs of an increasing section of the population, especially of the new middle classes. These countries swing back and forth between equalitarian and elitist regimes; and elitist rulers often revert to downright oppression and totalitarianism to maintain their position.

Stavig and Barnett (1977) have demonstrated across 75 nations that one of the measures of domestic conflict we used (Rummel's scores) also correlates with the country's population size; the same is true for *foreign* conflict. This fits with the correlation found between PDI and population size. In larger countries, consensus between citizens is less easily achieved, and for outside relations, the use of power is more easily considered. Levinson (1977: 760), reviewing anthropological cross-cultural studies, relates the frequency of aggression to a warm climate; this fits with the correlation between PDI and latitude.

The relationship with PDI should be found not only in the occurrence of instability, however. For countries in which a more or less stable parliamentary system exists, this too will reflect the country's power distance norm. In high PDI parliamentary countries such as France, Italy and Japan we see a polarization between left and right with a weak center (just as with the preferences for managers' decision-making styles in HERMES discussed earlier); in lower PDI countries such as Sweden, Germany, and Britain we see more votes to center parties or support to center tendencies within broad left and right parties. Also, in France, Italy, and Japan the government parties have nearly always been right of the middle; in which "right" stands for not stressing equality and "left" for stressing equality. Most low PDI countries have frequently had left-wing-dominated governments. In France and Italy, administrative elites are distinctively *unrepresentative* of the total population as far as their social origins are concerned, much more so than in Great Britain, Germany, the Netherlands, and the United States (Aberbach and Putnam, 1977). An outcome of this pattern may be that in France and Japan taxation has less of an equalizing effect on incomes than in most other countries (in France, it has an *un*equalizing effect—see Figure 3.17). Such differences based on legislation ("positive law," see Northrop, 1962:427) only reflect differences in societal norms ("living law"). We finally can trace the PDI norm also in the kind of labor movement a country has; many high PDI countries have no free labor unions at all, but unions are organized by government. In such countries as France and Italy which have free labor unions, these tend to be ideologically based and involved in politics more than in lower PDI countries, where unions tend to be more pragmatically oriented toward earnings, working conditions, and employment security. Maurice et al. (1978), comparing France and Germany, show that the different industrial relations systems of the two countries are part of the total pattern that maintains and is maintained by greater inequality in France than in Germany.

PDI and Religion, Ideology, and Theories of Power

Power distance norm differences are definitely associated with aspects of religious life, but it is doubtful whether religion can "explain" PDI; power distances and religion should be seen rather as results of a common cause. In Europe, there is a striking similarity between the limits of the Roman Empire and the limits of the Roman Catholic Church[33]; with few exceptions, the various reformations have been successful only in countries or areas not once under Roman rule.[34] We see this even in Germany and the Netherlands.[35] For power distance (and other cultural dimensions) the Empire appears to have been more decisive than the Church, as can be seen by the fact that Ireland (Catholic but not Latin) scores similar to Britain (mainly Protestant but also not Latin). However, once a religion has been established in a country, it will reinforce the values that led to its being adopted. Catholicism with the supreme authority of the Pope and the intermediate authority of the priest corresponds more to a large power distance than Protestantism with its general priesthood of the believers. Max Weber (1930, [1976]: 224) quotes a seventeenth-century Puritan Protestant text about "the sinfulness of the belief in authority, which is only permissible in the form of an impersonal authority." In *The Protestant Ethic and the Spirit of Capitalism,* Weber links Protestantism with the capitalist modernization of countries; this fits the low PDI side of Figure 3.8.

In Asia, I have used religion as a factor to explain the difference in power distance between Muslim Pakistan and Hindu India: Islam is more equalitarian. However, this religious difference was merely the outcome of a historical development in which certain castes embraced Islam, so that the Muslim part of the population was more homogeneous caste-wise. In present-day India, the caste system with its power distance aspect is a more fundamental element of society than the Hindu religion; Christians and Muslims have become absorbed in it and accepted the status of new castes (Srinivas, 1969). In Japan, Confucianism was imported from China; it helps to explain the respect for a vertical hierarchy (Yochimori, 1976: 6), but it is questionable whether it would have been imported if the hierarchical norm did not already exist (Kawasaki, 1969: 208).

In ideological and philosophical thinking, we find different theories about power in high PDI and in low PDI countries. Among the classics, Machiavelli (1517 [1955]) has given us the picture *par excellence* of the high PDI society. Machiavelli identified with the powerful; more recent authors who did the same are Mosca (Delle Piane, 1968) and Pareto (1976), Italians like Machiavelli, and Michels with his "iron law of oligarchy" (1915) (the latter, although German, lived and worked in Italy). I referred earlier to another classical author, de la Boétie (1548 [1976]), who also wrote from a high PDI viewpoint but identified with the powerless. Not infrequently, authors from a high PDI background identified with the powerless when they were young (de La Boétie was 16 when he wrote his *Discours de la Servitude Volontaire*), but switched to the powerful when they grew old. All these authors are "elitists." To them, power is a zero-sum entity; one can only obtain it by taking it from someone else.

In the low PDI countries, we tend to find "pluralist" theories. The phenomenon of polarization between the powerful and the powerless, between wealthy and poor, is considered a fact, but an undesirable one. The pluralists usually assume that power can be shared and that power distances can be reduced. This presupposes a range of intermediate strata between the powerful and the powerless; these strata tend to exist in the small PDI countries. We find in this category Thomas More (*Utopia,* 1516 [1965]) and, among modern social scientists, Mulder (1976, 1977) and A. Tannenbaum (1968). The latter explicitly defends a non-zero-sum theory of power in which all parties can gain. Within the group of pluralists we may also place those who try to reduce power distance by formal means (as in the case of the German *Mitbestimmung*)—we find these in Germany. I would classify in this category Marx and Engels (1848 [1974]) and Weber (Gerth and Mills, 1948). Marx believes that once the powerless replace the powerful, power distribution will be equal. Weber pictures a system of impersonal rules to which the use of power is tied and which protects both the more and the less powerful. Pluralists who want to reduce power distance by informal means are found in the United States ("participative management"; Likert 1967) or in Britain (sociotechnical systems; Miller, 1976). I shall come back to the formal-informal distinction in Chapter 4.

In the terminology of Machiavelli, the high PDI countries apply a "lions" approach to the exercise of power; the low PDI countries, a "foxes" approach. To Pareto, only the "lions" approach led to stability; but it must be recognized that Pareto came from a "lions" country. To authors like Mulder and Likert, only a "foxes" approach leads to stability; but they come from "foxes" countries. Where "lions" and "foxes" value systems clash within the same society it becomes unstable, as we have seen in the previous section.

PDI and Organizations

People familiar with organizations in different countries are often struck by the variety of organizational solutions to the same task problem. That is, organizational structures, other factors being equal, vary between countries. Yet there is a lack of empirically tested data on how national culture affects organizational structure. Studies of a broad spectrum of countries—essential for generalization—are lacking completely; what is available is comparisons of organizations in two or three countries at a time.

Organizational structures are in themselves very complex phenomena. The study of organizational structures has been influenced considerably by the work since 1961 of a group of researchers originally concentrated at the University of Aston in Birmingham, Great Britain, who developed standardized measuring methods (Pugh, 1976; Pugh and Hickson, 1976; Pugh and Hinings, 1976; see also Chapter 2). Basing their study on data from a large number of work organizations, first in Britain and later in other countries, the Aston group researchers established an empirical taxonomy of organizational structures. The two main dimensions of this taxonomy are "structuring of activities" (including standardization, specialization, and formalization) and "concentration of authority" (which includes centralization). These two dimensions seem to apply across all kinds of organizations in all kinds of environments. The Aston researchers related their structural dimensions to various aspects of what they call the "organizational context" (including organizational size and technology). In a later stage of the Aston research, when it spread to other countries, the issue was raised of the relationship between and the relative influence of contextual versus cultural influences on organizational structures. This issue is known as the "culture-free thesis" (Child and Kieser, 1979), a somewhat misleading term because the Aston authors do not claim that culture does not affect structure, only that relationships between context and structure will be stable across societies. "Simply stated, if Indian organizations were found to be less formalized than American ones, bigger Indian units would still be more formalized than smaller Indian units" (Hickson et al. 1974: 59). So the issue is whether the effects of culture and context are additive or interactive; whether culture affects the *degree* to which structural characteristics are present or (also) the *relationship* between structural characteristics and organizational context factors.

The Power Distance norm as measured by the PDI is clearly conceptually related to the Aston dimension of "concentration of authority." A values complex as pervasive as Power Distance would be very unlikely not to affect organizational structures. Some evidence is present in the data reported by Brossard and Maurice (1974) about carefully matched industrial manufacturing plants in France (a high PDI country) and Germany (a low PDI country). These authors clearly show a difference between the two countries on variables related to the "concentration of authority" dimension, with greater concentration in France. French plants tended to have five hierarchical levels against the German's three; French plants had an average of 26 percent of personnel in management and specialist roles; German plants, 16 percent. A similar difference in number of hierarchical levels was reported by Negandhi and Prasad (1971: 60) between Indian-owned and American-owned plants in India, which is also in line with the PDI difference between India and the United States. On page 125 I referred to the wage differentials in the French and German plants reported by Brossard and Maurice, which were considerably larger in France (the lowest French plant had a larger wage differential between top percentile and bottom decile than the highest German plant). The lower strata in the German plants are both better paid and more qualified.

Granick (1962), in an impressionistic study of French, Belgian, German, and British executives seen from an American viewpoint, found least centralization in Britain. French, Belgian, and German companies were more centralized, but in Germany the central authority tended to be a *team;* in France and Belgium, a *person*.

The higher proportion of managerial and specialist personnel in France goes together with a greater appreciation for white-collar work in general. Vlassenko (1977) shows that the high income inequality scores for France and Italy (which are visible in Figure 3.17) are mainly due to the salary gap between blue-collar and white-collar workers, which is wider in these countries than in the remaining ones on the list. Whyte (1969: 35) reports from Latin America "a sharp line of social distinction between white collar and blue collar jobs." This is another form of inequality which seems to be associated with PDI and is bound to affect the division of labor in organizations.

The Aston studies have shown another dimension: structuring of activities. The search for a corresponding dimension of national culture led to the identification of "Uncertainty Avoidance" which will be the subject of the next chapter.

Figure 3.9 summarizes the "consequences" of national differences in PDI for political systems, religious life, and philosophical and ideological thinking, and for organizations, as described in the previous sections. The term "consequences" must be seen in the sense of the righthand box in the model of Figure 1.4, with a feedback loop to the societal norm (PDI) itself, so that it does not suggest only a one-way causality. If we stay with the model of Figure 1.4, for the PDI-case we find the origins (lefthand box) in Figure 3.8 and a description of the norm itself (middle box)

FIGURE 3.9   Consequences of National Power Distance Index Differences

Low PDI	High PDI

Consequences for Political Systems

Low PDI	High PDI
• Pluralist governments based on outcome of majority votes	• Autocratic or oligarchic governments
• No sudden changes in form of government (evolution and stability)	• Sudden changes in form of government (revolution and/or instability)
• Political parties exist and tend to be in the center with relatively weak left and right wings	• If political parties exist, there is a polarization between left and right with a weak center.
• Government is frequently led by parties stressing equality, usually social democrats	• If government is based on election results, it tends to be led by parties not stressing equality (rightwing).
• Tax system aims at redistributing wealth	• Tax system protects the wealthy
• Free labor unions exist and tend to be pragmatically oriented	• If free labor unions exist, these tend to be ideologically based and involved in politics.

Consequences for Religious Life and Philosophical and Ideological Thinking

Low PDI	High PDI
• Success of religions stressing equality	• Success of religions stressing stratification
• Ideologies of power equalization	• Ideologies of power polarization
• Pluralist theorists about society	• Elitist theories about society
• Non-zero-sum theories of power	• Zero-sum theories of power
• "Foxes" approach is seen as leading to stability	• "Lions" approach is seen as leading to stability
• More, Marx, Weber, Mulder, Tannenbaum	• Machiavelli, Mosca, Pareto, Michels

Consequences for Organizations

Low PDI	High PDI
• Less centralization	• Greater centralization
• Flatter organization pyramids	• Tall organization pyramids
• Smaller proportion of supervisory personnel	• Large proportion of supervisory personnel
• Smaller wage differentials	• Large wage differentials
• High qualification of lower strata	• Low qualification of lower strata
• Manual work same status as clerical work	• White-collar jobs valued more than blue-collar jobs

in Figure 3.7. The PDI level of a country is fairly strongly related to a country's level of economic development, as we saw, but the value differences go beyond economic differences: A considerable range of PDI values is possible for countries at the same level of economic development.

As a conclusion I paraphrase from George Orwell's *Animal Farm*—which I discovered Parkin (1971) did before me—"All societies are unequal but some are more unequal than other."

STATISTICAL ANALYSIS OF
DATA USED IN CHAPTER 3

Calculating the Power Distance Index
by Country

The detailed calculation of the PDI for the 40 countries can be found in an earlier publication (Hofstede, 1977c). The following remarks are important:

(1) The "employees afraid" question (B46). Normally, as described in Chapter 2, country scores from HERMES data are a mean across seven occupational categories: two categories of managers and five of nonmanagers. In the case of the "employees afraid" question, the answers from *managers* have been excluded, as managers' perceptions of employees' fear to disagree are not the same as employees' perceptions: they may be distorted by low sensitivity or wishful thinking precisely in those cases where employees are very afraid. The values found are listed in Appendix 2. The range of means between the most "afraid" country, Greece, and the least "afraid," Austria, is $(3.64 - 2.49) = 1.15$ points on a scale from 1 to 5, or 29 percent of the total scale width; for mean scores across large numbers of respondents (between about 50 and about 10,000 per country) such a range is considerable. With a standard deviation of individual scores within countries of 1.20 points (usually it is less), a difference in means of about .50 points between the smallest country samples and of .03 points between the largest country samples is statistically significant at the .05 level.

(2) The "perceived manager" question (A55). This time the data for all seven occupational categories, including those from managers, were used. Managers in this case have described the behavior of *their* boss, and there is evidence that their perceptions of their boss' behavior do not differ much from employees' perceptions of their own (Sadler and Hofstede, 1972).

In the lower part of Figure 3.10 we see the distribution of answers over the five categories used for this question (manager type 1, 2, 3, 4, or none of these), by survey round (1967–1969 and 1971–1973) for the 28 countries surveyed in both rounds. It is clear that the change in definition of manager type 4 (democratic to participative) has not influenced the answers very much. We also see in the lower part of Figure 3.10 the rank correlations between the "employees afraid" question and the choices of a particular type of perceived manager. In countries where employees are more frequently seen as afraid to disagree with their bosses (lower "afraid" scores), managers are more frequently seen as autocratic and, to a lesser extent, persuasive; managers are less frequently seen as consultative. There are no significant correlations between "employees afraid" and the percentage of those perceiving a democratic, participative, or "none of these types" manager. On the basis of Figure 3.10 I feel justified in averaging the "perceived manager" data for 1967–1969 and 1971–1973. I shall use the mean percent *manager 1 + 2* between both survey rounds as a country measure of perceived manager type (correcting for trend effects in the case of countries surveyed only once, as in the case of the "employees afraid" scores). The combined percentage of the perceived manager 1 + 2 has been shown in Figure 2.5 to be quite stable over time (stability coefficient .82). The mean combined percentage

FIGURE 3.10   Questions A54 and A55

A54. Preferred manager		manager type :				
		1	2	3	4	
Mean % choosing this type	1967-'69	4	23	57	16^d	
	1971-'73	3	20	50	27^p	
Spearman rank ecological correlation with B46 : employees afraid	1967-'69	-.34*	-.31*	.76***	-.28^a	
	1971-'73	-.34*	-.31*	.44*	-.03	

A55. Perceived manager		manager type :				
		1	2	3	4	none
Mean % choosing this type	1967-'69	18	30	32	7^d	13
	1971-'73	17	28	31	11^p	13
Spearman rank ecological correlation with B46 : employees afraid	1967-'69	-.62***	-.34*	.60***	.01	-.07
	1971-'73	-.73***	-.32*	.67***	.25	.15

Preferred and perceived type of manager: 1. autocratic, 2. persuasive, 3. consultative, and 4. democratic (1967–'69) or participative (1971–'73). Mean percent distributions of answers across seven occupations and across 28 countries surveyed twice, and ecological correlations with question B46: employees afraid to disagree.

d = democratic   p = participative
For significance levels see Figure 2.4.
a = significant at .07 level

manager 1 + 2 over both survey rounds rank-correlates (Spearman) −.66*** with the mean "employees afraid" score over both survey rounds. The data by country can be found in Appendix 2.

(3) The "preferred manager" question (A54). The upper part of Figure 3.10 shows that whereas the perceptions (lower part) were more or less equally distributed over types 2 and 3, preferences concentrate more on type 3. There is, however, a considerable shift between the two survey rounds toward preferring the manager 4 new style (the participative, rather than democratic, manager). In this case, a "none of these" category was not included in the questionnaire; everyone was asked to express a preference for one of the four types. The non-responses (which were treated as invalid) constituted less than five percent.

In the same way as for the perceived manager, I have rank-correlated the country "preferred manager" percentages with country "employees afraid" scores (Figure 3.10). We now see a remarkable picture for the 1967–1969 scores. The country level of preference for a type 3 (consultative) manager is strongly correlated with "employees less afraid"; all three other types are weakly correlated with "employees more afraid" (the .05 significance level for 32 cases is at rho = .30). This effect is much less pronounced in the 1971–1973 data, obviously due to the reformulation of manager 4.

The correlation coefficients in Figure 3.10 suggest that the preference or lack of preference for a consultative manager in the 1967–1969 data can be used as a (negative) measure of power distance, but that 1967–1969 and 1971–1973 data should not be combined in this case. I therefore regret the change in the description of manager 4 introduced in 1970; I have not been able to use the 1971–1973 data now. The country data can be found in Appendix 2, separately for manager 1 + 2 (both survey rounds combined), 3A (1967–1969), 3B (1971–1973), and 4B (1971–1973). Column 3A has been used for computing the Power Distance Index.

(4) In computing the Power Distance Index by country out of the three question scores, according to the formula given earlier, some missing data had to be filled in. I have extrapolated these according to the regression line of the variable on the sum or difference of the two other variables. Thus, for example, the missing value for the United States on "employees afraid" is filled up by drawing the regression line of "employees afraid" scores against the difference (% perceived manager 1 + 2)–(% preferred manager 3—1967) based on the available country data and finding the point where the United States value for the latter difference intersects with this regression line.

Figure 3.11 shows the correlations between the three items that form the Power Distance Index across individuals, countries, and occupations. The correlations across individuals within groups (countries × occupations) are virtually zero. These individual correlations were computed for the five subpopulations used for developing the 1971 core questionnaire (see Chapter 2). Each of these covers one occupation in one country; their size varies from 200 to 458 respondents. For the "perceived" and "preferred" manager questions, one difference between the scores used for the individual and the aggregate correlations should be noted. In the individual correlations, the scores used for these questions are values on ordinal scales (1-2-3-4); for the perceived manager, the answer "none of these" was treated as invalid and missing.

FIGURE 3.11   Product Moment Correlations Among Scores on Three
                Questions Composing the Power Distance Index, Across
                Individuals, Countries, and Occupations

Pairs of questions	Correlation of individual scores in five homogeneous groups (200-458 respondents)			Correlation of mean scores across 40 countries	Correlation of mean scores across 38 occupations
	Minimum	Maximum	Median		
a x b (B46 x A55) employees (not) afraid x perceived manager autocratic/persuasive	-.08	.05	-.05	-.67***	-.77***
a x c (B46 x A54) employees (not) afraid x preferred manager consultative	-.11*	.08	.03	.57***	.68***
b x c (A55 x A54) perceived manager autocratic/persuasive x preferred manager consultative	-.07	.12**	.07	-.54***	-.69***

Country scores are means of mean scores for seven occupational groups.
Occupation scores are means of mean scores for three large countries (France, Germany, and Great Britain).

For the perceived manager, substituting percent manager 1 or 2 by a scale value does not affect the correlations very much. For the preferred manager, however, substituting percent manager 3 by a scale value *does* affect the correlations. For another subpopulation (a test population of 1.075 professionals and technicians from all European countries) a dichotomous variable has been created: preferred manager 3/not manager 3. This "pure" variable correlates .03 with "employees afraid." It does not seem, therefore, that the correlations of the preferred manager would have been much higher had we used the pure variable in all cases.

The correlations of the three questions across the 40 countries and across 38 occupations are all well over .50 and justify the calculation of country and occupation Power Distance Indices. The correlations of the three questions with PDI across the 40 countries are −.87, .85, and −.84, respectively.

Power Distance Index Scores by Occupation

The calculation of occupational PDI scores, using the same formula as for country PDI scores but averaging between the occupational means for the three countries France, Germany, and Great Britain, is shown in Hofstede (1977c). For occupations surveyed both in 1967–1969 and 1971–1973, the data for "employees afraid" and the "perceived manager" are the mean of the two survey scores.

Two problems had to be overcome in the calculation. First, half of the occupations were only surveyed since 1970, after the text of question A54, the preferred manager 4, had been changed. The scores, however, should be based on the 1967–1969 version of question A54. Fortunately, the 15 occupations surveyed twice (four were only surveyed in all three countries in 1967–1969) showed a very clear, somewhat curvilinear relationship between 1967–1969 and 1971–1973 scores on question A54. The best-fitting curve has been used to transpose, for those occupations for which no 1967–1969 data existed, the 1970–1973 data into 1967–1969 type scores.

Second, I have argued above that the answers by *managers* on question B46 (are employees afraid to disagree with their managers?) should be taken with a grain of salt. This is because the way question B46 is formulated, it deals with employees in general, who for the nonmanagerial respondents are their colleagues, but for the managers are their subordinates. The answers to this question by managers therefore are not equivalent to the answers by nonmanagers, although they probably also reflect, to some extent, the managers' own power distance with their bosses. In the cross-country comparison I have not used the answers on question B46 by managers, only by nonmanagers. The above objection does not exist in the case of the preferred and perceived manager, for in the responses to these questions, everyone refers to his own superior.

To determine the extent to which managers' responses to question B46 differ systematically from nonmanagers' responses, I have studied the regression lines between the scores (A55–A54) and the scores B46 for managerial and nonmanagerial occupations separately. It appears that the two regression lines run about parallel, but that for a given score (A55–A54) managers tend to score about .16 points higher on B46 than nonmanagers, indicating that they perceive less fear to disagree. To make managers' scores comparable with nonmanagers' scores, I have therefore reduced all scores on B46 for managers by .16 points to determine the PDI for the managerial occupations. After these corrections, the occupational PDI values could be calculated. The correlations of the three questions with PDI across the 38 occupations are −.85, .89, and −.93, respectively.

Results of Other Survey Studies
Significantly Correlated with PDI

(1) Managers at IMEDE answering HERMES questions. Two of the PDI questions were answered by 362 managers in the courses at IMEDE. The samples per country are small; in

order not to lose all information, I used data for as few as seven participants per country and combined participants from some countries assumed to be culturally close; in this way I could use data from 352 managers.

Figure 3.12 shows the comparisons between IMEDE and HERMES, weighting HERMES scores in the case of country combinations. We find a positive but not significant correlation for "employees afraid to disagree" (B46), and a positive and highly significant correlation for the preferred manager (A54). It is remarkable that the IMEDE managers, who, on the average, have *less* preference for autocratic or paternalistic bosses than the HERMES employees, on the average *more* frequently perceive employees as afraid. One reason could be that on the whole they tend to work with less highly educated employees than the HERMES population consists of: We saw that employees' fear to disagree depends strongly on their educational level.

(2) Managers at IMEDE answering L.V. Gordon's Value Surveys. For a population of 372 IMEDE participants (partly overlapping with the one referred to in the previous section), scores were collected on two values tests developed in the United States by L. V. Gordon, called the Survey of Personal Values (SPV: Gordon, 1967) and the Survey of Interpersonal Values (SIV: Gordon, 1976; see Chapter 2). These tests were developed in the United States on a test population of American students. Either test has six scales and 90 items to be scored, grouped in 30 triads from which the respondent must choose the item most and least important to him or her; the answers on a "scale" combine an average of 15 items. There is no proof that these items intercorrelate sufficiently for any but the U.S. test population. The use of such tests for cross-cultural research is ethnocentric and commits the reverse ecological fallacy deplored in Chapter 1. What can be said in favor of the Gordon tests is that their items do not carry strong local American connotations (such as is the case, for example, for the well-known Allport-Vernon-Lindzey Study of Values). In an earlier publication I showed that on the basis of the Gordon test results obtained at IMEDE, countries could be grouped into meaningful clusters (Hofstede, 1976a). If we accept again a minimum of seven cases per country, data are available from 14 countries (1976a: Table 1, taking the two parts of Switzerland together); for each country, we have 12 mean scale values (six for SPV, six for SIV). In order to avoid the reverse ecological fallacy, we should not study scales but item values by country and group them according to their ecological, not their individual, dimensions. Data on item scores by individual respondent, however, have not been kept on file. I have now chosen a next best solution, which is to see to what extent the *scales* can be lumped together into cultural clusters through an ecological factor analysis using the 14 countries as cases. In this factor analysis, it appeared that three factors explained respectively 29, 24, and 21 percent of the variance in country means, together 74 percent. The six scales of the Survey of Personal Values are Practical-Mindedness, Achievement, Variety, Decisiveness, Orderliness, and Goal Orientation. The six scales of the Survey of Interpersonal Values are Support, Conformity, Recognition, Independence, Benevolence, and Leadership. After orthogonal rotation with three factors, the rotated factors found are as follows (all loadings of .40 and over are shown):

Factor 1 (factor variance 27%)
.92 Conformity (SIV)
.82 Orderliness (SPV)
versus
−.83 Leadership (SIV)
−.89 Variety (SPV)

Factor 2 (factor variance 25%)
.93 Recognition (SIV)
.69 Achievement (SPV)
.69 Support (SIV)
versus

−.86 Independence (SIV)
−.48 Goal Orientation (SPV)

Factor 3 (factor variance 22%)
.80 Decisiveness.(SPV)
.76 Benevolence (SIV)
versus
−.86 Practical-Mindedness (SPV)
−.53 Support (SIV; second loading)
−.42 Orderliness (SPV; second loading)

FIGURE 3.12   Comparison of Scores for Two PDI Questions Obtained from 15 Nationality Groups at IMEDE with Scores Obtained in HERMES

Countries	Number of IMEDE respondents	B 46 : employees afraid to disagree (mean score)		A 54 : preferred autocratic and paternalistic (% 1 + 2)	
		Managers IMEDE 1971-'73	Employees HERMES 1967-'69 and 1971-'73	Managers IMEDE 1971-'73	Employees HERMES 1967-'69 and 1971-'73
India, Thailand	15	2.33	2.63	40	35
France, Belgium	15	3.00	2.69	7	27
Brazil, Argentina	19	3.18	2.71	21	31
Iran, Turkey	14	3.00	2.81	36	22
Italy, Spain	20	2.60	2.92	15	24
Japan	7	2.86	3.16	14	38
U.S.A.	18	3.00	(3.18)[a]	33	27
Australia, Canada	14	3.21	3.27	14	27
Netherlands	8	2.75	3.28	0	17
Germany F.R.	41	3.09	3.33	7	15
Great Britain	39	3.31	3.36	13	29
Switzerland	88	2.88	3.33	13	20
Norway	18	3.61	3.17	0	15
Sweden	23	2.96	3.29	0	19
Denmark	14	3.00	3.42	0	15
Total and mean	353	2.99	3.10	14	24
Spearman rank correlation coefficient		.27		.71***	

[a]extrapolated value (see text).

Figure 3.13 lists the factor scores of the 14 countries on each of these three factors and their rank correlations with PDI and the other HERMES indices. By far the strongest correlation (rho = .79***) is between PDI and the "Decisiveness versus Practical-Mindedness" factor.

(3) Students answering L.V. Gordon's S.I.V. For one of Gordon's two tests, the Survey of Interpersonal Values (SIV), the new test manual contains mean scores for male student samples from 24 countries (Gordon, 1976: 4, 55). Eighteen of these countries occur both in the manual and in the HERMES study. In this case I did not factor-analyze the scores because this technique of data reduction is hardly meaningful for only six variables. The student samples are considerably larger than the IMEDE manager samples: a total of 3.887 respondents for 17 countries, with a minimum of 62 for Germany and a maximum of 874 for the Netherlands (I omitted Israel from the Gordon data because its scores are based on only 15 cases and therefore are of a different order of reliability).

The country mean scores for each scale can be found in the Gordon manual. Their correlations, across the 17 countries, with the four HERMES indices are listed in Figure 3.14. We find several significant zero-order correlations, of which the highest are of PDI with Conformity (r = .80***) and negatively with Independence (r = −.79***). There is also a negative correlation of PDI with Support (r = −.70***); Support with negative sign is also part of the "Decisive-

FIGURE 3.13   Factor Scores for 14 Countries Based on Responses of 315 Managers at IMEDE on Gordon's SPV and SIV

Country	Number of respondents	PDI	Factor score of country on factor no		
			1. conformity vs. variety	2. recognition vs. independence	3. decisiveness vs. practical mindedness
India	7	77	1.02	.72	2.20
Brazil	9	69	−.81	−1.18	.81
France	10	68	−.13	−1.87	.71
Iran	9	58	2.66	−.03	−.27
Japan	11	54	1.08	.60	−.18
Italy	16	50	−.55	−.23	.57
U.S.A.	16	40	−.99	1.40	.26
Netherlands	.9	38	−.20	−.09	−.34
Germany F.R.	39	35	−.68	−.37	−.44
Great Britain	33	35	−.58	.68	−.01
Switzerland	99	34	−.30	−.86	.38
Norway	22	31	.15	.87	−1.16
Sweden	22	31	−.90	1.41	−.39
Denmark	13	18	.21	−1.06	−2.14
Spearman rank correlation with	PDI		.21	−.19	.79***
	UAI		.15	−.50*	.39
	IDV		−.42[a]	.27	−.19
	MAS		−.01	−.16	.42[a]

[a]p = .07; for other significance levels see Figure 2.4.
For country mean scores on individual test scales see Hofstede (1976a: Table 1).

FIGURE 3.14   Zero-Order, Multiple, and Stepwise Correlations of Six
Gordon SIV Scales (Male Student Data) for 17 Countries,
Against Four Ecological Indices

Gordon's SIV scale	Zero order product moment correlations across 17 countries with ecological index				Squared multiple correlation with all four indices R^2	Order of indices in stepwise regression, cumulative R^2 and sign of coefficient	
	PDI	UAI	IDV	MAS		1st	2nd
Support	-.70 ***	.14	.68 ***	-.08	.64	.49 - PDI	
Conformity	.80 ***	.34	-.76 **	.44 *	.74	.64 + PDI	
Recognition	.28	.11	.17	.50 *	.47	.25 + MAS	
Independence	-.79 **	-.17	.41 *	-.54 *	.71	.63 - PDI	
Benevolence	.10	-.49 *	-.29	-.59 **	.61	.35 - MAS	.51 + PDI
Leadership	.12	-.28	.23	.15	.32		

The 17 countries are AUL, BRA, CAN, DEN, FIN, GER, HOK, IND, ITA, JAP, NET, PHI,
SAF, SPA, SWE, TAI, USA.

ness versus Practical-Mindedness" factor found for IMEDE managers and correlated with PDI
in their case.

Stepwise multiple regression is a technique in which independent variables are added one at
a time, in the order in which they make a maximum additional contribution to the dependent
variable. It is particularly useful where independent variables are correlated with one another.
In our case the stepwise regression shows also a positive association of PDI with Benevolence,
after eliminating the effect of the MAS index. Benevolence is equally part of the "Decisiveness
versus Practical-Mindedness" factor found at IMEDE.

(4) Managers answering Haire et al.'s (1966) management attitudes and assumptions. This 14-country questionnaire survey of "Managerial Thinking" has been expanded to
Australia by Clark and McCabe (1970) and to seven Southeast Asian countries by Redding and
Casey (1976). The part of Haire et al.'s questionnaire that can be expected to relate to the Power
Distance Index is "attitudes and assumptions underlying management practices" (1966: chap.
2). This uses eight items which are merged into area indices two by two. The items are as
follows (1966: 19–20):

(1) *Capacity for leadership and initiative*
   (a)   The average human being prefers to be directed, wishes to avoid responsibility, and has relatively little ambition (1 = strongly agree).
   (b)   Leadership skills can be acquired by most people regardless of their particular inborn traits and abilities (1 = strongly disagree).
(2) *Sharing information and objectives*
   (a)   A good leader should give detailed and complete instructions to his subordinates, rather than giving them merely general directions and depending upon their initiative to work out the details (1 = strongly agree).
   (b)   A superior should give his subordinates only that information which is necessary for them to do their immediate tasks (1 = strongly agree).

(3) *Participation*
- (a)   In a work situation, if the subordinates cannot influence me then I lose some of my influence on them (1 = strongly disagree).
- (b)   Group goal-setting offers advantages that cannot be obtained by individual goal-setting (1 = strongly disagree).

(4) *Internal control*
- (a)   The use of rewards (pay, promotion, etc.) and punishment (failure to promote, etc.) is *not* the best way to get subordinates to do their work (1 = strongly disagree).
- (b)   The superior's authority over his subordinates in an organization is primarily economic (1 = strongly agree).

In Chapter 1 of this book another part of the Haire et al. study was referred to as an example of the reverse ecological fallacy and of an ethnocentric approach to cross-cultural study.This applies to their "attitudes and assumptions underlying management practices" as well. The eight items have been combined into four subscales, without proof that the items making up one subscale correlate across countries. Only subscale scores by countries are reported, and it is with these that I shall have to work. Combining the Haire et al. data (1966: 22) with the supplementary data from Clark and McCabe and from Redding and Casey, I find 19 countries for which the data can be compared with the HERMES data.

The relevant statistical data are assembled in Figure 3.15, which is composed in the same way as Figure 3.14. In the scoring of the Haire et al. items, a low score always means agreement with a more "traditional" viewpoint, a high score with a more "modern" viewpoint. The obvious hypothesis is that countries with higher PDI levels would show more "traditional" viewpoints. We find, however, that a high PDI for a country is significantly correlated (r = .54**) with the more *"modern"* optimistic viewpoint on "capacity for leadership and initiative" and nonsignificantly (between r = −.32 and r = −.37) with the more "traditional" pessimistic viewpoints on "sharing information and objectives," "participation," and "internal control" (two of the latter three subscales, however, are significantly correlated with Individualism; see Chapter 5).

Two items in the Haire et al. list were used in more or less the same form in the HERMES questionnaire. Item 1a resembles B61, "Most employees in industry prefer to avoid responsibility, have little ambition, and want security above all." Both items derive from McGregor's Theory X (1960: 34). Across 19 countries, the Spearman rank correlation of scores on this item with the *combined* subscale 1 (1a + 1b) of Haire et al. is .37. Question 2a resembles C9, "A good manager gives his employees detailed and complete instructions," which was modeled after it. Across 16 countries the Spearman rank correlation of this item with subscale 2 is also .37. Both stay below the .05 level of statistical significance, but we do not know to what extent this is the effect of Haire et al.'s combining two different questions into one index.

PDI versus Seven Geographic, Economic, and Demographic Indicators

In Chapter 2 I identified seven geographic, economic, and demographic indicators of countries for which it is likely that they show systematic relationships to the value systems revealed by the survey data. An analysis of the literature and common-sense reasoning allows us to hypothesize the following relationships of the seven indicators with PDI (for the definition of the indicators see Figure 2.7).

Wealth (GNP) should be negatively correlated with PDI, because wealth goes together with the growth of middle strata in society which can form a bridge between the powerful and the powerless in society (Adelman and Morris, 1967: 151, 255).

Economic growth (GNG) could be related to PDI in different ways: Some hold that the relationship should be positive because authoritarian coordination of the economy is necessary

FIGURE 3.15 Zero-Order, Multiple, and Stepwise Correlations of Four Haire et al. Management Attitude Subscales for 19 Countries, Against Four Ecological Indices

Haire et al. subscale	Zero order product moment correlation across 19 countries with HERMES index				Squared multiple correlation with all four indices R^2	Order of indices in stepwise regression, cumulative R^2 and sign of coefficient		
	PDI	UAI	IDV	MAS		1st	2nd	3rd
Capacity for leadership and initiative	.54**	-.33	-.49**	.35	.60	.29 + PDI	.45 - UAI	.55 + MAS
Sharing information and objectives	-.33	.12	.63**	-.13	.49	.40 + IDV		
Participation	-.32	.41*	.48*	.14	.41	.23 + IDV	.40 + UAI	
Internal control	-.37	.10	.37	-.17	.21			

The 19 countries are ARG, AUL, BEL, CHL, DEN, FRA, GBR, GER, HOK, IND, ITA, JAP, NOR, PHI, SIN, SPA, SWE, THA, USA.

for growth (Tugwell, 1972). Some hold that the relationship should be negative because authoritarian systems do not innovate (Hagen, 1962: 79). Dick (1974) has found empirically for 59 less-developed countries a curvilinear relationship between economic development and the concentration of power in a few hands: The authoritarian states do either very well or very poorly. To the extent that the authoritarianness of the state is reflected in the PDI, the relationship between GNG and PDI also should be curvilinear.

Geographical latitude (LAT) should be negatively related with PDI because, impressionistically, there is more power inequality in warm countries.

Population size (POP) should be positively related with PDI because larger social systems mean by definition a larger distance between the top and the bottom.

Population growth (PGR) is one of the factors in economic growth; economic growth per capita (this is our indicator GNG) is negatively affected by population growth. Various hypotheses were given for the relationship GNG-PDI; the same would apply to PGR-PDI, but in the opposite sense.

Population density (PDN) may be positively related with PDI because in densely populated countries people are forced to interact more, which could mean a need for authority to settle conflicts.

Organization size (ORG) should be negatively related with PDI because greater size enforces decentralization (Pugh, 1976: 74; Pugh and Hickson, 1976: 88).

The actual correlations of PDI with the seven indices are shown in Figure 3.16. I have computed these across all 40 countries, but also separately across the 19 economically more-developed countries (1970 GNP/capita over $1300) and the 21 less-developed ones. For all 40 countries together, we find significant correlations in the expected direction with GNP, LAT, POP, and ORG; the correlation with PGR is positive, and the remaining two are nonsignificant. If we divide the countries into poorer and wealthier ones, the correlations fall, which is no wonder, as we deliberately restrict the range of one of the two strongest correlates. The only surprise is that ORG for the wealthy countries correlates positively with PDI. However, this can be explained because for these countries, POP and ORG correlate .93; if we control for POP, the partial correlation of PDI and ORG becomes negative ($-.34$) also for those countries.

If we compare the pattern of zero-order correlations across 40 countries for PDI with the intercorrelation pattern of the seven indicators (see page 89), we see that PDI is associated with the cluster of five variables, in the sense that these variables are correlated with each other, except for POP. The fact that the indicators are correlated fairly strongly among themselves makes it desirable to use a stepwise multiple regression technique. This shows that the seven indicators contribute to the prediction of PDI in the following order (lower part of Figure 3.16):

(1) Latitude (LAT)	r = .65	r² = .43
(2) Population size ((POP)	R = .72	R² = .51
(3) Wealth (GNP)	R = .76	R² = .58

(The squared multiple correlation coefficient R^2 indicates the fraction of the total variance explained). The other four indicators do not add substantially to the prediction of PDI; for example, the contribution of ORG is explained completely by ORG's correlations with POP and GNP. The correlation pattern for PDI means that if we know nothing more about a country than its geographical position, number of inhabitants, and 1970 GNP per capita, we can predict fairly accurately the mean answers of HERMES employees in that country on paper-and-pencil questions about power distances.

PDI versus Some Other
Characteristics of Societies

(1) Income inequality. Data on income inequality by country have been published by Kravis (1960), Kuznets (1963), and Bégué (1976). The data come from a variety of sources,

FIGURE 3.16   Product Moment Correlations and Multiple and Stepwise
Regression Across Countries of PDI Scores with Seven
System-Level Indicators

Indicator	Zero-order correlations with PDI scores across		
	All 40 countries	21 poorer countries	19 wealthier countries
GNP	$-.65^{***}$	$-.21$	$.11$
GNG	$.05$	$-.18$	$.35$
LAT	$-.65^{***}$	$-.39^{*}$	$-.03$
POP	$.38^{**}$	$.07$	$.58^{**}$
PGR	$.51^{***}$	$.29$	$-.24$
PDN	$.11$	$.11$	$.36$
ORG	$-.30^{*}$	$.04$	$.52^{**}$
Squared multiple correlation with all seven R^2	$.60$	$.23$	$.43$
Order of indicators in stepwise regression, cumulative R^2, and sign of coefficient	1. .43 − LAT	1. .15 − LAT	1. .34 POP
	2. .51 + POP		
	3. .58 − GNP		

The 19 countries are AUL, AUT, BEL, CAN, DEN, FIN, FRA, GBR, GER, IRE, ISR, ITA, JAP, NET, NOR, NZL, SWE, SWI, USA.
For definition of indicators see Figure 2.7.

often from income tax returns, and are therefore of doubtful reliability. Figure 3.17 shows the data and their correlations with the HERMES indices. I also computed correlations with wealth per se, in order to see whether income inequality could be explained economically rather than through the intermediary of value systems. Figure 3.17 shows significant positive rank correlations of PDI with inequality except for Bégué before tax data. Bégué used OECD data; in fact, the purpose of his article is to criticize these for the case of France. Applying the corrections he suggests, however, has virtually no effect on the correlations with PDI. The correlations of the before-tax data are greatly affected by the data from Japan: The lowest income groups in Japan receive a considerably higher share of national income than in any other country, which strongly influences the ratios. If we exclude Japan, the correlations of PDI with the four Bégué columns become .60*, .66*, .87***, and .84***; the correlations of 1970 GNP/capita with the same four columns become .62*, .55, .13, and .13. Figure 3.17 shows considerable inconsistencies from one study to the other which are due to the different sets of countries in each study and to the different origins of the data; the only index consistently correlated with inequality in the same direction (positively) is PDI. We can take the data as proof that income inequality is larger in high PDI than in low PDI countries.

The Bégué (OECD) data in Figure 3.17 (last four columns) show also the effect of taxation on inequality. If the data are correct, taxation in France *increases* income inequality; it does not affect it in Australia, and reduces it in the other countries, the most so in Norway. We can compute a rate of inequality reduction by taxation which in itself is rank-correlated with PDI across the 10 countries for which data are given: $-.37$ for the top and bottom 10 percent of incomes, and $-.47$ for the top and bottom 20 percent (not significant for this number of countries). This is only the effect of the *official* taxation and does not take into account the unofficial ways in which higher incomes may escape taxation (which are likely to be more

FIGURE 3.17   Comparison of HERMES Indices with Data on Income Inequality

Country	P D I	Kravis[a] : share of top 20% compared to USA=100	Kuznets[b] share of top 5% expressed in % of total	Bégué [c] share of bottom in % of share of top		Bégué [c] share of bottom in % of share of top	
				Income inequality before tax		Income inequality after tax	
				bottom 10%	bottom 20%	bottom 10%	bottom 20%
				top 10%	top 20%	top 10 %	top 20%
Mexico	81		40.0				
India	77		33.4				
France	68			20.7	10.9	21.7	10.9
Colombia	67		41.6				
Spain	57					12.7	7.1
Japan	54	104		9.9	5.6	9.1	5.2
Italy	50	114	24.1			18.2	9.1
U.S.A.	40	100	20.4	23.7	11.8	17.7	9.5
Canada	39	100		22.6	10.1	16.7	8.2
Netherlands	38	100	24.6	13.5	7.8	10.7	6.6
Australia	36			11.3	.5.9	11.3	5.9
Germany F.R.	35		23.6	12.4	7.9	10.8	7.1
Great Britain	35	100	20.9	11.8	7.5	9.4	6.1
Norway	31			14.4	8.3	9.7	5.9
Sweden	31		20.1	12.2	6.8	9.7	5.6
Denmark	18	89	20.1				
Israel	13	96					
Spearman rank correlation with : PDI		.89 **	.86 ***	.25	.30	.57 *	.54 *
UAI		.40	.80 **	−.19	−.07	.21	.15
IDV		.02	−.60 *	.26	.25	.29	.29
MAS		.77 *	.41	−.35	−.13	.02	.13
1953 GNP/capita		−.75 *	−.88 ***				
1970 GNP/capita				.72 *	.67 *	.21	.22

[a]Data from Kravis (1960: 409) based on the early 1950s.
[b]Data from Kuznets (1963: 13) based on different years between 1948 and 1953.
[c]Data from Bégué (1976: 98) based on different years between 1966 and 1974 (OECD study).

plentiful in high PDI countries). We can therefore safely assume that in higher PDI countries the tax systems, rather than reducing the greater income inequalities, in fact increase them.

(2) Balance of power in government. I dichotomized the 40 countries into 20 with "balanced power" and 20 with "unbalanced power." The "balanced power" countries since at least 1950 have had government systems in which the majority of the population could elect periodically the persons or parties it wanted in power, whereby history has shown that peaceful changes in the ruling coalition could indeed take place. These are the 19 wealthiest countries, plus Turkey as a borderline case. The other 20 since 1950 had at least one period of unbalanced government power (autocratic or oligarchic), often after revolutions or periods of political instability. The classification is shown in Figure 3.18.

FIGURE 3.18   A Classification of 40 Countries According to Balance of
             Power in Their Government System and Power Distance
             Scores

Number of countries with	PDI	
	11 – 55	57 – 94
Balanced power since 1950	17[a]	3[b]
Periods of unbalanced power since 1950	3[c]	17
Chi-square	16.9*** (1 d.f.)	

[a]AUL, AUT, CAN, DEN, FIN, GBR, GER, IRE, ISR, ITA, JAP, NET, NOR, NZL, SWE, SWI, USA
[b]BEL, FRA, TUR
[c]ARG, PAK, SAF
For country abbreviations see Figure 2.2.

With chi-quare = 16.9*** and one degree of freedom, the association between balanced power in government and PDI is highly significant. As all 19 wealthiest countries are on the "balanced power" side, GNP per capita is even a better predictor of balanced power than PDI— but I believe the link with PDI helps to account for the relationship between GNP and balanced power. I shall come back to this issue in Chapter 5.

(3) Domestic political violence. Quantitative studies of domestic political violence have been done for 77 nations (1955–1957 data) by Rummel (1963), separately for 71 noncommunist and 11 communist nations by Nesvold (1969; based on 1948–1961 data), and 10 noncommunist and mostly western nations by Schneider and Schneider (1971; based on 1948–1968 data). Political violence includes events like antigovernment demonstrations, riots, coups d'état, assassinations, and civil war.

The rank correlations of the country scores for domestic political violence found in these studies with the HERMES indices are listed in Figure 3.19. All correlations with PDI are highly significant statistically; the correlations with the other HERMES indices (UAI, IDV, MAS), if significant at all, are lower. That the correlation with Rummel's data is not higher is probably because he used a measurement period of only three years, very short for a measure using "events" as a basis.

NOTES

1. Earlier versions of this chapter can be found in Hofstede (1977b, 1979b).

2. For the anthropologists see Bohannan (1969: chap. 11) and Balandier (1972: chap. 4); for the sociologists, Bendix and Lipset (1966), Lenski (1966), Parkin (1971), and Béteille (1977).

FIGURE 3.19   Comparison of HERMES Indices with Data on Domestic
               Political Violence

Countries in order of PDI-score		Rummel[a] 1955-'57	Nesvold[b] 1948-'61	Schneider & Schneider[c]	
				1948-'58	1959-'68
Philippines		-2.14	26		
Mexico		- .82	36	6.0	9.7
Venezuela		1.30	78		
India		5.47	76		
Yugoslavia		-2.14			
Brazil		2.04	28		
France		7.67	97	8.0	9.2
Colombia		- .02	80		
Turkey		1.70	47		
Belgium		- .09	14	2.0	5.0
Peru		- .16	48		
Thailand		.31	54		
Chile		2.70	40		
Portugal		-2.14	29		
Greece		-2.14	22		
Iran		-1.48	59		
Taiwan		- .82	6		
Spain		.64	58		
Pakistan		4.17	46		
Japan		- .16	27	4.0	5.0
Italy		3.50	32	7.0	6.0
South Africa		4.08	83		
Argentina		7.27	109		
U.S.A.		.64	30		
Canada		-2.14	7		
Netherlands		-2.14	1		
Australia		-2.14	5		
Germany F.R.		-2.14	8	2.0	3.0
Great Britain		.71	21	.5	2.0
Switzerland		-2.14	6		
Finland		-1.07	6		
Norway		-2.14	4	.0	.0
Sweden		-1.07	4	.0	.5
Ireland		-2.14	1		
New Zealand		-2.14	5		
Denmark		-2.14	3		
Israel		- .09	5		
Austria		5	5	1.0	.5
Spearman	PDI	.39**	.71***	.79**	.93***
rank	UAI	.23	.44**	.73*	.70*
correlation	IDV	-.22	-.52****	-.10	-.10
with :	MAS	.10	.11	.43	.32

[a]Rummel's (1963: 44) "turmoil" factor score.
[b]Nesvold's (1969: 181) "political violence" score.
[c]Schneider and Schneider's (1971: 81) "political violence" score.

    3. Boulding (1978: 240ff) argues that status and wealth lead to power. In fact, he distin-
guishes between (1) threat power or force, (2) exchange power or wealth, and (3) integrative
power, related to legitimacy and status. Not all status and not all wealth leads to power,
however.

    4. The Christian Church has not escaped the force toward status consistency either. Monks'
orders have collectively become wealthy and powerful. A study by George and George (1966)
has shown that from 2489 official Roman Catholic Saints and Beati living between the first and
twentieth centuries, 78 percent belonged to the upper classes of their time and only 5 percent to
the lower classes.

    5. "The fundamental treaty substitutes moral and legal equality for any physical inequality
between men which nature may have caused; and while they may be unequal in force or

intelligence, they become all equal by agreement and by law" (Rousseau, 1762 [1972]: 122–123; my translation). See also Bottomore (1976).

6. Freedom, equality, brotherhood.

7. Even as an ideological statement it was weak because it did not take into account that equality imposes restrictions on freedom and vice versa.

8. Evan (1977) suggests that hierarchical structure is negatively related to organizational effectiveness. However, he fails to take the cultural environment into account (although he refers to the need for it).

9. Even Stinchcombe (1965: 181) relates the nature of the relationship between superiors and inferiors solely to the ideology of superiors, not of inferiors.

10. About role power Boulding (1978: 248) writes: "It is the images of roles in the minds of the human race that give them [the roles] their power and nothing else."

11. Mathematically, Power Distance could be represented by a ratio as well as by a difference, but as the "extents" involved can be measured only in very approximate terms, this distinction is not relevant. A ratio, however, corresponds better with Blais' (1974) term of "slope," which he uses in a way similar to my use of "Power Distance."

12. Results obtained with the early version in six countries have been published in Sadler and Hofstede (1972). Results obtained with the later version in eight countries have been collected in Schaupp (1973: chap. IV).

13. I have illustrated the dependence, counterdependence, and interdependence mechanisms in the case study "Confrontation in the Cathedral" based on a school incident in Lausanne, Switzerland, in 1972 (Hofstede, 1977a).

14. For evidence see Sadler and Hofstede (1972: 50) and Hofstede (1974b: 16).

15. Inkeles (1969) has constructed a "modernity scale" based on the answers of survey respondents in six developing countries, and shows that across individuals in these countries, "modernity" relates to educational level. Every year longer in school leads to two to three points of gain on a modernity scale of zero to 100. In our case the theoretical length of the PDI scale is 300 points; a gain of 18 points per year on a 300-point scale means 6 points' gain per year on a 100-point scale. Lower power distances are one aspect of Inkeles' modernity. PDI, however, is an aggregate, not an individual index.

16. This is in spite of the correction of managers' scores for B46 described in the statistical section.

17. Lee and Alvares (1977) found in a laboratory study with American psychology students that female subordinates tended to describe the same supervisor as being higher in "consideration" than did male subordinates. If this were a general phenomenon, women should score lower percentages for question b than men. On the other hand, it would be consistent with their answers on questions a and c for them to score higher percentages on b. It is possible that these two tendencies have canceled each other out.

18. This list does not include questions for which the ecological correlation with IDV is higher than the correlation with PDI. The rationale for this will be explained in Chapter 5.

19. The positive association of PDI with managers' answers on "capacity for leadership and initiative" can be compared with the relationship between PDI and McGregor's Theory X, to which I referred before. We found that across countries, employees' agreement with "Most employees have an inherent dislike of work and will avoid it if they can" (C13) was positively correlated with PDI; this was interpreted as a lower work ethic in these countries. Employees' agreement with "Most employees in industry prefer to avoid responsibility, have little ambition, and want security above all" (B61) was unrelated to PDI. In the Haire et al. data we have found evidence that *managers'* answers on a scale comprising the latter item are *negatively* correlated with PDI. Unfortunately, we do not know whether this really applies to both items of the scale separately. In any case, it confirms that work ethic and ambition should be sharply distinguished.

20. The behavior validity of the F-scale in the United States has also been disputed (Ray, 1976).

21. See Stinchcombe (1965: 149) on the ability to trust relative strangers as a cultural trait of vital importance to organizational innovation.

22. The other concepts are anger, courage, fear, laughter, peace, truth, punishment, crime, knowledge, progress, success, death, defeat, love, sympathy, and trust.

23. In Moulin's Nobel Index, Great Britain and its former dominions are taken together. There are therefore no separate data for Australia, Canada, Ireland, and New Zealand. Israel is missing because it was only established in 1948.

24. Norway was a part of Sweden until 1905.

25. The values of the Nobel Index are: SWI 2.62, DEN 1.43, AUT 1.19, NET 1.15, SWE 1.13, GER .71, GBR .67, USA .41, FRA .40, FIN .29, BEL .26, ITA .10, JAP .01, NOR .00.

26. This is significant at the .05-level. The Spearman rank correlations of the Nobel Index with the other HERMES indices are: UAI −.46*, IDV .04, MAS −.02; the rank correlation with 1970 GNP/capita is .42.

27. "Cadres—higher educated employees—think in terms of efficiency; lower educated employees think in terms of protest."

28. See also the answers on question B46 by managers at IMEDE.

29. A very Latin proverb is *"Quod licet Iovi, non licet bovi"* (What is allowed to Jupiter is not allowed to an ox).

30. The effect of inheritance laws on population was already suggested by Le Play in the nineteenth century; see Pitts (1968: 86).

31. Austria is also the only country among the 40 for which employees rate themselves on question B46 as *less* afraid to disagree with their bosses than these bosses rate them. In Switzerland, employees and their bosses break even in this respect. See also Chapter 7 for data on Austria.

32. Stinchcombe (1965: 171) lists an intuitive ranking of some countries according to their means of resolving political conflict which follows perfectly the PDI sequence.

33. Pirenne (1939: 397) sees the Roman Catholic Church in many respects as a continuation of the Roman Empire.

34. Ireland and Poland are Catholic countries without a Latin past; both used their Catholicism as a source of identity to protect them against powerful non-Catholic enemies.

35. The borderline of the Roman Empire ran through present-day Germany and the Netherlands. The southern parts of both countries which once were Roman are still in majority Catholic, the northern parts Protestant. In the Federal Republic of Germany, the 1976 Bundestag elections showed that the ex-borderline of the Roman Empire is also a political dividing line: The (more conservative) Christian Democrats obtained an absolute majority only in the two southern states of Bavaria and Baden-Württemberg.

Chapter 4

UNCERTAINTY AVOIDANCE

SUMMARY OF THIS CHAPTER

The second dimension of national culture found in the data has been labeled "uncertainty avoidance." Uncertainty about the future is a basic fact of human life with which we try to cope through the domains of technology, law and religion. In organizations these take the form of technology, rules, and rituals. The pervasive share of ritual behavior in organizations is only rarely recognized, and most organization theories, except those of March, have no place for it. Data from HERMES show that the tolerance for uncertainty varies considerably among people in subsidiaries in different countries; the three indicators used are rule orientation, employment stability, and stress. The three together produce a country Uncertainty Avoidance Index (UAI). The same index cannot be used for distinguishing between occupations, however. Sex differences in uncertainty avoidance are negligible, but there is a clear relationship between UAI and the average age of respondents in the subsidiary. The chapter is further devoted to a study of the other questions in the HERMES questionnaire with which UAI correlates across countries, and with data from other studies which correlate significantly with UAI. The most important correlations are with national anxiety level, as found in national medical statistics by Lynn, and negatively with need for achievement, as measured in children's stories from 1925 by McClelland.

These and ten other cross-national survey studies allow the composition of a coherent picture of the UAI syndrome as related to anxiety, need for security, and dependence upon experts. The country UAI scores are then correlated with seven national geographic, economic, and demographic indicators; the correlates differ strongly for wealthy and for poor countries; the one consistent correlate is faster economic growth with higher UAI. A relationship is drawn between UAI and historical factors as well as countries' political systems, citizen competence, and legislation. Wealthy, high UAI countries allow cars to drive faster, have more accidents, and oblige citizens to carry identity cards. UAI scores are also related to dominant religions and to the prevalent approaches to scientific activity: more theoretical for high UAI countries, more empirical-pragmatic for low UAI countries; this is explained by a need for absolute truth on the high UAI side. The data supply only few suggestions as to the origins of UAI differences between countries, but more about their consequences for society at large, for ideology, and for organizations.

THE CONCEPT OF
UNCERTAINTY AVOIDANCE

Time, Future, Uncertainty, and Anxiety

A basic fact of life is that time only goes one way. We are caught in a present which is just an infinitesimal borderline between past and future. We have to live with a future which "cannot begin" because "it moves away if we try to approach it;" but which "serves as a projection screen for (our present) hopes and fears" (Luhmann, 1976b: 143). In other words, we are living with uncertainty and we are conscious of it.

Extreme uncertainty creates intolerable anxiety, and human society has developed ways to cope with the inherent uncertainty of our living on the brink of an uncertain future. These ways belong to the domains of technology, law, and religion; I use the terms in a broad sense. Technology includes all human artifacts; law, all formal and informal rules that guide social behavior; religion, all revealed knowledge of the unknown. Technology has helped us to defend ourselves against uncertainties caused by nature; law, to defend against uncertainties in the behavior of others; religion, to accept the uncertainties we cannot defend ourselves against. The knowledge of a life after death is the ultimate certainty of the believer which allows him to face uncertainties in this life.[1] The borderline between "defending against uncertainties" and "accepting them" is fluid; many of our defenses aiming at creating certainty are not really doing so in an objective sense, but they allow us to sleep in peace.

Different societies have adapted to uncertainty in different ways. These ways not only differ between traditional and modern societies, but even among modern societies. Ways of coping with uncertainty belong to the cultural heritage of societies and they are transferred and reinforced through basic institutions like the family, the school, and the state. They are reflected in collectively held values of the members of a particular society. Their roots are non-rational, and they may lead to collective behavior in one society which may seem aberrant and incomprehensible to members of other societies. Fromm (1965) explained fascism and Nazism by a need to "escape from freedom," a response to the anxiety which freedom created in societies with a low tolerance for such anxiety. Freedom implies uncertainty in the behavior of oneself and of others. Totalitarian ideologies try to avoid this uncertainty. Psychologists, especially after World War II and especially in Great Britain and the United

States, have devoted much research to personality dispositions which would make it easier or more difficult for persons to live with uncertainty. The "authoritarian personality syndrome" as described by Adorno et al. (1950) has been investigated by many others since.[2] Attitudes correlated with the "authoritarian personality" (at least in the United States), include intolerance of ambiguity, rigidity, and dogmatism, intolerance of different opinions, traditionalism, superstition, racism, and ethnocentrism next to pure dependence on authority. I shall use the terms "uncertainty" and "ambiguity" as synonyms; the first is more common in organizational theory; the second, in psychology.

We have met the "authoritarian personality" syndrome in Chapters 1 and 3. I have argued, following Kagitcibasi (1970) that attitudes associated across individuals in the United States (or even in other countries) are not necessarily associated across cultures. In cross-cultural studies, we find a component of *norm authoritarianism* which I related to the Power Distance Index; but there is no reason why intolerance of ambiguity, dogmatism, and the rest should be related to PDI across cultures. In the present chapter I shall try to show that on the level of national cultures, norms for (in)tolerance of ambiguity exist which are independent of the norms for dependence on authority. On the cultural level, tendencies toward rigidity and dogmatism, intolerance of different opinions, traditionalism, superstition, racism, and ethnocentrism all relate to a norm for (in)tolerance of ambiguity rather than to the norm for dependence on authority. The norm for (in)tolerance of ambiguity is measured by the Uncertainty Avoidance Index (UAI), which will be described in the present chapter.

Uncertainty in Organizations

Uncertainty is a key concept in modern organizational theories. The concept of uncertainty is often linked to the concept of environment; the "environment" which usually is taken to include everything not under direct control of the organization is a source of uncertainty for which the organization tries to compensate.

Theories of how organizations deal (or should deal) with uncertainty can be divided into those only assuming rational behavior and those also allowing for non-rational behavior. I use the words "rational" and "non-rational" in the same sense as Pareto's *Treatise on General Sociology* (first published 1916) used "logical" and "non-logical." Logical behavior consists of activities "which are logically linked to an end, not only in respect to the person performing them but also to those other people who have more extensive knowledge." Non-logical behavior consists of other activities (Pareto, 1976: 184). What is non-logical or non-rational to a larger public may seem logical or rational to the actor. What is rational for people sharing the same culture may be non-rational to people not sharing that culture.[3]

Theories assuming rational behavior tend to be normative (describing how organizations *should* deal with uncertainty). They include (1) theories of decision-making under uncertainty, (2) contingency theories, and (3) theories of strategic behavior. In the case of *decision-making under uncertainty,* operational research offers statistical tools to put certainty back into decisions, by making one certain of how uncertain one is. This presupposes, however, a continuity of events—that is, a relatively certain environment. The *contingency theories* consider uncertainty as an input which should affect the structure and functioning of the organization (Burns and Stalker, 1961; Lawrence and Lorsch, 1967). What I called *theories of strategic behavior* (strategic planning, strategic management) are normative approaches to the management of organizations in very *un*-certain environments; environments that are called "turbulent" or "discontinuous" (Ansoff, 1978).

Theories allowing for non-rational behavior tend to be descriptive rather than normative. Important contributions to theories about non-rational ways of dealing with uncertainty have been made over the past 20 years by James G. March and his colleagues. In March and Simon (1958: 138) it is recognized that "in the case of uncertainty, the definition of rationality becomes problematic." This same study suggests that organizations maintain an environment which looks relatively certain to their members by "uncertainty absorption": they absorb uncertainty through a limitation of the concepts available for analyzing and communicating about the organization's problems:

> The world tends to be perceived by the organization's members in terms of the particular concepts that are reflected in the organization's vocabulary [March and Simon, 1958: 165].

Cyert and March, in their *Behavioural Theory of the Firm* (1963), use the expression "uncertainty avoidance." Organizations avoid uncertainty in two major ways. First,

> they avoid the requirement that they correctly anticipate events in the distant future by using decision rules emphasizing short-run reaction to short-run feedback rather than anticipation of long-run uncertain events. They solve pressing problems rather than develop long-run strategies. Second, they avoid the requirement that they anticipate future reactions of other parts of their environment by arranging a negotiated environment. They impose plans, standard operating procedures, industry tradition, and uncertainty-absorbing contracts on that situation by avoiding planning where plans depend on prediction of uncertain future events and by emphasizing planning where the plans can be made self-confirming by some control device [1963: 119].

These theories were developed in the relatively certain environment of the U.S. business firm in the 1950s and 1960s. More recently, March's attention has turned to organizations dealing with considerably greater uncertainties, not only in their environment but also within the organization itself—for example, with goals that are unclear, technologies that are imperfectly understood, histories that are difficult to interpret, and participants who wander in and out. Cohen et al. (1972) and March and Olsen (1976) focus on educational institutions (universities and schools) which they present as "organized anarchies." In these, "choices" are made rather than "decisions" in a "garbage can" process in which collections of choices look for problems, issues and feelings look for decision situations in which they might be aired, solutions look for issues to which they might be an answer, and decision makers look for work. Choices are made as well by oversight or flight as by resolution. Elements of this can be found in earlier work by political scientists who always were more accustomed to dealing with uncertain situations; a classical paper by Lindblom (1959) describes the activities of the public administrator as "The Science of Muddling Through"; administrators rarely resolve problems by a rational-comprehensive (root) method but usually by a successive limited comparison (branch) method which takes account of the limited intellectual capacities and sources of information of the administrator, and of the conflicts of values even within the administrator himself. Non-rational aspects of organizing are also described in Weick's *Social Psychology of Organizing* (1969): "Imputing to organizations and their members the disposition towards "rationality" reduces the unease of the theorists but in reality it says very little about the members themselves" (p. 10).

The situation of the business manager in the 1980s is one of increasing environmental and internal uncertainty, and concepts like "muddling through" and "garbage can processes" are becoming relevant also to business organizations—if this was not already the case.

The way in which organizations deal with uncertainty does not depend on some objective amount of uncertainty, but on the way in which uncertainties are *perceived* within the organization. Duncan (1972) studied the perceptions of uncertainty in 22 decision units in the United States. He related these to the perceived complexity and dynamics of the environment. However, he stresses that uncertainty, complexity, and dynamics

> are dependent on the perceptions of organization members and thus can vary in their incidence to the extent that individuals differ in their perceptions. Some individuals may have a very high tolerance for ambiguity and uncertainty so they may perceive situations as less uncertain than others with lower tolerances [1972: 325].

Downey et al. (1977) have shown for a sample of 51 U.S. business division managers that their perceptions of uncertainty related more to personality variables (their cognitive processes) than to their perception of environmental conditions.

If perceptions of uncertainty are affected by personality variables, it is more than likely that they will also be affected by cultural variables. If different societies deal with uncertainty in different ways, this should affect the ways in which they build organizations that react to uncertainty. Faucheux (1977) has shown that strategy formulation is a cultural process: That American approaches to strategic management do not apply to Latin countries in general and to France in particular. Horowitz (1978), in a comparison of 175 British, French, and German top managers, shows that the French and Germans focus much more on short-term feedback than do their British counterparts: The French and Germans show to a much larger extent the behavior which Cyert and March have labeled "uncertainty avoidance" (see their quote above). The cultural element in the way organizations deal with uncertainty merits more attention than it has so far received. The exposition in this chapter of an Uncertainty Avoidance Index with values for nations may help to achieve this.

Technology, Rules, and Rituals in Organizations

In the same way as human societies at large use technology, law, and religion to cope with uncertainty, organizations use technology, rules, and rituals. Technology (such as the automation of a process) obviously creates short-term predictability as to its outcomes (perhaps at the cost of long-term risks of complete breakdown, which are often overlooked). The use of technology looks extremely rational but even this hides several implicit non-rational value choices.

Organizations reduce internal uncertainty—caused by the unpredictability of the behavior of their members and stakeholders—by the setting of rules and regulations. "Rules stem from past adjustments and seek to stabilize the present and future" (Perrow, 1972: 29). "A multitude of rules and regulations appears to be the very essence of a bureaucracy" (1972: 24). Bureaucracy has become a bad word, and "rules are the scapegoats for a variety of organizational problems" (p. 30), but this is because bad rules are more likely to be noticed than good ones; and rules do hold organizations together.

Rules are semirational. They try to make the behavior of people predictable. As people are both rational and non-rational, rules should take account of both aspects of people. Good rules lead to the desired outcome if they are kept (their rational side) and concur with the values of the people whose behavior they try to influence, which means they are likely to be kept (their non-rational side). Bad rules fail on either or both of these criteria.

Bad rules may arise out of differences in values between those who make them and those who have to follow them. People in accounting, planning, and control roles tend to stress the *form* of activities, while people in operating roles tend to stress *content* (Hofstede, 1978b: 453). Baker (1976) found that scores on a values test discriminated among U.S. students majoring in accounting and others; accounting majors, for example, attributed higher value to being "clean" and "responsible" and lower to being "imaginative." This suggests that people in accounting, planning, and control roles have a higher need to avoid uncertainty than others; their scores as students show that they may be self-selected on this characteristic. However, the rules they set may not correspond to other people's needs and values.

Good rules can set energies free for other things: they are not necessarily constraining. Inkson et al. (1970) showed that British executives in more structured organizations (those with more rules) did more innovative work than did executives in less structured ones. Kohn (1971), in a cross-national sample of over 3000 American men, showed that employees of more "bureaucratic" organizations (larger organizations, government organizations, and non-profit organizations) tended to be more intellectually flexible than employees of less bureaucratic organizations, counter to the public image of bureaucracies.

Rules, on the other hand, may destroy people's autonomous judgment and lead them to do things they would have considered bad without the rules. We can think of the behavior of soldiers at war, but also, for example, of the outcome of Milgram's (1974) experiments with obedience to authority. Ordinary U.S. citizens were led to torture others (at least they thought they were doing so) by the mere fact of the experimenter telling them that this was part of the rules of the experiment. In this case the rule is used as an alibi in order to avoid the uncertainty of an independent judgment. In more uncertainty-avoiding environments, people will have a greater need for the authority of rules.

The authority of rules is something different from the authority of persons. The first relates conceptually to uncertainty avoidance, the second to power distance. The German *Befehl ist Befehl* (an order is an order) refers to the authority of the rule: The person who gives the order is irrelevant, as long as he occupies the position to whom the rule assigns the giving of orders. The French *bon plaisir* (literally, "good pleasure": used to describe the arbitrary will of the ruler in the seventeenth century), which Crozier (1964a: 222) still finds in modern French bureaucracies, puts the authority of the person above the system of rules. The first suggests high uncertainty avoidance, the second high power distance.

Rituals, such as sacrificing to the gods, are prescribed by primitive religions to ensure the season's crop or the winning of a war. Unbelievers smile at such practices because they think they know that on the logical level the rituals do not change anything. But this is immaterial; the rituals are functional because they allow the members of that society to continue their lives as peasants or warriors together in the face of otherwise intolerable uncertainty. Of course, rituals may also be cruel and destructive, as in the case of human sacrifices.

Modern society is less different from primitive society than we sometimes think. Its basic ingredient is man, and there is no evidence that human nature has changed much in the process of modernization. In any case, we share with primitive man a need for social cohesion and a limited tolerance for uncertainty. We dispose of infinitely better technological means to defend ourselves against risks, but unfortunately these means themselves always bring new risks; and we still feel the future to be very uncertain indeed. Like the social systems of primitive man, ours have developed their rituals to make uncertainty tolerable.

Rituals in traditional and modern society serve many other purposes besides making uncertainty tolerable. They play an important role in our establishing relationships with our fellow man and in giving meaning to our lives.[4] Rituals in modern society are recognized in religions and state ceremonies, in the family, in youth movements and countercultures. They are less easily recognized, but equally present, in pragmatic business and public organizations.

Rituals in organizations are non-rational. They include social rituals and uncertainty avoidance rituals. They are neither silly nor superfluous; they are, moreover, omnipresent. There are good and bad organizational rituals. Good rituals support social cohesion and relieve stress because they concur with the values of the people involved, and they have no negative consequences for the organization or any of its members (modern society knows its human sacrifices, too).

Social rituals in organizations, for example, are found in various types of meetings. Meetings partly serve a ritual purpose in all cases and serve no other purpose in many cases. Business meetings usually have their own liturgy, sacred language, and taboos. To the social rituals also belong various training programs, especially management development programs which serve as initiation rites for the organization's leaders.

Uncertainty-avoiding rituals in organizations do not make the future more predictable, but they relieve some of the stress of uncertainty by creating a pseudo-certainty within which organization members can continue functioning. To the category of uncertainty avoiding rituals we can count the following items.

(1) Memos and reports which often contain no information that anyone will act upon, but which are a device to "stop time" for a moment.

(2) Certain parts of the accounting system. Accounting is an "uncertainty-absorbing" process in the sense meant by March and Simon (1958: 4.5). It may absorb uncertainty to such an extent that it absorbs all usable information as well. In an amusing series of comparisons between business and primitive society, Cleverley (1973: 38) calls the accountants the "priests" of business. Gambling (1977) draws a

parallel between accounting and magic, and gives many examples showing that accounting information is often after-the-fact justification of decisions that were taken for non-logical reasons in the first place. The main function of accounting information is to maintain morale in the face of uncertainty. "In short, the accountant is the person who enables a distinctly demoralized modern industrial society to live with itself, by reassuring it that its models and data can pass for 'truth'" (1977: 18–19).[5]

(3) A considerable part of planning systems. In the face of growing uncertainty, organizations sometimes try to be more rational, and they follow the frequent calls in the literature or from consultants for better and more elaborate planning. However, a more sophisticated planning system does not necessarily guarantee more effective operations if the latter are affected by unforeseeable events. Very few planning systems have helped firms to cope with the 1973 oil crisis, for example. When the event hit the firms, the planning systems were simply bypassed. Cleverley calls planning the "fertility rites" of business (1971: 67). Primitive cave dwellers already pictured the animals they *planned* to kill. Weick (1969: 102) suggests that as no one can anticipate future contingencies and we can only look back, random trial and error is more likely than planning to produce results; it furnishes data that can be viewed retrospectively and made meaningful. Having a planning system, however, allows managers to sleep more peacefully, even if it does not really work. It may also help members of an organization to believe in what they are doing, which is an essential element of success in overcoming crisis. Jönsson and Lundin (1977), using case studies from Sweden, show the importance of collectively accepted myths and wishful thinking in creating waves of enthusiasm among members which keep the organization going, even if the dreams do not come true; they are in due time replaced by new myths.[6]

(4) A very considerable part of control systems. Most control systems use a cybernetic philosophy, which presupposes some kind of standard, measurability of accomplishment, and a possibility to use feedback. If one or more of these conditions is not fulfilled, cybernetic control cannot work; but the market offers many techniques which still try to enforce it, such as management by Objectives (MBO) for nonmeasurable tasks, or Planning-Programming-Budgeting (PPBS; for a more extensive analysis of these attempts to enforce the impossible see Van Gunsteren, 1976; Hofstede, 1978b). Such rituals can be harmful, as they can cloud real issues by false pseudo-certainties and make things less "discussable" that should remain open for discussion. Even when the conditions for cybernetic control are fulfilled, control systems still may be entirely or mainly ritual; for example, the minute checking of the figures of travel accounts where there is no possibility to judge the necessity of the trip. Control systems also become rituals when those whose activities are controlled receive the message that correct figures are more important than correct facts. Weir (1975) calls this "control overkill." It is one of several forms of "pseudo-control." Other forms of pseudo-control are the automatic adaptation of the standard when there is a variance between measurement and standard and the excessive stress on those aspects of a process visible in the control system at the expense of the invisible elements—which could lead, for example, to balancing cost at the expense of quality. Crozier (1964a: 185,191) sees "ritualism" as contributing to the dysfunctions

of bureaucracies, and finds its origins in the French case in a need for self- and peer-group-protection among officials. It stresses the needs of the individual and of the group, but not of the organization.

(5) A final uncertainty-avoiding ritual is the nomination of experts. Experts used by an organization may be in-house specialists or outside consultants. Whether the expert can apply more information, insight, or skill to solving the problem is often immaterial, as long as the organization members see him as transforming uncertainty into certainty. Cleverley compares consultants with the "sorcerers" of primitive societies (1971: 53). Outside consultants are often used when various persons within the organization cannot reach consensus, to absorb this inside uncertainty. Modern people-processing organizations such as social welfare agencies resort to an increasing degree to professionalization in order to make the uncertainties inherent in this type of organization tolerable. The belief in experts, however, is strongly determined by the national norm for uncertainty avoidance. Great Britain which, as we will see later, has a low uncertainty avoidance norm, is known for its preference for a generalist, nonspecialized education for managers. A British ex-executive (Marks, 1977) states that "the more difficult it is to plan, the less you need full-time professional planners." In such countries as France and Germany (higher uncertainty avoidance norm), this statement definitely would not be endorsed; the opposite probably would be defended.[7]

MEASURING NATIONAL DIFFERENCES IN UNCERTAINTY AVOIDANCE IN HERMES

An Uncertainty Avoidance Index for HERMES Countries

The previous paragraphs have argued that coping with the inevitable uncertainties in life is partly a non-rational process which different individuals, organizations, and societies resolve in different ways. The main underlying dimension is the tolerance for uncertainty (ambiguity) which can be found in individuals and which leads some individuals in the same situation to perceive a greater need for action for overcoming the uncertainty than others. This tolerance for uncertainty is partly a matter of personality, partly a matter of culture. Societies differ in their societal norms (Figure 1.4) for uncertainty avoidance, and members of these societies are socialized in the society's institutions toward this norm.

Chapter 2 has described how three questions in the HERMES data bank were selected from which the country scores could be used to form a country Uncertainty Avoidance Index. The three questions refer to three components of national levels of uncertainty avoidance: rule orientation, employment stability, and stress. It is likely that other and perhaps better survey indicators of national levels of uncertainty avoidance can be developed, but I had to use the data available in the HERMES archives; and uncertainty avoidance had not been a familiar concept to us when, in 1967, we composed the HERMES questionnaire.

The "rule orientation" item in the HERMES questionnaire is: "Company rules should not be broken—even if the employee thinks it is in the company's best interests" (B60 in Appendix 1 with a five-point answer scale from "strongly agree" to "strongly disagree"). The selection of this item was guided by the findings of the Aston group in Great Britain (Pugh, 1976; Pugh and Hickson, 1976). The Aston group found, among different organizations in Britain, three dimensions of organizational structure of which the third was relatively weak. The two strong dimensions are "concentration of authority"—conceptually related to power distance—and "structuring of activities." The item in the HERMES questionnaire most closely conceptually related to "structuring of activities" is the item just mentioned.[8]

It will be evident that disagreement with the "rule orientation" statement indicates a higher level of tolerance for uncertainty: It is acceptable that employees break company rules if they believe this is in the company's interest. The opposite position, agreement with the "rule orientation" statement, avoids the uncertainty of employees deciding themselves whether or not a rule should be followed.

The "employment stability" item in the HERMES questionnaire is: "How long do you think you will continue working for this company?" Answers are: (1) Two years at the most; (2) From two to five years; (3) More than five years (but I probably will leave before I retire); (4) Until I retire (A43). It had long been noticed that this question showed considerable and consistent differences in answer distributions among countries. What was not evident from the start is that country scores on this question would be correlated with "rule orientation" country scores, which, however, appeared to be the case (r = .59 across 40 countries; see the statistical analysis). The link between the two questions is that a low percentage of employees planning to leave within five years and a low "rule orientation" score (= strong rule orientation) both indicate a strong Uncertainty Avoidance norm in a country: Employment stability and rule orientation are two ways of avoiding uncertainty.

There is evidence that the answers on the employment stability question do reflect actual behavior. An unpublished study in HERMES showed that across 14 countries, country scores on this question in the 1968 survey of technical experts correlated highly with 1967 turnover rates among technical experts.[9]

The "stress" question in the HERMES questionnaire is: "How often do you feel nervous or tense at work?" Answers range from 1. "I always feel this way" to 5. "I never feel this way" (A37). This question was taken from earlier surveys of managers in HERMES U.S.A. run by the company medical department, which also included questions on medical symptoms; it could be shown to be correlated with answers on medical symptom questions (see the statistical analysis on page 190).

The "stress" question taps a fundamental phenomenon in human life. There is probably no human being who does not feel stressed at times. Stress is a state of mind and body which corresponds to the state of preparation for aggression in primitive man, released through acts of aggression. When social norms forbid overt aggression, modern man must cope with his stress in different ways.

Stress is a subjective experience. "Stress is in the eye of the beholder. If you think you are under stress, you are under stress" (Pettigrew, 1972). The same objective situation may be felt as stressful by one person and as relatively stress-free by another. However, in spite of its "soft" subjective character, stress has "hard" objective consequences. Stress affects the metabolism of the body, as various medical studies have shown (Selye, 1974; Friedman and Rosenman, 1975; a popular summary can be found in Toffler, 1971: chap. 15). This is not necessarily bad; a certain amount of stress is indispensable for activity, for a feeling of satisfaction in life, for physical and mental health, and for performance. An excess of stress without adequate opportunities for release, however, may lead to various physiological and mental disorders, although the exact causal relationship between a particular stressful condition and a particular complaint is often difficult to prove (Levine and Scotch, 1970; Gross, 1970).

The following are some of the most frequent physiological and mental disorders that have been shown in different studies to be related to forms of stress:

(1) diseases of the heart and the blood vessels (Jenkins, 1971; Friedman and Rosenman, 1975);
(2) diseases of the stomach and the intestines (Vertin, 1954; Dunn and Cobb, 1962);
(3) nervous breakdowns and disruption of interpersonal relations, in extreme cases leading to suicide (Levinson, 1964, 1975); and
(4) reduced intellectual performance; a reduced ability to perceive alternatives in decision-making (Kalsbeek, 1967), and a tendency to use negative rather than positive evidence (Wright, 1974).

Kets de Vries et al. (1975) explain stress reactions from a combination of four kinds of variables[10]:

(1) a personality with his personal history, traits, and so on;
(2) a nonwork (for example, family) environment;
(3) an organizational (work) environment; and
(4) a sociocultural, larger environment, in which the personality, his nonwork life, and the organization in which he works are all embedded.

In the HERMES data, we can identify stress differences due to the socio-cultural environment (in the form of differences among nationalities) and due to one organizational environmental factor: occupation.[11] The differences in stress due to other organizational environmental factors,[12] to the nonwork environment, and to personality will be treated as random error. This, however, does not mean they are unimportant; other studies have dealt with these factors. For example, in the area of personality, Friedman and Rosenman (1975) have created the distinction between persons showing "Type A" and "Type B" behavior. The typical Type A person tries to do more and more things in less and less time, while the Type B person is unhurried and patient. Type A persons are more likely to suppress fatigue (Carver et al., 1976). Friedman and Rosenman found that for American men between the ages of 35 and 60, Type A persons were seven times more likely to develop coronary heart disease than were Type B persons. In the area of the nonwork aspects of life (or the interaction between work and non-work aspects), Holmes and Rahe (1976) have developed their "Social Readjustment Rating Scale," allocating point values to stressful life events such as the death of the spouse, getting married, or losing a job. In the United States, Japan (Masuda and Holmes, 1967), Sweden, and Denmark these authors and their associates have shown that if the sum of the point values of crucial life events within a certain period exceeds a certain level, a person is highly likely to suffer physical and/or mental disorders.

It now appears that on the country level, higher mean stress goes together with stronger rule orientation and greater employment stability, and vice versa. We find in the statistical analysis that stress, rule orientation, and employment stability form one societal "Uncertainty Avoidance" syndrome. The conceptual link among the stress question and the other two questions is the mean level of anxiety in a country. When this is higher, people feel more stressed; but at the same time they try to cope with the anxiety by a greater need for security, which is visible in both rule orientation and employment stability. The association between anxiety and rule orientation was already postulated by Van Gunsteren (1976); the HERMES data provide statistical evidence for it.

An Uncertainty Avoidance Index for each of the 40 countries has therefore been compiled on the basis of the country mean scores for the three questions:

(a) Rule orientation: Agreement with the statement "Company rules should not be broken—even when the employee thinks it is in the company's best interest" (B60).

(b) Employment stability: Employees' statement that they intend to continue with the company (1) for two years at the most, or (2) from two to five years; this, of course, taken with a negative sign (A43).

(c) Stress, as expressed in the mean answer to the question "How often do you feel nervous or tense at work?" (A37).

The actual computation of the Uncertainty Avoidance Index (UAI) uses mean percent values for question b, and mean scores on five-point scales for questions a and c. These mean scores have been multiplied by 30 (for a) and 40 (for c) to make their range, and therefore their contribution to UAI, roughly equal to the range in percentage values of question b. The actual formula used is:

$$\text{UAI} = 300 - 30 \text{ (mean score rule orientation)} - (\% \text{ intending to stay less than 5 years}) - 40 \text{ (mean stress score)}.$$

The constant 300 brings country index values in a range between eight (lowest uncertainty avoidance country: Singapore) and 112 (highest uncertainty avoidance country: Greece). The mean over 40 countries is 64. The theoretical range of the index is from -150 (all think that rules can be broken, no one wants to stay, no one ever feels nervous) to $+230$ (all think that rules should not be broken, everyone wants to stay more than five years, everyone always feels nervous). Of the theoretical range of the UAI (380 points), 104 points, or 27 percent, are really used for differentiating among countries.

The computation of the UAI values for the 40 countries has been shown in an earlier publication (Hofstede, 1977d). The resulting values are summarized in Figure 4.1 (first column). The ranking of the countries in Figure 4.1 suggests certain clusters of similar countries, but it differs from the ranking we found for the Power Distance Index in Figure 3.1: For example, many Asian countries score on the lower part of the UAI scale. A comparison between countries' Power Distance Index and Uncertainty Avoidance Index positions will be given in Chapter 7.

Occupation and Sex Differences in the Scores on the Uncertainty Avoidance Items

In the statistical section of this chapter it is shown that the three items comprising the Uncertainty Avoidance Index *for countries* are uncorrelated across occupations. Therefore, the calculations of occupational Uncertainty Avoidance Index values makes no sense; this in contrast to what we saw for the Power Distance Index

FIGURE 4.1   Country Uncertainty Avoidance Index (UAI)

Country	UAI Actual	UAI Controlling for age [a]	Country	UAI Actual	UAI Controlling for age[a]
Greece	112	98	Finland	59	54
Portugal	104	102	Switzerland	58	62
Belgium	94	80	Netherlands	53	45
Japan	92	112	Australia	51	47
Peru	87	91	Norway	50	38
France	86	73	South Africa	49	62
Chile	86	66	New Zealand	49	60
Spain	86	89	Canada	48	55
Argentina	86	74	U.S.A.	46	36
Turkey	85	61	Philippines	44	45
Mexico	82	86	India	40	48
Israel	81	73	Great Britain	35	43
Colombia	80	77	Ireland	35	54
Venezuela	76	78	Hong Kong	29	61
Brazil	76	74	Sweden	29	23
Italy	75	58	Denmark	23	32
Pakistan	70	82	Singapore	8	31
Austria	70	77	Mean of 39 countries (HERMES)	64	64
Taiwan	69	73			
Germany (F.R.)	65	53			
Thailand	64	73			
Iran	59	59	Yugoslavia (same industry)	88	77

NOTE: Values based on the scores on three attitude survey questions for a stratified sample of seven occupations at two points in time. Actual values and values obtained after controlling for the average age of the country sample.

[a]For age scores see Appendix 2, Question A57.

(Chapter 3), where correlations across occupations were even higher than across countries. The statistical analysis also shows that an occupation's mean level of *rule orientation* is mainly dependent on the occupation's average formal educational level (higher-educated occupations tend to show less rule orientation).

An occupation's mean *employment stability* level is a combined function of (1) the average age of its incumbents (the older, the more stability); (2) their average educational level (the higher, the less stability); and (3) the occupation's percentage of female incumbents (the more women, the less stability).

An occupation's mean *stress level* depends somewhat on its hierarchical level (managers higher than nonmanagers). Differences in stress level by occupation have consequences for the physical and mental health of the occupations' incumbents. However, it appears that this health effect is modified by the incumbents' level of job satisfaction. The HERMES data bank supplies interesting data about the stress-satisfaction balance of various types of occupations; these have been described elsewhere (Hofstede, 1978c).

The fact that rule orientation, employment stability, and stress relate quite differently to the demographic factors of educational level, hierarchy, age, and percent female represents another reason why for occupations the three uncertainty avoidance questions should not be integrated into one index.[13]

There is some tendency for occupations with more women to show higher stress scores, after we have eliminated the effect of hierarchy on stress (Figure 4.8). This does not mean, however, that women *within the same occupations* are necessarily under higher stress than men. For two occupations with sizable numbers of both men and women who do about the same work, Figure 4.2 lists the scores on the three Uncertainty Avoidance Index items separately for women and for men (compare Chapter 3, Figure 3.4).

FIGURE 4.2   Scores on UAI Questions for Men and Women in the Same Occupations

Occupations (2 surveys, total world data)	(a) Rule orientation mean score	(b) Employment stability % stay less than 5 years	(c) Stress mean score
Branch Office technical experts			
men (n = 9917)	2.94	34	3.21
women (n = 591)	2.94	45***	3.14
Head Office clerks			
men (n = 7665)	2.78	19	3.08
women (n = 5496)	2.77	31***	3.06

The differences between men and women in questions (a) and (c), tested by the t-test for difference of means, do not reach statistical significance.

The differences between men and women in question (b), tested with the Kolmogorov-Smirnov test, are significant at the .001 level for both groups.

We see that women and men score equally on rule orientation and that on stress women produce slightly lower scores—that is, higher stress—but the difference in stress scores between women and men is not statistically significant (not even with these very large numbers of respondents). The stress difference is therefore negligible.[14] On employment stability, women score significantly less "stable" than men; this has nothing to do with their attitude to uncertainty, but with their family role.[15] The computation of a UAI by sex therefore does not make sense. As a whole, sex and uncertainty avoidance are unrelated.

**Country Uncertainty Avoidance Index Scores
and Other HERMES Survey Questions**

The average scores by country on several other questions used in the HERMES questionnaire are also statistically significantly correlated with the Uncertainty Avoidance Index. Figure 4.9 in the statistical part of this chapter lists these questions.

First, there is a strong relationship of a country's UAI level and the average age of the HERMES respondents in the country. To check whether the country differences in UAI cannot be due entirely to these average age differences, I have in the second column of Figure 4.1 listed the UAI values that would be obtained if we control for age—that is, if all countries had the same average age. The various country clusters remain essentially the same, but some countries shift somewhat; the separation between the Asian countries (except Japan) and the Latin-Mediterranean countries becomes slightly less sharp. The country differences in UAI certainly cannot be accounted for by an average age artifact. We cannot claim, either, that the age-correlated UAI scores are more "correct" than the uncorrelated ones. The average age of HERMES employees in a country is partly a *consequence* of a high UAI norm. A higher UAI implies, among other things, a hesitation to change jobs; therefore, the average seniority in such a country will be higher and, with it, the average age, which reinforces the tendency to stay. I shall therefore continue to use the "raw" UAI values in order to characterize countries, not the values corrected for age.

In addition to the age question, respondents in high UAI countries tend to differ from those in low UAI countries on the following issues:

(1) a lower ambition for advancement (A15) and a preference for specialist over manager positions (B9);

(2) a preference for large over small organizations (C17), and more approval for loyalty to those organizations (C12), while the more senior managers are considered to be the better ones (C11);

(3) a tendency to avoid competition among employees (B54) and to prefer group decisions (B57) and consultative management (B55) over individual decisions and more authoritative management (note that question B55 is correlated in opposite ways with PDI and UAI);

(4) dislike of working for a foreigner as a manager (B44);

(5) resistance against change (C16);

(6) a pessimistic outlook on the motives guiding companies (C10: in spite of admiration for loyalty to companies);

(7) finally, the level of overall satisfaction scored (A58) in a country is positively related to UAI.

If in a country there is a high level of uncertainty avoidance as evidenced by the UAI items rule orientation, employment stability, and stress, then we also find that advancement to a manager position, working for small organizations, competition among employees, individual decisions, working for a foreign manager, and a high rate of organizational change tend to be felt as risky situations which fewer people are willing to face. In such countries people are more pessimistic about employers in general, but they produce higher satisfaction scores. This looks paradoxical; it suggests that the satisfaction score levels in a country reflect partly an element of avoidance of "cognitive dissonance" (Festinger, 1957). If people do not consider "leaving the organization" as a feasible alternative, they will have a tendency to convince themselves that they like being in it.

The ecological correlation of UAI with a dislike of competition among employees does not mean that there will be, in effect, less competition among employees in high UAI countries; there may even be more. The correlation of UAI with a preference for group decisions reminds us strongly of the Japanese *ringi* system of collective decision-making; in fact, Japan scores very high on UAI, although Japanese HERMES employees do *not* score high on the group decisions item (B57 in Appendix 2).[16] Group decision-making can be seen as a way of avoiding risk for the individual.

COMPARING THE HERMES
UNCERTAINTY AVOIDANCE INDEX VALUES
WITH OTHER DATA

UAI and Anxiety: The Lynn Studies

The analysis of national differences in anxiety-related behavior goes back to Durkheim (1897 [1937]). He showed systematic and stable differences in suicide rates between the countries on which he had data, next to systematic differences between other societal categories, such as men and women, married and divorced. Durkheim used his analysis of the suicide phenomenon to demonstrate how a highly individual act could be caused by social forces. He discarded purely psychological explanations: Although some people may be psychologically more predisposed to suicide than others, the force which really determines whether they will commit the act, according to Durkheim, is social.[17] Psychologists have related anxiety to stress. Kahn et al. (1964: part 5) established a link between stress reactions and the personality dimensions of neurotic anxiety, extraversion-introversion, flexibility-rigidity and achievement verses security orientations. Popular wisdom and stereotypes attribute to people from different countries different levels of stress-related behavior, such as aggressiveness, expressiveness, talkativeness, and patience. Tannenbaum et al. (1974: 156ff), in a study of five countries, show differences among countries in levels of "psychological adjustment," which includes depression, resentment, and low self-esteem.

Differences in anxiety levels among countries or subcultures in countries have been revealed by medical studies of body reactions (Dunn and Cobb, 1962; Levinson, 1964; Jenkins, 1971; Zaleznik et al., 1977; Hofstede, 1978c). A major source of information on country differences in such reactions is the death rate statistics published by the Statistical Office of the United Nations, and several authors have built theories on the basis of these (for example, Rudin, 1968; Barrett and Franke, 1970).

The most extensive and serious study of country-level medical and related statistics that came to my attention has been done by Lynn (1971, 1973, 1975) and Lynn and Hampson (1975, 1977). In the later version of their work, Lynn and Hampson (1975) factor-analyzed 12 variables for 18 developed countries[18] and found two factors (accounting for 57 per cent of the variance in the data). They labeled their first factor "neuroticism," or "anxiety." It combined the following variables (the figures are factor loadings)

  −.79 low chronic psychosis (number of patients per 1000 population)
   .78 high suicide death rate
  −.69 low caffeine consumption
   .68 high alcoholism (liver cirrhosis death rate)
  −.68 low daily calorie intake

−.66 low coronary heart disease rate
.66 high accident death rate
.51 high punished crime rate (number of prisoners per 10,000 population).

They labeled their second factor "extraversion," combining

.73 high divorce rate
.65 high murder rate
.61 high cigarette consumption
.61 high punished crime rate (also loading on factor 1)
.60 high coronary heart disease rate (loading on factor 1 with opposite sign)
.53 high "illegitimacy" (percentage of births extramarital).

Lynn's first factor can also be seen as a "stress" factor. Its negative correlation with the coronary heart disease rate may be puzzling because it has been shown in U.S. studies that stress and coronary heart disease are *positively* correlated (Jenkins, 1971; Friedman and Rosenman, 1975). However, this is a correlation across *individuals;* the correlation in the Lynn data is an *ecological* one, across countries, and the two may well have opposite signs. The factors which lead to correlations across individuals are psychological (characteristics of persons); the factors which lead to correlations across countries are sociological and cultural (characteristics of social systems). Jenkins (1971) quotes a number of studies which show that the effects of stress on the cardiovascular system are conditioned by people's ability to show emotions. One study (Jenkins, 1971: 309) shows that mortality from coronary disease in Japan is much lower than among American citizens of Japanese ancestry; this is attributed to the cultural institutions in Japan that encourage the free expression of emotions and provide social support for the individual. This suggests that in certain countries with higher national anxiety levels, social systems have developed which allow for emotions to be expressed and therefore prevent stress from leading to coronary death. Latins are more anxious—but because the Latin environment allows them to be more talkative and expressive, Latins in Latin countries are less prone to coronary conditions. This and other social systems characteristics can overcompensate for the negative effect of stress on the heart.

The statistical analysis shows that Lynn and Hampson's "neuroticism" (anxiety) factor scores for 18 countries are strongly correlated (rho = .73) with the HERMES Uncertainty Avoidance Index (and also with the HERMES stress scores). This high correlation of UAI and "neuroticism" is encouraging for the validity of the HERMES data in general and the Uncertainty Avoidance Index in particular. There is—at least among these 18 countries—a national syndrome which relates to neuroticism, anxiety, stress, uncertainty avoidance, or whatever we want to call it, which differentiates between modern nations and affects HERMES employees as much as anyone else.

Independently of Lynn's work and unaware of it, Millendorfer (1976) did a similar analysis of data on suicides, psychoses, accidents, and divorces from 15 countries and also found differences in stress levels among countries (p. 10). Across the 12 countries studied by both Lynn and Millendorfer, their country rankings correlate with .69; and Millendorfer's stress ranking rank-correlates .71 with the HERMES UAI.[19] Interesting are Millendorfer's stress scores for the Eastern European countries Hungary, Czechoslovakia, and Poland, for which I have no data. The three countries do not cluster: Hungary scores high, Czechoslovakia medium, and Poland low in stress.

Another cross-national study of anxiety which, however, covered only the four Nordic countries (Sweden, Norway, Denmark, and Finland) was published by Kata (1975). He used questionnaires administered by public opinion research to about 1000 respondents in each country. In spite of the difference in data collection methods, Kata and Lynn rank the four countries in the same order of anxiety— Sweden lowest, then Norway, then Denmark, and Finland highest (except that for Lynn, Sweden and Norway break even). The HERMES stress and UAI data also put Finland highest of the four countries, but in this case Denmark scores lower than Sweden and Norway. The number of countries is too small to make the comparison conclusive.

UAI and Achievement Motivation:
McClelland's Data

A now classic source of data about social norms—although its author would not call them that—is David McClelland's *The Achieving Society* (1961). McClelland argues that differences in social action among societies can be explained by different dominant motive patterns in the populations of those societies.[20] He distinguishes three types of motives: achievement motives, affiliation motives, and power motives. In order to measure the strength of these motives for a number of modern nations, McClelland content-analyzed stories appearing in school books to be read by second-to fourth-grade elementary schoolchildren. These were for modern nations what comes closest to folk tales for primitive nations; and folk tales have been widely used by anthropologists to infer motive patterns of primitive tribes.

McClelland's research team content-analyzed 21 children's stories dating from 1925 from each of 25 countries and 21 children's stories from 1950 from each of 41 countries and determined scores for each country on Need for Achievement, Need for Affiliation, and Need for Power. In his book *The Achieving Society,* McClelland focuses on Need for Achievement (n_{Ach}). He shows a relationship of a country's n_{Ach} scores for 1925 with that country's growth in per capita electric power production from 1929 to 1950, and of n_{Ach} scores for 1950 with growth of absolute electric power production from 1952 to 1958. On the basis of his theories, McClelland has developed methods for achievement motivation training for developing countries. Recently, McClelland's attention has turned more to the Need for Power as a motive (McClelland, 1975; McClelland and Burnham, 1976).[21]

McClelland's work has had considerable influence, both in the development of the psychology of motivation and on certain areas of policy-making in development aid. However, his original findings about a relationship between achievement motives in children's readers and some measures of economic growth afterward have raised questions. An unfortunately unpublished study by Barrett and Franke (1971) comparing McClelland's scores with various measures of economic growth over various periods has shown that the relationship on which McClelland built his economic growth theory is fortuitous; it is an artifact of the particular measures and measuring periods that were chosen. The period 1929–1950, which includes a world war, is also not an ideal one in which to isolate the effects of inner motives on economic performance: Outside influences during these years have played a considerable role in what happened to nations. Another puzzling fact about McClelland's motive scores is that from 1925 to 1950 there is no consistency among country scores (the Spearman rank correlations between 1925 and 1950 scores across the 25 countries studies twice are .16 for n_{Ach}, .21 for n_{Ach}, and even negative, -.14, for n_{Pow}). Is it likely that something as fundamental as a basic motive pattern can change completely in one generation? Or has the measurement been unreliable?

The statistical analysis (Figure 4.11) shows that across 22 countries there is a strong negative correlation (rho = −.64) between HERMES UAI scores and *1925* n_{Ach} scores, but none (across 31 countries) between any HERMES dimension and any of McClelland's *1950* scores. The multiple correlation of McClelland's 1925 n_{Ach} with HERMES UAI *plus* MAS (Masculinity Index, see Chapter 6) is even higher ($R^2 = .54$, $R = .74$).[22] A high score for Need for Achievement in 1925 children's stories tends to be found in countries in which HERMES respondents show low uncertainty avoidance and high masculinity.

Two questions must now be resolved: Why are HERMES scores correlated with McClelland's 1925, not his 1950, data? Why are low UAI and high MAS associated with high n_{Ach}? As for the first question, the average HERMES respondent learned to read between 1945 and 1947; and if people's values reflect what they learned at school, we should rather expect the HERMES data to be correlated with 1950 than with 1925 children's stories content. However, it is likely that around 1925 children's stories were more traditional; they were more like the anthropologist's folk tales which McClelland tried to match, and more likely to express basic themes of a country's subconscious norm pattern. In 1950, education in many countries had been modernized, so more frequently stories were produced that deliberately stressed the values of innovative educators rather than the traditional ones. This means that as measures of a country's underlying culture pattern, the 1925 stories were more reliable than the 1950 stories. This also explains the lack of correlation between 1925 and 1950 scores. In fact, the underlying patterns, found in the 1925 stories, were still present in people's mental programs around 1970 when the HERMES surveys took place.

A low UAI means by definition a greater willingness to take risks. High MAS, as we shall see in Chapter 6, means assertiveness or ambitiousness. The two together match the picture of McClelland's achievement-motivated individual. The countries that show both low UAI and high MAS are primarily the Anglo countries, in particular Great Britain, Ireland, and the United States. Indeed, these did relatively well economically in the 1929–1950 period because they suffered less from the war than did countries that were occupied. However, they definitely did *not* do as well economically as some other countries after 1950 (we shall go deeper into this later in this chapter). It is therefore doubtful whether McClelland's achievement motive should be offered as a *universal* model for economic success in countries, as it has been. McClelland, an American, has been describing a typical Anglo-American value complex—the one present in his own environment—and offered it as a model to the world. A Frenchman, Swede, or Japanese would have been unlikely to discover a worldwide achievement motive (even the word "achievement" is difficult to translate in most languages other than English).

UAI and the Generation Gap

Earlier in this chapter it was demonstrated that UAI correlates with the average age of the HERMES respondent population. In a more uncertainty-avoiding society, older people will wait longer before leaving responsibility in the hands of younger people, and in such a society its members will more often disapprove of the behavior of young people.

Reader's Digest (1970) conducted an interview study of representative samples of a total of over 17,500 persons in 16 European countries which dealt with consumption patterns but which also covered attitudes toward younger and older generations. The statistical analysis in Figure 4.12 shows that across 15 countries, favorable attitudes toward younger people are strongly negatively correlated with UAI ($r = -.77$). This suggests a greater generation gap in high UAI countries. That it also means a greater de facto age difference between leaders and led is shown by data collected by de Bettignies and Evans (1977). They published the average ages of top leaders in the business community in 11 European countries around 1970; as the statistical analysis shows, these are strongly positively correlated ($r = .75$) with UAI. This complements the *Reader's Digest* data on attitudes toward younger people. It is likely that older leaders understand the young less; but the lower level of approval of the young is found in the *entire population* of high UAI countries; and these countries have the older leaders who fit with their value pattern. In higher UAI countries there is more of a "gerontocracy" (old people's rule).

UAI Scores and Other Survey Studies
Outside HERMES

(1) Managers on course at IMEDE, answering Gordon's Value Surveys. Figure 3.13 in the statistical analysis section of Chapter 3 shows that across 14 countries, UAI is significantly negatively correlated (rho $= -.50$) with a factor "recognition versus independence." This factor includes on the plus side a score for "achievement." We thus find for the IMEDE participants an indication of a negative association between high UAI and need for achievement, which supports the relationship we found with McClelland's Need for Achievement scores earlier in this chapter.

(2) Samples of managers in 19 countries, answering to Haire et. al.'s (1966) management attitudes and assumptions questions. In the statistical analysis on page 196, I show that these indicate for countries higher in UAI

(a) a stronger preference for group decisions and consultative management, which can be interpreted as a way of avoiding risk for the individual decision maker; and

(b) a tendency to agreement, at the same time, with statements taken from McGregor's "Theory X": less optimism about people's ambition and leadership capacities.

(3) Managers from 16 countries on course at IMEDE, answering Fiedler's Least Preferred Co-worker questionnaire. Fiedler's (1967) LPC has been referred to in Chapter 1 as an original test of values: The values of a respondent are inferred from the way in which he or she describes a third person; that is, the one other person with whom he or she could work least well. High LPC scorers describe their least preferred co-worker in relatively favorable terms, and Fiedler interprets this as interpersonal orientation: Low LPC scorers describe their least preferred co-worker in very

unfavorable terms, and this is interpreted as task orientation. We can also, however, interpret high LPC scores as a high tolerance for ambiguity and low LPC scores as the reverse. This would mean that in high UAI countries LPC score levels should be lower. As the statistical analysis in Figure 4.13 shows, in spite of the small samples of respondents used, we find a significant negative correlation ($r = -.44$) between UAI and LPC.

Fiedler explains leadership effectiveness by a combination of the leader's LPC score and the difficulty of the situation (Fiedler, 1967; Fiedler and Chemers, 1974). Differences in LPC levels among countries would mean that a person can be an effective leader in one country and not in another, which of course is an entirely reasonable proposition.[23]

(4) Samples of managers on management courses from 10 countries, surveyed by Laurent (1978). We find (Figure 4.13) a high correlation between UAI and the scores on five items all expressing a low tolerance for ambiguity in hierarchical structures. Laurent draws consequences from this about the acceptability of a "matrix organization" philosophy in a country: A successful application of matrix organization presupposes a tolerance for ambiguity in the hierarchy, as one subordinate will have two (or three) bosses. Therefore, matrix organization-type structures should be less acceptable in high UAI countries. I shall come back to this issue in Chapter 9. A later analysis I performed on more extensive data from Laurent has shown UAI to be highly correlated (rho = .77) with an ecological factor which at its positive pole stands for a highly formalized conception of management.

(5) More or less representative samples of the population in nine countries, surveyed about their "Images of the World in the Year 2000" (Ornauer et al., 1976). I selected the Ornauer study in the context of UAI because if there is such a thing as a national norm for uncertainty avoidance, this would very likely be reflected in issues related to the future. Out of 20 items conceptually related to uncertainty avoidance, four are shown (Figure 4.14) to be significantly correlated across countries with UAI. These four items express that in countries lower in UAI more people believe they themselves can do something to contribute to peace; more people believe that compromising with opponents is not dangerous[24]; more people are prepared to live by the day; and a somewhat larger fraction of the respondents are prepared to live abroad. These items express for the countries lower in UAI a lower level of alienation of the citizens from what happens in the world, greater tolerance of other opinions, less fear for tomorrow, and less fear of the unknown.

(6) Representative samples of the population in five countries, surveyed by Almond and Verba (1963). Based on their survey questions, these authors developed an index of "subjective competence" in dealing with local government: the extent to which respondents believe they can participate in political decisions at the local level. The concept of subjective competence is somewhat similar to the issue in Ornauer et al.'s survey whether respondents believe they can contribute to peace in the world. We find a strong ($r = .96$) correlation between UAI and subjective competence (Figure 4.14). This shows that in higher UAI countries, citizens tend to feel less able to participate in political decisions at the local level.[25] Taken with the correlations with pessimism about the interest of companies in employees' welfare (HERMES data, question C10 in Figure 4.9) and with pessimism about people's capacity for leadership and initiative (Haire et al.; data, Figure 3.15), these data suggest a higher level

of individual alienation in organizational participation, in the sense of powerlessness of the individual against the system. It is likely that these feelings are in turn fed by the organizational systems found in the higher UAI countries, which in effect respond less to members' attempts to influence the system because such attempts are not expected. One should see the embarrassed reaction of a (good and progressive) Belgian teacher when the parents of her English and Dutch pupils want to raise an issue not on her agenda (Belgium is a high UAI country, Britain and Holland are much lower). More in general, the data suggest that a country's UAI level is negatively correlated with the amount of control people believe they have over the world, including their own lives.

(7) A survey of samples of engineers in the United States and Germany by Preiss (1971). He found that the U. S. engineers were more oriented toward the company, administrative careers, and their private lives. The German engineers were more oriented toward anxiety avoidance and toward a professional career, earnings, cooperation, and security. The anxiety avoidance and the preferences for a professional (specialist) career and for employment security in Germany versus a manager career in the United States fit the Uncertainty Avoidance Index difference between the two countries.

(8) Before Preiss, Fridrich (1965) surveyed 80 U.S. and 94 German middle managers, using, among other questions, several of those used by Haire et. al.(1966). Fridrich concluded that the Germans more than the Americans stressed high economic performance and expertise; they were more concerned with security and showed greater status anxiety. Finally, Germans stressed more than Americans the value of stability in their society and its institutions. This confirms, of course, the picture found by Preiss and the UAI difference between the two countries.

(9) A final study I want to quote is actually not a comparative survey but a comparative laboratory experiment with Belgians and Americans by McClintock and McNeel (1966). I referred to this study in Chapter 1 (note 23) because it led to a reaction by Faucheux, who showed that the author's conclusions (that Belgians are more competitive than Americans) could be reversed if one started from a different value position. The study used a two-player "Maximizing Difference Game" in which players could get a maximum payoff by cooperating but a competitive advantage over the other by not cooperating. It appeared that American students cooperated more frequently than did Belgian students, which led to the author's conclusion of greater competitiveness on the Belgian side. However, in his comment, Faucheux (1976: 286) dwells on another finding by the experimenters: that Belgians prefer the competitive strategy especially when they are behind their adversary (and know it), whereas Americans prefer it more when they are ahead. Belgians want to avoid losing, while Americans want to win; therefore, Faucheux calls the Americans more competitive. Faucheux interprets the Belgian behavior as "legalistic," valuing equity more than efficiency, and the Americans as more "realistic." Belgium has a considerably higher UAI score (94) than the United States (46), and the "legalistic" versus "realistic" distinction fits well with this UAI difference. We saw in the HERMES questionnaire data that in higher UAI countries, competition between employees is disliked. The McClintock and McNeel experiment shows how this attitude can go together with a behavior which is actually less cooperative. It also suggests that the

source of achievement motivation in the high UAI countries is more "fear of failure," while in the low UAI countries it is more "hope of success."

A Summary of Connotations of
the Uncertainty Avoidance Index
Found in Surveys and Related Material

In the same way as was done for the PDI in Figure 3.6, in Figure 4.3 I have interpreted the connotations of UAI found in the various survey data. As in the case of PDI, it should be remembered that (1) the "low UAI" and "high UAI" sides of Figure 4.3 are extreme ideal-types between which country cultures are somewhere placed on a continuum; (2) not all connotations apply with equal strength to a given country; and (3) individuals in countries vary widely around a country's norms.

The data on which Figure 4.3 is based derive from surveys of narrow samples in countries (HERMES employees, students, managers), but also from representative sample surveys of entire populations (*Reader's Digest,* Ornauer et al., Almond and Verba) and from systematically collected nonsurvey data (McClelland, Lynn). They are from a much broader set of sources than the HERMES data bank alone. As such they represent a "triangulation" (Chapter 1) which suggests that we are not just dealing with an idiosyncrasy of HERMES people but, indeed, with nations' modal personalities.

THE UNCERTAINTY AVOIDANCE NORM,
ITS ORIGINS AND CONSEQUENCES

Economic Growth and Political Systems

Before trying to describe the general societal norm which is behind the "high UAI" and "low UAI" syndromes, I shall explore the relationship between uncertainty avoidance and a number of characteristics of societies. The statistical analysis in Figure 4.15 shows the correlations of UAI with seven economic, geographic, and demographic indicators which were identified in Chapter 2 and correlated with the Power Distance Index in Chapter 3. The resulting pattern of correlations for UAI is less clear than in the case of PDI and differs considerably for wealthy and for poor countries. For wealthy countries, the strongest relationship found is between UAI and economic growth in the 1960–1970 period (the higher the UAI, the faster the economic growth). A reverse relationship is found, however, if we take the same countries' economic growth figures over the 1925–1950 period (the higher the 1970 UAI, the slower the 1925–1950 economic growth; see Figure 4.16). This is because this earlier period included World War II, and the high UAI countries tend to have lost more because of war damages. The positive relationship between uncertainty avoidance and economic growth therefore only applies within specific historical conditions.

For the Power Distance Index, it appeared to make sense to divide countries into those with a political system with "balanced power" (since 1950) and "unbalanced power": the "balanced power" countries tend to show much lower PDI values. For uncertainty avoidance, the statistical analysis (Figure 4.17) shows that it makes

FIGURE 4.3   A Summary of Connotations of Uncertainty Avoidance Index
             Differences Found in Survey Research

See page	*Low UAI Countries*	*High UAI Countries*
169	• Lower anxiety level in population.	• Higher anxiety level in population.
173	• Greater readiness to live by the day.	• More worry about the future.
164	• Lower job stress.	• Higher job stress.
	• Less emotional resistance to change.	• More emotional resistance to change.
164	• Less hesitation to change employers.	• Tendency to stay with the same employer.
167	• Loyalty to employer is not seen as a virtue.	• Loyalty to employer is seen as a virtue.
167	• Preference for smaller organizations as employers.	• Preference for larger organizations as employers.
172	• Smaller generation gap.	• Greater generation gap.
167 172	• Lower average age in higher level jobs.	• Higher average age in higher level jobs: gerontocracy.
167	• Managers should be selected on other criteria than seniority.	• Managers should be selected on the basis of seniority.
171 172	• Stronger achievement motivation.	• Less achievement motivation.
175	• Hope of success.	• Fear of failure.
171	• More risk-taking.	• Less risk-taking.
167	• Stronger ambition for individual advancement.	• Lower ambition for individual advancement.
167	• Prefers manager career over specialist career.	• Prefers specialist career over manager career.
199	• A manager need not be an expert in the field he manages.	• A manager must be an expert in the field he manages.
173	• Hierarchical structures of organizations can be by-passed for pragmatic reasons.	• Hierarchical structures of organizations should be clear and respected.
201	• Preference for broad guidelines.	• Preference for clear requirements and instructions.
164	• Rules may be broken for pragmatic reasons.	• Company rules should not be broken.

FIGURE 4.3   Continued

199	• Conflict in organizations is natural.	• Conflict in organizations is undesirable.
167	• Competition between employees can be fair and right.	• Competition between employees is emotionally disapproved of.
167 172	• More sympathy for individual and authoritative decisions.	• Ideological appeal of consensus and of consultative leadership.
199	• Delegation to subordinates can be complete.	• However, initiative of subordinates should be kept under control.
173	• Higher tolerance for ambiguity in perceiving others (higher LPC).	• Lower tolerance for ambiguity in perceiving others (lower LPC).
173	• More prepared to compromise with opponents.	• Lower readiness to compromise with opponents.
167	• Acceptance of foreigners as managers.	• Suspicion toward foreigners as managers.
173	• Larger fraction prepared to live abroad.	• Fewer people prepared to live abroad.
167	• Higher tolerance for ambiguity in looking at own job (lower satisfaction scores).	• Lower tolerance for ambiguity in looking at own job (higher satisfaction scores).
173	• Citizen optimism about ability to control politicians' decisions.	• Citizen pessimism about ability to control politicians' decisions.
167	• Employee optimism about the motives behind company activities.	• Employee pessimism about the motives behind company activities.
172	• Optimism about people's amount of initiative, ambition, and leadership skills.	• Pessimism about people's amount of initiative, ambition, and leadership skills.

sense to divide the 20 "balanced power" countries into "old" and "young" democracies. The young democracies (which developed their present form of government after World War I or later)—Austria, Finland, France, Germany, Ireland, Israel, Italy, Japan, and Turkey—tend to show higher UAI scores than the old democracies—Australia, Belgium, Canada, Denmark, Great Britain, the Netherlands, New Zealand, Norway, Sweden, Switzerland, and the United States. All the young democracies acquired their present form of government after losing or winning a war in which they played a more or less aggressive role. Lynn and Hampson have proved the continuity of their anxiety factor from 1935 to 1978 (see Chapter 8). This means that the stress levels were not caused by the war, but rather a force contributing to countries taking part in it. We also just saw that the correlation of UAI with economic growth in the 1960–1970 period was reversed for economic growth in the 1925–1950 period, which includes World War II. In other words, the uncertainty avoidance syndrome is associated with aggressive belligerence and economic disaster during the first half of the twentieth century, and economic success during its second half.

Political systems cannot survive for long if they are not in harmony with the mental programming of the citizens. Almond and Verba (1963), through their public opinion study in five countries (Germany, Great Britain, Italy, Mexico, the United States) have made a major contribution toward showing how different "political cultures" are rooted in different mentalities. We saw earlier that their measure of "citizen competence" is highly correlated with UAI: This was the extent to which respondents believe they can participate in local political decisions. Almond and Verba also show how these mentalities are fostered in the family, school, and job relationships. For example, for a question "remembered freedom to protest decisions" on the percent "free to protest" the five countries are ranked in an order which is identical to the rank order of their UAI-scores; the same is true for the percent who claim they have actually ever protested about decisions on the job (p. 343). It is a reasonable assumption, supported by history, that (1) political systems in countries in which citizens feel they cannot participate will be less stable, and (2) younger balanced-power political systems following periods in which citizens were deliberately kept incompetent will not show the same level of subjective citizen competence as old and established political systems.

More recently, another comparative study about political attitudes of citizens was one by Kaase and Marsh (1976), who used representative samples of the populations of Austria, Germany, Great Britain, the Netherlands, and the United States. They measured "protest potential" (the acceptability of unorthodox political behavior such as boycotts and occupations) and "repression potential" (the desirability of repression of such behavior by the authorities). On both dimensions, the higher UAI countries Austria and Germany oppose the lower UAI countries, Great Britain, the Netherlands, and the United States. In Austria and Germany, fewer respondents declare themselves prepared to go beyond the more classical forms of protest such as petitions, demonstrations, and boycotts; and more respondents favor repression of political demonstrations by the government. This fits with the lower citizen competence in higher UAI countries found by Almond and Verba; citizens are not only more dependent on government but *want it that way;* citizen attitudes and behavior of officials in both high and low UAI countries reinforce and confirm the societal norm.

Putnam (1973) has published results of a survey of political attitudes not among the public at large but among high civil servants in Germany, Great Britain, and Italy who were interviewed in 1970–1971. The main conclusion is that civil servants can be distinguished into "classical bureaucrats" who are negative toward politics and "political bureaucrats" who are positive. On an "Index for Tolerance of Politics" (ITP) 94 percent of the Italian civil servants ranked below the mean, 38 percent of the Germans, and 7 percent of the British. This follows, of course, the three countries' UAI rank and shows that alienation about the political process exists not only among citizens, but also among those who are supposed to represent the system.[26] In a later publication using some of the same material, Aberbach and Putnam (1977) compared the backgrounds of civil servants in five countries: the three previous ones plus the Netherlands and the United States. Of special interest to us are the percentages of higher civil servants with a law education: choosing law graduates for the civil service can be seen as a form of uncertainty avoidance. These percentages are: Great Britain, three percent; the United States, 18 percent; the Netherlands, 39 percent; Italy, 53 percent; and Germany, 65 percent. This sequence is almost identical to the sequence of UAI scores.[27]

There is a certain resemblance between the uncertainty avoidance dimension of societies and the distinction made by anthropologists between "tight" and "loose" societies. Definitions of these concepts are rather vague and vary from one author to another. According to Pelto (1968), in loose societies:

—norms are expressed with a wide range of alternative channels;
—deviant behavior is easily tolerated; and
—values of group organization formality, permanence, durability, and solidarity are un-
    developed.

In tight societies, the opposite is the case. These discrepancies fit well with some of the connotations of "low UAI countries" in Figure 4.3. Pelto measures the tightness of a number of traditional societies with a (Guttman) scale which uses characteristics of the society's political system, in which "theocracy" (government by priests claiming to rule with divine authority) is at the "tight" end and political control without legitimate use of power is at the "loose" end. This scale is not applicable to modern nations; however, Pelto also describes Japan and Israeli kibbutzim as "tight" and Thailand as "loose." In the HERMES data the Thai UAI score is not low (64), but it is considerably lower than the UAI scores for Japan (92) and Israel (81); (whereas the kibbutz will be "tighter" than Israeli society as a whole, I assume they reflect partly the same norms). UAI can thus be seen as an operationalization of "tightness" for modern societies. Many modern societies are even "looser" than those Pelto considered.

Uncertainty Avoidance, History, and Legislation

In the analysis of power distance differences, the cultural inheritance of the Roman Empire was shown to coincide with high PDI scores. It also coincides with high UAI scores (Latin Europe, Latin America). The Roman Empire, by establishing an effective system of formal control of its territories and a unified legal system, set an uncertainty-avoiding pattern which seems to have survived as a societal norm in the countries most affected by the empire's inheritance.

Laws and by-laws are the form par excellence in which societal norms are expressed: We find "legislation" as one of the consequences of societal norms in the diagram of Figure 1.4; it serves, in its turn, to reinforce the norm. Uncertainty-avoiding countries will have a greater need for legislation than will less uncertainty-avoiding countries. We can, for example, oppose Germany (UAI 65) to Great Britain (UAI 35). Germany has an extensive set of laws even for emergencies that *might* occur *("Notstandgesetz")*; Great Britain does not even have a written constitution. Attempts to codify labor-management relations in Britain (the Industrial Relations

Act) failed because they are too much against societal norms. One of the ways in which the inheritance of the Roman Empire perpetuates itself is through its legal systems.

An interesting example of how "positive law" (actual regulations) reflects "living law" (unwritten societal norms; the terms are taken from Northrop, 1962: 427), is the following: After the 1973 oil crisis, the governments of all Western European countries felt a need—or had an excuse in the face of public opinion—to establish or at least consider maximum speeds on highways. Whether these speeds are actually respected is irrelevant here; the concern is with formal law, not the practice (although practice will be affected to some extent by formal law). In the statistical analysis in Figure 4.18 we see across 14 Western European countries a significant correlation (rho = .59) of the maximum speeds adopted with the countries' UAI-scores. Maximum speeds are also a means to reduce fatal accidents on highways. We could assume, naively, that the countries with the highest traffic death rates before the oil crisis would have chosen the lowest maximum speeds. The statistical analysis has also explored the relationship between maximum speeds, HERMES indices, and traffic deaths. The naive logic about maximum speeds does not hold; countries with higher accident mortality have not tended to adopt lower maximum speeds. Governments do not legislate just on the basis of facts, but at least as much on the basis of prerational values. I have also observed that in countries which allow high speeds, experts prove regularly that speed reduction will not make traffic safer; in countries which allow lower speeds, experts prove the opposite. Expertise is not value-free either. I interpret the higher maximum speeds in higher UAI countries as a higher value attributed to saving time than to saving lives.

We saw that UAI scores in some countries correlated with citizen competence; this is one aspect of the relationship of the citizen versus the authorities. One issue on which modern nations differ and which, for example, cuts right through the 14 Western European countries considered above, is whether a citizen is obliged to carry an identity card or document which he or she must produce at the request of the police or other authorities. In the lower UAI countries (Denmark, Sweden, Ireland, Great Britain, Norway, the Netherlands, and Finland) this obligation does not exist (although many people do carry credit cards and other material for convenience): Not being able to identify oneself to a policeman is no offence. In the higher UAI countries (Belgium, France, Spain, Italy, Austria, Germany, and Switzerland) this obligation exists and is usually maintained very strictly.[28]

The identity card obligation splits the countries almost perfectly according to UAI level.[29] The relationship of the citizen to the authorities and vice versa is different in the two kinds of countries; in lower UAI countries the citizen feels more competent, and if the authorities want to identify him or her, the burden of proof is on the authorities; in countries where the societal norm is one of greater uncertainty avoidance, the citizen feels more at the mercy of the authorities and his or her dependency is accentuated by the continuous need to be able to justify his or her identity by carrying a document.

Another sign of the norms prevalent in a country is the relative priority given to the training of experts versus lay personnel for certain tasks. We can expect that countries higher in UAI will be more likely to train experts. This can be proved on data published by Gaspari and Millendorfer on the number of nurses per doctor in 15 countries (Figure 4.19). The average number of nurses to one doctor in a country correlates strongly with the countries' UAI ($r = -.80$). There are many activities in hospitals which can be done either by doctors or by nurses. It is clear that in more uncertainty-avoiding countries, there is a greater tendency to have doctors carry out these activities. I interpret this as a consequence of the stronger belief in expert knowledge.

Religions, Games and Risk-Taking

In trying to account for differences in power distance, I argued that differences in religion by themselves did not account for differences in power distance; both the adoption of a certain religion and a dominant value for power distance should be seen rather as a result of a common cause; but once a religion has been established in a country, it will reinforce the values that led to its being adopted. Power distance deals with the relationship between man and his fellowmen, in which the supernatural is only indirectly involved. In the introductory section to this chapter, religion has been referred to as one of the three fundamental ways for human society to cope with uncertainty. We can postulate now that in countries with a greater need for uncertainty avoidance, we will find more often religions that stress absolute certainties and that are intolerant of other religions.

In the statistical analysis in Figure 4.20, I show that for the 29 countries in my sample of 40 which are predominantly Christian, there is a strong tendency for the more Catholic (Roman Catholic or Orthodox) countries to show higher UAI values than the more Protestant countries. Catholicism puts a much stronger accent on life after death and the believer's ability to ensure his participation in it than do most Protestant groups; also, Catholicism stresses certainties like the infallibility of the Pope and the uniqueness of the Church. Protestantism, and especially Calvinism, encourages worldly ways to cope with uncertainty (technology and law) as willed by God rather than ritual ways (see Weber, 1930: [1976] 224). On the UAI scale, 15 out of the 19 highest-scoring countries are Catholic. With them Japan seems out of line, although a Chinese writer states that "it is not generally realized how much more important religion and religious affiliation are to the Japanese than to the Chinese" (Hsu, 1971: 40). Ancestor worship in Japan can be seen as a form of religious coping with uncertainty. With the Catholic countries, but somewhat on the lower side as far as their UAI scores go, we also find three Moslem countries (Turkey, Pakistan, and Iran), and one Judaic country. These other two great revelation religions, while claiming absolute truths, show greater tolerance toward others than does official Roman Catholicism.

On the low side of the UAI scores, besides the mixed Catholic-Protestant and the Protestant countries, we find four Buddhist countries (Taiwan, Thailand, Hong Kong, and Singapore) and Hindu India. The Eastern religions are less concerned with the absolute and are more tolerant; certainties are not imposed from the outside but may come through meditation. The Chinese have been described as showing an "exceedingly relativistic sense of morality" (Inkeles and Levinson, 1969: 481–482).

In summary, religion and uncertainty avoidance appear to be meaningfully related. Whether religion is the root cause of UAI differences is unclear; the fairly low

UAI scores for Catholic Ireland and the Philippines suggest that other influences are at work as well. However, religion certainly reinforces uncertainty avoidance differences.

What applies to religions also applies to ideologies, which are secular religions. Dogmatic, intolerant ideological positions are more likely in countries with a higher UAI norm. In general, we can expect that problems more often will be looked at ideologically in higher UAI countries and pragmatically in lower UAI countries.

Another form in which uncertainty avoidance can be manifested is the kinds of games played in a certain culture. An anthropological study of games in traditional cultures (Roberts et al., 1959) distinguishes three kinds of games: games of physical skill, which aim at mastery of the self and the environment; games of strategy, which aim at mastery of the social system; and games of chance, which aim at mastery of the supernatural. These resemble the three categories to which I referred in the introduction to this chapter: technology, law, and religion. It is very likely that differences in uncertainty avoidance among countries will be reflected in the frequency and the types of game-playing behavior. The study by Roberts et al. (1959: 602) suggests that games of chance are more often present in primitive tribes when the gods are seen as less aggressive and more benevolent. If the ascribed aggressiveness of the gods reflects the aggressiveness of the particular society, we can hypothesize that games of chance will be played more often in countries with low uncertainty avoidance. Unfortunately, I have not yet been able to locate data on the frequency of chance games in modern nations. In comparing Great Britain and Germany, at least, the relationship between low uncertainty avoidance and the frequency of chance games seems to hold.

An interest in chance games as part of a national culture is likely to correlate with greater willingness in managers to make risky business decisions. For the time being, I have no data on this issue, but, impressionistically, at least British and U.S. managers seem more willing to make risky decisions than, for example, German and French managers.

UAI and Theory Versus Empiricism

In Chapter 3 I argued that a country's PDI norm affects the type of theories about power that will be developed in that country; elitist theories in high PDI countries, pluralist theories in low PDI countries. A country's UAI norm affects the type of intellectual activity in the country in an even more fundamental way. In high UAI countries, scholars look for certainties, for Theory with a capital T, for Truth.[30] In low UAI countries they take a more relativistic and pragmatic stand and look for usable knowledge. The Nobel Index described in Chapter 3 correlates nearly as highly (negatively) with UAI as with PDI (−.46), which means more Nobel prizes in the applied physical sciences for lower UAI countries. The difference between the high UAI and low UAI approach is even more pronounced in the social sciences. The great theoreticians and philosophers of the west tend to come from higher UAI countries, especially Germany and Austria: Kant, Marx, Freud, Weber, and Popper, to mention but a few. On the other hand, up to the present day empirical studies in the social sciences in such high UAI countries as Germany and France are rare; in a society with a high Uncertainty Avoidance norm, it seems that scholars cannot run the risk of exposing their truths to experiments with unpredictable outcomes. On the other hand, lower UAI countries like the United States and Great Britain show a multitude of empirical studies. The orthodox methodological justification of such studies is that the progress of scientific knowledge passes through the falsification of hypotheses in testing them on reality; but to actually attempt to falsify one's hypotheses means a large tolerance for uncertainty. Of course, good hypotheses presuppose good theory. Social science research in the Anglo-American tradition often suffers from a lack of such theory. A lot of energy is wasted in fishing expeditions equipped with powerful computing tools which are doomed to find only trivialities because they do not know what to look for (see also my critique of "catch-all" ecological factor analysis in Chapter 1 and my own search for a theory-first approach described in Chapter 2). A marriage between a high UAI concern for theory and a low UAI tolerance for empiricism seems a promising solution.[31] In general, collaboration and exchange among scholars of different national backgrounds, and therefore different scientific approaches, can only benefit all.[32]

The Uncertainty Avoidance Norm
and Its Origins

An integrated picture of what the general societal norm behind the "low UAI" and "high UAI" syndromes stand for is presented in Figure 4.4, which uses inferences from the survey data summary of Figure 4.3 and from the subsequent analysis of correlations of UAI with country-level characteristics.

As in the case of the Power Distance norm (Figure 3.7), the Uncertainty Avoidance norm is meant to be a value system shared by the majority in the middle classes in a society. The UAI norm deals with the level of anxiety about the future in a country and the consequent need to protect society through three kinds of measures: technology, rules, and rituals. The higher anxiety leads to higher stress and a more hurried social life, but also to higher energy release, which means an inner urge to work hard, and to a stronger superego needed to control dangerous impulses. On the high UAI side, anxiety is released more through the showing of aggressiveness and emotions for which society has created outlets; on the low UAI side, anxiety is released more through passive relaxation, and showing of aggressiveness and emotions is not approved of socially. On the other hand, the higher aggressiveness level on the high UAI side makes conflict and competition between people into something more threatening than is the case in the low UAI countries. People in high UAI countries feel a greater need for consensus; group decisions are ideologically popular, although not necessarily more frequent. Tolerance toward people with different ideas or showing deviant behavior and toward people from other countries is more present on the low UAI side. This tolerance also stretches to young people and their ideas, which are believed to be more of a potential threat in high UAI countries. Change in these countries is resisted more emotionally; there is a greater tendency to conservatism and a desire for law and order. Achievement in life on the high UAI side is more sharply defined in terms of acquired security, which is quite different from the "achievement motive" described by McClelland; the latter is related more to social recognition and fits the low UAI syndrome; it also implies more willingness to take risks. The high UAI side looks for the absolute, both in science and in legislation; relativism and pragmatism belong more on the low UAI side. The ritual element in the high UAI societies is represented in a belief in experts who, like "priests," are

FIGURE 4.4   The Uncertainty Avoidance Societal Norm

Low UAI	High UAI
• The uncertainty inherent in life is more easily accepted and each day is taken as it comes.	• The uncertainty inherent in life is felt as a continuous threat that must be fought.
• Ease, lower stress.	• Higher anxiety and stress.
• Time is free.	• Time is money.
• Hard work is not a virtue per se.	• Inner urge to work hard.
• Weaker superegos.	• Strong superegos.
• Aggressive behavior is frowned upon.	• Aggressive behavior of self and others is accepted.
• Less showing of emotions.	• More showing of emotions.
• Conflict and competition can be contained on the level of fair play and used constructively.	• Conflict and competition can unleash aggression and should therefore be avoided.
• More acceptance of dissent.	• Strong need for consensus.
• Deviance is not felt as threatening; greater tolerance.	• Deviant persons and ideas are dangerous; intolerance.
• Less nationalism.	• Nationalism.
• More positive toward younger people.	• Younger people are suspect.
• Less conservatism.	• Conservatism, law and order.
• More willingness to take risks in life.	• Concern with security in life.
• Achievement determined in terms of recognition.	• Achievement defined in terms of security.
• Relativism, empiricism.	• Search for ultimate, absolute truths and values.
• There should be as few rules as possible.	• Need for written rules and regulations.
• If rules cannot be kept, we should change them.	• If rules cannot be kept, we are sinners and should repent.
• Belief in generalists and common sense.	• Belief in experts and their knowledge.
• The authorities are there to serve the citizens.	• Ordinary citizens are incompetent versus the authorities.

beyond uncertainty. A consequence of the belief in experts and expertise is that lay citizens are not encouraged to take the initiative in their jobs. There is more of a feeling of incompetence among ordinary members of organizations toward issues not within their immediate activity range.

The UAI norm reflects on the societal level some of the components of Adorno et al.'s (1950) Authoritarian Personality and Eysenck's (1954) Tough-Mindedness. The latter stands, among other things, for intolerance of ambiguity.[33] However, not all aspects of an individual personality syndrome are necessarily reflected in a societal norm. The UAI norm also reflects a number of values which Eckhardt (1971) found to be associated with people—both wealthy and poor—who placed themselves politically to the "right" in 18 different countries: personal conformity, no personal benevolence, resistance to social change, lack of political interest, never writing to a newspaper to express a point of view, interest in national rather than international affairs, national loyalty, and wanting national leadership.

The origins of the UAI syndrome are much less clear than were the origins of the PDI syndrome; it is not possible to develop a "causal chain" that leads to a high or low UAI norm with any degree of plausibility (compared with Figure 3.8). Whatever indications the data provide about origins of UAI are collected in Figure 4.5. The origins mentioned are in the areas of modernization, population density in relation to wealth, religion, and the history of legislation; additional factors are the mean age of the population, especially of its leaders, and the size of organizations.

FIGURE 4.5 Origins of National Uncertainty Avoidance Index Differences

Low UAI	High UAI
• Advanced modernization	• Beginning modernization: high rate of change in society
• Older democracies	• Younger democracies
• Dense populations in poor countries; sparse populations in wealthy countries	• Sparse populations in poor countries; dense populations in wealthy countries
• Tolerant religions stressing relativity	• Intolerant religions stressing absolute certainties, the hereafter, and sin
• Historical events: less legislation, more settlement of disputes by negotiation and/or conflict	• Historical events: inheritance of developed system of legislation
• Low mean age of population leaders	• High mean age of population leaders
• Smaller organizations	• Larger organizations

Consequences of Different UAI Levels

Figure 4.6 assembles the various suggested consequences of high and low UAI levels. The potential consequences for society at large and for religious life and philosophical and ideological thinking have been discussed in the previous pages. The greater popularity of ideological thinking which I attribute to higher UAI countries also means that the tolerable size of discrepancies between the desirable and the desired and between the desired and actual behavior is larger in high UAI countries than in low ones (compare Figure 1.3 and page 20).

The consequences for organizations follow from the role which uncertainty plays in determining organization structures and processes. In general, a greater need for uncertainty avoidance should lead to what Pugh (1976: 68) in the Aston studies subsumes under the heading "structuring of activities": formalization, specialization, and standardization. A certain amount of cross-national comparative data on organization structures has been collected with the Aston methods: in Britain and the United States (Inkson et al., 1970); in Britain, the United States, and Canada (Hickson et al., 1974); in Britain and Japan (Azumi and McMillan, 1975); in Britain, Japan, and Sweden (Horvath et al., 1976); and in Britain and Germany (Child and Kieser, 1979); an overall comparison is given in Hickson et al. (1979). These studies show a wide variance of structures within each country; whatever systematic difference in structuring of activities (or concentration of authority) may exist among countries is hidden by this within-country variance. Proving systematic differences in degree of structuring of activities between countries will demand either data on far more organizations per country or better-matched samples. In this respect it should be interesting to apply Aston-type measures to subsidiaries of the same multinational

FIGURE 4.6   Consequences of National Uncertainty Avoidance Index
                         Differences

See page	Low UAI	High UAI
	Consequences for Society at Large	
175	• Slower economic growth after World War II	• Faster economic growth after World War II
185	• Weaker nationalism	• Stronger nationalism
177	• Less aggressiveness versus other nations	• Greater aggressiveness versus other nations
179	• "Looser" societies	• "Tight" societies
178 180	• Stronger feelings of citizen competence	• Greater dependence of citizens on authorities
178	• More tolerance for citizen protest	• Less tolerance for citizen protest
178	• Civil servants positive toward politics	• Civil servants dislike politics

FIGURE 4.6   Continued

179	• More casuistic approach to legal issues	• More elaborate legal system
180	• Lower speed limits and fewer fatal road accidents	• Faster car-driving admitted and more fatal road accidents
181	• Stronger accent on lay competence: more nurses per doctor	• Stronger accent on expertise: fewer nurses per doctor

Consequences for Religious Life and Philosophical and Ideological Thinking

181	• Either no state religions or more de facto religious tolerance	• More intolerant state religions
181	• Pragmatic or introvert, meditative religions	• Activist religions
182	• Relativism	• Search for absolute truth
182	• Practical contributions to knowledge	• Theoretical contributions to knowledge
183	• Empiricism in social sciences	• Theoricism in social sciences
182	• Pragmatic thinking popular	• Ideological thinking popular

Consequences for Organizations

186	• Less structuring of activities	• More structuring of activities
188	• Fewer written rules	• More written rules
188	• More generalists or amateurs	• Larger number of specialists
188	• Organizations can be pluriform	• Organizations should be as uniform as possible (standardization)
188	• Managers more involved in strategy	• Managers more involved in details
188 189 .	• Managers more interpersonal oriented and flexible in their style	• Managers more task-oriented and consistent in their style
182	• Managers more willing to make individual and risky decisions	• Managers less willing to make individual and risky decisions.
167	• High labor turnover	• Lower labor turnover
167	• More ambitious employees	• Less ambitious employees
167	• Lower satisfaction scores	• Higher satisfaction scores
189	• Less power through control of uncertainty	• More power through control of uncertainty
189	• Less ritual behavior	• More ritual behavior

companies in various countries. Those applying the Aston approach to different countries run the risk of a reverse ecological fallacy (Chapter 1). Structure variables, even if they are correlated within different countries, are not necessarily correlated across societies. Whereas the main dimensions—that is, "structuring of activities" and "centralization of authority"—probably are found universally, the individual measurements used to locate organizations on these dimensions may have to be changed if the purpose is comparison across countries.

In comparing Britain and the United States Inkson et al. (1970) could not use "structuring of activities" as a homogeneous dimension for international comparison because, while no differences were found in specialization and standardization, Britain was systematically lower on one aspect of formalization: reliance on written rules. Only an analysis of structural data from a number of societies—for example, 15 or 20—could reveal in what way structural variables are clustered across societies. Child and Kieser (1979) found that whereas most decisions were made at higher management levels in Germany than in Britain, some key decisions were made at higher levels in Britain. Obviously, the decisions selected determine on which side one finds more centralization. Child and Kieser also find more managerial job descriptions in Britain than in Germany; but it is unlikely that German organizations are overall less formalized than British ones. Other variables may interact with the measurements: For example, Heller et al. (1976: 24) show that in their sample in Great Britain older managers centralized their decisions less than younger ones, whereas in Germany older managers centralized more.

It is in line with the greater rule orientation and with the more elaborate legal system for organizations in higher UAI countries to have more structuring of activities and more written rules—other factors being equal. It is also in line with the value differences found for organizations in higher UAI countries to appoint more specialists (see the evidence for the greater popularity of specialized roles in higher UAI countries on page 167). Finally, I assume for organizations in higher UAI countries greater standardization: We can expect the ideal model of an organization on the higher UAI side to be uniform; on the lower UAI side, more diverse.

We can relate the UAI scores to the findings of Horowitz (1978) in his interviews with executives in France, Germany, and Great Britain. He found that French and German top managers want to be better informed of the details of their business than do British top managers: The latter engage more in strategic activities. Keeping an eye on details is a clear sign of uncertainty avoidance.

Managers in higher UAI countries are likely to be more task-oriented, as was manifested by their lower LPC scores. An illustrative incident is that in one phase of the HERMES survey, two questions about whether managers were seen as task-oriented were suppressed in the two higher UAI countries Japan and Germany, although they belonged to the compulsory core of the questionnaire. Local management considered these questions superfluous and/or unacceptable. When the questions were used in Germany in another survey phase, it appeared that, contrary to managers in other countries, managers in Germany seen as representing different leadership styles did not receive significantly different scores on these task-orientation issues.

Heller et al. (1976: 15) compared samples of managers from eight countries as to the degree to which they centralized decisions for 12 different problems; both according to their subordinates and according to themselves. From the eight countries, the Germans had the most consistent decision style across the 12 problems, the British the most flexible one. It seems that once a style is set, Germans tend to stick to it throughout.[34]

The UAI norm in a country may also affect the exercise of power in organizations. "Power" in organizations is not just power among people whose exercise is affected by a PDI norm. Power in organizations is also exercised among groups and subsystems of organizations, and this type of power is strongly affected by the control of uncertainty (Crozier, 1964a: 107ff; Hickson et al., 1971; Hinings et al., 1974).[35] "Coping with uncertainty is the variable most critical to power, and is the best single predictor of it" (but not the only one; quoted from Hinings et al., 1974: 40). If the societal norm is one of lower tolerance of uncertainty, those who control uncertainty will be more powerful than if uncertainty is more easily tolerated. This explains the difference between Indian, French, and German "authoritarianism." In India it is pure personal power ("a basic fact of society which antedates good or evil"; see Figure 3.7). In France it is the same, *plus* the fact that power holders control uncertainties, to confront which would be too threatening to many people. In Germany "the use of power should be legitimate" (Figure 3.7), but the impact of formal power is strong because of the uncertainties it controls, which corresponds to many people's profound needs.

Finally, it is likely that the various forms of ritual behavior in organizations described in the beginning of this chapter will be found more frequently in organizations in high UAI societies. The variations in UAI among countries and their various correlated phenomena illustrate the non-rational component in the structuring of activities in human institutions, organizations, and society. This structuring of activities serves a deep-seated human need for avoiding the uncertainties inherent in human life, but the strength of this need for uncertainty avoidance differs among nations, groups within nations, and individuals.

Structuring of activities is, both in theory and in practice, usually defended on rational grounds. On the other hand, there is in organizational folklore and in daily life, in jokes, anecdotes, and humorous literature, much evidence that the rational purposes often are not achieved. Theories which explicitly recognize the non-rational element in structuring of activities are rarer, and their consequences for the validity of other theories and for practice often are not drawn. A further development of such non-rational theories (like the work of March and Olsen, 1976) should be strongly encouraged. In this regard, studies across different cultures with different subjective "rationalities" can be useful.

STATISTICAL ANALYSIS OF
DATA USED IN CHAPTER 4

Calculating the Uncertainty Avoidance
Index by Country

A detailed calculation of the UAI by country can be found in an earlier publication (Hofstede, 1977d). The country data for the three questions B60, A43, and A37 can be found in

Appendix 2. For question A43 (employment stability) I have used the combined percentage of answers 1 + 2 because these were more strongly correlated with the two other UAI questions than the combined answers 1 + 2 + 3 (= 100 − answer 4).

The answers for question A43 for the United States and Yugoslavia, although available, have been treated as missing. The reason is that I use the question as a measure of *values* and that I should therefore exclude answers differentially affected by situational influences. The data for the 38 countries that have been used were obtained from people working for a subsidiary of a foreign company which in their own country was not a major employer. As the United States is the home country of HERMES, U.S. respondents refer to a domestic company which is moreover a major employer. It is likely that the attraction for a long-term career of a large domestic employer is of a different order of magnitude from the attraction of a foreign company, one of many foreign employers in the host country. For Yugoslavia, the different societal context and relationship to the company of the Yugoslav respondents should be taken into account. Contrary to respondents in the 39 other countries, they did not refer to a large, worldwide employer, but to a small, self-managed trade firm under Yugoslav law. This is likely to affect considerably the attraction of the company as a long-term employer; thus, the Yugoslav data should not be compared with HERMES' subsidiary data. Consequently, for both the United States and Yugoslavia I have not used the existing data, but considered them as missing; the values to be used in the computation of the Uncertainty Avoidance Index have been extrapolated on the regression line of "employment stability" scores with the sum of the two other UAI question scores, for the 38 countries for which data are complete. The extrapolated data are: United States 30, Yugoslavia 11; the actual data (not used) were: United States 15; Yugoslavia 35.

The "stress" question, as mentioned earlier in this chapter, was taken from earlier surveys of managers in HERMES U.S.A., run by the company medical department. Unfortunately, the results of the earlier medical surveys were never fully published, and the data on file do not contain the correlation coefficients that led to the decision to include the question in the later attitude surveys. What is available from one medical survey are mean scores for 13 organizational divisions, into which the almost 1500 respondents were divided. These show that mean scores on the "How often nervous or tense" question differ significantly among divisions (chi-square = 41.3*** with 12 degrees of freedom, significant beyond the .001 level) and that these mean scores are significantly rank-correlated with mean scores on "How often are you bothered by having an upset stomach?" (rho = .49*, significant at .05 level) but not with "Headaches" or "Trouble getting to sleep or staying asleep." Interestingly, mean scores on the "How often nervous or tense" question were negatively correlated with mean scores on "Do you have any particular physical or health problems now?" (rho = −.48*), suggesting that denial of health problems could be part of the stress syndrome.

Figure 4.7 lists the correlations among the three questions that make up the Uncertainty Avoidance Index across individuals, countries, and occupations. For country scores, the three intercorrelations are between .40 and .59, somewhat lower than for PDI (compare Figure 3.11); nevertheless, the correlations of the three items with UAI across countries are −.80, −.81, and −.80, respectively.

Calculating Differences in Item Scores by Occupations

Figure 4.7 also shows that the three UAI-items are *not* correlated across occupations. This means that we cannot use them to measure the "uncertainty avoidance level" of an occupation. We can look only at occupational differences in the scores of the three items separately.

For the correlations of the three items across individuals, an interesting picture appears. As in the case of PDI (Figure 3.11), these individual correlations were computed for the five one-country, one-occupation subpopulations used in developing the 1971 core questionnaire. We see that across individuals:

FIGURE 4.7 Product Moment Correlations Among Scores on Three
Questions Composing the Uncertainty Avoidance Index:
Across Individuals, Countries, and Occupations

Pairs of questions	Correlation of individual scores in five homogenous groups[a] (200-458 respondents)			Correlation of mean scores across 40 countries[b]	Correlation of mean scores across 38 occupations[c]
	min.	max.	median		
a x b (B 60 x A 43) rule orientation x employment stability	.02	.26***	.14***	.59***	-.11
a x c (B 60 x A 37) rule orientation x stress	-.03	.05	.00	.40***	.23
b x c (A 43 x A 37) employment stability x stress	-.18**	.04	-.11***	.44***	-.09

[a]Correlations with question A43 for *individuals* are with score values (1-2-3-4). In order to make them comparable with the country and occupation correlations which are based on % answer 1 + 2, the sign of the correlation coefficient has been reversed.
[b]Country scores are means of mean scores for seven occupational groups.
[c]Occupational scores are means of mean scores for three large countries (France, Germany, and Great Britain).

(1) Rule orientation and employment stability tend to be significantly positively correlated (just as across countries).
(2) Rule orientation and stress are uncorrelated.
(3) Employment stability and stress tend to be *negatively* correlated—that is, within the subpopulations those people who perceive more stress tend also to be those who think of leaving the company early.

The relationship between employment stability and stress is an example of the fact that individual and ecological correlations of the same variables can have opposite signs (compare Chapter 1). The reason for the sign difference is that at the country (ecological) level, a societal norm (Figure 1.4) intervenes which pushes everyone toward a higher overall level of employment stability in higher stress countries, even if within each country the higher stressed individuals may intend more often to leave the company.

Coming back to the differences of UAI items by occupations, while the items should not be integrated into an occupational index, it is still worthwhile to investigate what determines an occupation's mean level of rule orientation, employment stability, and stress. Across 38 occupations, rule orientation is strongly correlated with the occupation's PDI ($r = -.72***$; as a low score on the question means *more* rule orientation, this indicates a higher occupational rule orientation for a higher occupational PDI, which is plausible). Employment stability is uncorrelated and stress only weakly correlated with the occupation's PDI.

The correlations of occupational rule orientation, employment stability, and stress with the four "demographic" indicators average educational level of the occupation, hierarchy level (1 = nonmanagers, 2 = managers), average age, and percent female are listed in Figure 4.8.

Figure 4.8 shows that the amount of rule orientation for an occupation is mainly related to its educational level (negatively); the amount of employment stability to its average age, and the

FIGURE 4.8 Zero-Order, Multiple, and Stepwise Correlations of UAI Items for 38 Occupations, with Four Demographic Items

Question	Zero order product moment correlation across 38 occupations with demographic items :				Squared multiple correlation with all four R^2	Order of indices in stepwise regression, cumulative R^2 and sign of coefficient		
	Average formal education level years	Hierarchy level	Average age years	% Female		1st	2nd	3rd
d (B60) rule orientation	-.73***	-.17	-.01	.26	.60	.53-Educ.		
e (A43) employment stability	-.21	.56***	.70***	-.62***	.80	.49+Age	.61-Educ.	.79-Fem
f (A37) stress	-.19	.40**	.34*	.13	.32	.16+Hier	.25+Fem	

The signs of all correlations have been reversed so that a positive correlation stands for a positive association between the two concepts.

amount of stress is somewhat related to its hierarchical level. In the interpretation of the zero-order correlations we should, however, take into account that an occupation's average age is strongly correlated with its hierarchy level (r = .83) and negatively with its percent female (r = .55). It is therefore more meaningful to look at the righthand side of Figure 4.8, where I show the results of a stepwise regression on all four demographic items: the cumulative R^2 indicates what part of the variance is cumulatively explained by 1, 2, or 3 demographic items. We see that besides education, other demographics contribute little to occupational differences in rule orientation. An occupation's level of employment stability depends to a sizable extent on three different factors: age (positively), education (negatively), and percent female (negatively); but not on hierarchical level per se. An occupation's stress level relates besides to its hierarchical level (managers higher stress) somewhat to its percent female.

Country UAI and the Average Age of the HERMES Sample

We shall now return to our analysis at the country level, the only aggregate level at which an overall index of uncertainty avoidance is meaningful. Besides the three items used to form the UAI, a number of other questions in the HERMES questionnaire are correlated on the country level with UAI.

Figure 4.9 lists the other survey questions (A + B numbers) which in the country-level factor analysis with 32 variables (Chapter 2) load on the UAI factor, plus the C questions (which were used only in the first survey round and were not factor-analyzed) for which the country scores are significantly correlated with UAI.

In the earlier country-level factor analysis with 48 variables (for which the results were not shown in Chapter 2), the highest factor loadings were .74 for the average age of the sample (A57) and .68 for its average seniority in HERMES (A2). These variables were not used in the 32-variable factor analysis. Age and seniority are, of course, highly intercorrelated across the 40 countries (r = .72***). Age and UAI correlate .52*** across countries. Age correlates separately with rule orientation scores (−.45***), with employment stability scores (−.46***) and with stress scores (−.36*). We should investigate whether the differences among countries in uncertainty avoidance level are not just an artifact of the age difference in the HERMES sample. The average age scores (Appendix 2, A57) vary from 3.01 in Hong Kong (corresponding to an age of 27.1 years) to 4.63 in Turkey (35.2 years). In order to test how strong the effect of age differences on the UAI country scores really is, I have in the second column of Figure 4.1 listed the UAI values which result when age differences are controlled for. The formula of the regression line is:

$$UAI = 7 \times (\text{average age in years}) - 157,$$

which means that one year of increase in the average age of a country sample corresponds to a UAI increase of seven points.

Across *individuals* (rather than across countries) age relates to two of the three UAI questions. If we take the median correlation across individuals for the five subpopulations (one country, one occupation) on which the 1971 questionnaire was developed, we find .00 for age versus stress, −.13* for age versus rule orientation scores (older people more rule-oriented), and, not surprisingly, −.32*** for age versus employment stability scores (older people more stable).

Results of Other Studies Significantly Correlated with UAI

(1) Country neuroticism and extraversion factor scores according to Lynn and Hampson. The data are listed in Figure 4.10. Lynn and Hampson's factor scores have been correlated with the HERMES scores on stress and on the four indices PDI, UAI, IDV, and MAS. The occurrence of extreme scores on Lynn's list has led me to use Spearman rank correlations instead of product moment correlations. Lynn's "neuroticism" factor is highly significantly rank-correlated with UAI (.73***) and also with the "stress" scores separately

FIGURE 4.9   Other Questionnaire Items Ecologically Related to UAI

Factor loading	Item N°	Questionnaire item and sense in which related to UAI
–	A57	Average age of country sample.
–	A2	Average seniority in HERMES of country sample.
–.56	B9	If you had a choice of promotion to either a managerial or a specialist position and these jobs were at the same salary level, which would appeal to you most ? (specialist).
.50	B57	Decisions made by individuals are usually of higher quality than decisions made by groups. (disagree)
–.49	A58	Considering everything, how would you rate your overall satisfaction in this company at the present time? (more satisfied).
–.49	B44	How do you feel or think you would feel about working for a manager who is from a country other than your own? (prefer own nationality).
–.46	A15	How important is it to you to have an opportunity for advancement to higher level jobs? (less important).
.46	B55	Employees lose respect for a manager who asks them for their advice before he makes a final decision. (disagree)
–.45	B54	Competition between employees usually does more harm than good. (agree).
Correlat. coeff.		C-items (only used in first survey round)
–.72***	C17	A large corporation is generally a more desirable place to work than a small company. (agree).
–.52**	C16	By and large, companies change their policies and practices much too often. (agree)
.45**	C10	Most companies have a genuine interest in the welfare of their employees. (disagree).
–.44**	C11	In general, the better managers in a company are those who have been with the company the longest time. (agree).
–.40**	C12	There are few qualities in a man more admirable than dedication and loyalty to his company. (agree).

(a) A +B—items loading on the UAI factor analysis of 32 items; (b) C items correlated with UAI.
For factor analysis see Chapter 2 (factor 3; signs of coefficients reversed).
For correlations with C items see Appendix 2.
All factor loadings of .45 and over and correlations of .40 and over are shown.

($-.72***$): As low stress scores stand for high stress, high neuroticism goes with high stress and high UAI. Lynn's "extraversion" factor correlates moderately ($-.47*$) with PDI, in the sense that "introvert" countries tend to score high on PDI and extravert countries score low. The correlation of "extraversion" with UAI is just a by-product of the correlation with PDI.

(2) McClelland's scores for dominant motives found in children's stories from different countries (see page 170). Twenty-two of McClelland's 1925 countries and 31 of his 1950 countries are among the HERMES data set. The correlations between McClelland's and HERMES data are presented in Figure 4.11. The most obvious hypothesis is a correlation between HERMES PDI scores and McClelland's 1950 Need for Power. However, this correla-

FIGURE 4.10   Factor Scores for 18 Countries on Two Factors Found by
Lynn and Hampson in Medical and Related Statistics,
Versus Four Indices

Country	Factor score on :	
	Neuroticism	Extraversion
Austria	3.73	1.61
Japan	2.95	−2.37
France	2.37	− .94
Germany (Fed. Rep.)	2.11	− .19
Italy	1.05	−1.61
Finland	.61	1.73
Switzerland	.28	.47
U.S.A.	.18	4.56
Belgium	.15	−1.29
Canada	− .29	.15
Denmark	− .55	.41
Australia	− .75	.36
Norway	− .86	−2.03
Sweden	− .86	.99
Netherlands	−1.52	−2.30
New Zealand	−1.61	.29
Great Britain	−2.41	.30
Ireland	−4.58	− .17
Spearman rank corr. with :		
stress score	− .72***	.39
•PDI	.35	− .47*
UAI	.73***	− .44*
IDV	− .53*	.08
MAS	.41*	− .02
Squared multiple correlation with all four indices R^2	.63	.29

A stepwise regression shows no sizable second-order correlations.
SOURCE: Lynn and Hampson (1975: 237).

tion is not significant (.20). In addition, the correlation of PDI with $n_{Pow}-n_{Aff}$ (which, according to McClelland [1961: 168] might be an important measure) is not significant (.25; this figure is not shown in Figure 4.11).

Instead, however, we find an unexpected and highly significant correlation of (1970) HERMES indices with McClelland's *1925* scores for n_{Ach}. The highest correlation is with UAI (−.64***). The correlations with PDI and IDV can be shown to be by-products of the correlation with UAI, but the stepwise regression shows that there is a sizable contribution to the variance in 1925 n_{Ach} by MAS, the masculinity score (which in the zero-order correlation pattern is suppressed by the correlation with UAI). In fact, the best predictor of McClelland's 1925 n_{Ach} is *low* UAI plus *high* MAS (see Chapter 6). There is, besides, a weaker correlation of 1925 n_{Aff} with IDV, to which I shall come back in Chapter 5.

(3) Reader's Digest's *(1970) data on attitudes of the public toward younger and older people*. The questions are (*Reader's Digest*, 1970: 202, questions 22 and 23); "Considering young people today between 16 and 25 years old, would you say that, in the main, you have a *favorable* or an *unfavorable* impression of them, or neither one nor the other?" (three-point answer scale). "And what about people over 45, would you say that, in the main, you have a favorable or unfavorable impression of them or neither one nor the other?" (three-point answer scale).

The comparison between the *Reader's Digest* data and the four indices for 15 countries (all except Luxemburg, for which I do not have data) is shown in Figure 4.12. The correlation between attitudes toward young people and UAI is a highly significant −.77***. The correlation with PDI is a by-product of this. However, the stepwise regression with the four indices shows that the individualism index IDV contributes to an explanation of the variance (in a sense *opposite* to the zero-order correlation!); after we have controlled for UAI, more "individualistic" countries are less favorable toward younger people. The attitudes toward *older* people correlate somewhat with both PDI and UAI: favorable attitudes toward older people tend to be found in countries with lower power distances and lower uncertainty avoidance.

(4) De Bettignies and Evans' (1977) data on the average age of top executives in 11 countries. The data are listed in the last column of Figure 4.12. The correlations with PDI and UAI are of about equal strength (both .75**); as the correlation with UAI is marginally stronger, this is the one to show up in the stepwise regression. There is no sizable second-order correlation.

(5) Haire et al.'s (1966) data on management attitudes and assumptions. The correlations with the HERMES index values for 19 countries were shown in Chapter 3 (Figure 3.15). The stepwise regression with the four indices (which is a more meaningful criterion than the zero-order correlations, because the four indices are intercorrelated) shows UAI to be positively correlated with "Participation" (after controlling for IDV) and negatively with "Capacity for leadership and initiative" (after controlling for PDI). "Participation" consists of the following two items (of course, we do not know whether both items separately show ecological correlations with UAI!):

(a) In a work situation, if the subordinates cannot influence me then I lose some of my influence on them (agree).

(b) Group goal-setting offers advantages that cannot be obtained by individual goal-setting (agree).

In the HERMES data, too, we found that higher UAI countries prefer group decisions and consultative management (Figure 4.9). I interpreted it as a way of avoiding risk for the individual decision maker.

"Capacity for leadership and initiative" consists of the following two items:

(a) The average human being prefers to be directed, wishes to avoid responsibility, and has relatively little ambition (disagree).

FIGURE 4.11 Zero-Order Correlations, Multiple and Stepwise Regression
of McClelland's Motivation Scores

Mc Clelland's motivation standard scores for : [a]	Zero-order Spearman rank correlations across 22 (31) countries with :				Squared multiple correlat. with all four indices R^2 [b]	Order of indices in stepwise regression, cumulative R^2, and sign of coefficient	
	PDI	UAI	IDV	MAS		1st	2nd
1925 Achievement	-.58***	-.64***	.44*	.31	.56	.41-UAI	.54+MAS
1925 Affiliation	-.02	-.31	.46*	.19	.31	.21+IDV	
1925 Power	-.05	.13	-.24	.05	.09		
1950 Achievement	.08	.03	-.07	.05	.01		
1950 Affiliation	-.07	.10	.16	-.07	.11		
1950 Power	.14	-.04	-.00	.27	.12		

Based on the content of children's readers dated 1925 for 22 countries, and dated 1950 for 31 countries, against four HERMES indices.
[a] SOURCE: McClelland (1961: 461–462).
[b] Multiple and stepwise correlations have been computed after a transformation replacing both variables by rank-order numbers.

FIGURE 4.12   Attitudes of the Public Toward Younger and Older People, and Average Age of Top Business Executives, Versus Four Indices

Countries in order of UAI score	Readers Digest Survey[a] % favourable attitudes towards		De Bettignies[b] average age of top executives
	Younger people	Older people	
Portugal	40	55	
Belgium	42	64	58
France	40	51	59
Spain	48	58	
Italy	28	45	54
Austria	49	61	
Germany (Fed. Rep.)	48	75	57
Finland	64	78	51
Switzerland	56	63	
Netherlands	45	56	56
Norway	64	69	52
U.S.A.			55
Great Britain	55	65	55
Ireland	69	70	
Sweden	67	71	50
Denmark	64	70	52
Mean of all countries	52	63	54
Zero-order product moment correlation with :			
PDI	-.65**	-.56*	.75**
UAI	-.77***	-.56*	.75**
IDV	.17	.14	.22
MAS	-.35	-.21	.58*
Squared multiple correlation with all four R^2	.72	.39	.67
Order of indices in stepwise regression, cumulative R^2 and sign of coefficient	1 .59-UAI 2 .72-IDV	1 .31-PDI	1 .57+UAI

[a]SOURCE: *Reader's Digest* (1970: 191)
[b]SOURCE: De Bettignies and Evans (1977: 286)

(b) Leadership skills can be acquired by most people regardless of their particular inborn traits and abilities (agree).

The combination of these two items was positively ecologically correlated with PDI, which looked paradoxical (see the discussion on page 113). The negative correlation with UAI is easier to interpret. In higher UAI countries, there is less optimism about people's ambition and leadership capacities; there is a stronger tendency toward McGregor's "Theory X." In the HERMES data, the correlations of "Theory X-Theory Y" items (B61, C13, and C14) with UAI are in the same direction, but they do not reach statistical significance. A rather pessimistic philosophy of life for higher UAI countries was found, however, in the HERMES scores in the disagreement with C10: "Most companies have a genuine interest in the welfare of their employees" (Figure 4.9).

(6) Fiedler's (1967) Least Preferred Co-Worker questionnaire (LPC). Although there is a body of literature about the use of LPC, I have not found any studies comparing LPC score levels between countries, with the exception of a small study I did at IMEDE in the period 1971–1973 (Hofstede, 1974b). The LPC-questionnaire was administered to 154 managers participating in management courses. Figure 4.13 lists the mean scores for those countries from which I had at least three participants (a very small sample, but if I do not use small samples in this case, hardly any data are left).

It appears that in spite of the extremely small sample sizes, UAI does correlate significantly negatively with the country LPC level. Moreover, the stepwise regression shows that the correlation with UAI suppresses a second-order correlation with PDI in the sense that if we control for UAI, countries with higher power distance levels tend to score *higher* on LPC. This would mean that in high PDI countries relationships between people play a more important role and in low PDI countries tasks play a more important role.

(7) Laurent's (1978) survey data of attitudes of managers in management courses. Laurent's questionnaire contained 56 value statements about organizational issues. The first published results show answers from 635 managers in 10 countries on the following five statements:

(1) Most organizations would be better off if conflict would be eliminated forever.
(2) It is important for a manager to have at hand precise answers to most of the questions that his subordinates may raise about their work.
(3) If a manager gives his subordinates more freedom of initiative, he must at the same time reinforce the extent to which he controls their activities.
(4) In order to have efficient work relationships, it is often necessary to bypass the hierarchical line (scored *negatively*).
(5) An organizational structure in which certain subordinates have two direct bosses should be avoided at all costs.

Answers were scored on the usual five-point scale. The five statements form an ecological dimension, that is, differences in percentages of agreement among countries are in the same direction for all five. Average agreement ("strongly agree" and "agree") across the five questions varied from 24 percent in the United States to 63 percent in Italy (Figure 4.13). All statements express a low tolerance for ambiguity in hierarchical structures. We see in Figure 4.13 that the level of agreement with Laurent's statements in the 10 countries correlates significantly with UAI (r = .78**; the correlation with PDI is a by-product of the correlation with UAI).

Just before finalizing the manuscript for this book, I did an ecological factor analysis of Laurent's scores on 56 value statements for 11 countries (those in Figure 4.13 plus Japan, which was added later). I found three factors; the first and strongest, after rotation, correlated with UAI with rho = .77**. This factor showed loadings over .60 for 17 statements, among which

FIGURE 4.13   Scores of Managers on Fiedler's LPC and Laurent's
Acceptability of Matrix Organization, Versus Four Indices

Countries in order of UAI score	Fiedler's LPC scores collected at IMEDE[a]		Laurent's scores on accepta-bility of matrix organiza-tion philosophy[b]	
	N° of res-pondents	Average LPC score	N° of res-pondents	Average % agree-ment with clari-ty of hierarchy items
Belgium			35	57
Japan	4	2.70		
France	5	3.42	179	54
Spain	4	3.00		
Brazil	7	3.69		
Italy	6	2.95	24	63
Germany (Fed. Rep.)	15	3.53	47	47
Iran	7	3.60		
Switzerland	34	3.85	48	45
Netherlands	3	3.78	29	36
Australia	4	4.10		
Norway	7	3.50		
U.S.A.	7	3.78	44	24
India	3	5.30		
Great Britain	14	3.49	150	38
Sweden	10	2.92	43	30
Denmark	6	3.79	36	40
Total and mean	136	3.59	635	43
Product moment correla-tion with :				
PDI		.21		.61*
UAI		-.44*		.78**
IDV		.01		-.47
MAS		-.03		.40
Squared multiple correla-tion with all four R^2		.56		.69
Order of indices in step-wise regression,cumulative R^2,and sign of coëfficient		1 .19-UAI 2 .53+PDI		.60+UAI

aSOURCE: Hofstede (1974b: 10)
bSOURCE: Laurent (1978: 11)

were four of the five statements in Laurent's earlier analysis (1, 2, 4, and 5). Below are some of the other statements loading on the factor:

(1) A good manager is able to express his feelings and emotions in the majority of situations. (disagree)

FIGURE 4.14 Percent Answers on Public Opinion Studies by Ornauer et al. and by Almond and Verba, Versus Four Indices

Countries in order of UAI score	Ornauer et al.[a] % answers on questions				Almond & Verba[b]
	1.Can you yourself contribute?	2.Compromise is not dangerous	3.Take one day after another	4.Like to live in foreign country	citizen competence score
	%	%	%	%	%
Japan	18	28	15	6	
Yugoslavia	6	21	24	9	
Spain	19	21	36	5	
Mexico					38
Italy					40
Germany (Fed.Rep.)	18	31	22	10	46
Finland	13	41	41	10	
Netherlands	27	44	21	13	
Norway	28	38	49	7	
U.S.A.					65
India	28	39	52	16	
Great Britain	21	48	49	15	63
Mean	20	35	34	10	50
Product moment correlation with :					
PDI	−.25	−.55	−.06	.06	−.66
UAI	−.64*	−.90***	−.71*	−.80**	−.96***
IDV	.55	.81**	.28	.41	.79*
MAS	−.04	−.11	−.22	03	−.86*
Squared multiple correlation with all four R^2	.46	.87	.62	.82	.99
Order of indices in stepwise regression, cumulative R^2, and sign of coëfficient	1 .46-UAI	1 .81-UAI	1 .51-UAI	1 .63-UAI 2 .77+PDI	1 .93-UAI

[a]SOURCE: Ornauer et al. (1976: 674, 682, 685, 695)
[b]SOURCE: Almond and Verba (1963: 233)

(2) It is desirable that management authority can be questioned. (disagree)

(3) If you want a competent person to do a job properly, it is often best to provide him with very precise instructions on how to do it.

(4) When the respective roles of the members of a department become complex, detailed job descriptions are a useful way of clarifying.

These items represent a highly formalized conception of management.

(8) Ornauer et al.'s (1976) 11-country survey study, Images of the World in the Year 2000. In all, nearly 10,000 persons were interviewed or reached by mail questionnaires in more or less representative samples of the population. The data were collected in 1967. Nine

of the countries also appear in the HERMES sample (see Figure 4.14). The book lists mean answer percentages for the 11 countries for 187 questions: I have tested ecological correlations with UAI for 20 of these questions for which such correlations would make sense conceptually. I found significant correlations with UAI for the following items:

> (1) (II/49, 1976: 674): Do you think that there is anything you yourself can do to contribute to the realization of this proposal (that is, a proposal which is likely to lead to peace)? Answer: No.
> (2) (III/13, 1969: 682): To compromise with our opponents is dangerous because it usually leads to the betrayal of our own side. Answer: Agree.
> (3) (III/27, 1969: 685): The future is so uncertain that the best thing one can do is to take one day after the other. Answer: *Dis*agree.
> (4) (III/61, 1969: 695): Would you like to live the *main part* of your life in a foreign country or would you prefer to live most of your life in your native country? Answer: Most in native country.

The ecological correlations of these four items with the four indices are shown in Figure 4.14. As I tried 20 items, I could expect one of them to be statistically correlated with UAI at the .05 level by pure chance: However, four were found to correlate statistically on this level (the interpretation of these four items has been given on page 173).

(9) Almond and Verba's (1963) extensive study of political attitudes of representative samples of the population in five countries: Great Britain, Germany, Italy, Mexico, and the United States (about 1000 respondents in each country). One of their key concepts is "subjective political competence": the extent to which respondents believe they can participate in political decisions. Almond and Verba have designed a five-point Guttman scale of subjective competence in dealing with *local* government. This scale puts the United States and Great Britain highest in subjective competence and Germany, Italy, and Mexico lower in this order. As we see in Figure 4.14, the scores correlate –.96,*** with UAI (and not appreciably with the other indices after we have controlled for UAI).

(10) Preiss (1971) has surveyed by mail 345 U.S. and 227 German engineers working in five more or less matched companies in either country. Forty-seven of his questions are in the format of "work goal importance" items (such as A5–A18 in the HERMES questionnaire, Appendix 1). As the scores for the German and the U.S. samples have almost identical overall means across all goals (2.39 for Germany and 2.42 for the United States) and identical ranges (2.42 points in both cases), the data can be compared without standardization. Preiss finds several significant differences: U.S. engineers score as more important (1) six goals dealing with contributing to the interest of the company, (2) working for a successful company, (3) five goals dealing with becoming an administrator or manager, (4) personal time, and (5) living in a desirable area. German engineers score as more important (1) three goals dealing with anxiety avoidance, (2) challenge, (3) freedom, (4) earnings, (5) advancement in general, (6) training, (7) up-to-dateness and professional learning, (8) employment security, (9) cooperation (but not friendly atmosphere), and (10) physical conditions. The text of the three anxiety avoidance goals which Germans score as significantly more important than do Americans are:

> (1) "Work in a well defined job situation where the requirements are clear" (mean score U.S. 3.06, Germany 2.03 on a scale from 1 = number of utmost importance to 5 = of very little or no importance. This is the largest difference found for any goal from the 47 questions.).
> (2) "Be given clear, detailed instructions as to how to proceed with the job" (mean score U.S. 3.81, Germany 3.58).
> (3) "Have little tension and stress on the job" (mean score U.S. 3.46, Germany 3.31).

In HERMES, Germany scores considerably higher on UAI (65) than the United States (46). Preiss' findings on differences in anxiety avoidance confirm this difference. In fact, his anxiety avoidance work goals (which were not used in HERMES) might turn out to be suitable cross-cultural measures of uncertainty avoidance; possibly even more suitable than some of the items now in the UAI. I am suggesting Preiss' first and third items for an improved Values Survey Module (Appendix 4).

The UAI Versus Seven Geographical, Economic, and Demographic Indicators

The same seven indicators identified in Chapter 2 (Figures 2.7 and 2.8) and correlated with PDI in Chapter 3 (Figure 3.16) will now be correlated with UAI (the indices GNP, GNG, LAT, POP, PGR, PDN, and ORG). Only a few specific hypotheses about the direction of the correlations can be made.

Inkeles (1969), in his six-country study of modernization, found no relationship between stress and modernity; modernity is closely related to GNP/capita. This suggests that UAI is probably unrelated to the "GNP" index.

Lynn (1971: 92ff) has found for his 18 developed countries a .67*** Spearman rank correlation between anxiety level and economic growth in the period 1950–1965. This suggests a positive correlation between UAI and our "Economic Growth" measure (GNG) which covers the 1960–1970 period. However, McClelland (1961) found a positive correlation of n_{Ach} in 1925 with economic growth (measured in terms of per capita electric power production) in the period 1929–1950. As 1925 n_{Ach} is negatively correlated with UAI, this suggests a relationship which is the opposite of Lynn's.

A positive correlation between UAI and Population Density (PDN) would be in line with evidence of a positive relationship between Population Density and stress, summarized in Levi and Andersson (1974: 80–88). This is partly based on extrapolations from animal life (deer, monkeys, fish, birds, rats). The biological need for space leads to aggression when others come too near. In the case of humans, the data are less consistent, but large cities can be dehumanizing and stress-generating. Levi and Andersson (1974: 80) suggest that the relationship between density level and individual and social psychological costs for humans may be U-shaped, with an optimum for a medium level of density.

Finally, the size of the HERMES subsidiary in a country (ORG) should be positively correlated with UAI because greater size has been found to be associated with greater formalization (Pugh, 1976: 74) and this corresponds with rule orientation, one of the components of UAI.

For the relationship of uncertainty avoidance to Latitude (LAT), Population Size (POP), and Population Growth (PGR) I did not find any indications in the literature.

Figure 4.15 lists the actual correlations and regressions of UAI with the seven indicators. As in the case of PDI, I have computed these for all 40 countries, for the 19 wealthier countries (1970 GNP/capita over $1300) and for the 21 poorer ones.

We see that across all 40 countries, the correlations with UAI are much weaker than those with PDI (Figure 3.16). Only the zero-order correlation of UAI with GNP is significant. This unpredicted relationship shows that wealthier countries tend to be less uncertainty-avoiding. In the introduction to this chapter I referred to technology as one of the fundamental ways human society copes with uncertainty. It seems that in more technologically developed countries, uncertainty has become more tolerable. As the correlation between UAI and GNP is negative for the high GNP countries but positive for the low GNP countries, the overall relationship of UAI and GNP is somewhat curvilinear. In the middle-range countries, which are generally caught in a fast rate of societal change, uncertainty avoidance is relatively highest.

In general, when we divide the countries into poor and wealthy, most correlations with UAI become stronger, and they have different signs for the two groups of countries. The most

FIGURE 4.15   Product Moment Correlations, Multiple and Stepwise
Regressions Across Countries of UAI Scores with Seven
System-Level Indicators

Indicator	Zero-order correlations with UAI scores across		
	All 40 countries	21 poorer countries	19 wealthier countries
GNP	$-.30^*$	.15	$-.34$
GNG	.13	$-.10$	$.57^{**}$
LAT	$-.07$	$.51^{**}$	$-.44^*$
POP	.20	.07	.25
PGR	.03	$-.41^*$	.18
PDN	$-.24$	$-.65^{***}$	$.43^*$
ORG	$-.05$	.25	.12
Squared multiple correlation with all seven R^2	.36	.66	.60
Order of indicators in stepwise regression, cumulative R^2, and sign of coefficient	1. .09-GNP 2. .16+ORG 3. .22-PDN 4. .33+GNG	1. .42-PDN 2. .60-PGR 3. .64+GNG	1. .32+CNG 2. .41-LAT 3. .48+PDN

For definitions of indicators see Figure 2.7.

pronounced differences occur for latitude (LAT) and Population Density (PDN). The hypotheti-
cal positive correlation between UAI and PDN is found only for the wealthier countries. UAI
tends to be lower in poor, tropical, and densely populated and in wealthy, cold, and sparsely
populated countries; higher in poor, moderate climate, and sparsely populated and in wealthy,
moderate climate, and densely populated countries. However, these correlations are strongly
influenced by some extreme scores, especially the low UAI values for Singapore (on the
equator and very densely populated) and Sweden (high latitude and sparsely populated). In
general, the high correlations with latitude and population density for the poorer countries
reflect the complete split on UAI between Asian countries (average latitude 21 degrees, average
density 230 per square km) and Latin American plus Mediterranean countries (average latitude
28 degrees, average density 39 per square km). The factors explaining UAI differences are not

necessarily latitude and population density but could be other dimensions differentiating Asia, Latin America, and parts of Europe, such as history and religion, as discussed elsewhere in this chapter.

The predicted relationship between UAI and economic growth is significantly present in the 19 wealthier countries ($r = .57**$). Extreme cases are Great Britain (low GNG) and Japan (high GNG). The striking thing about these two countries is that they have so much in common (Kassem, 1974); both are insular, traditionally governed states of about the same size and climatic zone. What differentiates them and has led to the large difference in economic growth after 1945 must be in the minds of the people; I have now identified it as uncertainty avoidance. The stepwise regression shows that for the poorer countries and for all countries together, economic growth also contributes to the prediction of UAI. I interpret this correlation as a greater energy release in higher UAI countries (aggressiveness invested in work). Moreover, in order for this energy release to lead to real economic growth, it is first necessary that the country reach a minimum level of modernization; for the poorer countries, this is not the case, and most of the energy is wasted. The period over which the economic growth was measured is 1960–1970. I assume uncertainty avoidance to be a relatively stable characteristic of societies, which therefore should change only slowly; differences in uncertainty avoidance should survive for decades, if not for centuries. However, country economic growth rates have been less stable historically. For 13 western countries, Kuznets (1971: 38) supplied data on economic growth since about 1865.

In Figure 4.16 these have been correlated with UAI scores for these countries: We see that UAI (measured around 1970) is strongly correlated with recent economic growth, but as strongly *negatively* correlated with economic growth for the 1925–1950 period (which includes the 1929 depression and World War II). There is no correlation with economic growth over a 100-year period. UAI therefore only relates positively to economic growth in wealthy countries under post-World War II conditions. UAI also correlates with aggressive belligerence in World War II, a condition which over the 1925–1950 period led to *low* economic growth because of the damages of the war.

The sign reversal between correlations with 1925–1950 and 1960–1970 economic growth explains how UAI can be *negatively* correlated with McClelland's 1925 n_{Ach}, while McClelland found his n_{Ach} to be *positively* correlated with (1929–1950) economic growth, while UAI is also positively correlated with economic growth (but over 1960–1970). The ranking of countries on economic growth has changed drastically from 1925–1950 to 1960–1970.

FIGURE 4.16 Spearman Rank Correlations Across 13 Western Countries Between UAI and Economic Growth Rates

Average economic growth over period	UAI scores around 1970	Average Economic growth 1865-1965 (Kuznets)
1960-1970 (World Bank Atlas, 1972)	.62*	.52
1950-1967 (Kuznets, 1971)	.43	.48
1925-1950 (Kuznets, 1971)	-.62*	.52
ca1890-1950 (Kuznets, 1971)	-.08	.79
ca1865-1965 (Kuznets, 1971)	-.14	1.00

The countries are: AUL, BEL, CAN, DEN, FRA, GBR, GER, ITA, JAP, NET, NOR, SWE, USA.

McClelland's n_{Ach} scores have also changed drastically, but not in the same way. I tested the correlation of McClelland's 1950 n_{Ach} with 1960–1970 economic growth (GNG) and found it to be rho = –.07 (across 35 countries for which data for both n_{Ach} and GNG existed). Again, the data do not support McClelland's claim that n_{Ach} has been measured reliably for 1925 *and* 1950 and that both measurements relate to subsequent economic growth.

In all, the seven indicators used predict only a small part of the variance in UAI; they do not, as in the case of PDI, explain how levels of uncertainty avoidance in countries have become so different. Other and less measurable factors must have played a major role in the genesis of country uncertainty avoidance differences.

UAI Versus Some Other Characteristics of Societies

(1) Age of the political system. PDI appeared to be strongly related to a country's political system (balanced power since 1950 versus periods of unbalanced power since 1950: see Figure 3.18). UAI does not discriminate between balanced power and unbalanced power countries (chi-square = 2.5 with one degree of freedom: not significant). However, if we divide the "balanced power" countries according to the age of their present political system (uninterrupted/not uninterrupted since before World War I) we get the picture of Figure 4.17. The relationship between age of political system and UAI for these countries is highly significant (however, there is no relationship with PDI: chi-square = 0.1 with one degree of freedom).

(2) Maximum speeds on highways and traffic deaths. The maximum speeds allowed on the highways of 14 European countries in 1975 are listed in Figure 4.18. We see that these correlate with rho = .67** with Lynn's neuroticism scores, .62* with the HERMES country scores on the "stress" question, .59* with UAI, and .52* with MAS. It is in the higher stressed, more uncertainty avoiding countries (and the more masculine ones) that drivers are allowed to drive faster.

Naive logic would suggest that countries with the highest accident rates before the oil crisis would have established the lowest maximum speeds, as speeds affect accident rates. The 1971 accident death rates are also listed in Figure 4.18; they are uncorrelated with maximum speed but positively correlated with UAI, stress, neuroticism, and MAS. Moreover, the highest correlation of accident rates is (negative) with the Individualism index IDV. We shall meet it again in Chapter 5; one factor involved is the greater wealth of countries with higher IDV scores.

FIGURE 4.17   Classification of 20 "Balanced Power" Countries According to the Age of Their Present Political System, Together with UAI Scores

Number of balanced power countries in which present political system exists	UAI	
	23–53	58–92
Uninterrupted since before World War I[a]	9	2
Not uninterrupted since before World War I[b]	1	8
Chi-square	9.9** (1 d.f.)	

[a]AUL, BEL, CAN, DEN, GBR, NET, NZL, NOR, SWE, SWI, USA
[b]AUT, FIN, FRA, GER, IRE, ISR, ITA, JAP, TUR

FIGURE 4.18   Maximum Speeds on Highways and Traffic Deaths in 14
European Countries, Versus Four Indices

Countries in order of UAI score	1975 maximum speeds on highways[a] kilometers/hour	1971 traffic deaths per 1000 vehicles[b]
Belgium	120	1.21
France	140	.72
Spain	130	1.28
Italy	120	1.02
Austria	130	1.66
Germany (Federal Republic)	none	1.21
Finland	80	1.38
Switzerland	130	1.13
Netherlands	100	.99
Norway	90	.55
Great Britain	112	.56
Ireland	96	1.18
Sweden	110	.51
Denmark	110	.89
Spearman rank correlation with 1971 traffic deaths,	.26	
HERMES stress score,	.62**	.54*
Lynn's neuroticism score[c]	.67**	.48*
PDI	.43	.00
UAI	.59*	.56*
IDV	-.21	-.62**
MAS	.52*	.51*
Squared multiple correlation with four HERMES indices R^2	.53	.67
Order of indices in stepwise regression, cumulative R^2, and sign of coefficient	1. .34+UAI 2. .45+MAS	1. .38-IDV 2. .56+MAS

[a]SOURCE: ANWB Handbook (1975).
[b]SOURCE: United Nations Demographic Yearbook (1973).
[c]See Figure 4.10. Not available for Spain.

(3) Number of nurses per doctor. Statistics of the ratio between the number of nurses and the number of doctors in 22 countries in 1971 are shown by Gaspari and Millendorfer (1978: 199). The data for 15 countries also in the HERMES sample are presented in Figure 4.19. The correlation with PDI was quoted on page 126. The correlation with UAI, however, is much stronger (−.80***). Wealth per se is a less accurate predictor of nurses per doctor than the PDI, UAI, or IDV; in itself it is curious that the correlation with wealth should be positive, because a poorer country should be better able to pay for nurses than for doctors!

(4) The Catholic/Protestant ratio in Christian countries. For the 29 Christian countries in my sample, I have in Figure 4.20 correlated a measure of the Catholic/Protestant ratio with the four HERMES indices and with GNP. As on the Catholic side we have many poor countries which could be said to disturb the picture, I have also considered in the righthand column only the wealthy countries (1970 GNP/capita over $1300). In both cases, however, the

FIGURE 4.19   Number of Nurses per Doctor in 1971 in 15 Countries,
Versus GNP/Capita and Versus Four Indices

Countries in order of UAI scores	Number of nurses per doctor in 1971[a]
Greece	.4
Portugal	1.1
Spain	.8
France	2.6
Austria	1.5
Germany (Fed. Rep.)	1.7
Finland	5.3
Switzerland	1.4
Netherlands	3.2
Norway	3.2
U.S.A.	3.3
Great Britain	2.7
Ireland	5.5
Sweden	3.7
Denmark	3.3
Mean of 15 countries	2.6
Zero-order product moment correlation of rank order of number of nurses per doctor with	
1970 GNP/capita	$.48^{*}$
PDI	$-.52^{*}$
UAI	$-.80^{***}$
IDV	$.63^{**}$
MAS	$-.34$
Squared multiple correlation with all four R^2	.68

[a]Read from graph in Gaspari and Millendorfer (1978: 199).
NOTE: A stepwise regression shows no sizable second-order correlations.

strongest correlate of the Catholic/Protestant ratio is uncertainty avoidance. The stepwise regression shows that Catholic countries tend to score more uncertainty-avoiding and more masculine; Protestant countries tend to score less uncertainty-avoiding and more feminine.

FIGURE 4.20   Catholic/Protestant Ratio on Christian Countries, Versus
Four HERMES Indices

Countries	$\dfrac{\% \text{ catholic } - \% \text{ protestant}}{\% \text{ catholic } + \% \text{ protestant}}$ [a]	
	29 Christian countries	17 wealthy countries only
Argentina	.96	
Australia	-.45	-.45
Austria	.85	.85
Belgium	.98	.98
Brazil	.80	
Canada	.16	.16
Chile	.76	
Colombia	.98	
Denmark	-.98	-.98
Finland	-.96	-.96
France	.95	.95
Great Britain	-.75	-.75
Germany (Federal Republic)	-.06	-.06
Greece	1.00	
Ireland	.90	.90
Italy	1.00	1.00
Mexico	.95	
Netherlands	.03	.03
Norway	-1.00	-1.00
New Zealand	-.65	-.65
Peru	.98	
Philippines	.74	
Portugal	1.00	
Spain	1.00	
Sweden	-1.00	-1.00
Switzerland	-.01	-.01
U.S.A.	-.09	-.09
Venezuela	.98	
Yugoslavia	.98	
Product moment correlation with		
PDI	.68***	.48*
UAI	.76***	.68***
IDV	-.63***	-.19
MAS	.40*	.58**
GNP	-.68***	-.36
Squared multiple correlation with PDI,UAI, IDV,MAS R^2	.75	.68
Order of indices in stepwise regression, cumulative R^2 and sign of coefficient	1. .58+UAI	1. .46+UAI
	2. .68+MAS	2. .60+MAS

[a]SOURCE: Taylor and Hudson (1972: Table 4.16).
All non-Protestant Christians have been classified as Catholics (these are Roman Catholics and
Orthodox believers).
South Africa has been omitted as HERMES indices refer to whites only.

NOTES

1. "Above all we want release from fear. . . And in the end most fears . . . are forms of fear of the unknown. So we are all the time pressing for assurances that the unknown is known really, and that what it contains is something we are going to want anyway. We embrace religions which assure us that we shall not die, and political philosophies which assure us that society will become perfect in the future". (Magee, 1975: 88, based on Karl Popper).

2. For a review of 27 paper-and-pencil instruments measuring attitudes related to the "authoritarian personality syndrome" see Shaver (1973).

3. Non-rational and non-logical is not the same as irrational and illogical. The former are meant to be value-free statements describing the origins of behavior; the latter have negative value connotations implying that a behavior is wrong.

4. "Ritual is a stereotyped, symbolically concentrated expression of beliefs and sentiments regarding ultimate things. It is a way of renewing contact with ultimate things, of bringing more vividly to the mind through symbolic performances certain centrally important processes and norms" (Shils, 1975: 154)—this is part of a clarifying article on ritual in modern society. For a study of rituals in modern Britain see Bocock (1974).

5. Hampton (1977) proposed an anthropological study of accounting in Great Britain which takes these ritual aspects into consideration.

6. Another attempt at uncertainty reduction is found in the construction of "world models" which try to describe what will happen to the world, given certain assumptions. For a fundamental critique of such models see Faucheux et al. (1976). Their basic argument is that social systems are different from physical systems: People in the system adapt to changing situations to an extent which makes extrapolation useless. They advocate using models in a normative rather than in a descriptive way, to show what should be done in order to get somewhere.

7. Marks only compares British with U.S. industry and argues that adoption of U.S. organizational structures in Britain is often ill-advised: The United States is a centralist and federalist society with checks and balances, while in Britain the tradition is one of consensus. The United States scores somewhat higher than Britain on both power distance and uncertainty avoidance.

8. Two other questions in the HERMES questionnaire were also tried: B39 (manager insists on rules and procedures") and B47 ("unclear on what duties and responsibilities are"). As Figure 2.5 shows, both had to be dropped due to low stability of country scores from 1968 to 1972.

9. Rho = .73*** for "stay less than 2 years," and rho = .77*** for "stay less than 5 years." The survey answers were thus correlated with *past* turnover levels in countries. Their correlation with *future* turnover levels unfortunately has not been tested in HERMES; but turnover level differences for this occupation tended to be fairly stable, and studies in other organizations (Mangione, 1973; Kraut, 1975a; Price and Bluedorn, 1977) have shown that for individuals within countries, answers on similar survey questions did predict their actual turnover in the period following the survey.

10. See also Zaleznik et al. (1977). A review of the American literature on social-psychological factors in stress can be found in McGrath (1970).

11. A variance analysis of the scores on the "stress" question can be found in Chapter 2, Figure 2.4. The variance in stress scores due to country and due to occupation are both significant, but the country effect is much stronger than the occupational effect. The same was found by Kraut and Ronen (1975).

12. The variance in stress scores due to other organizational factors may be considerable: For example, in one large office with about 350 persons divided into 23 working groups, group mean scores on the "nervous or tense" question varied between 2.69 and 3.56. The differences between the extreme groups are statistically significant in spite of the small size of the groups (nine and 13 persons, difference of means, tested by t-test, two-tailed, significant at .05 level).

Discovering such differences on this and other questions and feeding them back to the manager and members of the groups is, in fact, one of the main reasons for the corporation in question to conduct surveys. However, departmental pressures leading to such stress differences are diverse and do not lend themselves to a macro-analysis.

13. Two more reasons why a UAI by occupation makes no sense are that (1) occupational differences in rule orientation can be shown not to be stable from 1968 to 1972, and (2) the range of scores for stress across occupations is much smaller than across countries. Kraut and Ronen (1975: 675) also found that stress scores depend more on country than on occupation; employment stability scores, more on occupation than on country.

14. In the analysis of variance data for the manufacturing personnel analyzed in Chapter 2 (Figure 2.4) we found also no sex effect on stress and only a weak sex effect in rule orientation.

15. See also the strong sex effect for this question in the analysis of variance of Figure 2.4.

16. Interestingly, employees' employment stability answers for HERMES' subsidiary in Japan are not very different from those in other industrial countries: Only about 40 percent of respondents state that they want to stay until retirement. Abroad, the myth is widespread that all Japanese work under a system of permanent employment (*nenko*). It is likely that in purely Japanese companies the percentage of employees wanting to stay until retirement is higher; but even there, the *nenko* system is used less often than non-Japanese believe; and actual labor turnover in Japan is not so low (Azumi, 1974; Oh, 1976; Marshall, 1977).

17. See also Aron (1970:33–45). For a recent confirmation of the validity of Durkheim's analysis see Besnard (1976). Recent comparative studies of suicide in different cultures are reviewed in Hippler (1969), and 16 papers are collected in Farberow (1975). Murphy et al. (1970) report on a study among psychiatrists in 30 countries about symptoms of depression. They find differences, but consider their data insufficiently reliable to draw clear conclusions.

18. A study like Lynn's only makes sense for developed countries where a certain level of medical care and a certain accuracy of statistics exist. Haas (1969) has factor-analyzed medical variables for 72 countries (including less-developed ones) together with political variables. In this case, all death causes tend to converge on a "medical development" factor which runs parallel with economic development.

19. Both correlations are statistically significant at the .01 level.

20. Le Vine (1973: 51) argues that this is a "psychological reductionist" theory of society.

21. McClelland's later work compared with his earlier publications shows a shift in the connotations of the power motive. In his original study (1961:168) he suggests that "a combination of high n_{Pow} and low n_{Aff} is very closely associated with the tendency of a nation to resort to totalitarian methods in governing its people." More recently, McClelland applied measures of need strength to more and less successful business managers in the United States and concluded that the "better managers we studied are high in power motivation, low in affiliation motivation" (McClelland and Burnham, 1976: 103). Should this explain why some successful business managers sympathize with totalitarian regimes?

22. There is a correlation between 1925 n_{Ach} and PDI, but it can be shown to be a by-product of the correlation with UAI. A cross-cultural review of achievement motivation studies by Schludermann and Schludermann (1977: 155) describes something like a curvilinear relation between PDI and n_{Ach}, but this is not found—at least not on the level of countrywide data.

23. Bennett (1977b) has shown that among managers working for U.S. banks, a low LPC was functional in the Philippines but not in Hong Kong.

24. Inkeles and Levinson (1969: 476) write about Germany (which is above average in UAI): "[A] major contributing power in the fall of the Weimar republic was the inability of large numbers of Germans to tolerate the necessity for political compromise."

25. Seeman (1977: 775), comparing 450 French with 450 U.S. workers, found the former much more frequently believing that "experts" should make political decisions; this fits with the UAI score differences between these countries.

26. In Putnam's study, attitudes of German civil servants are most polarized. SPD-sympathizing civil servants who mostly arrived on the scene later tend to be more "politically" oriented than CDU-sympathizing employees who more frequently take a "classical" stand. Putnam's study contains questions more conceptually related to PDI and others more related to UAI; on the first, Germany and Great Britain produce more similar answers.

27. Rho = .90, significant at the .05 level.

28. During World War II, the German occupants introduced identity cards in the Netherlands. This was the first procedure to be abolished when the Germans left.

29. Rho = .85, significant at the .001 level.

30. Theories based on unfalsifiable hypotheses, such as those by Freud and Marx, will be more popular in high UAI countries (see Magee, 1975: 44 on Karl Popper).

31. This explains the influence of German social scientists like Lewin and Adorno who emigrated to the United States.

32. For an analysis of different national interests in the area of organization theory see Hofstede and Kassem (1976: 22).

33. Eysenck (1954: 178) used a distinction based on work by Guilford between two personality factors: Neuroticism and Extraversion. He related (for individuals) Tough-Mindedness to Extraversion. Eysenck's student, Lynn, operationalized the factors of Neuroticism and Extraversion on the societal level. As I showed (Figure 4.10), UAI is correlated in this case with Neuroticism and *not* with Extraversion.

34. A detailed comparison of Germany with Great Britain is found in Heller and Wilpert (1977: 69).

35. This is one of the points of critique on Mulder's (1977) Power Distance Reduction theory. Ng (1977) reports on an extension of Mulder's experiments in which structural properties of organizations are shown to affect Power Distance Reduction tendencies.

Chapter 5

INDIVIDUALISM

SUMMARY OF THIS CHAPTER

The third dimension of national culture is called Individualism. It describes the relationship between the individual and the collectivity which prevails in a given society. It is reflected in the way people live together—for example, in nuclear families, extended families, or tribes; and it has all kinds of value implications. In some cultures, individualism is seen as a blessing and a source of well-being; in others, it is seen as alienating. Sociology has provided us with a variety of distinctions associated with the individualism dimension, of which the best known is probably Tönnies' *Gemeinschaft* (low individualism) versus *Gesellschaft* (high individualism).

The HERMES data bank has allowed the computation for each of the 40 countries of a country Individualism Index (IDV): It opposes in particular the importance of time for personal life on the high IDV side versus the importance of being trained by the company on the low IDV side. The same index is not suitable for distinguishing among occupations, sexes, age groups, or individuals, however. The Individualism Index is negatively correlated with the Power Distance Index, but some countries (the Latin European ones) show both high individualism and high power distances. The stronger a country's individualism, the less the tendency of HERMES respondents to say "yes" to questions in the survey ("acquiescence"). Individualism is related to a variety of other questions in the HERMES questionnaire. The individualism dimension is also found in work goal scores by managers attending courses at IMEDE. It is associated with the answers on Gordon's Surveys of Values for manager and student samples, and with various questions in Haire et al.'s 14-country study on

"Managerial Thinking." An individualism ecological dimension can be shown to exist in Bass' exercise "Life Goals," in Bass and Franke's Organizational Success Questionnaire, and in Morris' Ways to Live. IDV is correlated significantly with Need for Affiliation in McClelland's content analysis of 1925 children's readers. All these and some other correlates of IDV are integrated into a coherent list of connotations of individualism as a country characteristic.

It also appears that IDV is correlated with several country-level indicators; it correlates .82 with GNP per capita, and also with geographical latitude, with the size of the HERMES subsidiary, and with various characteristics of political and economic systems (such as occupational mobility, sectoral equality, and press freedom). From this, a picture of the Individualism-Collectivism dimension of societal norms can be drawn, as well as some inferences about its origins and consequences. The latter are separated into consequences (1) for society at large; (2) for religion, ideology, and theory; and (3) for organizations.

THE INDIVIDUAL AND THE COLLECTIVITY

Individualism in Society

Some animals, like wolves, are gregarious, and others are solitary, like tigers. The human species should no doubt be classified with the gregarious animals, but different human societies show gregariousness to different degrees. Here again, then, we have a fundamental dimension on which societies differ: the relationship between the individual and the collectivity.

If we look across a broad range of human societies, traditional as well as modern, we recognize differences in gregariousness through, for example, differences in the complexity of the family units in which people live and which affect their day-to-day behavior. Some people live in nuclear families: husband, wife, and children; others in (patrilineal or matrilineal) extended families, or clans with grandparents, uncles, aunts, and cousins[1]; others in tribal units based on kinship ties of an even more distant nature. Blumberg and Winch ((1972) support a "curvilinear hypothesis" for the relationship between family complexity and the complexity of societies as they develop from traditional to modern. Very traditional hunting-gathering tribes tend to live in nuclear families. In more complex agricultural societies, people tend to live in extended families, clans, or tribal units. However, as agricultural societies develop toward still more complex urban-industrial societies, family complexity decreases again and extended families disintegrate into nuclear families[2], while grandparents are sent to homes for the aged and single relatives lead solitary lives. Thus, modern industrial man in this respect reapproaches the state of the hunter-gatherer. In several cases in modern society even the nuclear family is threatened with disintegration; but attempts to replace it by some other institution which takes account of the fundamental gregariousness of human nature so far have not been very successful.

The relationship between the individual and the collectivity in human society is not only a matter of ways of living together, but it is intimately linked with societal norms (in the sense of value systems of major groups of the population: see Figure 1.4). It therefore affects both people's mental programming and the structure and functioning of many other types of institutions besides the family: educational, religious, political, and utilitarian. The central element in our mental programming involved in this case is our self-concept. "The tradition-directed person. . .hardly thinks of himself as an individual" (Riesman et al., 1953: 33). A different self-concept is evident when we compare western with Chinese thinking. Hsu (1971) shows that the western concept of "personality" does not exist in the Chinese tradition. In our concept of "personality," we consider it as a separate entity distinct from society and culture. Hsu sees this as a reflection of western individualist thought. The Chinese use the word *jen* (*jin* in Japanese) for "man" in order to describe a "human constant" which includes the person himself plus his intimate societal and cultural environment which makes his existence meaningful. The Chinese will modify their views more easily in terms of their environment. Later in this chapter it will be shown that the Chinese-majority countries Taiwan, Hong Kong, and Singapore score considerably lower on individualism than the countries of the western world.

An example of the consequence of a more individualistic or more collectivistic self-concept is the case of religious or ideological conversion. In western individualist society, converting oneself is a highly individual act[3]; if I would convert myself to, for example, Catholicism or Communism, it is unlikely that even my closest relatives would follow me. However, the history of all great religions is one of collective rather than individual conversions. "Then he . . . got baptized instantly, *he and all his family . . .* overjoyed *like all his household* at having believed in God" (Acts 16: 33–34, New Testament, translation by J. Moffatt). Similarly, in modern China ideological conversions tend to take place collectively. This is not just a matter of deference to more powerful persons; rather, people have a sense of collective identity which makes it only natural that they should change together.

Because they are tied to value systems shared by the majority, issues of collectivism versus individualism carry strong moral overtones. Americans see their own culture as very individualistic; and this individualism is interpreted as a major contributor to the greatness of the United States. In their classic study *The Lonely Crowd,* Riesman et al. (1953) distinguish between "tradition-directed types," who are typical for traditional societies with high birth rates and high death rates, and "inner-directed types" who are typical for societies in periods of transitional growth: For example, the United States in the eighteenth through twentieth centuries. Inner-directed types have no stable traditions to go by; rather, they are guided by a "psychological gyroscope" (1953: 31) which is set during their early education and keeps them on a steady track in a turbulent environment. Riesman et al. quote a gravestone inscription of an eighteenth-century American, Thomas Darling: "A gentleman of strong mental powers . . . habituated to contemplation and reading . . . in moral reasoning . . . of deep penetration and sound judgement . . . with a rational and firm faith in his God and Saviour: he knew no other master" (1953: 133). Riesman et al. do not restrict their concept of inner-directedness to people brought up in the "Protestant Ethic"; they find it equally present in, for example, descendants of Catholic cultures. In fact, Riesman et al.'s concern is that the "inner-directed" type is disappearing in the United States and that an incipient decline of population stimulates a new stabilization around another dominant type, the "other-directed" American: a new kind of collectivist who takes his bearings from his peer group and from the mass media. The data in this chapter will show, however, that at least inside the

HERMES corporation a comparison of U.S. employees with their counterparts from other nations shows the former around 1970 still scoring higher on individualism than all others.

A very different moral stance is found in China. For Mao Tse-tung, individualism is evil. Individualism and liberalism, for Mao, are manifest in the selfishness and aversion to discipline characteristic of the petty bourgeoisie. The selfish behavior which Mao condemns is not necessarily behavior at the expense of others. It is sufficient to place personal interests above those of the group or simply to devote too much attention to one's own things (Ho, 1978b: 395–396). Mao's anti-individualistic, pro-collectivistic ethos is deeply rooted in the Chinese tradition. Collectivism does not mean a negation of the individual's well-being or interest; it is implicitly assumed that maintaining the group's well-being is the best guarantee for the individual (Ho, 1978a: 2). In the collectivistic Chinese society (and in other Asiatic societies, such as Japan, as well), the individual is not "inner-directed" at all but controlled by a need for not losing face. "Face"—a literal translation of the Chinese *lien* and *mien-tsu*—"is lost when the individual, either through his action or that of people closely related to him, fails to meet essential requirements placed upon him by virtue of the social position he occupies" (Ho, 1976: 867).

Not all western thinkers are happy with individualism, of course, and not all eastern thinkers with collectivism. There is a certain symmetry between the criticism of western society by Brittan (1977) and the criticism of Japanese society by Kawasaki (1969). The first stresses the alienation of the "privatized" individual; the second the tyranny of the collectivity. They represent the devil and the deep blue sea, between which societies and man within them have to steer their course.

The different forms of society that go with more collectivistic and more individualistic self-concepts were recognized early by sociologists. Tönnies (1887 [1963]) introduced the distinction between *Gemeinschaft* and *Gesellschaft* (translated in the English version of his book as "community" versus "society"). These terms describe two types of social entities. *Gemeinschaft* entities result from mutual sympathy, habit, or common beliefs and are "willed" for their intrinsic value to their members; *Gesellschaft* entities are intended by their constituents to be means to specific ends (Heberle, 1968: 100). Tönnies further noted in history a transition from a predominantly *Gemeinschaft*—like to a predominantly *Gesellschaft*—like social order, which he attributed to increasing commercialization, the rise of the modern state, and the progress of science (1968: 101).

An association between the degree of collectivism or individualism in a society and its degree of modernity is suggested by at least three of the sources quoted above: by Blumberg and Winch, who associate modernity with lower familial complexity[4], by Riesman et al., who associate transitional growth with inner-directedness, and by Tönnies, who associates the modern state with *Gesellschaft*. In Chapter 1 I have referred to other studies that suggest that a society's degree of economic evolution or modernity is a major determinant of societal norms. This chapter will show that among the four dimensions of national culture found empirically in the HERMES data, it is the individualism-versus-collectivism dimension which relates most closely to a country's level of economic development.

Triandis (1971: 8) summarizes psychological studies on the effect of modernization on attitudes as follows:

> Modern man . . . is open to new experiences; relatively independent of parental author-
> ity; concerned with time, planning, willing to defer gratification; he feels that man can
> be the master over nature, and that he controls the reinforcements he receives from his
> environment; he believes in determinism and science; he has a wide, cosmopolitan
> perspective, he uses broad ingroups; he competes with standards of excellence, and he is
> optimistic about controlling his environment. Traditional man has narrow ingroups,
> looks at the world with suspicion, believes that good is limited and one obtains a share of
> it by chance or pleasing the gods; he identifies with his parents and receives direction
> from them; he considers planning a waste of time, and does not defer gratification; he
> feels at the mercy of obscure environmental factors, and is prone to mysticism; he sees
> interpersonal relations as an end, rarely as means to an end; he does not believe that he
> can control his environment but rather sees himself under the influence of external,
> mystical powers.

In Chapter 1 I also referred to Parsons and Shils' (1951: 77) "pattern variables"
which are part of their "General Theory of Action." From the five pattern variables
suggested, it is especially number 2, "Self-orientation versus Collectivity orientation," that calls for association with our individualism-collectivism dimension. Parsons and Shils wrote:

> The high frequency of situations in which there is a disharmony of interests creates the
> problem of choosing between action for private goals or on behalf of collective goals.
> This dilemma may be resolved by the actor either by giving primacy to interests, goals
> and values shared with other members of a given collective unit of which he is a
> member, or by giving primacy to his personal or private interests without considering
> their bearing on collective interest [1951: 80– 81]

In his later work, Parsons dropped "Self-orientation versus Collectivity orientation" as a pattern variable: It did not fit into the tight paradigm he developed (Rocher,
1974: 52, 43). In Parsons' theory of the evolution of societies (Parsons, 1977), the
self-versus-collectivity orientation distinction is not used. Parsons' other pattern
variables are less clearly conceptually related to the individualism-collectivism dimension. However, it will appear later on in this chapter that pattern variable number
3, "Universalism versus Particularism," is statistically related to individualism. This
variable refers to whether or not value systems should take particular relationship
systems of the actor into account (such as family or friendship ties). The individualist
society also tends to be universalist (particular relationships should *not* be counted).

Individualism in Organizations

The norm prevalent in a given society 'as to the degree of individualism/
collectivism expected from its members will strongly affect the nature of the relationship between a person and the organization to which he or she belongs. More
collectivist societies call for greater emotional dependence of members on their
organizations; in a society in equilibrium, the organizations should in return assume
a broad responsibility for their members. Whenever organizations cease to do that—
as in the incipient capitalism in nineteenth-century Europe, and today in many less-
developed countries—there is disharmony between people's values and the social
order; this will lead to either a shift in values toward more individualism, or pressure
toward a different, more collectivist social order (such as state socialism), or both.

The level of individualism/collectivism in society will affect the organization's members' reasons for complying with organizational requirements. Following the terminology introduced by Etzioni (1975), we can assume more "moral" involvement with the organization where collectivist values prevail, and more "calculative" involvement where individualist values prevail. Etzioni distinguishes between "pure" and "social" moral involvement: "Pure" moral involvement tends to develop in vertical relationships, such as those between teachers and students, priests and parishioners, leaders and followers. 'Social' involvement tends to develop in horizontal relationships like those in various types of primary groups. Both pure moral and social orientations might be found in the same relationships, but as a rule, one orientation predominates" (1975: 11). We can relate pure moral involvement to the values of the subordinate in a high power distance society, and social involvement to the values of the organization member in a collectivist society. As we will see later in this chapter, high power distance and collectivism go together in most, but not all, societies.

The level of individualism/collectivism in society will also affect what type of persons will be admitted into positions of special influence in organizations. A useful distinction in this case is Merton's "locals" versus "cosmopolitans" (Merton, 1968: 447, first published in 1949; the terms derive from a translation of Tönnies' work). The local type is largely preoccupied with problems inside the organization; this type is likely to become influential in a more collectivist climate. The cosmopolitan type must maintain a minimum set of relations within the organization, but he or she considers him or herself as an integral part of the world outside it. We would rather find cosmopolitans in positions of influence in organizations where a more individualist norm prevails. We shall see evidence for this in the HERMES data.

The degree of individualism in organizations obviously will depend on many other factors besides a societal norm: We can expect effects of employee educational level and of the organization's own history and subculture. Also predictable is a relationship with organization size. In a study among workers of large and small production firms in Bradford, England, Ingham (1970: 117ff) found more moral involvement in the smaller firms, more calculative in the larger. This suggests a positive correlation between organization size and individualism, which, as we shall see later in this chapter, is supported by the HERMES data.

There is an obvious relationship between the organization's technology and the position of its members on the individualism-collectivism continuum. Technologies developed in western individualist settings more or less presuppose an individualist mentality in entrepreneurs, managers, and workers which is part of "modernity" (Stinchcombe, 1965: 145ff; Triandis, 1973: 166). Introducing such technologies in more collectivist countries represents one of the main forces toward a shift of societal norms in those countries (Figure 1.4). On the other hand, the collectivist value pattern in more traditional societies sets a limit to the technology transfer possibilities; this is one of the dilemmas of the economic development of poor countries. One solution is sought in the transfer of "intermediate" or "appropriate" technologies which are better adapted to what already exists in the traditional collectivist societies. Another solution is the local design of political and organizational structures which allow collectivism and modern technology to co-exist. Examples are Japan, China, the Soviet Union, and Yugoslavia. To what extent these designs will be effective barriers against increased individualism if technology advances only history will tell. In spite of the successful integration of modern technology with more traditional Japanese and Chinese values, there are definite signs of increasing individualism in these countries as well. I shall deal with shifts in individualism at greater length in Chapter 8.

The individualism-collectivism dimension is also visible in the normative organization theories coming from different countries. The United States is the major exporter of modern organization theories, but its position of extreme individualism in comparison to most other countries makes the relevance of some of its theories in other cultural environments doubtful. As we saw, in the United States there is a strong feeling that individualism is good and collectivism bad. Riesman et al. were concerned about the "inner-directed" type being replaced by an "other-directed" one. In his now classic bestseller *The Organization Man,* William H. Whyte Jr. (1956) accused the modern big U.S. organization of destroying individualism and exhorted the individual to defend himself against collectivist organizational pressures. Among other things, Whyte supplied a practical guide "How to Cheat on Personality Tests" (1956: 449).[5] The strong feelings about the desirability of individualism in the United States make it difficult for some Americans to understand that people in less individualistically oriented societies want to resolve societal and organizational problems in ways other than the American one.[6]

One of the rare non-American collections of organization theory literature is a volume of European contributions co-edited by the present author (Hofstede and Kassem, 1976). In it, Hjelholt, who is from Denmark, argues for the importance of the organization and its external and internal boundaries as sources of collective identity for the members:

> I think the identity of groups and systems is important. Without identity the system or the group is neither productive nor satisfying as a place to live. And if we have to get our identity from other systems and just be a prisoner in the working organization, we create a society which is clearly asking for trouble.

> From this outburst you can guess my attitude toward the predominantly American organization theories advocating the organization structure as matrix-organizations or temporary systems. I think that the theories which try to get away with or loosen boundaries are attacking the group identities, and in this way, while temporarily ensuring flexibility inside the organization, they export problems to the outside, where we get a society of alienated, rootless individuals. I feel much more in accordance with the moves of groups to extend or redefine their boundaries, trying to let their values influence the organization as a whole. I refer to the unions' demand for a better work environment, their demand to be included in decision-making for the whole organization, and the like [Hjelholt, 1976: 241–242].

Of course, American unions do not as a rule demand to be included in this type of decision-making; unions in some European countries do. This is no accident; union-management relationships, too, reflect dominant value systems. The quote from Hjelholt shows that a normative stance in favor of individualism is not the only possibility for the organization theorist and that a different value position leads to a different theory.

MEASURING NATIONAL DIFFERENCES
IN INDIVIDUALISM IN HERMES

An Individualism Index for HERMES Countries

In the statistical analysis section of this chapter the calculation of a country Individualism Index is described. This index and the Masculinity Index, with which we shall deal in Chapter 6, use country mean answer scores on the 14 "work goals" questions: questions of the format "How important is it to you to . . ."; for example, "How important is it to you to have an opportunity for high earnings?" or "How important is it to you to fully use your skills and abilities on the job?" For the 14 questions, see A5 through A18 in Appendix 1. They are resumed in Figure 5.8 in the statistical analysis section, together with the short names which I shall use for the sake of convenience to refer to them.

The Individualism Index and the Masculinity Index are based on the two main factors that explain the country differences in HERMES employees' answers to the 14 work goals questions.[7] A factor analysis showed that almost one-half of the variance in country mean scores on the two questions could be accounted for by just two factors. The Individualism Index is based on the first of these factors, which accounts for 24 percent of the variance in the country mean "work goals" scores. It is mainly composed of the following six work goals:

Loading	Work goal
.86	personal time
.49	freedom
.46	challenge
−.63	use of skills
−.69	physical conditions
−.82	training

The "loading" represents the correlation coefficient across the 40 countries between the factor score and the country mean score for each work goal. Thus, the Individualism Index is strongly related to the mean importance attached in a country to "personal time" ("have a job which leaves you sufficient time for your personal or family life") and sharply *negatively* related to "training" ("have training opportunities—to improve your skills or learn new skills").

Psychologists, and especially American psychologists, have done a considerable amount of research using "work goals" questions (Hofstede, 1976b). Since the publication of a seminal book by Herzberg et al. (1959), it is customary to divide such goals into "intrinsic" (work-related) and "extrinsic" (non-work-related). The factor which we found (empirically) in the country mean work goals scores opposes three goals with positive loadings (personal time, freedom, and challenge) to three goals with negative loadings (use of skills, physical conditions, and training). This is *not* a split according to the intrinsic-extrinsic distinction; Herzberg et al. probably would have classified "freedom," "challenge," "use of skills," and "training" as intrinsic job aspects; "personal time" and "physical conditions" as extrinsic. The factor does *not* oppose the intrinsics to the extrinsics. What the three goals with positive loadings have in common is that they stress the actor's independence from the organization. Even "challenge"("have challenging work to do—work from which you can get a personal sense of accomplishment"), although it takes place within the organization, stresses the individual's *personal* accomplishment. The three goals with negative loadings rather stress things the organization should do for the individual: provide him or her with training, with working conditions, allow him or her to use his or her skills. The latter goals reflect a more "local" mentality, whereas the former goals reflect a more "cosmopolitan" mentality.

The distinction between "challenge" and "use of skills" may look trivial to a western-educated reader. In fact, across *individuals* within each country and occupational group the importance of "challenge" and "use of skills" are always highly correlated (Hofstede et al, 1976: 29). Yet, this distinction discriminates sharply between national cultures; "challenge" (with its stress on a "personal sense of accomplishment") appeals more in one kind of culture and "use of skills" (with no mention of accomplishment) appeals more in others.

The opposing of goals stressing independence from the organization to goals not stressing independence has been the argument for calling this factor "individual-collective" and using the country factor scores as the basis for a country Individualism Index. The index, by a simple mathematical transformation, has been brought in a range between zero and 100: Its values for the 40 countries are listed in the first column of Figure 5.1.[8]

The highest Individualism Index (IDV) values are found for the United States (91), Australia (90), and Great Britain (89); the lowest for Venezuela (12), Colombia (13), and Pakistan (14). This suggests immediately a correlation of IDV with the Power Distance Index, which also tends to place these countries on opposite sides of the scale. The relationship between PDI and IDV is shown graphically in Figure 5.2.

The PDI-IDV plot shows that there is a broad overall correlation between the two dimensions. Its value is $r = -.67$. In Chapter 2, in the factor analysis of all HERMES value questions, PDI and IDV showed up (with opposite signs) on the same factor. In this book I have nevertheless dealt with power distance and individualism separately for the following reasons:

(1) They are conceptually different. Power distance refers to emotional dependence on more powerful people; individualism to emotional (in)dependence on groups, organizations, or other collectivities.

(2) Although most high PDI countries are also low IDV countries and vice versa, this is not always the case. The Latin European countries (and in particular France and Belgium) combine large power distances with high individualism; Austria and Israel combine small power distances with only medium individualism. Collapsing PDI and IDV into one dimension would obscure the unique value patterns of these country clusters.

People in HERMES subsidiaries in the Latin European cluster (to which also South Africa marginally belongs) have a need for strict authority of hierarchical superiors, but *at the same time* stress their personal independence from any collectivity: They are dependent individualists. This culture pattern of dependent individualism has been recognized in the case of France by, for example, Crozier. In *The Bureaucratic Phenomenon,* he writes:

Face-to-face dependence relationships are . . . perceived as difficult to bear in the French cultural setting. Yet the prevailing view of authority is still that of universalism

FIGURE 5.1   Country Individualism Index (IDV) Values Based on the
Factor Scores of the First Factor Found in a 14-Work Goals,
40-Country Matrix

Country	IDV actual	predicted	Country	IDV actual	predicted
U.S.A.	91	95	Argentina	46	47
Australia	90	62	Iran	41	34
Great Britain	89	74	Brazil	38	37
Canada	80	80	Turkey	37	35
Netherlands	80	71	Greece	35	41
New Zealand	79	58	Philippines	32	23
Italy	76	62	Mexico	30	33
Belgium	75	71	Portugal	27	42
Denmark	74	75	Hong Kong	25	29
Sweden	71	85	Chile	23	38
France	71	80	Singapore	20	15
Ireland	70	52	Thailand	20	19
Norway	.69	73	Taiwan	17	27
Switzerland	68	73	Peru	16	22
Germany (F.R.)	67	81	Pakistan	14	22
South Africa	65	38	Colombia	13	18
Finland	63	68	Venezuela	12	28
Austria	55	61	Mean of 39 countries		
Israel	54	47	(HERMES)	51	50
Spain	51	51			
India	48	34	Yugoslavia (same		
Japan	46	60	industry)	27	44

Work goal scores were computed for a stratified sample of seven occupations at two points in time.
Actual values and values predicted on the basis of multiple regression on wealth, latitude, and
organization size.

and absolutism . . . . The two attitudes are contradictory. However, they can be recon-
ciled within a bureaucratic system since impersonal rules and centralization make it
possible to reconcile an absolutist conception of authority and the elimination of most
direct dependence relationships [Crozier, 1964a: 222].

The opposite pattern (no strict authority but relative personal dependence on the
collectivity) as found in Austria and Israel could be called "independent collectivism." An Austrian psychologist interprets this as follows:

The political structure of this country is based on a more primitive organization of
society, in which the family model is more clearly present than, for example, in France,
where political superstructures prevail . . . At the same time, our society is sufficiently
advanced not to be threatened by this family model in personal relationships. The easy-
going relationship between superiors and individuals in private and public organizations
is interpreted by the German as "Austrian charm." Yet I believe that this friendly
relationship pattern applies only to face-to-face relationships, such as personally known
superiors [Traugott Lindner, personal communication, my translation].

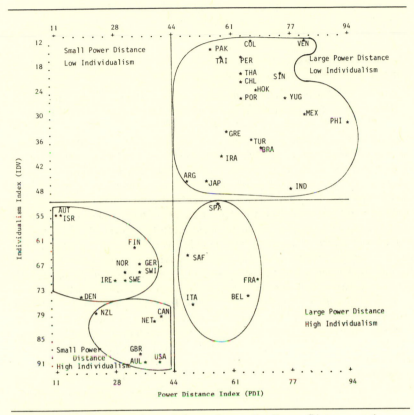

FIGURE 5.2   Position of the 40 Countries on the Power Distance and
Individualism Scales

Individualism and Occupation, Sex, and Age

The IDV values were based on the result of a factor analysis of work goals *across
countries*. The statistical section, which supplies the details on this factor analysis,
also shows the results of a factor analysis of mean work goals scores *across 38
occupations,* holding country constant. In this occupational factor analysis there is
no trace of an individual-collective dimension: We cannot label one occupation as
more "individualist" than another. Instead, for occupations we do find a factor which
corresponds fairly well to the "intrinsic-extrinsic" dichotomy according to Herzberg.
This factor opposes freedom and challenge on the "intrinsic" side to benefits, physical conditions, and personal time on the "extrinsic" side.[9]

The sex differences in work goals will be shown to be closely related to the issue
of "masculinity" in value systems and will therefore be treated in Chapter 6. In that
chapter it will be shown that we cannot speak of "Individualism" as being systematically better linked to the male or to the female role.

Age differences in work goals obviously are associated with generation differences; they will be discussed, together with other trend data on values, in Chapter 8.[10]

Country Individualism Index Scores
and Other HERMES Survey Questions

The statistical analysis indicates that, first, the country Individualism Index IDV is correlated r = .64 with the mean raw Work Goal Importance scores *across all 14 goals* ("IMP"). A low value of IMP means that respondents in the country tend to score all goals—regardless of content—as "more important."[11] I consider this as a measure of "acquiescence"; that is, the tendency to say "yes" to whatever question. Within countries, we found that acquiescence depends strongly on occupation: lower educated occupations show more acquiescence than higher educated ones (Figure 2.6). I attributed this both to a desire to please the author of the questionnaire (a yielding to the perceived "demand characteristics" of the questions) and to a less differentiated cognitive map among the respondents (see Chapter 2). We now find that the strong acquiescence which is found in less educated occupations (holding country constant) is also found in more collectivist, less individualist countries (holding occupation constant). The respondent in a more collectivist culture is more sensitive to the social pressure he or she perceives to be emanating from the questionnaire.[12] We also find a correlation between the Individualism Index and the mean number of years of formal education in a country, keeping occupation constant. In less individualist (poorer) countries, HERMES employees on the average have gone to school *longer* for a particular occupation (but the education probably has been less practical).

In addition, respondents in more individualist countries, compared with those in more collectivist countries, tend to endorse significantly more frequently the following items in the questionnaire:

(1) Staying with one company is *not* desirable (B59), and the better managers in a company are *not* those that have been in the company the longest time (C11).
(2) A larger corporation is generally *not* a more desirable place to work than a small company (C17), and respondents are also less happy about the fact that HERMES is a foreign company (B24).
(3) A corporation is *not* responsible for its employees (B52).
(4) Interesting work is *not* as important as earnings (B53).[13]
(5) For getting ahead in industry, knowing influential people is usually more important than ability (C15).
(6) Decisions made by individuals are usually of higher quality than decisions made by groups (B57).
(7) In the first survey round (1967–1970), the HERMES questionnaire included 22 rather than 14 work goals. Two of the goals discontinued in 1971 were particularly characteristic of the "collectivist" side of the individual-collective dimension: the importance of working in a successful company (C4) and in a modern company (C5).

Points 1, 2, 3, and 7 confirm the lesser dependency of the individual on the company in more individualist cultures. Point 4 suggests that on the more individualist side, respondents defend more a calculative involvement with the organization, according to Etzioni's terminology. The skeptical attitude about careers in point 5 confirms this calculative, rather than moral, involvement. Point 6, finally, is not surprising: Individual decisions are more ideologically appealing in more individualist cultures.

COMPARING THE HERMES
INDIVIDUALISM INDEX VALUES
WITH OTHER DATA

Sample Survey Studies

(1) Managers at IMEDE answering HERMES questions (see this item in Chapters 2 and 3). Three hundred and sixty-two managers in courses at IMEDE scored the 14 work goals questions in their English version. The statistical analysis (Figure 5.13) shows that across 15 countries, in spite of (1) the small and poorly matched IMEDE samples, (2) the fact that the respondents at IMEDE were all managers whereas those in HERMES were mostly rank-and-file, and (3) the fact that at IMEDE all people answered in English, in HERMES in their native tongue, we do find significant agreement between the two surveys on the following points:

(a) The acquiescence pattern (the tendency to rate *all* goals as more important: rho = .62);
(b) the presence of the same two factors in the IMEDE data as we found in the HERMES data: an individual-collective and an ego-social factor;
(c) the scores of the 15 countries on the IMEDE individual-collective factor agree with those on the HERMES Individualism dimension (rho = .64); and
(d) for five out of the 14 goals separately, countries at IMEDE rank themselves significantly like countries at HERMES: for 12 out of the 14 goals, the rank orders of countries at IMEDE are positively correlated with those at HERMES (Figure 5.14).

(2) Managers at IMEDE answering Gordon's Surveys of Personal and Interpersonal Values. In Chapter 3 we saw how IMEDE participants also supplied scores on L.V. Gordon's Surveys of Personal and Interpersonal Values and how these scores were subjected to an ecological factor analysis (Figure 3.13). One of the three factors found, "Conformity versus variety," is weakly negatively correlated with IDV (r = −42), in the sense that IMEDE managers from more individualist countries tend to stress leadership and variety, while those from less individualist countries tend to stress conformity and orderliness.

(3) Samples of managers in 19 countries answering Haire et al.'s "attitudes and assumptions underlying management practices." The classical "comparative management" study by Haire et al. (1966) has already been quoted several times in this book. One part of this 14-country study dealt with "attitudes and assumptions underlying management practices"; it consisted of eight items which are listed in Chapter 3. I have expressed my methodological misgivings about combining the items into subscales at face value; in addition, the choice of the items reflects strongly the American frame of mind of the authors, and their formulation is not always foolproof. Yet, across 19 countries (14 from the original study plus five from replications by Clark and McCabe and Redding and Casey), two subscales correlate significantly with IDV (Figure 3.15). ·

The highest correlating subscale is "Sharing information and objectives" (r = .63).

In more individualist countries, managers tend to *disagree* with the statements that a good leader should give detailed instructions and only information necessary for their immediate tasks.

The other subscale significantly correlating with IDV (r = .48) is "participation." In more individualist countries, managers tend to agree with the statements that if subordinates cannot influence them, they as managers lose some influence; and that group goal-setting offers advantages.

In both cases, the subscales correlate more with IDV than with PDI; they seem to be less associated with the immediate power relationships people are in, but more with the country's general level of modernity (IDV being closely associated with economic development).

(4) Samples of managers in 14[14] *countries answering to Haire et al.'s "managerial motivations and satisfactions" questions.* This is another part of the survey referred to in the previous section. This part can also be criticized on methodological grounds, for a "reverse ecological fallacy" (see Chapter 1) and for ethnocentrism. The authors combined the country scores on 11 "need importance" items (which I would call "work goals") into five categories based on the theory of Maslow, without statistical proof (through ecological correlations) that this combining was justified.[15] As the statistical analysis shows, Haire et al.'s published scores for 14 countries and five "need categories" show the following significant similarities with the HERMES results:

> (a) The acquiescence (the tendency to rate *everything* as more or less important) in Haire et al.'s country data correlates with the HERMES acquiescence scores ("IMP") with rho = .59, and also with the HERMES individualism Index scores (IDV) with rho = −.59, (more individualist countries less acquiescence).
>
> (b) In countries which the HERMES data show to be more individualist (higher IDV), Haire et al. find a stronger need for autonomy and a weaker need for security (r = .60 in both cases).[16]

(5) Samples of managers from 12 countries doing the exercise "Life Goals" (one of the exercises distributed by IRGOM). This exercise asks respondents to rank 11 goals in order of importance; they are not strictly work goals but cover a somewhat broader area. The 11 goals are labeled self-realization, leadership, expertness, wealth, independence, prestige, affection, service, duty, security, and pleasure. Using unpublished data for 3082 managers from 12 countries (which were kindly made available by Bernard M. Bass), I performed an ecological factor analysis; the result can be found in the statistical analysis. There are two strong factors, of which one (labeled by me "hedonism-skill") is strongly correlated (rho = .76) with the Individualism Index, and the other (labeled by me "assertiveness-service") is strongly correlated (rho = .84) with the Masculinity Index. This means that the two main factors found in the IRGOM Life Goals are virtually identical to the two main factors found in HERMES work goals. This occurred in spite of the differences in samples (managers from a variety of organizations versus employees of one company), the different data collection periods (the IRGOM data were collected between 1978 and 1976), the different data collection setting (training versus employee survey), the different questions used, and the different methods of scoring (ranking versus rating).

The convergency between the factors in the two studies means that individualism (personal time, freedom, challenge) is associated also with hedonism (pleasure, security, affection); collectivism (training, physical conditions, use of skills) also with skill (expertness, prestige, duty). The social or feminine value cluster which we shall further explore in Chapter 6 (manager, cooperation, desirable area, employment security) is associated also with service; the ego or masculine value cluster (earnings, recognition, advancement, challenge, use of skills) also with assertiveness (leadership, independence, self-realization).

(6) Samples of students from six countries answering Bass and Franke's (1972) "Organizational Success Questionnaire." I quoted this study in Chapter 1 as an illustration of the reverse ecological fallacy. The 12 items in the questionnaire were grouped into a "social" and a "political" index based upon correlations found across U.S. individuals, whereas the ecological correlations pointed to a quite different clustering of items on the basis of country means.

The statistical analysis shows that on the basis of country means we find *three* dimensions, of which one, "openness vs. secrecy," is significantly negatively correlated with the Individualism Index ($r = .91$). This means that in more individualist countries, students confronted with Bass and Franke's items are more inclined to score themselves as "withholding information" and less inclined to score "sharing in decision making," "openly committing themselves," and "making political alliances." It does *not* mean, of course, that when put in the situation they would actually *show* these behaviors (they may or they may not), but it does illustrate the different social desirability of these behaviors in the different cultures. In more individualist countries, students describe themselves more easily as *going their own way without minding others*.

(7) Samples of male students from six countries answering Morris' (1956) "Ways to Live" questionnaire. Morris' 13 "Ways to Live" are terminal values: fundamental attitudes toward life, each of which is described in a fairly lengthy paragraph. The respondents are required to score on a seven-point scale how much they would like or dislike living according to each of the 13 ways. In an ecological reanalysis of Morris' published data,[17] I found two main dimensions which are described later in this chapter: I labeled them "enjoyment versus duty" and "engagement versus withdrawal." It appears that the first factor is significantly ($r = .73$) correlated with the Individualism Index. In more individualist countries, students prefer the "enjoyment" ways to live; in less individualist countries, they tend toward the "duty" side. The second dimension is dominated by a high score of the Chinese on "obeying the cosmic purposes"[18] and has no significant correlations with HERMES indices.

The presence in these seven very different sample survey studies of dimensions correlated with the Individualism Index shows the pervasiveness of individualism as a dimension of culture. The last two cases demonstrate that even with only six countries, it makes sense to use ecological factor analysis to reduce the data to meaningful dimensions.

Other Multicountry Studies

(1) McClelland's need for Affiliation (n_{Aff}). The statistical analysis part of Chapter 4 showed in Figure 4.11 a significant correlation (rho = .46 across 22 countries)

between the Individualism Index and the scores for nAff, based on 1925 children's readers (we find again that it is McClelland's 1925, not his 1950, data which correlate with a HERMES index; which speaks in favor of the greater reliability of the 1925 data). The implication of the correlation is that in the more individualist countries, there is more of a stress on affiliation in the stories. McClelland defines affiliation as "establishing, maintaining, or restoring a positive affective relationship with another person. This relationship is most adequately described by the word friendship" (1925: 160). Thus, in less individualist countries where traditional social ties, like those with extended family members, continue to exist, people have less of a need to make specific friendships. One's friends are predetermined by the social relationships into which one is born. In the more individualist countries, however, affective relationships are not socially predetermined, but must be acquired by each individual personally. Thus, making friendships becomes more of an issue for the individual.

(2) Traffic deaths. We also saw in Chapter 4 (Figure 4.18) that there is a more significant (rho = −.62) negative correlation between individualism and traffic deaths (across 14 European countries). In the more individualist countries, traffic is safer. These countries tend to be wealthier, which is likely to increase the numbers of vehicles available and to decrease the number of kilometers per vehicle; also, roads are probably better adapted to heavier traffic in the wealthier countries. Nevertheless, the Spearman rank correlation between wealth (GNP/capita) and traffic deaths is only −.51, so there is more to the correlation between IDV and traffic safety than just greater wealth. If we expand Etzioni's distinction between a "calculative" and a "moral" involvement to the traffic situation, it is likely that drivers in more individualist countries show a more calculative involvement in traffic, and that this leads to safer driving.

(3) Time use. Converse (1972) summarizes the findings of a 12-country comparative study of their citizens' time use. Using both multi-dimensional scaling and smallest space analysis, he finds that the major differences in overall time use among the countries separate themselves into two dimensions, which he calls "North-South" and "East-West" (1972: 151). Because this study includes six East European countries not in the HERMES sample, I can only compare it with HERMES data across six countries: Belgium, France, Germany, Peru, U.S.A., and Yugoslavia.

Across these six countries, Converse's North-South dimension rank correlates 1.00 with the HERMES Individualism Index (significant at the .01 level). The "North" countries spend more time watching TV, shopping, as members in voluntary organizations, in personal care, in religious activities, and reading papers. This corresponds with high Individualism Index scores. The "South" countries spend more time resting, cooking, tending animals, gardening, being outdoors, sleeping, and eating. This corresponds with low Individualism Index scores. It obviously reflects the "modernity" of the society.[19]

Differences in Individualism
Found in Two Country Studies

The statistical analysis shows a comparison between HERMES work goal data and data collected by Preiss (1971) on American and German engineers. The data strongly support the greater individualism in the United States which is also reflected in the HERMES Individualism Index scores (91 for U.S.A., 67 for Germany).

Another "comparative" study of work goals was done by Singh and Wherry (1963) among 200 Indian metal workers; 10 goals were ranked, and the results were compared with those of six studies carried out in the United States between 1932 and 1950. The Indians' goal-ranking resembled more that of the Americans in the thirties than in the fifties. The United States became considerably wealthier in this period; if the goals of Indians resemble more the goals of Americans when they were poorer, this supports the relationships between goal pattern and wealth.

In chapter 3 I referred to a study by Williams et al. (1966) among workers in Peru and the United States. They established a relationship between a high Power Distance Index value and low "faith in people" or interpersonal trust. High PDI tends to be associated with low individualism, but it seems paradoxical that low individualism should be associated with low interpersonal trust, and vice versa (Peru scores 16 on IDV and the United States 91). Williams et al. (1966: 117) suggest on this issue that we should distinguish between individualism as the taking of individual initiative and individualism as the nonidentification with a group. The Individualism Index measures the taking of individual initiative. Identification or nonidentification with a group is rather related to the distribution of power—that is, to PDI. High PDI leads to low trust in others—that is, to nonidentification with a group. I would add, however, that we should also distinguish between ingroups and outgroups. In low individualism cultures, the contrast between the two is particularly strong. It is because the Peruvian work groups studied by Williams et al. remained outgroups to the worker that interpersonal trust did not develop. In low individualism cultures one just does not trust a "somebody"—one only trusts "us."

Another comparison between the United States and a Latin American country, this time Mexico, is found in a paper by Zurcher et al. (1965). They administered a questionnaire to 38 Mexican-American, and 149 Anglo-American bank employees near the border between the two countries; the questions were aiming at measuring the endorsement of values of "universalism" (institutionalized obligations to society) versus "particularism" (institutional obligations to friendship). This distinction is one of Parsons and Shils' pattern variables (Chapter 1). They showed Mexicans to be more particularist, Anglo-Americans more universalist. Zurcher et al. (1965: 54) link the Mexican particularism to the maintenance of an extended kinship system. They quote Oscar Lewis: "Without his family, the Mexican individual stands prey to every form of aggression, exploitation and humiliation." This family becomes extended through a large number of compadres, or godparents. Zurcher et al. conclude that individuals in this type of society perceive social situations in terms of close personal bonds, where Americans would perceive them impersonally. Mexico scores 30 on IDV, the United States 91; the association between low IDV and particularism, through the extended kinship system, makes sense.

A Summary of Connotations of
the Individualism Index Found in
Survey and Related Material

As was done for PDI in Figure 3.6 and for UAI in Figure 4.3, in Figure 5.3 I have integrated the connotations of low and high individualism found so far. The warnings given in Chapter 3 should be remembered when reading this table; countries may be anywhere in between the two extremes pictured; not all connotations apply in all countries; and individuals within countries vary from societal norms.

The data upon which Figure 5.3 is based are mostly from narrow samples in countries; some of them not even very well matched. The samples, however, were at least all *different* ones. The fact that the same individualism dimension shows up in these different samples speaks in favor of the ubiquity of the dimension. It is very likely that a more thorough search of the literature on comparative representative samples studies of entire populations will yield more evidence of an IDV dimension in these studies too; I simply have not got that far.

FIGURE 5.3   Summary of Connotations of Individualism Index Differences Found in Survey and Related Research

See page	Low IDV Countries	High IDV Countries
220	Importance of provisions by company (training, physical conditions).	Importance of employees' personal life (time).
224	Emotional dependence on company.	Emotional independence from company.
224	Large company attractive.	Small company attractive.
224	Moral involvement with company.	Calculative involvement with company.
220	More importance attached to training and use of skills in jobs.	More importance attached to freedom and challenge in jobs.
227	Students consider it less socially acceptable to claim pursuing their own ends without minding others.	Students consider it socially acceptable to claim pursuing their own ends without minding others.
225	Managers aspire to conformity and orderliness.	Managers aspire to leadership and variety.
226	Managers rate having security in their position more important.	Managers rate having autonomy more important.
226	Managers endorse "traditional" points of view, not supporting employee initiative and group activity.	Managers endorse "modern" points of view on stimulating employee initiative and group activity.
224	Group decisions are considered better than individual decisions.	However, individual decisions are considered better than group decisions.
227	Duty in life appeals to students.	Enjoyment in life appeals to students.
227	Managers choose duty, expertness, and prestige as life goals.	Managers choose pleasure, affection, and security as life goals.

FIGURE 5.3 Continued

229	Individual initiative is socially frowned upon; fatalism.	Individual initiative is socially encouraged.
224 225 226	More acquiescence in responses to "importance" questions.	Less acquiescence in responses to "importance" questions.
229	People thought of in terms of ingroups and outgroups; particularism.	People thought of in general terms; universalism.
228	Social relations predetermined in terms of ingroups.	Need to make specific friendships.
224	More years of schooling needed to do a given job.	Fewer years of schooling needed to do a given job.
228	More traffic accidents per 1000 vehicles.	Fewer traffic accidents per 1000 vehicles.
228	More traditional time use pattern.	More modern time use pattern.

THE INDIVIDUALISM NORM
ITS ORIGINS AND CONSEQUENCES

The Relationship Between
Individualism and National Wealth

The statistical analysis in Figure 5.20 explores the relationship of the Individualism Index (IDV) with seven economic, geographic, and demographic indicators which were identified in Chapter 2 and already used in the Chapters 3 and 4. Across all 40 countries, there is a striking .82 correlation between IDV and wealth (1970 GNP per capita). If we take into account the large error margins of IDV (composed from answers of HERMES employees to translated paper-and-pencil questionnaires) and of GNP (World Bank data based on imprecise statistics and shaky exchange rates), this level of correlation is really remarkable: The two measures share $.82^2 = 68\%$ of their variance! The strong correlation between IDV and GNP per capita is illustrated in the graph of Figure 5.4.

Countries to the righthand side of the regression line are less individualistic than their 1970 wealth would predict; those to the left are more individualistic.[20] We notice that the three Chinese countries Singapore, Hong Kong, and Taiwan score well to the right side of the regression line: They are less individualistic than their wealth would warrant, which is in agreement with the *jen* philosophy referred to earlier.

The statistical analysis shows that, besides wealth, geographical latitude and HERMES organization size in the country contribute significantly to predicting IDV (colder countries and countries with larger HERMES subsidiaries are more individualist). By using the three predictors of wealth, latitude, and organization size simultaneously, we get an even more accurate prediction of IDV, which has been listed with the actual values in Figure 5.1. Differences of more than 10 points between actual and predicted value of IDV are found for the following:

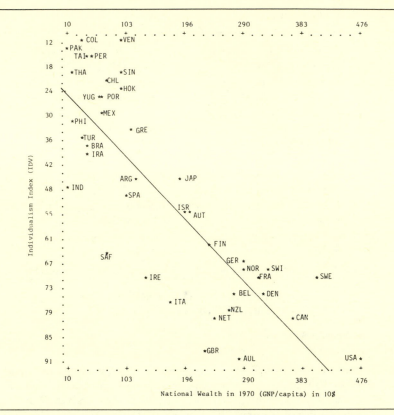

FIGURE 5.4   Position of the 40 Countries on Their Individualism Index
(IDV) Versus Their 1970 National Wealth

more individualistic	less individualistic
+28 Australia	−17 Yugoslavia
+27 South Africa	−16 Venezuela
+21 New Zealand	−15 Chile
+18 Ireland	−15 Portugal
+15 Great Britain	−14 Sweden
+14 India	−14 Japan
+14 Italy	−14 Germany

These differences represent the variance in Individualism Index scores not related to wealth, latitude, or the size of the HERMES subsidiary, but, for example, to historical or traditional factors. The positive score for South Africa is partly due to the IDV score being based on the answers of white respondents only, while the GNP per capita refers to the total population. However, we do find at the "more individualistic" side a "British Culture" cluster in which only Canada and the United States are conspicuously absent.

One particularity which distinguishes these countries from others is an exceedingly atomized trade union system (especially in Great Britain, which has been the model for the other British-culture countries) with craft unions that compete with each other and find it very difficult to undertake integrated action; we can see this as an outcome of an exceedingly individualistic value system. Worker self-management is not a popular theme in these countries.

On the "less individualistic" side we find Yugoslavia with its worker self-management system; Chile and Portugal, in which forms of worker self-management were tried in the recent past; Sweden, which is known for its keen interest in worker participation; and Japan and Germany , which both carry the image of countries in which collective efforts are popular. These show that the residual variance in IDV does relate to differences in the work organization tendencies among countries which cannot be explained by differences in wealth.

For the 19 wealthier countries, 1960–1970 economic growth is *negatively* related to individualism. This fact (wealth is positively associated with individualism, but lower individualism with faster growth of wealth) logically should lead to a certain balancing of wealth among wealthy countries: If they become too wealthy they become too individualist to grow any more. This, of course, assumes a causality which the data do not prove; and over time, other factors may enter. But the theory of a balancing of wealth among wealthy countries has a certain plausibility.

Individualism and Political Systems

Béteille (1977: 162ff) stresses the correspondence, both historical and geographical, among political democracy, capitalism, competition, and individualism. The capitalist market economy fosters individualism and in turn depends on it. On the other hand, various socialist types of economic order foster collectivism and in turn depend on it, although to various degrees.

In Chapter 3 I related power distance to the difference between "balanced power" and "unbalanced power" in political systems. Figure 3.18 showed that 17 countries in the upper half of the Power Distance Index range show unbalanced power, 17 in the lower half show balanced power since 1950, and there are three exceptions on either side (France, Belgium, and Turkey high PDI and balanced power; Argentina, South Africa, and Pakistan lower PDI and unbalanced power). If we make a similar 2×2 table for IDV, we find that it is even closer associated with balanced power: 18 countries in the upper half of the IDV-range have balanced power and vice-versa; the two exceptions on either side are Turkey and Japan (balanced power but lower IDV; both are marginal cases as the balance of power in Turkey is precarious and Japan is just in the lower half of the IDV range) versus South Africa and Spain (unbalanced power but higher IDV).

I used the power distance explanation of balanced versus unbalanced political power in Chapter 3 because it makes conceptual sense to relate power to power. Why does individualism predict balanced political power even more accurately? The key to this question must be in the two exceptional countries, Belgium and France, which show high PDI *and* high IDV (Figure 5.2) and balanced political power. If these two countries, in spite of strong authoritarian elements in their national value systems, have continued to respect certain rules of political pluralism, it is certainly because of their individualism: A dictator in these countries simply cannot obtain sufficient passive compliance to survive. The universalist norm which we found associated with individualism also resists a regime based entirely on particularism (although there is a lot of de facto particularism in these countries).

We saw in Chapter 3 that GNP per capita per se is an almost perfect predictor of balanced political power: 19 countries in the upper range of GNP show balanced power and vice versa, and there is only one exception on either side—Turkey versus Argentina, both in some way marginal cases. If GNP predicts the balance in the political system in the period we are considering (since 1950), it must be because it affects political events in other ways than through dominant value systems (Power Distance and Individualism) as well. In Chapter 3 I drew a suggested causal path (Figure 3.8) for PDI in which social mobility and the development of a middle class is the central factor contributing directly to GNP and indirectly to decentralization of political power and questioning of authority in general (PDI). It is likely that individualism, too, is associated with the development of a middle class: Individualist values tend to be middle-class values; individualism is even more closely conceptually related to the development of a middle class than is low power distance.

The development of a middle class presupposes social mobility. In the statistical analysis, Figure 5.21, we see the correlations of the Individualism Index with two measures of social mobility, one (Cutright, 1968) across 12 countries, the other (Miller, 1960) across 11 countries. Both indicate to what extent sons of fathers in manual occupations have access to nonmanual occupations, and vice versa. Both correlate with IDV (rho $= -.71$ and $-.50$); the correlation indicates greater social mobility for more individualist countries.

Individualism and balanced political power—that is, political stability—can be related in still another way: through the distribution of the national wealth across sectors of the economy (such as, between farming and manufacturing workers). Sectoral equality or inequality is something other than equality or inequality of individual incomes; the latter in Figure 3.17 was shown to be associated with PDI. In the statistical analysis in Figure 5.22 we find significant correlations among the Individualism Index and two measures of sectoral inequality, from Cutright (1967) and from Taylor and Hudson (1972), in both cases across 33 countries (r $= -.60$ and $-.71$); they indicate greater sectoral equality in more individualist countries. I interpret this as the outcome of a universalist attitude among both decision makers and population; but it will definitely increase political stability; as underprivileged economic sectors are a threat to the stability of any regime. In his article, Cutright shows for 44 countries a relationship between equality of sectors of the exonomy and "political representativeness"; the latter resembles my "balanced power" criterion. He argues that political representativeness decreases inequality because it forces the political elites to respond to the needs of the nonelite classes for a greater share of the national product (1967: 565).

The statistical analysis (Figure 5.22) also shows a correlation across 19 countries between the Individualism Index and an (intersubjective) measure of press freedom (Taylor and Hudson, 1972): rho $= .51$. It makes sense that greater press freedom is the outcome of a more individualist, universalist value system with a stronger approval of individual initiative. However, per capita GNP per se is an even better predictor of the Press Freedom Index, which suggests that apart from values, there are purely economic reasons which push toward more press freedom in wealthier countries: more newspapers, more interest groups that want their opinions to be known and have the means for it. In Chapter 4 I referred to a public opinion study in five countries by Kaase and Marsh (1976) about "protest potential." The results of the study oppose Austria and Germany (low protest potential, high repression potential) to Great Britain, the Netherlands and the United States (the opposite). I interpreted this as a difference in UAI, but the two groups of countries are also separated on IDV; high protest potential and low repression potential is found in higher IDV, lower UAI countries. This is in agreement with the findings on the value components in press freedom shown above.

The Individualism Norm and Its Origins

In the same way as I did earlier for PDI and UAI, I have in Figure 5.5 composed an integrated picture of the general societal norm behind the "low IDV" and "high IDV" syndromes. It goes back to the summary of survey findings in Figure 5.3 and some of the correlations with country-level indices discussed afterward.

FIGURE 5.5   The Individualism Societal Norm

Low IDV	High IDV
• In society, people are born into extended families or clans which protect them in exchange for loyalty.	• In society, everyone is supposed to take care of him or herself and his or her immediate family.
• "We" consciousness.	• "I" consciousness.
• Collectivity-orientation.[a]	• Self-orientation.[a]
• Identity is based in the social system.	• Identity is based in the individual.
• Emotional dependence of individual on organizations and institutions.	• Emotional independence of individual from organizations or institutions.
• Emphasis on belonging to organization; membership ideal.	• Emphasis on individual initiative and achievement; leadership ideal.
• Private life is invaded by organizations and clans to which one belongs; opinions are predetermined.	• Everyone has a right on a private life and opinion.
• Expertise, order, duty, security provided by organization or clan.	• Autonomy, variety, pleasure, individual financial security.
• Friendships predetermined by stable social relationships; but need for prestige within these relationships.	• Need for specific friendships.
• Belief in group decisions.	• Belief in individual decisions.
• Value standards differ for ingroups and outgroups; particularism.[a]	• Value standards should apply to all; universalism.[a]

[a]Parsons and Shils (1951).

Again, we should see the individualism norm as a value system shared especially by the majority in the middle classes in a society.

As far as the origins of national differences in individualism are concerned, according to the diagram in Figure 1.4 we have to look for these in ecological factors. In Figure 5.6 I have listed those we met in the previous pages as being statistically associated with IDV, with some inferences that make the pattern more coherent.

There are similarities between the origins of IDV and the origins of PDI as pictured in the proposed "causal chain" of Figure 3.8. However, for differences in IDV we have to put economic development first, as it correlates so highly. Climate in this case is a secondary factor, and it is supposed to either support or discourage individual initiative. The nuclear rather than extended family structure is supposed to be a central element in breeding individualism. The smaller population growth (Figure 5.20) means that also, on the high IDV side, parents tend to have fewer children; the child from a small family, other factors being equal, learns to be more individualist than the child from a large family. The longer education for a given job on the low IDV side (discussed earlier in this chapter) suggests a more traditional educational system with more rote learning of revealed truths; also, this educational system will cover a smaller part of the population than the more pragmatic education on the high IDV side. Then, apart from all these systematic characteristics, we should take idiosyncratic historical factors into account.

Consequences of Different
Individualism Index Levels

As in the two previous chapters, I have collected in Figure 5.7 the consequences of low and high IDV levels: for society at large; for religion, ideology, and theory; and for organizations. On the low IDV side, this table presents a problem: Some statements apply to all societies studied, which means that "low IDV" stands for "less economically developed." Others presuppose a certain level of economic development, so that "low IDV" stands for "relatively low IDV given a certain level of economic development." I have nevertheless maintained the two types of statements in one column because they show a certain coherence.

The religious-ideological-political consequences merit further study. Individualism reminds us of the "Protestant Ethic" of Max Weber, but as Figure 4.20 shows, the Catholic/Protestant ratio in wealthy countries is unrelated to individualism (but related to UAI and MAS); we are rather dealing with a "modernist ethic" versus a "traditionalist ethic." The Chinese *jen* philosophy of man described at the beginning of this chapter (Hsu, 1971) is the best formulation of the low IDV sentiment I found so far; the worship of the independent actor in Whyte's (1956) *Organization Man* the best formulation of the high IDV sentiment.

With regard to organizations, in stable low IDV societies, members will transfer part of their extended-family or clan allegiances to the organization they belong to. Japan is the one example of a society that has shaped its utilitarian organizations to cater to people's needs in this respect, although both values and organizations in Japan are shifting fast to the more individualist side. In the history of capitalism, we find many examples of employers who attempted to look after their employees from the cradle to the grave, from Robert Owen in early nineteenth-century Britain to

FIGURE 5.6   Origins of National Individualism Index Differences

Low IDV	High IDV
• Less economic development.	• Greater economic development.
• Less social mobility and weak development of middle class.	• Greater social mobility and strong development of middle class.
• Tropical and subtropical climates.	• Moderate to cold climates.
• Survival less dependent on individual initiative.	• Survival more dependent on individual initiative.
• More traditional agriculture, less modern industry, less urbanization.	• Less traditional agriculture, more modern industry, more urbanization.
• Extended family or tribal structures.	• Nuclear family structure.
• More children per nuclear family.	• Fewer children per nuclear family.
• Traditional educational systems, for minority of population.	• Pragmatic educational systems, for majority of population.
• Historical factors: tradition of collectivist thinking and action.	• Historical factors: tradition of individualist thinking and action.
• Smaller, particularist organizations.	• Larger, universalist organizations.

Philips Lamp in the Netherlands and IBM in the United States in the 1930s; the latter even had its company songs, as some Japanese companies still have today. One of the challenges of multinational organizations today is to adapt themselves to the very different levels of individualism of their employees in different parts of the world; in Chapter 9 I shall go deeper into this.

STATISTICAL ANALYSIS OF
DATA USED IN CHAPTER 5

Calculating the Individualism Index
by Country

The Power Distance Index and Uncertainty Avoidance Index described in Chapters 3 and 4, respectively, were each based on the country means for three questions in the HERMES questionnaire. As I explained in Chapter 2 the two remaining indices, for individualism and masculinity, were arrived at in a different fashion. Both are based on the scores among HERMES subsidiary employees in 40 countries on the same 14 "work goals" questions. I made a separate study of the validity of these questions (what it actually is that the scores measure) which can be found in Hofstede (1976b). The 14 questions are listed in Figure 5.8, together with the short names which I shall use throughout this and the next chapter to refer to them. Eight more "work goals" questions used only in the first (1968–1971) survey round are listed in Figure 5.9.

Scores for all goals were standardized for each one-country, one-occupation subset of the data, in order to eliminate acquiescence (Chapter 2). They were subsequently averaged across seven occupational groups. Two matrices were composed: one of all 22 goals used for 1968–1971, for 19 countries only (data for the other countries are missing). The second matrix

FIGURE 5.7   Consequences of National Individualism Index Differences

See page	Low IDV Countries	High IDV Countries

Consequences for Society at Large

216	• *Gemeinschaft* (community-based) social order.	• *Gesellschaft* (society-based) social order.
233	• For wealthy countries, a relatively low IDV helps economic growth.	• After a certain level of wealth has been obtained, slower economic growth.
233	• Unbalanced power political systems.	• Balanced power political systems.
234	• Less occupational mobility.	• Greater occupational mobility.
234	• Income inequality between sectors of the economy.	• Income equality between sectors of the economy.
234	• Less press freedom.	• More press freedom.
235	• Repression potential.	• Protest potential.
233	• Labor movement more united.	• Labor movement more atomized.
233	• Labor unions more interested in sharing management responsibility; appeal of worker self-management.	• Labor unions less interested in sharing management responsibility.
228	• More road accidents.	• Safer driving.

Consequences for Religious Life and Philosophical and Ideological Thinking

215	• Collective conversions.	• Individual conversions.
215	• *Jen* philosophy of man.	• Personality philosophy of man.
219	• Stress on identity and roots.	• Worship of the independent actor.
215	• Traditionalist ethic.	• "Protestant" (modernist) ethic.

Consequences for Organizations

218 225	• Involvement of individuals with organizations primarily moral.	• Involvement of individuals with organizations primarily calculative.
217 236	• Employees expect organizations to look after them like a family— and can become very alienated if organization dissatisfies them.	• Organizations are not expected to look after employees from the cradle to the grave.
216 224	• Organization has great influence on members' well-being.	• Organization has moderate influence on members' well-being.
221	• Employees expect organization to defend their interests.	• Employees are expected to defend their own interests.
229	• Policies and practices based on loyalty and sense of duty.	• Policies and practices should allow for individual initiative.

218	• Promotion from inside.	(localism)	• Promotion from inside	(cosmo-
224	• Promotion on seniority.		and outside.	poli-
			Promotion on market	tanism)
			value.	

226	• Less concern with fashion in management ideas.	• Managers try to be up-to-date and endorse modern management ideas.

217	• Policies and practices vary	• Policies and practices apply to all
229	according to relations (particularism).	(universalism).

FIGURE 5.8   Fourteen Work Goals Used in All Questionnaires 1968–1973

Number[a]	Short name	Full questionnaire wording
A5 (15)	Challenge	Have challenging work to do - work from which you can get a personal sense of accomplishment
A6 (18)	Desirable area	Live in an area desirable to you and your family
A7 (1)	Earnings	Have an opportunity for high earnings
A8 (6)	Cooperation	Work with people who cooperate well with one another
A9 (9)	Training	Have training opportunities (to improve your skills or learn new skills)
A10 (4)	Benefits	Have good fringe benefits
A11 (12)	Recognition	Get the recognition you deserve when you do a good job.
A12 (11)	Physical conditions	Have good physical working conditions (good ventilation and lighting, adequate work space, etc.).
A13 (7)	Freedom	Have considerable freedom to adapt your own approach to the job.
A14 (2)	Employment security	Have the security that you will be able to work for your company as long as you want to.
A15 (17)	Advancement	Have an opportunity for advancement to higher level jobs.
A16 (19)	Manager	Have a good working relationship with your manager.
A17 (21)	Use of skills	Fully use your skills and abilities on the job.
A18 (5)	Personal time	Have a job which leaves you sufficient time for your personal or family life.

[a]See Appendix A. Numbers between parentheses indicate the order of the questions in the 1968–1971 questionnaires.

FIGURE 5.9   Eight Work Goals Used in the 1968–1971 Questionnaires
             Only

Number [a]	Short name	Full questionnaire wording
C1 (3)	Position security	Have the security that you will not be transferred to a less desirable job.
C2 (8)	Efficient department	Work in a department which is run efficiently
C3 (10)	Contribute to company	Have a job which allows you to make a real contribution to the success of your company.
C4 (13)	Successful company	Work in a company which is regarded in your country as successful.
C5 (14)	Modern company	Work in a company which stands in the forefront of modern technology
C6 (16)	Friendly atmosphere	Work in a congenial and friendly atmosphere.
C7 (20)	Up-to-dateness	Keep up to date with the technical developments relating to your work.
C8 (22)	Day-to-day learning	Have a job on which there is a great deal of day-to-day learning.

[a]See Appendix 1. Numbers between parentheses indicate the order of the questions in the 1968–1971 questionnaires.

contains 14 goals used for 1968–1973 for all 40 countries; scores, after standardization, were averaged over the two survey rounds. The two matrices are reproduced in Appendix 3, Table A3.2 and A3.1.

Factor analysis of the 22-goals, 19-country matrix produces only two interpretable factors, together explaining 43 percent of the variance. After orthogonal rotation, the loadings over .35 are as follows:

Factor 1 (factor variance 23%)
Ego-social

Positive
.90 advancement
.68 earnings
.61 challenge
.50 recognition (second loading)
.45 use of skills
.44 modern company

Negative
−.79 friendly atmosphere
−.78 desirable area
−.70 manager
−.66 cooperation

Factor 2 (20%)
Individual-company

Positive
.79 freedom
.69 personal time
.65 up-to-dateness
.48 training
.43 cooperation (second loading)
.40 physical conditions

Negative
−.88 successful company
−.83 contribute to company
−.53 recognition
−.43 modern company (second loading)

No loading of .35 or over on any factor:
  benefits (−.32 on factor 2)
  efficient department (−.31 on factor 1)
  employment security (−.22 on factor 1)
  position security (.21 on factor 2)
  day-to-day learning (.20 on factor 2).

Factor 1 opposes Austria, Germany, and Ireland to Sweden, Yugoslavia, and Norway; factor 2 opposes Finland, Spain, and Denmark to Greece, Turkey, and Sweden.

 Factor analysis of the 14 goals, 40-country matrix also produces two factors, together explaining 46 percent of the variance. The two factors are of virtually equal strength even before rotation; the orthogonal rotation does not change much in the loadings. We find the following:

Factor 1 (factor variance 24%)	*Factor 2* (22%)
Individual-collective	Social-ego
Positive	*Positive*
.86 personal time	.69 manager
.49 freedom	.69 cooperation
.46 challenge (second loading)	.59 desirable area
.35 desirable area (second loading)	.48 employment security
Negative	*Negative*
−.82 training	−.70 earnings
−.69 physical conditions	−.59 recognition
−.63 use of skills	−.56 advancement
−.40 benefits	−.54 challenge
−.37 cooperation (second loading)	−.40 use of skills (second loading)

All goals load .35 or over on one of the two factors. High scorers on factor 1 are U.S.A., Australia, and Great Britain; low scorers are Venezuela, Colombia, and Pakistan. High scorers on factor 2 are Sweden, Norway, Netherlands, and Denmark; low scorers are Japan, Austria, and Venezuela.

 Factor 2 in the 14-goals, 40-country matrix (with reversed sign) and factor 1 in the 22-goals, 19-country matrix are identical (except for a reversal in sign). In fact, the factor scores for the 19 countries appearing in both matrices (columns "SOC" in Table A3.1 and "EGO" in A3.2) correlate with rho = .92. In Chapter 6, I relate this factor to masculinity (ego pole) and femininity (social pole); the factor scores for the 14-goals, 40-country matrix are the basis for computing the Masculinity Index (MAS).

 Factor 1 in the 14-goals, 40-country matrix differs from factor 2 in the 22-goals, 19-country matrix because in the former the three "company" goals which form one pole of the 22-goal factor are missing. In the 14-goal solutions, personal time and freedom now oppose training plus some other goals which have a somewhat passive, being-looked-after flavor (see the opposition between "challenge" and "use of skills"). Rather than "individual-company." I have labeled the 14-goals, 40-country factor 1 "individual-collective." Factor scores on this axis have been used as a basis for computing the Individualism Index (IDV). These factor scores are listed in Table A3.1 in the column "INV."

 The "individual-collective" factor scores for 14 goals, 40 countries differ from the "individual-company" factor scores for 22 goals, 19 countries (the latter can be found, with reversed sign, in the column "ING" in Table A3.2). Across the 19 countries appearing in both matrices, the factor scores (correcting the sign) only correlate with rho = .19. However, the 19 countries form an extremely selective sample out of the 40: they are nearly all European and nearly all wealthy; as wealth and individualism are highly correlated, the 19 have a very restricted range of IDV scores—in fact, 16 out of the 19 score above average in IDV. This restricted range explains the low correlation between the "individual" factors in the two different work goals data matrices.

In order to bring the values for the Individualism Index (IDV) in a range between zero and 100, I used the following formula: IDV = 50 + 25 INV, in which INV is the factor score. The values found for the Individualism Index are listed in Figure 5.1.

Nine work goals have loadings of .35 and over on the individual-collective factor: on the positive side personal time, freedom, challenge, and desirable area; on the negative side training, physical conditions, use of skills, benefits, and cooperation. As the zero-order contribution of each work goal to the variance in the factor is determined by the square of the loading, the goals with the lower loadings hardly affect the dimension. In the analysis earlier in the chapter I have therefore only considered the six goals with loadings over .45.

Work Goal Dimensions by Occupation

In the HERMES surveys, between 1968 and 1971, the same list of 22 work goals was scored by more than 50,000 employees in virtually all occupations occurring in the company. The matrix of standardized mean scores on the 22 goals for 38 major occupational groups is shown in Appendix 3, Table A3.3. The data in this table are based on totals for 15 European countries (the non-European countries were surveyed in 1967 with a slightly different list of work goals). For Plants B and Laboratories, worldwide data are used, which means that some non-European data are included in the totals (15 percent and 8 percent of respondents, respectively); their influence is too small to warrant the additional data-processing cost for eliminating them. The occupation data on power distance and uncertainty avoidance were taken from the three large countries France, Germany, and Great Britain only. Unfortunately, for several occupations German data on the 22 goals are missing. Therefore, in this case I preferred using European totals, which differ only slightly from weighted means of the large countries.

In a factor analysis of the occupational work goal data, two factors explain 54 percent of the variance. After orthogonal rotation, the following loadings over .35 are found:

Factor 1 (factor variance 27%)   *Factor 2* (27%)
Intrinsic-extrinsic   Social-ego

Positive   *Positive*
.80 freedom   .88 manager
.73 challenge   .86 cooperation
.68 contribute to company   .84 friendly atmosphere
.55 successful company   .74 efficient department
.54 use of skills   .58 physical conditions (second loading)
.40 day-to-day learning   .41 position security

Negative   *Negative*
−.79 benefits   −.76 up-to-dateness
−.72 physical conditions   −.68 modern company
−.65 personal time   −.67 advancement
−.62 employment security   −.59 training
−.59 desirable area   −.50 earnings (second loading)
−.50 earnings   −.40 day-to-day learning (second loading)
−.37 recognition

All goals load over .35 on one of the two factors. Factor 1 is not an individual-collective factor as we found across countries, but predominantly an "intrinsic" versus "extrinsic" factor: job content on the positive pole, job context on the negative. High-scoring occupations on this factor are sales department managers A and headquarters managers; low-scoring occupations are unskilled plant workers B and skilled plant workers. It is evident that this factor is related to educational level.

Factor 2 is about the same social-ego factor as we found across countries. High-scoring occupations are laboratory clerks A and office typists and secretaries; low scorers are branch office service technicians A and branch office technical experts.

Figure 5.10 plots the 38 occupations according to their factor scores on the two dimensions. We find similar occupations close together:

Sales representatives are both intrinsic and ego-oriented.

Managers are generally intrinsic-oriented and vary between social (the clerical managers) and ego-oriented (the sales department managers).

Professionals are ego-oriented and more to the intrinsic side.

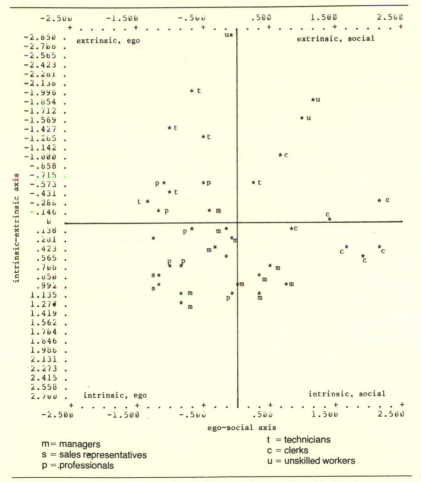

FIGURE 5.10   Factor Scores for 38 Occupations on Two Factor Axes:
Intrinsic-Extrinsic and Social-Ego

Technicians tend to be ego-oriented and are all to the extrinsic side.

Clerks are all social-oriented and more intrinsic than extrinsic.

Unskilled workers tend to be both extrinsic and social.

This two-dimensional picture of the work goal orientation of the various occupations is richer than the one-dimensional distinction common in the U.S. literature: for example, in Inkeles (1960: 10); Friedlander (1965), Centers and Bugenthal (1966), Shepard (1971: 101–102), and Quinn (1973: 244). These other studies apply a ranking of occupations from upper right to lower left in Figure 5.10, combining the extrinsic and social dimensions.

The Individualism Index and
Other HERMES Survey Questions

The other HERMES survey questions correlated with IDV can be identified in the factor analysis of all HERMES values questions, as shown in Chapter 2. However, as PDI and IDV load on the same factor, it is necessary to separate the questions into those more related to PDI and those more related to IDV.

More related to IDV than to PDI is the mean raw Work Goal Importance score across 14 goals (IMP, see Appendix 3, Table A3.1). I consider it as a measure of the respondents' acquiescence, a yesmanship in answering the work goal questions; and I have treated it as another variable in the analysis. IMP correlates with $r = .64^{***}$ with IDV and with $r = -.53^{***}$ with PDI; if we keep IDV constant, the correlation between IMP and PDI drops to an insignificant $r = -.18$. About equally strongly related to PDI ($r = .44^{***}$) and to IDV ($r = .41^{***}$) is A56, the mean number of years of formal education for the occupations compared in the different countries. For an explanation see pages 111 and 224.

All other survey questions loading on the IDV-PDI factor are listed in Figure 5.11 divided into those primarily related to individualism, to power distance, or to both. The split has been made on the basis of partial correlations, holding either IDV or PDI constant. The questions primarily related to power distance were referred to in Chapter 3.

The correlations of IDV with the work goals A18, A9, A12, A17, A5, and A13 are obvious because these are the goals the IDV score is based on. This leaves only the questions B24, B59, B52, and B53 as additional correlates of IDV. In addition, we can read in Appendix 2 that question B57 (which in the factor analyses loads on other factors) is in fact more strongly correlated with IDV ($r = .-44^{**}$) than with any other of the four indices.

As for the C questions (discontinued in 1971 or before), the following have their highest correlations with IDV (Appendix 2): C11 ($r = .70^{***}$), C15 ($r = .63^{***}$), and C17 ($r = .70^{***}$).

Earlier Studies of Work Goals in HERMES

In 1971, Sirota and Greenwood published HERMES work goal data for three occupations and 25 countries on 14 goals. Acquiescence was eliminated by *ranking* the goals on the basis of their mean scores from one to 14. Sirota and Greenwood did not use their data for computing ecological dimensions, but they performed a cluster analysis of countries which divided the 25 countries into five clusters with more or less similar goal rankings, and some leftover countries which did not fit any cluster. It so happens that their set of countries contains 16 of the 19 wealthy countries in my set of 40, and only 9 of the 21 poorer ones. The individualism dimension therefore shows up in their analysis only where they compare the poor Latin American clusters with the rich countries and notice that the former stress individual achievement less and benefits more. Their data reflect more clearly the masculinity-femininity distinction (see Chapter 6).

Schaupp (1973) in a doctoral dissertation in the United States used 1971 HERMES data from manufacturing plants in eight countries. His data treatment shows several weaknesses

FIGURE 5.11 Correlations Across 40 Countries of Country Scores for Questions Loading on Factor 1

Question number	Question	correlation with	
		IDV Individualism Index	PDI Power Distance Index
	correlated with Individualism, not with Power Distance :		
A 18	Importance personal time	.86 (.75)	−.64 (−.16)
A 9	Low importance training	−.83(−.75)	.50 (−.15)
A 12	Low importance physical conditions	−.69(−.60)	.43 (−.06)
B 24	Does not prefer foreign company	.68 (.55)	−.48 (−.04)
A 17	Low importance use of skills	−.63(−.49)	.47 (.09)
B 59	Staying with one company not desirable	.61 (.45)	−.48 (−.12)
A 5	Importance challenge	.46 (.38)	−.28 (.05)
	correlated with Power Distance, not with Individualism :		
B 46	Employees not afraid to disagree	.58 (.00)	−.87 (−.80)
A 55	Low percentage perceived manager 1 or 2	−.50 (.18)	.85 (.80)
A 54	High percentage preferred manager 3 (1967−'69)	.66 (.25)	−.84 (−.72)
B 56	Employees should not participate more	.41(−.05)	−.65 (−.57)
B 55	Employees don't lose respect for consultative manager	.35 (.03)	−.49 (−.38)
B 58	Corporation not responsible for society	.16(−.10)	−.34 (−.32)
	equally correlated with Individualism and with Power Distance :		
B 52.	Corporation not responsible for employees	.62 (.35)	−.63 (−.37)
B 53	Interesting work not as important as earnings	.60 (.31)	−.63 (−.38)
A 13	Importance freedom	.49 (.24)	−.50 (−.27)
A 15	(Low importance advancement)	−.19(−.07)	.21 (.11)

For 40 cases, the .05 significance level for r is at .27. Figures without parentheses are zero-order correlations; figures between parentheses are partial correlations: for IDV, while controlling for PDI; for PDI, while controlling for IDV.

(reverse ecological fallacy, neglect of occupational differences, sign errors in the analysis) but he did recognize an inverted relationship between a country's degree of economic development and the importance of "training" and "company" goals; that is, the negative pole of the Individualism axis (1973: 168).

In an earlier publication (to which I referred in Chapter 2), I used work goal data in order to show the profile of one particular country, the Netherlands, in comparison to a European mean (Hofstede, 1973). The comparison of the Netherlands versus Europe was done separately for all 21 occupations for which data were available. The sign test on the 21 occupational score differences between the Netherlands and Europe showed that for 18 out of the 22 work goals, the Dutch scored consistently different from the European mean, regardless of their occupation. I afterwards repeated this procedure for two other countries, Norway and Sweden, but the results of this comparison were never published. I have now assembled the results for the Netherlands, Norway, and Sweden, shown in Figure 5.12.

FIGURE 5.12   Comparison of Work Goal Importance Scores
(Standardized) for 22 Goals, Between Each of Three
Countries and the European Average (Across 15 Countries)

Individualism goals	Sign of differen- ce with European average			Masculinity goals	Sign of differen- ce with European average		
	NET	NOR	SWE		NET	NOR	SWE
positive pole				positive pole			
Freedom	+		−	Advancement	−	−	−
Personal time	+		−	Earnings	−	−	−
Up-to-dateness	−		−	Challenge	−		−
Training				Recognition	−	−	
Cooperation	+	+	+	Use of skills	−		−
Physical conditions	+	+		Modern company	−	−	
Position security		+	+	Employment security	−		
Day-to-day learning			+	Efficient department	−	+	
Benefits	+		+	Cooperation	+	+	+
Modern company	−	−		Manager	+	+	+
Recognition	−	−	−	Desirable area	+	+	+
Contribute to company	−	−	+	Friendly atmosphere			+
Successful company	−	−	+				
negative pole				negative pole			

Significance has been determined by comparing all available occupations separately and applying the sign test for consistency across occupations.
Number of occupations compared:
   Netherlands   21
   Norway   15
   Sweden   26
The classification of goals into "Individualism" and "Masculinity" goals follows the result of the ecological factor analysis for 22 goals and 19 (mostly European) countries.
Source of Netherlands data: Hofstede (1973: 345).
Norway and Sweden data were not published before.

Figure 5.12 illustrates in detail what we can find out in broader terms from the cultural dimension scores: that compared with other European countries, the Netherlands score relatively individualistic and Sweden relatively collectivistic, with Norway in between (on our IDV measure which is based on 14 goals, Norway has a slightly lower score than Sweden, but the difference between the two will become evident when we correct for national wealth; see Figure 5.4). On the masculinity dimension, all three countries score definitely to the low—that is, feminine—side (see Chapter 6). The importance of this way of analyzing the data is that it uses the data for *all* available occupations, not only for the matched sample of seven occupations on which the present study is based.

Results of Sample Survey Studies Correlated with IDV

(1) Managers at IMEDE answering HERMES questions. While attending courses at IMEDE, 362 managers *not* from the HERMES Corporation but from 40 different countries and a variety of organizations took the work goals questionnaire in English. For analysis, I grouped the participants in 15 countries or combinations of countries, with a minimum of seven respondents per country; in this way I could use 359 of the 362 cases (see Figure 5.13).

FIGURE 5.13   Comparison of Acquiescence Trends and Ecological Factor Scores Found in Work Goals Data Collected at IMEDE, with Indices Found in HERMES

Countries	Number of IMEDE respondents	Acquiescence mean raw score across all 14 goals	Ecologial factor scores found in IMEDE data	
			Individual-collective	Ego-social
Australia, Canada	14	2.30	1.25	-1.38
Great Britain	39	2.32	1.15	-.03
Italy, Spain	20	2.26	1.13	.33
U.S.A.	18	2.32	.68	.61
Brazil, Latin America	22	2.12	.45	1.33
Denmark	14	2.29	.42	-.41
Sweden, Finland	24	2.39	.29	-.39
France, Belgium	15	2.48	.27	1.39
Norway	18	2.29	.18	-1.94
Switzerland	88	2.27	.01	-.23
India, Thailand	15	2.19	-.41	.92
Germany FR, Austria	43	2.31	-.42	.90
Netherlands	8	2.22	-1.50	-.61
Japan	7	2.34	-1.57	-1.15
Iran, Turkey	14	2.16	-1.94	.68
Total and mean	359	2.28	0	0
Spearman rank correlations with HERMES indices:				
IMP (acquiescence)		.62**		
PDI			-.21	.63**
UAI			-.32	.30
IDV		.52*	.64**	.36
MAS			.09	.12

Of course, the IMEDE samples are very small; there is some mixing of countries; and the samples are not perfectly matched. The group of Swiss managers that comes to IMEDE is definitely *not* functionally equivalent to the group of, for example, Japanese or U.S. managers. Yet we find that:

(a) When we compare the mean raw scores across all 14 goals in the IMEDE data (a measure of acquiescence) with the corresponding scores for HERMES (which we called IMP), we find a rank correlation of .62**.

(b) When we subject the mean scores for the 15 IMEDE countries on the 14 goals to an ecological factor analysis, we find again two strong factors which explain each 23 percent of the variance. Although the combination of goals differs somewhat from the HERMES factor analysis, the IMEDE factors can also be labeled "Individual-collective" and "Ego-social." Their loadings are: *Individual-collective*: .91 personal time; .46 challenge; .44 advancement (second loading); −.54 recognition; −.64 cooperation; −.88 use of skills. *Ego-social*: .71 advancement; .57 training; .48 earnings; .41 freedom; −.44 desirable area; −.81 manager; −.82 benefits. The factor scores on these two factors are listed in Figure 5.13. The Individual-collective factor is significantly (.64**) rank-correlated with IDV in HERMES; thus, the Individualism dimension is common to both populations.

The Ego-social factor at IMEDE is *not* correlated with MAS, the Ego-social factor in HERMES, but with PDI in HERMES. The Ego-social dimension is related to, among other things, career ambitions; it is quite likely that the selection for an international management course in Switzerland has different consequences for the careers of participants from different countries and therefore leads to unmatched samples as far as career ambitions are concerned. As the IMEDE factor scores on the ego-social axis are significantly related to the Power Distance Index, in the sense that managers from higher PDI countries stress advancement and training while those from lower PDI countries stress benefits and manager, we can conclude that in authoritarian cultures the ambitious assertive manager has been selected or selected himself for this course abroad, while in less authoritarian cultures it is rather the relationship-oriented, less ambitious man who has been selected.

A final comparison between the work goal data of IMEDE and of HERMES is possible by rank-correlating *for each of the 14 goals separately* the mean scores for the 15 countries on the IMEDE list (see Figure 5.13; the mean scores per goal are *not* shown, however) with the mean scores per goal for these same 15 countries in HERMES. The resulting 14 Spearman rank correlations are listed in Figure 5.14. Twelve of the 14 rank-order correlations are in the expected positive direction, which in itself is a significant finding at the .01-level**, according to the sign test. Five of the 14 goal rankings are significant by themselves. This is probably as good an agreement as could be expected under the circumstances (small samples, different population, and so on).

(2) Samples of managers in 14 countries answering to Haire et al.'s "managerial motivations and satisfactions" questions. The data are unfortunately only available in the form of combined "need category" scores.

A direct comparison is possible between the acquiescence in the Haire et al. and HERMES studies. In fact, this is also about the only aspect of the country differences in "need category" scores for which Haire et al. find an interpretation: the tendency in the developing countries Argentina, Chile, and India to rate *everything* as more important. The authors also attribute this to an acquiescence response set (Haire et al., 1966: 105). However, they do not correct their data for acquiescence. In their data table (1966: 100), the "security" column is based on one questionnaire item, "social" and "autonomy" each on two, and "esteem" and "self-actualization" each on three. The acquiescence score is the mean raw score across all 11 items; it can be reconstructed by taking the published values for security 1 × , social and autonomy

FIGURE 5.14   Comparison of Country Mean Scores on 14 Work Goals:
              IMEDE Managers Versus HERMES Employees

Work goal	Spearman rank correlation of standar-dized country mean scores across 15 countries : HERMES vs. IMEDE
Challenge	.42
Desirable area	.52*
Earnings	.31
Cooperation	.15
Training	.81***
Benefits	−.04
Recognition	−.06
Physical conditions	.47*
Freedom	.10
Employment security	.14
Advancement	.59**
Manager	.18
Use of skills	.08
Personal time	.63*
Median for 14 goals	.25

For numbers of respondents in IMEDE see Figure 5.13.

$2 \times$, esteem and self-actualization $3 \times$, and dividing by 11. The results are thus: DEN 5.30; GER 5.61; NOR 5.29; SWE 5.53; BEL 5.60; FRA 5.51; ITA 5.74; SPA 5.88; GBR 5.53; USA 5.62; ARG 6.34; CHL 6.16; IND 6.06; JAP 5.82. Higher scores mean greater acquiescence. If we rank the countries in order of acquiescence, we find a Spearman rho of .59* with the acquiescence levels (IMP scores) in HERMES (in HERMES, lower scores mean greater acquiescence, so I have reversed the sign of the correlation). The Haire et al. acquiescence level also rank-correlate − .59* with IDV (high IDV, less acquiescence). It seems, therefore, that the acquiescence phenomenon is reasonably stable across different populations and questionnaire items.

It is possible to clean the Haire et al. need importance scores from acquiescence. After doing this, I have correlated them in Figure 5.15 with the four HERMES indices. Only IDV is strongly correlated: In more individualist (and more developed) countries, security ("the feeling of security in my management position") is less important and autonomy ("the authority connected with" and "the opportunity for independent thought and action in my management position") is more important ($r = .60*$ in both cases). The pattern probably would have been richer had I been able to go back to the country mean scores *per item* and to group the items according to their own ecological dimensions, rather than to the Maslowian straitjacket.

(3) Samples of managers in 12 countries doing the IRGOM exercise "Life Goals." Earlier, Alexander et al. (1971) published U.S. mean goal rankings for 450 managers from six countries; we see, for example, that U.S. managers score relatively high on "leadership" and "wealth" but low on "affection," "service," and "duty."

From the material for a forthcoming book, Dr. Bass kindly made available to me the "Life Goals" scores for 3082 managers from 12 countries (Hofstede, 1978e, Table 4). The samples

FIGURE 5.15   Zero-Order and Multiple Correlations of Five Haire et al.
Need Importance Subscales for 14 Countries, After
Standardization, Across Four Ecological Indices

Haire et al. subscale	Zero-order product moment correlation across 14 countries with ecological index				Squared multiple correla- tion with all four indices R^2
	PDI	UAI	IDV	MAS	
security (1 item)	.34	.12	-.60*	.13	.48
social (2 items)	-.05	.15	-.03	-.09	.08
esteem (3 items)	.09	.04	.05	.18	.04
autonomy (2 items)	-.46*	-.55*	.60*	-.14	.45
self-actualization (3 items)	.07	.29	-.04	-.14	.21

The 14 countries are ARG, BEL, CHL, DEN, FRA, GBR, GER, IND, ITA, JAP, NOR, SPA, SWE, USA.
A stepwise regression shows no sizable second-order correlations.

are of a very respectable size. There is no problem of acquiescence, as the goals were ranked by the respondents; the data are therefore ipsative (that is, they add up to a constant for each country). I performed on the data matrix an ecological factor analysis; there were two strong factors (eigenvalues 3.2 and 2.8), together explaining 54 percent of the variance. After orthogonal rotation I obtained the following results:

Factor 1 (factor variance 28%)   *Factor 2* (factor variance 26%)
hedonism-skill   assertiveness-service

Positive   *Positive*
.87 pleasure   .86 leadership
.77 security   .85 independence
.72 affection   .57 self-realization

Negative   *Negative*
-.74 expertness   -.92 service
-.58 prestige
-.56 duty

No loading of .40 or over on either factor:
     wealth (-.20 on factor 1).

The labels "hedonism-skill" and "assertiveness-service" are, of course, mine. "Security" in the Life Goals exercise is formulated as "to achieve a secure and stable position in work and financial situation," so it pertains to individual financial security.

Figure 5.16 lists the factor scores for the 12 countries or areas and their Spearman rank correlations with the HERMES indices (where Bass combined countries into areas, I have weighted the HERMES index scores according to the population sizes of the countries). We find

FIGURE 5.16   Factor Scores Found in an Ecological Analysis of IRGOM
Life Goals Data,Correlated with HERMES Indices

Country or area	Bass IRGOM data.- factor scores on:	
	hedonism-skill	assertiveness - service
U.S.A.	.32	.58
Great Britain	1.42	-.17
Netherlands	.02	-1.14
Belgium	-.31	-.18
Germany, Austria	-.27	1.71
Scandinavia	1.35	-.54
France	.10	-.30
Italy	1.40	.49
Spain, Portugal	-.42	-1.02
Latin America	-.92	-.44
India	-1.72	-.92
Japan	-.97	1.92
Spearman rank correlation with :		
PDI	-.66***	-.24
UAI	-.49	.15
IDV	.76***	.18
MAS	-.03	.84***

Signs of factor scores for IRGOM data have been reversed so that positive scores mean high
importance of goals with positive loading on the factor.
The matrix of base data has been taken from Hofstede (1978e: Table 4). Since then, the base data
were published also in Bass and Burger (1979).

that hedonism-skill correlates strongly with IDV (rho = .76***) and assertiveness-service with
MAS (rho = .84***).

*(4) Samples of students in 6 countries answering Bass and Franke's (1972)
organizational success questionnaire (total number of respondents 1009).* The matrix
of country mean scores on the 12 items shows no evidence of differences in acquiescence level
among countries, so it is not necessary to control for this. A factor analysis of the six-country,
12-item matrix shows that there are three strong factors in the data (with a matrix of this type in
which the number of variables exceeds the number of countries, the percentage of variance

"explained" tends to be inflated; however, the analysis does show the structure in the data. Rather than reporting the amount of variance "explained" by each factor, I list below the strength of the ecological intercorrelations of the variables associated with the factor). The factors are:

(1) Sharing in decision-making, openly committing oneself, making political alliances, and *not* witholding information (ecological intercorrelations between .28 and .86 with a median of .71). I have called this "openness versus secrecy."
(2) Establishing mutual objectives, leveling with others, arranging group discussions, *not* bluffing, *not* maintaining social distance (ecological intercorrelations between .39 and .90 with a median of .58). I have called this "group versus distance."
(3) Fostering mutual trust, *not* compromising-but-delaying, *not* initiating-but-retarding actions (ecological intercorrelations between .36 and .75 with a median of .54). I have called this "trust versus delay."

There is therefore, no "social" versus "political" dichotomy in the ecological data, as Bass and Fanke assumed. Figure 5.17 shows factor scores for the six countries on the three factors which have subsequently been correlated with the four HERMES indices. We find one significant correlation: of individualism with the "secrecy" end of the "openness versus secrecy" dimension (r = −.91***).

(5) Samples of students in six countries answering Morris' (1956) "Ways to Live" questionnaire. Data from a total of over 3700 male students are available for Canada, China (collected in 1948), India, Japan, Norway, and the United States; the smallest sample, for

FIGURE 5.17   Country Scores on Three Factors Found in Bass and Franke's (1972) Organizational Success Study, Correlated with HERMES Indices

Countries	Openness versus secrecy	Group versus distance	Trust versus delay
France	1.14	.45	−.97
Great Britain	−1.17	.39	−.83
Germany (Federal Rep.)	.41	.05	−.69
Netherlands	−.40	−1.93	.13
Sweden	1.00	.10	1.41
U.S.A.	−.99	.95	.95
product moment correlation with :			
PDI	.41	.20	−.48
UAI	.45	−.01	−.63
IDV	−.91**	.17	.16
MAS	−.46	.59	−.55

For data see Bass and Franke (1972).

Norway, is 149. I have cleaned the 6 × 13 (six countries, 13 ways) matrix from acquiescence (the tendency to score everything as more of less important) by standardizing the 13 scores for each country. I then factor-analyzed the "ways." The factor analysis shows that there are two clear factors in the matrix:

(1) Ways 4, 7, 8, and 12: "Experience festivity and solitude in alteration," "Integrate action, enjoyment and contemplation," "Live with wholesome, carefree enjoyment," and "Chance adventuresome deeds," as opposed to ways 2, 3, 6, and 10: "Cultivate independence of persons and things," "Show sympathetic concern for others," "Constantly master changing situations," and "Control the self stoically" (ecological intercorrelations between .38 and .95 with a median of .73). I have called this dimension "enjoyment versus duty".

(2) Ways 5 and 13: "Act and enjoy life through group participation" and "Obey the cosmic purposes," as opposed to ways 1, 9, and 11: "Preserve the best that man has obtained," "Wait in quiet receptivity," and "Meditate on the inner life" (ecological intercorrelations between −.23 and .73 with a median of .46). I have called this dimension "engagement versus withdrawal."

Figure 5.18 shows factor scores for the six countries on the two factors, with their correlations with the HERMES indices, taking "Hong Kong" for "China." We find again one significant correlation: of IDV with "enjoyment" (r = .73).

FIGURE 5.18 Country Scores on Two Dimensions Found in Morris' (1956) Ways to Live Study, Correlated with HERMES Indices

Countries	Enjoyment versus duty	Engagement versus withdrawal
Canada	1.14	−.48
China (Hong Kong)	−.14	2.02
India	−.65	−.24
Japan	−1.39	−.59
Norway	−.11	−.52
U.S.A.	1.15	−.19
product moment correlation with :		
PDI	−.53	.49
UAI	−.52	−.59
IDV	.73 *	−.65
MAS	−.33	.03

For data see Morris (1956: Table 8).

(6) Samples of engineers in the United States and Germany studied by Preiss (1971). See Chapter 4. Figure 5.19 lists the differences in scores between countries which Preiss obtained using 12 out of the 14 HERMES work goal items. The goals loading on the "Individualism" factor have been underlined. On the IDV index, HERMES respondents in the United States score considerably higher (91) than in Germany (67). If we compare the HERMES United States-Germany differences with those found by Preiss in Figure 5.19, we see, first, that they tend to follow the same order (rank correlation .68**). Six goals in Preiss' data show United States-Germany differences in agreement with the IDV difference between the countries; two goals with moderate loadings on IDV, challenge and freedom, are more important in Germany, whereas the IDV difference would predict the opposite. But then in the HERMES data (on which the IDV dimension is based), even for three goals (including freedom) the United States-Germany difference does not follow the overall IDV pattern. Preiss' data therefore support the stronger individualism in the United States even more than the HERMES data themselves.

FIGURE 5.19   Work Goal Importance Score Differences Between the
                United States and Germany According to HERMES Data
                and to the Study of Engineers by Preiss (1971)

Work goal	HERMES, 1967-'73 standard scores (Appendix 3)	Preiss, 1971 p. 33-37 raw scores
Desirable area	+ 216 (a)	+.27 (a)
Personal time	+ 80 (a)	+.24 (a)
Challenge	+ 77 (a)	-.14 (c)
Cooperation	+ 38 (c)	-.30 (a)
Use of skills	+ 17 (c)	-.07 (a)
Recognition	− 7	-.07
Manager	− 11	+.18
Training	− 50 (a)	-.58 (a)
Earnings	− 54	-.34
Physical conditions	− 69 (a)	-.14 (a)
Freedom	− 84 (c)	-.41 (c)
Employment security	− 118	-.30
Spearman rank correlation	.68**	

+ more important in the United States.
− more important in Germany.
Work goals loading on the Individualism factor have been underlined.
(a) = a difference between the United States and Germany corresponding to the difference in IDV scores between the two countries.
(c) = a difference between the United States and Germany in a sense counter to the difference in IDV scores between the countries.

The IDV Index Versus Seven Geographical,
Economic, and Demographic Indicators

Our seven standard indicators (GNP, GNG, LAT, POP, PGR, PDN, and ORG; see Figure 2.7) should now be correlated with IDV. We have already found the suggestion of a positive relationship between individualism and economic development (GNP) in various classical studies; we also found a positive relationship between individualism and Organization Size (ORG) suggested in the work of Ingham (1970). I find no theoretical base to predict any other correlation with IDV, except that if IDV correlates with GNP and ORG, it will most likely also correlate with the other variables in the GNP-ORG cluster (see page 89): Latitude (LAT) and (with negative sign) Population Growth (PGR).

Figure 5.20 lists the actual correlations and multiple and stepwise regressions with the seven indicators, again for all 40 countries, for the 19 wealthier ones (1970 GNP/capita over $1300) and for the 21 poorer ones.

FIGURE 5.20   Product Moment Correlations and Multiple and Stepwise Regression Across Countries of IDV Scores with Seven System-Level Indicators

Indicator	Zero-order correlations with IDV scores across		
	All 40 countries	21 poorer countries	19 wealthier countries
GNP	.82***	.19	.45*
GNG	.12	.01	-.66***
LAT	.75***	.51**	.06
POP	-.03	.34	.23
PGR	-.63***	-.30	-.01
PDN	-.07	-.25	-.15
ORG	.72***	.56**	.37
Squared multiple correlation with all seven R^2	.80	.55	.74
Order of indicators in stepwise regression, cumulative R^2, and sign of coefficient	1. .68 +GNP	1. .31 + ORG	1. .45 - GNG
	2. .75 + LAT	2. .50 + LAT	2. .66 + POP
	3. .78 + ORG		

For definition of indicators see Figure 2.7.

If we compare Figure 5.20 with the corresponding table for PDI, Figure 3.16, we see (not surprisingly) that IDV is mostly correlated (with opposite sign) with the same indicators as PDI, only more so. The .82*** correlation between IDV and GNP is the highest between any of the HERMES indices and any of the seven indicators.

Geographical latitude (LAT), in the stepwise regression for 40 countries adds another seven percent to the prediction of IDV. Colder countries tend to be more individualistic even if we control for wealth; this is especially true for the poorer countries, not for the 19 that are already wealthy. We can argue, in the same way as was done in Figure 3.8, that colder climates force people to show more individual initiative in order to survive.

Organization size (ORG), as predicted, contributes independently to the prediction of IDV across the full set of countries and in the poorer countries; the effect is not noticeable in the wealthier ones. ORG is one indicator which correlates in the stepwise regression with IDV only, not with PDI; organization size affects (negatively) the dependence on the organization, not the dependence on the boss.

In the wealthier countries we find IDV to be negatively related to economic growth (GNG). This was not predicted. It seems that once a country has obtained wealth, having remained *less* individualistic helps it to develop faster. Economic growth, of course, has been measured over the 1960–1970 period; Figure 4.16 showed that for other periods we find different figures, especially if major wars are included. Therefore, the relationship between individualism and slower economic growth is a short-term relationship, linked to specific historical conditions. On the other hand, it is very likely that the relationship between wealth and individualism is long-term and more universal. The negative correlation with GNG shows that at least over the 1960–1970 period, wealth preceded individualism, and not the other way around.

The relationship with Population Size (POP), which we found for PDI, does not repeat itself for IDV, except as a second-order effect for the wealthier countries; population size is associated more with dependence on the bosses than with dependence on the organization, which is contrary to what we saw for organization size.

Correlation of IDV with
Other National Indicators

(1) Cutright's (1968) data on social mobility. For 12 countries, Cutright published coefficients of "Occupational Inheritance" between fathers and sons based on the 1950s (between 1949 and 1963). The coefficients (Yule's Q) express the shift from fathers in manual occupations to sons in nonmanual occupations and vice versa, controlling for structural changes (that is, for mobility that is simply the result of a shift in the overall distribution of occupations to manual and nonmanual strata between generations). The coefficient is 1.000 when all sons, to the extent that the overall distribution of occupations allows it, are in their father's stratum; it is 0.000 when sons choose their occupations regardless of their father's stratum.

Figure 5.21 (first column) demonstrates that Cutright's occupational inheritance rank correlates –.71** with IDV and much more so than with either PDI or GNP per se. This means that more individualistic countries tend to show lower coefficients—that is, greater mobility. Cutright's data do not refer to the mere numerical strength of the middle class (which coincides mostly with the nonmanual occupations); in fact, the influence of this is eliminated in his coefficient. His data show the *ease of access* to middle-class positions for people, regardless of their father's profession: individual careers not being constrained by family background.

(2) Miller's (1960) data on social mobility. A more primitive measure, not controlling for structure changes, of social mobility in 11 countries is Miller's Index of Inequality of opportunity, which measures the ease of access of sons to the category of nonmanual workers if their father is either a nonmanual or a manual worker. The index is 100 for perfect equality of access and increases with greater inequality. It correlates –.50 with IDV, which stays just below the .05 level of significance (Figure 5.21, second column).

FIGURE 5.21   Country Index Scores for 12 Countries on Occupational
Inheritance, Versus Four HERMES Indices

Countries in order of IDV-score	Cutright[a] occupational inheritance score	Miller[b] index of inequality
U.S.A.	.685	275
Great Britain	.614	234
Netherlands	.684	290
Italy	.878	747
Denmark	.689	262
Sweden	.735	284
France	.759	256
Norway	.709	308
Germany (Federal Republic)	.777	355
Finland	.883	691
Japan	.768	297
Yugoslavia	.846	
Spearman rank correlations with HERMES indices		
PDI	.29	-.00
UAI	.64 *	.45
IDV	-.71 **	-.50[c]
MAS	.27	.15
GNP	-.44	-.45
Squared multiple correlation with PDI, UAI, IDV, MAS : R^2	.62	.67

[a]From Cutright (1968: 412), total population data.
[b]From Miller (1960: 36).
[c]The .05 significance limit is at .52.
A stepwise regression shows no sizable second-order correlations.

(3) Cutright's (1967) and Taylor and Hudson's (1972) data on sectorial inequality. Cutright's data, dating from the early 1950s, are reproduced in the first column of Figure 5.22. Data from the early 1960s listed in Taylor and Hudson's *World Handbook of Political and Social Indicators* are reproduced in the middle column of Figure 5.22.

The measure of income inequality between sectors of the economy used by both studies (and originally developed by Kuznets) compares the percentage of the labor force in eight sectors with the percentage of Gross Domestic Product produced by these sectors. Its numerical value is a "Gini coefficient" based on the "Lorenz curve," a graphical method used by economists to express inequality in distribution. Its minimum is zero (complete equality) and its maximum 100 (one sector gets all, others get nothing). Figure 5.22 shows, in both cases across 33 countries, the Gini coefficients to be primarily correlated with IDV (-.60***), more than with PDI or GNP per se.

(4) Taylor and Hudson's (1972) data on press freedom. These are based upon a doctoral dissertation by R. L. Lowenstein. The data measure the situation in the mid-1960s according to both native and nonnative judges, and were published by Taylor and Hudson (1972: Table 2.7). For 39 countries from the HERMES set they appear in the third column of

FIGURE 5.22   Country Index Scores on Sectoral Inequality and Press
Freedom, Versus Four HERMES Indices

Countries in order of IDV score	Cutright[a] sectoral inequality	Taylor–Hudson[b] sectoral inequality	Taylor–Hudson[c] press freedom
U.S.A.	12	12.2	2.72
Australia	8	8.5	2.53
Great Britain	6	5.0	2.37
Canada	12	19.9	2.78
Netherlands	15	10.2	3.02
New Zealand	11	–	2.24
Italy	15	22.2	1.98
Belgium	5	11.9	2.53
Denmark	13	15.4	2.65
Sweden	––	5.6	2.83
France	22	21.3	1.92
Ireland	6	24.7	2.37
Norway	19	23.7	3.06
Switzerland	–	–	3.06
Germany (Federal Republic)	11	12.2	2.43
South Africa	–	35.1	1.07
Finland	9	25.6	2.72
Austria	14	16.4	2.10
Israel	6	5.7	1.75
Spain	12	18.6	-.99
India	21	22.5	.98
Japan	9	14.9	2.44
Argentina	20	15.7	.92
Iran	–	–	-1.02
Brazil	29	36.4	1.25
Turkey	21	24.7	1.66
Greece	10	19.5	1.37
Philippines	16	37.9	2.66
Mexico	–	45.7	1.46
Yugoslavia	43	–	.08
Portugal	19	26.3	-1.42
Chile	23	37.1	1.19
Singapore	–	–	1.81
Thailand	34	43.0	.70
Taiwan	18	–	.61
Peru	45	39.8	2.76
Pakistan	17	21.2	-.01
Colombia	12	–	2.21
Venezuela	30	48.7	2.54

product moment correlation (sectoral inequality) and Spearman rank correlation (press freedom)				
PDI	.54 ***	.67 ***	-.38 **
UAI	.27	.22	-.40 **
IDV	-.60 ***	-.71 ***	.51 ***
MAS	-.34 *	.08	.10
GNP	-.49 ***	-.65 ***	.67 ***

squared multiple correlation with four indices R²	.51	.65	.30

order of indices in stepwise regression, cumulative R² and sign of coefficient	1. .36 −IDV 2. .45 −MAS	1. .51 −IDV 2. .60 +PDI	1. .26 +IDV

[a]Cutright (1967: 577). Period early 1950s. Figures are Gini indices—min. score 0, max. score 100.
[b]Taylor and Hudson (1972: Table 4.13). Period 1960–1965. Figures are Gini indices—min. score 0, max. score 100.
[c]Taylor and Hudson (1972: Table 2.7). Period mid-1960s. Figures are ratings by judges. Max. score 4.00, min. score −4.00.

Figure 5.22. Among the four HERMES indices, the Press Freedom Index rank-correlates primarily with IDV (.51***). However, the rank correlation with national wealth per se (GNP) is even stronger: 67.

NOTES

1. Differences in family structure are reflected in the words available in a language to describe kinship ties. See Chapter 1, note 31.

2. Across 74 less developed nations, Adelman and Morris (1967: 151) show a close relationship between their level of economic development and their "basic social organization": from strong tribal allegiances to extended family to nuclear family.

3. This applies to the twentieth century. For example, the time of the Reformation (sixteenth century) western countries, too, were collectivistic and were converted collectively.

4. And by the corresponding statistical data of Adelman and Morris; see note 2.

5. Others, such as Sayles (1964), have tried to defend U.S. big business against Whyte's attacks. Sayles is as much in favor of individualism as is Whyte, but he claims that big business fosters individualism rather than the opposite.

6. Martin and Lodge (1975) report on a survey among over 1800 readers of *Harvard Business Review,* on which "ideology" will prevail in the United States in 1985: the traditional individualistic one, or a new communitarian ideology. Of the respondents, 70 percent prefer individualism, but 73 percent expect that communitarianism will prevail in 1985. The survey expresses a fear of collectivism as an alien but inescapable force.

7. After standardization of the raw country mean scores: see Chapter 2.

8. Unlike in the case of PDI and UAI, a theoretical maximum and minimum score for IDV cannot be given. IDV is not based on scores for separate questions but on factor scores; through the factor analysis computation, the factor scores are automatically brought within a range which rarely exceeds ± 2.00; this corresponds to an index value range of 0–100.

9. For a goal-by-goal analysis of work goal differences between occupations see Hofstede (1979a).

10. In Chapter 2, Figure 2.4, the results are shown of an analysis of variance, carried out on the scores of individuals in HERMES manufacturing plants, of the difference between the importance of personal time and the importance of training (the reason for taking the difference is that this eliminates acquiescence). Besides the strong country effect, there are a weak occupation effect but strong sex and age effects. This, however, does not allow us to conclude on the relevance of the "individualism" concept for sex and age differences, as it uses only two of the goals and these combined.

11. A small study by Slocum et al. (1971) compares importance scores of Mexican versus U.S. glass workers. The Mexicans score everything much more important, which is in line with my data.

12. The IMP data (first column in Appendix 3, Table A3.1) show the highest scores, and so the least acquiescence, for Finland (IMP = 2.33). To Professor Osmo Wiio from Finland, who has done extensive survey research, I owe the remark that Finns seem to be a nation of flip-flops; they readily choose extreme answers on survey questions.

13. There is no correlation between the country mean scores for this belief (which is formulated as an ideological statement) and the importance of "earnings" as a personal work goal (A7). We see again the difference between a "value as the desirable" and a "value as the desired."

14. "Need importance" data were collected afterwards with the Haire et al. questionnaire or translations of it by Mozina (1969) in Yugoslavia and by Redding (1977) in eight Southeast Asian countries. I have not used the data from these studies because in Mozina's case I am not sure that the sample matches Haire et al.'s samples. Redding unfortunately only presents his

data in graphical form which makes them difficult to read; also, his data were collected through interview rather than by questionnaire.

15. I have written to Dr. Haire and Dr. Porter to gain access to the mean country data *per item*. Very unfortunately, Dr. Porter believes these data have been destroyed. It is my firm conviction that raw data for this type of study should always remain accessible to secondary analyses by others, if we take our contribution to scientific discovery seriously. What would happen if someone wanted to do a trend study over a 20-, 50-, or 100-year period?

16. Ajiferuke and Boddewyn (1970b) have tried ecological correlations of Haire et al. data with various national indicators. They used the total score on "attitudes and assumptions underlying management practices," however, (which I believe does not mean much, for some of its items are countercorrelated—see Figure 3.15) and the total score on "need importance" (which only measures acquiescence). The first correlates positively, the second negatively with national wealth and some related indices.

17. A fair amount of statistical research has been done on Morris' data. For example, Morris and Jones (1955) have shown that factor analyses of the scores of Americans show the same factors as those of Indians. Morris (1956: 194) relates these factors to Parsons and Shils' five pattern variables (see Chapter 1). In Chapter 1 we also saw that Osgood et al. (1961) analyzed the 13 "ways" with the semantic differential. Finally, Dempsey and Dukes (1966) have studied the coherence of Morris' lengthy formulation of the "ways" and proposed more coherent, shorter formulations.

18. This "way" is defined in the English version of the questionnaire as follows: "A person should let himself be used. Used by other persons in their growth, used by the great objective purposes in the universe which silently and irresistably achieve their goal. One should be a serene, confident, quiet vessel and instrument of the great dependable powers which move to their fulfillment." This statement, apparently, appealed very much to the Chinese students in 1948.

19. Converse's "East-West" dimension rank correlates .89* with PDI. This is not as easy to interpret; it opposes more book reading, movies, and radio and more time at work and traveling to it in higher PDI countries; more magazine reading, TV watching, social activities, home chores, conversation, and sleep in lower PDI countries. Converse sees in it a work-versus-free-time dimension (1972: 155).

20. The fact that GNP is expressed in dollars leads to predicting higher IDV scores for countries with relatively overvalued currency in 1970 (the United States and Switzerland) and the reverse for countries with undervalued currency (Great Britain and Italy).

Chapter 6

MASCULINITY

SUMMARY OF THIS CHAPTER

The fourth dimension along which national cultures can be shown to differ systematically has been called masculinity, with its opposite pole femininity. The duality of the sexes is a fundamental fact with which different societies cope in different ways; the issue is whether the biological differences between the sexes should or should not have implications for their roles in social activities. The sex role distribution common in a particular society is transferred by socialization in families, schools, and peer groups, and through the media. The predominant socialization pattern is for men to be more assertive and for women to be more nurturing. In organizations, there is a relationship between the perceived goals of the organization and the career possibilities for men and women; business organizations have "masculine" goals and tend to promote men; hospitals have more "feminine" goals and, at least on the nursing side, tend to promote women.

A review of survey data on the importance of work goals shows near consistency on men scoring advancement and earnings as more important, women interpersonal aspects, rendering service, and the physical environment as more important. The same kind of differences were found in HERMES data. Differences in work goal importance in HERMES among occupations and among countries contain a component or factor which opposes "masculine" to "feminine" goals. The factor score of the 40 countries on this factor has been used as the basis for a country Masculinity Index (MAS) which measures to what extent HERMES respondents in a country (of both sexes) tend to endorse goals usually more popular among men (high MAS) or among women (low MAS). Countries with higher MAS values also show greater differences in values between men and   women in the same jobs. The MAS index scale is correlated across countries with other questions in the HERMES questionnaire, with an indirect measure of work centrality in HERMES, and with survey data collected outside HERMES. MAS is correlated, together with low uncertainty avoidance, with need for achievement as measured by McClelland in a content analysis of 1925 children's books.

The various correlates of MAS have been assembled into a coherent picture of the "masculine" and "feminine" types of national culture. MAS is significantly negatively correlated with the percentage of women in professional and technical jobs, at least in the wealthier countries, and positively with the segregation of the sexes in higher education. It is also positively correlated both with allowed traffic speeds and with traffic deaths; and in Christian countries with Catholicism rather than with Protestantism. Finally, across wealthy countries it is correlated negatively with the percentage of GNP spent on government aid to third world countries. From all these data, an integrated picture has been developed of the masculinity and femininity societal norms, their likely origins, and their consequences for society at large, for ideology, and for organizations.

SEXES AND SEX ROLES

Absolute, Statistical, and Social Sex Differences

If the duality of life and death is nature's number one law, the duality of female and male, which governs procreation in all higher vegetal and animal species, is number two law and follows very closely. In human societies of all ages and levels of complexity, this nature-given fact has been one of the very first issues with which the society had to cope in its own specific way, and which profoundly affected a multitude of societal institutions: "The sex-role system is at the core of our cultural norms" (Chetwynd and Hartnett, 1978: 3).

The only difference between women and men which is absolute is that women bear children and men beget them. The biological differences between the sexes not immediately related to their roles in procreation are statistical rather than absolute: men are *on the average* taller and stronger (but many women are taller and/or stronger than many men), women have *on the average* greater finger dexterity and, for example, faster metabolism which makes them recover faster from fatigue.[1] These absolute and statistical biological differences are the same for all human societies; but these differences leave a wide margin for the actual division of roles in most activities between women and men. In a strict sense, only behaviors directly connected with procreation (childbearing and child-begetting) are "feminine" or "masculine." Yet, every society recognizes many other behaviors as more suitable to females or more suitable to males; however, these represent relatively arbitrary choices, mediated by cultural norms and traditions.

Of course, there is a common trend among the vast majority of societies, both traditional and modern, as to the distribution of sex roles apart from procreation: men must be more concerned with economic and other achievements and women must be more concerned with taking care of people in general and children in particular. It is not difficult to see how this role pattern fits with the biological sex roles: women first bear children and then breast-feed them, so they must stay with them. Anthropologist

Margaret Mead explains the dominant concern for achievement in men by the fact that men cannot bear children. She argues that women in every society attain a "sense of irreversible achievement" in giving birth to their children.[2] However, "the recurrent problem of civilization is to define the male role satisfactorily enough—whether it be to build gardens or raise cattle, kill game or kill enemies, build bridges or handle bank-shares—so that the male may in the course of his life reach a solid sense of irreversible achievement" (Mead, 1962a: 158).

The common pattern of male assertiveness and female nurturance leads to male dominance at least in matters of politics and, usually, of economic life; within the household, whether this be a nuclear or an extended family group, different societies show different distributions of power over the sexes.

Antropology, psychology, and political science confirm the male assertiveness-female nurturance pattern. For example, Barry et al. (1957) found in a secondary analysis of anthropological reports of 110 mostly nonliterate societies that, in the vast majority of cases, girls are socialized toward nurturance and responsibility and sometimes obedience; boys are socialized toward achievement and self-reliance. McClelland (1975: chap. 3) reviewed the U.S. psychological literature for evidence of psychological differences between the sexes. Universally in the U.S. data, boys and men tend to be more assertive; girls and women are more sensitive to social interdependence. Spenner and Featherman (1978: 395ff.) reviewed the U.S. sociological literature, which invariably shows a strong relationship between sex and achievement ambitions, in the sense of lower ambitions for women. Williams et al. (1977) report on a comparative study of sex-role stereotypes in Great Britain, Ireland, and the United States; they show close agreement between male and female judges and among the three countries. Male behavior is associated with autonomy, aggression, exhibition, and dominance; female behavior with nurturance, affiliation, helpfulness, and humility. The pervasiveness of the common sex role pattern is shown in cases where deliberate attempts were made to abolish it, as in Israeli kibbutzim; even here, quite a bit of it has survived—kibbutz women prefer maternal activities to participating as fully as men in the general assembly and kibbutz committees (Quinn, 1977: 191–192).

On the other hand, there is evidence of variations on the common sex role pattern. Mead gives the example of the Iatmul and the Tchambuli, two New Guinea tribes living close to one another, of which the first shows the usual pattern of male aggressiveness and female nurturance, while the second presents a reverse pattern of female initiative in practical matters while the nonaggressive males concentrate on art and theater (Mead, 1962a: 102–107).

Le Vine (1966), when discussing the influence of male labor migration on African family relationships, show how in East and South African families the absent husbands still tend to control the larger share of family income while placing an increased burden of work on the wives; the traditional dominance of the males has not been challenged. In parts of West Africa, however, there always was a tradition of an independent role of the women in trading products; on the basis of this, male labor migration allowed wives to attain independent incomes and seriously challenged the ideal of male dominance in marital relations. In these societies we find expressions of male fears of female witchcraft, antifeminism, envy of women, and feelings of sexual inadequacy among men (1966: 192).[3]

Bem (1974) has developed a Sex Role Inventory of adjectives which a sample of male and female U.S. students judged to be more socially desirable in American society for one sex than for the other. Bem's Inventory contains both a "feminine" and a "masculine" scale. In later studies (Bem, 1975; Bem et al., 1976), self-descriptions of U.S. students on these scales were collected and validated in laboratory experiments. On the basis of their self-descriptions, students are divided into four types: "masculine," "feminine," "androgynous" (scoring both types of characteristics) and "undifferentiated" (scoring neither). From 444 male students, 55 percent scored masculine only and 11 percent feminine only; from 279 female students, 54 percent scored feminine only and 20 percent masculine only; the others were androgynous or undifferentiated. Thus, only just over half of these respondents correspond in their own eyes to the sex trait stereotype (Bem, 1975: 636). Typical items from the masculine scale are "aggressive," "ambitious," and "competitive"; typical items from the feminine scale are "affectionate," "compassionate," and "understanding." Masculine and androgynous persons yielded less to pressure to conform than did feminines; feminine and androgynous persons showed more supportive behavior toward a lonely fellow student than did masculines. Bem's studies show that actual behavior need not correspond to the stereotype, and that differences, here too, are statistical rather than absolute. It may be that the U.S. student population of the mid-1970s is more tolerant of non-sex-typical behavior than are many others; Newson et al. (1978: 47), citing their experiences in Nottingham, England, state that "experimentation with novel sex-role relationships is . . . likely to be taken seriously only by a minority in the highly educated middle class."

However, the fact that an active feminist movement exists in a number of countries (albeit predominantly the wealthy ones) shows that some women, at least (and some men, too) no longer take the traditional pattern of male dominance for granted, and try to develop alternative role distributions.

In human thinking, the issue of the equality or inequality between the sexes is as old as religion, ethics, and philosophy themselves. In Genesis, the first book of the Judao-Christian Old Testament which contains the myths of creation (and which was codified in the fifth century B.C.), we find *two* conflicting versions of the creation of the sexes. The first, Genesis 1: 27–28, states:

> So God created man in his own image, in the image of God created he him; male and female created he them. And God blessed them, and God said to them, Be fruitful, and multiply, and replenish the earth, and subdue it.

This text suggests equal partnership between the sexes. In the second version, Genesis 2: 8ff (which is supposed to have derived from a different source document), we find the story of the garden in Eden, in which God first put "the man" alone. Then, in Genesis 2: 18, it states:

> And the Lord God said, It is not good that the man should be alone: I will make him a help meet for him.[4]

Then follows the story of the Woman being made from one of Adam's ribs. This text gives clear priority to the male partner and defines the woman as "a help meet" (that is, appropriate) for him; it justifies a society in which there is a male dominance.

In *The Republic*, Plato in the fourth century B.C. offers a design for an ideal state. In this state there is an elite class, the Guardians, who are the best warriors. In selecting Guardians, Plato does not want to discriminate between men and women. He lets Socrates (to whom the dialogue is ascribed) argue at length that of course there is a great natural difference between men and women, but that this difference is irrelevant to the criteria that should be applied to Guardians:

> We never meant that natures are the same or different in an unqualified sense, but only with reference to the kind of sameness or difference which is relevant to various employments . . . Then if men or women as a sex appear to be qualified for different skills or occupations . . . we shall assign these to each accordingly; but if the only difference apparent between them is that the female bears and the male begets, we shall not admit that it is a difference relevant for our purpose, but shall still maintain that our male and female Guardians ought to follow the same occupations [Lee, 1974: 232–233].

It must be admitted that the actors in Plato's dialogues are all men. Also, Plato argues later that

> In general the one sex [he means the male] is much better at everything than the other. A good many women, it is true, are better than a good many men at a good many things. But the general rule is as you stated it [he means that men do things better; 1974: 234].

But at least Plato sees the social role of the sexes as equal in principle, and he reduces inequality to a statistical issue.[5] In this respect he comes closer to modern feminist positions than, for example, the Roman Catholic church even today.

Sex-Role Socialization

Socialization is the process by which culture patterns are transferred from one generation to the next (Figure 1.4). As only such a small part of sex role differentiation is biologically determined, the stability of sex role patterns is almost entirely a matter of socialization. Socialization means that both men and women learn their place in society and, once they have learned it, the majority of them *want it that way*. We find the same process here as we found in Chapter 3 for the relationship between superiors and subordinates (de La Boétie's "voluntary servitude"): in male-dominated societies, most women are accessary to the male dominance.

A very important part of sex role socialization takes place in the family, whether this be the nuclear family of the modern industrial society, the extended family of more traditional societies, the one-parent family more and more common in "post-industrial" society, the commune, or even the day nursery which partly replaces the family. In all these institutions, children see adults of different sexes (but mostly females) fulfill certain roles; they more or less quickly become aware of their own sex category, and look for adults to identify with. Parsons and Bales (1955) describe the American nuclear family as the functional socialization center of American middle-class society in which boys are socialized to perform "instrumental" tasks and girls to do "expressive" tasks. Feminists who want to change sex roles criticize the family (and Parsons) for this supposed built-in traditionalism (Rapoport, 1978: 66ff). The problem is, however, that traditional patterns in a society are transmitted in alternative institutions as well; it is not the family as such that transfers a certain role pattern but the specific kind of values and behaviors of each of the adult members—and this holds equally in nonfamily socializing institutions which do not automatically work out differently. Weinreich (1978: 26–27) quotes studies about the backgrounds of women who came to adopt nontraditional roles (feminists and professional women): "The single most consistent feature of the backgrounds of both groups of women is having a mother who worked or who was at least orientated to a life beyond the wife and mother role." But just the fact that a woman has a job does not necessarily change a traditional sex role pattern; and a "housewife" role does not necessarily mean socializing the children toward male dominance.

McClelland (1975) illustrates the importance of the total set of values of the adult family members, women and men alike, on the sex role socialization in the following quote about his own experiences when as a young man he came into contact with the American Quaker subculture:

> [T]he women seemed to be so much more self-assured and important in the community than even the career-oriented feminists I had known at Illinois Woman's College. They were vigorous, self-confident, and obviously influential. They were wives and mothers, for the most part, and not career women, but many had strong intellectual and artistic interests, even though few of them had gone to college. I realized that my feminist upbringing had led me to take it for granted that the "housewife" role would be weak or passive, a second best that many women had to choose. But here were women who gloried in their role, regarding it in no way as a hindrance: yet I could not dismiss them as simple homebodies. As I wondered how this could be, I realized that Quakerism as a religion gives strong support to the sharing rather than the assertive life style . . . I found the emphasis on career muted among both men and women . . . The life goal was to develop a certain character and to live in a simple, harmonious way rather than to achieve a career of great significance. It is the only society I have ever entered in America in which the first question asked of a man is not "What do you do?", but "Who are you?". In fact I discovered that many of the women seemed to have only a very vague idea of what their men did. Though they realized of course that it was necessary to have an occupation and to earn money, that was not the most salient or valued feature of a person's life, as it is nearly everywhere else in contemporary America [McClelland, 1975: 108–109].

In this case the entire subculture, women and men alike, endorses values that elsewhere in United States would be seen as more "feminine." Greater sex role equality cannot be attained only when women are more assertive or instrumentally oriented, but also when men are more nurturing or expressive oriented.

Sex-role socialization of course continues in peer groups and in schools. The latter have received a lot of attention as socializing agencies (Lobban, 1978), because school results show so clearly the effect of sex role socialization: Girls and boys enter primary schools with equal intellectual endowment, but at the end of secondary schools girls stay behind or drop out; which appears to be a matter of lower ambition, not lesser abilities. A recurrent theme in U.S. research is the fear of success in academic achievement which is frequent among girls and almost absent among boys; it seems to develop between ages 13 and 16 (1978: 51). From Norway, Gjesme (1973) reports among seventh-grade girls a tendency to collectively underestimate their abilities. Again in the United States, Deaux and Emswiller (1974) did a laboratory study with undergraduate students who were observing male and female actors perform a traditionally masculine task. Both male and female observers tended to attribute success to skill for the male actors and to luck for the females. This asymmetry of sex roles in the later part of the school education is partly attributed to a "hidden curriculum" (Lobban, 1978: 52) which represents the unofficial and often unintentional aspects of learning, present not so much in the course content as in the behaviors of teachers and, I would add, probably even more of class peers and parents. I tend to believe that the asymmetry at school is to a considerable extent a retarded effect of early socialization in the family. If there are opposing socializing forces in families and school, the family usually wins.

Sex-role socialization, finally, is furthered through the media; starting with a children's literature which usually pictures children and adults in traditional sex roles, and reinforced by TV and the press; Women's journals, in particular, are obvious sex role socializers.

Sex-role socialization is not necessarily consistent. A study by Komarovsky (1976) among male U.S. students shows considerable strain between new equalitarian sex-role norms on the one side and a deeper need for adhering to a traditional male role on the other: Men want women to be intellectual companions, but at the same time some feel threatened by women if they are really intelligent and assertive; many men want wives who are intellectually inferior to them. It is likely that these more traditional role concepts are the residues of early life socialization.

Sex Roles in Organizations

All organizations have a division of labor, and most have members of both sexes. In organizational practice, the division of labor and the division of sex roles tend to be linked in ways which Plato would have considered irrelevant (see the earlier quote); the "proper" division of labor over the sexes is largely a matter of convention (Acker and Van Houten, 1974; Hartnett, 1978). Jobs are given stereotypes of being "masculine" or "feminine" but these may differ from one country or even organization to another and over time; examples are policeman, soldier, dentist, pharmacist, nurse.

The goals of organizations affect the distribution of labor over the sexes. Business organizations have goals of achievement which concur with the achieving role of the male. It is not surprising that they are almost always led by men, and that their climate is set by men.

> The model of the successful manager in our culture is a masculine one. The good manager is aggressive, competitive, firm, just. He is not feminine; he is not soft or yielding or dependent or intuitive in the womanly sense. The very expression of emotion is widely viewed as a feminine weakness that would interfere with effective business processes [McGregor, 1967: 23].

This implies a bias against female managers; and it also fits with the general pattern of male dominance in most societies that "males are higher than females and are not expected to take orders from females" (Acker and Van Houten, 1974: 152; Kroeber-Keneth, 1955: 161–162). Perceptions and evaluations of manager behavior by observers are affected by the manager's sex: Bartol and Butterfield (1976) showed two

versions of descriptions of manager behavior to (male and female) American business students, in which the managers' names indicated males or females, but no other
differences were present. Students (regardless of their sex) evaluated managers with
men's names more positively on "initiating structure" and managers with women's
names more positively on "consideration."

In contrast to business organizations, hospitals have a quite different set of goals,
which concurs more with the traditional, nurturing female role. Women do take, and
always have taken, management positions in hospitals, at least on the nursing side. A
study in the Netherlands by Philipsen and Cassee (1965) compares scores of leadership styles as rated by subordinates for matrons in hospitals, middle managers in
industrial companies, and section heads in government offices. Hospital matrons
receive the highest scores on "initiating structure" and the lowest on "consideration"
from their subordinates (of course, "initiating structure" for nurses may be seen as
"considerate" toward patients). The data from Philipsen and Cassee show the con-
text-dependence of the association of "masculine" with "initiating structure" and
"feminine" with "consideration." Similar resistance as can be found against female
managers in business organizations sometimes exists against male "matrons" in
hospitals (although in the Netherlands the prejudice against male *nurses* has in recent
years disappeared).

The management literature of the 1950s and 1960s stresses the importance of a
manager's "consideration" toward subordinates in certain types of jobs. In such jobs,
female managers statistically should be more effective than men, if they ever get the
chance to prove it. Sex bias which bars women (or men) from certain jobs because of
tradition obviously affects the functioning of the organization (Acker and Van
Houten, 1974). Hartnett (1978: 90), writing in Great Britain, aptly remarks:

> It is not a little fascinating that, when the language of expertise is translated, it transpires
> that improvements in the climate and structure of organizations, recently being sug-
> gested by organization development experts . . . bear an uncanny resemblance to the
> characteristics specified by a member of the Women's Liberation Movement as being
> necessary, from the other end of the spectrum, in the organization to which she belongs.

Organization Development (O.D.) where it stresses openness and expression of
emotion represents a counter-culture in the modern business world which fits traditional feminine values better than masculine ones.

The effect of the mixing up of the division of labor and of sex roles is an uneven
distribution of men and women over the different levels of the work force and pay
scales. Hartnett (1978: 83) criticizes the "gatekeeper" activity of males in personnel
departments in selection and promotion (in Great Britain), but this looks like an
oversimplification, making one group the scapegoat for an almost worldwide cultural phenomenon to which even the victims are accessary. The economic systems of
many countries are kept in balance only by women doing menial jobs and being paid
less than men even if they do the same jobs. In wealthier countries, they are often
considered "cake-winners" rather than breadwinners (1978: 82). As stated earlier,
the fact that women have jobs rather than stay at home in itself means no reversal of a
traditional sex role distribution pattern; it may even reinforce it.

SEX DIFFERENCES IN WORK GOALS

Data from the Literature

Earlier in this book I referred several times to the measurements of "work goal importance" which are part of the HERMES research but are also found in the literature. When the answers of men and women on "work goal importance" scores are compared, significant differences tend to appear. A review of research in the area of job attitudes by Herzberg et al. (1957) summarizes the results of nine U.S. studies about sex differences in work goals (1957: 52):

More important for men   *More important for women*
Advancement   Supervision
Earnings   Social aspects of the job
                                   Working conditions
                                   Working hours
                                   Ease of work

Crowley et al. (1973) quote Herzberg et al. plus four U.S. studies from the 1960s, and conclude the following:

1. Women are more concerned than men with the social aspects of their jobs, particularly with having good relationships with co-workers.

2. It is often said that women are less intrinsically oriented than men [the authors mean that they attach less importance to such things as job content] but the empirical support for this is slight and inconsistent.

3. Sex differences in work goal importance are small and tend to disappear when the confounding effects of educational and/or occupational level are removed [Crowley et al., 1973: 446].

Crowley et al. then analyze the data from the 1969–1970 U.S. Survey of Working Conditions on sex differences in work goal importance. They find for this representative sample of the U.S. working population the following significant differences:

More important for men   *More important for women*
Freedom   Co-workers
                                   Clearly defined responsibilities
                                   Working hours
                                   Working conditions
                                   Convenient travel to and from work

For the question "my co-workers are friendly and helpful" a control was tried on whether the job *demanded* significant interaction (which was more the case for women than for men); but even after this control, the observed sex difference in the desire for friendly and helpful co-workers remained (1973: 454).

The analysis by Crowley et al. does not include a work goal question on "promotion" which was eliminated from the report on the 1969–1970 Survey of Working Conditions because it did not load on any of the five major "work goals" factors. However, on another question (not in the work goal importance format) Crowley et al. found that significantly more women than men answered that they never wanted to be promoted.[6]

Manhardt (1972) surveyed 365 male and 301 female college graduates who were hired by the Prudential Insurance Company of America between 1966 and 1970—a group well matched by educational level. He found the following differences:

More important for men

Advancement

Supervising others

Responsibility

Working on problems central
    to the organization

Earnings

Creativeness

More important for women

Congenial associates

Ample leisure time

Relationship with superiors

Physical conditions

Variety

Through a factor analysis of total data, Manhardt divided his 25 goals into three factors: (1) careers, which included the first five goals of the above list of "more important for men"; (2) working environment and relationships, which included the first four goals of the above list of "more important for women"; and (3) autonomy and self-actualization, which included mostly items which did not differentiate between women and men, plus "creativeness" and "variety" which differentiate in opposite directions. Manhardt also found that "when the female sample was restricted to only those who rated a career first among their major life satisfactions, the sex differences, including those in job characteristics not directly related to career orientation, were almost completely eliminated" (1972: 367).

Bartol (1976) collected work goal importance scores on 25 goals from 175 male and female U.S. business students and female psychology students. Again, females scored interpersonal relationship and a comfortable environment as more important than did men, but differences between female business and female psychology students were larger than between business males and business females.

A random survey of 329 Dutch youths between age 14 and 24 in November 1976 conducted by McCann-Erickson (1977) asked, among other things, about the most important factors in choosing a job. Girls and boys did not differ in the frequency of their first choice: interesting work. Girls more than boys chose "helping others" and "able to make friends"; boys more than girls chose "exciting, challenging work"; "advancement opportunities"; "money"; and "long-term security."

In a survey of a representative sample of 1450 French youths between age 14 and 24 in the summer of 1977 conducted by IFOP (1977: 47–48) a question was included about work goals. Girls and boys again did not differ in the frequency of their first choice: interesting work. Girls more than boys chose a congenial working atmosphere and rendering service to others; boys more than girls chose high earnings and responsibility.

So far, the literature suggests the following:

(1) Sex differences in work goal importance may easily be confounded with educational and/or occupational differences.
(2) In samples from the United States, the Netherlands, and France we find that women compared with men tend to score the interpersonal aspects, rendering service, and sometimes the physical environment as more important, and advancement, sometimes independence, responsibility, and earnings as less important; as far as job content is concerned, women score no different from men, although they may value different detail aspects.

There is no indication that it makes sense to translate the sex differences in work goal importance in Herzbergian terms (one sex is not more "intrinsic-oriented" than the other) or in Maslowian terms (one sex is not further advanced in a hierarchy of human needs, although there may be differences at the intermediate levels of "social" and "esteem" needs)—this in case anyone would like to apply these popular categories of need classification. They simply do not apply to sex differences (as little as they apply to national cultures, see Chapter 1).

All the literature quoted deals with cross-sections of the population or with women in nonmanagerial roles. J.S. Herrick (1973) compared two samples of male and female U.S. government executives on 13 work goals (mostly taken from Haire et al., 1966). His results are reported by clusters of one to four goals at a time, and in nonstandardized form. His samples of female executives are small (40 and 13, respectively) and the differences between men and women which he finds are significant only in one out of 10 cases. However, it is interesting that in both cases, after a rough standardization carried out by me, women executives score self-actualization goals as more and *social goals as less important* than do men. This suggests that the selection mechanism is for those women to be promoted who are more "masculine" in their goals than the average male executive; those who beat the men at their own game.

Sex Differences in Work Goals: HERMES Data

In HERMES, work goal importance was measured in all surveys, first with 22 and later with 14 questions (see Figures 5.8 and 5.9). If we want to analyze the scores obtained with these questions for sex differences, we should avoid confusing the latter with occupational differences. We should therefore only compare men and women in the same occupations. Among the 38 occupations in HERMES for which data are available, only a few are (1) performed by both men and women in sufficient numbers to allow statistical treatment of data, and (2) not subject to an internal division of labor in which the women still perform tasks different from men. Altogether, I found seven occupations surveyed with the 22 goals set and two with the 14 goals set which more or less satisfy these conditions. Work goal importance scores for men and women in these occupations (taking a number of countries together) were standardized as usual, and the differences between standardized scores for women and men are tabulated in Figure 6.1.

FIGURE 6.1 Differences of Standardized Mean Scores for the Importance of 22 (14) Work Goals Between Men and Women in the Same Occupations

WORK GOALS	1968–69 Data[a] Europe, Selected Countries						1970–73 Data[a] Total World				Sign Test Numbers of Cases	
	Head Office Managers FRA, GBR, SWE	Head Office Professionals FRA, GBR, SWE	Branch Office Technical Experts Tot. Europe	Data Processing Profes. FRA, GBR, GER, SWE	Head Office Clerks FRA, GBR, ITA, SWE, SWI	Branch Office Clerks FRA, GBR, ITA, SWE	Unskilled Plant Workers B	Branch Office Technical Experts	Head Office Professionals & Clerks	Mean all Occupations[b]	+	−
Number of Respondents Women	20	48	92	76	710	207	1184	379	2155			
Men	356	382	2015	744	1467	298	3658	6041	4009			
JOB CONTENT AND LEARNING												
Challenge	− 17	+ 31	− 8	− 39	+ 44*	+ 64*	+ 6*	− 16	+135*	+ 22*	5	4
Use of skills	+ 20	− 4	0	− 11	+ 19*	+ 41	+ 93*	− 25	+ 62*	+ 22*	5	3
Training	+ 39	− 36	+ 42	+ 96*	+132*	+ 35	+226*	+ 4	+116*	+ 73*	8	1
Up-to-dateness	+ 84*	+ 7	+ 35	+ 88*	+ 93*	+ 16	+ 95*	—	—	+ 60*	7	—
Learning	+ 16	+ 17	− 37	+ 41	0	− 31	+ 63*	—	—	+ 10	5	2
REWARD												
Recognition	− 42	− 12	+ 25	− 39	− 5	+ 18	− 34*	− 15	− 13	− 13	2	7
Advancement	+164*	+ 73*	+131*	+128*	+187*	+230*	+124*	+102*	+232*	+152*	9	—
Earnings	+182*	+ 55	+ 71*	+146*	+101*	+ 85*	+ 71*	+108*	+ 93*	+101*	9	—
INTERPERSONAL RELATIONS												
Manager	− 43	− 26	− 50	− 63*	− 56*	− 49*	− 70*	− 29	−129*	− 57*	—	9
Cooperation	+ 7	− 28	− 68*	− 87*	+ 42*	− 80*	− 40*	− 49*	− 78*	− 52*	1	8
Freedom	− 15	+ 65	− 15	− 1	+ 19	− 27	− 42*	+ 6	+ 13	0	4	5
Friendly atmosphere	−122*	− 89*	− 93*	−112*	−115*	−117*	− 62*	—	—	−101*	—	7
Efficient department	+ 11	+ 19	− 35	− 54	− 26*	− 25	− 42*	—	—	− 22	2	5

[272]

Figure 6.1 Continued

SECURITY												
Employment security	+ 3	− 79*	+ 34	+ 16	− 20	− 14	+ 42*	− 38*	− 45*	− 11	4	5
Benefits	−132*	− 61	+ 12	+ 6	− 50*	− 91*	− 10	− 1	−100*	− 47	2	7
Position security	−106	− 50	− 59*	− 53	− 72*	−171*	− 80*	—	—	− 84*	—	7
COMFORT												
Personal time	+ 69	+ 11	+ 47	+ 8	− 40*	+ 43	− 77*	− 12	− 70*	− 2	5	4
Desirable area	+ 48	+ 49	+ 30	+ 3	− 29*	+ 6	+ 16*	+ 33*	− 39*	+ 13	7	2
Physical conditions	−120*	− 78*	− 31	− 68*	−114*	− 10	− 24*	− 69*	−177*	− 77*	—	7
COMPANY												
Contribution to company	+ 23	+ 42	+ 13	+ 20	+ 56*	+124*	− 5	—	—	+ 39	6	1
Modern company	+ 12	+ 34	− 18	+ 21	+ 10	− 10	− 58*	—	—	− 1	4	3
Successful company	− 79	+ 60	− 26	− 46	− 91*	− 38	−195*	—	—	− 59	1	6
Years of Formal — Women	12.0	14.9	16.0	14.8	12.5	11.5	10.4	15.6	13.0			
Education — Men	14.1	14.8	15.8	14.9	13.1	12.0	11.0	15.8	13.6			

Number of respondents 18,970 men, 4871 women, 23,841 total.

+ scores: more important for men; − scores: more important for women.

[a]Significance of these differences has been tested with the t-test, two-tailed, for differences in means, taking account of the ratio by which the means were increased in the standardization process. All differences marked + are significant at the .05 level or beyond.

[b]Significance of overall mean differences has been tested with the sign test on the 9 (7) subpopulation scores.

We find across the occupations the following significant sex difference trends:

More important for men   *More important for women*
Advancement   Friendly atmosphere
Earnings   Position security
Training   Physical conditions
Up-to-dateness   Manager
                                  Cooperation

No significant sex differences are found for job content goals (challenge, use of skills) and for private life goals (personal time, desirable area). However, Figure 6.1 suggests that there may be an interaction betweeen sex and education, in that in the higher educated occupations the women would be relatively more job-content-oriented than the men, while in the lower educated occupations the opposite would be the case. The bottom lines of Figure 6.1 show the actual years of formal education of men and women in the various occupations; in the professional groups, women are at least as educated as men, but in the clerical and unskilled groups they tend to be less educated and may therefore still not do exactly the same work. Remarkable is the large educational differences between male and female headquarters managers; here the two sexes are definitely not equivalent (but it was the only sizable group of female managers in the population).

The international HERMES data largely confirm the results of the national studies reported in the previous section. The sex differences for advancement, earnings, atmosphere plus cooperation, physical conditions, and manager were already reported in the 1957 review of Herzberg et al. It seems that the differences in sex roles which determine the reference groups of these women and men when they score their goal importances are pervasive in our modern industrialized world.

Among the "interpersonal relations" goals we have used two formulations with closely related meanings: "cooperation" and "friendly atmosphere" (the latter was dropped after 1971). It appears (Figure 6.1) that "friendly atmosphere" leads to greater score differences between the sexes than "cooperation." Among head office managers, "cooperation" is even scored marginally *less* important by women than by men (compare the finding by Herrick that female executives scored lower on social needs than men). It seems that "atmosphere" has more a nurturing and "cooperation" more an assertive flavor.[7]

We saw earlier that the "component structures" in the HERMES work goal data depend on whether we compare individuals, occupations, or countries. On the previous page, we found a "clustering" of goals based on the comparison of sexes. To what extent does this clustering on the basis of sex differences agree with or differ from the clustering on the basis of individual, occupational, or country differences?

When we cluster goals on the basis of differences between *individuals* within more or less homogeneous subsets of the data (one occupation, one country) we generally find, according to Chapter 2, six clusters or factors; these are the ones used for categorizing goals in Figure 6.1. There is a trend (but not a perfect one) for the "Job content and learning" and the "Reward" factors to be scored more important by men, the "Interpersonal relations," "Security," "Comfort," and "Company" factors more important by women.

When we cluster goals on the basis of differences between *occupations* (taking total Europe data), we find, according to Chapter 5, two factors, each with some goals on the positive and some on the negative side. I called these "intrinsic-extrinsic" and "social-ego." The goals related to the intrinsic-extrinsic factor do not differ significantly in importance for the sexes (the reader can check the statistical analysis section of Chapter 5) that on the positive side of the "intrinsic-extrinsic" factor we find no goals significantly discriminating between men and women, and on the negative side we find both "earnings": more important for men, and "physical conditions": more important for women. However, the social-ego factor contains four goals significantly more important to women on the "social" side (manager, cooperation, friendly atmosphere, physical conditions) and four goals significantly more important to men on the "ego" side (up-to-dateness, advancement, training, earnings). It is virtually identical with a female preference-male preference factor.

One reason for a female-male factor to appear across occupations could be that some occupations are filled mainly by women, others mainly by men. It is true that when the HERMES occupations are located on the social-ego factor axis (Figure 5.10) the most "social" occupations are the clerks and unskilled workers; that is the groups employing sizable percentages of women (from 18 percent women for unskilled plant workers A to 99 percent women for office typists and secretaries). The "ego" occupations generally employ less than 10 percent women, or no women at all. However, this does not yet mean that it is the *women* in the "social" occupations who are solely responsible for the occupation's high "social" score. In order to test this, I compare in Figure 6.2 the "intrinsic-extrinsic" and "social-ego" factor scores for two occupations, separately for the women and the men in these occupations (for the method of calculation of these scores see the statistical analysis part of this chapter).

Head office clerks are a typical "social" occupation; branch office technical experts a typical "ego" occupation, as the mean scores for both sexes on the Social-Ego factor show. Within both occupations, women score considerably more to the

FIGURE 6.2   Factor Scores on Occupational Factors, for Two Occupations, Separated by Sex, 1968–1969 Data for 22 Goals

Occupation	Factor 1 Intrinsic-Extrinsic	Factor 2 Social-Ego
Head Office Clerks		
5 countries		
Both sexes	.52	1.10
Men only (n = 1467)	.48	.45
Women only (n = 710)	.61	2.43
Branch Office Technical		
Experts, Total Europe		
Both sexes	.27	−1.42
Men only (n = 2015)	.23	−1.49
Women only (n = 92)	1.10	.12

For a description of the factors see Chapter 5.

"social" side than men; and the sex difference in scores is larger for the less educated group (clerks) than for the more educated (experts). Still, between male clerks and male experts, and betweeen female clerks and female experts, there are also large differences. Female experts have lower social scores than male clerks. This confirms the findings of Bartol that goals differ by sex and occupation, but that occupation differences outweigh sex differences.

The scores on the "intrinsic-extrinsic" factor in Figure 6.2 illustrate that male and female clerks hardly differ in this respect, but the (college-educated) female experts tend to be more intrinsically oriented than males (compare previous pages). It may be that women only choose a technical expert job if they are really interested in it, while at least some of the men choose such a job arbitrarily.

When we cluster goals on the basis of differences between *countries* (taking our standard sample of seven occupational groups) we find again two factors. When we use the data for 40 countries and 14 goals, the two factors can be labeled (see Chapter 5) "individual-collective" and "social-ego." The goals related to the individual-collective factor do not differ systematically in importance for the sexes (goals belonging to this factor with significant sex differences are "training" and "physical conditions," but both appear on the "collective" side, while the first is more important to men, the second to women). However, the social-ego factor contains two goals significantly more important to women on the "social" side (manager, cooperation) and two goals significantly more important to men on the "ego" side (earnings, advancement). If we look at the factor analysis across countries for 22 goals (which, however, is only available for 19 countries; see the statistical analysis section of Chapter 5) we find that also "friendly atmosphere" belongs to the "social" side of the "social-ego" factor. Again, the "social-ego" factor closely resembles a female preference-male preference factor.[8]

In the same way as the social-ego factor across *occupations* has something to do with the percentage of women in these occupations, the social-ego factor across *countries* is related to the percentage of women in the seven standard occupational groups in each country. In fact, the "social" factor score and the percentage of women per country (across the 40 countries) are correlated with r = .43. However, the percentage of women in the country samples does not *account* for the "social" factor score; in all countries women form only a minor fraction of the respondents in the seven occupational groups (between 4.0 percent in Pakistan and 16.2 percent in Finland: see Appendix 2, question A1; see also the second column in Figure 6.3 in which percentage of women has been controlled for). The "social" factor score of a country rather expresses a value complex which makes it more likely that women will be hired for some occupations; we shall come back to this below.

MEASURING NATIONAL DIFFERENCES
IN MASCULINITY/FEMININITY IN HERMES

A Masculinity Index: Country Scores

In the previous chapter I explained how I used the factor scores of countries on the first main factor ("individual-collective") in the 14-goals, 40-country factor analysis, to arrive at an Individualism Index (IDV).

The second main factor in this case, as we saw above, was labeled "social-ego." It accounts for 22 percent of the variance in the country mean "work goals" scores. The work goals which together compose this factor are the following (see Chapter 5; I excluded the second loading for "use of skills"):

Loading	Work goal (see Figure 5.8)
.69	manager
.69	cooperation
.59	desirable area
.48	employment security
−.54	challenge
−.56	advancement
−.59	recognition
−.70	earnings

As the (zero-order) contribution of each work goal to the variance in the factor is determined by the square of the loading, the "social-ego" factor is mainly characterized by *high importance of manager and cooperation and low importance of earnings*. Essentially the same factor was found in the factor analysis of the 22 goals, 19 country matrix (the two factors are rank correlated with rho = .92, see page 241); the 22 goals analysis adds "friendly atmosphere" on the positive side of the factor. We saw in the previous section that for these goals there is a significant difference in the preference of men and women in the same occupations, in the sense of women scoring more "social" and men more "ego."

In the same way as I measured the individualism dimension of national cultures with an index based on "individual-collective" factor scores, I shall measure the fourth and last dimension with an index based on "social-ego" factor scores. Reversing the sign of the scores, I have called this dimension "Masculinity." This label needs some explanation.

The English language (unlike, for example, Dutch) distinguishes between male/female and masculine/feminine. The first pair of words usually refers to what is biologically determined and I shall use it in this sense. The second pair usually refers to what, in a given environment, is deemed suitable for members of one sex rather than the other:

> [T]he words *masculine* and *feminine* do not refer in any simple way to fundamental traits of personality, but to the learned styles of interpersonal interactions which are deemed to be socially appropriate to specific social contexts, and which are imposed upon, and sustain and extend, the sexual dichotomy [Newson et al., 1978: 28].

"Masculinity" and "femininity," in the sense in which I shall use these terms, refer to the dominant sex role pattern in the vast majority of both traditional and modern societies as described in the early part of this chapter: that of male assertiveness and female nurturance. It is by no means necessary that men always actually behave more "masculine" than women and women more "feminine" than men, as Bem's experiments have shown; statistically, however, men as a rule will, be more on the "masculine" side and women more on the "feminine."

As demonstrated above, I found both occupations and countries in the "HERMES" data to differ along a "social-ego" dimension of work goals, opposing the interpersonal relations goals "(relationship with) manager," "cooperation," and "friendly atmosphere" to "earnings" and "advancement." This dimension is related to the percentage of women within the occupation or country sample, but not *due* to the presence of women only; we find it also in the responses by men in these occupations or countries. The fact that the social-ego difference appears on a worldwide ecological level means that it must be associated with a fundamental dilemma of mankind. This dilemma is the relative strength of nurturance interests (relation with manager, cooperation, atmosphere) versus assertiveness interests (earnings, advancement): of interests which in nearly all traditional and modern societies are traditionally more "feminine" versus those that are traditionally more "masculine." The ecological dimension we are dealing with measures to what extent the HERMES respondents in a country (mainly men) show less or more a traditionally "masculine" interest pattern. The fundamental dilemma behind this dimension then, can be no other than the distribution of roles over the sexes: and this sex role distribution differs among the 40 nations. I have therefore interpreted it as a femininity-masculinity dimension (using the words in the sense described earlier, of learned styles of interpersonal interaction). Because the respondents were mainly men, I have called the dimension *Masculinity,* thereby reversing its sign.

Like the Individualism Index (IDV), the Masculinity Index (MAS) has been brought in a range between zero and 100. The values of the Masculinity Index found for the 40 countries are listed in Figure 6.3.

The second column of figures in Figure 6.3 shows the effect on MAS scores of controlling for the percentage of women in the HERMES sample: the scores that would have been obtained if all country samples included the same percentage of female respondents. We see that the basic ordering of the countries is hardly affected. The biggest differences occur for Finland and Yugoslavia, which both have relatively high percentages of women; but the percentage of women in these occupations in the country is not only a cause but can also be seen as partly an *effect* of the country's relatively low masculinity norm.

The list of countries in order of Masculinity Index shows Japan at the top. German-speaking countries (Austria, Switzerland, and Germany) tend to score high; so do the Caribbean Latin American countries Venezuela, Mexico, and Colombia, and Italy. The Anglo-American countries (Ireland, Great Britain, South Africa, the United States, Australia, New Zealand, and Canada) all score above average. Asian countries, other than Japan, are rather in the middle. On the lower side we find other Latin countries (France, Spain, Peru, Portugal, and Chile) and Yugoslavia; at the lowest end are the four Nordic countries Finland, Denmark, Norway, and Sweden, and the Netherlands.

The Individualism Index (IDV) could only be used to compare countries, not occupations, because in the factor analysis of work goals by occupations (Chapter 5) there is no such thing as an individual-collective factor. However, across occupations we *do* find a social-ego factor which is largely similar to the social-ego factor that we find across countries (compare pages 240, 241, and 242. In all three cases we find "manager" and "cooperation" opposing "earnings" and "advancement"; there is some variation in the additional goals that load on the factor). Thus, we can identify

FIGURE 6.3   Country Masculinity Index (MAS)

Country	MAS Actual	MAS Controlling for % Women[a]	Country	MAS Actual	MAS Controlling for % Women[a]
Japan	95	87	Brazil	49	44
Austria	79	75	Singapore	48	52
Venezuela	73	70	Israel	47	41
Italy	70	72	Turkey	45	53
Switzerland	70	67	Taiwan	45	38
Mexico	69	64	Iran	43	52
Ireland	68	74	France	43	41
Great Britain	66	66	Spain	42	35
Germany (F.R.)	66	59	Peru	42	32
Philippines	64	58	Thailand	34	45
Colombia	64	56	Portugal	31	32
South Africa	63	60	Chile	28	26
U.S.A.	62	—[b]	Finland	26	51
Australia	61	59	Denmark	16	22
New Zealand	58	55	Netherlands	14	—[c]
Greece	57	73	Norway	8	10
Hong Kong	57	61	Sweden	5	6
Argentina	56	50	Mean of 39 countries (HERMES)	·51	51
India	56	47			
Belgium	54	53	Yugoslavia (same industry)	21	42
Canada	52	53			
Pakistan	50	40			

[a]For % women see Appendix 2, question A1.

[b]Only data for occupations filled by men available.

[c]Sex identification not asked in surveys.

Values based on the factor scores of the second factor found in a 14 work goals, 40-country matrix. Work goal scores were computed for a stratified sample of seven occupations at two points in time. Actual values and values obtained after controlling for % women in the country sample.

occupations as more "masculine" (ego) or more "feminine" (social); the MAS index can be used to describe occupations.

As for other demographic criteria, the MAS index can, of course, be used for discriminating between the sexes; this is why it was given its name. Age group differences in work goals will be described in Chapter 8.

Masculinity and Sex Role Differentiation

Most HERMES respondents were men, and the differences in Masculinity Index values listed in Figure 6.3 reflect therefore mainly the values of *men* in these countries. What about the "masculinity" or "feminity" of women's values in these countries? Two of the occupational categories used for the 40-country comparison contain minorities of women (doing the same work as the men) of a size that permits statistical treatment: head office clerks (35 percent women in 1971–1973) and branch office technical experts (6 percent women). The first is a group which usually has secondary school education, the second usually has a higher (college) education. In Figure 6.4 I have computed separate MAS scores for men and women in these occupations for those countries in which there are at least 20 female respondents in either occupation. I used 1971–1973 survey data (which generally show larger numbers of respondents than the earlier survey round).[9]

In order to widen the range of social class and educational level within the data, I have also entered in Figure 6.4 the MAS scores for male and female unskilled workers B in HERMES manufacturing plants, which are available for six countries.

Several conclusions can be drawn from Figure 6.4. If we look first to the rank correlations with country MAS scores, we see that country differences in "masculinity" are present in the scores of men and women separately and in all three occupations. The men's scores follow the MAS ranking somewhat more closely than the women's scores, not surprisingly, as the MAS scores are mainly based on men's answers. However, we also see from the bottom line of Figure 6.4 that the score differences between men and women (a measure of sex role differentiation) are themselves positively correlated with MAS. For experts and clerks, the correlations of "Δ men-women" with MAS are significant. For unskiled workers, the data for Japan are out of line; but the sample of women in Japan is just 20, the lowest limit of what is acceptable. Without Japan, the rank correlation of "Δ men-women" with MAS for the unskilled would be .83. This means that in the more "masculine" countries, the values of men and women in the same occupations tend to be more different than in the more "feminine" ones. Our measure of masculinity in a country is also a measure of sex role differentiation. The two most "feminine" countries, Sweden and Norway, even show a reversal of sex role values: in these countries, the women score more "masculine" than the men in the same occupations. In the right-hand part of Figure 6.4 I show the occupational differences in MAS, taking men and women together. Experts distinguish themselves considerably from the two other groups: They are more "masculine" (compare Figure 6.2). The average female expert scores more "masculine" than the average male clerk or unskilled worker. Occupation stands also for education plus social class; in all countries for which I have data, except Japan, the higher educated, upper-middle-class experts score more masculine, assertive values than the others. In Japan there is no systematic occupation/education difference (or at least it goes one way for men, the other way for women). The largest occupation/education differences are visible for Germany, Sweden, and Australia.

Occupation/education and sex difference interact, as we can see by comparing the Δ scores between women and men for unskilled, clerks, and experts.[10] In France, Great Britain, and Germany, female experts score almost as "masculine" as their male colleagues. Swedish female experts and female unskilled score even more "masculine" than their male colleagues. The women experts pursue a career in an essentially male world. Whereas this career is primarily technical, not managerial, the following quote from a British female executive may still apply:

> Underlying most of the controversy about women's suitability for management is the narrow and single minded conception of the ideal manager. This is almost entirely male in character: aggressive, competitive, firm, rational and vigorous. And against this women are seen to fall short by being characterized as not competitive: valuing social

skills; intuitive, dependent and person orientated, rather than objective; cooperative; creative but in a small domestic way rather than visionary. To the extent that one is talking about the population as a whole, these sex defined characteristics are no doubt valid; they have been demonstrated in studies at a very general level and accord with observations of Western societies as they exist. However, these are largely irrelevant when dealing with a self-selected universe: women sufficiently motivated to pursue a career [Lannon, 1977: 10].

The female experts belong to this self-selected universe. However, not in all countries do their values approach those of their male colleagues: In Japan, Australia, and Brazil the female experts differ even more from their male colleagues than do the female clerks from theirs. Most likely, in these countries they do not feel themselves as seriously competing with the men.

The French pattern is extreme in that sex value differences are virtually zero for the experts: Both men and women "cadres" score average on the masculinity-femininity scale. For the "non-cadre" clerks however, the men and women score wide apart and show the widest gap for any of the 14 countries between male assertiveness and female nurturance. This latter gap concurs with the results of a study on broad samples of the populations in 12 countries dealing with family time budgets for child care (Stone, 1972). As "non-cadres" are much more numerous than "cadres," this study reflects primarily the non-cadre situation. It concludes:

> The French pattern of child rearing is particularly different from all others. French housewives give the most time to young children, yet do not show a large reduction in time spent with the child as he grows older. French men spend very little time with children apart from time spent also with the spouse . . . In France, periods of child time and adult time appear to be strictly identified [Stone, 1972: 263].

This suggests that the French (non-cadre) child is socialized to sharply differentiated sex roles.

The German female experts score the most "masculine" of any of the samples of women except the Japanese unskilled. These German college-graduate women show an assertiveness which bypasses many groups of men in other countries.

Country Masculinity Index Scores and Other HERMES Survey Questions

HERMES respondents in more masculine countries, compared with those in more feminine countries, tend to endorse significantly more frequently the following items in the questionnaire (see the statistical analysis):

(1) High stress (A37).
(2) Decisions made by individuals are usually of higher quality than decisions made by groups (B57).
(3) A large corporation is generally a more desirable place to work than a small company (C17); a corporation is responsible for its employees (B52) and for society (B58); and the private life of an employee is properly a matter of direct concern to the company (C19).
(4) Most employees have an inherent dislike of work and will avoid it if they can (C13); and for getting ahead in industry, knowing influential people is usually more important than ability (C15).

FIGURE 6.4 Masculinity Index (MAS) Scores for Men and Women Separately, in 3 Occupations and 15 Countries

Country	Country MAS score	Unskilled plant workers B			Head office clerks			Branch office technical experts			Δ scores between occupations (men & women)		
		men	women	Δ men−women	men	women	Δ men−women	men	women	Δ men−women	clerks−unskilled	experts−clerks	experts−unskilled
Number of respondents		3211	1169		3388	1807		4123	260				
Japan	95	89	92[a]	(− 3)	99	77	22	102	73	29	(− 3)	− 1	(− 3)
Austria	79				69	34	35						
Great Britain	66	63	13	50	80	28	52	80	69	11	16	21	37
Germany (F.R.)	66	45	18	27	47	16	31	83	79	4	0	50	50
South Africa	63				52	19	33						
Australia	61				35	19	16	74	52	22		36	
Argentina	56				75	37	38						
Belgium	54				61	33	28						
Brazil	49				35	18	17	59	39	20		23	
France	43	28	0	28	71	− 6	77	55	51	4	19	21	39
Spain	42				43	38	5						
Denmark	16				4	−10	14						
Netherlands	14	− 8	−21	13	−12	− 9	− 3						
Norway	8												
Sweden	5	−14	3	−17	−30	−28	− 2	7	19	−12	−24	42	19

FIGURE 6.4 Continued

Mean of 5 countries (JAP, GBR, GER, FRA, SWE)	55	42	25	17	53	17	36	65	58	7	2	27	28
Mean of all available country scores	48	34	18	16	45	19	26	66	55	11	2	27	28
Spearman rank correlation with MAS		.99**	.81	.33	.73***	.63**	.61**	.99***	.90***	.71*	.11	−.29	−.13

Number of respondents: 10,722 men, 3,236 women, 13,958 total.

[a]Based on answers of 20 women only.

The association of masculinity with higher stress is interesting because in Chapter 4 we saw that there is no evidence of systematic differences in stress between men and women in the same jobs. The conclusion is that stress is not in the *sex* but in the *sex role*. Le Vine (1966: 255) quotes data from Africa showing that "separated and widowed women, who have become family heads involuntarily, have a significantly higher frequency of high blood pressure than married women": Their more masculine new role is associated with more stress symptoms. In all developed countries, women on the average live four to eight years longer than men; differences in stress during life are a likely contributor to this.[11] The higher ambition of the men is paid for in years of life.[12] One aspect of the sex role patterns is that usually "masculinity" is associated with being tough and not showing emotions, while "femininity" means that emotions may be shown (Jourard, 1968; Levinson, 1970a: 181; Bartolomé, 1972). Showing emotions is an excellent way of reducing the negative effect of stress on long-term health (see Chapter 4).

The association of masculinity with "individual decisions better than group decisions" confirms the picture of the masculine decision maker who is *not* socially oriented.

Masculinity in a country is also.(weakly) associated with support for the large, responsible corporation which has a right to interfere in its employees' lives; while the "feminine" pattern is more to prefer the smaller company (small is beautiful), to leave social responsibility to other institutions, and to reject company interference with their private lives. The corporation belongs to the masculine world.

Finally, in more "masculine" countries, people tend to show a more skeptical view of others, which is demonstrated by their lesser rejection of Theory X ("most employees dislike work") and their agreement that knowing people is more important for getting ahead than ability.

Masculinity and Work Centrality in HERMES

Earlier studies of the HERMES survey data (Hofstede, 1976b, 1979a) have compared two measures of the importance of work goals. One is the set of direct questions ("how important is it to you to . . .") used for computing the Country Individualism and Masculinity Indices. I have called this measure a "sociological" measure because the answers reflect the respondents' social frame of reference and feelings of social desirability. The other measure is the strength of the correlation between the satisfaction with each individual work goal and a score of the respondents' "overall satisfaction in the company" (see the statistical analysis). I have called this a "psychological" measure because it is unconscious and unaffected by social desirability.

It can be shown (Hofstede, 1976b: 28) that the psychological measure always leads to about the same ordering of work facets. Regardless of country or occupation, "challenge" and "earnings" tend to be the two work facets whose satisfaction is most strongly correlated with overall satisfaction. That is, within any category of HERMES employees, those scoring more satisfaction with their "challenge" and their "earnings" are also usually the ones scoring more satisfaction with their job in general.

The sociological measure, as we saw in Chapter 5 and in this chapter, is strongly affected by the occupation and the country of the respondents. It appears (albeit in a comparison of only five countries, see the statistical analysis) that in three high MAS countries the sociological measure is much more similar to the psychological, unconscious measure than in two low MAS countries. In these high MAS countries (Japan, Germany, and Great Britain) HERMES employees rate as personally and socially desirable in their job mainly those facets that go together with high overall job satisfaction. In the lower MAS countries (France and the Netherlands) they rate other job facets as personally and socially desirable (important). In rating work goal "importance" respondents choose their own reference frame. They are not told in the questionnaire that their ultimate criterion should be maximal *job* satisfaction. It is obvious that in the lower MAS countries, the ultimate criterion is *not* maximal job satisfaction. If we accept the hedonistic principle that people always try to maximize some kind of satisfaction, this leads to the conclusion that respondents in the lower MAS countries try to maximize a "life satisfaction," which is seen as socially desirable but does not overlap with "job satisfaction." That is, in the higher MAS countries, the job takes a more central position in the respondents' total life space than in the lower MAS countries. This same reasoning can be applied to occupational differences: We also find that only the higher educated occupations (managers and professionals) rate as personally and socially desirable those facets that go together with high overall job satisfaction; the job *does* occupy a more central position in the life space of managers and professionals than in that of lower status employees.

If this analysis is correct, it means that there is a relationship between MAS and national levels of "work centrality." This is a concept that has been used in sociology since Dubin's (1956) study of "Central Life Interests" of U.S. workers. Another related concept in the literature is "Job Involvement" (Lodahl and Kejner, 1965). Unfortunately, so far I have not been able to trace any systematic cross-national studies of work centrality.

Vroom (1964: 43) quotes U.S. research findings pertaining to a difference in work centrality by sex: "Job satisfaction is more highly correlated with general satisfaction among employed men than among employed women." This, of course, supports a positive association between work centrality and masculinity. Whyte (1969: 31) uses a quote from American businessman Charles F. Kettering to illustrate the cultural boundedness of the meaning of work.

> I often tell my people that I don't want any fellow who has a job working for me: What I want is a fellow whom a job has. I want the job to get the fellow and not the fellow to get the job. And I want that job to get hold of this young man so hard that no matter where he is the job has got him for keeps. I want that job to have him in its clutches when he goes to bed at night, and in the morning I want that same job to be sitting on the foot of his bed telling him it's time to get up and go to work. And when a job gets a fellow that way, he's sure to amount to something.

It is no accident that Kettering refers to a "young man" only—his is a masculine ideal. If we also take into account the correlation referred to on page 281 between the Masculinity Index and "the private life of an employee is properly a matter of direct concern to his company," we can postulate that people in more "masculine" countries, other factors being equal, "live to work," while people in more feminine countries "work to live." I am waiting for more extensive cross-national studies of work centrality to confirm this distinction, which at present has the status of a hypothesis.

COMPARING THE HERMES
MASCULINITY INDEX VALUES
WITH OTHER DATA

Sample Survey Studies

(1) Samples of students from 17 countries answering L.V. Gordon's Survey of Interpersonal values (Figure 3.14). Higher masculinity in a country is associated with higher recognition (importance of being looked up to and admired, being considered important, attracting favorable notice, achieving recognition: r = .50). Higher masculinity is associated with lower benevolence (importance of doing things for other people, sharing with others, helping the unfortunate, being generous: r = −.59). This clearly shows the association of masculinity with assertiveness and of femininity with nurturance.

(2) Samples of managers in 12 countries answering Bass' IRGOM Life Goals Exercise (Figure 5.16). An ecological factor analysis of the "Life Goals" scores showed the existence of two factors. The first ("hedonism-skill") was related to individualism (see Chapter 5). The second factor (labeled "assertiveness-service") is correlated with masculinity: rho = .84. This factor opposes leadership, independence, and self-realization to service. These goals are defined in the exercise as follows:

> *Leadership:* "To become an influential leader; to organize and control others; to achieve community or organizational goals."

> *Independence:* "To have the opportunity for freedom of thought and action; to be one's own boss."

> *Self-realization:* "To optimize personal development; to realize one's full creative and innovative potential."

> (These three are associated with the masculine end of the scale.)

> *Service:* "To contribute to the satisfaction of others; to be helpful to others who need it."

> (This is associated with the feminine end of the scale.)

We find again, and on a very different sample, the assertive goals to be associated with masculinity, the service (nurturing) goal with femininity.

(3) Large representative samples of the public in six European countries answering a poll on preferences for free versus nationalized enterprises (McGee, 1977; see the statistical analysis in Figure 6.11). A measure of the *size* of the enterprise in which people would prefer to work is strongly correlated with MAS (rho = .84). This confirms that in lower MAS countries people think more frequently that "small is beautiful."

(4) Large representative samples of the public in eight European countries answering a poll on attitudes toward retirement issues (CCE, 1978; see Figure 6.12). A general question about preferences for more salary or for shorter working hours shows answer percentages which correlate strongly with MAS (rho = .86), in the sense that more masculine countries prefer more salary while more feminine ones strongly prefer shorter working hours. This reminds us of the "live to work" versus "work to live" dilemma discussed earlier.

Masculinity and the Content Analysis of Children's Books

McClelland (1961) derived national measurements of Need for Achievement (n_{Ach}) from a content analysis of children's readers. Across 22 countries, we found in Chapter 4, Figure 4.11, a strong negative correlation (rho = −.64) between the countries' Uncertainty Avoidance Index and Need for Achievement as identified by McClelland in 1925 children's reakers. However, there is a sizable second-order positive correlation with the Masculinity Index (multiple correlation coefficient with UAI + MAS: R = .74). In the statistical analysis in Figure 6.13 I demonstrate that the order of Need for Achievement as found by McClelland can be predicted to a large extent from UAI and MAS. High Need for Achievement according to McClelland's definition (as a national characteristic) stands for the combination of a willingness to take risks (low UAI) and of masculine assertiveness (high MAS).

This is a way of defining human accomplishment which is specific to a certain cultural and economic environment: In particular, to the economic environment of early capitalism. If we take "achievement" in a wider sense, in the spirit of the quote from Margaret Mead at the beginning of this chapter, it can apply to anything irreversible a human being can accomplish. In Chapter 4, Figure 4.4, I suggested that both high UAI and low UAI national cultures have their achievements, but while those in low UAI cultures tend to be defined in terms of (social) recognition, those in high UAI cultures tend to be measured in terms of the security they offer. In the same way, both high MAS and low MAS national cultures have their achievements, but these will be defined differently: In high MAS cultures, achievement is defined more in terms of recognition and of wealth[13]; we can call this "ego accomplishment." In low MAS cultures it is defined more in terms of the quality of human contacts and of the living environment; this is "social accomplishment."

Denmark and Waters (1977) content-analyzed children's readers from different countries (France, Rumania, Spain, Sweden, and the USSR) for the sex roles of their main characters. Spain and France showed few females and pictured both males and females in sex-traditional roles only; Rumania and the USSR showed more females, but still fewer than males; some females were pictured in traditionally male roles. Sweden only showed more female than male leading characters and had some of both in nontraditional sex roles—for example, a boy as a babysitter.[14] This fits well with the extreme position of Sweden on the feminine side of the MAS scale; but Spain and France also score on the "feminine" side of the midpoint. More data on other countries will be necessary to explore this further; intuitively, I would suggest that the role of women in society as reflected by the children's readers reflects the interaction of both masculinity *and* power distance.

A Summary of Connotations of the Masculinity Index Found in Survey and Related Material

In analogy with Figures 3.6, 4.3, and 5.3, Figure 6.5 integrates the connotations of low and high MAS scores found so far. Again, this presents a polarized picture; actual values often will be somewhere between the extremes described.

FIGURE 6.5   Summary of Connotations of Masculinity Index Differences Found in Survey and Related Research

See page	Low MAS Countries	High MAS Countries
277	• Relationship with manager, cooperation, friendly atmosphere, living in a desirable area, and employment security relatively more important to HERMES employees.	• Earnings, recognition, advancement, and challenge relatively more important to HERMES employees.
286	• Managers relatively less interested in leadership, independence, and self-realization.	• Managers have leadership, independence, and self-realization ideal.
284	• Belief in group decisions.	• Belief in the independent decision maker.
286	• Students less interested in recognition.	• Students aspire to recognition (admiration for the strong).
287	• Weaker achievement motivation.	• Stronger achievement motivation.
287	• Achievement defined in terms of human contacts and living environment.	• Achievement defined in terms of recognition and wealth.
285	• Work less central in people's lives.	• Greater work centrality.
287	• People prefer shorter working hours to more salary.	• People prefer more salary to shorter working hours.
281	• Company's interference in private life rejected.	• Company's interference in private life accepted.
284	• Greater social role attributed to other institutions than corporation.	• Greater social role attributed to corporation.
284	• HERMES employees like small companies.	• HERMES employees like large corporations.
286	• Entire population more attracted to smaller organizations.	• Entire population more attracted to larger organization.
284	• Lower job stress.	• Higher job stress.
281	• Less skepticism as to factors leading to getting ahead.	• Skepticism as to factors leading to getting ahead.

FIGURE 6.5   Continued

286	• Students more benevolent (sympathy for the weak).	• Students less benevolent.
286	• Managers have more a service ideal.	• Managers relatively less attracted by service role.
284	• "Theory X" strongly rejected.	• "Theory X" (employees dislike work) gets some support.
276	• In HERMES, more women in jobs with mixed sex composition.	• In HERMES, fewer women in jobs with mixed sex composition.
280	• Smaller or no value differences between men and women in the same jobs.	• Greater value differences between men and women in the same jobs.
287	• Sex role equality in children's books.	• More sex role differentiation in children's books.

The number of different studies on which Figure 6.5 is based is smaller than in the case of the other dimensions (PDI, UAI, IDV). Besides the HERMES data we have two other narrow sample studies (Gordon and IRGOM), two studies of representative samples of entire populations (McGee and CCE), and one content analysis study (McClelland) which supply significant correlations with MAS. A more extensive literature search will probably lead to the discovery of other related studies. However, it is also likely that the masculinity-femininity dimension in national cultures is not as easily recognized by researchers as for example, the power distance or individualism dimensions. Researchers will therefore be less likely to ask the relevant questions. There is room for more cross-cultural studies in this area. As it is, the few studies that are available supply a picture supportive of the masculinity-femininity syndrome.

Masculinity and Some Anthropological and Psychological Concepts

The one concept from the anthropological literature which can be directly associated with masculinity is "*machismo*" (a need for ostentatious manliness) which is usually attributed to Latin American countries, especially Mexico (De Vos and Hippler, 1969: 365; Lewis, 1966: XXVII). The Latin American female counterpart to *machismo* is "*Marianismo*": a combination of near-saintliness, submissiveness, and frigidity (Stevens, 1973). In the HERMES data, some Latin American countries score far to the masculine side—Venezuela, Mexico, and Colombia—which fits with the *machismo* image. Argentina and Brazil, however, score in the middle, while Peru and Chile score more feminine. Private discussions with Latin American spokesmen confirm that *machismo* is more present in the countries around the Caribbean than in the remainder of South America. However, it has also been signaled in, for example, British working-class youngsters (compare Figure 6.4).

There are case descriptions in the anthropological literature which fit the masculinity scores. For Iran (MAS = 43), Hall (1965: 50) writes:

> In Iran . . . men are expected to show their emotions. Iranian men read poetry; they are sensitive and have well-developed intuition and in many cases are not expected to be too

logical. They are often seen embracing and holding hands. Women, on the other hand, are considered to be coldly practical. They exhibit many of the characteristics we associate with men in the United States. A very perceptive Foreign Service Officer . . . . once observed "If you will think of the emotional and intellectual sex roles as reversed from ours, you will do much better out here."

And this in a country where the *formal* role of women, under the influence of Islam, is one of submissiveness!

A fascinating development in cross-cultural psychology is the study of "psychological differentiation" across cultures, whose chief protagonists are H.A. Witkin and J.W. Berry. Witkin has worked in the United States in the area of test development for nearly four decades. He noticed a consistency in the differences in performance of individuals on a number of tests of perceptual ability, such as the Embedded Figures Test, Rod and Frame Test, and Body Adjustment Test (Cronbach, 1970: 240ff, 627ff). It became clear that these tests, next to pure ability, measure a personality component. Witkin introduced the distinction between "field-dependent" and "field-independent" persons. Field-dependent persons are influenced in their perception by characteristics of their physical and social environment. Field-independent" persons are more "psychologically differentiated": In carrying out perceptual tasks, they are better able to keep an object and its environment apart. Field-dependent persons tend to rely on external frames of reference as guides to behavior; field-independent persons rely more on internal frames of reference (Witkin, 1977: 85). Field-dependent people generally can be shown to have better social skills; field-independent people have better analytical skills (Witkin and Goodenough, 1977: 682).

Psychological differentiation is related to sex.

> Many studies in Western settings have shown that, starting around early adolescence, women tend to be more field-dependent than men. The difference between the sexes is slight, even though persistent: the range within each sex is vastly larger than the mean difference between the sexes [Witkin, 1977: 88].[15]

Psychological differentiation is also related to age; data from both nonliterate and western settings seem to indicate a U-shaped relationship, with maximum field independence between 21 and 40 (Witkin and Berry, 1975: 37ff).

Berry (1976) has carried the study of psychological differentiation to the ecological level. Between 1964 and 1974, he tested more than 1000 members of 21 different communities in Africa, Australia, Europe, and North America with a battery of psychological differentiation tests. He found systematic differences in field-dependence levels which he related to factors in the ecological and cultural situations of these communities.

The research findings on psychological differentiation, though impressive, stop short of the comparison of modern societies. One exception is an unpublished Dutch master's thesis referred to by Van Leeuwen (1978:110) which found sex differences on two tests of psychological differentiation to be insignificant for Dutch undergraduates; earlier studies on American undergraduates had shown significant sex differences.[16]

Berry's discovery of significant differences in psychological differentiation among nonliterate societies makes it highly likely that there will be systematic differences among modern societies as well (Ember, 1977: 48–49; Triandis, 1977: 117–118). In order to show these we should, obviously, have well-matched samples of the populations, as the range of variation within countries is likely to exceed the mean score differences among countries. I venture the hypothesis that such studies will show levels of of field-independence in countries to be correlated with the countries' Masculinity Index, because:

(1) As we saw above, in western settings women tend to be more field-dependent than men;

(2) as we also saw above, people over 40 tend to be more field-dependent than younger people; in Chapter 8 I shall show that for the mainly male HERMES samples, work goals associated with the "masculine" cluster tend to decrease in importance and those associated with the "feminine" cluster tend to increase in importance with age;

(3) also shown above, Dutch (low MAS) undergraduates showed smaller sex differences in psychological differentiation than U.S. (high MAS) undergraduates;

(4) conceptually, valuing social relationships ("femininity") converges with relying on external frames of reference as guides to behavior ("field-dependence"); valuing ego-gratification ("masculinity") converges with relying more on internal frames of reference ("field independence"); and finally,

(5) Kohn (1971), in a cross-national sample of over 3000 American men, found a significant positive correlation between field-independence and the size of the organization in which the men worked. We found an association of masculinity with a preference for larger organizations.

A feasible setting for such cross-cultural studies of psychological differentiation would be participants in international training courses or students of international schools.

THE MASCULINITY NORM,
ITS ORIGINS AND CONSEQUENCES

Masculinity, Latitude,
Population Growth, and Bigness

The statistical analysis in Figure 6.14, in analogy with the previous chapters, explores the relationship of the Masculinity Index (MAS) with seven economic, geographic, and demographic indicators. The correlations are weaker than in the case of individualism. The highest (zero-order) correlation of MAS is with geographical latitude, in the sense that countries closer to the equator tend to be more masculine, countries closer to the poles more feminine ($r = -.31$); the relationship becomes stronger when we consider the poorer countries and the wealthier countries separately. We have to speculate on the explanation of the relationship between latitude and femininity. Latitude can only be an independent variable, so causality must run somehow from lower latitude to greater masculinity. We found earlier (Chapter 3) a negative relationship between latitude and power distance, which I interpreted as the result of a greater need for technology for survival in more moderate climates, which imposes a certain level of education and equality upon people. We can extend this argument to equality between the sexes. In more moderate climates, survival presupposes the mastery of complex skills by both men and women, which makes extreme inequality between the sexes unlikely.

A complex relationship shows up between MAS and population growth: It is negative for the wealthier countries and positive for the poorer ones. The overall picture is that the feminine end of the scale is associated with slower population growth in poorer countries and faster population growth in wealthier countries. Population growth depends strongly on the average family size (and, of course, on the level of medical care); thus, femininity means smaller families in poorer countries and larger families in wealthier countries. This is precisely what we would expect in those cultures in which the woman has a say in the number of children she bears: She will adapt the family size to the available wealth. Where male choice prevails in matters of family size, we find (too) large families in poor countries and small families in wealthy countries.[17]

There are positive correlations between MAS and a country's population size, as well as with the size of the HERMES organization in the country. In both cases, bigness and masculine values go together. We saw earlier a relationship between femininity and the feeling that "small is beautiful"; the "small is beautiful" value is more likely in smaller countries and smaller organizations.

Masculinity and the
Role of Women in Society

If the degree of masculinity or femininity of a country's dominant value system is related to sex role differentiation in HERMES (see earlier), it should be related in a more general way to the role of women in society.

We could try to determine the role of women in society from their participation in the paid work force. However, being allowed—or forced—to work for money is not necessarily a sign of greater independence: it may just be another form of slavery.[18] Whether women do paid work does not determine the weight of their role, but what job they fill and how they are paid for it.

Data shown in the statistical analysis part of this chapter (Figure 6.15) prove that the Masculinity Index is negatively correlated ($r = -.64$) with the percentage of all working women who are in professional and technical jobs (at least across the wealthier countries, where there exist sufficient professional and technical jobs). It is also correlated ($r = .56$) across the wealthier countries with an "index of segregation" for higher education (Figure 6.16): the degree to which it is customary that men and women choose *different* types of higher education. Thus, in more feminine countries more working women are in the more qualified jobs, and in higher education the *same* courses tend to be taken by women and men.

There is also some evidence that in more masculine countries fewer men are positive toward the idea of seeing women in leading positions (see page 308: this is based on a survey study in six countries by Bártová, 1976). Aberbach and Putnam (1977) report on the percentage of women in parliament in six countries; while low all over, it still varies between four percent in Italy and Great Britain (high MAS) and 14 percent in the Netherlands (low MAS), with Germany, the United States, and France in between. Maurice et al. (1978: 5) compare wage differentials in France and

Germany. While wage differentials between hierarchical levels are lower in (lower PDI) Germany, wage differentials between men and women are lower in (lower MAS) France.

Masculinity and Religion, Development Aid, and Traffic Habits

In Chapter 4 we found for countries with a Christian majority a correlation between uncertainty avoidance and the Catholic/Protestant ratio, indicating a tendency toward more Catholicism in more uncertainty-avoiding countries. However, the statistical analysis (Figure 4.20) also showed a second-order positive correlation between the Catholic/Protestant ratio and the Masculinity Index. In fact, Christianity takes many cultural forms, both between and within countries and even within the larger churches. It is my personal feeling that the message of the Old Testament is more "masculine" (eye for eye, tooth for tooth) and the New Testament more "feminine" (turn the other cheek); thus, perhaps Christians have their choice in finding biblical support for more masculine or feminine norms. Catholicism has produced some very masculine tough currents (Templars, Jesuits) but also some feminine tender ones (Franciscans); and some Protestant groups defend strongly masculine values (Mormons, most fundamentalist sects). However, on the average, the data show that countries with a Catholic culture tend to be more masculine and those with a Protestant culture more feminine. A fact which supports this is that many Protestant churches now practice equality between men and women in their leadership and clergy, while the Catholic churches are led entirely by men.

A greater benevolence and need for helping the weak in more feminine countries, as found earlier in the chapter, could express itself for the wealthier countries in the percentage of the Gross National Product which governments spend on development assistance to third world countries. The statistical analysis in Figure 6.17 shows that, indeed, across the 15 wealthy countries for which data have been published, the mean annual official development assistance (over 1967–1976) in percentage of 1970 GNP is strongly negatively correlated with the Masculinity Index (rho = −.81). It is virtually uncorrelated with national wealth (GNP/capita) per se, so that it is evident that a value complex (femininity rather than masculinity) and not an economic condition (wealth) determines governments' willingness to give development assistance. The data also show no evidence that former colonial powers now give more (or less) development aid than countries which had no colonies.[19]

We saw earlier (Chapter 4, Figure 4.18) that maximum allowed speeds on highways in Europe were related to uncertainty avoidance. They were not related to traffic death rates; the latter were negatively correlated with individualism (see Chapter 5). However, the statistical analysis (page 206) showed that there also exists a sizable (second-order) correlation between masculinity and *both* allowed speeds on highways *and* traffic death rates. In more masculine countries drivers are allowed to drive faster, *and* more people die in traffic accidents per 1000 vehicles. Both phenomena are consistent with a societal norm of greater assertiveness; in the more "feminine" countries there is not only more of a feeling that "small is beautiful," but also that "slow is beautiful." A lesser urge to show off in driving is certainly consistent with fewer traffic deaths.[20]

The Masculinity Norm and Its Origins

Figure 6.6 presents an integrated picture of the general societal norm behind the "low MAS" and "high MAS" syndromes, in analogy with Figures 3.7, 4.4, and 5.5. Figure 6.6 draws upon the summary of survey findings in Figure 6.5 and the correlations with country-level indices discussed afterward. As with the other three societal norms described in the previous chapters, the masculinity norm should be seen as a value system shared especially by the majority in the middle classes of a society.

Some suggested origins of Masculinity Index differences between countries are listed in Figure 6.7.

The correlations of the Masculinity Index with the various ecological indicators are not very conclusive and explain at best only a small part of the variance in MAS. Much of societal masculinity-femininity differences must be historically and traditionally determined, in the same way as anthropologists report differences in sex role differentiation between otherwise quite similar tribes, which can only have historical/traditional origins. However, the mechanisms for the conservation of such differences (Figure 1.4) are solid; as Chapter 8 will show, there is no sign of convergency in the direction of masculinity or femininity among modern nations. One possible explanation of the strongly feminine score of the Scandinavian countries is that this is inherited from the Viking society in which the women had to manage the villages when the men were away on their long trips. However, the next question becomes,

FIGURE 6.6   The Masculinity Societal Norm

Low MAS	High MAS
• People orientation.	• Money and things orientation.
• Quality of life and environment are important.	• Performance and growth are important.
• Work to live.	• Live to work.
• Service ideal.	• Achievement ideal.
• Interdependence ideal.	• Independence ideal.
• Intuition.	• Decisiveness.
• Sympathy for the unfortunate.	• Sympathy for the successful achiever.
• Levelling: don't try to be better than others.	• Excelling: try to be the best.
• Small and slow are beautiful.	• Big and fast are beautiful.
• Men need not be assertive but can also take caring roles.	• Men should behave assertively and women should care.
• Sex roles in society should be fluid.	• Sex roles in society should be clearly differentiated.
• Differences in sex roles should not mean differences in power.	• Men should dominate in all settings.
• Unisex and androgyny ideal.	• *Machismo* (ostentative manliness) ideal.

FIGURE 6.7   Origins of National Masculinity Index Differences

Low MAS	High MAS
• More necessary in colder climates in which more equal partnership of men and women improves chances of survival and population growth.	• More easily maintained in warmer climates in which survival and population growth are less dependent on man's intervention with nature; women can be kept ignorant.
• More necessary if country is very poor. More easily maintained if country is very wealthy.	• Less likely if country is very poor or very wealthy.
• Controlled family size: relatively small when country is poor, relatively large when country is wealthy.	• Uncontrolled family size: relatively large when country is poor, relatively small when country is wealthy.
• Stronger position of the mother in the family.	• Weaker position of the mother in the family.
• Both father and mother used as models by boys and girls.	• Father used as model by boys; mother by girls.
• Same as high MAS.	• Traditions going back several generations, reinforced or weakened by historical events.

Why did these men travel so far and so long—was it because they had women who were able to manage the home front? In this way the Viking phenomenon has to be traced to even earlier roots.

As argued in the beginning of this chapter, the crucial link in the transfer of sex role patterns must be the family, in which children model their sex role self-concepts after the values-in-use which they notice in the adults of both sexes with whom they are in contact. The sex role pattern is transferred together with other values. Power distance, for example, is also transferred in the family; I assume it to reflect the degree of absoluteness of the authority of adults, but mostly of the fathers, over the children. Masculinity or femininity is then related to the difference in roles between the parents or other male and female adults. For the transfer of power distance the role of the father is most crucial; for the transfer of masculinity the role of the mother is crucial.

Consequences of Different MAS Levels

The presumed consequences of differences in the norm for masculinity/ femininity in societies are listed in Figure 6.8; they are partly based on the correlations found in this chapter and partly expanded on the basis of impressions and reasoning.

The different importance of achievement in more masculine versus more feminine societies is definitely reinforced by a difference in rewards. A Norwegian colleague once explained to me that in his society "you shouldn't suppose you are better than anybody else," and a Spanish author writing about my own country, the Netherlands, wrote that "the Dutchman . . . is perpetually leveling everything and

FIGURE 6.8   Consequences of National Masculinity Index Differences

See pages	Low MAS Countries	High MAS Countries

Consequences for Society at Large

See pages	Low MAS Countries	High MAS Countries
295	• Trying to be better than others is neither socially nor materially rewarded.	• There are rewards in the form of wealth or status for the successful achiever.
297	• Social adaptation-oriented school system.	• Performance-oriented school system.
293	• More benevolence versus the third world.	• Less benevolence versus the third world.
297	• Conservation of the environment is seen as a more important problem than economic growth.	• Economic growth is seen as a more important problem than conservation of the environment.
284 286	• Small-scale enterprises, projects, etc. popular.	• Large-scale enterprises, projects, etc. popular.
292	• Men and women follow the same types of higher education.	• Men and women follow different types of higher-level education.
268	• Men and women can both be breadwinners.	• Men are breadwinners, women are cakewinners.
268	• Less occupational segregation: e.g., male nurses.	• Some occupations are considered typically male, others female.
293	• Slower car driving, fewer accidents.	• Faster car driving, more accidents.

Consequences for Religious Life and Philosophical and Ideological Thinking

See pages	Low MAS Countries	High MAS Countries
293	• In Christianity, greater affinity to Protestantism.	• In Christianity, greater affinity to Catholicism.
293 266	• Appeal of "tender" religious currents, philosophies, and ideologies.	• Appeal of "tough" religious currents, philosophies, and ideologies.
293	• Belief in equality of the sexes.	• Belief in inequality of the sexes.
298	• More moderate women's liberation movements.	• Aggressive women's liberation movements.

Consequences for Organizations

See pages	Low MAS Countries	High MAS Countries
278	• Some young men and women want careers, others do not.	• Young men expect to make a career; those who don't see themselves as failures.
284	• Organizations should not interfere with people's private lives.	• Organizational interests are a legitimate reason for interfering with people's private lives.
292	• More women in more qualified and better-paid jobs.	• Fewer women in more qualified and better-paid jobs.

FIGURE 6.8   Continued

281	• Women in more qualified jobs not particularly assertive.	• Women in more qualified jobs are very assertive.
284	• Lower job stress.	• Higher job stress.
298	• Less industrial conflict.	• More industrial conflict.
298	• Appeal of job restructuring permitting group integration.	• Appeal of job restructuring permitting individual achievement.

everyone" (de Baena, 1968: 115). These are both very feminine-scoring countries; and in such countries, the social rewards for excellence are slight. The material rewards are reduced by equalitarian tax systems.

The differences in stress on achievement are also present in the school system. For example, school performance in Germany is an important issue; there is a strong pressure for performance, which in extreme cases can lead to suicide attempts among students who fail. In the Netherlands, for example, the amount of pressure for performance is much less; anything that looks like competitive pressure is socially disapproved of. Suicides among young people occur, but rarely because of failed exams.

One inferred consequence of differences in MAS which I mention in Figure 6.8 has to do with what both citizens and politicians in a country consider top priority issues. Two potential top priority issues are economic growth and conservation of the environment; and they are in conflict. Whoever watches the international political scene cannot avoid noticing that different countries use different priorities in the issue of economic growth versus environment. The point is that the essential choices are not rational. In a lucid analysis, Douglas (1970) shows that we are far from being the first civilization to realize that our environment is at risk, although the dangers differ. Every society has its ideas about things that pollute and argues about measures against it in terms of "time, money, God, and nature." The dangers of pollution today are certainly very real, but their evaluation is still not a rational process. In a discussion between Wildavsky (1976) and Coppock (1977), the former argues that the search for environmental quality contains many ritual, rather than rational, elements; and the latter answers that the non-rationality is as much on the side of the economists who oppose the environmentalists as of the environmentalists themselves. I suggest that the main non-rational value issue that opposes economists and environmentalists in this discussion is based on the masculinity-femininity dimension.[21] We have seen evidence in this chapter that the feminine values syndrome puts greater weight on the environment ("living in a desirable area"), while the masculine values syndrome puts greater weight on earnings—and the various correlates found throughout this chapter confirm that this difference reflects something quite fundamental that stretches beyond the work situation. Applied to the growth-versus-environment controversy, a more feminine value position will put higher priority on environmental conservation and a more masculine one on economic growth. Of course, events may shift the priorities too; but the value conflict will always be present. Currently, more feminine countries like Sweden and the Netherlands take a more "environmentalist" position; more masculine such as Germany and Belgium put more priority on economic growth. In Asia, masculine Japan has huge pollution problems with which it seems to be unable to cope, while China, in its development, attaches a greater priority to pollution control (Tsurumi, 1977). The masculinity scores of Hong Kong, Singapore, and Taiwan make it likely that the Chinese value system is considerably less masculine than the Japanese.

Among the consequences for ideological thinking I have put the suggestion that more masculine and more feminine countries have different types of women's liberation movements. Those in more masculine countries tend to be more aggressive; the ideal of women's liberation is that women can be as assertive as men: women try to beat men at their game. In more feminine countries, we find women's liberation movements which defend the reform of the entire society along traditionally "feminine" lines.

Most other entries in Figure 6.8 refer to aspects of the masculinity dimension discussed earlier in this chapter. However, two lines under "consequences for organizations" need more explanation. I suggest that a relationship can be expected between the strength of the masculinity norm and the tendency to resolve issues in industrial relations by open conflict. The masculinity-femininity dimension is the only one which sharply separates the Nordic from the Anglo countries; one of the most visible differences between, for example, Sweden and Great Britain is their different ways of handling industrial conflict issues, which in Sweden tend to be resolved by dialogue and in Britain by strikes (whether this really means a resolution is, of course, doubtful).

A final issue which I also associate with masculinity is the type of "humanization of work" or "job restructuring" popular in a country. In Chapter 5 I suggested that differences in individualism affect preferences for different forms of employee participation and worker self-management. Masculinity affects another trend in work organization reform: humanization of work. What is a "humanized" job depends on one's definition of what is human. In a masculine culture a humanized job should give opportunities for recognition, advancement, and challenge. In a feminine culture, the stress will more be on cooperation and the working atmosphere. This is illustrated by a most fascinating case study.[22] In 1974, six U.S. automobile workers (two women and four men) worked three weeks in the Saab-Scania plant in Soedertaelje, Sweden, where a new "humanized" system of group assembly had been installed. Journalist Robert B. Goldmann (1975) went with them, and at the end of the third week he asked them whether they preferred the Detroit (U.S.) or the Soedertaelje (Swedish) system. *The only American who clearly preferred the Swedish system was a woman.* The other five chose the U.S. system, though two would accept the Swedish system under certain conditions. About the woman who chose the United States Goldmann writes:

> Lynette Stewart chose Detroit. In the Cadillac plant where she works, she is on her own and can make her own challenge, while at Saab-Scania she has to consider people in front and behind her [1975: 48].

Goldmann also noticed that this very feature had been mentioned by a Swedish woman he interviewed as a point of attraction. This is clearly a value issue. Humanization of work, too, is a matter of values: of the "masculinity" or the "femininity" of one's point of departure.

STATISTICAL ANALYSIS OF
DATA USED IN CHAPTER 6

Calculating Factor Scores for New Cases

In Figure 6.2 factor scores are shown for the work goals factor analysis across 38 occupations, for men and women separately in two of the occupations. However, the four cases involved (male and female clerks, male and female experts) were not part of the original set of 38 cases on which the factor analysis was based.

Computing factor scores for cases which were not part of the original factor analysis is possible if we have the "factor score coefficient" for each factor on each variable. The procedure is then as follows: We start with the scores on each variable (in this case the standardized score on each of the 22 goals) for each new case (in this case, male clerks, female clerks, male experts, and female experts). We now replace these scores by standard scores in terms of the mean and standard deviation of the cases that were in the original factor analysis (in this case, the 38 occupations). Then, each standard score is multiplied by its factor score coefficient and the products are summed. This is how the factor scores for men and women only in Figure 6.2 were determined.

The scores for men and women in Figure 6.4 were computed in a similar way, however now using as a basis the work goals factor analysis for 14 goals across 40 countries. The means and standard deviations used for computing the standard scores can be read from the bottom lines of Appendix 3, Table A3.1. The factor score coefficients for IDV and MAS are listed in Figure 6.9. The resulting factor scores must be transposed into IDV and MAS scores through multiplying by 25 and 20, respectively, and adding 50 (see below).

The Country Masculinity Index
and Its Correlations with Other
HERMES Survey Questions

The Masculinity Index, like the Individualism Index, is based on a factor score. This factor score was found in the 40-country, 14 work goals factor analysis (Appendix 3, Table A3.1); it is labeled SOC (social-ego). SOC scores have been transposed into Masculinity Index (MAS) scores by a linear transformation: $MAS = 50 - 20 \, SOC$, which brings MAS into a range between zero and 100 and reverses its sign. Across the 40 countries, MAS is correlated $-.43$ with the percentage of female employees in the country's HERMES subsidiary (A1 in Appendix 2).

In order to find the other questions in the HERMES survey ecologically correlated with MAS, we can use the ecological factor analysis of all value-related A and B questions (Chapter 2). In this factor analysis, "masculinity" appears as a factor by itself. Not surprisingly, we find that the various work goals on which the MAS index is based all load on the MAS factor (A5, A6, A7, A8, A11, A14, A15, A16, and A17). We find four other questions which also load on other factors: A37, which also loads on uncertainty avoidance, B57, which also loads on the opposite pole of uncertainty avoidance, and B52 and B58, which also load on the negative pole of individualism.

As for the C questions (discontinued in 1971 or before), significant but weak correlations with MAS are found (Appendix 2) for C13 ($r = -.45$), C17 ($r = -.41$), and C19 ($r = -.48$), as well as for C15 after controlling for acquiescence ($r = -.40$).

MAS is finally correlated .40 with A58, the "overall satisfaction" score (see Appendix 2), although in the factor analysis of all questions A58 loads highest on UAI (see page 84). In more masculine countries, respondents tend to score *less* overall satisfied.

FIGURE 6.9   Factor Score Coefficients for the 14 Work Goals, 40-
Countries Factor Analysis, to be Used for Computing IDV and
MAS Scores for Cases not in the Original Factor Analysis

	Factor score for	
Work goal	IDV	MAS
challenge	.12	.17
desirable area	.09	-.19
earnings	-.01	.22
cooperation	-.12	-.22
training	-.27	.00
benefits	-.14	-.03
recognition	.05	.18
physical conditions	-.22	.00
freedom	.14	.00
employment security	-.04	-.16
advancement	-.08	.17
manager	.04	-.22
use of skills	-.20	.13
personal time	.23	-.01

**Masculinity and Femininity in
Earlier HERMES Studies**

The 1971 study of HERMES data by Sirota and Greenwood for 14 goals, 25 countries, and three occupations, was mentioned in Chapter 5. These authors noticed in the goal profiles for their clusters of countries an opposition between getting-ahead goals and concern with the immediate environment, which is the same distinction which I, on more extensive data, labeled masculinity-femininity.

In Chapter 5 I also referred to my earlier (Hofstede, 1973) study of HERMES work goals in 21 occupations in the Netherlands, compared with Europe; a study which was afterwards extended to Norway and Sweden. The results (Figure 5.12) show that where the three countries are similar is in their relatively low scores on advancement and earnings, their high scores on cooperation, manager, and desirable area. This is why all three show up on the low end of the MAS scale (Figure 6.3). The 1973 study was based on *all* available occupations and not just on the seven occupations on which the MAS index has been founded; it illustrates that the MAS dimension is present in the other occupations as well.

**Masculinity and the Similarity of
Two Measures of the Importance of Work Goals**

In a preliminary study (Hofstede, 1976b, 1979a: 28ff) reference was made to two measures of the importance of work goals. One is the measure through direct questions: "How important is it to you to . . . ." (for example, "have an opportunity for high earnings"). The other is an indirect measure that can be used only for a *group* of respondents, not for an individual respondent. This second measure uses the answers on a set of other questions in the HERMES questionnaire: "About the satisfaction of your goals" (A19–A32 in Appendix 1)—the 14 work aspects (facets) covered in these questions are the same as those on covered by the direct "work goal importance" questions (A5–A18). Also, the second measure uses the answer on question A58 "Considering everything, how would you rate your overall satisfaction in this company at the present time?" For the group of respondents we want to study, the "facet satisfaction" questions A19–A32 have been correlated with the "overall satisfaction" question A58. We can now use the strength of the correlation between facet and overall satisfaction as a second, indirect measure of work goal importance for the group.

In the preliminary study it was shown that this second, indirect measure leads to largely the same ordering of work goals as the first, direct measure for the higher educated occupations, but to a very different ordering of work goals for clerks and unskilled workers. However, the similarity between the two measures depends also on the nationality of the respondents.

For 18 more or less homogeneous categories of HERMES employees, representing five countries (France, Great Britain, Germany, Japan, and the Netherlands) and four groups of occupations, I have compared the rank order of 22 work facets on the basis of the direct measure with the rank order of the same work facets on the basis of the second, correlation measure. The results, expressed in the Spearman rank correlation coefficients between the two measures, are tabulated in Figure 6.10.

Figure 6.10 shows positive and sometimes significant rank correlations for Japan, Germany, and Great Britain (high MAS countries) and correlations around zero for France and The

FIGURE 6.10 Spearman Rank Correlation Coefficients Between Self-Rated Work Goal Importance and Facet Vs. Overall Satisfaction Correlations, Across 22 Work Facets for 15 Subpopulations of HERMES Respondents

	Japan	Germany	Great Britain	France	Netherlands	Rank order of occupations according to correlation
Laboratory managers and professionals	no data	.59***	.31	.05	.27	1-2
Manufacturing plant managers and professionals	.53**	.64***	.54**	-.01	.01	1-2
Laboratory technicians and clerks	no data	.47*	.41*	-.14	-.26	3
Manufacturing plant technicians, clerks & unskilled operators	.45*	.29	.19	.02	-.35	4
Rank order of countries according to correlation	1-2	1-2	3	4-5	4-5	

Total number of respondents 11,352.
SOURCE: Hofstede (1976b: Table 6), completed with some additional data.

Netherlands (low MAS countries). The strength of the correlation diminishes for the lower educated occupations in all countries, as was found before.

Results of Other Studies Significantly Correlated with MAS

(1) McGee (1977) reports on a public opinion survey with about 7000 respondents in six European Common Market countries; the purpose of the survey was to find out about the public's preferences for free versus nationalized enterprises. One question asked respondents in what *size* of enterprise they would prefer to work. The results are tabulated in Figure 6.11. In the table I have computed a mean size score, giving the value 1 to the smallest size category used and the value 4 to the largest. The mean size scores for the six countries are correlated with MAS with rho = .84.

(2) The European Commission sponsored a public opinion survey in the nine European Common Market countries in October/November 1977, about issues related to retirement, with a total of nearly 9000 respondents (CCE, 1978). One question from this survey was the following:

> "If the economic situation were to improve so that the standard of living could be raised, which of the following two measures would you consider to be better:
> —increasing the salaries (for the same number of hours worked)
> —or reduce the number of hours worked (for the same salary)?"

Across the eight countries also represented in the HERMES survey (all except Luxemburg), the mean percentages of answers on this question are listed in Figure 6.12. The percentages do not add up to 100 because of "no opinion" answers. The third column shows the differences

FIGURE 6.11   Results of a Public Opinion Poll in Six European Countries Held in December 1976

Countries in order of MAS		% preferring to work in enterprise of				Mean score
		< 50 employees (1)	50–100 employees (2)	100–500 employees (3)	> 500 employees (4)	
Italy		23	8	12	29	2.65
Great Britain		35	12	14	20	2.23
Germany (Fed.Rep.)		33	19	19	17	2.23
Belgium		41	12	13	19	2.12
France		35	16	15	20	2.23
Netherlands		59	12	8	12	1.70
Spearman	PDI					.04
rank	UAI					.09
correlation	IDV					-.09
with :	MAS					.84[*]

Total number of respondents 6833.
SOURCE: McGee (1977: Table 3).

FIGURE 6.12 Results of a Public Opinion Poll in Eight European Countries
Held in October/November 1977

Countries in order of MAS		% preferring :		
		more salary (1)	shorter working hours (2)	difference (1) - (2)
Italy		54	39	15
Ireland		62	31	31
Great Britain		45	49	- 4
Germany Federal Republic		36	49	-13
Belgium		35	48	-13
France		40	52	-12
Denmark		23	66	-43
Netherlands		28	64	-36
Spearman rank correlation with	GNP			.78*
	PDI			-.04
	UAI			.11
	IDV			-.14
	MAS			.86**

Total number of respondents 8936.
SOURCE: CCE (1978: 37).

between the percentage in favor of more salary and the percentage in favor of less working hours. These differences are correlated with MAS with rho = .86. They are also correlated with the country's GNP/capita: Not surprisingly, the poorer countries stress more the need for increasing the salaries. However, the correlation with the subjective value syndrome of masculinity is stronger than with the objective national wealth.

MAS and McClelland's Need for Achievement

In Chapter 4, Figure 4.11, a negative rank correlation was shown between UAI and the scores on Need for Achievement (n_{Ach}) which McClelland (1961) derived from a content analysis of 1925 children's readers from 22 countries. Figure 4.11 also shows a sizable positive second-order rank correlation of 1925 n_{Ach} with MAS, which increases the cumulative percentage of variance explained, R^2, from .41 to .54 and the multiple correlation coefficient R from .64 to .73.

The discussion in Chapter 4 suggests a possible explanation why McClelland's 1925 data (and not his data for 1950) correlate with the HERMES indices. The actual n_{Ach} scores are shown in Figure 6.13, together with the UAI and MAS scores and the ranking of n_{Ach} that would be predicted from UAI plus MAS. Five of the seven highest n_{Ach} countries are Anglo countries; five of the seven lowest n_{Ach} countries are Latin or Mediterranean countries. These are the clusters that also appear in the HERMES data for most indices. In the upper part of the table we generally find UAI < MAS (except for Sweden and Denmark); in the lower part, UAI > MAS (except for South Africa).

FIGURE 6.13   McClelland's Need for Achievement Scores for 1925,
              Compared with UAI and MAS

Country	n_{Ach} standard scores 1925	UAI	MAS	Rank order of n_{Ach} predicted on basis of UAI + MAS
Ireland	2.29	35	68	1
Australia	·1.77	51	61	9
Canada	1.58	48	52	7
Sweden	.92	29	5	8
Great Britain	.79	35	66	2
Denmark	.66	23	16	5
U.S.A.	.52	46	62	3
Argentina	.47	86	56	17
Japan	.34	92	95	13
Austria	.07	70	79	10
New Zealand	−.06	49	58	6
Germany	−.19	65	66	11
Norway	−.26	50	8	12
Chile	−.32	86	28	20
Finland	−.38	59	26	14
South Africa	−.64	49	63	4
Belgium	−.71	94	54	22
France	−.97	86	43	18
Spain	−.97	86	42	19
Greece	−1.56	112	57	21
Brazil	−1.68	76	49	16
Netherlands	−1.68	53	14	15

**The MAS Index Versus Seven Geographical,
Economic, and Demographic Indicators**

Like the other indices PDI, UAI, and IDV, MAS has been correlated with the seven standard ecological indicators listed in Figure 2.7. The only prediction that can be made is a positive correlation between MAS and ORG, the size of the HERMES subsidiary in the country, as we found people in higher MAS countries to prefer larger organizations (Figure 6.11).

The actual correlation coefficients in Figure 6.14 show that across all 40 countries, the multiple correlation of MAS with these ecological indicators is low: $R^2 = .30$. It is higher if we split the countries, as we did in the previous chapters, into poorer and wealthier ones. For the poorer countries, the multiple correlation pattern is complicated: the seven indicators suppress

FIGURE 6.14   Product Moment Correlations and Multiple and Stepwise
Regression Across Countries of MAS Scores with Seven
System-Level Indicators

Indicator	Zero-order correlations with MAS scores across		
	All 40 countries	21 poorer countries	19 wealthier countries
GNP	-.09	.13	-.33
GNG	.05	-.18	.23
LAT	-.31*	-.48*	-.63**
POP	.29*	.11	.42*
PGR	.14	.47*	.05
PDN	.10	-.00	.19
ORG	.20	.24	.23
Squared multiple correlation with all seven R^2	.30	.62	.78
Order of indicators in stepwise regression, cumulative R^2, and sign of coefficient	1. .10-LAT 2. .25+ORG 3. .28-PGR	1. .23-LAT 2. .34+ORG 3. .36+PGR	1. .40-LAT 2. .71-PGR

For definition of indicators see Figure 2.7.

each other's contribution to MAS. In the multiple regression of MAS on the seven indicators for the 21 poorer countries, the two that contribute significantly to the variance in MAS are GNP and POP (both with positive sign), but these show negligible zero-order correlations and do not appear in the first three steps of the stepwise regression. For the wealthier countries, the picture is much clearer, with LAT and PGR as the indicators mainly explaining MAS.

The hypothesized positive relationship between ORG (the size of the HERMES organization in the country) and MAS is indeed found (step 2 in the stepwise regression for 40 countries).

The correlation of MAS with PGR (population growth) is positive for the poorer countries; for the wealthier ones, PGR shows up with *negative* sign in the stepwise regression, while the zero-order correlation between MAS and PGR for the wealthier countries is about zero. This is because MAS correlates negatively with LAT, but LAT and PGR are also strongly negatively correlated: therefore, the zero-order correlation is suppressed.

MAS and the Role of Women in Society

(1) Data on the position of women in society in different modern nations have been assembled by Boulding et al. (1976) in their *Handbook of International Data on Women*. The data were collected from several sources, often from United Nations documents, and their reliability is variable. From this source book I have taken data on (1) sex role differentiation in higher level jobs and (2) sex role differentiation in higher education.

Two different tables in the handbook express the participation of women in professional and technical work[23]: one as a percentage of all professional and technical workers, and the other as a percentage of all working women. The figures are presented in Figure 6.15.

The correlations with all indices are considerably higher for the percentage of working women than for the percentage of professional and technical workers. Either the former figures are more reliable or they are more meaningful (they implicitly contain information about the

FIGURE 6.15   Indices of Female Activity in Professional and Technical Work, Versus GNP/Capita and Four HERMES Indices

Countries	Professional and technical women as % of all prof. and tech. workers[a]		Professional and technical women as % of all working women[b]	
	All countries	Wealthy countries only	All countries	Wealthy countries only
Argentina	59		18	
Australia	42	42	14	14
Austria	40	40	7	7
Belgium	42	42	11	11
Canada	42	42	18	18
Chile	48		11	
Colombia	47		10	
Denmark	51	51	12	12
Finland	52	52	-	-
France	43	43	12	12
Great Britain	38	38	11	11
Germany (Fed.Rep.)	33	33	10	10
Greece	34		7	
Hong Kong	44		7	
India	16		1	
Iran	26		6	
Ireland	51	51	15	15
Israel	49	49	-	-
Italy	37	37	-	-
Japan	37	37	6	6
Mexico	38		-	
Netherlands	39	39	19	19
Norway	37	37	13	13
New Zealand	44	44	17	17
Pakistan	10		1	
Peru	46		9	
Philippines	20		3	
Portugal	50		11	
South Africa	42		7	
Singapore	37		10	
Spain	33		10	
Sweden	43	43	23	23
Switzerland	32	32	13	13
Thailand	34		1	
Turkey	21		-	
U.S.A.	39	39	14	14
Venezuela	43		20	
Yugoslavia	46		10	
Product moment correlation with :	GNP	.29*	-.18	.62*****	.44*
	PDI	-.33*	-.31	-.41	-.14*
	UAI	.08	-.24	-.13**	-.57*
	IDV	.17	-.09	.46**	.50*
	MAS	-.17	.35	-.24	-.64**

[a]Table 28
[b]Table 37
SOURCE: Boulding et al. (1976).

average educational level of working women). Also, it makes a considerable difference whether we take all countries, wealthy and poor alike, or only the wealthy ones. Across all countries, wealth (GNP per capita) is the strongest correlate of the percentage of professional and technical women versus all working women. This suggests that in less developed countries the few professional and technical jobs go first to men, regardless of societal values. If we limit our analysis to the 19 wealthy countries (1979 GNP/capita over $1300), the masculinity norm

FIGURE 6.16   Indices of Female Participation in Higher Education, Versus GNP/Capita and Four HERMES Indices

Countries	Female students in higher education as % of total students[a]		Index of segregation for five types of higher education[b]	
	All countries	Wealthy countries only	All countries	Wealthy countries only
Argentina	42		37	
Australia	30	30	60	60
Austria	29	29	41	41
Belgium	35	35	27	27
Brazil	37		34	
Canada	39	39	50	50
Chile	40		55	
Colombia	23		50	
Denmark	34	34	41	41
Finland	49	49	33	33
France	42	42	42	42
Great Britain	32	32	44	44
Germany (Fed.Rep.)	26	26	56	56
Greece	32		27	
Hong Kong	31		59	
India	21		64	
Iran	25		35	
Ireland	34	34	44	44
Israel	50	50	38	38
Italy	38	38	45	45
Japan	28	28	38	38
Mexico	18		38	
Netherlands	27	27	37	37
Norway	30	30	16	16
New Zealand	29	29	39	39
Pakistan	16		66	
Peru	34		33	
Philippines	55		39	
Portugal	44		43	
South Africa	26		55	
Singapore	29		53	
Spain	26		45	
Sweden	37	37	25	25
Switzerland	22	22	-	-
Thailand	42		44	
Turkey	19		26	
U.S.A.	41	41	49	49
Venezuela	33		15	
Yugoslavia	40		28	
Product moment correlation with :	GNP	.17	.06	-.10	.03
	PDI	-.03	.04	-.01	.01
	UAI	.06	.13	-.31*	-.06
	IDV	.08	-.06	.03	.34
	MAS	-.24	-.26	.28*	.56**

[a]Table 54
[b]Table 60
SOURCE: Boulding et al. (1976).

FIGURE 6.17   Average Yearly Official (Government) Development
              Assistance 1967–1976, Expressed in % of 1970 GNP,
              Versus GNP/Capita and Four HERMES Indices

Countries in order of MAS		Development assistance in % of GNP
Japan		.37
Austria		.20
Italy		.15
Switzerland		.24
Great Britain		.45
Germany F.R.		.48
U.S.A.		.35
Australia		.79
Belgium		.75
Canada		.61
France		.83
Denmark		.68
Netherlands		.99
Norway		.74
Sweden		.79
Spearman rank correlation with	GNP	.24
	PDI	.14
	UAI	−.13
	IDV	.22
	MAS	−.81***

SOURCES:
   Development assistance 1967–1968: U.N. Statistical Yearbook 1972: Table 198.
                        1969–1972: U.N. Statistical Yearbook 1974: Table 199.
                        1973–1976: U.N. Statistical Yearbook 1977: Table 204.
   1970 GNP: World Bank Atlas, 1972

of the country becomes the strongest correlate of the percentage of professional and technical women (the more masculine the culture, the lower the share of professional and technical women). The correlation of $-.64***$ is sizable.

In the field of higher education, I show in Figure 6.16 data from two tables from Boulding et al.The first is the percentage of female students in all kinds of higher (third-level) education taken together. The second is an Index of Segregation which measures the proportion of males (or females) that would have to change their field of study for there to be equality in the distribution of the sexes in the study of education, law, social sciences, engineering, and agriculture (Boulding et al., 1976: 346). The second measure produces the higher correlations. Across all countries, the segregation index is weakly but significantly correlated with UAI and MAS: If we limit ourselves again to the wealthier countries, a stronger correlation with MAS remains (.56**); more "masculine" countries tend to show greater segregation in higher education.

(2) In the context of the 12-country study Images of the World in the Year 2000 (Ornauer et al., 1976; see page 173), Bártová has analyzed the images of the position of the woman and the family. The questions of interest to us in the context of "masculinity" are: (1) "Do you think that by the year 2000 it will be more common or less common with women in leading positions than it is today?" and (2) "Do you hope . . . ?" We find that country mean scores across six countries which can be compared are correlated with MAS as follows:

Thinks women in leading positions (answers by men)	rho $= -.37$
Thinks women in leading positions (answers by women)	rho $= -.37$
Hopes women in leading positions (answers by men)	rho $= -.54$
Hopes women in leading positions (answers by women)	rho $= .03$

For six cases, none of these correlations reaches significance; but the negative correlations show a trend that, in particular, men in more masculine countries do *not* hope to see more women in leading positions.

MAS and Official Development Assistance

The amounts of money spent by wealthier countries in development assistance to third world countries, both from official (government) and from private funds, is published by the United Nations.Figure 6.17 lists the results of a computation of the mean annual *official* development assistance over a 10-year period (1967–1976), expressed in percentage of 1970 GNP, for the 15 countries from the HERMES sample for which full data have been published. We find a rho $= -.81***$ between official development assistance and MAS; the correlation between development assistance and national wealth (GNP/capita) is very weak: rho $= .24$.

NOTES

1. See Kroeber-Keneth (1955: 47) and Heberer et al. (1970: 283).

2. A French duchess at the court of Louis XIV is supposed to have said to her husband: "I can produce peers of France without you—you cannot without me." In the same vein is the following quote from a story from eighteenth-century Denmark by Isak Dinesen: "The ladies . . . carried the future of the name in their laps. . . . They were . . . conscious of their value. . . . For how free they were, how powerful! Their lords might rule the country, and allow themselves many liberties, but when it came to that supreme matter of legitimacy which was the vital principle of their world, the centre of gravity lay with them" (Dinesen, 1942: 32).

3. Many other examples of cross-cultural variability of sex role distribution in traditional societies are found in Quinn (1977: 198–219).

4. The quotations are from the Authorized Version of the British and Foreign Bible Society (1954).

5. In the Roman Empire, the dominant philosophical trends considered males as superior (*sexus melior*), but for example the philosopher C. Musonius Rufus (first century A.D.) defended the equality of the sexes and, in particular, the study of philosophy by women and men alike (Eyben, 1976).

6. Brief et al. (1977) compared samples from the U.S. population in the 1974 General Survey conducted by the National Opinion Research Center, matched for occupational category, on the ranking of five goals: Feelings of accomplishment, high pay, advancement, security, and short hours. They found no significant differences between the sexes; both rated accomplishment, pay, and advancement as much more important than security and short hours. However, the list of goals used was excessively short; no social goals were present, and it is these, in other studies, which were placed high on the female priority list. The selection of five items tells us more, in fact, about the survey designers' values than about the U.S. population.

7. "Friendly atmosphere" also discriminates more between *occupations* than cooperation (Appendix 3, Table A3.3). On the other hand, the two formulations show hardly any difference in discrimination between *countries*, and "cooperation" discriminates better between age groups. The fact that different formulations of apparently almost the same concept discriminate differently among sexes, occupations, countries, and age groups is one of the reasons why ecological factors differ according to the criterion of aggregation used (for example, occupation or country: see page 81).

8. The fact that I associate the "social-ego" factor with female-male preference (and not the "individual-collective" factor) seems to contradict the results of the variance analysis in Figure 2.4. In that case, I find a strong sex effect for earnings minus cooperation (= ego-social) but an even stronger sex effect for personal time minus training (= individual-collective). However, the variance analysis is based on different data: five other occupations (all from manufacturing plants) in only 10 countries; and only two of these occupations (clerks and unskilled workers) have sizable numbers of female incumbents.

9. The minimum limit of 20 female respondents per country is based on Hofstede (1975b) in which it is shown that work goal importance rank orders became less reliable for groups smaller than 20.

10. In the United States, Mack (1974) found in a laboratory experiment with married couples that working-class husbands exerted more power over their wives than did middle-class husbands. However, the class effect only applied for a relatively "intellectual" task (jointly filling out a questionnaire).

11. Thomas (1973) reports an exceptionally wide age gap between the sexes for France. However, Boulding et al. (1976: Table 70) show a much higher life expectation (72 instead of 68 years) for French men than does Thomas, so that the information is contradictory.

12. The ambition of women may be channeled toward *their husband's* career. In a study of the Dutch lower middle class, Berting (1968: 138–139) found that "in many cases, the wife is the motor behind the husband's aspirations for promotion."

13. In no country does wealth have so strong a symbolic value as in the United States (Kluckhohn, 1950: 392; Beteille, 1977: 85). That country, of course, is a low UAI, High MAS country *and* McClelland's home culture.

14. Sweden has a deliberate educational policy for training both girls and boys in nontraditional sex roles. See Fredriksson (1969).

15. For a more extensive survey of sex differences in psychological differentiation see Van Leeuwen (1978).

16. The thesis was written by O.C. Wit in 1955. In another study, Witkin et al. (1974) compared pairs of villages (one traditional, one nontraditional) in Italy, Mexico, and the Netherlands, and showed that children in traditional villages tend to produce more field-dependent test scores than do children in nontraditional villages. However, the samples were taken to show within-country differences and do not allow any conclusion on between-country differences.

17. Levinson (1977: 763), reviewing anthropological studies of primitive cultures, concludes that population increases where females are subservient to males.

18. A crude labor force participation rate for women can be computed from the Yearbook of Labour Statistics (ILO, 1976: Table 1). Across 38 countries, this rank correlates −.01 with MAS. A similar rate is shown in Boulding et al. (1976: Table 1).

19. For evidence of the lack of support for development aid in public opinion in (high MAS) Great Britain see Bowles (1978).

20. Galtung et al. (1976: 34) summarize a paper by Stang which describes the car as a "materialized ideology" representing, among other things, an "actionist" value orientation, "an ideal of extravert efficiency, of conquering ever new challenges, new horizons." This is a masculine value orientation. The car has often been identified as a phallic symbol.

21. Gray (1973) links the impossibility in the United States to imagine a future without growth to the "masculine consciousness" in that country.

22. Also in Gohl (1977: 267ff).

23. Boulding et al. also show tables for "administrative and managerial work." I suspect, however, that several countries have mixed up "administrative" and "clerical" (which was another category). It is extremely unlikely that 87 percent of all administrators and managers in the Philippines are women, or 48 percent in Switzerland, as Boulding et al.'s Table 29 indicates.

Chapter 7

INTEGRATING THE FOUR DIMENSIONS

SUMMARY OF THIS CHAPTER

The four dimensions of national culture described and analyzed in the Chapters 3 through 6 relate to basic problems of humanity. Some of the dimensions interact in their effects upon cultures. The combination of PDI and UAI affects in particular organization structures and functioning through the implicit models of the ideal organization which people carry. It also affects which theories of organization will gain popularity in a country.

The interaction of UAI and MAS is shown to relate to the dominant motivation pattern, thereby refuting the universality of the American motivation theories of McClelland and Maslow.

This chapter summarizes the significant correlations that were found between the HERMES indices and non-HERMES data: data from narrow surveys, from representative surveys, and from country-level indicators. For the seven geographical, economic, and demographic indicators used in each of the Chapters 3 through 6, the regression of each indicator on the four indices is shown.

The values of the four indices for the 40 countries can be used to form clusters of countries with similar index profiles. The literature is reviewed for other studies using quantitative data to form country clusters; those using a theoretical "catch-all" sets of variables do not arrive at clusters which make much sense. Those using political or values data lead to more meaningful clusterings. For a cluster analysis on the basis of the HERMES data, a hierarchical grouping method has been used which shows the overall closeness or distance of the country cultures. On the basis of the resulting "dendrogram" and with some reordering of clusters, the 40 countries are divided into eight culture areas: More Developed Latin, Less Developed Latin, More Developed Asian, Less Developed Asian, Near-Eastern, Germanic, Anglo, and Nordic.

A special analysis is done for two countries in which the HERMES surveys were taken in two languages each: Belgium and Switzerland. In Belgium, the two language areas are culturally very similar and belong to the same (More Developed Latin) culture area; in Switzerland, the two language areas show wide cultural differences and clearly belong to different culture areas.

The Four HERMES Dimensions Relate to Universal Problems of Mankind

Power Distance, Uncertainty Avoidance, Individualism and Masculinity satisfy Kluckhohn's criteria for "universal categories of culture" (see page 44): they form "a generalized framework that underlies the more apparent and striking facts of cultural relativity." They come close to the "standard analytic issues" distilled from the literature on "National Character" by Inkeles and Levinson (1969: 447ff; see page 47).

> (1) Relation to authority: This obviously corresponds to the power distance dimension.
> (2) Conception of self: Under this heading, Inkeles and Levinson mention first "the individual's concepts of masculinity and feminity" (1969: 450). This is the Masculinity dimension. Then they refer to the relationship between ego and society, quoting the work of E. H. Erikson on "ego identity" and by A. Kardiner on the "individual security system." This, obviously, is the Individualism dimension.
> (3) Primary dilemmas or conflicts, and ways of dealing with them: Under this heading, Inkeles and Levinson refer to the control of aggression, the expression versus inhibition of affect, and the dilemma of trust versus mistrust. These are issues that we found to be particularly associated with the Uncertainty Avoidance dimension.

In short, the four dimensions that were empirically found in the HERMES data are theoretically relevant. They describe basic problems of humanity with which every society has to cope; and the variation of country scores along these dimensions shows that different societies do cope with these problems in different ways. On each of these problems there is not just one possible answer; but a range of possible answers,[1] even for modern industrial nations.

The four dimensions deal with issues that are equally relevant to psychologists (and psychoanalysts) and to sociologists. Some psychological connotations of Power Distance are dependency and the impact of the father on one's personality; of Uncertainty Avoidance, anxiety, aggression versus apathy, stress, and superego; of Individualism, ego identity; of Masculinity, assertiveness, sexual identity, and the impact of the mother on one's personality. Some sociological connotations of Power Distance are social stratification and inequality; of Uncertainty Avoidance, the need for structure and formalization; of Individualism, the relationship among individuals, institutions, and society; of Masculinity, social sex role differentiation.

The four dimensions, however, are not necessarily exhaustive; they do not represent the final word on dimensions of national culture. First, it may be that there exist other dimensions related to equally fundamental problems of mankind which were not found in the HERMES research because the relevant questions were simply not asked. Some suggestions for other dimensions can be found in the review of the literature in the final pages of Chapter 1. Second, these dimensions were based on one specific set of 40 modern nations, excluding, for example, all countries under state socialism and the smaller poor countries; adding these might change the range of values covered and affect the dimensions necessary to describe this range. Third, the four dimensions represent a compromise between comprehensiveness and attention to detail. I could have added more dimensions in order to account for differences among countries which are evident in the data but are not explained by the present set of four indices. In that case, I would have done more justice to the variety of individual country cultures but at the same time would have lost part of the overall picture; I would have favored the trees at the expense of the forest.

Country Scores and Score Intercorrelations

In Figure 7.1, the scores for the 40 countries on the four indices have been summarized. In Figure 7.2, the intercorrelations are shown among the four indices; across all 40 countries, across the 21 poorer ones (1970 GNP/capita below $1300) and across the 19 wealthier ones. Across all countries, we find the −.67 correlation between the Power Distance Index and the Individualism Index, which explained why the two load on one factor (Chapter 5); a plot of PDI versus IDV which illustrates this negative correlation is shown in Figure 5.2. The correlation between PDI and IDV does not subsist for either the poorer or the wealthier countries separately.

Across all 40 countries, we also find weak correlations between PDI and UAI and between UAI and IDV.[2] Across the 21 poorer countries there are no significant correlations between the indices at all; they are mutually independent. Across the 19 wealthier countries, however, UAI is significantly correlated with PDI, IDV, and MAS, in spite of the fact that these three other indices do not show significant intercorrelations. Across the 19 wealthier countries, UAI functions as a kind of summary index; comparative studies which are limited to wealthy countries will easily distinguish only one dimension, Uncertainty Avoidance, which subsumes also Power Distance, Masculinity, and the inverse of Individualism.

In Chapters 3 through 6 I have considered one dimension at a time, thereby isolating each from the other dimensions (except in Chapter 5, where I considered PDI and IDV together in order to separate them). Isolating dimensions is a useful intellectual exercise in order to structure our observations; but in the reality of each country situation the four dimensions interact with each other. The effect of interaction of dimensions is particularly evident for PDI × UAI, and the next section of this chapter will be devoted to it. Later I shall also devote attention to the interaction of UAI × MAS.

Power Distance Versus Uncertainty Avoidance

In Figure 7.3 I have plotted the position of the 40 countries on a PDI-versus-UAI axis. The axes and cluster lines in Figure 7.3 have been drawn arbitrarily in order to obtain maximum separation of geographically or historically distant groups of countries. We find a Latin plus Mediterranean cluster including *all* Latin countries in the high PDI, high UAI quadrant; in addition, this cluster includes Japan. All other Asian

FIGURE 7.1   Values of the Four Indices for the 40 Countries

Country	PDI	UAI	IDV	MAS
Argentina	49	86	46	56
Australia	36	51	90	61
Austria	11	70	55	79
Belgium	65	94	75	54
Brazil	69	76	38	49
Canada	39	48	80	52
Chile	63	86	23	28
Colombia	67	80	13	64
Denmark	18	23	74	16
Finland	33	59	63	26
France	68	86	71	43
Great Britain	35	35	89	66
Germany (F.R.)	35	65	67	66
Greece	60	112	35	57
Hong Kong	68	29	25	57
India	77	40	48	56
Iran	58	59	41	43
Ireland	28	35	70	68
Israel	13	81	54	47
Italy	50	75	76	70
Japan	54	92	46	95
Mexico	81	82	30	69
Netherlands	38	53	80	14
Norway	31	50	69	8
New Zealand	22	49	79	58
Pakistan	55	70	14	50
Peru	64	87	16	42
Philippines	94	44	32	64
Portugal	63	104	27	31
South Africa	49	49	65	63
Singapore	74	8	20	48
Spain	57	86	51	42
Sweden	31	29	71	5
Switzerland	34	58	68	70
Taiwan	58	69	17	45
Thailand	64	64	20	34
Turkey	66	85	37	45
USA	40	46	91	62
Venezuela	81	76	12	73
Yugoslavia	76	88	27	21
Mean	52	64	50	50
Standard Deviation	20	24	25	20

countries are found in two clusters with high PDI but medium to low UAI. On the low PDI side we find a mainly German-speaking cluster higher in UAI, which includes Israel and Finland; and two Anglo-Scandinavian clusters which include the Netherlands in the low PDI, low UAI quadrant.

FIGURE 7.2   Correlations among the Four Indices Across All Countries, Poorer Countries Only and Wealthier Countries Only

	Product moment correlations across		
Pair of indices	All 40 countries	21 poorer countries	19 wealthier countries
PDI × UAI	.28*	−.28	.52*
PDI × IDV	−.67***	−.30	.16
PDI × MAS	.10	.26	.16
UAI × IDV	−.35*	−.05	−.51*
UAI × MAS	.12	−.26	.43*
IDV × MAS	.00	.10	−.16

In their impact on a society, power distance and uncertainty avoidance will interact. A high UAI score was related (Figure 4.4) to a strong superego. However, in a high PDI environment this superego will be personified in the form of a powerful person (the father, the leader, the boss). People will be able to blame the powerful

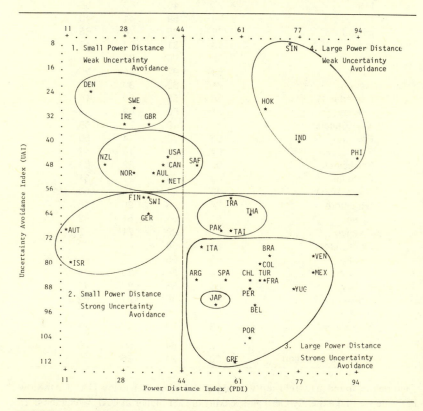

FIGURE 7.3   Positions of the 40 Countries on the Power Distance and Uncertainty Avoidance Scales

people for their ills (a favorite pastime in the Latin countries) and will feel relatively free to sin if the boss isn't looking. In the higher UAI, low PDI countries this escape is not available, and the superego is internalized. It is no accident that the concept of "superego" was invented by an Austrian, Sigmund Freud; we find Austria (and Israel) in the high UAI, low PDI corner. A reason for the very low PDI score in Austria (which means, among other things, that employees claim not to be afraid of disagreeing with superiors) may be that the idea of disagreeing with lawful superiors simply does not occur; it would make them feel guilty toward themselves.

In the low UAI countries there seems to be greater freedom of experimentation with alternative behaviors (except that if PDI is high, it is the powerful person who decides what happens, but that person is not supposed to embody any rules or moral imperatives). There is a well-known joke in Britain that everything is permitted except that which is forbidden; in Germany everything is forbidden except that which is permitted; and in France everything is permitted, even that which is forbidden. The German word *verboten* has even found its way into the American language.

The HERMES data also indicate that the sources of stress people are under may differ according to the PDI-UAI configuration. To show this, I shall exceptionally look at correlations of questionnaire items *across individual respondents,* not across countries (thus, this time I use individual rather than ecological correlations). For 33 subpopulations in HERMES (each representing one occupation in one country) I computed the correlations across individuals of the "stress" scores (question A37) with the scores for *satisfaction* with two work facets: personal time (question A32) and cooperation (question A22). Satisfaction with personal time and satisfaction with cooperation are the two satisfaction items that across all available HERMES data show the highest negative correlations with "stress."

FIGURE 7.4   Product Moment Correlation Coefficients of the Scores of Individual Respondents in 33 HERMES Subpopulations on Stress Versus the Satisfaction with Personal Time and with Cooperation

Subpopulations by country cluster	Median correlation of stress (A37) vs. satisfaction with personal time (A32)	Median correlation of stress (A37) vs. satisfaction with cooperation (A22)
High PDI, high UAI: France (4 groups), Japan (2), Latin America (2), Belgium, Italy, Spain (each 1)	$-.20^{***}$	$-.22^{***}$
Low PDI, low UAI: Great Britain (4 groups), Netherlands (4), Norway, Sweden, South Africa (each 1)	$-.18^{**}$	$-.14^{*}$
Low PDI, high UAI: Germany (6 groups), Austria (3), Switzerland (2)	$-.26^{***}$	$-.07$
All 33 subpopulations	$-.23^{***}$	$-.17^{**}$

In Figure 7.4 I show the median correlations found in the 33 subpopulations, separately for high PDI, high UAI countries, low PDI, low UAI countries, and low PDI, high UAI countries.[3] The correlations demonstrate that the relationship between stress and satisfaction with personal time is about equally strong in the three country clusters. However, the relationship between stress and satisfaction with cooperation is strongest in the high PDI, high UAI cluster and insignificant in the low PDI, high UAI cluster; the low PDI, low UAI cluster is in between. Stress in high PDI, high UAI countries (the Latin countries and Japan) has a social component; in low PDI, high UAI countries (the German language area) it has not. This fits with the earlier suggestion that the superego is personalized in the Latin countries and impersonal (becoming a true superego) in the German language area.

Something like a PDI × UAI matrix was impressionistically produced earlier by Van der Haas (1967: 90) for six countries. One dimension is "accepting or refuting ultimate authority in interpersonal relations," which looks like PDI except that the author puts France with Netherlands and the United States on the "rejects" side and Germany in the "accepts," with Great Britain and Sweden in between. The other dimension is "prevailing of ultimate versus functional values"; this can be seen as related to uncertainty avoidance; Van der Haas put France and Germany on the "ultimate" side. The prevalence of functional values presupposes a greater tolerance for uncertainty (what is functional in one case may not be so in another), and Van der Haas put the United States on this side and Great Britain, Sweden, and the Netherlands in between. The separation between France and Germany on the one side and the remaining four countries on the other is consistent with the UAI scores. However, ultimate values interact with the exercise of authority. Where ultimate values are *not* tied to large power distances, the individual must accept authority; he has nothing to revolt against (Germany). Where ultimate values *and* large power distance occur together, conflict at some time or another is unavoidable, and people will revolt (France).[4]

The difference between ultimate values and functional values finds confirmation in more classic studies. Lewin (1936 [1948]: 13) compared the United States and Germany and concluded, for example, "In America, two scientists or politicians may emerge from a hard theoretical fight and yet be on cordial terms with each other. In Germany, for most persons, a political or even a scientific disagreement seems to be inseparable from moral disapproval." McClelland et al. (1958) compared 155 18-year-old boys in the United States and Germany on TAT (Thematic Apperception Test) and questionnaire scores and interpreted the results as indicating more obligations to *self* in America and more to *society* in Germany. This points to a difference in individualism between the two countries (see Figure 5.5), and this difference is confirmed in our data. However, McClelland et al. go on to interpret German "authoritarianism" as a form of obligation to society by way of an abstract code, which fits with the "ultimate values," high uncertainty avoidance pattern.[5]

Power Distance, Uncertainty Avoidance, and Organizations

In their impact on the structure and functioning of organizations, power distance and uncertainty avoidance interact as well. In cultures where PDI is high, power is the leading principle which keeps the organization together and which protects it against uncertainty. In cultures where PDI is low, there are two possibilities. If people have an inner need for living up to rules (high UAI), the leading principle which keeps the organization together can be formal rules. If people do not have an inner need for living up to rules (low UAI), the organization has to be kept together by more ad hoc negotiation, a situation which calls for a larger tolerance for uncertainty from everyone.

Earlier (Chapter 2, page 76; Chapter 3, page 134; Chapter 4, page 186) I associated power distance and uncertainty avoidance with the two main dimensions of organization structure revealed by the Aston studies in Great Britain: power distance with "concentration of authority" and uncertainty avoidance with "structuring of activities." Pugh (1976: 70) uses a fourfold typology for describing organizations with high and low concentrations of authority and high and low structuring of activities. In Figure 7.5 I apply this typology to indicate the type of organization that fits best in a certain group of countries.

We should read Figure 7.5 in such a way that *ceteris paribus* (task, size of organization, etc., being equal) the countries in the fourth quadrant would tend more toward creating "implicitly structured" organizations, and, for example, those in the second quadrant more toward creating "full bureaucracies." In the full bureaucracy, the relationships both among people and between people and the work processes tend to be rigidly prescribed, either in formal rules and laws or in traditions. In the personnel bureaucracy, relationships among people are prescribed but not the work processes; in the workflow bureaucracy, the opposite is the case. Finally, in the

FIGURE 7.5   Connotations of the Four Combinations of Power Distance and Uncertainty Avoidance Levels

(4)	(1)
Small Power Distance Weak Uncertainty Avoidance	Large Power Distance Weak Uncertainty Avoidance
Countries: Anglo, Scandinavian, Netherlands	Countries: Southeast Asian
Organization type: implicitly structured[a]	Organization type: personnel bureaucracy
Implicit model of organization: market	Implicit model of organization: family
(3)	(2)
Small Power Distance Strong Uncertainty Avoidance	Large Power Distance Strong Uncertainty Avoidance
Countries: German-speaking, Finland, Israel	Countries: Latin, Mediterranean, Islamic, Japan, some other Asian
Organization type: workflow bureaucracy	Organization type: full bureaucracy
Implicit model of organization: well-oiled machine	Implicit model of organization: pyramid

[a]For the Aston types of organization see Pugh (1976: 70).

implicitly structured organizations, neither the relationships among people nor those between people and the work processes are strictly prescribed.

In Figure 7.5 I also refer to "implicit models" of organizations in different countries which derive from unfortunately unpublished studies by Professor O. J. Stevens with French, German, and British management students at INSEAD, Fontainebleau. In one of a series of different experiments, he let students of the three nationalities individually analyze the same case study of an organizational conflict. The majority of the French tended to resolve the problem by referring to the hierarchy; the British, by horizontal negotiation; the Germans, by the establishment of procedures. Stevens identified the implicit model of a well-functioning organization for the French as a pyramid; for the British as a (village) market; for the Germans as a well-oiled machine. This fits the types of full bureaucracy, implicitly structured organizations, and workflow bureaucracy.[6]

Stevens did not have Asian students available, but, based on the work of Kumar and Singh (1976) on Indian managers, I chose the "family" as the implicit model for an Indian organization. The "personnel bureaucracy" means that relationships among people are strictly determined by the hierarchical framework; but that the workflow is not at all codified to the same extent. The main continuous principle of Chinese administration has been described as "Government of Man" in contrast to the western idea of "Government by Law" (Chang, 1976).

In another of his studies with French, German, and British students, Stevens also drew attention to the different meaning of time in the three countries. For the Germans, it is a source of pressure; they are constantly aware of its passing. For the French, time is a resource which should be controlled and utilized. For the British, time is a tool for orienting oneself.

There are various other studies about differences among organizations in France, Germany, and Great Britain. Graves (1971, 1972) compared data from small samples of managers within a multinational corporation (not HERMES) in Great Britain (lower PDI) and France (higher PDI). In spite of the common corporation subculture, the attitudes and communication patterns of the managers differed sharply. In England, the organization tended to be held together by ties of personal or general loyalty (1971: 83). The French tended to have a clear conception of authority: they either accepted authority absolutely or rejected it entirely (1972: 54).

In HERMES, question A55 in the surveys asked respondents how they perceived their boss: as (1) autocratic, (2) persuasive, (3) consultative, (4) democratic (1967–1969) or participative (1970– 1973), or (5) as none of these (see Chapter 3). For two occupations in France, Great Britain, and Germany, I have tested how those perceiving their boss as representing each of these styles evaluated him or her in other respects. For these "other respects" I looked at 20 questions in the questionnaire.[7]

Figure 7.6 shows how may times (out of 20) each of the five subgroups (those who perceived their manager as representing one of the five decision-making styles) came up with the most favorable answer.[8] For example, we see that among branch office service technicians in France the subgroup perceiving their manager as persuasive-paternalistic gave the most favorable evaluation (of the five subgroups) in 15 out of the 20 questions; two questions were answered most favorably by those seeing their boss as consultative, and three by those seeing him as democratic (using

FIGURE 7.6   How Two Categories of HERMES Employees in France,
Great Britain, and Germany Evaluate Their Bosses

	Number of questions (out of 20) answered most favorably by those who perceive their boss to be:				
Branch office service technicians A. 1968	*autocratic*	*persuasive paternal- istic*	*consulta- tive*	*democratic*	*none of these*
France	—	15	2	3	—
Great Britain	—	8	10	2	—
Germany	—	4	2	14	—
Plant technicians 1970	*autocratic*	*persuasive paternal- istic*	*consulta- tive*	*participa- tive*	*none of these*
France	—	17	3	—	—
Great Britain	—	11	9	—	—
Germany	—	1	2	17	—

Total number of respondents = 2386.

majority vote). The data in Figure 7.6 tell us that for both occupations (technicians), French employees are most satisfied with a persuasive-paternalistic boss, Germans are most satisfied with a participative boss (slightly less with the "democratic," majority vote boss). British technicians divide their sympathies over the persuasive-paternalistic and the consultative boss. The (more uncertainty-avoiding) French and German technicians prefer a boss with a theoretically pure, unambiguous style of resolving problems: through hierarchy in high power distance France, and through consensus in low power distance Germany. The give-and-take intermediate "consultative" style demands a greater tolerance for uncertainty among subordinates, which is found only in Britain.

The industrial relations structures (labor-management relations) or France, Germany, and Great Britain support impressionistically the typology of Figure 7.5. The German labor unions are the most orderly and united; they do not like to strike (uncertainty avoidance), but they have achieved considerable formal co-determination (low power distance). The British are disorderly and have successfully resisted codifying industrial relations rules (no uncertainty avoidance). The French unions are politically oriented, reasonably orderly (predictable strike behavior), and in majority not very interested in formal co-determination.

As for the first quadrant (Asian countries), we have data from Negandhi and Prasad (1971) comparing 17 Indian organizations with 17 U.S. subsidiaries in India. The Indian organizations tend to have more layers in the hierarchy (1971: 60), but less formal control systems (p. 85), which fits with a distinction on both the power distance and uncertainty avoidance scales (although in the case of control systems, differences in modernization may have played a more important role).

Parsons (1951: 182ff) developed a 2 × 2 classification of "principal types of social structure" in which he puts China, Latin America, Germany, and the United

States in the four cells (compare Figure 7.3, reading "Hong Kong" for China). The dimension in Parsons' taxonomy which corresponds to power distance in mine is "universalistic" (low PDI) versus "particularistic" (high PDI); the dimension which corresponds to uncertainty avoidance is "achievement" (low UAI) to "ascription" (high UAI). In Chapter 5 I have associated the universalistic-particularistic distinction rather with individualism (but for the four countries which Parsons considers, high power distance and low individualism coincide). In Chapter 4 I showed the relationship between low uncertainty avoidance and achievement motivation.

Stressing the cultural element in organizational structure and functioning does not represent an attempt to reduce all differences among organizations to culture. It is only—and I believe this is necessary—a warning that the structure and functioning of organizations are not determined by a universal rationality. Making shoes, producing electricity, or treating the sick in Germany as opposed to France calls for organizational structures and processes that differ in several respects. Technology contributes to the shaping of organizations; but it is insufficient for explaining how they work. There is no "one best way" which can be deduced from technical-economical logic (Brossard and Maurice, 1974; Crozier and Friedberg, 1977: 168).

Culture and Organization Theory

The cultural relativity of the laws that govern human behavior had been recognized as early as the sixteenth century in the skepticism of Montaigne (1533– 1592). The quote from Pascal (1623– 1662) at the beginning of this book is in fact taken from Montaigne: *"Quelle vérité que ces montagnes bornent, qui est mensonge au monde qui se tient au delà?"* [9]

The founding parents of the theory of modern organizations, such as Tolstoy (1828–1910), Fayol (1841–1925), Taylor (1856–1915), Weber (1864–1920), and Follett (1868– 1933), and most of their successors up to the present day, have not followed Montaigne, but have typically looked for universal principles. The paradox is that in their theories the influence of their own cultural environment is clearly recognizable.

Let us take the issue of the exercise of authority. Weber, who was German (and, as his other work shows, quite sensitive about the role of values in society), wrote about authority in a bureaucracy—by which he meant any large organization, public, voluntary, and private: "The authority to give the commands required for the discharge of these duties is distributed in a stable way and is strictly delimited by rules concerning the coercive means . . . which may be placed at the disposal of officials" (from *Wirtschaft und Gesellschaft,* 1921; Part III, chapter 6; 650; English version in Weber, 1970: 196). For Weber, authority is in the office, not in the man.

Fayol, who was French, put it differently:

> We distinguish in a manager his *statutory* authority which is in the office, and his *personal* authority which consists of his intelligence, his knowledge, his experience, his moral value, his leadership, his service record, etc. For a good manager, personal authority is the indispensable complement to statutory authority [Fayol, 1916 (1970): 21; my translation].

Mary Parker Follett was American. She wrote:

> How can we avoid the two extremes: too great bossism in giving orders, and practically no orders given? . . . My solution is to depersonalize the giving of orders, to unite all concerned in a study of the situation, to discover the law of the situation and obey that. . . . One *person* should not give orders to another *person*, but both should agree to take their orders from the situation [from a paper presented in 1925; in Metcalf and Urwick, 1940: 58–59].

For the same issue of the exercise of authority, Weber stresses the office; Fayol, the person; Follett, the situation. We recognize the different positions of these three authors' national cultures on the Power Distance × Uncertainty Avoidance matrix. Between the American and the French view, a direct dispute was started elsewhere by Fayol when he took issue with Taylor's proposition of eight functionally specialized superiors for one person. Fayol (1916 [1970]: 84) calls this idea "wrong and dangerous," as it "flagrantly violates" the principle of unity of command. This principle, however, is much more holy in France than in the United States. It must be admitted that U.S. practitioners were not eager to try this idea of Taylor's either; but some of it can be recognized in the modern trend toward matrix organization, which was developed in United States and, not surprisingly, lacks popularity in France (Laurent, 1978; see page 385).

What is available as organization theory today is mostly written by Americans, and as such reflects the cultural context of one specific society. A collection of 15 new contributions by leading Europeans (Hofstede and Kassem, 1976) shows remarkable differences in focus by culture area. Authors from Latin Europe focus on power; from Central Europe, including Germany, on truth; from Eastern Europe, on efficiency; from Northern Europe, on change; while the Western Europeans, in this case British and Dutch, have a bit of all of these but show more than the others a concern with data collection which we also find in the United States.

Theorizing is only a semirational activity. "There are large sections of culture that act as a bar to the free exercise of rationality" (Kluckhohn, 1951a: 91, after E. Sapir). Or, as I would rather put it, there is no such thing as absolute rationality; there are different rationalities colored by different culturally influenced values, and your rationality differs from mine; while there is no standard to determine which of the two is more "rational." Culture affects in particular those ideas that are taken for granted without further proof because no one in our environment ever challenges them. Only comparison among cultures can show that other ideas are possible. It has been said that the last thing the fish will discover is water; it only finds out about water when it has landed on the fishmonger's cart. Douglas (1973b) has collected documentary evidence on the relevance of an "anthropology of everyday knowledge": our reality is manmade. We also have a natural tendency to choose our environment such that certain of our basic ideas are not challenged. Ideas are entangled with our values and our interests[10]; a fact which we recognize more easily in others than in ourselves. Ideas and theories become popular or unpopular at a certain time not because they are more or less "true" but because the value systems that support them are activated or suppressed by ecological and institutional developments (more or less in the way pictured by the diagram in Figure 1.4). Thus, Bartell

(1976) showed why the "Human Relations Ideology" in the United States developed there at the time it did (the 1930s), putting it in the context of such factors as traditional American values, labor union expansion, the economic depression, the New Deal, and the bureaucratization of industrial organizations.

Motivation Patterns:
Uncertainty Avoidance Versus Masculinity

The 40 countries have been positioned in a UAI × MAS diagram in Figure 7.7. The combination of UAI and MAS was found to be the best predictor of Need for Achievement, as identified by McClelland in his content analysis of 1925 children's readers (Figures 4.11 and 6.13). The upper righthand quadrant in Figure 7.7 (weak Uncertainty Avoidance and Masculine) corresponds to the highest n_{Ach} as measured by McClelland. The countries of "masculine risk-takers" appear to be the entire "Anglo" cluster, plus, however, some Asian countries: India, Philippines, Hong Kong, and (marginally) Singapore (interestingly, all these are former U.K. or U.S. colonies).[11]

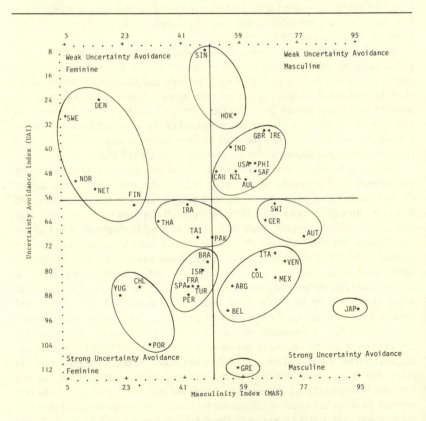

FIGURE 7.7   Positions of the 40 Countries on the Uncertainty Avoidance and Masculinity Scales

The clustering of the Anglo countries in Figure 7.7 suggests the cultural limitation of McClelland's achievement motivation concept and, at the same time, of other American theories of human motivation, such as those by Maslow or Herzberg (see also Chapter 9). The societal norms for uncertainty avoidance and masculinity affect what will motivate people in different cultures. McClelland's achievement motive or Maslow's hierarchy of human needs are based on one special set of societal norms (the first quadrant).

Basically, the vertical axis in Figure 7.7 (UAI) opposes motivation by success to motivation by security; at the extremes, hope of success to fear of failure. The horizontal axis opposes ego needs to affiliation needs. Combining the two axes, we get four quadrants, in each of which we need a different hierarchy to explain people's motives, rather than one universal hierarchy, as Maslow suggests. I have elaborated the dominant motivation patterns in each of the four quandrants in Chapter 9. Theories of human motivation should take account of the relativity of societal norms.

Other Combinations of Indices

Of the six possible combinations of the four indices, three have been plotted: PDI × IDV (Figure 5.2), PDI × UAI (Figure 7.3), and UAI × MAS (Figure 7.7). The combination of power distance and masculinity can be hypothesized to show authority relations and role patterns between parents in the family (Chapter 6). PDI in this case stands for the authority of the father and MAS for the dependence of the mother. However, I have not yet found any evidence from other sources which would support classifying cultures according to a PDI × MAS matrix.

The combination of uncertainty avoidance and individualism reminds us of Douglas' (1973a: chap. 4) taxonomy of "grid and group" (see Chapter 1). "Group" clearly corresponds to individualism, in the sense that high Group ("ego increasingly controlled by other people's pressure) represents the collectivist end of the scale. "Grid" resembles uncertainty avoidance: high Grid stands for a "system of shared classifications." However, as Douglas' taxonomy stands at present, she uses it to distinguish the subcultures of small units in societies, not the cultures of entire societies.

The combination of individualism and masculinity, by the very way in which these two dimensions were arrived at, characterizes people's work goals (what they want from a job). The kind of groupings of work goals found have been extensively described in Chapter 5.

A Summary of Correlations of the
Four HERMES Indices with External Data

In Chapters 3 through 6 I cited about 80 external (non-HERMES) comparative studies in support of the cultural differences pictured by the HERMES indices. Many of these external studies cover only a few countries at a time, so that the support they give to the picture found within HERMES is illustrative rather than statistical. Those that do show statistically significant correlations with the HERMES indices are listed in Figures 7.8 and 7.9.

Figure 7.8 assembles all significant correlations with data collected in 14 different surveys. It has been divided into two parts: narrow samples and representative

(text continues page 332)

FIGURE 7.8 Summary of Significant Correlations of HERMES Indices with Data from Surveys with Different Instruments Outside HERMES

Survey and Scales	See Fig.	No. of countries	Zero-order correlation with HERMES index				Sizable contributions in multiple regression
			PDI	UAI	IDV	MAS	
Narrow samples:							
Haire et al. (1966)	3.15	19					
Capacity leadership			.54**		-.49*		PDI, -UAI, MAS
Sharing information					.63**		IDV
Participation					.48*		IDV, UAI
Haire et al. (1966)	5.15	14					
Security			-.46*		-.60*		-IDV
Autonomy				-.55*	.60*		IDV
Gordon students (1976)	3.14	17					
Support			-.70***		.68***		-PDI
Conformity			.80***		-.76***	.44*	PDI
Recognition						.50*	MAS
Independence			-.79***		.41*	-.54*	-PDI
Benevolence				-.49*		-.59**	-MAS, PDI
Hofstede IMEDE (1974[b])	4.13	16					
LPC score				-.44*			-UAI, PDI
Hofstede IMEDE (1976[a])	3.13	14					
Recognition vs. independence							(a)
Decisive vs. practical minded			.79***	-.50*			(a)
Bass IRGOM managers	5.16	12					
Hedonism vs. skill			-.66***		.76***		(a)
Assertiveness vs. service						.84***	(a)

FIGURE 7.8 Continued

Laurent matrix (1978)	4.13	10					
Clarity of hierarchy			.61*	.78**			UAI
Bass and Franke (1972)	5.17	6			.91**		(a)
Openness vs. secrecy							
Morris ways to live (1956)	5.18	6			.73*		(a)
Enjoyment vs. duty							
Representative samples:							
Reader's Digest (1970)	4.12	15					
Attitude to younger people			−.65**	−.77***			−UAI, −IDV
Attitude to older people			−.56*	−.56*			−PDI
Ornauer et al. Year 2000 (1976)	4.14	9					
Contribute yourself				−.64*			−UAI
Compromise not dangerous				−.90***	.81*		−UAI
Take one day after another				−.71*			−UAI
Like living abroad				−.80**			−UAI, PDI
CCE, Retirement (1978)	6.12	9				.86**	MAS
Prefer salary over shorter working							
McGee, Free Enterprise (1977)	6.11	6				.84*	MAS
Preferred size of enterprise							
Almond and Verba (1963)	4.14	5				−.86*	−UAI
Citizen competence				−.96***	.79*		

(a) For factor scores, no multiple regressions were computed.

FIGURE 7.9 Summary of Significant Correlations of HERMES Indices with Various Country-Level Indicators

Indicator and source	See Fig.	No. of countries	Zero-order correlation with HERMES index				Sizable contributions in multiple regression
			PDI	UAI	IDV	MAS	
Press freedom, Taylor & Hudson	5.22	39	-.38**	-.40**	.51***		IDV
Segregation higher education, Boulding	6.16	38		-.31*		.28*	-UAI
same, wealthy countries only		18				.56**	MAS
Percent professional women, Boulding	6.15	33	-.41**		.46**		IDV
same, wealthy countries only		16		-.57*	.50*	-.64**	MAS
Domestic political violence, Rummel	3.19	37	.39**				PDI
same, Nesvold		37	.71***	.44**	-.52***		PDI
same, Schneider & Schneider		10	.93***	.70*			PDI
Sectorial inequality, Cutright	5.22	33	.54***		-.60***	-.34*	-IDV, -MAS
same, Taylor & Hudson		32	.67***		-.71***		-IDV, PDI
Catholics vs. Protestants, Taylor & Hudson	4.20	29	.68***	.76***	-.63***	.40*	UAI, MAS
same, wealthy countries only		17	.48*	.68***		.58**	UAI, MAS
1925 Children's readers, McClelland	4.11	22					
Need for Achievement			-.58***	-.64***	.44*		-UAI, MAS
Need for Affiliation					.46*		IDV
Medical statistics, Lynn & Hampson	4.10	18					
Neuroticism				.73***		.41*	UAI
Extraversion			-.47*	-.44*	-.53*		-PDI
Nurses per doctor; Gaspari-Millendorfer	4.19	15	-.52*	-.80**	.63**		-UAI
Government development assistance, UN yearbook	6.17	15				-.81***	-MAS

FIGURE 7.9 Continued

Nobel prize index, Moulin	p.126	14	-.50*	-.46*			-PDI
Identity card obligation	p.180	14		.85***			UAI
Maximum speeds, ANWB	4.18	14		.58*	.52*		UAI, MAS
Traffic deaths, UN yearbook.	4.18	14		.56*	.51*	-.61**	-IDV, MAS
Occupational inheritance, Cutright	5.21	12		.64*		-.71**	-IDV
Income inequality, Bégué	3.27	12	.57*				PDI
same, Kuznets		10	.86***	.80**		-.60*	PDI
same, Kravis		8	.89**		.77*		PDI
Age of executives, de Bettignies	4.12	11	.75**	.75**	.58*		UAI
Time use pattern, Converse	p.228	6				1.00**	IDV
Law degrees for civil servants, Aberbach & Putnam	p.179	5		.90*		-.90*	UAI

FIGURE 7.10 Summary of Significant Correlations of HERMES Indices with Seven System-(Country-)Level Indicators, Including Multiple and Stepwise Regression on the Four Indices

System-level indicators	Abbreviation	Zero-order correlation with HERMES index				Squared multiple correlation with all four R^2	order in stepwise regression cumulative R^2 & sign	
		PDI	UAI	IDV	MAS		1st	2nd
All 40 countries								
Wealth	GNP	-.65***	-.30*	.82***		.70	.68 + IDV	
Economic growth	GNG					.03		
Latitude	LAT	-.65***		.75***	-.31*	.76	.57 + IDV	.67 - MAS[a]
Population size	POP	.38**			.29	.32	.15 + PDI	.25 + IDV
Population growth	PGR	.51***		-.63***		.48	.39 - IDV	
Population density	PDN					.11		
HERMES org. size	ORG	-.30*		.71***		.63	.51 + IDV	.57 + PDI
21 poorer countries								
Wealth	GNP					.11		
Economic growth	GNG					.09		
Latitude	LAT	-.39*	.51**	.51**	-.48*	.73	.26 + IDV	.56 - MAS[b]
Population size	POP					.17		
Population growth	PGR		-.41*		.47*	.44	.22 + MAS	.34 - IDV
Population density	PDN		-.65***			.54	.42 - UAI	
HERMES org. size	ORG			.56**		.53	.31 + IDV	.39 + UAI
19 wealthier countries								
Wealth	GNP			.45*		.30	.20 + IDV	
Economic growth	GNG		.57**	-.67***		.67	.44 - IDV	.66 + PDI
Latitude	LAT		-.44		-.63**	.58	.40 - MAS	

FIGURE 7.10 Continued

Population size	POP	.58**	.42*	.51	.34 + PDI	.45 + MAS
Population growth	PGR					
Population density	PDN	.43*		.21	.18 + UAI	
HERMES org. size	ORG	.52**		.41	.27 + PDI	

For definitions of indicators see Figure 2.7.

Zero-order correlations have been taken from Figures 3.16, 4.15, 5.20, 6.14.

aThird-order correlation: .72 + UAI.

bThird-order correlation: .73 + UAI.

samples of entire populations (see page 85). The number of countries covered varies from five to 19. All four indices are represented in the correlations, so that none of them appear irrelevant. The few sizable second- and third-order correlations in the multiple regression do not suggest that we could substantially simplify the picture by subsuming any pair of indices into one.

Figure 7.9 groups the significant correlations with various indicators, from 24 different sources, measured at the country level. Again, all indices are represented. Altogether, Figures 7.8 and 7.9 represent 38 sources of data external to HERMES which show significant correlations with the HERMES indices; studies which only in rare cases had been related to each other in the past. These 38 sources represent, for the time being, the synergy harvest of the HERMES study. I hope and expect that other relevant data, either already collected but unknown to me or still to be collected in the future, can be added later to strengthen the picture of these four dimensions of national culture.

In each of the Chapters 3 through 6, the four indices were correlated with seven country-level indicators (Figures 2.7, 3.16, 4.15, 5.20, and 6.14). In Figure 7.10 I summarize the significant correlations found. In the previous chapters, multiple regressions were computed of PDI, UAI, IDV, and MAS on the seven indicators. In Figure 7.10 I now show the result of multiple regression the other way around: of the seven indicators on the four indices. This shows whether the indicators predict combinations of PDI, UAI, IDV, and MAS better than each index alone.

Figure 7.10 shows that especially geographical latitude has a rich multiple regression pattern, being related to IDV and UAI (positively) and MAS (negatively). The negative relationship between latitude and MAS is the only significant correlation consistent across all countries, poorer and wealthier alike. Colder countries tend to be less masculine, and this trend is not affected by the countries' wealth. Altogether, in the stepwise regression, we meet IDV 10 times and PDI, UAI, and MAS each five times: Individualism through its strong relationship with modernity is the culture dimension most clearly linked to the state of the geographic-demographic-economic system as measured by these indices.

Country Clusters

In principle, whenever we have a data matrix containing the levels of a number of variables for a number of countries as cases we can simplify this matrix in two ways. The first way is to summarize the *variables* into a smaller number of compound dimensions. The most common statistical tool used for this purpose is factor analysis. Factor analyses using countries as cases were described in Chapters 1, 2, and 5.

The second way of simplifying a countries × variables matrix is to summarize the *countries* (cases) into a smaller number of country clusters, whereby clusters consist of countries with similar levels of the variables: The differences within clusters should be minimal, those betweeen clusters maximal. To this end we can use a Q-analysis, which is nothing more than a factor analysis in which variables and cases have been exchanged; but there exist a number of other statistical clustering techniques.

The literature quoted earlier in this book contains several cases of country clustering on the basis of Q-analysis or other methods. From the factor analytic studies cited in Chapter 1, those of Cattell (1950), Russett (1968), and Rummel (1972: 307ff) also created country clusters.[12] Russett, for example, found five clusters: Afro-Asia, Western, Latin America, Semi-Developed Latin, and Eastern Europe. On the basis of HERMES data, Sirota and Greenwood (1971; see pages 244 and 300) did a cluster analysis on 25 countries and found an Anglo, French, Northern Europe, Southern Latin America, and Northern Latin America cluster. On the basis of IMEDE data, I (Hofstede, 1976a; see page 112) clustered 14 countries using the answers of 315 managers to Gordon's Surveys of Personal and Interpersonal Values. Five clusters were found: Nordic, Germanic, Anglo, Latin, and Asian. Finally, within the study of *Images of the World in the Year 2000* Siciński (1976) clustered 10 countries on the basis of their survey responses and found, for example, that Finland, the Netherlands, and Norway fitted closely together: As we shall see, this is confirmed in the HERMES findings.[13]

The matrix of country scores on the four HERMES indices PDI, UAI, IDV, and MAS (Figure 7.1) can be used for clustering the 40 countries. Rather than a Q-analysis, I have used in this case a hierarchical cluster analysis which produces a "dendrogram."[14] The advantage of this method is that the configuration of countries for various numbers of clusters can be seen at a glance.

The dendrogram in Figure 7.11 should be read from right to left. A split into two large clusters cuts off Colombia through Philippines from Israel through Finland. Next, the lower cluster splits into Israel through South Africa and Denmark through Finland, and so on.

In order to obtain a meaningful separation of countries with different historical backgrounds and/or geographical positions, I have cut the dendrogram at an error sum of squares of 12 percent of total, which leads to 11 clusters (numbered 1 through 11 in the lefthand column of Figure 7.11).

Most countries which we find together in the same cluster in Figure 7.11 were also together in the clusters drawn impressionistically in the two-dimensional plots of Figures 5.2, 7.3, and 7.7. Exceptions are Italy and South Africa, which were always separated from Germany and Switzerland, as they could also be considered marginal members of more historically related clusters (Latin for Italy and Anglo for South Africa). The computer analysis does not respect historical considerations.

The cluster configuration found depends partly on the statistical method used, and it depends very definitely on the variables used (in the case of the dendrogram, the four indices PDI, UAI, IDV, and MAS). I have also tried a smallest space analysis (Guttman, 1968)[15] performed on the basis of the country scores on 12 questions from the HERMES questionnaire (the three highest correlated questions for each of the four dimensions). This technique is not intended for cluster analysis, but rather for the identification of dimensions in the data (as for factor analysis); however, it produces two-dimensional plots for the 40 countries. One of these largely reproduces a PDI × UAI plot (Figure 7.3) with Latin, Asian, and Germanic-Anglo-Nordic superclusters, but it puts Italy (and also Japan) closer to the Germanic countries.

Culture Areas

By culture areas I mean groups of countries with common or similar histories, on the basis of which we can explain a partly similar mental programming of their citizens. Some of the clusters in Figure 7.11 can be considered culture areas by

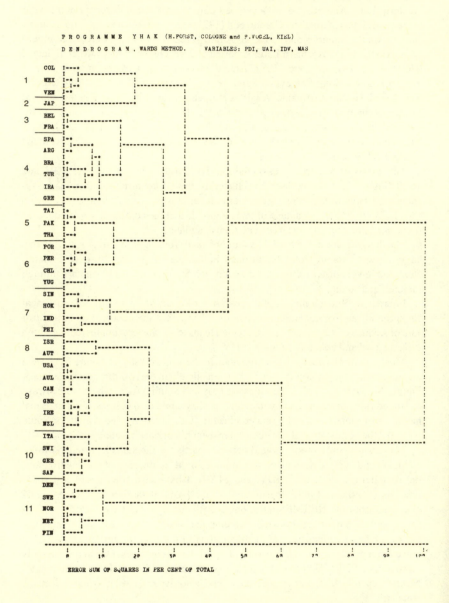

FIGURE 7.11   Country Clusters

themselves (numbers 1, 2, 3, 8, 9, and 11), but the others represent combinations of culture areas, probably brought together in the same cluster by other than historical factors (such as comparable economic development levels and/or political conditions). If we want to subdivide all clusters into culturally similar groups of countries, we arrive at at least 20 different countries or country groups,[16] only a modest reduction of complexity from the original 40 countries.

In Figure 7.12 I have therefore regrouped the clusters into eight culture areas by splitting one cluster from the dendrogram (number 4) and combining four times two clusters. Three countries—Italy, Yugoslavia, and South Africa—have been added in parentheses to the culture areas where historically they fit best, which means a deviation from the dendrogram in these three cases. Japan represents a culture area by itself.

Culture and Language:
The Cases of Belgium and Switzerland

In three of the 40 countries the surveys were administered in two languages each: in Belgium, Switzerland, and Yugoslavia. For Belgium and Switzerland, a separate analysis of the two language areas in the data has been possible. The resulting index values for the language areas, as well as those of the neighboring countries with the same languages, are listed in Figure 7.13.[17]

In order to show the similarities and differences among countries and language areas more clearly, the lower part of Figure 7.13 contains the summed absolute differences across the four indices for each pair of countries or areas.

Both Belgium and Switzerland combine Germanic and Latin languages. In Belgium, about 54 percent of the population speaks Dutch, 45 percent French, and 1 percent German. In Switzerland, the figures are about 75 percent German, 20 percent French, 4 percent Italian, and 1 percent Raeto-Romanic.

The index values for the main language areas in Belgium and Switzerland show that in Belgium the two language areas share basically the same culture, which closely resembles the French culture. Both parts of Belgium, the French-speaking as well as the Dutch-speaking part, belong to the "More Developed Latin" culture area. The culture gap between the Netherlands and Dutch-speaking Belgium is somewhat smaller than between the Netherlands and French-speaking Belgium, but it is still very wide. In fact, no two countries in the HERMES data with a common border and a common language are so far culturally apart, according to the HERMES indices, as Belgium and the Netherlands. The gap occurs in Power Distance, Uncertainty Avoidance, and Masculinity; only in Individualism do Belgium and the Netherlands come together.

A completely different picture is found for the other bilingually surveyed country, Switzerland. In this case, German-speaking Switzerland is clearly culturally associated with Germany and French-speaking Switzerland with France; there is a wide culture gap between the two language areas, in particular on the dimension of Power Distance. The two parts of Switzerland belong to different culture areas, the German-speaking part to the "Germanic" area and the French-speaking part to the "More

FIGURE 7.12 Culture Areas Based on a Regrouping of Country Clusters

Clusters 3 + 4A: *More Developed Latin* high PDI high UAI medium to high IDV medium MAS	*Clusters 1 + 6:* *Less Developed Latin* high PDI high UAI low IDV low to high MAS	
Belgium France	Colombia Mexico Venezuela	
Argentina Brazil Spain	Chile Peru Portugal	
(Italy)		
Cluster 2 *More Developed Asian* medium PDI high PDI medium IDV high MAS	*Clusters 5 + 7* *Less Developed Asian* high PDI low to medium UAI low IDV medium MAS	*Cluster 4 B* *Near Eastern* high PDI high UAI low IDV medium MAS
Japan	Pakistan Taiwan Thailand	Greece Iran Turkey
	Hong Kong India Philippines Singapore	(Yugoslavia)
Clusters 8 + 10 *Germanic* low PDI medium to high UAI medium IDV medium to high MAS	*Cluster 9* *Anglo* low to medium PDI low to medium UAI high IDV high MAS	*Cluster 11* *Nordic* low PDI low to medium UAI medium to high IDV low MAS
Austria Israel	Australia Canada Great Britain	Denmark Finland Netherlands
Germany (F.R.) Switzerland	Ireland New Zealand U.S.A.	Norway Sweden
	(South Africa)	

Developed Latin" culture area. The fact that in the cluster analysis for total countries Switzerland as a whole is part of the Germanic area is simply due to the greater numerical strength of German-speaking respondents in the HERMES sample.

Curiously, the language split is an extremely "hot" political issue in Belgium (where, according to the data, the two areas share largely the same culture) and not in

FIGURE 7.13   Index Values for Bilingual Countries by Language Area, and
              Their Differences

A. Values of the four indices for language groups in bilingual and
neighboring countries

	PDI	UAI	IDV	MAS
Belgium total	65	94	75	54
Netherlands	38	53	80	14
Belgium Dutch	61	97	78	43
Belgium French	67	93	72	60
France	68	86	71	43
Switzerland total	34	58	68	70
Germany (F.R.)	35	65	67	66
Switzerland German	26	56	69	72
Switzerland French	70	70	64	58
France	68	86	71	43

B. Summed absolute differences

	BEL-D	BEL-F	FRA
NET	98	123	111
BEL-D		33	25
BEL-F			26

	SWI-G	SWI-F	FRA
GER	26	51	81
SWI-G		77	103
SWI-F			40

Switzerland (where cultures differ). This is undoubtedly due to the political structure
of the countries, which is monolithical in Belgium (an attempt at regionalization is
being carried out) but federal in Switzerland, with more than 20 generally monolingual cantons (provinces) with a large amount of internal independence. In one case,
where a Swiss canton was bilingual (Berne), this led in the 1960s to political conflicts
not unlike those in Belgium, but these were resolved by splitting the canton (creating
the new canton Jura). The political structures of the two countries are in their turn the
outcome of historical events: For centuries Belgium was a distant dependent·prov-
ince of foreign powers (successively of Spain, Austria, France, and the Netherlands)
and only gained its independence in 1831. Switzerland was created in 1291 by a
voluntary federation of three cantons and grew gradually by the more or less voluntary addition of 19 other cantons, reaching its present size in 1815.

    The common French culture of the two language areas of Belgium can be ex-
plained by their common history and by the fact that since Belgium split from the
Netherlands in 1831, French was the language of government, the upper classes, and
secondary and higher education for more than 100 years. The emancipation movement of the Dutch-speaking majority in Belgium gained momentum only in the
1950s. In one of the rare studies comparing Dutch- and French-speaking Belgians
culturally, Leplae (1955) surveyed 300 Belgian elementary school teachers and in a

second study (1956) compared them with Dutch elementary school teachers. It appeared that as far as values were concerned (for example, which qualities should be developed in children) the two groups of Belgians were more similar than any of them and the Dutch; also, when it came to similarity with the Dutch, the French-speaking Belgians in several cases were the ones most resembling the Dutch, not the Dutch-speaking Belgians. I attribute this to the influence of traditional Roman Catholicism, which at that time was strong in Dutch-speaking Belgium but less influential in either French-speaking Belgium or the Netherlands (at least in a national sample). Aiken and Bacharach (1979) compared local government bureaucracies in the two language areas of Belgium and found a more impersonal approach and more use of universalistic criteria (see page 217) in the French-speaking part; however, their study does not contain comparisons with either France or the Netherlands so that the relative size of the language area difference cannot be identified. The HERMES data suggest that in both language areas, bureaucracies will function more like those in France than like those in the Netherlands.

As far as Switzerland is concerned, remarkable attitude differences between the German- and French-speaking areas were found in a representative sample survey of 1000 Swiss youth between 15 and 25 years old (La Suisse, 1972). Figure 7.14 reproduces in summarized form some of the results of this survey. On three key questions about attitudes toward society, parents, and working, the French-speaking Swiss score considerably more negative than the German-speaking Swiss. The question about parents suggests a greater counterdependence in the French-speaking area, which fits well with a higher PDI norm. The critical attitude toward society can be interpreted as a reaction to both a higher PDI and a higher UAI norm (external authority rather than "superego" authority). The lower work ethos fits with a lower

FIGURE 7.14   Attitudes of Random Samples of Swiss Youth Aged 15–25, Collected Through Interviews, by Language Area

	SWI-G n = 771	SWI-F n = 229	χ^2
Attitude toward present-day society[a]			
positive	41	20	43.4*** (2 d.f.)
negative	26	45	
Attitude toward parents[b]			
positive	49	44	14.2*** (2 d.f.)
negative	13	23	
Attitude toward working[c]			
positive	64	43	40.2*** (2 d.f.)
negative	14	31	

SOURCE: La Suisse (1972).
[a]Table 51
[b]Table 52
[c]Table 53

MAS norm. These survey results confirm the cultural gap between the two Swiss language areas.

In my own study with L. V. Gordon's Values Surveys of the values of 315 managers in courses at IMEDE (Hofstede, 1976a), the size of the Swiss sample allowed dividing it into German-speaking Swiss (n = 69) and French-speaking Swiss (n = 30). In the cluster analysis (see earlier pages), German-speaking Switzerland was part of the Germanic cluster and French-speaking Switzerland part of the Latin cluster. This is the same division as obtained in HERMES. In the IMEDE study all respondents used the same language (English); thus, language alone cannot be the reason for the splitting of the Swiss data in HERMES.

Culture Areas as a Basis for
an Emic Study of Cultures

The identification of four dimensions of national culture and the attribution of an Index value on each dimension to each country represent an approach to the study of culture which, in the terminology of Chapter 1, is entirely nomothetic-etic. Using the distinction which I attributed to Lammers (page 41) Chapters 3 through 6 have concentrated on "lawlike theories," while the present chapter looks for "configurations." The culture areas of Figure 7.12 represent to a certain extent ideal-types of national culture.

If we were to take an entirely idiographic-emic view of national cultures, we would consider each culture as an integral whole, which only makes sense from the inside—and we would condemn any attempt at classification across cultures as denying the uniqueness of each culture's *Gestalt*. The identificaion of culture areas as ideal-types represents an in-between solution between the purely emic position and the extreme etic of the index values. Rather than considering each country culture as an entirely different whole, we recognize that some cultures are more alike than others. The *Gestalt* of national cultures from the same area will present more of the same features than the *Gestalt* of national cultures from different areas.

At this point, it would be desirable to insert a number of "emic" descriptions of organization-related values in the various culture areas identified in Figure 7.12; or at least of one "typical" country from each culture area. The limits to the size of this book, however, prevent this. Instead, I refer the reader to the existing literature.[18]

NOTES

1. *Many Answers* is the title of a reader in cultural anthropology collected by Alger (1974).

2. The correlation between IDV and MAS must be .00 because these indices are based on orthogonal factors (Chapter 5). In the factor analyses of all questions (Chapter 2) we find three orthogonal factors, of which one represents a mixture of PDI and IDV and the others are not identical with, but approach closely, UAI and MAS. Thus, it is evident that the correlation across 40 countries for UAI and MAS must be low.

3. The correlations in Figure 7.4 are much lower than most ecological correlations found in this book, but correlations across individuals are nearly always much lower, as the data contain more random error.

4. The Power Distance × Uncertainty Avoidance matrix also shows some similarity to a matrix developed by Basil Bernstein for describing culture patterns, whose dimensions are "speech restriction" and "family control" (Douglas, 1973a: chap. 2). Speech restriction (elab-

orated versus socially restricted) reminds us of Power Distance: family control (personal versus positional), of Uncertainty Avoidance. However, this taxonomy was developed for distinguishing the subcultures of individual British families, not of societies.

5. Another impressionistic two-dimensional matrix of countries is shown by Wildavsky (1975: 246) when he deals with the specific issue of conflict in public budgeting. His first dimension is "support-on-spending," which relates to tax rates and their increase (highest increase in Britain, medium in the United States, lowest in France and Japan); his second dimension is "containment of conflict," which relates to citizen consensus and deference to the government (greater ability to contain conflict in Britain, least in France). Wildavsky shows how high containment of conflict is a condition for survival with low support on spending (high tax rates). His arguments are mainly rational-economic, but his classification of countries coincides with one obtained by PDI (support-on-spending) and UAI (reverse of containment of conflict). His theory of the need for a balance between the two suggests that low PDI, high UAI systems must be less stable.

6. To Peter Kessler, doctoral student at the European Institute for Advanced Studies in Management, I owe the observation that the French developed mercantilism (central control of foreign trade by the state) and that Great Britain produced Adam Smith with his idea of the market as an invisible hand.

7. Twelve of these questions became part of the Recommended Questionnaire (Appendix 1): A30, A38, A44, A49, A50, A52, B31, B33, B35, B36, B37, and B38. Seven others are described in Sadler and Hofstede (1972: Tables 6 and 7), and the last one deals with whether a complaint to the direct superior would be helpful (compare question A47).

8. The least favorable answers in France and Germany are always given by those perceiving their managers as representing "none of these" styles. This means inconsistent manager behavior (Sadler and Hofstede, 1972) which especially in strongly uncertainty-avoiding cultures is difficult to support. In Great Britain, the least favorable answers are mostly given by those who perceive their managers as "no style," but in a few cases by those with an autocratic or democratic manager.

9. Montaigne, Essais II, XII, 34: "What kind of a truth is this that is bounded by a chain of mountains and is falsehood to the people living on the other side?" (my translation)

10. The stress on interests as the source of ideas is found throughout the works of Marx and Engels, but they focus almost exclusively on the modes of production; Merton (1968: 516ff) shows how Marx's ideas have been broadened by Scheler and Mannheim to include other institutional structures and group formations as existential bases of ideas.

11. See also my comments about McClelland's Achievement Motivation Training in India on page 377.

12. Other studies clustering countries are Tsantis (1969) and Sethi and Holton (1973).

13. Siciński's countries were FIN, GBR, IND, JAP, NET, NOR, SPA, YUG plus Czechoslovakia and Poland.

14. Ward's grouping method (Rummel, 1972: 304). The actual computations were done with the program YHAK by Forst and Vogel (1977). This analysis, like the ANOVA in Chapter 2, was made possible through the kind help of Professor Klaus Brockhoff of Kiel University, Germany, and his computer staff.

15. Thanks are due for the kind help of Dr. Zvi Maimon of Tel Aviv University.

16. COL + MEX + VEN; JAP; BEL + FRA; SPA + ARG + BRA; TUR + IRA + GRE; TAI; PAK; THA; POR; PER + CHL; YUG; SIN + HOK; IND + PHI; ISR + AUT; USA + AUL + CAN + GBR + IRE + NZL; ITA; SWI + GER; SAF; DEN + SWE + NOR + NET + FIN.

17. For the computation of IDV and MAS in these cases see Chapter 6.

18. Some literature contributing to the kind of "emic" insight I mean, both by natives and nonnatives of the country in question follow. On *France:* Crozier (1971), Peyrefitte (1976),

Schonfeld (1976), and Marceau (1977). On *Latin America:* Lewis (1966), Heath (1974), Sanchez-Albornoz (1974), and Chaliand (1976). On *Japan:* Whitehill and Takezawa (1968), Kawasaki (1969), Dore (1973), and Hsu (1975). On *China and India:* Hsu (1971), Chang (1976), Moddie (1968), and Kumar and Singh (1976). On *Greece and Turkey:* Mead (1953), Lewis (1961), Triandis and Vassiliou (1972), and Ari (1977). On *Germany:* Lewin (1936 [1948]), Lowie (1954), McClelland et al. (1958), and Lütz (1976). On the *United States:* Spindler (1948), McGiffert (1970), Krishnan (1974), and Inkeles (1977). On the *Netherlands and Sweden:* Goudsblom (1967), de Baena (1968), Fleisher (1969), and Palm (1977).

Chapter 8

TRENDS OVER TIME

SUMMARY OF THIS CHAPTER

One reason for culture change is the proliferation of the results of scientific discoveries, but this does not mean that all cultures will become more and more similar. Different dimensions of culture in different countries may follow different trends, although some trends will be felt worldwide. The HERMES data bank contains data from two points in time (around 1968 and around 1972) and thus can be used to show trends at least for this period. These trends may be due to maturation, seniority, generation, and/or *Zeitgeist* effects; using both longitudinal data and breakdowns by the respondents' age bracket, these can, at least partly, be separated.

It appears that the answers on the three questions composing the Power Distance Index do not shift together over the four-year period, nor do those composing the Uncertainty Avoidance Index; the trend analysis for these two dimensions has therefore been limited to one question in each case, the preferred manager for PDI, and on-the-job stress for UAI. Both show a combined age and *Zeitgeist* effect. The latter points to a decrease of the desired power distance worldwide; only in the low PDI countries is this matched by a corresponding shift in perceived managerial behavior. There is also a worldwide trend toward an increase in stress. The two remaining dimensions, Individualism and Masculinity, show both an increasing trend, which in particular for IDV is quite sharp. There is no sign of convergency between extreme countries (except for the preferred manager); rather, the reverse.

This chapter shows graphically the relationships of preferred manager type, stress, individualism, and masculinity to age, by occupational category, for each of the two survey rounds. Higher-educated employees (managers and professionals) mature later, but they remain sensitive to the developments in society (the *Zeitgeist*) to a later age than lower-educated employees (techniciams, clerks, and unskilled workers) whose value systems tend to become more rigid after the age of 40. The relationship of individualism and masculinity with age is based on age effects in work goal importance which correspond with those found in the literature.

Finally, a speculative attempt is made to indicate possible longer-term trends; it is suggested that individualism will increase and the Power Distance norm will decrease as long as national wealth increases, that uncertainty avoidance—or at least its anxiety component—fluctuates over time with a 25–40-year wave length, and that masculinity differences among countries will remain large.

The Process of Culture Change

In the first chapter of this book, I pictured in Figure 1.4 how the stability of culture patterns over long periods of time can be explained from their reinforcement by the institutions which themselves are products of the dominant value systems. The system in Figure 1.4 is in a self-regulating quasi-equilibrium: It does change, but generally only slowly. The forces toward change come from the outside, in the form of forces of nature or forces of man: trade, conquest, or scientific discovery.

Scientific discovery, of course, may also take place within the system. Culture itself within a system affects both the inquisitiveness of the members of society and their tolerance for new ideas and therefore the rate of discovery and innovation (Wallace, 1970: 170ff). Until 100–200 years ago, this rate usually was extremely low. Today, the products of scientific discovery (including the mass media) represent the major force of culture change, and for most countries in the world they come mainly or exclusively from outside; that is why in Figure 1.4 I have listed "scientific discovery" as an outside influence (in a strict sense, it also could be put in the "origins" box).

As all countries are gradually exposed to the products of the same scientific discoveries in the form of modern technology, and as they play an important role in culture change, some authors have concluded that all societies will become more and more similar. In the "comparative management" literature of the 1960s we find the "convergency theory," which implies that management philosophy and practice around the world will become more and more alike (see Chapter 1). Kerr et al. (1960) stated it even stronger: "The logic of industrialism will eventually lead us all to a common society where ideology will cease to matter." Such a statement strikes us now as naive and as wishful thinking; a more realistic evaluation of the situation is made by Feldman and Moore (1965), who point out that "the inconsistent elements of pre-industrial systems do not simply disappear, lost without trace" (1965: 262). They are found in particular in the political field: "The political order, almost by operational definition, is the residuary legatee of unsolved social problems." Feldman and Moore conclude that "surely most of the changes in industrial societies, and certainly the major ones by any crude scale, are disequilibrating rather than equilibrating (1965: 265)—so that we should not expect a kind of end-state equilibrium to which all countries evolve."

A more sober statement about the process of culture change is therefore that technological modernization is an important force toward change which leads to partly similar developments in different societies.[1] However, it does not wipe out differences among societies and may even enlarge them; as on the basis of preexisting value systems societies cope with technological modernization in different ways.

Studies of the evolution of the culture of modern nations always have to cope with the dichotomies of similarity versus uniqueness and of stability versus change, and usually stress one side of either dichotomy at the expense of the other. The convergency theorists stressed similarity and change. Students of the developments within specific countries stress uniqueness and stability. Peyrefitte (1976) traces most of the problems of present-day France back to Louis XIV (seventeenth century); Hofstede (1973) shows that quotes of eighteenth-century visitors to the Netherlands still apply to the Dutch of today; Béteille (1977: 25) refers to the remarkable stability over time of the basic structure of ideas and values in India and China; Inkeles (1977) finds continuity in the American national character ever since the descriptions by de Crèvecoeur dating from 1782. The latter is particularly interesting because the United States is a country of immigrants; it shows with amazing clarity that culture is learned, not inborn.[2]

A qualitative approach to the assessment of "culture" change was tried by Cattell (1953). He factor-analyzed time series data on 48 variables for Great Britain from 1837–1937. In Chapter 1 I criticized Cattell's analyses for being atheoretical and his set of variables for being "catch-all." The same criticism applies to his time series data. He does find four factors (out of 10) which can be interpreted. Even if they do not necessarily refer to cultural evolution, they illustrate that over time, different dimensions of national indices shift in different ways, which is relevant to the present study. Cattell's four interpretable dimensions are the following:

(1) "Cultural Pressure"—basically, a modernization factor whose strength increases more or less monotonously over the total time span.
(2) "War Stress"—basically, the effect of wars on the national economy, etc.; peaks during war periods.
(3) "Emancipation"—mainly related to Universal suffrage; low until about 1920, then steps up.
(4) "Slum morale"—a poverty factor which peaks between 1860 and 1880.

Cattell later tried a similar analysis for the United States and found partly the same factors, but with a different timing.

Measuring Culture Change
Through Shifts in Values

In the present study I have tried to quantify both the similarities and the uniqueness of cultures; I shall now in the same way try to quantify both stability and change. For this purpose, I can analyze the HERMES data longitudinally (comparing the 1967–1973 survey cycle) as well as by the age brackets of the respondents.

Differences in values among respondents of different ages and/or at different points in time may be due to four different kinds of causes:

(1) maturation,
(2) seniority,
(3) generation, or
(4) *Zeitgeist*

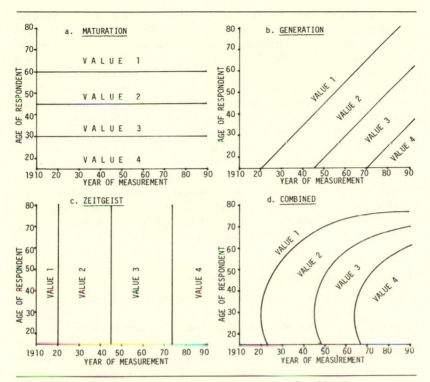

FIGURE 8.1 Maturation, Generation, *Zeitgeist,* and Combined
Effects in Values Change

The difference between 1, 3, and 4 is illustrated in Figure 8.1.

Maturation effects simply mean that respondents' values shift as they grow older.
This is pictured in Figure 8.1a. Shifts over time are due only to the aging of respondents; if we choose respondents of the same age, nothing changes.

Generation effects occur when values are fixed in the youth from a certain period
and then stay with their age cohort over its lifetime. If the conditions of life during
youth have changed drastically; this may lead to different generations having different fixed values (Figure 8.1b).

Zeitgeist effects occur when drastic system-wide changes in conditions cause
everyone's values to shift, regardless of age (Figure 8.1c).

In practice, these effects probably will occur in combination; an example is given
in Figure 8.1d in which the *Zeitgeist* affects only the younger people and older
people's values tend to be determined more by their age and/or generation.

Senority effects occur when we recruit our respondents from one particular
organization, for those values that shift not so much because people have physically
aged but because they have become more senior in their organization and have
acquired, for example, greater commitment, greater frustration, or a lower market
value elsewhere. Seniority and age effects are not easy to separate; for a sample of 12

subgroups from the HERMES data, seniority and age were correlated across individuals between .52 and .76, with a median of .61. Seniority and age can be separated only by comparing cross-tabulations of either variable with the dependent variable, or, even better, by separating the values of young junior, older senior, and older junior respondents.

Maturation and generation effects are often confused. Complaints of older people about "young people today" have been found on an Egyptian papyrus manuscript. One of the oldest Greek texts preserved, Hesiod's *Works and Days* dated toward the end of the eighth century B.C., contains a pessimistic paragraph on the new generation in which "father will have no common bond with son" and "men will dishonour parents . . . and will blame and criticize with cruel words" (Hesiod, 1973: 64).

In data collected at one moment in time, maturation and generation effects cannot be separated. In longitudinal data (from at least two points in time) but without age differentiation of respondents, generation and *Zeitgeist* effects cannot be separated (this will be immediately clear from Figures 8.1a, b, and c). Only in longitudinal data with age differentiation can we separate the three effects.

Value Shifts in HERMES: Time Effects

For the 36 questions in the HERMES questionnaire that were asked both in 1967–1969 and 1971–1973 and for which country differences were reasonably stable (Figure 2.5), the score shifts over time can be read in Figures 8.2 and 8.3.

The data in these tables are not yet differentiated by the age group of the respondents. The questions have been classified into four groups, according to the index (PDI, UAI, IDV, or MAS) with which they have the strongest ecological correlation. Under IDV I also show the shift in the mean raw work goal importance score across 14 goals (IMP).

In Figures 8.2 and 8.3 a plus or minus sign indicates the direction in which the total index (PDI, UAI, IDV, or MAS) would shift due to the shift of answers on each question, taking into account the sign of the correlation between the question and the index. The significance of the shifts (that is, whether they can be considered worldwide shifts) has been determined by the sign test across all countries surveyed twice; for example, scores on question A18 in Figure 8.3 shifted positively in *all* 19 countries surveyed twice and question A9 shifted negatively in 18 out of 19 countries, the exception being Pakistan.

The shifts in the answers of HERMES respondents may, of course, be due to situational (HERMES-specific) causes as well as to shifts in values in the societies outside HERMES. From 1968 to 1972, HERMES' growth rate was considerably reduced. This meant less opportunities for advancement and more competition for resources within the company. We see (Figure 8.2, question A58) that the overall satisfaction of employees with the company, measured on a 7-point scale, was reduced in virtually all countries. The company climate became less benevolent.

Figures 8.2 and 8.3 show shifts on individual questions; we are not allowed, without further analysis, to summarize these into a shift "on PDI," "on UAI," and so on. This would mean a reverse ecological fallacy as described in Chapter 1. Let us take the case of PDI in Figure 8.2. From the three questions that have been used to compose PDI (B46, A55, and B54), one shifts significantly in the direction of a larger power distance and two in the direction of a smaller power distance. This means that, as far as the shift over time is concerned, PDI is not a homogeneous index, and it should not be used for expressing time shifts. We can read from Figures 8.2 and 8.3 that only IDV and MAS show more or less homogeneous shifts, so that we can, as a whole, speak of shift toward "stronger individualism" and "stronger masculinity." We shall now study the questions related to each index and look at age bracket data as well.

Trends of Questions Related to Power Distance

Writing about social inequality, which we found in Chapter 3 (Figure 3.7) to be the core of the Power Distance societal norm. Béteille (1969) states:

> In spite of the great diversity of patterns, certain trends seem to emerge from a consideration of the events of the last hundred and fifty years. Everywhere there seems to have come about a steady erosion in the legitimacy accorded to social inequality. If social inequality continues to exist as a fact, it is no longer accepted by all as a part of the natural order but is challenged, or at least questioned, at every point. . . . The decline of the legitimacy of social inequality did not start everywhere at the same time and has not proceeded equally far in every society. But today there are few societies in the world where an ideology of inequality would be allowed to pass unchalleged [1969: 366–367].

This statement would lead to a prediction of a worldwide reduction in PDI. Obviously, the time span over which the trends in the HERMES data can be measured is very short: only four years (1968 to 1972). Still, if there is an overall decreasing trend, some of it should be visible even over so short a period.

The data in the upper half of Figure 8.2 show that from the three questions on which PDI is based, two indeed point to a decrease in the Power Distance norm worldwide. From the correlated questions, another three point in the same direction. However, questions B46 (How frequently does it occur that employees are afraid to express disagreement with their managers?) and A52 (How often is your manager concerned about helping you get ahead?) show significant shifts in the opposite direction—that is, toward larger power distance. It may be that the shift on these questions is situationally determined: It can well be understood from the decrease of HERMES' growth rate (fewer actual possibilities for getting ahead) and the unfavorable shift in climate described above.

The phenomenon of the combination of negative and positive shifts in power distance can be better understood if we consider the countries with large PDI values (49 and over) separately from those with smaller PDI values (40 and under). This has been done in Figure 8.4.

From Figure 8.4 we read that the increase in fear to disagree is virtually limited to the high PDI countries; on the other hand, the decrease in the perception of autocratic or persuasive behavior on the part of the manager is virtually limited to the smaller PDI countries. The only phenomenon that is common to both groups of countries is the decrease of respondents' preference for an autocratic or persuasive manager.[3]

These figures bear resemblance to recent figures about the economic development of the world: All countries want development, but those which already have it are developing further at a faster rate than those which do not yet have it. As a result, the gap between wealthy and poor countries increases. In the case of power distance,

(text continues page 353)

FIGURE 8.2   Shifts Between the 1967–1969 and the 1971–1973 Survey Round of Questions Associated with PDI and UAI

Question number	Question	Mean score[a]		Corresponding shift in index[b]	Number of countries		Countries shifting in opposite direction	Range of scores between highest and lowest country	
		1967–69	1971–73		total surveyed twice	shifting in same direction[c]		1967–69	1971–73
	primarily correlated with PDI:								
B46	employees afraid to disagree	3.09	2.93	+	26	18*	AUT, BRA, GER, ISR, NET, PAK, TUR	.98	1.51
A55	perceived manager, % 1 + 2	47.9	45.4	–	29	22**	ARG, BRA, ISR, GRE, PER, PHI	28	36
A54	preferred manager, % 1 + 2	27.1	22.9	–	29	22**	AUT, FIN, SPA	33	27
B55	employees lose respect	4.02	4.10	–	20	15**	FIN, GER, GRE, SPA	.95	.87
A52	manager helps ahead	2.34	2.52	+	29	23***	ARG, AUT, BRA, PAK, PER	.91	.95
A13	importance freedom	529	544	–	19	16***	GBR, ISR, NOR	223	181
B52	corporation responsible	1.74	1.72	0	22	11	many	1.14	1.36
B53	interesting work important	1.78	1.84	–	23	16*	FIN, GER, MEX, PAK, SAF, TUR, VEN	.65	.75

[348]

FIGURE 8.2 Continued

primarily correlated with UAI:

Code	Item			0(−)					
B60	rules shouldn't be broken	2.80	2.87	0(−)	20	12	many	1.04	1.03
A43	continue with company, % 1 + 2	20.0	20.7	0(−)	28	12	many	33	32
A37	stress	3.19	3.10	+	29	24***	ARG, NET, PAK, PHI, VEN	1.15	1.35
B9	prefer specialist career	3.09	3.23	−	13	11*	FRA, ISR	.69	1.04
B44	prefer manager own nationality	1.73	1.68	+	21	14*	IRE, ISR, NET, PHI, VEN	.54	.47
B54	competition harmful	3.02	2.84	+	21	17**	AUT, GER, PAK, PHI	1.08	.97
B57	individual decisions better	3.53	3.64	+	17	13*	ARG, COL, FRA, PER	.71	.84
B61	most employees avoid responsibility	3.36	3.38	0	20	11	many	.74	.87
A10	importance benefits	376	392	+	19	14*	FRA, GER, IRA, NET, SAF	281	261
A15	importance advancement	546	510	+	19	17***	IRA, ISR	219	253
A58	overall satisfaction	2.79	3.14	−	28	27***	PAK	1.05	1.15
A2	seniority in company	3.10	3.27	+	29	22**	ARG, BRA, COL, ISR, JAP, PAK, SWI	1.20	1.09
A57	age	3.87	4.03	+	29	24***	ARG, BRA, IRE, ISR, JAP	1.06	1.54

[a] Expressed in % for A43, A54 and A55; in standardized scores (App. 3) for A10, A13, and A15; and in points on the scale used (3, 5, or 7) for all other questions.

[b] Sign of shifts multiplied by sign of correlation between this question and the index (PDI or UAI).

[c] Tested with sign test, one-tailed.

FIGURE 8.3 Shifts Between the 1967–1969 and the 1971–1973 Survey Round of Questions Associated with IDV and MAS

Question number	Question	Mean score[a]		Corresponding shift in index[b]	Number of countries		Countries shifting in opposite direction	Range of scores between highest and lowest country	
		1967–69	1971–73		total surveyed twice	shifting in same direction[c]		1967–69	1971–73
	primarily correlated with IDV:								
A18	importance personal time	438	484	+	19	19***	none	212	227
A9	importance training	578	526	+	19	18***	PAK	120	79
A12	importance physical conditions	363	348	0(+)	19	13	many	125	89
A17	importance use of skills	555	530	+	19	17***	NET, SWE	97	94
B24	prefer foreign company	1.79	1.88	+	22	15*	ISR, MEX	.52	.63
B25	other job available?	1.85	1.87	0	25	15	many	.61	.82
B59	staying one company desirable	3.19	3.06	–	21	16**	AUT, FRA, ISR, JAP	1.23	1.14
IMP	mean raw goal importance	197.2	199.7	0	19	13	many	58	62

FIGURE 8.3 Continued

primarily correlated with MAS:

A7	importance earnings	501	525	+	19	14*	FIN, SWE, PAK, SAF, SPA	141	230
A16	importance manager	566	531	+	19	16***	GER, IRE, ISR	134	146
A8	importance cooperation	554	542	0(+)	19	11	many	133	138
A11	importance recognition	480	486	+	19	14*	BEL, GRE, ISR, PAK, TUR	231	191
A6	importance desirable area	433	468	–	19	14*	GRE, IRA, PAK, SPA, TUR	305	347
A5	importance challenge	587	619	+	19	17***	NET, SWE	129	136
A14	importance employment security	496	495	0	19	11	many	172	187
A1	sex (% female)	7.0	7.3	0	26	16	many	10.9	14.7

[a]Expressed in % for A1; in standardized scores (App. 3) for A5 through A18; and in points on the scale used (3, 4, or 5) for B24, B25, and B59.

[b]Sign of shift multiplied by sign of correlation between this question and the index (IDV or MAS).

[c]Tested with sign test, one-tailed.

FIGURE 8.4   Shifts Between the 1967–1969 and the 1971–1973 Survey Round of Questions Used to Compose the PDI, for High and Low PDI Countries

| Question number | Question | Mean Score | | Corresponding shift in index | Number of countries | | Countries shifting in opposite direction |
		1967–69	1971–73		total surveyed twice	shifting in same direction	
	for countries with PDI = 49 − 94						
B46	employees afraid to disagree	2.92	2.69	+	17	13*	BRA, PAK, TUR
A55	perceived manager, % 1 + 2	52.7	51.6	0(−)	15	9	many
A54	preferred manager, % 1 + 2	31.5	27.5	−	15	11**	SPA
	for countries with PDI = 11 − 40						
B46	employees afraid to disagree	3.42	3.40	0(+)	9	5	many
A55	perceived manager, % 1 + 2	42.9	38.8	−	14	13**	ISR
A54	preferred manager, % 1 ÷ 2	22.3	17.9	−	14	11*	AUT, FIN

For explanation of columns see Figure 8.2.

all want it to be reduced; but only in countries in which it is already lower subordinates experience a reduction in power distance in their bosses' behavior; the others experience an increase in fear to disagree. Again, the gap between low PDI countries and high PDI countries increases rather than decreases; and it is, of course, no accident that the low PDI countries tend to be the wealthier ones as well. There is no support for a convergency theory according to which all countries move to a low PDI stable state. The last two columns in Figure 8.2 also show that the range of scores on the various questions from 1967–1969 to 1971–1973 shows an increase rather than a decrease (for the % preferred manager 1 + 2 there is actually a modest decrease in range). Inequality perpetuates itself (Kohn, 1969: 200; Béteille, 1977: 132ff).

Using the causal chain of Figure 3.8 we can understand the shift to a desire for more equality by the increase of technology which is indispensable for the survival of an increasing world population and the corresponding increase in education and development of middle classes. However, only in the low PDI countries does the system seem able to cope with the new middle-class values; in the high PDI cluster the rigidity of existing structures usually seems to resist change, and the shift to less directive relationships is slight, leading to an increase of frustration on the part of the middle strata. Studies like Crozier's (1971) about France[4] and Chaliand's (1976) about the less developed countries confirm this. It should be no surprise that PDI is ecologically correlated to domestic political violence (Figure 3.19).

Earlier I argued that the difference in shifts among the three questions used to compose the PDI makes it undesirable to compute PDI shifts over time: These would represent a summation of heterogeneous elements. In order to study the shifts in the Power Distance societal norm, I shall use only question A54: the percentage of respondents preferring an autocratic or persuasive manager, which, according to Figure 8.4, has decreased as much in the high PDI as in the low PDI countries.

According to the distinction introduced earlier in this chapter, we should now investigate whether the shifts in the percentage preferring a certain type of manager are due to a maturation, generation, or *Zeitgeist* effect. For this purpose, I show in Figure 8.5 the percentage preferring manager 1 + 2 separately for seven large categories of employees (world totals), by age groups, by survey round (1967–1969 and 1971–1973).

In a diagram like Figure 8.5, a mere *maturation* (or perhaps *seniority*) shift would manifest itself in an overlap of the 1968 and 1972 curves: people in, for example, the 30–39 age bracket in 1972 would score exactly like those who were in the 30–39 age bracket in 1968. A *generation* shift would manifest itself in a horizontal shift of the curves by four years: The 30–39 age bracket of 1968 would have become a 34–43 age bracket in 1972, but it would have maintained its score level. A *Zeitgeist* shift would manifest itself in a vertical shift of the curve from 1968 to 1972, affecting all age brackets equally.

What Figure 8.5 shows is a combination of maturation and a *Zeitgeist* effect with little evidence of a generation effect[5]; something like Figure 8.1d. The *Zeitgeist* effect varies by age bracket. It is lower for the very young (clerks and secretaries under 20) and for those over 40 (see the dotted vertical lines in the "managers"

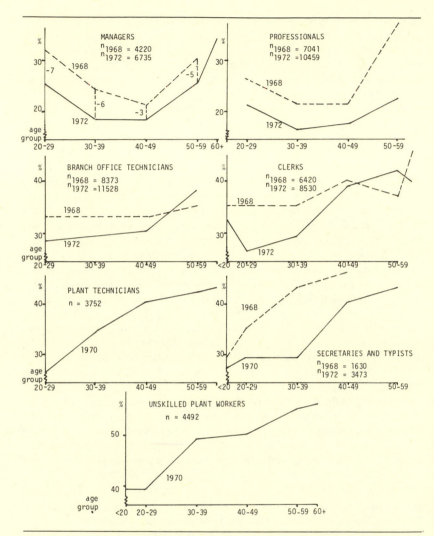

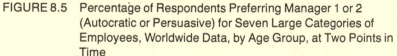

FIGURE 8.5   Percentage of Respondents Preferring Manager 1 or 2
              (Autocratic or Persuasive) for Seven Large Categories of
              Employees, Worldwide Data, by Age Group, at Two Points in
              Time

diagram of Figure 8.5 as an example). For the (relatively small) groups over 50, the
higher educated employees (managers and professionals) still show a reduction in
preference for an autocratic or persuasive manager from 1968 to 1972, but the less
educated employees (technicians and clerks) show a small *increase* rather than a
reduction. If we compare the curves for higher educated employees to those of lower
educated employees, we find that the former reach maturity (in the sense of a low

need for dependence) later, but as they grow older they remain in touch with the *Zeitgeist* (the trends in society) longer. Less educated employees when they grow older even shift their values in a sense opposite to the trend in society.

As could be expected (compare Chapter 3, Figure 3.2, the overall level of preference for an autocratic or persuasive manager differs among employee categories: It is lowest for professionals and managers, medium for technicians, clerks, and secretaries, and highest for unskilled workers.

The increase in preference for an autocratic or persuasive boss for the higher age brackets points to a relationship between age and conservatism which is not surprising and which is, moreover, confirmed by other surveys. For example, Inglehart (1971) used a representative sample (the total number of respondents was about 10,000) from the populations of Belgium, France, Great Britain, Germany, Italy, and the Netherlands. Relevant to us is a classification by age category of those in each country who chose "acquisitive values"—maintaining order in the nation and fighting rising prices—versus those who chose "post-bourgeois" values—giving the people more say in important political decisions and protecting freedom of speech. In each of the six countries the percentage of those choosing acquisitive values increased and that of those choosing post-bourgeois values decreased with age (1971: 1000).

Rokeach (1973) reports results obtained with the Rokeach Value Survey on a national U.S. sample of about 1400 respondents. This instrument (1973: 357–361) asks respondents to rank-order 18 "terminal" and 18 "instrumental" values. For the four age categories 20–29, 30–39, 40–49, and 50–59, we find the following clear value differences (monotonous increase or decrease and at least one full rank point of difference between youngest and oldest category; see Rokeach, (1973: 396–405).

More important with age	*Less important with age*
True Friendship (terminal)	Mature Love (terminal)
Cheerful (instrumental)	Freedom (terminal)
	Equality (terminal)

Feather (1977) applied the same survey to about 600 inhabitants of an Australian city aged 14 and above. He finds the following significant correlations between importance and age (1977: 243):

More important with age	*Less important with age*
Family Security (terminal)	An Exciting Life (terminal)
Self-Respect (terminal)	Freedom (terminal)
Polite (instrumental)	Equality (terminal)

In both the U.S. and the Australian sample, therefore, "freedom" and "equality" appeal less to older than to younger people, and Inglehart's data from Europe, obtained with another instrument, point in the same direction.

In a survey study of over 1000 Swedish workers, Gardell (1971: 386) found that claims to influence over decisions decrease with mounting age.

The HERMES data that were shown do not allow us to distinguish between *maturation* and *seniority*. For three large employee groups, cross-tabulations of the preferred type of manager against age group and seniority category are available; in all three, the age (maturation) effect is stronger than the seniority effect, so that we may assume that physical age, rather than length of service with the company, explains the differences in type of manager preferred.

Trends of Questions Related to Uncertainty Avoidance

Uncertainty Avoidance, as we saw in Chapter 4, is related to levels of anxiety. In Figure 4.10 I demonstrated a .73 rank correlation between UAI and a "neuroticism" or "anxiety" factor found by Lynn and Hampson in medical and related statistics for 18 countries. In a later phase of their research (Lynn, 1975; Lynn and Hampson, 1977) these authors did an analysis over time using data from 1935, 1950, 1955, 1960, 1965, and 1970.[6] The five countries with the highest anxiety scores in 1935 were Austria, Finland, Germany, Italy, and Japan: The World War II axis powers and two countries which became involved in the war on their side. From 1935 to 1950, all countries defeated or occupied during World War II increased in anxiety level, while six out of the nine countries not defeated or occupied decreased in anxiety level. The mean anxiety scores across all 18 countries developed as follows (Lynn and Hampson, 1977: Table 5):

1935	1950	1955	1960	1965	1970
50.6	51.3	50.6	49.0	48.6	50.4

We see that the postwar increase of 1950 had disappeared in 1955, and that 1960 and 1965 were years of relatively low anxiety; this applies also to individual countries.[7] From 1965 to 1970 there is a sharp increase in anxiety. It occurred in 14 out of the 18 countries; all except Finland, France, Japan, and Norway.[8]

The 1965–1970 period overlaps partly with the 1968–1972 period for which longitudinal HERMES data are available. In fact, the lower half of Figure 8.2 shows that question A37, the "stress" question which is one of the three used to compose the Uncertainty Avoidance Index, does show a significant worldwide shift toward higher stress over this period.[9] This shift occurs both in high UAI and in low UAI countries, although the countries with the highest stress in 1968 also show the largest increase, so that the gap between countries becomes wider (no convergency—see the last two columns of Figure 8.2).

On the other hand, the two other UAI questions "rule orientation" (B60) and "employment stability" (A43) do not show significant worldwide shifts, neither for all countries nor for either high or low UAI countries. In the case of rule orientation, we have seen (Figure 4.8) that across occupations this is strongly negatively correlated with educational level. From 1968 to 1972 the mean educational level of HERMES employees increased[10] (because of higher education requirements in hiring new employees) which would make a decrease in rule orientation likely (we see an insignificant decrease in Figure 8.2). It is possible that if we could control for educational level, we would actually find the increase in rule orientation, which we would expect with an increase in anxiety.

The shifts in the "employment stability" scores are more complex. Figure 8.2 shows a small increase in percentage wanting to continue with the company for not more than five years (answer 1 + 2). In Figure 8.6 we also see the shifts in the other answers.

Around 1972, fewer people wanted to stay until retirement, but most of these now state they want to stay for more than five years but not until retirement. The percentage of those who want to leave within two years has marginally decreased, and the *actual* labor turnover rate in a number of large countries also has decreased, but more substantially. If these figures reflect general values shifts in society, they reflect at the same time the changes specific to HERMES to which I referred earlier: The reduction of opportunities for advancement may have caused some people to rethink their long-term career plans; on the other hand, the increased average age and seniority in the company (see Figure 8.2) leads logically to a lower labor turnover.

Most questions listed in the lower half of Figure 8.2 which are correlated with UAI show shifts in the direction of greater uncertainty avoidance, except for B9, more people now preferring a manager career rather than a specialist career, and A58, lower overall satisfaction. Both can be explained from developments within HERMES.

All in all, there are indications of an increase in anxiety and related uncertainty avoidance attitudes in HERMES from 1968 to 1972, but UAI as computed for the comparison of countries at one moment in time does not seem to be the proper index to measure shifts over time; it is useless for this purpose as was PDI. In order to study the shifts in the Uncertainty Avoidance societal norm, I shall only use question A37, the "stress" question: "How often do you feel nervous or tense at work?" This is the only question to have shifted systematically worldwide. Rather than attributing these shifts to a change in a societal norm, we can postulate that they are also due exclusively to internal causes at HERMES (the less benevolent climate). However, two arguments speak against this: the fact that the shift confirms the increase in anxiety found by Lynn and Hampson for 1965–1970 on completely different data (see earlier pages) and the fact that, as we shall see below, the shift occurs across all employee

FIGURE 8.6   Shifts in Answers on the Employment Stability Question

A43. How long do you think you will continue with HERMES?	Mean % across 28 countries surveyed twice	
	1967–69	1971–73
two years at the most	6.1	5.8
from two to five years	13.8	14.9
more than five years—but leave		
before I retire	29.1	31.8**
until I retire	51.0	47.5***
total	100.0	100.0
	1968	1972
mean labour turnover rate in % in HERMES, 13 countries	7.1	5.4

Significance of shifts has been tested with the sign test, one-tailed, on 28 pairs of mean scores.

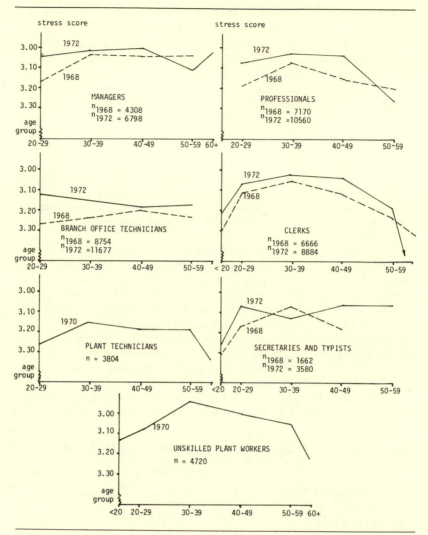

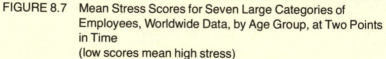

FIGURE 8.7   Mean Stress Scores for Seven Large Categories of
Employees, Worldwide Data, by Age Group, at Two Points
in Time
(low scores mean high stress)

categories which are, however, differently affected by the internal pressures of the
company.

Analogous to Figure 8.5, Figure 8.7 presents the "stress" scores separately for
seven large categories of employees (world totals) by age groups, by survey round
(1967–1969 and 1971–973). From Figure 8.7 we can read the following:

(1) There is a maturation and a *Zeitgeist* effect, but no sign of a generation effect.

(2) Most curves of stress against age are inverted U-shaped, which means that stress is highest for those in a middle age range (out of 12 curves, eight have their peak in the 30–39 age bracket).

(3) There is a difference in the absolute stress levels of the occupation categories: the highest stress is found among unskilled workers and managers, the lowest among technicians (Hofstede, 1978c).

(4) There is a systematic *Zeitgeist* difference between 1968 and 1972 data; with few exceptions, 1972 stress is higher for all occupational categories and all age brackets. The stress increase tends to be largest for the 20–29 and the 40–49 groups. In the case of those over 50, we find a decrease of stress for managers and professionals, but an increase for technicians and clerks. We saw on a previous page that the older, higher educated employees remain more in touch with the trends in society than do the older, lower educated employees. However, this does not seem to make their working lives more stressful. The decrease in stress for the managers and professionals in the 50–59 bracket shows that older people in higher qualified jobs have more opportunities to adapt their work situation to themselves than older people in less qualified jobs. However, for managers over 60 there is an increase in stress.

Trends of Questions Related to Individualism and Masculinity

The dimensions of Individualism and Masculinity have been measured through HERMES respondents' scores for the "work goal importance" questions (A5 through A18). Any shifts over time in individualism and/or masculinity should be visible in shifts in the importance of these work goals. In Figures 8.2 and 8.3 we can read that across the 19 countries surveyed twice with the same set of goals questions, 11 out of the 14 goals show significant worldwide shifts in importance between 1967–1969 and 1971–1973:

More important have become	*Less important have become*
personal time (+ 46)	training (−36)
desirable area (+ 35)	advancement (−36)
challenge (+ 32)	manager (−35)
earnings (+ 24)	use of skills (−25)
benefits (+ 16)	
freedom (+ 15)	
recognition (+ 6)	

No systematic shifts across the 19 countries are found for physical conditions (−15), cooperation (−12), and employment security (−1).

Again, there are in-company reasons for some of these shifts. The smaller rate of personnel growth which has reduced opportunities for advancement has definitely affected people's aspirations for advancement and channelled it toward other types of reward, such as earnings. The maturing of the company's technology, which was novel in the 1960s, has definitely reduced the importance of training to some extent. However, not all shifts in goals can be explained this way. A shift from the importance of "use of skills" to the importance of "challenge" is unlikely to have been generated by in-company reasons; nor is there a plausible in-company explanation for the universal shift in the importance of "personal time."

Although (as we saw in Chapter 2 and read again in Figure 8.2) some goals are associated more with PDI and UAI than with IDV and MAS, 13 out of the 14 goals relate to IDV and MAS as well. The pattern of association of the goals with "Individualism" and "Masculinity" as we found it in Chapter 5 is as follows:

Associated with IDV
personal time (factor loading .86)
freedom (.49)
challenge (.46)
use of skills (− .63)
physical conditions (− .69)
training (− .82)

Associated with MAS
earnings (factor loading .70)
recognition (.59)
advancement (.56)
challenge (.54)
employment security (− .48)
desirable area (− .59)
cooperation (− .69)
manager (− .69)

(We see that "challenge" appears for both IDV and MAS; "benefits" does not appear, but it is correlated − .40 with IDV).

From the six goals associated with IDV, five shifted significantly toward a larger IDV-score, and the sixth shifted toward a larger IDV, but not significantly so. Thus, there has been a strong tendency for goals to shift toward greater individualism in 1971–1973 than in 1967–1969 (we recognized this in the upper part of Figure 8.3). This shift can be interpreted from the quite strong association between individualism and national wealth (Figure 5.20). From 1967 to 1973, most countries (among the 19 surveyed twice with these goals questions) have become wealthier. This should have increased the individualism of their citizens.

Figure 8.8 shows the result of separate calculations of IDV for the 1967–1969 and for the 1971–1973 data.[11] There is, indeed, a drastic shift in IDV across the 19 countries (+ 20 points). However, the poorest country among the 19, Pakistan, which also had the lowest IDV score in 1969, shifted toward a *lower* IDV. Figure 8.8 shows no convergency in Individualism among countries over time: The gap between the two extreme countries in the set of 19 (Pakistan and Great Britain) increased from 60 to 89.

For the eight goals associated with MAS, four shifted significantly toward a larger MAS score, two shifted also toward a larger MAS (but not significantly so),

FIGURE 8.8   Shifts in IDV and MAS Scores Between Two Survey Rounds

	1967–'69	1971–'73	Difference
IDV-scores:			
19 countries[a]	50	70	+20
Great-Britain (high IDV)	75	101	+26
Pakistan (low IDV)	15	12	− 3
MAS-scores:			
19 countries[a]	43	48	+ 5
Austria (high MAS)	76	81	+ 5
Sweden (low MAS)	7	5	− 2

[a]AUT, BEL, DEN, FIN, FRA, GBR, GER, IRA, IRE, ISR, NET, NOR, PAK, SAF, SPA, SWE, SWI, TUR.

and two (advancement and desirable area) shifted significantly in the opposite direction. Neither of the latter is among those most strongly determining the Masculinity dimension, so we could still expect an overall shift toward greater masculinity. We recognized this in the lower part of Figure 8.3, and it is borne out by the separate calculations of MAS on 1967–1969 and 1971–1973 data shown in the lower part of Figure 8.8. However, the shift in MAS (+ 5 across 19 countries) is much weaker than the shift in IDV. We see again the phenomenon that the country lowest in 1968–1969 (Sweden) actually becomes (marginally) lower still, so that the gap between it and the highest country (Austria) increases slightly; once more, there is no sign of convergency. I do not find an easy explanation for an overall increase in masculinity, and the possible origins of high and low MAS scores identified in Chapter 6 (Figure 6.7) do not help to explain it. Compared with the shift in individualism, the shift in masculinity is relatively minor.

Shifts in Work Goal Importance as a Function of Age

We should still investigate whether the shifts in individualism and masculinity are due mainly to maturation, generation, or *Zeitgeist* influences—or to a combination of these. To this purpose we have to look at individualism and masculinity by age group; but in order to avoid a reverse ecological fallacy, we should first study to what extent the importance of individual work goals is affected by the age bracket of the respondents. Besides the HERMES data, there exists a fairly extensive literature on the relationship between age and work goal importance.

The classical review of research in the area of job attitudes by Herzberg et al. (1957) is brief about the relationship between age and work goals. Without specifying the number of studies upon which their data are based, they conclude only that the importance of *security* increases with age, while the importance of *earnings* first decreases and then increases again, with a minimum around the age of 40.

Friedlander (1966) summarizes the importance scores on 14 goals into three factors: social environment, intrinsic work, and recognition through advancement. For about 1000 white-collar U.S. government employees he shows in a diagram the importance of the three factors by age group (20–29, 30–39, 40–49, and 50 +). However, he does not correct for acquiescence (some of his groups of respondents rate *everything* more important). Recalculating Friedlander's data to eliminate acquiescence, I find both for lower paid and for higher paid white-collar employees that the importance of intrinsic (interesting and so on) work *decreases* with age and that of social environment *increases* with age. The latter includes interpersonal relations as well as job security and efficiency. It is not possible to see from Friedlander's published data whether the age differences in importance of "social environment" are due mainly to security or to interpersonal relations or to both; this is a reverse ecological fallacy.

The 14-country study of managerial thinking by Haire et al. (1966) includes a comparison of work goal importance responses by age groups (managers up to 39, and 40 and over; 1966: 167). Like Friedlander, these authors do not correct for acquiescence (they standardize across countries, not across goals); their data show that older managers tend to rate everything as more important. Also, they group 11 goals into five clusters whose relevance for age comparison is not proved (see pages 31 and 226). Their data show that the importance of "security" and, to a lesser extent, "social relationships" and "esteem" increases with age. However, *after correcting for acquiescence*, we see that the strongest age effects are a relative increase of the importance of security and a relative decrease of the importance of self-actualization (personal growth and development, using one's capabilities, accomplishment—that is, what others call intrinsic work).

Quinn (1973) and N. Q. Herrick (1973) used the data from the 1969–1970 Survey of Working Conditions, a representative sample of the entire U.S. working population aged 16 years and older. Quinn published a table of work goal importance indices for the age groups 16–29, 30–44, 45–54, and 55 + (1973: 244). The data suffer from the same weaknesses as those by Friedlander and Haire et al.: first, no correction for acquiescence and second, a clustering of 23 goals into five factors which are not necessarily relevant for age comparison. Quinn shows a relationship between age and the importance of *comfort* (which persists if we correct for acquiescence): comfort includes physical working conditions, hours, travel arrangements, and ease. There are no consistent relationships between other importance clusters and age. However, N. Q. Herrick (1973: 474–475) looks at the same data using scores for single goals, not clusters, for younger versus older respondents. Besides the differences in the importance of "comfort" goals he notices that to the young, interesting work, developing abilities, and opportunities for advancement were more important.

In one of the rare studies by other than U.S. researchers, Sand (1973) reports on a survey of about 2000 German workers. Their work goal importance scores (1973: 52) are shown by age category: 16–19, 20–29, 30–39, 40–59, and 60 +. If we limit ourselves to the three middle categories (excluding specific youth and retirement goal patterns) we find that among 14 goals only "security" increases consistently in importance with age, and "advancement opportunities" decreases.

One of the publications on results obtained with the IRGOM exercise "Life Goals" by Bass (1976) relates the importance of the life goals of over 2000 managers from France, Great Britain, Germany, Italy, the Netherlands, and the United States to their age bracket. In five out of the six countries, the life goal "service" (to contribute to the satisfaction of others; to be helpful to others who need it) is more important for the higher age groups, and "pleasure" (to enjoy life, to be happy and content, to have the good things in life) is less important for the older (1976: 166).

Combining the conclusions of the above seven references, we find that the following trends are suggested by one or more of them:

More important with age	Less important with age
security	intrinsic work
social relationships	developing abilities
comfort	advancement opportunities
service	pleasure

Some of these—for example, the increase in the importance of security and the decrease in the importance of developing abilities and advancement opportunities— are highly obvious correlates of age: it would be curious if we did not find them. In fact, we would have to wonder about the validity of our measuring instruments. The others, the increasing importance of social relationships and comfort and the decreasing importance of intrinsic work, are less obvious, although they correspond with psychological theories about interest shifts during life (for example, Lievegoed, 1976).

For HERMES, separate work goal importance scores for four age brackets (20–29, 30–39, 40–49, and 50–59) were computed for five large categories of employees covering the full range of status and educational levels: managers, professionals, branch office technicians, clerks, and unskilled workers (all 1971–1973 data).

For each goal and age bracket, the deviation from the mean of all four age brackets (expressed in standardized score points) has been calculated; first for the five employee categories separately, then means across the five categories have been computed. These means are shown in Figure 8.9, which therefore presents in concise form the relationship between age bracket and work goal importance, as found for about 40,000 HERMES employees from all countries and a wide range of occupations.

We see in Figure 8.9 the following trends in HERMES:

More important with age	*Less important with age*
employment security	advancement
benefits	training
manager	earnings
cooperation	challenge
	personal time

More or less fluctuating scores are found for desirable area, physical conditions, and use of skills, while virtually no age effect at all is visible for recognition and freedom.

The HERMES findings (based on an international respondent population) thus confirm largely the trends found in the literature. The "comfort" goals—desirable area and physical conditions,—do not increase monotonously with age, but they do increase. For "service" and "pleasure" the HERMES questionnaire has no items (but "pleasure," like "personal time," is part of the individualism syndrome). Had we looked at the five employee categories separately, we would have seen that lower educated employees worry about "employment security" at an earlier age and lose their interest in "challenge" and "training" earlier. Professionals and clerks show an interest in "cooperation," which is much less dependent on age than is the case for the other three employee categories. Living in a desirable area is particularly important for the 40–49 age bracket regardless of education and job level.

Individualism and Masculinity Shifts
by Age Group

The last column of Figure 8.9 shows whether each of the 14 work facets is primarily related to IDV or to MAS, and in what sense. We see that the age effects for all facets most closely related to MAS point in the direction of decreasing masculinity with increasing age (for "Recognition," the relationship is marginal). For IDV, the picture is more ambiguous. "Use of Skills" and "Training" point to increasing individualism with increasing age; "Benefits," "Personal Time," and "Physical Conditions" point to decreasing individualism with increasing age. The IDV score for a

FIGURE 8.9 Differences of Standardized Mean Scores for the Importance
of 14 Work Goals, Between Each of Four Age Groups and
Their Common Mean, Averaged Across Five Large
Employee Categories

Work goals	Standardized goal importance score differences—mean of five employee categories				Most closely asso- ciated di- mension and sign of corre- sponding age ef-
Age bracket	20-29	30-39	40-49	50-59	fect
JOB CONTENT AND LEARNING					
Challenge	+42	+28	−20	−51	−MAS
Use of skills	+28	−8	0	−21	+IDV
Training	+103	+4	−36	−72	+IDV
REWARD					
Recognition	+4	+7	−5	−5	±MAS
Advancement	+149	+50	−60	−140	−MAS
Earnings	+50	+45	−31	−64	−MAS
INTERPERSONAL RELATIONS					
Manager	−47	−19	+16	+50	−MAS
Cooperation	−27	−14	+13	+27	−MAS
Freedom	−5	+5	−1	+2	±IDV
SECURITY					
Employment security	−114	−22	+61	+74	−MAS
Benefits	−63	−29	+3	+88	−IDV
COMFORT					
Personal Time	+25	+13	−1	−37	−IDV
Desirable Area	−60	−5	+46	+19	−MAS
Physical Conditions	−31	−43	−7	+80	−IDV

The categories are: managers, professionals, branch office technicians, clerks, and unskilled
workers. Total number of respondents 39,973; worldwide data, 1971–1973.

given age group is therefore not a meaningful index; it is composed of a different mix
of goals for different age groups. I have computed it anyway and plotted it in Figure
8.10 because I see no other way of succinctly showing the age and trend effects of this
group of work goals in one diagram.

Figure 8.10 is analogous to Figures 8.5 and 8.7, except that (1) it shows on the
vertical axes an index score rather than the score for a single question, and (2) it
covers only the five employee categories that were surveyed twice. We find for all
five groups a relatively flat age curve, which, however, in most cases is inverted U-
shaped: The youngest and oldest age categories are less individualistic (but we have
seen in Figure 8.9 that this is due to *different* work goals for the young and for the
old). There is a strong *Zeitgeist* effect which has affected all age brackets for the

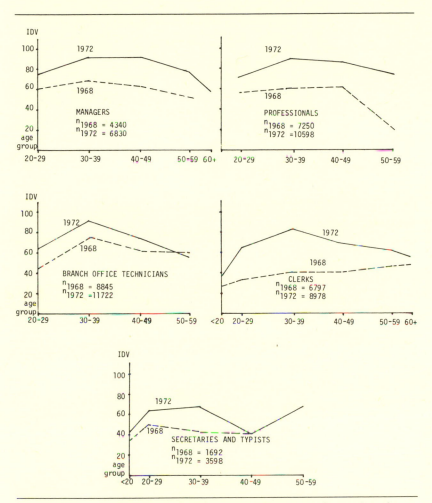

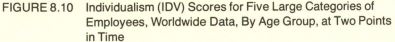

FIGURE 8.10   Individualism (IDV) Scores for Five Large Categories of
Employees, Worldwide Data, By Age Group, at Two Points
in Time

managers and professionals (they have all become much more individualist from
1967–1969 to 1971–1973) and the younger age brackets of technicians, clerks, and
secretaries; as in Figure 8.5, we see that the older, less educated employees have not
followed the trends in society so much, while the older, more educated employees
have followed them closely.

In Figure 8.11 I have plotted the MAS scores by age bracket for the same five
employee categories. The curves in Figure 8.11 contrast with those in Figure 8.10:
We see a strong dependency of masculinity on age: it reaches a peak for the 20–29
age bracket and then monotonously decreases; this is even true for the secretaries and

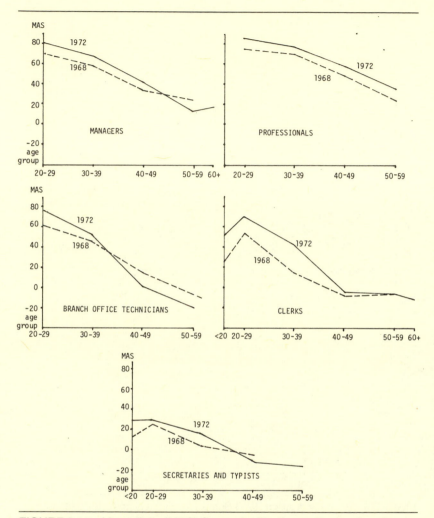

FIGURE 8.11   Masculinity (MAS) Scores for Five Large Categories of
Employees, Worldwide Data, By Age Group, at Two Points
in Time

typists (who are nearly all female). However, the *Zeitgeist* effect is much weaker than was the case for IDV, and it is negative for the older managers, technicians, and secretaries. Especially those in the 20–29 and 30–39 age brackets between 1967–1969 and 1971–1973 have become more masculine. Those over 40 were less masculine in 1967–1969, and they remained so or became even less masculine in 1971–1973.

Gradually, from age 25 to age 50, men and women at work reorient themselves with respect to the values which I associated with the Masculinity-

Femininity continuum. Self-assertion (advancement, earnings, challenging work) becomes less important; security, environment (desirable area), and social relationships (manager, cooperation) become more important. Moreover, differences in these values between men and women disappear. Let us compare from Figure 8.11 two employee categories with roughly equal educational levels: branch office technicians (all male) and secretaries and typists (all female). Comparing their 1971–1973 MAS scores for the 20–29 and the 50–59 age brackets, we find:

technicians, 20–29: MAS =   76,
secretaries, 20–29: MAS =   29,
technicians, 50–59: MAS = −19,
secretaries, 50–59: MAS = −17.

The gap of almost 50 points on the MAS scale between the male technicians and the female secretaries in the 20–29 age bracket has completely disappeared for the 50–59-year-olds. Lannon (1977: 11) remarks that sex role behaviors become blurred as men and women reach middle age. This can be felt as a liberation, especially for those who may have always wanted to engage in non-sex-typical behavior, but felt constrained by society to the traditional role: women who suppressed their professional talents in an ill-fitting housewife role, or men who like to care for others, cook, or knit.

Speculations on Longer-Term Trends

This chapter has so far shown that the indices PDI, UAI, IDV, and MAS which were designed to compare the societal norms of countries at one point in time are not necessarily the best indices for measuring trends over time, because the questions used to compose each index are about issues that do not necessarily shift together. In the case of PDI and UAI, I have therefore focused on the one question from each index which showed the largest shift in scores between the 1967–1969 and 1971–1973 HERMES data. I found clear evidence of decreasing preferences for an autocratic or persuasive superior (which suggests lower power distances) and increasing stress at work (which suggests higher uncertainty avoidance). In the case of IDV and MAS, the questions composing the indices shifted sufficiently homogeneously to allow using the indices themselves as trend indicators; we found a sharp increase in individualism and a weaker increase in masculinity. All these shifts occur in a sufficient majority of countries to consider them as dominant worldwide trends, although a few individual countries in each case show shifts in opposite directions. The effect of these is to widen the gaps among individual country scores. The HERMES data on the four trend indicators used show only for the preferred manager (PDI) a somewhat smaller gap between extreme countries in 1971–1973 than in 1967–1969; in the three other cases, country scores showed a divergency over time rather than a convergency; the differences between extreme countries in stress (UAI), individualism, and masculinity were larger in 1971–1973 than in 1967–1969.

The time span covered by the HERMES data—from around 1968 to around 1972—is four years, obviously a very short period for concluding about longer-term trends; a period marked by specific historical events (such as the 1968 student revolt in France and the Vietnam war) which may have affected societal norms in specific ways and made extrapolations less valid.

If I have to speculate about longer-term trends than just those for 1968–1972, the easiest dimension to extrapolate is Individualism. This showed a remarkably strong shift toward larger IDV scores in 1971–1973. I referred earlier to the strong association between IDV and national wealth. We can assume that as long as the wealth of nations increases, the individualism of their citizens will increase. The consequences for individualism of a levelling off into zero growth are more difficult to forecast. Individualism may continue to increase for some time, but it is also possible that it stabilizes; I find it less likely that it will decrease, as this would mean that differentiated societies would become less differentiated. The differentiation process may well be irreversible.

If national wealth increases, the causal chain of Figure 3.8 leads to predicting a reduction in PDI, or at least in some of the components of PDI, such as the need for dependence, which expresses itself in the preference for an autocratic or persuasive boss. However, we have seen that in countries in which at present large power distances are the norm, the desire for a less dependent subordinate-superior relationship is hardly honored. Unfortunately, this cannot but lead to power strife in many of these countries. Only the growth of the middle classes, with a concomitant reduction in the general Power Distance norm, offers perspectives of a gradual reduction in violence and repression.

The lower-PDI countries are better prepared to cope with a desire for power equalization, but they may increasingly face a different dilemma. The harmony and pluralist philosophy on which their societal relationships are based works well in a period of overall economic expansion (Scott, 1974), but may no longer apply in a zero-growth world. It has still to be proved whether in such a situation structures based on low power distances can continue to be functional. One "solution," well known in many abortive attempts at democratization, is to escape into bureaucracy: to shift on the dimension of uncertainty avoidance. Everything is fixed by formal rules until no one has any power left, except those who can anonymously twist the system (Crozier, 1964a; Luhmann, 1975: 94). Another possibility is a reversal into higher power distances according to the French example. A great deal of organizational ingenuity will be needed to create or maintain low power distances if the road to expansion is blocked.

As far as long-term trends in uncertainty avoidance are concerned, the data shown by Lynn and Hampson for the 1935–1970 period (page 356) suggest that at least the anxiety (stress) component in UAI may be subject to long-term oscillations. The wave-length of such oscillations may be somewhere between 25 and 40 years. According to Lynn and Hampson, 1935 and 1950 were years of high anxiety, and it is likely that in the intermediary World War II years anxiety reached a peak. The postwar period saw a reduction in anxiety, accompanied by optimism.[12] Lynn and Hampson show that since 1965, anxiety is again on the increase. A survey of images of the future in 10 European countries (both East and West) in 1967–1968 demonstrated deep pessimism (Galtung, 1976). The 1973 oil crisis and the 1974 recession are in themselves further anxiety-reinforcing phenomena; while the accompanying pessimism by itself reinforces the recession. ISR (1979) summarized the results of a longitudinal study of mental health in the United States comparing representative samples of the population in 1957 versus 1976. They show on average no decrease in the sense of happiness and well-being but more worry, especially among the young: sleeplessness, nervousness, headaches, loss of appetite, and upset stomachs.

One illustrative trend investigation covering a more recent period (1973–1977) was published for the Federal Republic of Germany by a market research firm, the Leo Burnett Company (Burnett, 1977). It used samples of 4400 men and women in 1973 and 6200 in 1977. The surveys are part of the firm's "Life Style Research." The following are some of the shifts that occurred in Germany between 1973 and 1977, which suggest a continued increase in uncertainty avoidance (compare the description of the Uncertainty Avoidance societal norm in Figure 4.4):

—Complaints about sleep trouble: increased for women from 17 to 22 percent (but decreased for men from 16 to 14 percent).

—"I am active and dynamic": increased for women from 34 to 42 percent, for men from 46 to 52 percent.

—"Occasional spanking of children is O.K.": increased for women from 36 to 53 percent and for men from 36 to 54 percent (!)

—"Feelings should not be shown": decreased for women from 33 to 29 percent, for men from 34 to 33 perent.

—In favor of reintroducing capital punishment: increase for women from 39 to 43 percent, for men from 41 to 44 percent.

—In favor of reintroducing the national hymn *"Deutschland, Deutschland über alles"*: increase for women from 24 to 31 percent, for men from 27 to 30 percent.

—Interest in contact with children: decrease for women from 75 to 67 percent, for men from 66 to 56 percent.

—Longing for the good old days: increase for women from 18 to 23 percent, for men from 18 to 21 percent.

—Ideal of never changing one's place of employment: increase for women from 37 to 44 percent, for men from 39 to 41 percent.

—"Regrets the loss of influence of the Church": increase for women from 38 to 41 percent, decrease for men from 30 to 29 percent.

—Regularly reads horoscopes: increase for women from 24 to 29 percent, for men from 15 to 16 percent.

—"It isn't worthwhile to get involved in politics, one cannot change anything": increase for women from 33 to 36 percent, for men from 25 to 28 percent.

We find shifts toward the "high UAI side" on virtually *any single element* of the Uncertainty Avoidance societal norm!

Other questions in the Burnett survey suggest that besides uncertainty avoidance, masculinity also continued to increase in the Federal Republic of Germany in the 1973–1977 period (compare the description of the Masculinity societal norm in Figure 6.6:

—"The father should be the Master in the house": agreement increased for women from 35 to 36 percent and for men from 45 to 47 percent.

—"Men usually have an easier life than women": agreement increased for women from 46 to 49 percent, for men from 32 to 36 percent.

—In favor of equal rights for women: decrease for women from 80 to 77 percent, for men from 74 to 69 percent.

—"When she likes it, a woman should go for success in her job": agreement decreased for women from 88 to 84 percent, for men from 82 to 80 percent.

—"A university education for women is a waste of money": increase for women from 11 to 12 percent, for men from 14 to 16 percent.

—"When the job demands it, the family should be prepared to come second": agreement increased for women from 43 to 44 percent, for men from 44 to 51 percent.

—"Success in the job is more important than one's private life": agreement increased for women from 14 to 15 percent, for men from 18 to 23 percent.

—"The only important thing for a job is the level of pay": agreement increased for women from 23 to 26 percent, for men from 29 to 30 percent.

—"I am willing to pay higher taxes if this would give us better schools and hospitals": decrease for women from 39 to 33 percent, for men from 42 to 33 percent.

—"The greatest danger for our country is the increasing pollution": decrease for women from 75 to 69 percent, for men from 73 to 67 percent.

—"I mind my own business; other people don't interest me": increase for women from 17 to 21 percent, for men from 20 to 23 percent.

—"I am much more independent than most others": agreement increased for women from 37 to 43 percent, for men from 48 to 54 percent.

—"If one has been successful and makes money, one should not be bashful about showing it": increase for women from 35 to 42 percent, for men from 37 to 42 percent.

—"Actually, I can be fairly proud of myself": increase for women from 38 to 48 percent, for men from 41 to 49 percent.

These shifts show an increase of masculinity, following the description of the Masculinity societal norm in Figure 6.6 almost to the letter. It is evident that both men *and women* in the Federal Republic of Germany between 1973 and 1977 shifted toward more masculine values, while at the same time the support for a traditional type of sex role differentiation has increased: No progress for women's liberation, or for men's liberation, for that matter.

On another issue related to masculinity,—foreign development aid—and for another (Masculine) country—Great Britain—Bowles (1978) shows a decrease of public support for development aid from 1969 to 1978. In a survey in 1969, 62 percent of respondents favored Britain aiding poorer nations; in 1978 this was reduced to 46 percent. This can be ascribed to Britain's economic difficulties; but it can also reflect an increase in masculinity (compare page 293).

At the present time, I do not dispose of other recent trend data that would justify expanding the conclusions to more countries and a longer period. I have no clues as to which way country masculinity norms will move in the long run; I suppose that the wide differences which we notice at present will continue to exist.

The combination of a continued increase in anxiety, combined with an increase in masculinity—if it were to apply to most nations in our world—offers a far from attractive perspective. Neither high anxiety nor a hypertrophy of masculine assertiveness in a nation is helpful in creating the conditions under which wise political decisions are made: the decisions about disarmament, stopping nuclear proliferation, saving scarce and irreplaceable resources, and a more equal distribution of wealth over the countries of the world which are prerequisites for our common survival. The phenomenon of the anxiety fluctuations is a painful example of the "inner limits of mankind" which threaten our existence more than the limits to growth imposed from the outside (Laszlo, 1978). More than by disasters of nature, human existence is threatened by "disasters of culture."

NOTES

1. The reviews of anthropological literature by Naroll (1970) and Driver (1973) and the theory of cultural evolution by Lomax and Berkowitz (1972) indicate the common elements in the evolutionary patterns of traditional societies. See Chapter 1.

2. Hines (1973, 1974) studied the phenomenon of the socialization of immigrants on the particular issue of achievement motivation (measured by the Lynn test). The persistence of values from the country of origin seems to depend on several factors (countries of origin and of immigration; occupation); in the case of Greeks having immigrated to the United States and New Zealand, Greek values persisted to the second generation.

3. As we saw in Chapter 3, PDI has not been computed from the percentage preferring manager 1 or 2 but from the percentage preferring manager 3 in the 1967–1969 formulation, reversing the sign. As this measure was only available for one survey round, it could not be used to show a trend over time. The description of manager 1 and 2 did not change from 1967–1969 to 1971–1973.

4. In France in the period 1954–1972, income inequalities increased (CERC, 1976).

5. These data do not confirm Mead's (1978) analysis of the Generation Gap as a one-time, worldwide shift for all those born after 1945. An example of a study that equally used longitudinal plus age cohort data and found a generation and *not* a maturation effect is Abramson (1971). The variable he analyzed was a different one, however: class-based voting in four large European countries.

6. Due to World War II, data for 1940 and 1945 were not available for several countries in their sample.

7. The year of highest anxiety per country was as follows: 1935: FIN, SWI, USA; 1950: AUT, DEN, FRA, GER, ITA, JAP, NET, NOR; 1955: BEL, SWE; 1960: none; 1965: none; 1970; AUL, CAN, GBR, IRE, NZL.

8. According to the sign test, this is a significant overall shift at the .95 level of probability.

9. Figure 4.10 shows that HERMES stress scores and Lynn's anxiety scores are rank correlated with .72***.

10. The increase in educational level is not shown in the survey data because of an incompatibility in the educational level scales used in the 1967–1969 and the 1971–1973 questionnaires. It is shown by unpublished company data.

11. For the method of calculation of these scores see Chapter 6.

12. Sauvy (1966: 137) attributes the increase of the birth rates in most developed countries after World War II (well beyond a short-term "baby boom") to a general spirit of optimism.

Chapter 9

CONSEQUENCES FOR POLICY AND RESEARCH

SUMMARY OF THIS CHAPTER

On behalf of policy makers in organizations, this chapter resumes the practical conclusions that can be drawn from the findings in this book. The main finding is that organizations are culture-bound. This applies not only to the behavior of people within organizations and to the functioning of organizations as a whole; even the theories developed to explain behavior in organizations reflect the national culture of their author, and so do the methods and techniques that are suggested for the management of organizations. The consequences of this cultural relativity are described for a number of areas: motivation, leadership, and decision-making, Management By Objectives, planning and control, organization design, Management Development and Organization Development, humanization of work, industrial democracy, company ownership and control, and, finally, the reaction of the local environment to organizations. The next part of the chapter is devoted to the management of multi-cultural organizations: in particular, multinational corporations and international bodies. The importance of a strong internal subculture of such organizations for their effective functioning is stressed. Possibilities of training people for productive collaboration across cultures are described. Finally, the chapter indicates areas for continued research into cultural differences among nations. It introduces a "Values Survey Module" which is an improved and shortened version of the HERMES values questions, and a questionnaire to the reader of this book.

There Are No Universal Solutions to
Organization and Management Problems

Chapters 3 through 6 have demonstrated four ways in which national cultures can be distinguished. They illustrate that different nations have different cultural heritages which are largely invisible. The invisible part consists of values, collectively held by a majority of the population (but possibly differentiated by social class), and transferred from generation to generation through education and early life experience in family and schools and through socialization in organizations and institutions. These values have thus grown into societal norms which, in their turn, determine to a large extent the political and organizational solutions which are feasible within that particular national culture. No political or organizational system can survive long without some degree of member consensus, unless it is continually supported by outside force.

I hold that the stability of national cultures over long periods of history is achieved through a system of constant reinforcement, because societal norms lead to particular political, organizational, and intellectual structures and processes, and these in turn lead to self-fulfilling prophecies in people's perceptions of reality,[1] which reinforce the societal norms. It is difficult to recognize this process in one's own culture. A deep and often painfully acquired empathy with other cultures is required before one becomes sensitive to the range of societal norms which our genus *homo sapiens* has been able to invent and to the relativity of our society's norms. We find this eloquently expressed in the quote from Pascal at the beginning of this book: "There are truths on this side of the Pyrenees which are falsehoods on the other."

Organization and management theorists have rarely taken Pascal's wisdom to heart. In the management literature there are numerous unquestioning extrapolations of organizational solutions beyond the border of the country in which they were developed. This is especially true for the exportation of management theories from the United States to the rest of the world, for which the non-U.S. importers are at least as responsible as the U.S. exporters. "Management" itself is very much an American concept, just as earlier the entire discipline of economics was very much an Anglo-Saxon discipline.[2] However, the empirical basis for American management theories is American organizations; and we should not assume without proof that they apply elsewhere. This assumption is not found only in the popular literature: In scholarly journals—even in those explicitly addressing an international readership—the silent assumption of universal validity of culturally restricted findings is frequent. Articles in such journals often do not even mention the country in which the data were collected (which usually is the United States as can be concluded from the affiliations of the author). As a matter of scientific etiquette, I suggest that any article written for an international public should mention the country—and time period—in which the data were collected.

A similiar naiveté with regard to foreign solutions is often found among journalists and political writers, whether they want to export German-type Mitbestimmung to France, Swedish job reform to Italy, Yugoslav worker self-management to Holland, or Mao communism to Angola. There exists a widespread tendency to underestimate the importance of deeply rooted societal norms for arriving at political or organizational solutions which will work and be stable. But, to rephrase a famous dictum: There is nothing as impractical as a bad theory.

This does not mean that countries cannot learn from each other: On the contrary, looking across the border is one of the most effective ways of getting new ideas in the area of management, organization, or politics. However, applying these in one's own setting calls for prudence and judgment.

In the present chapter I shall try to translate the conclusions of this book into recommendations for practical policy, on behalf of those trying to manage or control organizations in the widest sense of the word—public, voluntary, private, or informal. This means that I have to go two steps beyond the relatively safe ground of measured data. One step was made in the integrated interpretations of dispersed findings in Chapters 3 through 6. The second step has to be made now, and it implies a reinterpretation with a view toward applicability.[3]

Resistances to Cultural Relativism

Cultural relativism is not a popular subject.[4] I regularly participate in international discussion groups at scholarly meetings. After one has been sensitized to it, it is impossible not to recognize the cultural influence on the interest areas and points of view taken by Scandinavians, French, Americans, Germans, British, Italians, and Dutch participants, not to mention the cultural influence on their ways of presenting their ideas. Yet I noticed that drawing attention to the cultural component in our points of view is a risky strategy which polarizes the audience. Some think it highly enlightening; an *Aha-erlebnis*[5] which suddenly puts the entire discussion into perspective. Others, however, reject the notion of a cultural component rigorously, become upset, and feel threatened by it. "Possibly one of the many reasons why the culture concept has been resisted," Hall (1959: 50) writes, "is that it throws doubt on many established beliefs. Fundamental beliefs . . . are shown to vary widely from one culture to the next. It is easier to avoid the idea of the culture concept than to face up to it." In addition, "the concepts of culture . . . touch upon such intimate matters that they are often brushed aside at the very point where people begin to comprehend their implications" (1959: 165).

Yet I believe that the battle for the recognition of the cultural component in our ideas is worth being fought. More so now than a generation ago, most of us meet people with cultural backgrounds different from our own and are expected to work with them. If we maintain the naive assumption that because they look like us they also think like us, our joint efforts will not get very far. If we begin to realize that our own ideas are culturally limited, from that moment we need the others—we can never be self-sufficient again. Only others with different mental programs can help us find the limitations of our own. Once we have realized we are blind persons in front of the elephant we can welcome the exchange with other blind persons.

Acceptance of cultural relativism is in itself easier in some cultures than in others. On the level of intellectual discourse (not necessarily on the level of practice) the French have little difficulty. Montaigne and Pascal were French. I know of no other country where a violent criticism of national values like Alain Peyrefitte's *Le Mal Français* (1976) could, first, be written at all and, second, even by a cabinet minister of the majority party who rather than be publicly rebuked would then be admitted to the country's most illustrous intellectual club (the Academie Française). Perhaps, the French's sublime gift for separating theory and practice allows them to react this way. In Germany, by contrast, any type of relativism is digested with difficulty; the German tradition is to search for absolute truth, and in the sciences of man most of the great theorists of the western world were from the German culture area (Kant, Hegel, Marx, Freud, Weber, and Lewin). Germans can, however, accept the relativity of ideas as part of an absolute truth of a higher order, some *Unzulänglichkeit menschlichen Strebens''*.[6]

Sex was the great taboo of the Victorian age. At least in the organization literature, power was the great taboo until the 1960s. Both taboos have been more or less lifted since that time. Culture in the organization literature may be the great taboo of today. In all three cases, the taboo is on something we are all involved in but not supposed to speak about. If this book helps to break the culture taboo, it will have served its purpose.

Motivation

The founding father of motivation theory was Sigmund Freud; but he is rarely quoted in the U.S. management literature on "Motivation." Instead, the popular motivation theorists in the U.S. management literature are David McClelland, Abraham Maslow, Frederick Herzberg, and Victor Vroom.

Freud was Austrian; and there are good reasons in the culture profile of Austria in my data for explaining why his theory would be conceived in Austria rather than elsewhere. According to Freud, we are impelled to act by unconscious forces in us which he calls our "id." Our conscious self-conception, our "ego," tries to control our id; and an again unconscious inner pilot, our "superego," criticizes the thoughts and acts of our ego. Feelings of guilt and anxiety develop when the ego is felt to be giving in to the id. Freud sees the superego as the product of early socialization, mainly by our parents when we were small children. The Austrian culture is characterized by the combination of a very low power distance with a fairly high uncertainty avoidance (Figure 7.3).[7] The low power distance means that there is no powerful superior who will take away our uncertainties for us; we have to carry them ourselves. Freud's superego now comes natural by as an inner uncertainty-absorbing device, an interiorized boss. This is reinforced by the fairly low individualism score of Austria which implies an obligation to the ingroups we belong to. Finally, Austria's high masculinity score may have something to do with Freud's strong concern with sex.

The American culture profile differs from the Austrian by a much lower uncertainty avoidance score and a much higher individualism score. The high individualism implies a "calculative involvement" of the Americans in organizations (see page 218). This explains the popularity in the United States of "expectancy" theories of motivation, which see people as pulled by the expectancy of outcomes, mostly consciously (Vroom, 1964), rather than as pushed by unconscious drives. The low uncertainty avoidance, combined with fairly high masculinity, appeared earlier in this book to be associated with high scores on Need for Achievement according to McClelland (pages 171, 287, and 324). McClelland's achievement motive stands for the value pattern of the masculine risk taker, which corresponds with the U.S.

pattern; this explains the popularity in the United States of McClelland's motivation theory. The combination of high individualism, low uncertainty avoidance, and masculinity in the United States also explains the popularity of Maslow's Hierarchy of Human Needs. Maslow's supreme category, self-actualization, is a highly individualistic motive. In research done in the mid-1960s among managers from 14 countries by Haire et al., only the American managers ordered their needs almost exactly in the order of Maslow's hierarchy (security-social-esteem-autonomy-self-actualization; see page 32).

Herzberg's popular two-factor theory of motivation claims that there are "motivators" with positive but no negative motivation potential, and "hygienic factors" with negative but no positive motivation potential. The motivators are the "intrinsic" aspects of work—basically those related to Maslow's higher needs: esteem and self-actualization. The hygienic factors are the "extrinsic" aspects—basically those related to Maslow's lower needs: social and security. If Maslow's hierarchy is culturally determined, however, Herzberg's two-factor theory is to a greater degree. This has been argued before: For example, it has been shown not to apply to Dutch trainees (Hofstede, 1964) and not in a wide variety of work settings in New Zealand (Hines, 1976).

In Chapter 7 I interpreted the diagram of Figure 7.7 as follows: The vertical axis (Uncertainty Avoidance) opposes motivation by success to motivation by security; at the extremes, hope of success to fear of failure. The horizontal axis (Masculinity) opposes ego needs to affiliation needs. Combining the two axes, we get in quadrant:

(1) (U.S.A., Great Britain, and their former dominions and colonies): Motivation by personal, individual success, in the form of wealth, recognition, and "self-actualization." This is the classic McClelland-Maslow-Herzberg pattern.

(2) (Japan, German-speaking countries, some Latin countries, and Greece): Motivation by personal, individual security. This can be found in wealth and especially in hard work. Second-quadrant countries have grown fastest economically in the 1960–1970 period (contrary to McClelland's theory).

(3) (France, Spain, Portugal, Yugoslavia, Chile, and other Latin and Asian countries): Motivation by security and belonging. Individual wealth is less important than group solidarity. It is no accident that Yugoslavia, with its worker self-management system, is in this quadrant.

(4) (North European countries plus the Netherlands): Motivation by success and belonging. In this quadrant, success will be measured partly as collective success and in the quality of human relationships and the living environment.

We thus arrive at a motivational "map of the world" which is a far cry from a universal order of needs.

The implication of the different motivation patterns in different countries is that personnel policies aiming at motivating people will have different effects in different countries (they may also have different effects within the same country, for different classes of employees!). This is perhaps nowhere as clear as in the different reactions to *career opportunities*. Careers always mean trade-offs between risk and security, between success and family life, and people's career behavior is therefore very much a reflection of cultural values. In an earlier article (Hofstede, 1976c: 44) I told the story of three key executives of a large European corporation who resigned when they were in their early forties, in spite of outstanding career prospects, to accept bigger jobs in smaller local companies. What I did not mention then is that the president who ordered an investigation (because he was so shocked) was an American, and the three executives were Swedes. The Swedes complained about being frustrated by the company bureaucracy (which reflects a value position of not liking formalization and not liking bigness), but they also mentioned the importance of being able to live where their families wanted to live. Evidently, they were willing to give up prospects of increased earnings for this purpose.

Bartolomé and Evans (1979) published a study on the trade-off between professional and private life for 532 middle managers, mainly from Great Britain, France, and Scandinavia. They write about differences among countries:

> The French are slightly more sensitive to career tensions at all stages, possibly a reflection of working as middle managers in relatively structured and authoritarian organizations. Young British managers are particularly insensitive to their marriages, though this changes strongly in the mid-30's, while the Scandinavians are more preoccupied than other nationalities with their wives during their 20's and early 30's. . . . While French managers believe more in a rigid separation of professional and private life— work should not in principle be allowed to interfere with family and leisure—the British executive perceives a fluid and much less clear boundary between the two domains. . . . Their time in private life is spent differently. The British are more passive and companionable, spending time relaxing, doing chores, and simply being together. The French are more active—playing sports, spending time with children, friends, or the extended family. . . . The French feel most "tied down" in their careers, whereas the British and particularly the Scandinavians feel "free." . . . The career strategy of the Frenchman is necessarily more defensive and risk-avoidant, while that of his British counterpart is more aggressive and risk-taking [from Bartolomé and Evans, 1979].

We recognize in this quotation the difference in uncertainty avoidance (which opposes Britain and Scandinavia on the one side to France on the other) but also the differences in masculinity (which opposes Britain to Scandinavia, with France in between).

McClelland (1965) suggested that *achievement motivation training* would be an answer to the problems of underdevelopment in the Third World. He himself tried this in India. Interestingly, Figure 7.7 suggests that India (the Indian middle class) already shares American values about achievement, so McClelland could build on values already present. Pareek (1968), writing on the basis of Indian development practice, proposes, however, that next to achievement motivation his country needs "extension motivation" (concern for other people or the society as a whole) and a reduction of "dependence motivation." Extension motivation will be facilitated by low IDV and low MAS (relative to its wealth, India has a high IDV—see Figure 5.4). Dependence motivation is undoubtedly related to PDI, which is very high for India. All this suggests that "achievement motivation training" should not be seen as a psychological patent medicine against underdevelopment.[8]

Leadership

We saw in Chapter 3 that values about appropriate power distances are present among both superiors *and subordinates* in a country; therefore, trying to develop "leadership" as if it were an independent characteristic which a person could acquire is naive: Leadership is a complement to subordinateship. This is immediately clear in the political field: It is difficult to imagine that a Hitler would have been successful in Great Britain, a Churchill in France, or a de Gaulle in Germany. However, it applies equally well to other spheres of life.

In Chapter 7 we saw how HERMES technicians in France attribute the most positive characteristics to a boss seen as persuasive-paternalistic, those in Great Britain to a boss seen as either persuasive-paternalistic or consultative, and those in Germany to a boss seen as participative. Similar differences among countries have been reported elsewhere. For example, Williams et al. (1966: see page 115) showed that close supervision was associated with more positive attitudes to the boss among Peruvian workers, while the reverse was true for U.S. workers. Meade (1967) repeated in India the classic Lippitt and White (1958) U.S. experiments with school children subjected to authoritarian, democratic, and laissez-faire leadership. He found that both morale and productivity of the children in India were higher under authoritarian leadership, whereas the opposite had been found in the United States. What represents appropriate leadership in one setting does not have to be appropriate for a differently programmed group of subordinates.[9]

One of the oldest theorists of leadership in the world literature is Machiavelli (1469–1527). He described the most effective techniques for manipulation and remaining in power, including deceit, bribery, and murder, which has given him a bad reputation in the centuries afterwards. Machiavelli wrote in the Italy of his day, and what he describes is clearly a large power distance situation. We still find Italy on the larger power distance side of Figure 7.3 (with all other Latin and Mediterranean countries), and we can assume from historical evidence that power distances in Italy in the sixteenth century were still considerably larger.

American theories of leadership are written from a middle-range power distance background (the United States ranks 15 out of 40 on the Power Distance Index). Some of the most popular are McGregor's (1960) Theory Y versus Theory X, Likert's (1967) System 4, and Blake and Mouton's Managerial Grid (Blake et al., 1973). What these theories have in common is that they all advocate participation in the manager's decisions by his or her subordinates (participative management); however, the initiative toward this is supposed to be taken by the manager.

In countries with still lower Power Distance Index values—such as Sweden, Norway, Germany, and Israel—we find considerable sympathy with models of management in which even the initiatives are taken by the subordinates. I shall come back to this later in the section dealing with "Industrial Democracy." These models of management, however, meet little sympathy in the United States where maintaining certain "management prerogatives" is seen as essential. The concept of management prerogatives, again, is not popular in the low power distance countries. This is illustrated by a remark which a Scandinavian social scientist is supposed to have made to Herzberg in a seminar: "You are against participation for the very reason we are in favor of it—one doesn't know where it will stop. We think that is good" (Jenkins, 1973: 258).

If leadership is only a complement to subordinateship, a key to leadership is the type of subordinate expectations we are likely to find in a country. In Figure 9.1 I have listed these for three levels of power distance: the U.S. level is in the middle. American theories of leadership have been widely exported to all parts of the world, in a normative way, without cultural provisos. They have been taught to foreigners in business schools, they have been packaged into training kits and sold to companies and organizations abroad. However, neither McGregor nor Likert nor Blake and Mouton nor any other U.S. leadership theorist I know has taken the collective values of subordinates into account. We found evidence in the present study that agreement with McGregor's Theory X is more frequently found among subordinates in large power distance countries (page 110), that Likert's participative management is less popular in some countries than in others (Figure 7.6), and that the perceived leadership behavior between "task"- and "people"-orientation (Blake and Mouton) is a **function of the country's power distance level (page 109).** The only U.S. theory of leadership which allows for a certain amount of cultural relativity, although indirectly, is Fiedler's (1967) Contingency Theory of Leadership: Fiedler states that different leader personalities are needed for "difficult" and "easy" situations, and a

FIGURE 9.1   Subordinateship for Three Levels of Power Distance

Small Power Distance	Medium Power Distance (USA)	Large Power Distance
Subordinates have weak dependence needs.	Subordinates have medium dependence needs.	Subordiates have strong dependence needs.
Superiors have weak dependence needs toward their superiors.	Superiors have medium dependence needs toward their superiors.	Superiors have strong dependence needs toward their superiors.
Subordinates expect superiors to consult them and may rebel or strike if superiors are not seen as staying within their legitimate role.	Subordinates expect superiors to consult them but will accept autocratic behavior as well.	Subordinates expect superiors to act autocratically.
Ideal superior to most is a loyal democrat.	Ideal superior to most is a resourceful democrat.	Ideal superior to most is a benevolent autocrat or a paternalist.
Laws and rules apply to all, and privileges for superiors are not considered acceptable.	Laws and rules apply to all but a certain level of privileges for superiors is judged as normal.	Everyone expects superiors to enjoy privileges; laws and rules differ for superiors and subordinates.
Status symbols are frowned upon and will easily come under attack from subordinates.	Status symbols for superiors contribute moderately to their authority and will be accepted by subordinates.	Status symbols are very important and contribute strongly to the superior's authority with the subordinates.

cultural gap between superior and subordinates is one of the factors that makes a situation "difficult." However, his theory does not consider the *kind* of cultural gap.[10]

What happens in practice when U.S. theories are taught abroad—and this I infer from personal experience and observation—is that the theories preached are not practiced. The wise managers, however, still learn; but they perform a *cultural transposition* of the ideas to make them fit the values of their subordinates. The less wise managers who do not recognize the need for cultural transpositions may once try an unfitting approach, find out it does not work, and fall back into their old routine.

Attempts at the transfer of leadership skills which do not take the values of subordinates into account have little chance of success. This is a pity, because managers (and subordinates) all over the world need to learn, and we can learn much from other countries, including the American example. Countries at different levels of economic development, with different social structures, economic systems, institutions, *and* values try to take over the same new technologies. Technologies are not neutral with regard to values: In order to work, they assume that certain values are respected. Making these technologies work means that people in the receiving countries must learn new leadership and subordinateship skills, change old institutions, and shift their values. However, this will not be achieved by ignoring them. Cultural transposition, in the ideal case, means finding a new cultural synthesis which retains from the old local values those elements deemed essential but which allows the new technologies to function. Probably the country which has most successfully done this so far is Japan; a country where it has clearly failed is Iran.

The cultural limitations to leadership approaches have their consequence for the way company policies will work: for example, in the area of *grievance channels*, ways in which lower-level organization members can bring their complaints forward to those at the top of the organization. Grievance channels in large power distance environments will be difficult to establish: subordinates will fear retaliation (and superiors will in fact try to retaliate); there will be more unrealistic and exaggerated grievances, and the channels may be used for personal revenge against a superior who is not accessible otherwise.

What happens if within a multicultural organization managers move to other countries? The adaptation of a manager to a higher power distance environment does not seem to offer many problems. Managers in all settings probably learn to behave as autocratically as their subordinates allow them. Although this is an unpopular message and seldom professed in management development courses, managers moving to a large power distance culture soon learn that they have to behave more autocratically in order to be effective, and they do so: The colonial history of most western countries provides many examples of this. It is interesting that the western ex-colonial power which itself has the highest Power Distance norm—France— seems to be most appreciated by its former colonies and to maintain the best postcolonial relationships with most of them. This suggests that subordinates in a large power distance culture still feel more comfortable with superiors who are real autocrats than with those acting as autocrats for opportunistic reasons.

The operation of a manager in an environment with a Power Distance norm lower than his own is more problematic. It is easier to move toward more than to move toward less autocratic behavior. French and other Latin managers, unless they are exceptionally culturally sensitive, tend to have problems in Anglo or Nordic countries. American managers usually find it difficult to collaborate wholeheartedly in the "industrial democracy" process of countries like Sweden, Germany, or even the Netherlands. U.S. citizens tend to consider their country as the example of democracy and find it difficult to accept that other countries may want to develop forms of democracy for which they feel no need and which make major inroads into management prerogatives.

Leadership and decision-making styles are also affected by a country's position on the Masculinity Index. The following case is illustrative: A prestigious U.S. consulting firm was asked to analyze the decision-making processes in the large Scandinavian XYZ corporation. In their report, they criticized the corporation's decision-making style, which they characterized as, among other things, "intuitive"- and "consensus-based." They opposed "observations of traditional XYZ practices" to "selected examples of practices in other companies." These "selected examples" offered as a model evidently were taken from their U.S. clients and reflect the U.S. textbook norm: "fact-based" rather than intuitive management and "fast decisions based on clear responsibilities" rather than the use of informal, personal contacts and the concern for consensus.

Is this consulting firm doing its Scandinavian clients a service? Where the U.S. and the Scandinavian cultures most widely diverge is on the Masculinity dimension. The use of intuition and the concern for consensus in Scandinavia are "feminine" characteristics of the culture, well embedded in the total texture of these societies. Stressing "facts" and "clear responsibilities" fit the "masculine" U.S. culture. From a neutral viewpoint, there are as good reasons for criticizing the American decision-making style as the Scandinavian style. In complex decision-making situations "facts" no longer exist independently from the people who define them, so "fact-based management" becomes a misleading slogan; intuition may not be a bad method of deciding in such cases. And if, for their implementation, decisions need the commitment of many people, a consensus process, even if it takes more time, is an asset rather than a liability. However, the essential thing overlooked by the consultant is that decisions have to be made in a way that corresponds to the values of the environment in which they have to be effective. People in this consulting firm lacked insight into their own cultural biases. This does not mean that the Scandinavian corporation management need not improve its decision-making and that it could not learn from the consultant's experience. However, this can be done only through a mutual recognition of cultural differences, not by ignoring them. As one XYZ manager put it, "they looked at us through American glasses and discovered we don't operate the American way. What did they expect?"

Management By Objectives (MBO)

MBO may be the single most popular post-World War II American-born management technique. It is based on a cybernetic control-by-feedback philosophy. Probably its earliest advocate is Peter Drucker (1955: chap. 11). In the United States MBO has been a way of spreading a pragmatic results orientation throughout the organization. It has been considerably more successful where results are objectively measurable than where results are a matter of subjective interpretation (Hofstede, 1978b). It has also been criticized in the United States as industrial engineering with a new name, applied to higher management levels and with the same resistances (Levinson, 1970b). Of interest to us here is what has happened in the inevitable attempts to export MBO to other countries.

MBO reflects an American value position in that it presupposes the following:

- that the subordinate is sufficiently independent to negotiate meaningfully with his boss (not too large Power Distance);
- that both superior and subordinate are prepared to take some risks (weak Uncertainty Avoidance); and
- that performance is seen as an important criterion by both (Masculinity).

Let us now take the case of Germany. This is also a below-average power distance country, so the dialogue element in MBO should present no problem. However, Germany scores considerably higher on uncertainty avoidance; consequently, the tendency toward accepting risk and ambiguity will not be present to the same extent. The idea of replacing the arbitrary authority of the boss by the impersonal authority of mutually agreed-upon objectives, however, fits the small power distance, strong uncertainty avoidance cultural cluster very well. The objectives become the subordinates' "superego." In a book of case studies about MBO in Germany, Ferguson (1973: 15) states: "MBO has acquired a different flavour in the German-speaking area, not least because in these countries the societal and political pressure towards increasing the value of man in the organization on the right to co-determination, has become quite clear. Thence, MBO has been transposed into Management by Joint Goal Setting [*Führung durch Zielvereinbarung*]". According to Ferguson, MBO fits the ideological needs of these countries of the moment. The case studies in Ferguson's book show elaborate formal systems with extensive ideological justification; the stress on *team* objectives is quite strong, which is one way to reduce individual risk.

The other case on which specific information is available is France. In France, MBO was first introduced in the early 1960s, but it became extremely popular for a time after the 1968 students' revolt. People expected that this new technique would lead to the long-overdue democratizing of organizations. Instead of DPO (Direction Par Objectifs), the French name for MBO became DPPO (Direction *Participative* Par Objectifs). Thus, in France, too, societal developments affected the MBO system. However, in general DPPO remained as much a vain slogan as did "Liberté, Egalité, Fraternité" (Freedom, Equality, Brotherhood) after the 1789 revolt. Franck wrote in 1973: "I think that the career of DPPO is terminated, or rather that it has never started, and it won't ever start as long as we continue in France our tendency to confound ideology and reality." In a postscript to Franck's article, the editors of *Le Management* wrote: "French blue and white-collar workers, lower-level and higher-level managers, and 'Patrons' all belong to the same cultural system which maintains dependency relations from level to level. Only the deviants really dislike this system. The hierarchical structure protects against anxiety; DPO, however, generates anxiety."[11] The reason for the anxiety in the French cultural context is that MBO presupposes a depersonalized authority in the form of internalized objectives; but French people, from early childhood, are accustomed to large power distances, to an authority that is highly personalized; in spite of all attempts to introduce Anglo-Saxon management methods, French superiors do not easily decentralize and do not stop short-circuiting intermediate hierarchical levels, and French subordinates do not expect them to. The developments of the 1970s have severely discredited DPPO, which probably does injustice to the cases where, starting from less exaggerated expectations, individual organizations or units in France have benefited from it.[12]

Planning and Control

Planning represents an attempt to reduce uncertainty; control implies the exercise of power. Moreover, planning and control are complementary. It should be no surprise, then, that planning and control processes in organizations reflect the Power Distance and Uncertainty Avoidance norms of the dominant national culture. Planning and control systems are more than rational tools; they contain an element of ritual (see Chapter 4). Rituals are an indispensable but non-rational element in any human society, which helps to make uncertainty tolerable, to confirm our relationships with our fellow men, and to give meaning to our lives. However, different societies develop different rituals. Planning and control systems for management largely were made in the United States. That is, they reflect a below-average Power Distance, low Uncertainty Avoidance societal norm. In addition, they were developed in a particular socioeconomic-historical setting: competitive capitalism, political stability, unlimited resources, overall economic expansion, and nonintervention by government. Under these conditions, an entire family tree of planning and control systems has grown up from the groundworks by F.W. Taylor to the Strategic Management of the 1970s (Ansoff and Thanheiser, 1978: 8).

Even in the United States it is extremely difficult to know how effective planning and control really are. We can usually find avid defenders and violent critics for the same system. A particular example is the Planning-Programming-Budgeting System (PPBS) as tried in the 1960s in the U.S. government and elsewhere (see Hofstede, 1978b). The dean of a large U.S. business school writes "Despite all the talk about planning, it is still a primitive art. Very few organizations do as much as they claim to do, and few of those who do take planning seriously do it well" (Dill, 1979). I suggest that it is in particular the ritual element in planning and control which defies objective evaluation. Either one believes in it or one doesn't.

This means, however, that we have to be even more modest in our claims about identifying effective and ineffective planning and control systems in other cultures. I referred earlier to a study by Horovitz in France, Germany, and Great Britain (see Chapter 4). By the criteria set by the U.S. designers of modern planning and control systems, the British managers do a better job of strategic planning than their German and French counterparts; the latter focus on details and short-term feedback. Yet the average annual growth rate in GNP in the 1965–1974 period is highest for France (4.8 percent) followed by Germany (3.9 percent) and much lower for the U.S.A. (2.4 percent) and Great Britain (2.2 percent).[13] These figures do not encourage French and German top managers to plan the American way.

The art of management within a given culture is undoubtedly to strike a balance between faithfulness to the requirements of the local cultural, economic, and political environment and sensible innovation. In the latter, selective adoption of foreign management techniques can be useful, if again the need for cultural transposition is respected.

Relating planning and control systems to the national Power Distance and Uncertainty Avoidance norms leads to the following suggestions:

- A stronger Uncertainty Avoidance norm supports a need for more detail in planning and more short-term feedback.
- A stronger Uncertainty Avoidance norm makes it less likely that strategic planning activities are practiced, which may put question marks to the certainties of today.
- A stronger Uncertainty Avoidance norm supports a tendency to leave planning to specialists.
- A larger Power Distance norm supports "political" rather than "strategic" thinking (Faucheux, 1977).
- A larger Power Distance norm supports personal planning and control rather than impersonal systems. This often means no formal planning at all when power distances are large.
- A smaller power distance leads to the feasibility of control systems based on trust in subordinates; in larger power distance countries such trust is missing.[14]

Organization Design

The combination of power distance and uncertainty avoidance typical for a country's culture affects the structure of organizations that will work best in that country—next to the demands of technology and the traditions of the kind of activity that the organization exercises: whether it be a shoe factory, a municipal administration, a school, or a hospital. Several times in this book I referred to the Aston studies of organization structure (see Chapters 2, 3, 4, and 7). The Aston studies found the two main dimensions in the structure of a variety of organizations (but within one country, Great Britain) to be *concentration of authority* and *structuring of activities*. The first relates to power distance: Where subordinates are more dependent on superiors and superiors on their superiors, we get unavoidably greater centralization of authority. The second relates to uncertainty avoidance; in fact, the Aston results were one of the theoretical arguments that made me look for an Uncertainty Avoidance dimension (see page 76). Structuring of activities implies formalization (the need for written rules) and specialization (the assignment of tasks to experts). We find this translated in Figure 7.5 into different preferred organization types, and different implicit models in people's minds:

(1) For Southeast Asian countries: the "personnel bureaucracy" in which relationships among people are hierarchical, but the workflow is not codified to the same extent; with the "family" as its implicit model.
(2) For the Latin and Mediterranean countries, plus Japan: the "full bureaucracy" in which both relationships among people and work processes are rigidly prescribed; with the "pyramid" as its implicit model.
(3) For the German-speaking countries and Israel: the "workflow bureaucracy" in which work processes are rigidly prescribed but less the relationships among people; with the "well-oiled machine" as its implicit model.
(4) For the Anglo and Nordic countries plus the Netherlands: the "implicitly structured" organization in which neither work processes nor relations among people are rigidly prescribed, with the "village market" as its implicit model.

That societal norms affect organization structures even surreptitiously is shown by the following small case: An American-based multinational business corporation has a policy that salary increase proposals should be initiated by the employee's direct superior. In its French subsidiary, this policy was interpreted in such a way that the superior's superior's superior—three levels above the employee—was the one who initiated salary proposals. This way of working was seen as natural by both superiors and subordinates in France.

For the three countries France, Germany, and Great Britain, Maurice et al. (1980) show in more detail the mechanisms through which the national culture affects technologically similar organizations. Each of the three countries shows its own specific pattern on the following three blocks of variables:

(1) The configuration of the organization: The kind of categories the labor force is broken into varies from one country to the next, as well as the relative size of the categories when these are made comparable.
(2) Work structuring and coordination: the joining of individual tasks into work positions and the way in which work is coordinated.
(3) The qualification and career system: schooling, on-the-job-training, and the way individuals progress in typical careers.

The three blocks are interrelated; they form integrated systems of which the elements reinforce each other. It becomes evident that we cannot take just one element out of the whole and change it.

On the Power Distance x Uncertainty Avoidance map (Figure 7.3), the United States is fairly close to the center, which may be one reason for the success of U.S. businesses operating in very different cultures. However, the United States is still part of the "implicitly structured" quadrant: *Hierarchy is not a goal by itself* (as in France) *and rules are not a goal by themselves*; both are means toward obtaining results, to be changed if needed. Breaking with hierarchical and bureaucratic traditions is found in the development toward *matrix organizations* and similar temporary or flexible organization systems.

Laurent (page 173) showed that statements expressing tolerance for ambiguity in hierarchical structures are accepted more by managers from some countries than from others; the need for clarity in hierarchy appeared to be correlated with uncertainty avoidance. Matrix organizations implying a multiple hierarchy should thus be less acceptable in more uncertainty-avoiding cultures, even if people in these cultures feel at the same time that their present structures are ineffective. However, we can expect different types of problems for matrix organizations in high uncertainty avoidance, *high power distance* cultures and in high uncertainty avoidance, *low power distance* cultures. In the former, matrix organization violates the principle of unity of command, which is holy. We find this clearly expressed in Fayol's negative comments on Taylor's propositions of eight functionally specialized superiors for one person—a kind of supermatrix organization (see page 323). In high uncertainty avoidance, low power distance countries a matrix organization will be acceptable as long as roles in it can be defined without ambiguity (compare Preiss' data on Germany on page 202). As avoiding ambiguity is not always possible, this will detract from the popularity of the matrix system.

Laurent has suggested that to make matrix organization work in a high uncertainty avoidance, high power distance country like France it is desirable to translate it in hierarchical terms: that is, to leave the formal hierarchy intact and define the additional linkages in the system as nonhierarchical communication. This is, again, a way of "cultural transposition."

Another objection to matrix organization—or rather, to temporary organization systems—was mentioned in Chapter 5, where I quoted Hjelholt's plea for the importance of group identities, which points to differences with the United States on the dimension of Individualism. In less individualistic countries, the feasibility of temporary systems will depend to a large extent on whether organization members possess a sufficient basis for identity—for example, it will be likely to work well for groups of professionals, who, regardless of the organization structure they are in, identify with their professional reference group; less effective for nonprofessionals.

Management Development and Organization Development

It will be evident from all that is written in this book and, in particular, in this chapter that there is no single formula for management development to be used in different cultures. A meeting of International Labour Office Experts concluded in 1965 that

> one of the most important areas for research is the determination of exactly what is meant by managerial success and the identification of successful managers in different cultural settings. This would provide all those concerned with developing managers with clearer ideas of the sort of results they should aim at in attempting to provide knowledge and modify managerial attitudes and behaviour [ILO, 1966: 185].

Not only is success differently defined in different cultures, but systems of initial education in schools and training on the job are also very different.

Management development across cultural barriers could thus be seen as an impossible task, but fortunately it should not be judged exclusively from its cognitive content. It has other important functions which probably outweigh its cognitive role. It brings people from different cultures and subcultures together and by this fact only broadens their outlook. In many organizations it has become an essential *rite de passage* which indicates to the manager-participant as well as to his or her environment that from now on he or she belongs to the manager caste. It provides a socialization in the managerial subculture, either company-specific or in general. It also provides a break with the job routine which stimulates reflection and reorientation.

What applies to MD applies even more to OD. American-style organization development meets, for example, with formidable obstacles in Latin European countries.[15] It is felt that, to begin with, a Latin language like French is an ill-suited vehicle for discussing OD processes in which action is more important than the abstract definition of problems. Latin countries lack the equality ethos which is an important motor behind OD. Latins believe less in the possibility of self-development of people. OD processes create insecurity which in a high uncertainty avoidance culture is often intolerable. In fact, OD represents a counterculture in a

Latin environment. Whereas to some extent it may also represent a counterculture in the United States (it can be seen as introducing a feminine approach—group dynamics and caring for others—in an otherwise masculine organization culture), it has more elements in common with the dominant culture there; in the Latin world it will either be tolerated as a curiosity or rejected as subversive. Latin organizations are not changed that way—they are usually only changed by crisis and revolution.

To the extent that OD uses techniques of stimulating interpersonal openness and feedback, it meets with other problems. Cox and Cooper (1977) reported on the use of direct personal feedback in OD processes with managers in Great Britain and Japan. In Great Britain, the feedback, although not corresponding to daily British behavior, was accepted and appreciated. In Japan, the giving and receiving of personal feedback appeared virtually impossible, and, when tried, resulted in what the authors perceived as ritualized behavior: The receiver of feedback felt that he must have insulted the sender in some way. Japanese participants therefore tended to concentrate on task rather than interpersonal issues. My personal impression of OD activities with Germans is that talking about interpersonal issues tends to be seen as a wasteful deviation from task issues. French participants are more divided in this respect, but they will easily interpret interpersonal feedback competitively, unless it comes from a person seen as superior.

Humanization of Work

Since the late 1950s, a reaction has set in in many countries against what was seen as the continuing degradation of human work under the influence of extended Taylorism: simplification, specialization, and the separation of planning and execution. This reaction has been given many names: work (re-)structuring, job enlargement, job enrichment, quality of working life, sociotechnical job design. (semi-) autonomous groups. It has become evident that different approaches to humanization of work are popular in different countries. The main distinction is between individual job restructuring and group job restructuring; the first is more popular in, for example, the United States (job enrichment), the latter in Sweden (semiautonomous groups).

In Chapter 6 I related the preferred type of "humanization of work" to the Masculinity norm. We can say that what is seen as a "human" job depends on a society's prevailing model of man; as this model is more "masculine" in some societies and more "feminine" in some others, this leads to different forms of humanization. The United States can be said to practice more a "masculinization of work" and Sweden a "femininization of work." The latter, which we find in other low MAS countries as well, represents a stress on group rather than individual work and a deemphasis on competition.

Elsewhere (Hofstede, 1979a) I have referred to the dilemma with regard to humanization of work which arises out of the difference in values between those who take the initiative to humanization—usually college-trained managers and professionals—and the workers involved in simple unskilled and clerical work whose jobs are to be humanized. Jobs are "humanized" according to the models of man adopted by the "humanizers," not by the workers. I have argued that the humanizers should make an effort to understand the workers' value system which may differ considerably from their own—for example, as to the relative importance of earnings versus the intrinsic interest in the job. This caution applies to both more masculine and more feminine countries.

A special form of humanization is the introduction of *flexible working hours*—workers determining their own starting and finishing hours within certain constraints. These were invented in Germany and have their greatest success in Germany and Switzerland, but the idea has never become as popular in France, Britain, or the United States. In high uncertainty avoidance, low power distance countries like Germany and Switzerland, time rules are a source of considerable subjective stress, as they are difficult to *always* live up to: Therefore, a system which allows people relief from strict time rules is very attractive. Also, people have the "superego" that enables them to make the flextime system a success. In large power distance countries, flextime implies a loss of hierarchical control which will be resisted. In low uncertainty avoidance countries, the resistance is mainly directed against the reintroduction of time registration (clocking in and out) which the flextime system usually demands; also, the relief value of a less restrictive time rule system will be less, as the rules are probably already interpreted less strictly.[17] A manager from Hong Kong reported to me that the system is popular in Japan but not in Hong Kong; this would confirm its attractiveness being related to uncertainty avoidance.

Industrial Democracy

The term "industrial democracy" in this section should be seen as a collective heading for various types of efforts to make lower-level participants in organizations adopt a more active role in making certain decisions. It includes concepts like participative management, joint consultation, *Mitbestimmung*, worker directors, worker self-management, shop floor consultation, co-determination: in short, both formal and informal means of redistributing decision-making power and influence.

The feasibility of various forms of industrial democracy relates to the value system of the organization members—not only the leaders but, again, at least as much the subordinates. The first cultural dimension involved is obviously Power Distance. All forms of industrial democracy are in themselves ways of reducing power distance. They come more naturally to smaller power distance cultures than larger power distance cultures. On the other hand, we have seen in Chapter 3 that the ideological statement that "Employees in industry should participate more in the decisions taken by management" meets with stronger endorsement in *larger* power distance cultures; it seems that the ideological statement acts to some extent as a compensation for what happens on the pragmatic level. The consequence of this, as I suggested in Chapter 3, is that in higher power distance countries there will be a stronger ideological push toward models of formal participation (for example, through workers' council or boardroom representation), but also more de facto resistance against them because they are more at conflict with the present situation.

In addition, the chances and opportunities for more informal or more formal solutions to industrial democracy are affected by the country's level of uncertainty avoidance. We should thus take into account both power distance and uncertainty avoidance, and we can associate different preferred forms of industrial democracy with the four quadrants of the Power Distance x Uncertainty Avoidance matrix (Figures 7.3 and 7.5). In quadrant 4 of Figure 7.5 (Anglo countries, Scandinavia, Netherlands: small power distance and low uncertainty avoidance) we should find the greatest stress on informal and spontaneous forms of participation, such as shop-floor participation. In quadrant 3 (German-speaking countries: small power distance and high uncertainty avoidance) we should find more stress on formal, legally determined participation (*Mitbestimmung*). In Sweden we find, in fact, both the informal *and* the formal approach; but, unlike in Germany, the informal approach in the form of spontaneous experiments has preceded the legal arrangements (SAF, 1975).

In quadrants 2 and 1 of Figure 7.5 (large power distance), industrial democracy is basically a contradiction; it will meet with strong resistance from elites and some-times even from underdogs, or their representatives, such as labor unions. Where it is tried, it has to be pushed by a powerful leader; by a "father type" such as an enlightened entrepreneur in the large power distance, low uncertainty avoidance countries (quadrant 1), or by political leadership using legislative tools in the large power distance, high uncertainty avoidance countries (quadrant 2). Both mean "im-posed participation," which is, of course, a paradox. One way of making it function is to limit participation to certain spheres of life and to maintain tight control in others; this is the Chinese solution, in which participative structures in work organi-zations are combined with a strictly controlled hierarchy in ideological issues (Laaksonen, 1977). If total participation is to be created by imposition from above, it runs the risk of becoming self-destructive, because if it succeeds in reducing power distances, continued imposition is no longer possible. The supreme paradox is that in large power distance cultures unusually strong and enlightened leadership—that is, an unusually large power distance—is necessary to arrive at even a mild degree of power distance reduction, which is essential for self-management. Only exceptional leaders with long lives in power succeed in this—and by their very success they may breed new dependence in their subordinates, which means that they failed after all. This helps to explain why societal norms like power distance levels are so persistent over the centuries.

Company Ownership and Control

There is a close historical link between capitalism and individualism. The modern capitalist system, based on self-interest and the market mechanism, was "invented" in Great Britain and most successfully transferred to the United States. On the individualism scale of Chapter 5, Figure 5.1, the United States, Australia, and Great Britain are still the most individualistic countries among all 40. In the individualist value pattern, the relationship between the individual and the organization is *calcu-lative*; it is based on enlightened self-interest. In more collectivist societies, the link between individuals and their work organizations is *moral* by tradition (Chapter 5). It presupposes individuals' loyalty toward their ingroups in exchange for protection. In such societies, free-market capitalism with the supremacy of the profit motive and which considers the labor contract between employer and employee as a calculative bargain is an alien element. It can be imposed through the large power distances present in most such societies, but it is likely to have strongly disruptive effects on society. Various forms of state socialism or state capitalism are more likely to appeal to the collectivistic values of people in this case, regardless of whether these alternative economic orders actually protect their people effectively.

Capitalist organizations from individualistic countries (like the United States, Great Britain, and the Netherlands) that operate in more collectivistic environments (like Asian countries) are well advised to adapt their personnel policies to the local norm of mutual moral loyalty between organization and employee. A "hire and fire" approach, which is the usual image abroad of U.S. business corporations, is ill-perceived in less individualistic societies. Often, firing an employee is even prohibited by law. If it is not, the costs in terms of public image and goodwill with the authorities of firing redundant employees may exceed the benefits.

In whatever culture, the majority of small businesses are family businesses, and most capitalist business corporations have started as family-owned corporations. There has been a tendency in the western countries for family management and ownership to be gradually replaced by professional management and joint stock ownership, and in some cases by government ownership. Those companies continuing to be family-managed are often considered old-fashioned and less dynamic and effective. However, there is an influence of culture in this case as well. In cultures with large power distances (such as France and Belgium) the personalized power of the family members continues to fit the national value pattern very well. Family-controlled businesses remain numerous in these countries, and there is no reason why they should be less effective or dynamic than joint stock or government-owned businesses.[19]

Reactions of the Local Environment:
Public Opinion, Unions,
Authorities and Action Groups

Organizations moving to unfamiliar cultural environments are often badly surprised by unexpected reactions of the public or the authorities to what they do or want to do. Perhaps the effect of the collective values of a society is nowhere as clear as in this case. These values have been institutionalized partly in the form of legislation—and the way in which legislation is applied which may differ considerably from what is actually written in the law—in labor union structures, programs and power positions, and in the existence of organizations of stakeholders like consumers or environmentalists. The values are partly invisible to the newcomer, but they become all too visible in press reactions, government decisions, or organized actions by uninvited interest groups.

Being surprised by unfamiliar values in the environment may even occur to local organizations whose management has not followed the value shifts in their society due to the *Zeitgeist*. An extensive example is found in Hofstede (1980): the case of a large Dutch coffee roasting firm struck in 1972 by a consumer boycott because it refused to stop its coffee imports from Angola—then still a Portuguese colony. This firm had always proclaimed that "the consumer is the king"—but it never expected that consumers could have other preferences than for the taste of coffee. In the Netherlands, sympathy for the underdog has always been strong; this is one element of the feminine values pattern (Chapter 6). Improved communication media have brought international news into every household and created a possibility of collective feeling and action which the coffee firm's management had underestimated.

A few inferences from the value differences exposed in Chapters 3 through 6 with regard to the reactions of the local environment are listed below.

- Civic action groups are more likely to be formed in weak uncertainty avoidance, small power distance cultures than elsewhere (page 178).
- There will be more public sympathy and more effective legislation on behalf of the economically and socially weak members of society in the more feminine than in the more masculine countries (page 286).
- There will be more public sympathy and more public funding for aid to economically weak Third World countries, and in the case of disasters elsewhere in the world, in the affluent feminine than in the affluent masculine countries (page 293).
- There will be more public sympathy and more effective legislation on behalf of environmental conservation and maintaining the quality of life in affluent feminine than in affluent masculine countries (page 297).
- Business corporations will have to be more concerned with informing the public in weak uncertainty avoidance, small power distance cultures than elsewhere.[20]
- Conflicts between racial and/or linguistic groups are more a function of the relative size and social class composition of the groups than of any particular dimension of national culture. That is, they can occur in any culture.[21]

Multicultural Organizations:
The Importance of a Dominant National Culture

The twentieth century has seen a tremendous increase in the number and size of organizations that span national boundaries. These organizations pose their own type of management problems. An important distinction is between multinational or international organizations.

By *multinational* organizations I mean organizations active in several countries but in which there is one dominant "home" national culture to which most key decision makers of the organization belong. Examples are multinational business corporations like IBM (American), Volvo (Swedish), or Mitsubishi (Japanese), but also religious organizations like the Mormon Church (American) and, at least until recently, the Roman Catholic Church (Italian). A special category are those organizations in which there are *two* home national cultures; we find these in some large business corporations (for example, Unilever: British-Dutch) and in joint ventures between a local and a foreign company. I call these corporations *transnational*.

By *international* organizations I mean organizations without a home national culture, in which the key decision makers may come from any member country. Examples are the United Nations with its subsidiaries like UNESCO or UNIDO, the European Common Market, the International Labour Office, or the World Council of Churches.

Throughout this book we have seen evidence of the importance of shared value patterns for the functioning of organizations. It is primarily that which need not be said, that which all take for granted, which keeps an organization together. This is why multinational organizations which have a dominant home culture are much easier to run than international organizations which lack such a common frame of reference. In the multinational organizations, the values and beliefs of the home culture are taken for granted and serve as a frame of reference even for persons from other cultures who make a career in that organization. I have heard a French executive on the international staff of a U.S. multinational firm say, "in order to succeed in this job, I have to be bicultural."[22] It is my impression that the failure rate of non-home-culture executives in multinational business organizations is much higher than of home-culture executives, precisely because the non-home-culture executives frequently do not succeed in becoming sufficiently bicultural. Obviously, a prolonged period of working in the home culture environment is an asset in this respect.

The need for biculturality exists only for those non-home-culture members of multinational organizations who interact with the home office decision makers or their representatives abroad. National subsidiaries of multinational organizations function internally much more according to the value systems and beliefs of the host culture, even if they formally adopt many home culture ideas and policies; we see examples of this in the first part of this chapter, and the entire HERMES research project on which this book is based was possible only due to this phenomenon. Ordinary members of such national subsidiaries need not be bicultural; only those in "linking pin" roles between the national subsidiaries and the international superstructure need biculturality. This is necessary because these linking agents need a double confidence: from their home culture superiors and colleagues and from their host culture subordinates.

Biculturality obviously implies bilingualism. There is a difference in coordination strategy between most U.S. and most non-U.S. multinational organizations. Most American multinationals put the burden of biculturality on the foreign nationals. It is the latter who are bi- or multilingual (most American executives in multinationals are monolingual). This goes together with a relatively short stay of American executives abroad; two to five years per foreign country is fairly typical. These executives often live in "ghettos." The main tool of coordination is unified worldwide policies which can be maintained with a regularly changing composition of the international staff because they are highly formalized. Most non-American multinationals put the burden of biculturality on their own home country nationals. They are almost always multilingual (with the possible exception of the British, although even these are usually more skilled in other languages than the Americans). The typical period of stay in another country tends to be much longer, between five and 15 years or more, so that expatriate executives of non-American multinationals more often "go native" in the host country; they mix more with the local population, have their children in local schools, and live less frequently in ghettos. The main tool of coordination is these expatriate home country nationals, rather than many formal procedures.

Biculturality is extremely difficult to acquire after childhood, and the number of failures would even be much larger were it not that what is necessary for the proper functioning of multinational organizations is only *task-related biculturality*. Only with regard to the tasks at hand do the linking pin persons have to be bicultural. With regard to other aspects of life—their tastes, hobbies, religious feelings, and private relationships—they can afford to remain monocultural.

Perlmutter (1965) developed a typology of the multinational business corporation for which he distinguishes three conceptions:[23]

(1) Ethnocentrism
(2) Polycentrism
(3) Geocentrism

In ethnocentrism, the ways of working of the home culture are imposed abroad. In polycentrism, the maxim is "they know best," and operations abroad are left to the locals; the international links are mainly financial. Geocentrism, according to Perlmutter, is a kind of ideal end-state in which all countries within the worldwide organization are equivalent and positions in the global organization can be reached by anyone regardless of nationality, only on the basis of merit. He identified different parts of different corporations as in different stages of ethno-, poly-, or geocentrism. Perlmutter's geocentrism idea was a typical complement to the "convergency theory" of national culture of the 1950s and '60s (see page 343). As our belief in convergency has disappeared, geocentrism looks less a feasible or even desirable end-state; it would put multinational business corporations in the difficult bind that international organizations are in: that of the lack of a common cultural reference frame. In fact, the presence of a dominant national culture is an asset rather than a liability for the functioning of an organization, and it should be fostered carefully.

International organizations such as the United Nations or the European Common Market by definition can not fall back on one dominant national culture. This is less a problem for the political part of such organizations, in which people are supposed to act as representatives of their own countries and to settle their differences by negotia-tion. It is, however, a considerable problem within the administrative apparatus, in which people are *not* supposed to represent their countries but the organization as such. Organizations can function only if their members share some kind of culture—if together they can take certain things for granted. In the administrative part of international organizations the things that can be taken for granted have been reduced sometimes almost to nothing. No wonder that such organizations often function badly and wastefully.

Organizations like these are also frequently characterized by a quick turnover of members who may leave before they have learned their jobs; by selection, nomina-tion and promotion procedures in which many other arguments than suitability for the job play a role; by unclear objectives and, even where objectives are clear, unclear means-ends relationships.

The only way toward viability for such international organizations seems to be the creation of a strong organizational subculture based on professional rather than national identities; which means that considerable attention should be paid to the introduction, socialization, and follow-up of new members. I shall come back to this in the next section.

Managing Multicultural Organizations

Some common problems of the management of multicultural organizations are creating the organization's own subculture, choosing partner cultures, organizing international headquarters, forming international teams, and whether to accept or try to change local cultural habits in host countries.

Creating the organization's own subculture is a vitally important task of the management of any organization, but even more in those organizations dealing with cultural diversity among their own members. Every organization has its subculture, whether intended or not; this can also be labeled "character" (Harrison, 1972) or "style" (Hedlund, 1978). Organization subcultures, once established, are hard to change; just like national cultures, they tend to be very stable. They find their origin usually in the personalities and beliefs of the organization's founders and the history of its formation. Organizational subcultures are crystallized in the kind of phenomena that anthropologists study in primitive cultures and which acquire special meanings for the organization's members: symbols, a special language, rituals, and myths (Pettigrew, 1977). Organizational subcultures arise around task-relevant issues. A shared company subculture between people of otherwise different national cultures considerably facilitates communication and motivation. In general, we find that outstandingly successful organizations usually have strong and unique subcultures; the successes themselves contribute to the company mythology which reinforces the subculture. Unsuccessful organizations have weak, indifferent subcultures or old subcultures that became sclerosed and can actually prevent the organization's adaptation to changed circumstances. In-company management development programs have a subculture-building effect which is usually more important than the cognitive content of such programs. Employee introduction programs are a socialization to the organization's subculture, marking the boundary between those inside and those outside.

Choosing partner cultures is a problem for the organization which wants to start a foreign venture, alone or jointly, with a local partner. A key question, of course, is who controls the venture: whether control is shared or remains with one partner culture. For the case of shared control, we find examples of more and less successful partnerships in the transnational business corporations which were created by a merger of two partners of roughly equal strength but with different home cultures. The oldest and most successful date from long before World War II: Unilever and Shell (both British-Dutch). Post-World War II examples are Agfa-Gevaert (Belgian-German) and Estel Steel (Dutch-German). On the basis of the dimensions of national culture demonstrated in this book it is likely that some cultures can be combined more easily than others. The two British-Dutch mergers seem to function very well. The two cultures hardly differ on power distance and individualism, somewhat on uncertainty avoidance (Netherlands higher), but strongly on masculinity. Britain scores quite masculine and Netherlands quite feminine. The British-Dutch mergers thus represent true marriages. The Belgian-German merger of Agfa-Gevaert has not led to an integration of the two companies in the way this has happened in Unilever or Shell. In fact, the two companies have divided the product range between themselves and continue to function as independent entities; not even their management training is combined. In this case, the two countries show large differences on several dimensions—in particular, power distance—which means that they are likely to view the role of management completely differently. An integration must be difficult. The number of cases of transnational mergers discussed here is obviously small (three), but suggests that some combinations of countries work better than others.

For the case of unilateral control, an interesting study was published by McKinsey (1978) at the request of the Dutch Ministry of Economic Affairs. It deals with the attractiveness of the Netherlands for foreign investors, and used an informal polling of businessmen in various countries. The image of the Netherlands as an investment country appeared negative among American businessmen but positive among Norwegian and Swedish businessmen. In the family tree of cultures (Figure 7.11) Norway, Sweden, and the Netherlands belong to the same cluster, which explains why, as the report states, the management style developed in the Nordic countries works well in the Netherlands. The United States and the Netherlands differ sharply on the Masculinity dimension, and the societal consequences of this (less interest in performance, more in welfare) seem to discourage U.S. investors.

The country clusters on the basis of values in Figures 7.11 and 7.12 can be used as guidelines for the size of cultural conflicts to be expected. They can also help to define culturally homogeneous operating regions for multinational organizations already operating in many countries. Americans sometimes treat "Europe" or "Asia" as countries. In fact, these continents contain wide cultural divergencies and the differences within them are larger than between some of their countries and, for example, the United States. If cultural proximity (rather than geographic, economic, or political criteria) is a relevant criterion, the country clusters found suggest how to divide the world.

Organizing, staffing, and rewarding international headquarters operations for dealing optimally with cultural diversity: Earlier (Hofstede, 1976c) I used survey data from a multinational business corporation to show that personnel of the international headquarters felt considerable doubt about the usefulness of their contributions to the corporation's success; I identified these H.Q. people—managers, professionals, and clerical personnel—as relatively alienated compared with their counterparts in the country subsidiaries. The key to a reduction of alienation appeared to be in the ability to give effective support to the subsidiaries. As possible measures for a reduction of alienation, I suggested four Rs: Reflecting, Recruiting, Rewarding, and Restructuring. Reflecting means the creation of feedback channels by which the H.Q. departments can learn about the subsidiaries' point of view on the support they receive from headquarters. Recruiting means the establishment of such criteria as the ability to effectively support the subsidiaries and cross-cultural sensitivity as conditions for an H.Q. job. Rewarding of H.Q. staff is extremely crucial:

> The formal reward structure of headquarters operations often prevents the building up of a support relationship. Headquarters people typically face upward—they are magnetically drawn toward the power center of the organization, which is physically close to them and from which they expect their rewards in the form of decisions on their careers. It is important to be visible to one's headquarters boss and to the higher bosses, up to the president.

> A support relationship with the subsidiaries, however, means a facing outward and mostly downward in the hierarchy. Many headquarters people believe—with ample justification—they are not rewarded for that. They are not against support but, because their rewards lie elsewhere, they accord it low priority. Top management in headquarters communicates through its reward policy the kind of behaviour it considers desirable. If the way to be promoted is to serve your boss ("He needs this report before Monday") rather than serve your clients in the subsidiaries, this will be the headquarters' priority; but the price to be paid is alienation [Hofstede, 1976c: 58].

Restructuring, finally, means an elimination of H.Q. roles that appear to be alienating.

Forming international teams: When we compose task forces of people from different national cultures, or when we fill international H.Q. jobs, the question presents itself which nationals are likely to work well together and which are likely to be good at what tasks. Data about national cultures should be used with utmost modesty in predicting the behavior of individuals, because values vary widely within cultures, and even different national cultures overlap in many respects (see Figure 1.5). Given this caution, a few propositions can still be made:

- If people are to work together in hierarchical structures, differences in power distance are the most likely source of trouble (more so than on the other dimensions).
- For ambiguous tasks (like strategic planning), people from low uncertainty avoidance cultures perform better than from high uncertainty avoidance cultures. If an ambiguous task is given to a group, the chairman preferably should be chosen from a low uncertainty avoidance culture. At the INSEAD International Business School, discussion groups with British chairmen do better on average than with chairmen of other nationalities.
- For clearly defined and urgent tasks, people from high uncertainty avoidance cultures are likely to perform better.
- Other factors being equal, people from low uncertainty avoidance cultures can more easily acquire cross-cultural sensitivity than those from high uncertainty avoidance countries (see Edwards, 1978: 36). However, personal factors play an important role. In general, persons who have lived abroad, have parents from different nationalities, married a foreign wife or husband, or studied foreign languages are more likely to be culturally sensitive.
  Latin Europeans ("dependent individuals"—see page 221) are usually less productive in nonhierarchical monocultural peer groups: Such groups usually engage in a fight for leadership or the avoidance of such a fight; both go at the expense of task performance. However, Latin Europeans can be just as productive as anyone else in multicultural groups in which their initial reactions are not reinforced.

Accept or change local cultural habits? This is a major dilemma for the organization operating in a foreign culture. There are examples of successful changes. Laurent (1978; see Chapter 4) found that the mental maps of French managers make the introduction of matrix organization difficult in France. However, in one U.S.-based corporation with a long experience in matrix organization, their French managers had changed their mental maps; and in this organization's French subsidiary, matrix organization functioned quite well. Many Third World countries want to transfer new technologies from more economically advanced countries. In order to work at all, these technologies presuppose values that may be counter to local traditions, such as a certain discretion of subordinates versus superiors (lower power distance) or of individuals versus ingroups (more individualism). In this case the local culture has to be changed; but this is a difficult task which should not be taken lightly and which calls for a conscious strategy based on insight into the local culture, in which accultured locals should be involved. Often, the original policy will have to be adapted to fit the local culture in order to lead to the desired effect; we saw earlier in this chapter how in the case of Management By Objectives this has succeeded in Germany but mostly failed in France.

Training for Productive Collaboration
Across Cultures

Forced exposure to an alien cultural environment can put people under heavy stress. The phenomenon of "acculturative stress" is known from anthropology (Berry and Annis, 1974): Members of traditional cultures subject to sudden modernization and migrant workers and their families are likely to show an increase in mental disturbances. In the case of people working and living temporarily abroad we speak rather of "culture shock." An American book on the subject states:

> The symptoms of culture shock include excessive preoccupation with the cleanliness of one's drinking water, food and surroundings; great concern over minor pains; excessive anger over delays and other minor frustrations; a fixed idea that people are taking advantage of or cheating one; reluctance to learn the language of the host country; a feeling of hopelessness; and a strong desire to associate with persons of one's own nationality . . . . Victims of culture shock also experience a decline in inventiveness, spontaneity, and flexibility to the extent that it interferes with their normal behavior [Brislin and Pedersen, 1976: 13].[24]

Apart from its effect on the individuals, lack of adaptation when operating in alien cultural environments leads obviously to communication breakdowns and loss of effectiveness. Hall (1960) describes some of the cultural pitfalls for Americans trying to do business overseas; Smith and Jessee (1970), the dilemmas of UNESCO experts in Thailand, as seen by their Thai counterparts.

In the United States especially, since the early 1960s, considerable efforts have been spent to develop cross-cultural orientation and training programs. One driving force toward such training is the high rate of failure of assignments of American personnel overseas (Edwards, 1978). Often it is not so much the assignee as his wife and children who are unable to support the new environment (female assignees are rarely mentioned in the literature). Another driving force, especially in the case of U.S. military personnel abroad, is fighting the image of the "ugly American" in the host country. The Americans, however, are not necessarily the "ugliest" foreigners; Russians and Japanese seem to have even greater trouble adapting abroad (I proposed earlier that sensitivity abroad is negatively correlated with UAI). A review of cross-cultural orientation programs to date was presented by Brislin and Pedersen (1976), and a classification of approaches is found in Gudykunst et al. (1977).

The main distinction among cross-cultural training programs is between culture-general and culture-specific approaches. One of the oldest and best-tested culture-specific training approaches is the Culture Assimilator (Fiedler et al., 1970; O'Brien, 1978). Each Culture Assimilator is specific to *both* the sending and the receiving culture; so we cannot use it without adaptation to any other pair of countries. It consists of a programmed instruction using 75 to 100 critical incidents to which the trainees must respond with forced-choice answers. Developing one Culture Assimilator takes about 800 manhours. Other cross-cultural training programs are of widely varying content and quality. Kraemer (1978) warns against the hidden ethnocentrism of such programs: "Ethnocentrism is usually more difficult to recognize when it comes wrapped up in good intentions" (1978: 3). Amir (1978) draws attention to the selection and motivation of the trainees; frequently, these are self-selected, and "if motivation is really strong, even a placebo will do the trick" (Amir, 1978: 6).

There is no doubt that culture-specific training is to be preferred over culture-general training in those cases where it can be used—that is, when persons from one culture have to interact with one specific other culture. Culture shock phenomena are also culture-specific: Someone acculturated to one foreign culture may still experience culture shock in another. Culture-specific training should, where possible, be given with regard to the culture of the foreign country where a person will live, and it should include the members of that person's family as much as possible.

There is, however, a need for culture-general training for those persons who in their work interact with a multitude of foreign cultures: members of the international staffs of the multinational and international organizations referred to earlier. In this case, the very number of different contact cultures makes culture-specific training impossible. What can be attempted in these cases is the development of a number of general cross-cultural communication skills. Ruben (1977) suggests that these include:

(1) the capacity to communicate respect,
(2) the capacity to be nonjudgmental,
(3) the capacity to accept the relativity of one's own knowledge and perceptions,[25]
(4) the capacity to display empathy,
(5) the capacity to be flexible,
(6) the capacity for turn-taking (letting everyone take turns in discussions), and
(7) tolerance for ambiguity.

In fact, the reader will recognize that at least numbers 3, 5, and 7 are conceptually related to the UAI syndrome (Figure 4.4), suggesting, again, that people from lower UAI cultures will tend to do better in cross-cultural contacts.

Together with André Laurent, I have developed an experimental three-day course module on "Managing in the multi-cultural organization." Our main objective in this case is to increase cross-cultural communication skills by increasing awareness of the extent to which people are "programmed" by their own cultures. The latter may be a rather painful process which is likely to raise some defenses (Kraemer, 1978: 7). This course is intended for international staff members from multicultural organizations; participant groups are themselves a mixture of many nationalities. We try to make maximal use of this cultural variety in the groups, using cognitive inputs based on the research of others and ourselves, group discussions around culturally sensitive issues, case studies generated by the participants from their own experiences, and techniques derived from sensitivity training in which the question "How do I come through to you?" is replaced by "How would a person from my country behaving like me be perceived by most people in your country?"[26]

Six Areas for Continued Research

This book is, to a large extent, an exploration into new territory; specifically, the territory that lies between the various rather neatly defined disciplines of the sciences of man: anthropology, sociology, psychology, economics, political science, law, and medicine. I personally consider as the book's primary asset the development of a broad conceptual framework related to fundamental problems of human society, which allows qualitative analysis and quantitative measurement; in this way it is able to tie together a large number of studies by others, in the vast majority of cases hitherto unrelated (see page 332). Thus, it offers a beginning of synergy in a field where such synergy has been rare, in which individual studies are often like the proverbial needles in a haystack.

Most respectable research reports end with a call for more research, and in my case such a call is absolutely essential. This book has produced unfinished business, wrapped up because it should urgently be exposed to a wider readership. Below are listed the steps I feel must be taken next:

(1) The concept of dimensions of national culture in general and the particular four dimensions, Power Distance, Uncertainty Avoidance, Individualism, and Masculinity, should be further underpinned, criticized, and complemented by reference to additional literature—in particular to literature of non-Anglo-Saxon origins—and by exposure to the comments of scholars and practitioners from a variety of national backgrounds.

(2) The set of countries covered should be expanded from the present 40 to include others as well—the Socialist world, the smaller Third World countries. Eventually it should include all except the very small countries (the 1976 World Bank Atlas counts 125 countries with a population over one million).

(3) The time dimension should be expanded; both by historical analysis of meaningful indicators (such as those by Lynn and Hampson, see Chapter 8) and by repeat surveys. It is to be hoped that the HERMES corporation will repeat its surveys in the future, including the questions which this book revealed to be most relevant for cross-cultural comparison. However, other international organizations—public, private, and voluntary—can provide longitudinal attitude survey data about values.

(4) The analysis of differences in *national* cultures should be complemented with a further differentiation of regional, ethnic, occupational, and organizational subcultures. One aspect on which the present study provides no clues at all—which I know surprises many people—is the subculture of the HERMES corporation: for the simple reason that I have nothing to compare it against. I have only been able to compare HERMES employees in one country with those in another country. Surveys of other international organizations as suggested under point 3 above could contribute to the development of a typology of organizational subcultures—assuming, of course, that questions about values are included *and that a minimum set of identical questions* is used from one organization to another.

(5) Most important, the *consequences for organizational, national, and international policy* of a better insight into dimensions of national culture should be elaborated. My theory of cultural differentiation is like a product of the research laboratory, which awaits the efforts of the development technicians to elaborate it into something of practical use. The present chapter is clearly incomplete. I count on the critical support of enlightened and creative practitioners to, for example, learn about how the new insights can contribute to turning cultural conflict in multicultural organizations into cultural synergy.

(6) Beyond the consequences for policy—that is, for practice—the cultural relativism which my findings support calls for an effort at theory-building, especially in those countries in which theories of modern man, management, organization, and society must be imported wholesale from abroad. In the past 30 years there has been altogether too much reliance on American-made management and theories for countries in which neither the societal conditions nor the mental programming of the population were similar to those in the United States. There is a great lack of locally valid theories of management and organization in which the universally human, the globally imposed, and the culturally specific elements will be wisely recognized.

Two Questionnaires

My present modest contribution to continued research consists of two question-naires. One is a Values Survey Module, and I recommend it for cross-cultural survey studies. It is reproduced in Appendix 4. It contains the questions from the HERMES survey which proved most meaningful for cross-cultural differentiation, sometimes slightly reformulated. It is complemented with questions, either taken from other studies or newly developed, which cover issues which the HERMES questionnaire obviously missed. Items 3 and 18 are taken from Preiss (1971: see Chapter 4); item 23 was inspired by the different "Faith in People" scales (Robinson and Shaver, 1973: 612–618; see Chapter 3). Items 9, 12, 15, and 17 are "new" items (but about issues whose importance to some people, of course, was recognized before). I hope the new Values Survey Module is less ethnocentric than was the old HERMES questionnaire.

The use of the Values Survey Module is encouraged for studies which cover individuals in more or less equivalent situations but with different nationalities. Examples are employees of international organizations, members of international associations, and participants in international courses or conferences. *The results are meant to be analyzed ecologically, not individually* (see Chapter 1); the Values Survey Module is not, as, for example, the classical F-scale, an instrument for comparing the values of individuals within one country. Other language versions than the English are available through the author. The demographic questions about occupation (item 31) can, for most populations, be considerably simplified into a distinction between the relevant occupations occurring within that population. The nationality questions (items 32 and 33) are superfluous when respondents within a country are known to be all or almost all nationals; the questionnaires in this case can be preprinted with a nationality code.

The second questionnaire, reader, addresses itself to you personally.[27] You will find it in Appendix 6 and are welcome to copy it for your own use. These questions ask for your personal experience with differences in mental programming of other-wise comparable people from different nationalities, and about relevant research and theory of which the author so far has been unaware. You are kindly requested to do this if you feel you could contribute any experience or in any other way you want to give feedback to the author, in which case the questions may serve as guidelines. This book is about issues which no doubt many people have experienced but for which the systematic collection of this experience is difficult. Establishing a two-way com-munication between the author and the readers of the different language versions of the book will, I hope, be an additional way of collecting data from an interested population. It may lead to a new edition of the book which reflects your views next to mine. I know of no better way to transcend the limits imposed by our different mental programming.

NOTES

1. My colleague André Laurent uses the term "mental maps."
2. I owe this observation to Claude Faucheux.

3. Putting their findings in applicable form is not the strongest point of many social scientists. See Argyris (1972) for a criticism of U. S. sociologists in this respect.

4. Hall (1965: 31): "Even more unfortunate is the slowness with which the concept of culture has percolated through the public conscience. Compared to such notions as the unconscious or repression, to use two examples from psychology, the idea of culture is a strange one even to the informed citizen."

5. German: a revealing experience.

6. "Insufficiency of Human Endeavour"—the title of a song in Bertolt Brecht's *Beggars' Opera*.

7. It is likely that power distances all over Europe were higher in the days Freud grew up (second half of the nineteenth century). However, even then Austrian power distances must have been *relatively* low, as culture patterns shift only slowly.

8. Varga (1977) evaluated UNIDO-sponsored achievement motivation training projects in Indonesia, Iran, Pakistan, and Poland, but his results do not allow us to conclude whether the projects led to changes that would not have occurred without them.

9. Kakar (1971) found that Indian assistant foremen showed higher satisfaction and performance when working under "fraternal" foremen than under "assertive" or "nurturant" foremen. It is interesting that he uses a term based on a family relationship: compare page 320.

10. Triandis (1973: 165) argues that the Greek leadership style is dysfunctional in the United States and that the American leadership style is dysfunctional in Greece; he uses Fiedler's Contingency Theory to explain why this is so.

11. This paragraph and the previous quote from Franck represent my translation from the French original text.

12. For more information on MBO in France see Froissart (1971: "The Day Our President and MBO Collided") and Trépo (1973a, 1973b, 1975).

13. Data from *World Bank Atlas, 1976*.

14. I owe this observation to a remark by Claude Faucheux in a comparison between France and the Anglo-Saxon world.

15. This paragraph is inspired by unpublished documents by Anne-Marie Bouvy (Belgium) and Giorgio Inzerilli (Italy).

16. For a review of the development in Europe see Elbing et al. (1974); some reports from specific countries are for, respectively, Switzerland, Great Britain, France, and the United States: Willatt (1973), Evans and Partridge (1973), Le Berre (1976), Owen (1977).

17. This paragraph reflects ideas contributed by Torbjörn Stjernberg.

18. For an illustrative case from France (the Communauté de Travail "Boimondau") see de Bettignies and Hofstede (1977), or, seen through the eyes of the leader himself, Mermoz (1978).

19. Inspired by a study of the 200 largest corporations in France by Jacquemin and de Ghellinck (1977). Half of these are family-controlled.

20. This is partly inspired by a comparative study of corporate social reporting in France, Germany, and the Netherlands by Schreuder (1978).

21. I have added this proposition because it is obvious to look for a relationship between such conflicts and, for example, power distance and uncertainty avoidance; however, I have not been able to find any. Domestic political violence in general (not necessarily related to race or language) is correlated with PDI—see Figure 3.19.

22. J. Maisonrouge, IBM.

23. See Note 40 in Chapter 1.

24. Reddin and Rowell (1970) have developed a "Culture Shock Test" for North Americans which is supposed to measure something like culture shock-proneness. they are not very clear about the meaning of the test scores, however; the questions look rather superficial, and validation data are missing.

25. This is my reformulation of Ruben's "to personalize one's knowledge and perception."

26. For this element in our training, I acknowledge inspiration by Howard V. Perlmutter's "Personal and Managerial Feedback."

27. The idea of a questionnaire to the reader in this case came from Claude Faucheux.

APPENDIX 1

QUESTIONS FROM THE
"HERMES" ATTITUDE SURVEY QUESTIONNAIRE
REFERRED TO IN THIS BOOK

For the full questionnaire as standardized in 1971, see Hofstede et al. (1976).

A QUESTIONS (USED IN ALL SURVEYS,
1967–1973 OR 1968–1973):

A1 Are you:
  1. Male (married)
  2. Male (unmarried)
  3. Female (married)
  4. Female (unmarried)

A2 How long have you been employed by this company?
  1. Less than one year
  2. One year or longer, but less than three years
  3. Three years or longer, but less than seven years
  4. Seven years or longer, but less than fifteen years
  5. Fifteen years or longer.

A5–A18. About your goals:

   People differ in what is important to them in a job. In this section, we have listed a number of factors which people might want in their work. We are asking you to indicate how important each of these is to *you*.

   In completing the following section, try to think of those factors which would be important to you in an ideal job; disregard the extent to which they are contained in your present job.

   PLEASE NOTE: Although you may consider many of the factors listed as important, you should use the rating "of utmost importance" only for those items which are of the *most* importance to you.

With regard to each item, you will be answering the general question:

"HOW IMPORTANT IS IT TO YOU TO . . ."

(Choose one answer for each line across)

How important is it to you to:	of utmost importance to me	very important	of moderate importance	of little importance	of very little or no importance
A5 Have challenging work to do—work from which you can get a personal sense of accomplishment?	1	2	3	4	5

A6	Live in an area desirable to you and your family?	1	2	3	4	5
A7	Have an opportunity for high earnings?	1	2	3	4	5
A8	Work with people who cooperate well with one another?	1	2	3	4	5
A9	Have training opportunities (to improve your skills or to learn new skills)?	1	2	3	4	5
A10	Have good fringe benefits?	1	2	3	4	5
A11	Get the recognition you deserve when you do a good job?	1	2	3	4	5
A12	Have good physical working conditions (good ventilation and lighting, adequate work space, etc.)?	1	2	3	4	5
A13	Have considerable freedom to adopt your own approach to the job?	1	2	3	4	5
A14	Have the security that you will be able to work for your company as long as you want to?	1	2	3	4	5
A15	Have an opportunity for advancement to higher level jobs?	1	2	3	4	5
A16	Have a good working relationship with your manager?	1	2	3	4	5
A17	Fully use your skills and abilities on the job?	1	2	3	4	5
A18	Have a job which leaves you sufficient time for your personal or family life?	1	2	3	4	5

A19–A32. About the satisfaction of your goals:

In the preceding questions, we asked you what you want in a job. *Now, as compared to what you want, how satisfied are you at present with:*

		very satisfied	satisfied	neither satisfied nor dissatisfied	dissatisfied	very dissatisfied
A19	The challenge of the work you do—the extent to which you can get a personal sense of accomplishment from it?	1	2	3	4	5
A20	The extent to which you live in an area desirable to you and your family?	1	2	3	4	5
A21	Your opportunity for high earnings in this company?	1	2	3	4	5
A22	The extent to which people you work with cooperate with one another?	1	2	3	4	5

A23	Your training opportunities (to improve your skills or learn new skills)?	1	2	3	4	5
A24	Your fringe benefits?	1	2	3	4	5
A25	The recognition you get when you do a good job?	1	2	3	4	5
A26	Your physical working conditions (ventilation, lighting, work space, etc.)?	1	2	3	4	5
A27	The freedom you have to adopt your own approach to the job?	1	2	3	4	5
A28	Your security that you will be able to work for this company as long as you want to?	1	2	3	4	5
A29	Your opportunity for advancement to higher level jobs?	1	2	3	4	5
A30	Your working relationship with your immediate manager?	1	2	3	4	5
A31	The extent to which you use your skills and abilities on your job?	1	2	3	4	5
A32	The extent to which your job leaves you sufficient time for your personal or family life?	1	2	3	4	5

A37 How often do you feel nervous or tense at work?
1. I always feel this way
2. Usually
3. Sometimes
4. Seldom
5. I never feel this way.

A43 How long do you think you will continue working for this company?
1. Two years at the most
2. From two to five years
3. More than five years (but I probably will leave before I retire)
4. Until I retire

A48 If an employee did take a complaint to higher management, do you think he would suffer later on for doing this (such as getting a smaller salary increase, or getting the less desirable jobs in the department, etc.)?
1. Yes, the employee would definitely suffer later on for taking a complaint to higher management
2. Yes, probably
3. No, probably not
4. No, the employee would definitely not suffer later on for taking a complaint to higher management.

A52 How often would you say your immediate manager is concerned about helping you get ahead?
1. Always
2. Usually

3. Sometimes
4. Seldom
5. Never

The descriptions below apply to four different types of managers. First, please read through these descriptions:

Manager 1   Usually makes his/her decisions promptly and communicates them to his/her subordinates clearly and firmly. Expects them to carry out the decisions loyally and without raising difficulties.

Manager 2   Usually makes his/her decisions promptly, but, before going ahead, tries to explain them fully to his/her subordinates. Gives them the reasons for the decisions and answers whatever questions they may have.

Manager 3   Usually consults with his/her subordinates before he/she reaches his/her decisions. Listens to their advice, considers it, and then announces his/her decision. He/she then expects all to work loyally to implement it whether or not it is in accordance with the advice they gave.

Manager 4   Usually calls a meeting of his/her subordinates when there is an impor-
(version   tant decision to be made. Puts the problem before the group and invites
1967–   discussion. Accepts the majority viewpoint as the decision.
1969)

             Usually calls a meeting of his/her subordinates when there is an impor-
(version   tant decision to be made. Puts the problem before the group and tries to
1970–   obtain consensus. If he/she obtains consensus, he/she accepts this as the
1973)   decision. If consensus is impossible, he/she usually makes the decision him/
             herself.

A54   Now for the above types of manager, please mark the *one* which you would prefer to work under.
      1. Manager 1
      2. Manager 2
      3. Manager 3
      4. Manager 4

A55   And, to which *one* of the above four types of managers would you say your own manager *most closely corresponds?*
      1. Manager 1
      2. Manager 2
      3. Manager 3
      4. Manager 4
      5. He does not correspond closely to any of them.

A56   How many years of formal school education did you complete?
      1. 10 years or less   6. 15 years
      2. 11 years   7. 16 years
      3. 12 years   8. 17 years
      4. 13 years   9. More than 17 years
      5. 14 years

A57 How old are you?
    1. Under 20   5. 35–39
    2. 20–24   6. 40–49
    3. 25–29   7. 50–59
    4. 30–34   8. 60 or over

A58 Considering everything, how would you rate your overall satisfaction in this company at the present time:
    1. I am completely satisfied
    2. Very satisfied
    3. Satisfied
    4. Neither satisfied nor dissatisfied
    5. Dissatisfied
    6. Very dissatisfied
    7. I am completely dissatisfied

B QUESTIONS (USED IN ALL SURVEYS, 1967–1969 OR 1968–1969, BUT OPTIONAL AFTERWARD)

B9   If you had a choice of promotion to either a managerial or a specialist position and these jobs were at the same salary level, which would appeal to you most? (You may already have been promoted in either direction, but just assume you could start again).
    1. I would have a strong preference for being a specialist
    2. I would have some preference for being a specialist
    3. It does not make any difference
    4. I would have some preference for being a manager
    5. I would have a strong preference for being a manager.

B24 All in all, what is your personal feeling about working for a company which is primarily foreign-owned?
    1. All in all, I prefer it this way
    2. It makes no difference to me one way or the other
    3. I would prefer that it was not this way

B25 Suppose you quit this company. Do you think you would be able to get another job in your line of work at about the same income?
    1. Yes, definitely
    2. Yes, probably
    3. No, probably not
    4. No, definitely not

B39 How often would you say your immediate manager insists that rules and procedures are followed?
    1. Always
    2. Usually
    3. Sometimes
    4. Seldom
    5. Never

B44 How do you feel or think you would feel about working for a manager who is from a country other than your own?
1. In general, I would prefer to work for a manager of my own nationality
2. Nationality would make no difference to me
3. In general, I would prefer to work for a manager of a different nationality.

How frequently, in your experience, do the following problems occur?

	very frequently	frequently	sometimes	seldom	very seldom
B46 Employees being afraid to express disagreement with their managers	1	2	3	4	5
B47 Being unclear on what your duties and responsibilities are	1	2	3	4	5
B49 People above you getting involved in details of your job which should be left to you	1	2	3	4	5
B51 Some groups of employees looking down upon other groups of employees	1	2	3	4	5

B52–B61 about general beliefs:
Our company has employees in many countries and we are interested whether the personal opinions of employees differ from country to country. Listed below are a number of statements. These statements are *not* about the company as such, but rather about general issues in industry. Please indicate the extent to which you personally agree or disagree with each of these statements (mark one for each line across).

Remember: we want *your own opinion* (even though it may be different from that of others in your country).

	strongly agree	agree	undecided	disagree	strongly disagree
B52 A corporation should have a major responsibility for the health and welfare of its employees and their immediate families.	1	2	3	4	5
B53 Having interesting work to do is just as important to most people as having high earnings.	1	2	3	4	5
B54 Competition among employees usually does more harm than good.	1	2	3	4	5
B55 Employees lose respect for a manager who asks them for their advice before he makes a final decision.	1	2	3	4	5
B56 Employees in industry should participate more in the decisions made by management.	1	2	3	4	5

B57	Decisions made by individuals are usually of higher quality than decisions made by groups.	1	2	3	4	5
B58	A corporation should do as much as it can to help solve society's problems (poverty, discrimination, pollution, etc.).	1	2	3	4	5
B59	Staying with one company for a long time is usually the best way to get ahead in business.	1	2	3	4	5
B60	Company rules should not be broken— even when the employee thinks it is in the company's best interests.	1	2	3	4	5
B61	Most employees in industry prefer to avoid responsibility, have little ambition, and want security above all.	1	2	3	4	5

C QUESTIONS (DISCONTINUED IN 1971 OR BEFORE)
(C1–C8 WERE USED THROUGH 1971; C9 THROUGH 1970; C10–C14 THROUGH 1969; C15–C19 THROUGH 1968)

C1–C8 About your goals:
How important is it to you to:
(Mark one for each line across)

		of utmost importance to me	very important	of moderate importance	of little importance	of very little or no importance
C1	Have the security that you will not be transferred to a less desirable job?	1	2	3	4	5
C2	Work in a department which is run efficiently?	1	2	3	4	5
C3	Have a job which allows you to make a real contribution to the success of your company?	1	2	3	4	5
C4	Work in a company which is regarded in your country as successful?	1	2	3	4	5
C5	Work in a company which stands in the forefront of modern technology?	1	2	3	4	5
C6	Work in a congenial and friendly atmosphere?	1	2	3	4	5
C7	Keep up to date with the technical developments relating to your work?	1	2	3	4	5
C8	Have a job on which there is a great deal of day-to-day learning?	1	2	3	4	5

C9–C19 About general beliefs:
(Mark one for each line across)

	strongly agree	agree	undecided	disagree	strongly disagree
C9 A good manager gives his employees detailed and complete instructions as to the way they should do their jobs: he does *not* give them merely general directions and depends on them to work out the details.	1	2	3	4	5
C10 Most companies have a genuine interest in the welfare of their employees.	1	2	3	4	5
C11 In general, the better managers in a company are those who have been with the company the longest time.	1	2	3	4	5
C12 There are few qualities in a man more admirable than dedication and loyalty to his company.	1	2	3	4	5
C13 Most employees have an inherent dislike of work and will avoid it if they can.	1	2	3	4	5
C14 Most employees want to make a real contribution to the success of their company.	1	2	3	4	5
C15 For getting ahead in industry, knowing influential people is usually more important than ability.	1	2	3	4	5
C16 By and large, companies change their policies and practices much too often.	1	2	3	4	5
C17 A large corporation is generally a more desirable place to work than a small company.	1	2	3	4	5
C18 Even if an employee may feel he deserves a salary increase, he should *not* ask his manager for it.	1	2	3	4	5
C19 The private life of an employee is properly a matter of direct concern to his company.	1	2	3	4	5

APPENDIX 2
COUNTRY SCORES ON A, B, AND C QUESTIONS (EXCEPT A5-A32 AND C1-C8)

	NR OF RESP					A43			A54				A55			
CTR	67-69	71-73	A1	A2	A37	12	4	A52	12	3A	3B	4B	1-2	A56	A57	A58
ARG	543	602	53	355	275	17	53	253	27	59	49	25	440	493	429	296
AUL	805	1114	67	321	331	23	48	255	26	64	57	20	470	376	405	310
AUT	586	661	63	296	322	17	58	205	13	67	57	30	335	437	374	294
BEL	1057	1328	72	363	274	8	74	236	25	56	57	19	520	422	433	254
BRA	690	1884	57	329	309	16	59	258	22	46	39	43	475	556	399	308
CAN	715	2861	79	330	321	23	52	227	26	62	51	23	470	493	373	298
CHL	164		70	396	284	19	61	269	38	37			425	572	451	270
COL	175	252	46	346	285	25	44	250	34	54	40	28	515	565	403	312
DEN	567	737	98	296	368	23	45	212	15	67	55	35	355	357	368	282
FIN	377	425	162	333	322	26	41	270	17	58	33	50	360	392	409	316
FRA	4691	6646	69	350	302	12	66	248	29	52	46	26	525	503	432	259
GBR	3236	3731	77	281	333	33	32	249	29	61	60	15	445	465	370	318
GER	3477	7907	52	344	314	19	53	225	15	61	49	40	445	398	427	302
GRE	111	127	133	336	263	11	57	231	14	60	70	18	485	614	434	296
HOK		88	88	240	334	38	22	272	34		46	22	615	628	301	300
IND	231		45	297	353	26	46	250	30	53			595	656	371	328
IRA	115	116	108	290	361	13	65	272	22		50	31	485	495	394	312
IRE	119	132	95	251	332	32	32	260	22	65	59	23	420	466	340	322
ISR	142	215	54	298	313	20	26	202	27	68	59	16	370	529	416	276
ITA	1797		82	324	299	20	39	263	23	57			445	646	443	323
JAP	2345	4103	47	306	255	15	39	273	38	46	30	38	440	586	335	342
MEX	498	518	58	309	295	24	49	230	38	40	37	31	580	663	382	290
NET	593	1204		346	323	16	55	235	18	59	49	34	405	518	417	300
NOR	360	459	81	340	348	31	43	245	15	62	60	31	370	437	427	285
NZL	173	240	66	295	334	26	37	231	24	69	61	18	450	461	361	311
PAK	37	70	40	287	380	6	67	275	30	59	49	21	555	544	359	298
PER	138	152	42	346	282	18	57	245	34	46	47	22	460	582	383	290
PHI	158	161	55	317	326	28	39	248	41	40	49	14	655	616	392	313
POR		243	79	285	288	10	68	269	19		41	43	475	306	399	311
SAF	349	518	65	271	317	25	41	237	33	53	46	23	475	458	357	297
SIN		58	88	284	363	42	28	311	43		32	27		455	327	354
SPA	600	1202	50	291	300	14	65	250	25	57	51	23	530	542	384	303
SWE	1128	1304	79	342	350	37	25	266	19	58	46	37	360	366	410	255
SWI	951	1160	64	285	308	31	36	209	20	61	55	29	430	573	382	264
TAI		71	50	248	296	20	31	237	42		38	23	535	648	383	293
THA		80	114	282	322	21	33	207	27		46	30	525	648	367	267
TUR	106	62	105	351	309	9	78	289	22	52	52	25	555	330	463	269
USA	3967				331	15	60		29	65			495		423	290
VEN	217	318	65	338	296	22	53	244	33	49	39	30	610	467	389	309
YUG		248	150	269	292				38	37			530	515	426	
TOT	31218	40997														
MEA			75	312	315	21	48	248	27	56	49	28	480	507	393	298
PDI			-05	08	-29	-13	24	42	63	-84	-49	-08	85	44	01	14
UAI			-07	36	-80	-81	65	-10	03	-41	-05	05	11	21	48	-24
IDV			07	10	23	11	-07	-28	-51	66	50	-03	-50	-41	16	-11
MAS			-43	-18	-29	-04	-06	-08	25	01	-05	-30	27	30	-31	40

zero-order product-moment correlation × 100 with: (PDI, UAI, IDV, MAS)

Country scores are, where possible, the means of two survey rounds (1967–1969 and 1971–1973) and, for each survey round, of seven occupations. See Chapter 2. A1, A55 in ‰; A43, A54 in %; other questions in mean scores × 100. For country abbreviations see Figure 2.2. Significance levels for the product moment correlation coefficient for 40 cases: .05 level = .27; .01 level = .37; .001 level = .41.

TABLE A2.1 Country Scores on A Questions

CTR	B9	B24	B25	B44	B46	B52	B53	B54	B55	B56	B57	B58	B59	B60	B61
ARG	368	178	192	154	285	143	182	288	409	258	374	176	319	289	360
AUL	332	204	189	175	329	183	175	312	397		337	196	330	311	335
AUT	307	197	193	170	364	219	192	274	417	280	345	196	328	281	317
BEL	306	200	207	173	265	171	196	252	401		347		294	295	311
BRA	318	186	173	176	271	181	179	283	424	246	389	193	318	282	351
CAN		203	178	176	324	193	173	322	410		352		328	336	363
CHL		171	185	161	314	158	176	320	423		389		296	272	356
COL	304	168	165	176	263	143	165	294	390	230	374	203	314	269	335
DEN	321	203	194	175	342	225	192	288	433		370		331	357	359
FIN	290	196	188	165	322	243	205	272	417	244	354	247	351	288	312
FRA	317	182	210	176	271	224	196	274	400	249	360	229	299	270	307
GBR	346	196	188	175	336	209	191	318	397	253	316	209	345	330	325
GER	324	196	193	183	333	170	201	264	425	248	367		338	302	325
GRE	323	157	171	169	249	135	159	301	415	242	336	178	255	241	323
HOK	344	167	165	182	298	146	160	322	387	253	348	233	277	330	348
IND		181	195	200	257	144	157	301	383		316		278	311	327
IRA				180	277	128	150	395	372	241	386	205	226	280	352
IRE	359	186	174	183	335	208	207	305	402		332		340	335	352
ISR	294	160	160	157	363	181	215	331	435	306	329	298	306	245	334
ITA	351	204	182	179	290	194	215	268	418		372		329	285	318
JAP	304	196	221		316	143	160	297	344	235	334	153	337	305	383
MEX	320	168	149	161	287	143	157	335	391	231	364	160	296	255	330
NET	303	199	204	177	328	171	193	287	423	228	356	188	347	339	334
NOR	321	191	203	146	317	262	228	308	421		370		336	265	308
NZL	341	195	182	170	358	211	181	341	403		324	196	334	304	351
PAK	284	172	194	196	308	122	177	303	406	232	359	200	232	239	345
PER	312	161	172	172	285	157	173	314	399	249	379	206	311	273	336
PHI	301	181	195	160	265	124	152	327	372	218	373	175	328	327	357
POR	284	163	204	176	258	222	186	231	440	203	390	181	286	235	308
SAF	334	175	194	172	321	174	173	334	395	261	329	216	306	330	336
SIN	340	176	136	200	266	174	178	310	380	226	352	215	286	350	350
SPA	296	191	203	152	296	205	203	248	423	241	393	238	328	266	333
SWE	332	203	186	176	329	277	202	298	416		375		352	314	362
SWI	312	202	161	170	333	224	192	263	423	280	342	189	327	293	345
TAI	322	205	182	148	300	143	146	296	355	225	343	202	257	308	349
THA	301	186	162	168	275	145	135	273	383	240	380	177	234	287	280
TUR		194	187	168	291	154	178	301	415	247	353	227	273	275	353
USA			174			197	192	329	415		322		314	307	380
VEN	265	152	173	178	264	153	162	299	402	251	373	195	310	280	331
YUG		131			299	160	172	313	365	241	359		306	280	326
MEA	317	185	182	172	304	179	181	297	403	245	357	203	308	294	338

zero-order product moment correlation coefficient ×100 with:

	B9	B24	B25	B44	B46	B52	B53	B54	B55	B56	B57	B58	B59	B60	B61
PDI	−23	−48	−20	15	−87	−63	−63	05	−49	−65	34	−34	−48	−18	−07
UAI	−37	−44	02	−43	−35	−22	−05	−24	11	04	29	−12	−19	−80	−31
IDV	40	68	37	−02	58	62	60	−08	35	41	−44	16	61	41	06
MAS	12	−11	−01	20	−03	−37	−24	18	−30	−27	−41	−35	03	04	19

same but controlling for acquiescence (IMP)

	B9	B24	B25	B44	B46	B52	B53	B54	B55	B56	B57	B58	B59	B60	B61
PDI	−17	−22	−05	25	−82	−48	−52	−05	−59	−63	11	−27	−39	00	−01
UAI	−34	−30	15	−42	−22	−05	13	−33	11	13	15	04	−08	−77	−38
IDV	38	44	25	−12	40	44	45	03	47	35	−19	03	55	26	18
MAS	12	−11	−01	20	−03	−42	−27	18	−30	−28	−47	−36	03	04	19

See Table A2.1 for significance levels for the product moment correlation coefficient.
Scores for B46 exclude the answers of managers (see page 136).

TABLE A2.2 Country Scored on B Questions

CTR	C9	C10	C11	C12	C13	C14	C15	C16	C17	C18	C19
ARG	334	305	298	272	384	220	319	301	256	396	355
AUL	345	297	350	321	387	228	321	340	308	379	381
AUT	363	317	372	326	398	239	288	317	248	360	269
BEL	346	311	348	251	366	225	298	308	264	349	351
BRA	290	329	356	286	385	212	345	317	263	338	358
CAN	353	272	370	325	392	218	322	348	299	392	381
CHL	336	300	290	238	395	222	369	334	247	342	364
COL	303	291	277	229	382	225	355	326	236	379	338
DEN	344	299	378	352	412	234	335	341	314	378	360
FIN	354	299	367	357	394	228	316	316	295	384	422
FRA	253	339	347	293	376	229	314	322	241	386	420
GBR	361	295	365	356	380	239	281	334	286	390	381
GER	331	315	363	318	378	236	293	326	249	372	245
GRE	264	324	345	298	362	200					
IND	282	261	349	249	367	215	287	296	283	358	319
IRE	374	301	344	321	390	230	327	343	297	403	389
ISR	312	301	347	316	397	197					
ITA	343	335	366			242					
JAP	369	257	361	286	389	224	326	294	280	377	355
MEX	313	286	287	237	380	237	375	331	238	353	347
NOR	348	274	357	327	409	226	362	340	342	349	392
NZL	366	265	346	325	402	218	334	344	294	371	388
PER	352	333	302	214	379	246	374	320	246	389	356
PHI	354	274	358	236	356	188	333	305	254	304	307
SAF	327	261	352	285	382	219	330	342	283	339	339
SPA	337	349	354	289	392	226					
SWE	339	310	374	251	418	225	325	351	314	360	390
SWI	370	293	370	332	405	228	312	341	298	371	282
TUR	296	304	372	290	378	199					
USA	392	266	362	310	405	217	320	340	316	381	370
VEN	320	296	279	236	370	221	371	330	246	340	346
YUG	336										
MEA	335	299	345	291	387	223	328	327	277	367	354

zero-order product moment correlation coefficient × 100 with:

PDI	-47	04	-50	-78	-75	-27	38	-50	-61	-51	-08
UAI	-44	45	-44	-40	-43	-11	29	-52	-72	-06	-12
IDV	41	-14	70	73	44	24	-63	42	70	38	26
MAS	14	-21	-14	-06	-45	04	-25	-32	-41	05	-48

same but controlling for acquiescence (IMP)

PDI	-45	-09	-22	-66	-75	-40	-00	-56	-41	-38	07
UAI	-23	34	-59	-45	-32	22	16	-51	-71	04	-06
IDV	14	-10	45	50	25	-07	-32	52	51	17	15
MAS	20	-26	-09	02	-46	-04	-40	-32	-43	08	-47

Country scores for C9–C14 are the means of seven occupations, for C15–C19 the means of five occupations. See Chapter 2. Significance levels for the product moment correlation coefficient for 30 cases: .05 level = .31; .01 level = .43; .001 level = .47.

TABLE A2.3 Country Scores on C Questions

STANDARDIZED COUNTRY AND OCCUPATION SCORES FOR WORK GOALS (QUESTIONS A5-A18 AND C1-C8)

CTR	IMP	SD	A5	A6	A7	A8	A9	A10	A11	A12	A13	A14	A15	A16	A17	A18	INV	SOC
ARG	170	23	586	426	559	588	626	366	499	322	552	438	529	515	567	428	-15	-32
AUL	199	23	641	502	518	482	491	304	534	344	529	469	569	535	530	553	160	-53
AUT	201	36	629	317	578	523	585	363	517	373	584	452	574	492	553	462	21	-143
BEL	219	31	608	421	591	555	484	349	513	310	549	554	521	542	542	459	101	-21
BRA	164	17	602	466	474	614	658	349	508	353	466	356	566	532	572	486	-48	3
CAN	202	29	666	516	477	526	531	329	483	314	513	403	551	562	575	555	119	-12
CHL	171	17	552	440	505	601	604	455	384	441	460	608	431	484	561	474	-110	109
COL	162	31	610	454	532	566	640	435	502	389	490	414	530	502	634	299	-150	-71
DEN	195	31	579	562	452	606	543	328	436	372	608	488	432	565	534	497	94	170
FIN	233	31	624	470	477	571	584	370	365	383	560	513	485	566	521	511	53	120
FRA	213	24	602	452	523	563	587	310	489	322	558	513	506	543	527	505	83	34
GBR	207	28	624	492	563	494	499	278	525	321	555	471	588	520	536	533	156	-82
GER	203	28	611	336	607	496	525	444	500	336	576	572	548	510	504	436	69	-82
GRE	174	23	577	442	544	525	546	478	576	389	406	468	549	551	556	393	-60	-35
HOK	191	37	548	477	567	579	596	323	487	436	512	452	640	522	555	307	-99	-33
IND	191	25	616	345	468	510	561	377	562	404	507	509	580	576	558	427	-8	-31
IRA	180	30	582	450	501	599	584	411	480	326	521	482	609	551	549	256	-26	33
IRE	205	31	622	448	555	498	514	373	513	345	529	444	595	525	549	422	81	-89
ISR	182	29	629	373	471	559	584	442	483	313	548	455	557	580	563	444	15	15
ITA	197	31	628	470	528	528	546	390	639	367	561	290	505	520	524	498	103	-101
JAP	215	38	638	382	576	462	535	365	571	461	548	338	493	485	661	487	-18	-223
MEX	157	21	634	483	550	552	637	366	463	372	513	414	583	480	602	352	-81	-97
NET	190	24	573	617	445	585	505	481	437	318	561	449	464	561	498	505	118	181
NOR	212	25	586	603	492	554	544	395	385	382	516	512	388	617	528	499	75	209
NZL	209	33	604	474	511	520	507	283	525	424	565	363	565	550	540	572	117	-41
PAK	195	30	538	342	497	523	622	414	507	459	482	522	624	561	558	330	-145	2
PER	171	30	588	494	498	592	668	400	430	409	545	431	497	532	608	307	-135	40
PHI	170	21	603	468	544	491	571	381	438	424	488	517	630	506	580	361	-73	-71
POR	169	23	597	458	458	635	646	405	440	371	501	463	546	561	560	360	-94	96
SAF	194	25	641	443	549	491	547	329	504	337	513	477	576	566	573	456	60	-67
SIN	194	33	571	362	552	624	611	439	442	432	532	437	593	551	536	318	-122	12
SPA	184	30	579	437	475	583	612	225	485	426	537	505	518	526	567	524	2	38
SWE	192	24	595	613	427	572	506	397	443	346	479	578	456	605	516	467	85	223
SWI	216	32	670	346	530	533	553	473	473	339	595	407	513	484	552	534	71	-101
TAI	190	32	548	438	440	571	657	363	487	407	480	506	630	524	577	372	-133	27
THA	187	29	596	433	547	598	577	404	299	472	496	495	530	577	590	386	-120	82
TUR	177	30	591	403	469	585	557	432	546	357	516	547	532	536	581	349	-51	24
USA	192	22	688	552	553	534	475	382	493	267	492	454	575	499	521	516	164	-61
VEN	158	19	669	418	539	484	659	509	450	450	454	423	508	489	604	344	-154	-114
YUG	194	24	449	511	500	647	567	407	506	431	562	464	463	552	572	369	-92	147
MEA	191	28	602	453	516	553	571	383	483	376	524	466	539	537	558	438	0	0
SD	–	–	43	73	45	47	54	60	61	51	42	65	59	34	33	80	–	–

Country scores are, where possible, the mean of two survey rounds and, for each round, of the standardized values for seven occupations. Total number of respondents 65,378. All scores have been multiplied by 100. IMP, SD = mean and standard deviation of raw scores across all 14 goals × 100. INV, SOC = factor scores × 100 (see page 241).

TABLE A3.1   Standardized Work Goal Importance Scores for 40 Countries and 14 Goals (A5–A18)

TABLE A3.2 Standardized Work Goal Importance Scores for 19 Countries and 22 Goals (A5–A18 and C1–C8)

CTR	MEA	SD	A5	A6	A7	A8	A9	A10	A11	A12	A13	A14	A15	A16	A17	A18	C1	C2	C3	C4	C5	C6	C7	C8	ING	EGO
AUT	205	37	634	302	589	532	598	363	512	363	589	478	597	521	577	440	529	495	538	343	404	467	586	543	42	156
BEL	222	28	602	429	586	568	518	373	537	340	563	593	540	579	567	463	487	527	493	288	397	490	550	510	2	31
DEN	203	33	571	556	474	612	575	340	449	408	620	500	490	600	553	488	564	558	434	297	354	543	552	463	105	-106
FIN	235	36	596	473	495	595	591	371	389	398	564	547	505	615	547	507	570	535	453	292	349	555	593	461	120	-88
FRA	215	24	578	416	507	595	634	323	474	353	561	568	534	567	554	484	536	522	469	292	473	521	559	479	77	13
GBR	216	35	625	491	569	543	557	337	544	386	578	497	611	549	569	536	516	546	503	323	416	458	500	347	-4	95
GER	208	34	605	299	593	527	463	463	515	368	588	596	584	521	547	437	564	409	498	323	394	483	558	535	49	127
GRE	171	21	543	475	527	494	530	479	589	364	371	451	573	651	540	388	550	492	594	415	484	488	533	467	-256	-28
IRE	207	38	633	469	562	518	576	373	535	404	545	456	619	517	572	473	478	547	578	365	413	460	527	380	-55	113
ISR	191	33	618	393	440	589	597	422	528	392	576	484	550	594	591	466	543	580	515	375	429	488	535	295	-27	17
ITA	199	34	616	462	524	546	576	398	632	392	565	322	539	551	547	483	543	509	469	351	388	515	521	552	-8	36
NET	197	28	596	585	486	622	563	519	480	395	582	469	542	582	552	528	518	455	463	284	311	479	537	455	63	-45
NOR	215	36	572	561	506	561	577	437	523	427	527	514	520	549	552	501	558	551	457	306	292	533	549	521	68	-130
SAF	204	31	629	457	566	508	583	404	491	359	531	569	587	582	573	456	478	520	559	425	394	432	536	498	-96	97
SPA	191	25	609	591	479	575	629	280	436	436	469	574	520	630	591	538	440	573	500	285	392	545	613	540	117	-52
SWE	191	35	697	336	451	589	534	387	482	333	595	428	475	515	509	429	557	505	570	397	362	565	507	556	-121	-183
SWI	213	32	591	439	494	554	596	470	573	368	508	536	564	544	576	497	532	450	516	305	377	522	577	476	81	107
TUR	181				439	579	605	428					560		598	311	420	589	564	447	380	539	507		-150	-24
YUG	195	24	462	512	505	648	566	407	514	440	568	478	467	563	576	376	439	516	527	377	380	594	578	504	-7	-136
MEA	203	31	593	460	515	566	579	399	505	384	549	503	543	571	563	463	517	520	510	342	389	509	548	472	0	0
SD	—	—	52	85	50	41	30	59	61	31	55	67	48	40	21	58	47	46	47	52	46	42	31	73	—	—

Country scores are the mean of the standardized 1967–1969 values for seven occupations. Total number of respondents 18,052. All scores have been multiplied by 100. MEA, SD = mean and standard deviation of raw scores across all 22 goals × 100. ING, EGO = factor scores × 100 (see page 241).

ID	EDU	MEA	SD	A5	A6	A7	A8	A9	A10	A11	A12	A13	A14	A15	A16	A17	A18	C1	C2	C3	C4	C5	C6	C7	C8
21	104	186	14	453	475	579	601	408	579	534	653	445	682	445	631	505	527	549	534	394	305	327	557	438	379
46	105	182	14	474	525	628	555	467	614	570	672	400	650	496	562	481	533	511	459	378	290	334	584	393	422
49	109	186	13	517	493	581	605	446	533	501	621	470	454	454	533	557	557	549	501	415	254	254	581	414	382
47	110	187	13	549	490	676	557	512	542	542	579	460	691	535	549	535	468	564	468	415	214	341	482	497	393
11	112	202	20	615	430	545	570	385	430	430	285	600	695	530	585	540	415	550	500	575	305	415	485	565	430
12	113	198	22	570	399	565	534	660	462	462	295	529	669	592	538	574	457	556	439	462	278	394	484	610	484
50	115	197	17	579	424	620	561	489	477	519	513	519	644	555	579	543	507	567	477	442	162	334	513	543	436
51	115	201	19	576	432	607	576	509	499	566	550	540	566	504	602	504	504	576	520	391	227	269	576	412	432
19	116	196	23	656	373	519	638	497	373	453	417	537	566	528	652	541	387	523	523	581	289	378	537	577	409
64	116	204	24	550	492	500	616	475	446	554	570	545	545	438	669	506	533	550	570	446	310	269	628	364	372
31	117	204	27	577	431	483	641	506	423	540	540	562	483	487	641	479	479	604	581	412	292	284	634	374	461
14	118	198	22	572	423	513	654	509	382	536	536	572	509	513	636	450	450	581	581	450	282	287	618	409	416
7	119	214	26	643	361	527	593	574	380	489	292	597	647	531	593	454	454	535	500	547	292	400	492	558	450
63	121	209	23	580	461	523	588	593	378	588	496	518	549	527	593	571	553	523	518	440	181	313	562	596	418
8	122	213	26	604	433	550	561	627	402	476	312	530	485	555	662	561	492	511	456	452	230	378	491	490	479
9	123	190	23	633	277	492	568	659	368	498	299	589	561	611	542	571	453	520	520	563	377	503	490	596	472
74	123	213	29	570	349	603	529	529	483	543	469	485	561	478	569	566	536	612	510	359	271	326	621	437	529
10	124	190	25	611	311	623	546	545	368	543	267	575	561	520	560	560	471	560	518	478	244	348	604	554	461
18	124	198	19	577	362	539	641	614	432	532	523	485	544	571	571	392	392	546	534	380	242	342	473	532	464
73	127	215	20	570	349	527	514	612	446	505	505	558	599	514	563	453	453	496	460	411	146	297	593	496	451
26	129	200	20	580	417	496	649	545	407	535	511	550	599	520	575	536	536	496	590	417	244	348	491	451	466
41	133	209	21	679	399	560	579	499	371	532	399	579	598	556	624	575	471	560	527	565	242	342	473	554	461
13	133	210	29	655	455	533	585	529	340	511	389	596	518	596	626	537	484	533	566	544	289	300	470	532	423
24	141	208	26	660	380	511	599	557	302	504	389	591	496	565	611	572	511	496	569	479	289	300	477	485	385
43	143	213	27	662	432	607	519	578	358	545	449	593	490	574	574	462	462	534	490	479	298	336	477	553	416
15	144	209	24	675	432	523	613	605	338	506	412	506	506	556	613	505	505	502	552	539	211	350	494	578	497
42	144	210	24	698	420	535	580	498	330	506	338	593	506	556	535	543	457	490	552	620	264	322	494	531	424
25	148	209	30	642	423	531	578	629	304	531	423	578	396	547	575	535	420	477	535	503	293	400	473	522	461
17	152	213	28	634	430	546	578	658	367	497	441	571	451	564	595	497	497	500	554	487	261	355	500	588	490
2	156	211	29	638	363	597	552	658	325	514	304	571	438	588	549	574	507	535	500	427	219	339	497	592	500
1	156	216	29	671	370	568	575	589	309	517	304	571	469	617	542	572	421	528	493	504	339	438	469	572	514
62	156	222	30	638	557	516	533	589	517	567	309	640	469	606	567	558	425	524	493	589	350	418	466	524	490
61	156	222	30	671	370	607	575	309	309	567	452	567	519	519	573	573	573	526	496	479	198	333	502	553	421
5	158	215	30	642	557	549	533	327	327	567	352	595	555	488	598	555	508	515	548	535	255	389	475	538	392
6	159	219	31	654	406	549	536	655	343	555	330	615	443	572	555	555	502	490	459	461	277	386	486	602	519
71	159	227	30	696	486	572	570	661	309	557	348	564	377	612	528	590	509	490	519	461	306	416	509	574	483
72	159	228	34	664	454	547	509	615	332	597	372	621	492	572	565	519	535	476	526	503	250	345	516	496	424
82	165	227	44	722	432	500	580	446	363	551	439	631	366	455	537	544	388	580	480	457	208	407	519	649	569
MEA 132	207		24	616	429	552	578	555	397	528	431	558	545	542	587	559	483	535	514	477	268	355	521	519	450
SD —	—			61	61	43	37	70	78	39	111	54	87	51	40	25	51	34	39	69	55	54	52	72	46

For identification of occupations (ID) see Figure 2.6. Occupation scores are based on unweighted total Europe or world data 1968–1971. See Chapter 5. Total number of respondents 48,895. All scores have been multiplied by 100. EDU = years of education × 10. MEA, SD = mean and standard deviation of raw scores across all 22 goals × 100.

TABLE A3.3 Standardized Work Goal Importance Scores for 38 Occupations and 22 Goals (A5–A18 and C1–C8)

APPENDIX 4

VALUES SURVEY MODULE
(RECOMMENDED FOR FUTURE
CROSS-CULTURAL SURVEY STUDIES)

Please think of an ideal job—disregarding your present job. In choosing an ideal job, how important would it be to you to (please circle one answer number in each line across):

	of utmost importance	very important	of moderate importance	of little importance	of very little or no importance
1. Have sufficient time left for your personal or family life?	1	2	3	4	5
2. Have challenging tasks to do, from which you can get a personal sense of accomplishment?	1	2	3	4	5
3. Have little tension and stress on the job?	1	2	3	4	5
4. Have good physical working conditions (good ventilation and lighting, adequate work space, etc.)?	1	2	3	4	5
5. Have a good working relationship with your direct superior?	1	2	3	4	5
6. Have security of employment?	1	2	3	4	5
7. Have considerable freedom to adopt your own approach to the job?	1	2	3	4	5
8. Work with people who cooperate well with one another?	1	2	3	4	5
9. Be consulted by your direct superior in his/her decisions?	1	2	3	4	5
10. Make a real contribution to the success of your company or organization?	1	2	3	4	5
11. Have an opportunity for high earnings?	1	2	3	4	5
12. Serve your country?	1	2	3	4	5

13. Live in an area desirable to you and your
    family?   1   2   3   4   5

14. Have an opportunity for advancement to
    higher level jobs?   1   2   3   4   5

15. Have an element of variety and
    adventure in the job?   1   2   3   4   5

16. Work in a prestigious, successful
    company or organization?   1   2   3   4   5

17. Have an opportunity for helping other
    people?   1   2   3   4   5

18. Work in a well-defined job situation
    where the requirements are clear?   1   2   3   4   5

The descriptions below apply to four different types of managers. First, please read through these descriptions:

Manager 1 Usually makes his/her decisions promptly and communicates them to his/her subordinates clearly and firmly. Expects them to carry out the decisions loyally and without raising difficulties.

Manager 2 Usually makes his/her decisions promptly, but, before going ahead, tries to explain them fully to his/her subordinates. Gives them the reasons for the decisions and answers whatever questions they may have.

Manager 3 Usually consults with his/her subordinates before he/she reaches his/her decisions. Listens to their advice, considers it, and then announces his/her decision. He/she then expects all to work loyally to implement it whether or not it is in accordance with the advice they gave.

Manager 4 Usually calls a meeting of his/her subordinates when there is an important decision to be made. Puts the problem before the group and invites discussion. Accepts the majority viewpoint as the decision.

19. Now, for the above types of manager, please mark the *one* which you would prefer to work under (circle one answer number only):
    1. Manager 1
    2. Manager 2
    3. Manager 3
    4. Manager 4

20. And, to which *one* of the above four types of managers would you say your own superior *most closely corresponds?*
    1. Manager 1
    2. Manager 2
    3. Manager 3
    4. Manager 4
    5. He/she does not correspond closely to any of them.

21. How often do you feel nervous or tense at work?
    1. I always feel this way
    2. Usually
    3. Sometimes
    4. Seldom
    5. I never feel this way.

Please indicate your degree of agreement or disagreement with the following statements:

	strongly agree	agree	undecided	disagree	strongly disagree
22. A company or organization's rules should not be broken—even when the employee thinks it is in the organization's best interests.	1	2	3	4	5
23. Most people can be trusted.	1	2	3	4	5
24. Quite a few employees have an inherent dislike of work and will avoid it if they can.	1	2	3	4	5
25. A large corporation is generally a more desirable place to work than a small company.	1	2	3	4	5

26. How frequently, in your work environment, are subordinates afraid to express disagreement with their superiors?
    1. Very frequently
    2. Frequently
    3. Sometimes
    4. Seldom
    5. Very seldom

27. How long do you think you will continue working for this company or organization?
    1. Two years at the most
    2. From two to five years
    3. More than five years (but I probably will leave before I retire)
    4. Until I retire.

28. Are you:
    1. Male
    2. Female

29. How old are you?
    1. Under 20
    2. 20–24
    3. 25–29
    4. 30–34
    5. 35–39
    6. 40–49
    7. 50–59
    8. 60 or over.

30. How many years of formal school education did you complete? (Starting with primary school; count only the number of years each course should *officially* take, even if you spent less or more years on it; if you took part-time or evening courses, count the number of years the same course would have taken you full-time).
    1. 10 years or less
    2. 11 years
    3. 12 years
    4. 13 years
    5. 14 years
    6. 15 years
    7. 16 years

    8. 17 years
    9. 18 years or more

31. What kind of work do you do?
    a. I am a manager (that is, I have at least one hierarchical subordinate)—go to f.
    b. I am not a manager and I work most of the time in an office—go to e.
    c. I am not a manager and I do not work most of the time in an office—go to d.

    d. If you are not a manager and you do *not* work most of the time in an office, what do you do:
       1. Work for which normally no vocational training, other than on-the-job training, is required (unskilled or semi-skilled work).
       2. Work for which normally up to four years of vocational training is required (skilled worker, technician, non-graduate engineer, nurse, etc.)
       3. Work for which normally a higher-level professional training is required (graduate engineer, doctor, architect, etc.).

    e. If you are not a manager and you work most of the time in an office, what do you do:
       4. Work for which normally no higher-level professional training is required (clerk, typist, secretary, non-graduate accountant)
       5. Work for which normally a higher-level professional training is required (graduate accountant, lawyer, etc.).

    f. If you are a manager, are you:
       6. A manager of people who are not managers themselves (that is, a first-line manager)
       7. A manager of other managers.

32. What is your nationality? _____
33. And what was your nationality at birth (if different from your present nationality)?
    _____

Note: For other language versions of this module please contact the author.

APPENDIX 5

THE AUTHOR'S VALUES

In Chapter 1 I stated that research into values cannot be value-free. In fact, few human activities can be value-free. This book reflects not only the values of HERMES employees and IMEDE course participants, but between the lines the values of its author. It will, I hope, be read by readers with a variety of different values. In this Appendix I try as best I can to be explicit about my own value system.

First, in terms of some of the measures used in this book, among the "work goals" (A5-A18 and C1-C8), I would choose as:

1. Of utmost importance to me: freedom (A 13), personal time (A18).
2. Very important: challenge (A5), desirable area (A6), co-operation (A8).
3. Of moderate importance: earnings (A7), recognition (A11), physical conditions (A12), employment security (A14), manager (A16), position security (C1), efficient department (C2), contribute to "company" (C3), friendly atmosphere (C6), up-to-dateness (C7), and learning (C8).
4. Of little importance: training (A9), benefits (A10), advancement (A15), use of skills (A17).
5. Of very little or no importance: successful "company" (C4) and modern "company" (C5).

My "preferred manager" (question A54) is 3, the consultative manager.

Among the "general beliefs" I *strongly agree* with B58: "A corporation should do as much as it can to help solve society's problems (poverty, discrimination, pollution, etc.)." I *agree* with B52: "A corporation should have a major responsibility for the health and welfare of its employees and their immediate families" and with B56: "Employees in industry should participate more in the decisions made by management." I *disagree* with B59 "Staying with one company for a long time is usually the best way to get ahead in business," with B61: "Most employees in industry prefer to avoid responsibility, have little ambition, and want security above all," with C9: "A good manager gives his employees detailed and complete instructions etc.," with C10: "Most companies have a genuine interest in the welfare of their employees," with C13: "There are few qualities in a man more admirable than dedication and loyalty to his company," with C18: "Even if an employee may feel he deserves a salary increase, he should not ask his manager for it," and with C19: "The private life of an employee is properly a matter of direct concern to his company." I *strongly disagree* with B55: "Employees lose respect for a manager who asks them for their advice, etc.," with B60: "Company rules should not be broken, etc.," and with C13:

"Most employees have an inherent dislike of work and will avoid it if they can." I am undecided on the other "beliefs" (B53, B57, C11, C14, C15, C16, C17).

The origins of my value system, like everyone else's, are found in my national background, social class and family roots, education, and life experience. I was born in the Netherlands in 1928 and lived there until 1971. I was the youngest of three children of a high civil servant. Our family relationships were reasonably harmonious; my father had a modest but fixed income, so that we did not suffer from the 1930s economic crisis. There was enough of everything but not luxury; money was unimportant and rarely spoken of. What was important was knowledge and intellectual exercise, at which we were all quite good. I went to regular state schools and liked them. We lived through the German occupation (1940–1945) without physical suffering but detesting the occupants. I was too young at the time to understand the full scope of the ethical issues involved in Nazism, but I had seen my Jewish schoolmates being deported never to return. Only in the years after 1945 did I fully realize that for five years we had lived under a system in which everything I held for white was called black and vice versa; which made me more conscious of what were *my* values, and that it is sometimes necessary to take explicit positions. I completed a university education in the Netherlands and after that worked for half a year incognito as an industrial worker; thus, I learned to some extent how an organization looks from below. I am a Protestant Christian but I do not claim absolute truth for my faith: I know too well how conditioned we all are by our cultural environment. I believe in the equality to God of all mankind, and my image of the ideal world is one without fear. I am married and we have four sons; as will be clear from my "work goals" scores described above, our family life is very essential to me. It contains a certain tension between respecting each others' integrity and independence (including the children's) and at the same time maintaining close emotional links and liking to do things together. I hope our children will continue to go on well together without us. The distribution of sex roles in our family is rather classical; my wife has a university education and a broad intellectual interest, but so far has never built up any continuous career of her own. She has carried the main burden of educational and household chores and followed the geographic moves dictated by my successive jobs.

APPENDIX 6

QUESTIONS FOR THE READER

You are welcome to copy this and the next page from the book.

Dear Reader,

Usually, the communication between an author and the readers of his or her work is only one-way. However, in this particular case I should like very much to know your reaction and your experiences with regard to the issues this book deals with. I have therefore composed a short open-ended questionnaire which follows below. If you feel you could contribute reactions, ideas, or information to the author, please use these questions as a guideline and mail your answer to:

Dr. Geert Hofstede   % Sage Publications, Inc.
% Sage Publications, Ltd.   or   275 S. Beverly Drive
28 Banner Street   Beverly Hills, CA 90212
London EC1Y 8QE, England   U.S.A.

1. Please tell about examples *from your own experience* of differences in behavior among people, groups, or institutions which differ in their nationalities but are otherwise comparable. Please mention the year and the place of your observations and the precise nationalities involved.

2. Please describe any incidents *from your own experience* of cultural conflict: differences in mental programming of people from different national backgrounds which were misinterpreted by at least one of the actors and led to difficulties in productive collaboration.

3. Please describe any cases *from your own experience* of cultural synergy: the successful overcoming of differences in mental programming due to different national backgrounds, or even the use of different mental programs as a source of additional strength in a multicultural team.

4. I am interested in any characteristic quantitatively measured for five or more countries which conceptually could be expected to correlate significantly with the indices of Power Distance, Uncertainty Avoidance, Individualism, and/or Masculinity, whether or not it actually *does* show significant correlations (falsification is as important as verification!) If you have collected or discovered such measurements, please send either the data themselves or the full reference on where they can be found.

5. Any other comment on the content of this book is welcome too, as well as any reference to old or new literature that may be relevant for a revised version of the book.

6. The author would appreciate having your name and address so that he may write back to you if this proves desirable.
7. Anyway, please mention your:
   a. Nationality
   b. Nationality at birth (if different from a)
   c. Occupation or profession
   d. Sex (female or male)
   e. Age bracket (below 20, 20–29, 30–39, 40–49, 50–59, 60 and over)

Thank you very much for your contribution.

Geert Hofstede

REFERENCES

Aberbach, J. D., & Putnam, R. D. "Paths to the top: The origins and careers of political and administrative elites." Prepared for conference, "Frontiers in Comparative Analysis of Bureaucratic and Political Elites," Wassenaar, Netherlands, November, 1977.

Abramson, P. R. "Social class and political change in Western Europe: A cross-national longitudinal analysis." *Comparative Political Studies,* 1971, *4,* 131–155.

Acker, J., & Van Houten, D. R. "Differential recruitment and control: The sex structuring of organizations." *Administrative Science Quarterly,* 1974, *19,* 152–163.

Ackoff, R. L., & Emery, F. E. *On purposeful systems.* London: Tavistock Publications, 1972.

Adelman, I., & Morris, C. T. *Society, politics and economic development: A quantitative approach.* Baltimore: Johns Hopkins University Press, 1967.

Adler, F. "The value concept in sociology." *American Journal of Sociology,* 1956, *62,* 272–279.

Adorno, T. W., Frenkel-Brunswik, E., Levinson, D. J., & Sanford, R. N. *The authoritarian personality.* New York: Harper & Row, 1950.

Aiken, M., & Bacharach, S. B. "Culture and organizational structure and process: A comparative study of local government administrative bureaucracies in the Walloon and Flemish regions of Belgium." In C. J. Lammers & D. J. Hickson (Eds.), *Organizations alike and unlike: International and inter-institutional studies in the sociology of organizations.* London: Routledge & Kegan Paul, 1979.

Ajiferuke, M., & Boddewyn, J. "Culture and other explanatory variables in comparative management studies." *Academy of Management Journal,* 1970, *13,* 153–163. (a)

Ajiferuke, M., & Boddewyn, J. "Socioeconomic indicators in comparative management." *Administrative Science Quarterly,* 1970, *15,* 453–458. (b)

Albert, E. M. "Value systems." In D. L. Sills (Ed.), *International encyclopedia of the social sciences, volume 16.* New York: Macmillan/Free Press, 1968.

Alexander, R. A., Barrett, G. V., Bass, B. M., & Ryterband, E. C. "Empathy, projection and negation in seven countries." In L. E. Abt & B. F. Reiss (Eds.), *Progress in clinical psychology: Industrial applications.* New York: Grune and Stratton, 1971.

Alger, N. (Ed.), *Many answers: A reader in cultural anthropology.* St. Paul, MN: West Publishing, 1974.

Allerbeck, K. R. "Analysis and inference in cross-national survey research." In A. Szalai & R. Petrella (Eds.), *Cross-national comparative survey research.* Oxford: Pergamon Press, 1977.

Almasy, E., Balandier, A., & Delatte, J. *Comparative survey analysis: An annotated bibliography 1967–1973.* Beverly Hills, CA: Sage, 1976.

Almond, G. A., & Verba, S. *The civic culture: Political attitudes and democracy in five nations.* Princeton NJ: Princeton University Press, 1963.

Amir, Y. "Intercultural learning and training: Some critical comments from a friendly neighbor." Presented at the 19th Congress of Applied Psychology, Munich, August, 1978.

Anderson, R. B. W. "On the comparability of meaningful stimuli in cross-cultural research." *Sociometry,* 1967, *30,* 124–136.

Ansoff, H. I. *Planned management of turbulent change.* Working Paper 78-3. Brussels: European Institute for Advanced Studies in Management, 1978.

Ansoff, H. I., & Thanheiser, H. T. *Corporate planning: A comparative view of the evolution and current practice in the United States and Western Europe.* Working Paper 78-10. Brussels: European Institute for Advanced Studies in Management, 1978.

A. N. W. B. *A. N. W. B. Handboek.* The Hague: Koninklijke Nederlandsche Toeristenbond A.N.W.B., 1975.

Argyris, C. *The applicability of organizational sociology.* Cambridge, MA: Cambridge University Press, 1972.

Argyris, C., & Schon, D. A. *Theory in practice: Increasing professional effectiveness.* San Francisco: Jossey-Bass, 1974.

Ari, O. "Commitment and integration of the industrial labor force in two Turkish cities." In M. R. Haug & J. Dofny (Eds.), *Work and technology.* Beverly Hills, CA: Sage, 1977.

Aron, R. *Démocratie et totalitarisme.* Paris: Gallimard, 1965.

Aron, R. "Two definitions of class." In A. Béteille (Ed.), *Social inequality.* Harmondsworth, England: Pelican, 1970.

Aron, R. *Main currents in sociological thought 2: Durkheim—Pareto—Weber.* Harmondsworth, England: Pelican, 1970.

Azumi, K. "Japanese society: A sociological view." In A. E. Tiedemann (Ed.), *An introduction to Japanese civilization.* New York: Columbia Unicersity Press, 1974.

Azumi, K., & McMillan, C. J. "Culture and organization structure: A comparison of Japanese and British organizations." *International Studies of Management and Organization,* 1975, 5, 1, 35–47.

Baker, C. R. "An investigation of differences in values: Accounting majors versus nonaccounting majors." *Accounting Review,* 1976, *51,* 886–893.

Balandier, G. *Political anthropology.* Harmondsworth, England: Pelican, 1972.

Bandyopadhyaya, J. "Climate as an obstacle to development in the tropics." *International Social Science Journal, 1978, 30,* 339–352.

Banks, A. S., & Textor, R. B. *A cross-polity survey.* Cambridge, MA: MIT Press, 1963.

Bannock, G., Baxter, R. E., & Rees, R. *A dictionary of economics.* Harmondsworth, England: Penguin, 1972.

Banton, M. "Anthropological perspectives in sociology." *British Journal of Sociology,* 1964, *15,* 95–112.

Barnouw, V. *Culture and personality.* Homewood, IL: Dorsey Press, 1973.

Barrett, G. V., & Bass, B. M. "Comparative surveys of managerial attitudes and behavior." In J. Boddewyn (Ed.), *Comparative management: Teaching, training and research.* New York: Graduate School of Business Administration, New York University, 1970.

Barrett, G. V., & Franke, R. H. " 'Psychogenic' death: A reappraisal." *Science,* 1970, *167,* 304–306.

Barrett, G. V., & Franke, R. H. *Pyschological motivation and the economic growth of nations.* Rochester, NY: Management Research Center, University of Rochester, 1971. (mimeo)

Barry, H., Bacon, M. K., & Child, I. L. "A cross-cultural survey of some sex differences in socialization." *Journal of Abnormal and Social Psychology,* 1959, *55,* 327–332.

Bartell, T. "The human relations ideology: An analysis of the social origins of a belief system." *Human Relations,* 1976, *29,* 737–749.

Bartol, K. M. "Relationship of sex and professional training area to job orientation." *Journal of Applied Psychology,* 1976, *61,* 368–370.

Bartol, K. M., & Butterfield, D. A. "Sex effects in evaluating leaders." *Journal of Applied Psychology,* 1976, *61,* 446–454.

Bartolomé, F. "Executives as human beings." *Harvard Business Review,* 1972, *50,* 62–69.

Bartolomé, F., & Evans, P. A. L. "Professional lives versus private lives: Shifting patterns in managerial commitment." *Organizational Dynamics,* 1979, *7,*4, 2-29.

Bártová, E. "Images of the woman and the family." In H. Ornauer, H. Wiberg, A. Siciński, & J. Galtung (Eds.), *Images of the world in the year 2000: A comparative ten-nation study.* The Hague: Mouton, 1976.

Bass, B. M. "Life goals and career success of European and American managers." *Rivista Internazionale di Scienze Economiche e Commerciali,* 1976, *23,* 154–171.

Bass, B. M., & Burger, P. C. *Assessment of managers: A international comparison.* New York: Free Press, 1979.

Bass, B. M., & Franke, R. H. "Societal influence on student perceptions of how to succeed in organizations." *Journal of Applied Psychology,* 1972, *56,* 312–318.

Bégué, J. "Remarques sur une étude de l'OCDE concernant la répartition des revenus dans divers pays." *Economie et Statistique,* 1976, *84,* 97–104.

Bem, D. J. *Beliefs, attitudes, and human affairs,* Belmont, CA: Brooks/Cole, 1970.

Bem, S. L. "The measurement of psychological androgyny." *Journal of Consulting and Clinical Psychology,* 1974, *42,* 155–162.

Bem, S. L. "Sex role adaptability: One consequence of psychological androgyny." *Journal of Personality and Social Psychology,* 1975, *31,* 634–643.

Bem, S. L., Martyna, W., & Watson, C. "Sex typing and androgyny: Further explorations of the expressive domain." *Journal of Personality and Social Psychology,* 1976, *34,* 1016–1023.

Bendix, R., & Lipset, S. M. (Eds.), *Class, status and power: Social stratification in comparative perspective.* New York: Free Press, 1966.

Bennett, M. "Response characteristics of bilingual managers to organizational questionnaires." *Personnel Psychology,* 1977, *30,* 29–36. (a)

Bennett, M. "Testing management theories cross-culturally." *Journal of Applied Psychology,* 1977, *62,* 578–581. (b)

Berry, J. W. "On cross-cultural comparability." *International Journal of Psychology,* 1969, *4,* 119–128.

Berry, J. W. "An ecological approach to cross-cultural psychology." *Nederlands Tijdschrift voor de Psychologie,* 1975, *30,* 51–84.

Berry, J. W. *Human ecology and cognitive style: Comparative studies in cultural and psychological adaptation.* Beverly Hills, CA: Sage, 1976.

Berry, J. W., & Annis, R. C. "Acculturative stress." *Journal of Cross-Cultural Psychology,* 1974, *5,* 382–406.

Berthoud, R. *The disadvantages of inequality: A study of deprivation.* London: Macdonald and Jane's, 1976.

Berting, J. *In het Brede Maatschappelijke Midden.* Meppel, Neth.: Boom, 1968.

Besnard, P. "Anti- ou ante-durkheimisme?" *Revue Francaise de Sociologie,* 1976, *17,* 313–341.

Béteille, A. (Ed.). *Social inequality.* Harmondsworth, England: Penguin, 1969.

Béteille, A. *Inequality among men.* Oxford: Blackwell, 1977.

Bidney, D. "The concept of value in modern anthropology." In S. Tax (Ed.), *Anthropology today: Selections.* Chicago: University of Chicago Press, 1962.

Blais, A. "Power and causality." *Quality and Quantity,* 1974, *8,* 45–64.

Blake, R. R., Mouton, J. S., Barnes, L. B., & Greiner, L. E. "Breakthrough in organization development." In A. C. Bartlett & T. A. Kayser (Eds.), *Changing organizational behavior.* Englewood Cliffs, NJ: Prentice-Hall, 1973.

Blau, P. M. "Structural effects." *American Sociological Review,* 1960, *25,* 178–193.

Bloom, B. S. *Stability and change in human characteristics.* New York: John Wiley, 1964.

Blumberg, R. L., & Winch, R. F. "Societal complexity and familial complexity: Evidence for the curvilinear hypothesis." *American Journal of Sociology,* 1972, *77,* 898–920.

Bocock, R. *Ritual in industrial society: A sociological analysis of Ritualism in modern England*. London: George Allen & Unwin, 1974.

Boddewyn, J. (Ed.). *Comparative management and marketing*. Glenview, IL: Scott, Foresman, 1969.

Boddewyn, J. (Ed.). *Comparative management: Teaching, training and research*. New York: Graduate School of Business Administration, New York University, 1970.

Bohannan, P. *Social anthropology*. London: Holt, Rinehart & Winston, 1969.

Boulding, E., Nuss, S. A., Carson, D. L. & Greenstein, M. A. (Eds.). *Handbook of international data on women*. Beverly Hills, CA and New York: Sage/Halsted Press, 1976.

Boulding, K. E. "General systems theory: The skeleton of science." *Management Science,* 1956, *2,* 197–208. (a)

Boulding, K. E. *The image*. Ann Arbor, MI: University of Michigan Press, 1956. (b)

Boulding, K. E. *Ecodynamics: A new theory of societal evolution*. Beverly Hills, CA: Sage, 1978.

Bovenkerk, F., & Brunt, L. *Binnenstebuiten en Ondersteboven: De Anthropologie van de Industriele Samenleving*. Assen, Neth.: Van Gorcum, 1976.

Bowles, T. S. *Survey of attitudes towards overseas development*. London: HMSO, 1978.

Brace, C. L., & Livingstone, F. B. "On creeping Jensenism." In N. Alger (Ed.), *Many answers*. St Paul, MN: West Publishing, 1974.

Brief, A. P., Rose, G. L., & Aldag, R. J. "Sex differences in preferences for job attributes revisited." *Journal of Applied Psychology,* 1977, *62,* 645–646.

Bright, W. "Language and culture." In D. L. Sills (Ed.), *International encyclopedia of the social sciences, volume 9*. New York: Macmillan/Free Press, 1968.

Brislin, R. W. "Back-translation for cross-cultural research." *Journal of Cross-Cultural Psychology,* 1970, *1,* 185–216.

Brislin, R. W. (Ed.). *Translation: Applications and research*. New York: Goudner Press, 1976.

Brislin, R. W., & Pedersen, P. *Cross-cultural orientation programs*. New York: Gardner Press, 1976.

Brittan, A. *The privatised world*. London: Routledge & Kegan Paul, 1977.

Brossard, M., & Maurice, M. "Existe-t-il un modèle universel des structures d'organisation?" *Sociologie du Travail,* 1974, *4,* 402–426. (English translation: "Is there a universal model of organization structure?" *International Studies of Management and Organization,* 1976, *6,* 3, 11-45.)

Burnett, *Die Bundesdeutschen 1977: Irrational und konservativ. Ergebnisse einer Grossumfrage*. Frankfurt am Main: Leo Burnett Werbeagentur, 1977.

Burns, T., & Stalker, G. M. *The management of innovation*. London: Tavistock Publications, 1961.

Caplan, N., & Nelson, S. D. "On being useful: The nature and consequences of psychological research on social problems." *American Psychologist,* 1973, *28,* 199–211.

Carver, C. S., Coleman, A. E., & Glass, D. C. "The coronary-prone behavior and the suppression of fatigue on a treadmill test." *Journal of Personality and Social Psychology,* 1976, *33,* 460–466.

Cascio, W. F. "Functional specialization, culture and preference for participative management." *Personnel Psychology,* 1974, *27,* 593–603.

Cattell, R. B. "The dimensions of culture patterns by factorization of national characters." *Journal of Abnormal and Social Psychology,* 1949, *44,* 443–469.

Cattell, R. B. "The principal culture patterns discoverable in the syntal dimensions of existing nations." *Journal of Social Psychology,* 1950, *32,* 215–253.

Cattell, R. B. "A quantitative analysis of the changes in the culture pattern of Great Britain, 1837–1937, by P-technique." *Acta Psychologica,* 1953, *9,* 99–121.

Cattell, R.B., & Gorsuch, R.L. "The definition and measurement of national morale and morality," *Journal of Social Psychology*, 1965, *67*, 77-96.

Cattell, R.B., Breul, H., & Hartman, H.P. "An attempt at a more refined definition of the cultural dimensions of syntality in modern nations." *American Sociological Review*, 1952, *17*, 408–421.

CCE (Commission des Communautés Européennes). *Les Attitudes de la Population Active á l'Egard des Perspectives de la Retraite*. Brussels: European Economic Community, 1978.

Centers, R., & Bugenthal, D.E. "Intrinsic and extrinsic job motivations among different segments of the working population." *Journal of Applied Psychology*, 1966, *50*, 193–197.

CERC (Centre d'Etude des Revenus et des Coûts). "La dispersion et les disparités de salaires en France au cours des vingt derniéres années." *Economie et Statistique*, 1976, *Juillet–août*, 83–89.

Chaliand, G. *Mythes Révolutionnaires du Tiers Monde*. Paris: Seuil, 1976.

Chang, Y.N. "Early Chinese management thought." *California Management Review*, 1976, *19*, 71–76.

Chetwynd, J., & Hartnett, O. (Eds.). *The sex role system: Psychological and sociological perspectives*. London: Routledge & Kegan Paul, 1978.

Child, J., & Kieser, A. "Organization and managerial roles in British and West-German companies: An examination of the culture-free thesis." In C.J. Lammers & D.J. Hickson (Eds.), *Organizations alike and unlike: International and inter-institutional studies in the sociology of organization*. London: Routledge & Kegan Paul, 1979.

Christie, R. "Eysenck's treatment of the personality of communists." *Psychological Bulletin*, 1956, *53*, 411–430. (a)

Christie, R. "Some abuses of psychology." *Psychological Bulletin*, 1956, *53*, 439–451. (b)

Clark, A.W., & McCabe, S. "Leadership beliefs of Australian managers." *Journal of Applied Psychology*, 1970, *54*, 1–6.

Cleverley, G. *Managers and magic*. Harmondsworth, England: Pelican, 1973.

Cohen, M.D., March, J.G., & Olsen, J.P. "A garbage-can model of organizational choice." *Administrative Science Quarterly*, 1972, *17*, 1–25.

Collett, P., & O'Shea, G. "Pointing the way to a fictional place: A study of direction giving in Iran and England." *European Journal of Social Psychology*, 1976, *6*, 447–458.

Converse, P. "Country differences in time use." In A. Szalai (Ed.), *The Use of Time*. The Hague: Mouton, 1972.

Coppock, R. "Life among the environmentalists: An elaboration on Wildavsky's 'Economics and environment/rationality and ritual.'" *Accounting, Organizations and Society*, 1975, *2*, 125–129.

Cotta, A. "An analysis of power processes in organizations." In G. Hofstede & M.S. Kassem (Eds.), *European contributions to organization theory*. Assen, Neth.: Van Gorcum, 1976.

Cox, C.J., & Cooper, C.L. "Developing organizational development skills in Japan and the United Kingdom: An experimental approach." *International Studies of Management and Organization*, 1977, *6*, 72–83.

Cronbach, L.J. *Essentials of psychological testing*, New York: Harper & Row, 1970.

Crowley, J.E., Levitin, T.E., & Quinn, R.P. "Facts and fictions about the American working woman." In R.P. Quinn & T.W. Mangione (Eds.), *The 1969–1970 survey of working conditions*. Ann Arbor, MI: Institute for Social Research, University of Michigan, 1973.

Crozier, M. *The bureaucratic phenomenon*. Chicago: University of Chicago Press, 1964. (a)

Crozier, M. "Le contexte sociologique des relations hiérarchiques." *Organisation Scientifique*, 1964, *2, février*, 29–35. (b)

Crozier, M. *La Société Bloquée*. Paris: Seuil, 1971.

Crozier, M. "The problem of power." *Social Research*, 1973, *40*, 211–228.

Crozier, M., & Friedberg, E. *L'Acteur et le Systeme: Les contraintes de l'action collective.* Paris: Seuil, 1977.

Cutright, P. "Inequality: A cross-national analysis." *American Sociological Review,* 1967, *32,* 562–577.

Cutright, P. "Occupational inheritance: A cross-national analysis." *American Journal of Sociology,* 1968, *73,* 400–416.

Cyert, R.M., & March, J.G. *A behavioral theory of the firm.* Englewood Cliffs, NJ: Prentice-Hall, 1963.

Dahl, R.A., & Tufte, R. *Size and democracy.* Stanford, CA: Stanford University Press, 1974.

Dale, A. *Words, deeds, values and norms: A conceptual scheme.* Working Paper 74-9. Brussels: European Institute for Advanced Studies in Management, 1974.

Dale, A., & Spencer, E. *Sentiments, norms, ideologies and myths: Their relation to the resolution of issues in a state theatre company.* Working Paper 77-7. Brussels: European Institute for Advanced Studies in Management, 1977.

Davidson, A.R. "The emic-etic dilemma: Can methodology provide a solution to the absence of theory?" In Y.H. Poortinga (Ed.), *Basic problems in cross-cultural psychology.* Amsterdam: Swets and Zeitlinger, 1977.

Davis, S.M. *Comparative management: Organizational and cultural perspectives.* Englewood Cliffs, NJ: Prentice-Hall, 1971.

Deaux, K., & Emswiller, T. "Explanations of successful performance on sex-linked tasks: What is skill for the male is luck for the female." *Journal of Personality and Social Psychology,* 1974, *29,* 80–85.

de Baena, D. *The Dutch puzzle.* The Hague: Boucher, 1968.

de Bettignies, H.C., & Evans, P.L. "The cultural dimension of top executives' careers: A comparative analysis." In T.D. Weinshall (Ed.), *Culture and management.* Harmondsworth, England: Penguin, 1977.

de Bettignies, L.A., & Hofstede, G. "Communauté de Travail 'Boimondau': A case study on participation." *International Studies of Management and Organization,* 1977, *7,* 91–116.

de La Boétie, E. *Le Discours de la Servitude Volontaire.* Paris: Payot, [1548] 1976.

Delle Piane, M. "Gaetano Mosca." In D.L. Sills (Ed.), *International encyclopedia of the social sciences, vol. 10.* New York: Macmillan/Free Press, 1968.

Dempsey, P., & Dukes, W.F. "Judging complex value stimuli: An examination and revision of Morris' paths of life." *Educational and Psychological Measurement,* 1966, *26,* 871–882.

Denmark, F.L., & Waters, J.A. "Male and female in children's readers: A cross-cultural analysis." In Y.H. Poortinga (Ed.), *Basic problems in cross-cultural psychology.* Amsterdam: Swets and Zeitlinger, 1977.

Desplanques, G. "A 35 ans, les instituteurs ont encore 41 ans à vivre, les manoeuvres 34 ans seulement." *Economie et Statistique,* 1973, *49;* 3–19.

Despres, L.A. "Anthropological theory, cultural pluralism, and the study of complex societies." *Current Anthropology,* 1968, *9,* 3–26.

Deutscher, E. *What we say/what we do: Sentiments and acts.* Glenview, IL: Scott, Foresman, 1973.

De Vos, G.A., & Hippler, A.A. "Cultural psychology: Comparative studies of human behavior." In G. Lindzey & E. Aronson (Eds.), *The handbook of social psychology, vol. 4.* Reading, MA: Addison-Wesley, 1969.

Dick, G.W. "Authoritarian versus nonauthoritarian approaches to economic development." *Journal of Political Economy,* 1974, *July-August,* 817–827.

Dill, W.R. "Issues and alternatives for industrical democracy." In G. Hofstede (Ed.), *Futures for work.* Leyden, Neth.: Martinus Nijhoff, 1979.

Dinesen, I. *Winter's tales.* New York: Vintage, 1942.

Dore, W.R. *British factory-Japanese factory: The origins of national diversity in industrial relations.* Berkeley, CA: University of California Press, 1973.

Douglas, M. "Environments at risk." *The Times Literary Supplement,* 1970, Oct. 30, 1273–1275. 1273–1275.

Douglas, M. *Natural symbols: Explorations in cosmology.* New York: Vintage, 1973. (a)

Douglas, M. (Ed.), *Rules and meanings: The anthropology of everyday knowledge.* Harmondsworth, England: Penguin, 1973. (b)

Douglas, M. *Cultural bias.* Occasional Paper No. 35. London: Royal Anthropological Institute of Great Britain and Ireland, 1978.

Downey, H.K., Hellriegel, D., & Slocum, J.W. "Individual characteristics as sources of perceived uncertainty variability." *Human Relations,* 1977, *30,* 161–174.

Drever, J. *A dictionary of psychology.* Harmondsworth, England: Penguin, 1952.

Driver, H.E. "Cross-cultural studies." In J.J. Honigmann (Ed.), *Handbook of social and cultural anthropology.* Chicago: Rand McNally, 1973.

Drucker, P.F. *The practice of management.* London: Mercury Books, 1961.

Dubin, R. "Industrial workers' worlds: A study of the central life interests of industrial workers." *Social Problems,* 1956, *3,* 131–142.

Duncan, R.B. "Characteristics of organizational environments and perceived environmental uncertainty." *Administrative Science Quarterly,* 1972, *17,* 313–327.

Dunn, J.P., & Cobb, S. "Frequency of peptic ulcer among executives, craftsmen and foremen." *Journal of Occupational Medicine,* 1962, *4,* 343–348.

Durkheim, E. *Les Règles de la Méthode Sociologique.* Paris: Presses Universitaires de France, [1895] 1937.

Durkheim, E. *Le Suicide: Etude de Sociologie.* Paris: Presses Universitaires de France, [1897] 1930.

Eagly, A.H., & Himmelfarb, S. "Attitudes and opinions." *Annual Review of Psychology,* 1978, *29,* 517–554.

Eckhardt, W. "Conservatism, east and west." *Journal of Cross-Cultural Psychology,* 1971, *2,* 109–128.

Edwards, L. "Present shock, and how to avoid it." *Across the Board,* 1978, *15,* 36–43.

Eibl-Eibesfeldt, I. *Der vorprogrammierte Mensch: Das Ererbte als bestimmender Faktor im menschlichen Verhalten.* München: Deutscher Taschenbuch Verlag, 1976.

Eisenstadt, S.N. "Anthropological studies of complex societies." *Current Anthropology,* 1961, *2,* 201–222.

Eisenstadt, S.N. "Cultural models and political systems." *European Journal of Political Research,* 1974, *2,* 1–22.

Eitzen, D.S. "The use of Banks and Textor's 'A cross-policy survey' for the ranking of nations: A methodological note." *Social and Economic Studies,* 1967, *16,* 326–329.

Elbing. A.O., Gadon, H., & Gordon, J.R.M. "Flexible working hours: It's about time." *Harvard Business Review,* 1974, *54,* 1, 18–55.

Elder, J.W. "Comparative cross-national methodology." *Annual Review of Sociology,* 1976, *2,* 209–230.

Ember, C.R. "Cross-cultural cognitive studies." *Annual Review of Anthropology,* 1977, *6,* 33–56. 33–56.

England, G.W. *The manager and his values: An international perspective from the United States, Japan, Korea, India, and Australia.* Cambridge, MA: Ballinger, 1975.

Etzioni, A. *A comparative analysis of complex organizations: On power, involvement, and their correlates.* New York: Free Press, 1975.

Evan, W.M. "A data archive of legal systems: A cross-national analysis of sample data." *Archives Européennes de Sociologie,* 1968, *9,* 113–125.

Evan, W.M. "Measuring the impact of culture on organizations." *International Studies of **Management and Organization,** 1975, 5,* 1, 91-113.

Evan, W.M. "Hierarchy, alienation, commitment, and organizational effectiveness." *Human Relations,* 1977, *30,* 77–94.

Evans, M.G. "Conceptual and operational problems in the measurement of various aspects of job satisfaction." *Journal of Applied Psychology,* 1969, *53,* 93–101.

Evans, M.G., & Partridge, B.E. "Notes on the impact of flextime in a large insurance company." *Occupational Psychology,* 1973, *47,* 237–240.

Eyben, E. "Musonius Rufus: ook vrouwen moeten filosofie studeren." *Hermeneus, Tijdschrift voor de Antieke Cultuur,* 1976, *48,* 90–107.

Eysenck, H.J. "Primary social attitudes: A comparison of attitude patterns in England, Germany, and Sweden." *Journal of Abnormal and Social Psychology,* 1953, *48,* 563–568.

Eysenck, H.J. *The psychology of politics.* London: Routledge & Kegan Paul, 1954.

Eysenck, H.J. "The psychology of politics: A reply." *Psychological Bulletin,* 1956, *53,* 177–182. (a)

Eysenck, H.J. "The psychology of politics and the personality similarities between fascists and communists." *Psychological Bulletin,* 1956, *53,* 431–438. (b)

Farberow, N.L. (Ed.). *Suicide in different countries.* Baltimore, MD: University Park Press, 1975.

Farmer, R.N., & Richman, B.M. *Comparative management and economic progress.* Homewood, IL: Irwin, 1965.

Faucheux, C. "Cross-cultural research in experimental social psychology." *European Journal of Social Psychology,* 1976, *6,* 269–339.

Faucheux, C. "Strategy formulation as a cultural process." *International Studies of Management and Organization,* 1977, *7,* 2, 127–138.

Faucheux, C., Laurent, A., & Makridakis, S. "Can we model the wild world or should we first tame it?" In C.W. Churchman & R.O. Mason (Eds.), *World modeling: A dialogue.* New York: Elsevier North-Holland, 1976.

Fayol, H. *Administration Industrielle et Générale.* Paris: Dunod, 1970.

Feather, N.T. "Value importance, conservatism, and age." *European Journal of Social Psychology,* 1977, *7,* 241–245.

Feldman, A.S., & Moore, W.E. "Are industrial societies becoming alike?" In A.W. Gouldner and S.M. Miller (Eds.), *Applied psychology.* New York: Free Press, 1965.

Ferguson, I.R.G. *Management By Objectives in Deutschland.* Frankfurt: Herder und Herder. 1973.

Festinger, L. *A theory of cognitive dissonance.* Evanston, IL: Row, Peterson, 1957.

Fiedler, F.E. *A theory of leadership effectiveness.* New York: McGraw-Hill, 1967.

Fiedler, F.E., & Chemers, M.M. *Leadership and effective management.* Glenview, IL: Scott, Foresman, 1974.

Fiedler, F.E., Mitchell, T., & Triandis, H.C. *The culture assimilator: An approach to cross-cultural training.* Issue No. 5–156 C. New York: Experimental Publication System, American Psychological Association, 1970.

Fishbein, M., & Ajzen, I. *Belief, attitude, intention and behavior: An introduction to theory and research.* Reading, MA: Addison-Wesley, 1975.

Fishman, J.A. "A systematization of the Whorfian hypothesis." In J.W. Berry & P.R. Dasen (Eds.), *Culture and cognition.* London: Methuen, 1974.

Fleisher, F. *The new Sweden.* New York: David McKay, 1969.

Forst, H.T., & Vogel, F. *Hierarchisch-agglomerative Klassifikation von Merkmalstraegern bzw. Merkmalen.* Kiel FRG.: Institut für Betriebswirtschaft, 1977.

Franck, G. "Epitaphe pour la D.P.O." *Le Management,* 1973, *November.*

Fredriksson, I. "The future role of women." *Futures,* 1969, 532–540.

French, J.R.P., & Caplan, R.D. "Psychosocial factors in coronary heart disease." *Industrial Medicine and Surgery,* 1970, *39,* 383–397.

French, J.R.P., & Caplan, R.D. "Organizational stress and individual strain." In A.J. Marrow (Ed.), *The failure of success.* New York: Amacom, 1972.

French, J.R.P., & Raven, R. "The bases of social power." In D. Cartwright (Ed.), *Studies in social power*. Ann Arbor, MI: Institute for Social Research, University of Michigan, 1959.

Fridrich, H.K. *A comparative study of U.S. and German middle management attitudes*. Master's thesis. Cambridge, MA: Sloan School of Management, MIT, 1965. (unpublished)

Friedlander, F. "Comparative work value systems." *Personnel Psychology*, 1965, *18*, 1–20.

Friedlander, F. "Motivations to work and organizational performance." *Journal of Applied Psychology*, 1966, *50*, 143–152.

Friedman, M., & Rosenman, R.H. *Type A behavior and your heart*. Greenwich, CT: Fawcett, 1975.

Frijda, N., & Jahoda, G. "On the scope and methods of cross-cultural research." In D.R. Price-Williams (Ed.), *Cross-cultural studies*. Harmondsworth, England: Penguin, 1969.

Froissart, D. "The day our president and MBO collided." *European Business*, 1971, *Autumn*, 20–79.

Fromm, E. *Escape from freedom*. New York: Avon, 1965.

Galtung, J. "Rank and social integration: A multi-dimensional approach." In J. Berger, M. Zelditch, & B. Anderson (Eds.), *Sociological theories in progress*. Boston: Houghton Mifflin, 1966.

Galtung, J. *Theory and methods of social research*. London: George Allen & Unwin, 1967.

Galtung, J. "The future: A forgotten dimension." In H. Ornauer, H. Wiberg, A. Siciński, & J. Galtung (Eds.), *Images of the world in the year 2000: A Comparative ten-nation study*. The Hague: Mouton, 1976.

Galtung, J., Tägil, S., & Wiberg, H. (Eds.). *The first Nordic symposium on macroanalysis: Methods for macroanalysis of social change and social conflict*. Lund, Sweden: University of Lund, 1976.

Gambling, T. "Magic, accounting and morale." *Accounting, Organizations and Society*, 1977, *2*, 141–151.

Gardell, B. *Produktionsteknik och arbetsglädje*. Stockholm: Personal-administrativa Rådet, 1971.

Gaspari, C., & Millendorfer, J. *Konturen einer Wende: Strategien für die Zukunft*. Graz, Austria: Verlag Styria, 1978.

Gasse, Y. "Contextual transposition in translating research instruments." *Meta* (Montreal), 1973, *18*, 295–307.

Gasse, Y. *Technological uniformity and cultural diversity in organizational structure*. Working Papers 76-7 and 76-8. Sherbrooke, Québec: Faculté d'Administration, Université de Sherbrooke, 1976.

Geertz, C. *The interpretation of cultures: Selected essays*. New York: Basic Books, 1973.

George, K., & George, C.H. "Roman Catholic sainthood and social status." In R. Bendix & S.M. Lipset (Eds.), *Class, status and power*. New York: Free Press, 1966.

Gerth, H.H., & Mills, C.W. (Eds.). *From Max Weber: Essays in sociology*. London: Routledge & Kegan Paul, 1948.

Gjesme, T. "Sex differences in the connection between need for achievement and school preference." *Journal of Applied Psychology*, 1973, *50*, 270–272.

Glaser, W.A. "Cross-national comparisons of the factory." *Journal of Comparative Administration*, 1971, 83–117.

Glaser, W.A. "Cross-national comparisons of organizations." *International Studies of Management and Organization*, 1975, *5*, 1, 68–90.

Glennon, J.R., Owens, W.A., Smith, W.J., & Albright, L.E. "New dimension in measuring morale." *Harvard Business Review*, 1960, *38*, 1, 106–107.

Gohl, J. (Ed.). *Arbeit im Konflikt: Probleme der Humanisierungsdebatte*. Müchen: Goldmann, 1977.

Goldmann, R.B. *Work values: Six Americans in a Swedish plant*. New York. (mimeo)

Gordon, L.V. *Survey of personal values-manual*. Chicago: Science Research Associates, 1967.

Gordon, L.V. *The measurement of interpersonal values*. Chicago: Science Research Associates, 1975.

Gordon, L.V. *Survey of interpersonal values–revised manual*. Chicago: Science Research Associates, 1976.

Goudsblom, J. *Dutch society*. New York: Random House, 1967.

Granick, D. *The European executive*. New York: Doubleday, 1962.

Granick, D. *Managerial comparisons of four developed countries: France, Britain, United States and Russia*. Cambridge, MA: MIT Press, 1972.

Granick, D. "National differences in the use of internal transfer prices." *California Management Review*, 1975, *17*, 4, 28–40.

Graves, D. "Vive la management difference." *Management Today*, 1971, *April*, 81-83 + 128.

Graves, D. "The impact of culture upon managerial attitudes, beliefs and behaviour in England and France." *Journal of Management Studies*, 1972, *5*, 40–56.

Graves, D. (Ed). *Management research: A cross-cultural perspective*. New York-San Francisco: Elsevier North-Holland/Jossey-Bass, 1973.

Gray, E.D. "Masculine consciousness and the problem of limiting growth." In *Growth and its implications for the future*, Committee on Merchant Marine and Fisheries of the House of Representatives, Serial 93–29 Part 3. Washington DC: U.S. Government Printing Office, 1973.

Gregg, P.M., & Banks, A.S. "Dimensions of political systems: Factor analysis of a cross-polity survey." *American Political Science Review*, 1965, *59*, 602–614.

Gross, E. "Work, organization and stress." In S. Levine & N.A. Scotch (Eds.), *Social stress*. Chicago: AVC, 1970.

Gudykunst, W.B., Hammer, M.R., & Wiseman, R.L. "An analysis of an integrated approach to cross-cultural training." *International Journal of Intercultural Relations*, 1977, *1*, 99–110.

Guilford, R.R. *Personality*. New York: McGraw-Hill, 1959.

Guttman, L. "A general normative technique for finding the smallest coordinate space for a configuration of points." *Psychometrika*, 1968, *33*, 469–506.

Haas, M. "Toward the study of biopolitics: A cross-sectional analysis of mortality rates." *Behavioral Science*, 1969, *14*, 257–280.

Hagen, E.E. *On the theory of social change: How economic growth begins*. Homewood, IL: Dorsey Press, 1962.

Haire, M., Ghiselli, E.E., & Porter, L.W. *Managerial thinking: An international study*. New York: John Wiley, 1966.

Hall, E.T. *The silent language*. Greenwich, CT: Fawcett, 1965.

Hall, E.T. "The silent language in overseas business." *Harvard Business Review*, 1960, *38*, 3, 87–96.

Hampton, J. *An anthropological approach to accounting*. London: University College, 1977. (mimeo)

Haniff, G.M. "Politics, development and social policy: A cross-national analysis." *European Journal of Political Research*, 1976, *4*, 361–376.

Hanley, C., & Rokeach, M. "Care and carelessness in psychology." *Psychological Bulletin*, 1956, *53*, 183–186.

Harbison, F.H., & Burgess, E.W. "Modern management in Western Europe." *American Journal of Sociology*, 1954, *60*, 15–23.

Harbison, F.H., & Myers, C.A. *Management in the industrial world: An international analysis*. New York: McGraw-Hill, 1959.

Harrison, R. "Understanding your organization's character." *Harvard Business Review*, 1972, *52*, 3, 119–128.

Hartnett, O. "Sex-role stereotyping at work." In D. Chetwynd & O. Hartnett (Eds.), *The sex-role system*. London: Routledge & Kegan Paul, 1978.

Heath, D. B. (Ed.). *Contemporary cultures and societies of Latin America: A reader in the social anthropology of middle and South America*. New York: Random House, 1974.

Heberer, G., Schwidetzky, I., & Walter, H. (Eds.). *Anthropologie*. Frankfurt am Main: Fischer, 1970.

Heberle, R. "Tönnies, Ferdinand." In D. L. Sills (Ed.), *International encyclopedia of the social sciences, volume 16*. New York: Macmillan/Free Press, 1968.

Hedlund, G. *Organization as a matter of style*. Working Paper 78-15. Brussels: European Institute for Advanced Studies in Management, 1978.

Heginbotham, S. J. *Cultures in conflict: The four faces of Indian bureaucracy*. New York: Columbia University Press, 1975.

Heller, F. A., & Wilpert, B. "Limits to participative leadership: Task, structure and skill as contingencies—a German-British comparison." *European Journal of Social Psychology*, 1977, *7*, 61–84.

Heller, F. A., Mays, R., & Wilpert, B. "Methodology for multi-national study of managerial behaviour: The use of contingency theory." Presented at the 3rd Congress of Cross-Cultural Psychology, Tilburg, Netherlands, July, 1976.

Herrick, J. S. "Work motives of female executives." *Public Personnel Management*, 1973, *2*, 380–387.

Herrick, N. Q. "The now generation of workers." In R. P. Quinn & T. W. Mangione (Eds.), *The 1969–1970 survey of working conditions*. Ann Arbor, MI: Institute for Social Research, University of Michigan, 1973.

Herzberg, F., Mausner, B., Peterson, R., & Capwell, D. *Job Attitudes: Review of research and opinion*. Pittsburg, PA: Psychological Service of Pittsburg, 1957.

Herzberg, F., Mausner, B., & Snyderman, B. B. *The motivation to work*. New York: John Wiley, 1959.

Hesiod. *Theogony—Works and Days*. (D. Wender, trans.). Harmondsworth, England: Penguin, 1973.

Hickson, D. J., Hinings, C. R., McMillan, C. J., & Schwitter, J. P. "The culture-free context of organizational structure: A tri-national comparison." *Sociology*, 1974, *8*, 59–80.

Hickson, D. J., McMillan, C. J., Azumi, K., & Horvath, D. "Grounds for comparative organization theory: Quicksands or hard core?" In C. J. Lammers & D. J. Hickson (Eds.), *Organizations alike and unlike: International and inter-institutional studies in the sociology of organizations*. London: Routledge & Kegan Paul, 1979.

Hickson, D. J., Hinings, C. R., Lee, C. A., Schneck, R. E., & Pennings, J. M. "A strategic contingencies' theory of intraorganizational power." *Administrative Science Quarterly*, 1971, *16*, 216–229.

Hilton, G. *A review of the dimensionality of nations project*. Beverly Hills CA: Sage, 1973.

Hines, G. H. "The persistence of Greek achievement motivation across time and culture." *International Journal of Psychology*, 1973, *8*, 285–288.

Hines, G. H. "Achievement motivation levels of immigrants in New Zealand." *Journal of Cross-Cultural Psychology*, 1974, *5*, 37–47.

Hines, G. H. "Cultural influences on work motivation." In P. B. Warr (Ed.), *Personal goals and work design*. London: John Wiley, 1976.

Hinings, C. R., Hickson, D. J., Pennings, J. M., & Schneck, R. E. "Structural conditions of intraorganizational power." *Administrative Science Quarterly*, 1974, *19*, 22–44.

Hinrichs, J. R. "Value adaptation of new Ph.D.'s to academic and industrial environments: A comparative longitudinal study." *Personnel Psychology*, 1972, *25*, 545–565.

Hinrichs, J. R., & Ferrario, A. "A cross-national study of managers' job attitudes," Presented at the 18th Congress of Applied Psychology, Montreal, August, 1974.

Hippler, A. E. "Fusion and frustration: Dimensions in the cross-cultural ethnopsychology of suicide." *American Anthropologist,* 1969, *7,* 1074–1087.

Hjelholt, G. "Europe is different: Boundary and identity as key concepts." In G. Hofstede & M. S. Kassem (Eds.), *European contribution to organization theory.* Assen, Neth.: Van Gorcum, 1976.

Ho, D. Y. F. "On the concept of face." *American Journal of Sociology,* 1976, *81,* 867–884.

Ho, D. Y. F. "Psychosocial implications of collectivism: With special reference to the Chinese case and Maoist dialectics." Presented at the 4th Congress of Cross-Cultural Psychology, Munich, July, 1978. (a)

Ho, D. Y. F. "The concept of man in Mao-Tse-Tung's thought." *Psychiatry,* 1978, *41,* 391–402. (b)

Hofstede, G. H. "Arbeidsmotieven van volontairs." *Mens en Onderneming,* 1964, *18,* 373–391.

Hofstede, G. H. *The game of budget control.* Assen, Neth./London: Van Gorcum/Tavistock Publications, 1967.

Hofstede, G. H. *A comparison of four instruments for measuring values.* Research Working Paper No. 1. Lausanne: IMEDE, 1972. (a)

Hofstede, G. H. "The colors of collars." *Columbia Journal of World Business,* **1972,** *7,* **5, 72-80. (b)**

Hofstede, G. H. "The importance of being Dutch: Nationaliteits-en beroepsverschillen in werkorientatie." In P. J. D. Drenth, P. J. Willems, & C. J. de Wolff (Eds.), *Arbeids—en Organisatiepsychologie.* Deventer: Kluwer, 1973. (English version: "The importance of being Dutch: National and occupational differences in work goal importance." *International Studies of Management and Organization, 1976, 5,* 4, 5-28. (c)

Hofstede, G. H. *Experiences with G.W. England's personal values questionnaire in an international business school.* Working Paper 74-3. Brussels: European Institute for Advanced Studies in Management, 1974. (a)

Hofstede, G. H. *Experiences with F. E. Fiedler's least preferred co-worker questionnaire in an international business school.* Working Paper 74-5. Brussels: European Institute for Advanced Studies in Management, 1974. (b)

Hofstede, G. H. *Experiences with W.C. Schutz's FIRO-B questionnaire in an international business school.* Working Paper 74-22. Brussels: European Institute for Advanced Studies in Management, 1974. (c)

Hofstede, G. H. *Differences in value patterns between emigration and immigration countries in Europe.* Working Paper 74-56. Brussels: European Institute for Advanced Studies in Management, 1974. (d)

Hofstede, G. H. *Psephology in management or the art of using survey information.* Research Paper No. 147. Fontainebleau: INSEAD, 1975. (a)

Hofstede, G. H. *The stability of attitude survey questions: In particular those dealing with work goals.* Working Paper 75-45. Brussels: European Institute for Advanced Studies in Management, 1975. (b)

Hofstede, G. H. "Nationality and espoused values of managers." *Journal of Applied Psychology,* 1976, *61,* 148–55. (a)

Hofstede, G. H. *The construct validity of attitude survey questions dealing with work goals.* Working Paper 76-8. Brussels: European Institute for Advanced Studies in Management, 1976. (b)

Hofstede. G. H. "Alienation at the top," *Organizational Dynamics,* 1976, *4,* 3, 44–60. (c)

Hofstede, G. H. "Confrontation in the cathedral: A case study on power and social change." *International Studies of Management and Organization,* 1977, *7,* 1, 16–32. (a)

Hofstede, G. H. "Cultural elements in the exercise of power." In Y. H. Poortinga (Ed.), *Basic problems in cross-cultural psychology.* Amsterdam: Swets and Zeitlinger, 1977. (b)

Hofstede, G. H. *Cultural determinants of the exercise of power in a hierarchy.* Working Paper 77-8. Brussels: European Institute for Advanced Studies in Management, 1977. (c)

Hofstede, G. H. *Cultural determinants of the avoidance of uncertainty in organizations.* Working Paper 77-18. Brussels: European Institute for Advanced Studies in Management, 1977. (d)

Hofstede, G. H. "Businessmen and business school faculty: A comparison of value systems." *Journal of Management Studies,* 1978, *15,* 79–89 (a)

Hofstede, G. H. "The poverty of management control philosophy." *Academy of Management Review,* 1978, *3,* 450–46l. (b)

Hofstede, G. H. "Occupational determinants of stress and satisfaction." In B. Wilpert & A. R. Negandhi (Eds.), *Work organization research: European and American perspectives.* Kent, OH: C.A.R.I./Kent State University Press, 1978. (c)

Hofstede, G. H. "Culture and organization: A literature review study." *Journal of Enterprise Management,* 1978, *1,* 127–135. (d)

Hofstede, G. H. *Cultural determinants of individualism and masculinity in organizations.* Brussels: European Institute for Advanced Studies in Management, 1978. (e)

Hofstede, G. H. "Humanization of work: The role of values in a third industrial revolution." In C. L. Cooper & E. Mumford (Eds.), *The quality of working life in Eastern and Western Europe.* London: Associated Business Press, 1979. (a)

Hofstede, G. H. "Hierarchical power distance in forty countries." In C. J. Lammers & D. J. Hickson (Eds.), *Organizations alike and unlike: International and inter-institutional studies in the sociology of organizations.* London: Routledge & Kegan Paul, 1979. (b)

Hofstede, G. H. "Value systems in forty countries: Interpretation, validation and consequences for theory." In L. H. Eckensberger, W. J. Lonner, & Y. H. Poortinga (Eds.), *Cross-cultural contributions to psychology.* Lisse, Neth.: Swets and Zeitlinger, 1979. (c)

Hofstede, G. H. "Angola coffee—or the confrontation of an organization with changing values in its environment." *Organization Studies,* 1980, *1,* 21-40.

Hofstede, G. H., & Kassem, M. S. (Eds.). *European contributions to organization theory.* Assen, Neth.: Van Gorcum, 1976.

Hofstede, G. H., & Kranenburg, R. Y. "Work goals of migrant workers." *Human Relations,* 1974, *27,* 83–99.

Hofstede, G. H., & Van Hoesel, P. *Within-culture and between-culture component structures of work goals in a heterogeneous population.* Working Paper 76-26. Brussels: European Institute for Advanced Studies in Management, 1976.

Hofstede, G. H., Kraut, A. I., & Simonetti, S. H. *The development of a core attitude survey questionnaire for international use.* Working Paper 76-17. Brussels: European Institute for Advanced Studies in Management, 1976.

Hoijer, H. "The relation of language to culture." In S. Tax (Ed.), *Anthropology Today.* Chicago: University of Chicago Press, 1962.

Holmes, T. H., & Rahe, R. H. "The social readjustment rating scale." *Journal of Psychosomatic Research,* 1967, *11,* 213–218.

Horowitz, J. "Management control in France, Great Britain and Germany." *Columbia Journal of World Business,* 1978, *13,* 2, 16-22.

Horvath, D., McMillan, C. J., Azumi, K., & Hickson, D. J. "The cultural context of organizational control: An international comparison." *International Studies of Management and Organization,* 1976, *6,* 3, 60–86.

Hsu, F. L. K. "Psychosocial homeostasis and jen: Conceptual tools for advancing psychological anthropology." *American Anthropologists,* 1971, *73,* 23–44.

Hsu, F. L. K. *Iemoto: The heart of Japan.* Cambridge, MA: Schenkman, 1975.

IFOP. *Enquête auprès les Jeunes.* Paris: Institut Français de l'Opinion Publique, 1977.

ILO. "Social and cultural factors in management development: Extracts from the conclusions of a meeting of experts." *International Labour Review,* 1966, *94,* 175–185.

ILO. *Yearbook of labour statistics.* Geneva: International Labour Office, 1976.

Ingham, G. K. *Size of industrial organization and worker behaviour.* Cambridge: Cambridge University Press, 1970.

Inglehart, R. "The silent revolution in Europe: Inter-generational change in post-industrial societies." *American Political Science Review,* 1971, *65,* 991–1017.

Inkeles, A. "Industrial man: The relation of status to experience, perception, and value." *American Journal of Sociology,* 1960, *66,* 1–31.

Inkeles, A. "The modernization of man." In M. Weiner (Ed.), *Modernization.* New York: Basic Books, 1966.

Inkeles, A. "Making men modern: On the causes and consequences of individual change in the developing countries." *American Journal of Sociology,* 1969, *75,* 208–225.

Inkeles, A. "Continuity and change in the American national character." Prepared for American Sociological Association Annual Meeting, Chicago, September, 1977.

Inkeles, A., & Levinson, D. J. "National character: The study of modal personality and sociocultural systems." In G. Lindzey & E. Aronson (Eds.), *The handbook of social psychology, vol. 4.* Reading, MA: Addison-Wesley, 1969.

Inkson, J. H. K., Hickson, D. J., & Pugh, D. S. "Administrative reduction of variance in organizations and behaviour: A comparative study. Presented at the British Psychological Society Annual Conference, April, 1968.

Inkson, J. H. K., Schwitter, J. P., Pheysey, D. C., & Hickson, D. J. "A comparison of organization structure and managerial roles: Ohio, U.S.A. and the Midlands, England." *Journal of Management Studies,* 1970, *7,* 347–363.

ISR. "Americans seek self-development, suffer anxiety from changing roles." *ISR Newsletter,* 1979, *7,* 1, 4–5.

Jacquemin, A., & de Ghellinck, E. *Familial control, size and performance in the largest French firms.* Working Paper 77-25. Brussels: European Institute for Advanced Studies in Management, 1977.

Jahoda, G. "In pursuit of the emic-etic distinction: Can we ever capture it?" In Y. H. Poortinga (Ed.), *Basic problems in cross-cultural psychology.* Amsterdam: Swets and Zeitlinger, 1977.

Jenkins, C. D. "Psychologic and social precursors of coronary disease." *New England Journal of Medicine,* 1971, *284,* 244–255, 307–312.

Jenkins, D. *Blue and white collar democracy.* New York: Doubleday, 1973.

Jensen, A. R. "How much can we boost IQ and scholastic achievement?" *Harvard Educational Review,* 1969, *39,* 1–123.

Jönsson, S. A., & Lundin, R. A. "Myths and wishful thinking as management tools." In P. C. Nystrom & W. H. Starbuck (Eds.), *Prescriptive models of organizations.* New York: Elsevier North-Holland, 1977.

Jordan, T. G. *The European culture area: A systematic geography.* New York: Harper & Row, 1973.

Jourard, S. M. "Some lethal aspects of the male role." In A. G. Athos & R. E. Coffey (Eds.), *Behavior in organizations: A multi-dimensional view.* Englewood Cliffs, NJ: Prentice-Hall, 1968.

Kaase, M., & Marsh, A. "The matrix of political action: Protest and participation in five nations." Prepared for the 10th Congress of Political Science, Edinburgh, August, 1976.

Kagitcibasi, C. "Social norms and authoritarianism: A Turkish-American comparison." *Journal of Personality and Social Psychology,* 1970, *16,* 444–451.

Kahn, R. L., & Quinn, R. P. "Role stress: A framework for analysis." In A. McLean (Ed.), *Mental health and work organizations,* Chicago: Rand McNally, 1970.

Kahn, R. L., Wolfe, D. M., Quinn, R. P., Snoek, J. D., & Rosenthal, R. A. *Organizational stress: Studies in role conflict and ambiguity*. New York: John Wiley, 1964.

Kakar, S. "Authority patterns and subordinate behavior in Indian organizations." *Administrative Science Quarterly*, 1971, *16*, 298–307

Kalsbeek, J. W. H. *Mentale Belasting*. Assen, Neth.: Van Gorcum, 1976.

Kassem, M. S. "A tale of two countries: Japan and Britain." *Columbia Journal of World Business*. 1974, *9*, 2, 35–48.

Kata, K. "On anxiety in the Scandinavian countries." In I. G. Sarason & C. D. Spielberger (Eds.), *Stress and anxiety, volume 2*. Washington DC: Hemisphere Publishing, 1975.

Katerberg, R., Smith, F. J., & Hoy, S. "Language, time and person effects on attitude scale translations." *Journal of Applied Psychology*, 1977, *62*, 385–391.

Kawasaki, I. *Japan unmasked*. Rutland, VT: Charles E. Tuttle, 1969.

Kerr, C., Dunlop, J. T., Harbison, F. H., & Myers, C. A. *Industrialism and industrial man: The problems of labor and management in economic growth*. London: Heinemann, 1960.

Kets de Vries, M. F. R., Zaleznik, A., & Howard, J. H. *Stress reactions and organizations: The minotaur revisited*. Working Paper 75-30. Montreal: McGill University, Faculty of Management, 1975.

Kipnis, D. "Does power corrupt?" *Journal of Personality and Social Psychology*, 1972, *24*, 33–41.

Kipnis, D., Castell, P. J., Gergen, M., & Mauch, D. "Metamorphic effects of power." *Journal of Applied Psychology*, 1976, *61*, 127–135.

Klein, S. M., Kraut, A. I., & Wolfson, A. "Employee reactions to attitude survey feedback: A study of the impact of structure and process." *Administrative Science Quarterly*, 1971, *16*, 497–514.

Kluckhohn, C. "The study of culture." In D. Lerner & H. D. Lasswell (Eds.), *The policy sciences*. Stanford, CA: Stanford University Press, 1951. (a)

Kluckhohn, C. "Values and value-orientations in the theory of action: An exploration in definition and classification." In T. Parsons & E. A. Shils (Eds.), *Toward a general theory of action*. Cambridge, MA: Harvard University Press, 1951. (b)

Kluckhohn, C. "Universal categories of culture." In S. Tax (Ed.), *Anthropology today*, Chicago: University of Chicago Press, 1962.

Kluckhohn, F. R. "Dominant and substitute profiles of cultural orientation: Their significance for the analysis of social stratification." *Social Forces*, 1950, *28*, 376–393.

Kluckhohn, F. R., & Strodtbeck, F. L. *Variations in value orientations*. Westport, CT: Greenwood Press, 1961.

Koebben, A. J. F. "New ways of presenting an old idea: The statistical method in social anthropology." *Royal Anthropological Institute of Great Britain and Ireland Journal*, 1952, *82*, 129–146.

Kohn, M. L. *Class and conformity: A study in values*. Homewood, IL: Dorsey Press, 1969.

Kohn M. L. "Bureaucratic man: A portrait and an interpretation." *American Sociological Review*, 1971, *36*, 461–474.

Komarovsky, M. *Dilemmas of masculinity: A study of college youth*. New York: Norton, 1976.

Kornhauser, A. *Mental health of the industrial worker: A Detroit study*. New York: John Wiley, 1965.

Kraemer, A. J. "Cultural aspects of intercultural training." Presented at the 19th Congress of Applied Psychology, Munich, August, 1978.

Kraut, A. I. "Predicting turnover of employees from measured job attitudes." *Organizational Behavior and Human Performance*, 1975, *13*, 233–243. (a)

Kraut, A. I. "Some recent advances in cross-national management research." *Academy of Management Journal*, 1975, *18*, 538–549. (b)

Kraut, A. I., & Ronen, S. "Validity of job facet importance: A multinational, multicriteria study." *Journal of Applied Psychology*, 1975, *60*, 671–677.

Kravis, I. B. "International differences in the distribution of income." *Review of Economics and Statistics*, 1960, *42*, 408–416.

Krishnan, R. "Democratic participation in decision making by employees in American corporations." *Academy of Management Journal*, 1974, *17*, 339–347.

Kroeber, A. L., & Parsons, T. "The concepts of culture and of social system." *American Sociological Review*, 1958, *23*, 582–583.

Kroeber-Keneth, L. *Frauen unter Männern: Grenzen und Möglichkeiten der Arbeitenden Frau*. Düsseldorf: Econ-Verlag, 1955.

Kumar, U., & Singh, K. K. "Interpersonal construct system of Indian manager: A determinant of organizational behaviour." Presented at the International Congress of Applied Psychology, Paris, July, 1976.

Kunkel, J. H. *Society and economic growth: A behavioral perspective of social change*. New York: Oxford University Press, 1970.

Kuznets, S. "Distribution of income by size" (Quantitative aspects of the economic growth of nations, Paper no 8). *Economic Development and Cultural Change*, 1963, *11*, part 2, 1–80.

Kuznets, S. *Economic growth of nations: Total output and production structure*. Cambridge, MA: Belknap Press, 1971.

Kuznets, S. *Population, capital and growth: Selected essays*. London: Heinemann, 1973.

Laaksonen, O. J. "The power structure of Chinese enterprises." *International Studies of Management and Organization*. 1977, *7*, 1, 71–90.

Lammers, C. J. "Towards the internationalization of the organization sciences." In G. Hofstede & M. S. Kassem (Eds.), *European contributions to organization theory*, Assen, Neth.: Van Gorcum, 1976.

Lammers, C. J. *The contributions of organizational sociology*. Leyden: Institute for Sociology, University of Leyden, 1977. (mimeo)

Lammers, C. J. *Van Demokraten en Oligokraten*. Leyden: Universitaire Pers Leiden, 1978. (a)

Lammers, C. J. "The comparative sociology of organizations." *Annual Review of Sociology*, 1978, *4*, 485–510. (b)

Lammers, C. J., & Hickson, D. J. (Eds.). *Organizations alike and unlike: International and inter-institutional studies in the sociology of organizations*. London: Routledge & Kegan Paul, 1979.

Langbein, I. M., & Lichtman, A. J. *Ecological inference*. Beverly Hills, CA: Sage, 1978.

Lannon, J. M. "Male versus female values in management." *Management International Review*, 1977, *17*, 1, 9–12.

La Suisse. *La Suisse: Portrait de la Jeunesse*. Zurich: Société d'Assurances La Suisse, 1972.

Laszlo, E. "A systems philosophy of human values." *Behavioral Science*, 1973, *18*, 250–259.

Laszlo, E. *The inner limits of mankind: Heretical reflections on today's values, culture and politics*. Oxford: Pergamon Press, 1978.

Laurent, A. *Matrix organizations and Latin cultures*. Working Paper 78-28. Brussels: European Institute for Advanced Studies in Management, 1978.

Lawrence, P. R., & Lorsch, J. W. *Organization and Environment: Managing differentiation and integration*. Homewood, IL: Irwin, 1967.

Le Berre, M. "L'horaire variable individualisé dans la région Grenobloise." *Direction et Gestion des Entreprises*, 1976, *12*, 41–50.

Ledda, G. *Padre Padrone: l'Education d'un Berger Sarde*. Paris: Gallimard, 1977.

Lee, D. Plato: *The republic*. Harmondsworth, England: Penguin, 1974.

Lee, D. M., & Alvares, K. M. "Effects of sex on descriptions and evaluations of supervisory behavior in a simulated industrial setting." *Journal of Applied Psychology*, 1977, 405–410.

Lenski, G. E. *Power and privilege: A theory of social stratification.* New York: McGraw-Hill, 1966.

Leplae, C. "Différences culturelles entre instituteurs d'expression française et flamande." *Bulletin de l'Institut de Recherces Economiques et Sociales* (Louvain) 1955, *21*, 709–754.

Leplae, C. "Différences culturelles entre instituteurs flamands, francophones et hollandais." *Bulletin de l'Institut de Recherches Economiques et Sociales* (Louvain) 1956, *22*, 731–741.

Levi, L., & Andersson, L. *Population, environment and quality of life: A contribution to the world population conference.* Stockholm: Royal Ministry for Foreign Affairs, 1974.

Le Vine, R. A. "Sex roles and economic change in Africa." *Ethnology,* 1966, *5,* 186–193.

Le Vine, R. A. *Culture, behavior and personality: An introduction to the comparative study of psychosocial adaptation.* Chicago: AVC, 1973.

Levine, S., & Scotch, N. A. "Social stress." In S. Levine & N. A.Scotch (Eds.), *Social stress.* Chicago: AVC, 1970.

Levinson, D. "What have we learned from cross-cultural surveys?" *American Behavioral Scientist,* 1977, *20,* 757–792.

Levinson, H. *Emotional health in the world of work.* New York: Harper & Row, 1964.

Levinson, H. *Executive stress,* New York: Harper & Row, 1970. (a)

Levinson, H. "Management by whose objectives?" *Harvard Business Review,* 1970, *48,* 4, 125–134. (b)

Levinson, H. "On executive suicide." *Harvard Business Review,* 1975, *53,* 4, 118–122.

Levinson, H., & Weinbaum, L. "The impact of organization on mental health." In A. McLean (Ed.), *Mental health and work organizations.* Chicago: Rand McNally, 1970.

Levinson, H., Price, C. R., Munden, K. J., Mandl, H. J., & Solley, C. M. *Men, management and mental health.* Cambridge, MA: Harvard University Press, 1962.

Levitin, T. "Values." In J. P. Robinson & P. R. Shaver (Eds.), *Measures of social psychological attitudes.* Ann Arbor, MI: Survey Research Center, Institute for Social Research, University of Michigan, 1973, 489–502.

Lewin, K. "Some social-psychological differences between the United States and Germany." In K. Lewin, *Resolving social conflicts.* New York: Harper & Row, [1936] 1948.

Lewis, B. *The emergence of modern Turkey.* London: Oxford University Press, 1961.

Lewis, O. *La Vida: A Puerto Rican family in the culture of poverty: San Juan and New York.* New York: Vintage Books, 1966.

Lievegoed, B. *De Levensloop van de Mens.* Rotterdam: Lemniscaat, 1976.

Likert, R. *New patterns of management.* New York: McGraw-Hill, 1961.

Likert, R. "Trends towards a world-wide theory of management." *Proceedings of the CIOS XII International Management Congress,* 1963, *2,* 110–114.

Likert, R. *The human organization,* New York: McGraw-Hill, 1967.

Lindblom, C. E. "The science of muddling through." *Public Administration Review,* 1959, *19,* 78–88.

Lippitt, R., & White, R. K. "An experimental study of leadership and group life." In E. E. Maccoby, T. M. Newcomb, & E. E. Hartley (Eds.), *Readings in social psychology,* New York: Holt, Rinehart & Winston, 1958.

Lobban, G. "The influence of the school on sex-role stereotyping." In J. Chetwynd & O. Hartnett (Eds.), *The sex role system.* London: Routledge & Kegan Paul, 1978.

Lodahl, T., & Kejner, M. "The definition and measurement of job involvement." *Journal of Applied Psychology,* 1965, *49,* 24–33.

Lomax, A., & Berkowitz, N. "The evolutionary taxonomy of culture." *Science,* 1972, *177,* 228–239.

Lorenz, K. *On agression.* New York: Bantam Books, 1970.

Lowie, R. H. *Towards understanding Germany.* Chicago: University of Chicago Press, 1954.

Luhmann, N. *Macht.* Stuttgart: Ferdinand Enke, 1975.

Luhmann, N. "A general theory of organized social systems." In G. Hofstede & M. S. Kassem (Eds.), *European contributions to organization theory,* Assen, Neth.: Van Gorcum, 1976. (a)

Luhmann, N. "The future cannot begin: Temporal structures in modern society." *Social Research,* 1976, *43,* 130–152. (b)

Lütz, B. "Bildungssystem und Beschäftigungsstruktur in Deutschland und Frankreich." In H. G. Mendius (Ed.), *Betrieb, Arbeitsmarkt und Qualifikation, vol. 1.* Frankfurt am Main: Aspekte Verlag, 1976.

Lynn, R. *Personality and national character.* Oxford: Pergamon Press, 1971.

Lynn, R. "National differences in anxiety and the consumption of caffeine." *British Journal of Social and Clinical Psychology,* 1973, *12,* 92–93.

Lynn, R. "National differences in anxiety 1935–65." In I. G. Sarason & C. D. Spielberger (Eds.), *Stress and anxiety, volume 2.* Washington DC: Hemisphere, 1975.

Lynn, R., & Hampson, S. L. "National differences in extraversion and neuroticism." *British Journal of Social and Clinical Psychology,* 1975, *14,* 223–240.

Lynn, R., & Hampson, S. L. "Fluctuations in national levels of neuroticism and extraversion, 1935–1970." *British Journal of Social and Clinical Psychology,* 1977, *16,* 131–137.

Machiavelli, N. *The ruler* (P. Rodd, trans.). Chicago: Gateway, [1517] 1955.

Mack, D. E. "The power relationship in black families and white families." *Journal of Personality and Social Psychology,* 1974, *30,* 409–413.

Magee, B. *Popper.* Glasgow: Fontana/Collins, 1975.

Mangione, T. W. "Turnover—some psychological and demographic correlates." In R. A. Quinn & T. W. Mangione (Eds.), *The 1969–1970 survey of working conditions.* Ann Arbor, MI: Institute for Social Research, University of Michigan, 1973.

Manhardt, P. J. "Job orientation of male and female college graduates in business." *Personnel Psychology,* 1972, *25,* 361–368.

Marceau, J. *Class and status in France: Economic change and social immobility 1945–1975.* Oxford: Clarendon Press, 1977.

March, J. G., & Olsen, J. P. *Ambiguity and choice in organizations.* Bergen, Norway: Universitetsforlaget, 1976.

March, J. G., & Simon, H. A. *Organizations.* New York: John Wiley, 1958.

Marks, M. "Organizational adjustment to uncertainty." *Journal of Management Studies.* 1977, *14,* 1–7.

Marsh, R. M. *Comparative sociology: A codification of cross-societal analysis.* New York: Harcourt Brace Jovanovich, 1967.

Marshall, B. K. "Japanese business ideology and labour policy." *Columbia Journal of World Business,* 1977, *12,* 22–29.

Martin, W. F., & Lodge, G. C. "Our society in 1985—business may not like it." *Harvard Business Review,* 1975, *53,* 143–152.

Martyn-Johns, T. A. "Cultural conditioning of views of authority and its effect on the business decision-making process, with special reference to Java." In Y. H. Poortinga (Ed.), *Basic problems in cross-cultural psychology.* Amsterdam: Swets and Zeitlinger, 1977.

Marx, K., & Engels, F. "Manifest der Kommunistischen Partei." In K. Marx and F. Engels, *Werke, Band 4,* Berlin: Dietz, [1848] 1974.

Maslow, A. H. *Motivation and personality,* New York: Harper & Row, 1970.

Masuda, M., & Holmes, T. H. "The social readjustment rating scale: A cross-cultural study of Japanese and Americans." *Journal of Psychosomatic Research,* 1967, *11,* 227–237.

Maurice, M. "Theoretical and ideological aspects of the universalistic approach to the study of organizations." *International Studies of Management and Organization,* 1976, *6,* 3, 3–10.

Maurice, M., Sellier, F., & Silvestre, J. J. *Production de la Hiérarchie dans l'Entreprise: Comparaison France-Allemagne.* Aix-en-Provence: L.E.S.T., 1978.

Maurice, M., Sorge, A., & Warner, M. "Societal differences in organizing manufacturing units: A comparison of France, West Germany and Great Britain." *Organization Studies,* 1980, *1,* 59–86.

McCann-Erickson. *De Volwassen Jeugd van de Zeventiger Jaren.* Amsterdam: McCann-Erickson, 1977.

McClelland, D. C. *The achieving society.* Princeton, NJ: Van Nostrand Reinhold, 1961.

McClelland, D. C. "Achievement motivation can be developed." *Harvard Business Review,* 1965, *43,* 6, 6–24 and 178.

McClelland, D. C. *Power: The inner experience.* New York: Irvington, 1975.

McClelland, D. C., & Burnham, D. H. "Power is the great motivator." *Harvard Business Review,* 1976, *54,* 2, 100–110.

McClelland, D. C., Sturr, J. F., Knapp, R. H., & Wendt, H. W. "Obligations to self and society in the United States and Germany." *Journal of Abnormal and Social Psychology,* 1958, *56,* 245–255.

McClintock, C. G., & McNeel, S. P. "Cross-cultural comparisons of interpersonal motives." *Sociometry,* 1966, *29,* 406–427.

McGee, J. *The Europeans and free enterprise.* Press release. Brussels: J. McGee, 1977. (mimeo)

McGiffert, M. (Ed.). *The character of Americans: A book of readings.* Homewood, IL: Dorsey Press, 1970.

McGrath, J. E. "Settings, measures and themes: An integrative revision of some research on social-psychological factors in stress." In J. E. McGrath (Ed.), *Social and psychological factors in stress.* New York: Holt, Rinehart & Winston, 1970.

McGregor, D. *The human side of enterprise.* New York: McGraw-Hill, 1960.

McGregor, D. *The professional manager.* New York: McGraw-Hill, 1967.

McKinsey. *De Aantrekkelijkheid van Nederland voor Buitenlandse Investeerders: een opiniepeiling onder buitenlandse ondernemers.* Amsterdam: McKinsey and Company, 1978.

Mead, M. "Studies of whole cultures: Greece." In M. Mead (Ed.), *Cultural patterns and technical change.* Paris: UNESCO, 1953.

Mead, M. *Male and female: A study of the sexes in a changing world.* Harmondsworth, England: Penguin, 1962. (a)

Mead, M. "National character." In S. Tax (Ed.), *Anthropology today.* Chicago: University of Chicago Press, 1962. (b)

Mead, M. *Culture and commitment: The new relationships between the generations in the 1970's.* Garden City, NY: Anchor Books, 1978.

Meade, R. D. "An experimental study of leadership in India." *Journal of Social Psychology,* 1967, *72,* 35–43.

Meade, R. D., & Whittaker, J. D. "A cross-cultural study of authoritarianism." *Journal of Social Psychology,* 1967, *72,* 3–7.

Meltzer, L. "Comparing relationships of individual and average variables to individual response." *American Sociological Review,* 1963, *28,* 117–123.

Menzel, H. "Comment on Robinson's 'Ecological correlations and the behavior of individuals.'" *American Sociological Review,* 1950, *15,* 674.

Mermoz, M. *L'Autogestion c'est pas de la Tarte.* Paris: Seuil, 1978.

Merton, R. K. *Social theory and social structure.* New York: Free Press, 1968.

Metcalf, H. C., & Urwick, L. *Dynamic administration: The collected papers of Mary Parker Follett.* New York: Harper & Row, 1940.

Michels, R. *Political parties: A sociological study of the oligarchical tendencies of modern democracy.* New York: Free Press, [1915] 1962.

Milgram, S. *Obedience to authority —An experimental view.* London: Tavistock Publications, 1974.

Millendorfer, J. *Mechanisms of socio-psychological development.* Vienna: STUDIA (Studien-gruppe für Internationale Analysen), 1976.

Miller, E. J. "The open-system approach to organizational analysis with specific reference to the work of A. K. Rice." In G. Hofstede & M. S. Kassem (Eds.), *European contributions to organization theory.* Assen, Neth.: Van Gorcum, 1976.

Miller, S. M. "Comparative social mobility." *Current Sociology,* 1960, *9,* 1–89.

Moddie, A. D. *The brahmanical culture and modernity.* Bombay: Asia Publishing House, 1968.

More, T. *Utopia.* Harmondsworth, England: Penguin, [1516] 1965.

Morgenstern, O. "Does GNP measure growth and welfare?" *Business and Society Review,* 1975, *15,* 23–31.

Morris, C. *Varieties of human value.* Chicago: University of Chicago Press, 1956.

Morris, C., & Jones, L. V. "Value scales and dimensions." *Journal of Abnormal and Social Psychology,* 1955, *51,* 523–535.

Morris, D. *The naked ape: A zoologist's study of the human animal.* New York: McGraw-Hill, 1968.

Moulin, L. "La nationalité des prix Nobel de science de 1901 à 1960." *Cahiers Internationaux de Sociologie,* 1961, *31,* 145–163.

Mozina, S. "Management opinion on satisfaction and importance of psychosocial needs in their jobs." *Proceedings of the 16th Congress of Applied Psychology,* 1969, 788–794.

Mulder, M. "Power equalization through participation?" *Administrative Science Quarterly,* 1971, *16,* 31–38.

Mulder, M. "Reduction of power differences in practice: The power distance reduction theory and its applications." In G. Hofstede & M. S. Kassem (Eds.), *European contributions to organization theory.* Assen, Neth.: Van Gorcum, 1976.

Mulder, M. *The daily power game.* Leyden: Martinus Nijhoff, 1977.

Mulder, M., Ritsema van Eck, J. R., & De Jong, R. D. "An organization in crisis and non-crisis situations." *Human Relations,* 1971, *24,* 19–41.

Murdock, G. P. *Social structure.* New York: Free Press, 1949.

Murphy, H. B. M., Wittkower, E. D., & Chance, N. W. "The symptoms of depression—a cross-cultural study." In I. Al-Issa & W. Dennis (Eds.), *Cross-cultural studies of behavior,* New York: Holt, Rinehart & Winston, 1970.

Myrdal, G. *Asian drama: An enquiry into the poverty of nations.* New York: Twentieth Century Fund, 1968.

Nagi, M. H. "Language variables in cross-cultural research." *International Social Science Journal,* 1977, *29,* 167–177.

Naroll, R. "What have we learned from cross-cultural surveys?" *American Anthropologist,* 1970, *72,* 1227–1288.

Nath, R. "A methodological review of cross-cultural management research." *International Social Science Journal,* 1968, *20,* 35–61.

Negandhi, A. R. "Cross-cultural management studies: Too many conclusions, not enough conceptualization." *Management International Review,* 1974, *14,* 6, 59–67.

Negandhi, A. R., & Prasad, S. B. *Comparative management.* New York: Appleton-Century-Crofts, 1971.

Nesvold, B. A. "Scalogram analysis of political violence." *Comparative Political Studies,* 1969, *2,* 172–194.

Newson, J., Newson, E., Richardson, D., & Scaife, J. "Perspectives in sex-role stereotyping." In J. Chetwynd & O. Hartnett (Eds.), *The sex role system.* London: Routledge & Kegan Paul, 1978.

Ng, S. H. "Structural and nonstructural aspects of power distance reduction tendencies." *European Journal of Social Psychology,* 1977, *7,* 317–345.

Noesjirwan, J. "Contrasting cultural patterns of interpersonal closeness in doctors' waiting rooms in Syndney and Jakarta." *Journal of Cross-Cultural Psychology,* 1977, *8,* 357–368.

Northrop, F. S. C. "Cultural Values." In S. Tax (Ed.), *Anthropology today.* Chicago: University of Chicago Press, 1962.

Nowotny, O. H. "American versus European management philosophy." *Harvard Business Review,* 1964, *42,* 2, 101–108.

O'Brien, G. E. "The critical incident approach to cross-cultural training." Presented at the 19th Congress of Applied Psychology, Munich, August, 1978.

Oh, T. K. "Japanese management: A critical review." *Academy of Management Review,* 1976, *1,* 14–25.

Ornauer, H., Wiberg, H., Sicinski, A., & Galtung, J. (Eds.), *Images of the world in the year 2000: A comparative ten-nation study.* The Hague: Mouton, 1976.

Osgood, C. E., May, W. H., & Miron, M. S. *Cross-cultural universals of affective meaning.* Urbana, IL: University of Illinois Press, 1975.

Osgood, C. E., Suci, G. J., & Tannenbaum, P. H. *The measurement of meaning.* Urbana, IL: University of Illinois Press, 1957.

Osgood, C. E., Ware, E. E., & Morris C. "Analysis of the connotative meanings of a variety of human values as expressed by American college students." *Journal of Abnormal and Social Psychology,* 1961, *62,* 62–73.

Owen, J. D. "Flexitime: Some problems and solutions." *Industrial and Labor Relations Review,* 1977, *30,* 152–160.

Oxford Economic Atlas of the World. Oxford: Oxford University Press, 1972.

Palm, G. *The flight from work.* Cambridge: Cambridge University Press, 1977.

Pareek, U. "A motivational paradigm of development." *Journal of Social Issues,* 1968, *24,* 115–122.

Pareto, V. *Sociological writings: Selected and introduced by S. E. Finer.* Oxford: Basil Blackwell, 1976.

Parkin, F. *Class inequality and political order: Social stratification in capitalist and communist societies.* St. Albans Herts.: Paladin, 1971.

Parsons, T. *The social system.* London: Routledge & Kegan Paul, 1951.

Parsons, T. "Vilfredo Pareto: contributions to sociology." In D. L. Sills (Eds.), *International encyclopedia of the social sciences, volume 11.* New York: Macmillan/Free Press, 1968.

Parsons, T. (ed. and intro. by J. Toby). *The evolution of societies.* Englewood Cliffs, NJ: Prentice-Hall, 1977.

Parsons, T., & Bales, R. F. *Family, socialization and interaction process.* New York: Free Press, 1955.

Parsons, T., & Shils, E. A. *Toward a general theory of action.* Cambridge, MA: Harvard University Press, 1951.

Patchen, M. *Some questionnaire measures of employee motivation and morale.* Ann Arbor, MI: Institute for Social Research, Survey Research Center, University of Michigan, 1965.

Pelto, P. J. "The differences between 'tight' and 'loose' societies." *Trans-Action,* 1968, *April,* 37–40.

Perlmutter, H. V. "L'entreprise internationale: trois conceptions." *Revue Economique et Sociale, Lausanne,* 1965, *2,* 1–14.

Perrow, C. *Complex organizations: A critical essay.* Glenview, IL: Scott, Foresman, 1972.

Peterson, R. B. *Bibliography on comparative (international) management.* Seattle, WA: Graduate School of Business Administration, University of Washington, 1969.

Pettigrew, A. M. "Managing under stress." *Management Today.* 1972, *April,* 99–102.

Pettigrew, A. M. *The creation of organisational cultures.* Working Paper 77–11. Brussels: European Institute for Advanced Studies in Management, 1977.

Peyrefitte, A. *Le Mal Français.* Paris: Plon, 1976.

Philipsen, H., & Cassee, E. T. "Verschillen in de wijze van leidinggeven tussen drie typen organisaties." *Mens en Onderneming,* 1965, *19,* 172–184.

Phillips, D. L., & Clancy, K. J. "Some effects of 'social desirability' in survey studies." *American Journal of Sociology,* 1972, *77,* 921–940.

Pirenne, H. *A history of Europe from the invasions to the XVI century.* London: George Allen & Unwin, 1939.

Pitts, J. R. "Le Play, Frédéric." In D. L. Sills (Ed.), *International encyclopedia of the social sciences, volume 9.* New York: Macmillan/Free Press, 1968.

Playford, J. "The myth of pluralism." In F. G. Castles, D. J. Murray, D. C. Potter, & C. J. Pollitt (Eds.), *Decisions, organizations and society.* Harmondsworth, England: Penguin, 1976.

Poirier, J. "Aliénation culturelle et hétéroculture." In G. Michaud (Ed.), *Identité Collective et Relations Inter-Culturelles,* Paris: Presses Universitaires de France, 1978.

Porter, L. W., & Lawler, E. E. "Properties of organization structure in relation to job attitudes and job behavior." *Psychological Bulletin,* 1965, *64,* 23–51.

Preiss, G. W. *Work goals of engineers: A comparative study between German and U.S. industry.* Master's thesis. Cambridge, MA: Sloan School of Management, MIT, 1971. (unpublished)

Price, J. L., & Bluedorn, A. C. *Intent to leave as a measure of turnover.* Iowa City, IO: Department of Sociology, University of Iowa, 1977.

Przeworski, A., & Teune, M. *The logic of comparative social inquiry.* New York: John Wiley, 1970.

Pugh, D. S. "The Aston approach to the study of organizations." In G. Hofstede & M. S. Kassem (Eds.), *European contributions to organization theory.* Assen, Neth.: Van Gorcum, 1976.

Pugh, D. S., & Hickson, D. J. *Organizational structure in its context: The Aston programme I.* London: Saxon House, 1976.

Pugh, D. S., & Hinings, C. R. (Eds.), *Organizational structure: Extensions and replications. The Aston programme II.* London: Saxon House, 1976.

Putnam, R. D. "The political attitudes of senior civil servants in Western Europe: A preliminary report." *British Journal of Political Science,* 1973, *3,* 257–290.

Putnam, R. D. "Bureaucrats and politicians: Contending elites in the policy process." In W. B. Gwyn & G. C. Edwards (Eds.), *Perspectives on public policy making.* Tulane: Tulane University, 1975.

Putnam, R. D. "Elite transformation in advanced industrial societies: An empirical assessment of the theory of technocracy." *Comparative Political Studies,* 1977, *10,* 383–412.

Quinn, N. "Anthropological studies on women's status." *Annual Review of Anthropology,* 1977, *6,* 181–225.

Quinn, R. P. "What workers want: General descriptive statistics and demographic correlates." In R. P. Quinn & T. W. Mangione (Eds.), *The 1969–1970 survey of working conditions.* Ann Arbor, MI: Institute for Social Research, University of Michigan, 1973.

Quinn, R. P., & Mangione, T. W. "Evaluating weighted models of measuring job satisfaction: A Cinderella story." In R. P. Quinn & T. W. Mangione (Eds.), *The 1969–1970 survey of working conditions.* Ann Arbor, MI: Institute for Social Research, University of Michigan, 1973.

Rapoport, R. "Sex-role stereotyping in studies of marriage and the family." In J. Chetwynd & O. Hartnett (Eds.), *The sex role system.* London: Routledge & Kegan Paul, 1978.

Ray, J. J. "Do authoritarians hold authoritarian attitudes?" *Human Relations,* 1976, *29,* 307–325.

Reader's Digest. *A survey of Europe today.* London: The Reader's Digest, 1970.

Reddin, W. J., & Rowell, K. J. *Culture shock test.* Fredericton, New Brunswick: Organizational Tests Ltd, 1970.

Redding, S. G. "Some perceptions of psychological needs among managers in South-East Asia." In Y. H. Poortinga (Ed.), *Basic problems in cross-cultural psychology.* Amsterdam: Swets and Zeitlinger, 1977.

Redding, S. G., & Casey, T. W. *Managerial beliefs and behaviour in South-East Asia.* Working Paper. Hong Kong: Centre of Asian Studies, Hong Kong University, 1976.

Redfield, M. P. (Ed.). *Human nature and the study of society. The papers of Robert Redfield, volume I.* Chicago: University of Chicago Press, 1962.

Riesman, D., Glazer, N., & Denney, R. *The lonely crowd: A study of the changing American character.* New York: Doubleday, 1953.

Ritti, R. R. "Control of 'halo' in factor analyses of a supervisory behavior inventory." *Personnel Psychology,* 1964, *17,* 305–318.

Ritti, R. R. "Work goals of scientists and engineers." *Industrial Relations,* 1968, *7,* 118–131.

Roberts, J. M., Arth, M. J., & Bush, R. R. "Games in culture." *American Anthropologist,* 1959, *61,* 597–605.

Roberts, K. H. "On looking at an elephant: An evaluation of cross-cultural research related to organizations." *Psychological Bulletin,* 1970, *74,* 327–350.

Roberts, K. H. *International research related to organizational behavior: An annotated bibliography.* Technical Report No. 12. Stanford, CA: Graduate School of Business, Stanford University, 1972.

Roberts, K. H. "Symposium: Cross-national research—overview." *Industrial Relations,* 1973, *12,* 137–143.

Robinson, J. P., & Shaver, P. R. *Measures of social psychological attitudes.* Ann Arbor, MI: Survey Research Center, Institute for Social Research, University of Michigan, 1973.

Robinson, J. P., Athanasiou, R., & Head, K. B. *Measures of occupational attitudes and occupational characteristics.* Ann Arbor, MI: Survey Research Center, Institute for Social Research, University of Michigan, 1969.

Robinson, W. S. "Ecological correlations and the behavior of individuals." *American Sociological Review,* 1950, *15,* 351–357.

Rocher, G. *Talcott Parsons and American sociology.* London: Nelson, 1974.

Rokeach, M. *Beliefs, attitudes, and values: A theory of organization and change.* San Francisco: Jossey-Bass, 1972.

Rokeach, M. *The nature of human values.* New York: Free Press, 1973.

Rokeach, M., & Hanley, C. "Eysenck's tender-mindedness dimension: A critique." *Psychological Bulletin,* 1956, *53,* 169–176.

Rokkan, S., Verba, S., Viet, J., & Almasy, E. *Comparative survey analysis.* The Hague: Mouton, 1969.

Rosenberg, M. "Faith in people and success-orientation." In P. F. Lazarsfeld & M. Rosenberg (Eds.), *The language of social research.* New York: Free Press, 1955.

Rotterstøl, N. "Suicide in Norway." In N. L. Farberow (Ed.), *Suicide in different cultures.* Baltimore, MD: University Park Press, 1975.

Rousseau, J. J. *Du Contrat Social.* Oxford: Clarendon Press, [1762] 1972.

Ruben, B. D. "Guidelines for cross-cultural communication effectiveness." *Group and Organization Studies,* 1977, *2,* 470–479.

Rubenowitz, S. "Personnel management organization in some European societies." *Management International Review,* 1968, *8,* 4–5, 74–92.

Rudin, S. A. "National motives predict psychogenic death 25 years later." *Science,* 1968, *160,* 901–903.

Rummel, R. J. "Dimensions of conflict behavior within and between nations." *General Systems: Yearbook of the Society for General Systems Research,* 1963, *8,* 1–50.

Rummel, R. J. *The dimensions of nations.* Beverly Hills, CA: Sage, 1972.

Runciman, W. G. "The three dimensions of social inequality." In A. Béteille (Ed.), *Social inequality.* Harmondsworth, England: Penguin, 1969.

Russett, B. M. "Delineating international regions." In J. D. Singer (Ed.), *Quantitative international politics: Insights and evidence*. New York: Free Press, 1968.

Sadler, P. J., & Hofstede, G. "Leadership styles: Preferences and perceptions of employees of an international company in different countries." *Mens en Onderneming* (Leiden), 1972, 26, 43–63.

SAF. *Job reform in sweden: Conclusions from 500 shop floor projects*. Stockholm: Swedish Employers' Confederation, 1975.

Sanchez-Albornoz, N. *The population of Latin America: A history*. Berkeley, CA: University of California Press, 1974.

Sand, H. "Fragen zur Arbeitszufriedenheit." *Management International Review*, 1973, *13*, 4–5, 45–55.

Saunders, T. J. Plato: *The Laws*. Harmondsworth, England: Penguin, 1970.

Sauvy, A. *Théorie Générale de la Population: Volume II: La Vie des Populations*. Paris: Presses Universitaires de France, 1966.

Sawyer, J. "Dimensions of nations: Size, wealth and politics." *American Journal of Sociology*, 1967, *72*, 145–172.

Sawyer, J., & Le Vine, R. A. "Cultural dimensions: A factor analysis of the World Ethnographic Sample." *American Anthropologist*, 1966, *68*, 708–731.

Sayles, L. R. *Individualism and big business*. New York: McGraw-Hill, 1964.

Schachter, S., Nuttin, J., de Monchaux, C., Maucorps, P. H., Osmer, D., Duyker, H., Rommetveit, R., & Israel, J. "Cross-cultural experiments of threat and rejection: A study of the organization for comparative social research." *Human Relations*, 1954, *7*, 403–439.

Schaupp, D. L. *A cross-cultural study of a multinational company: Attitudes of satisfactions, needs and values affecting participative management*. Doctoral dissertation. Lexington, KY: University of Kentucky, 1973.

Scheuch, E. K. "Cross-national comparisons using aggregate data: Some substantive and methodological problems." In R. L. Merritt and S. Rokkan (Eds.), *Comparing nations*. New Haven, CT: Yale University Press, 1966.

Schludermann, S., & Schludermann, E. "Achievement motivation: Cross-cultural and development issues." In Y. H. Poortinga (Ed.), *Basic problems in cross-cultural psychology*. Amsterdam: Swets and Zeitlinger, 1977.

Schneider, P. L., & Schneider, A. L. "Social mobilization, political institutions, and political violence." *Comparative Political Studies*, 1971, *4*, 69–90.

Schollhammer, H. "The comparative management theory jungle." *Academy of Management Journal*, 1969, *12*, 81–97.

Schonfeld, W. R. *Obedience and revolt: French behavior toward authority*. Beverly Hills, CA: Sage, 1976.

Schreuder, H. *Facts and speculations on corporate social reporting in France, Germany and Holland*. Working Paper 78–42. Brussels: European Institute for Advanced Studies in Management, 1978.

Schuman, H. & Johnson, M. P. "Attitudes and behavior." *Annual Review of Sociology*, 1976, *2* 161–207.

Scott, W. G. "Organization theory: A reassessment." *Academy of Management Journal*, 1974, *17*, 242–254.

Seeman, M. "Role conflict and ambivalence in leadership." *American Sociological Review*, 1953, *18*, 373–380.

Seeman, M. "Some real and imaginary consequences of social mobility: A French-American comparison." *American Journal of Sociology*, 1972, *82*, 757–782.

Selye, H. *Stress without distress*. Philadelphia: J. B. Lippincott, 1974.

Sethi, S. P., & Holton, R. H. "Country typologies for the multinational corporation: A new basic approach." *California Management Review*, 1973, *15*, 3, 105–118.

Shaefer, J. M. "The growth of hologeistic studies 1889–1975." *Behavioral Science Research,* 1977, *12,* 71–108.

Shaver, P. R. "Authoritarianism, dogmatism and related measures." In J. P. Robinson and P. R. Shaver (Eds.), *Measures of social psychological attitudes.* Ann Arbor, MI: Institute for Social Research, University of Michigan, 1973.

Shepard, J. M. *Automation and alienation: A study of office and factory workers.* Cambridge, MA: MIT Press, 1971.

Shils, E. "Centre and periphery." In P. Worsley (Ed.), *Modern sociology: Introductory readings.* Harmondsworth, England: Penguin, 1970.

Shils, E. *Center and periphery: Essays in macrosociology.* Chicago: University of Chicago Press, 1975.

Sicinski, A. "The future: A dimension being discovered." In H. Ornauer, H. Wiberg, A. Sicinski & J. Galtung (Eds.), *Images of the world in the year 2000: A comparative ten-nation study.* The Hague: Mouton, 1976.

Singh, P. N., & R. J. Wherry, "Ranking of job factors by factory workers in India." *Personnel Psychology,* 1963, *16,* 29–33.

Sirota, D. "Why managers do not use attitude survey results." *Personnel* (A.M.A.), 1970, *Jan/ Feb.,* 24–35.

Sirota, D., & Greenwood, J. M. "Understand your overseas work force." *Harvard Business Review,* 1971, *49,* 1, 53–60.

Slocum, J. W., Topichak, P. M., & Kuhn, D. G. "A cross-cultural study of need satisfaction and need importance for operative employees." *Personnel Psychology,* 1971, *24,* 435–445.

Smith, D., & Jessee, M. "Barriers between expert and counterpart." *International Development Review,* 1970, *1,* 22–25.

Smith, J. C. "The theoretical constructs of western contractual law." In F.S.C. Northrop & H. H. Livingston (Eds.), *Cross-cultural understanding: Epistemology in anthropology.* New York: Harper and Row, 1964.

Spenner, K. I., & Featherman, D. L. "Achievement ambitions." *Annual Review of Sociology,* 1978, *4,* 373–420.

Spicer, E. H. "Persistent cultural systems: A comparative study of identity systems that can adapt to contrasting environments." *Science,* 1971, *174,* 795–800.

Spindler, G. D. "American character as revealed by the military: Descriptions and origins." *Psychiatry,* 1948, *2,* 275–281.

Srinivas, M. N. "The caste system in India." In A. Béteille (Ed.), *Social inequality.* Harmondsworth, England: Penguin, 1969.

Stavig, G. R., & Barnett, L. D. "Group size and societal conflict." *Human Relations,* 1977, *30,* 761–765.

Stevens, E. P. "Marianismo: The other face of machismo in Latin America." In A. Pescatello (Ed.), *Female and male in Latin America.* Pittsburgh, PA: University of Pittsburgh Press, 1973.

Stinchcombe, A. L. "Social structure and organizations." In J. G. March (Ed.), *Handbook of organizations.* Chicago: Rand McNally, 1965.

Stogdill, R. M., & Coons, A. E. (Eds.). *Leader behavior: Its description and measurement.* Research Monograph No 88. Columbus: Bureau of Business Research, Ohio State University, 1957.

Stone, P. J. "Child care in twelve countries." In A. Szalai (Ed.), *The use of time.* The Hague: Mouton, 1972.

Taft, R. "Cross-cultural psychology as a social science: Comments on Faucheux's paper." *European Journal of Social Psychology,* 1976, *6,* 323–330.

Tannenbaum, A. S. *Control in organizations.* New York: McGraw-Hill, 1968.

Tannenbaum, A. S., & Bachman, J. G. "Structural versus individual effects." *American Journal of Sociology*, 1964, *69*, 585–595.

Tannenbaum, A.S., Kavčič, B., Rosner, M., Vianello, M., & Wieser, G. *Hierarchy in organizations*. San Francisco: Jossey-Bass, 1974.

Tannenbaum, R., & Schmidt, W. H. "How to choose a leadership pattern." *Harvard Business Review*, 1958, *36*, 95–101.

Taylor, C. L., & Hudson, M. C. (Eds.). *World handbook of political and social indicators*. New Haven, CT: Yale University Press, 1972.

Taylor, R. N., & Thompson, M. "Work value systems of young workers." *Academy of Management Journal*, 1976, *19*, 522–535.

Thomas, C. "L'espérance de vie des hommes souvent tributaire des conditions climatiques." *Le Figaro*, 1973, *Jeudi 3 Mai*.

Thorndike, E. L. "On the fallacy of imputing the correlations found for groups to the individuals or smaller groups composing them." *American Journal of Psychology*, 1939, *3*, 122–124.

Toffler, A. *Future shock*. London: Pan Books, 1971.

Tönnies, F. *Community and society*. New York: Harper & Row, [1887] 1963.

Trépo, G. "Les racines du centralisme dans l'entreprise." *Le Management*, 1973, *Mai*. (a)

Trépo, G. "Management style à la française." *European Business*, 1973, *Autumn*, 71–79. (b)

Trépo, G. "Mise en place d'une DPO: Le rôle crucial de la Direction." *Direction et Gestions des Enterprises*, 1975, *1*, 25–34.

Triandis, H. C. *Some psychological dimensions of modernization.*" Presented at the 17th Congress of Applied Psychology, Liege, Belgium, August, 1971.

Triandis, H. C. (Ed.). *The analysis of subjective culture*. New York: John Wiley, 1972.

Triandis, H. C. "Subjective culture and economic development." *International Journal of Psychology*, 1973, *8*, 163–180.

Triandis, H. C. *Interpersonal behavior*. Monterey, CA: Brooks/Cole, 1977.

Triandis, H. C., & Vassiliou, V. "A comparative analysis of subjective culture (Greece-U.S.)." In H. C. Triandis (Ed.), *The analysis of subjective culture*. New York: John Wiley, 1972.

Triandis, H.C., Kilty, K.M., Shanmugam, A. V., Tanaka, Y., & Vassiliou, V. "Cognitive structures and the analysis of values." In H. C. Triandis (Ed.), *The analysis of subjective culture*. New York: John Wiley, 1972.

Tsantis, A. C. "Political factors in economic development." *Comparative Politics*, 1969, *2*, 63–78.

Tsurumi, K. "Some potential contributions of latecomers to technological and scientific revolution: A comparison between Japan and China." In R. Dahrendorf et al. (Eds.), *Scientific-technological revolution: Social aspects*. Beverly Hills, CA: Sage, 1977.

Tugwell, F. "The 'soft states' can't make it." *Center Report* (Center for the Studies of Democratic Institutions, Santa Barbara, CA), 1972, *December*, 15–17.

U.N. demographic yearbook. New York: Statistical Office of the United Nations, 1973.

Van der Haas, H. *The enterprise in transition*. London: Tavistock Publications, 1967.

Van Gunsteren, H. R. *The quest for control: A critique of the rational-central-rule approach in public affairs*, London: John Wiley, 1976.

Van Leent, J. A. A. "Sociologie en psychologie in interdisciplinair perspectief." In A. G M. Van Melsen, E. V. W., Vercruysse, J. C. W., Verstege, & J. A. A. Van Leent, *De moderne sociologie: Balans der methoden*. Utrecht: Spectrum, 1964.

Van Leeuwen, M. S. "A cross-cultural examination of psychological differentiation in males and females." *International Journal of Psychology*, 1978, *13*, 87–122.

Varga, K. "Who gains from achievement motivation training?" *Vikalpa*, 1977, *2*, 187–200.

Vertin, P. G. *Bedrijfsgeneeskundige Aspecten van het Ulcus Pepticum*. Doctoral dissertation. Groningen, Neth.: University of Groningen, 1954.

Vlassenko, E. "Le point sur la dispersion des salaires dans les pays du Marché Commun." *Economie et Statistique,* 1977, *93,* 64–72.

Von Bertalanffy, L. *General systems theory: Foundations, development, application.* New York: George Braziller, 1968.

Vroom, V. H. *Work and motivation.* New York: John Wiley, 1964.

Wallace, A. F. C. *Culture and personality.* New York: Random House, 1970.

Webb, E. J., Campbell, D. T., Schwartz, R. D., & Sechrest, L. *Unobtrusive measures: Non-reactive research in the social sciences.* Chicago: Rand McNally, 1966.

Webber, R. A. (Ed.). *Culture and management: Text and readings in comparative management.* Homewood, IL: Irwin, 1969.

Weber, M. *The Protestant ethic and spirit of capitalism.* London: George Allen and Unwin, [1930] 1976.

Weber, M. *Essays in sociology* (H. H. Gerth and C. W. Mills, eds.). London: Routledge & Kegan Paul, [1948] 1970.

Weick, K. E. *The social psychology of organizing.* Reading, MA: Addison-Wesley, 1969.

Weinreich, H. "Sex-role socialisation." In J. Chetwynd & O. Hartnett (Eds.), *The sex role system.* London: Routledge & Kegan Paul, 1978.

Weinshall, T. D. (Ed.), *Culture and management.* Harmondsworth, England: Penguin, 1977.

Weir, D. "Stress and the manager in the over-controlled organization." In D. Gowler & K. Legge (Eds.), *Managerial stress.* Epping, Essex; Gower Press, 1975.

Whitehill, A. M. and Takezawa, S. I. *The other worker: A comparative study of industrial relations in the United States and Japan.* Honolulu: East-West Center Press, 1968.

Whyte, W. F. "Culture and work." In R. A Webber (Ed.), *Culture and management.* Homewood, IL: Irwin, 1969.

Whyte, W. H. *The organization man.* New York. Doubleday, 1956.

Wildavsky, A. *Budgeting: A comparative theory of the budgetary process.* Boston: Little, Brown, 1975.

Wildavsky, A. "Economy and environment/rationality and ritual: A review essay." *Accounting, Organizations and Society,* 1976, *1,* 117–129.

Willatt, N. "Flextime at Sandoz." *European Business,* 1973, *Autumn,* 56–61.

Williams, J. E., Giles, H., & Edwards, J. R. "Comparative analysis of sex-trait stereotypes in the United States, England and Ireland." In Y. H. Poortinga (Ed.), *Basic problems in cross-cultural psychology.* Amsterdam: Swets and Zeitlinger, 1977.

Williams, L. K., Whyte, W. F., & Green, C. S. "Do cultural differences affect workers' attitudes?" *Industrial Relations,* 1966, *5,* 105–117.

Williams, R. M. "The concept of values." In D. L. Sills (Ed.), *International encyclopedia of the social sciences, volume 16.* New York: Macmillan/Free Press, 1968.

Wilmott, P. "Integrity in social science: The upshot of a scandal." *International Social Science Journal,* 1977, *29,* 333–336.

Witkin, H. A. "Theory in cross-cultural research: Its uses and risks." In Y. H. Poortinga (Ed.), *Basic problems in cross-cultural psychology.* Amsterdam: Swets and Zeitlinger, 1977.

Witkin, H. A., & Berry, J. W. "Psychological differentiation in cross-cultural perspective." *Journal of Cross-Cultural Psychology,* 1975, *6,* 4–87.

Witkin, H. A., & Goodenough, D. R. "Field dependence and interpersonal behavior." *Psychological Bulletin,* 1977, *84,* 661–689.

Witkin, H. A., Price-Williams, D., Bertini, M., Christiansen, D., Oltman, P. K., Ramirez, M. & Van Meel, J. "Social conformity and psychological differentiation." *International Journal of Psychology,* 1974, *9,* 11–29.

World Bank atlas. Washington, DC: International Bank for Reconstruction and Development, 1972.

Wright, P. "The harassed decision maker: Time pressures, distractions, and the use of evidence." *Journal of Applied Psychology,* 1974, *59,* 555–561.

Yoshimori, M. "Japanese management—A comparison with western management style." Presented at Japanese Management Seminars in Scandinavia, March, 1976.

Youngberg, C. F. X., Hedberg, R. & Baxter, B. "Management action recommendations based on one versus two dimensions of a job satisfaction questionnaire." *Personnel Psychology,* 1962, *15,* 145–150.

Zaleznik, A., Kets de Vries, M. F. R., & Howard, J. "Stress reactions in organizations: Syndromes, causes and consequences." *Behavioral Science,* 1977, *22,* 151–162.

Zaleznik, A., Ondrack, J., & Silver, A. "Social class, occupation and mental illness." In A. McLean (Ed.), *Mental health and work organizations.* Chicago: Rand McNally, 1970.

Zurcher, L. A., Meadow, A., and Zurcher, S. L. "Value orientation, role conflict, and alienation from work: A cross-cultural study." *American Sociological Review,* 1965, *30,* 539–548.

NAME INDEX

SUBJECT INDEX

About the Author

GEERT HOFSTEDE is presently Director, Human Resources, of Fasson Europe at Leiden, the Netherlands, and Visiting Professor of Organizational Behavior at INSEAD, Fontainebleau, France. He is a native of the Netherlands and holds an M. Sc. in mechanical engineering and a Ph. D. in social psychology from Dutch universities. His professional career includes experience as a worker, foreman, plant manager, chief psychologist on the international staff of a multinational corporation, and academic researcher. He has lived in Switzerland and Belgium, worked in France and Austria, and lectured in ten more countries. He has authored three books, edited two more, and published over 50 articles in the area of management, organization, and culture.